THE ENGAGED READER

Issues and Conversations for Composition

Editorial Committee:

William Breeze • Jane Dugan • Melanie Gagich
Alex Nielsen • Jessica Schantz

First Edition

VAN-GRINER

The Engaged Reader:
Issues and Conversations for Composition

2014–2015
Cleveland State University

Printed in the United States of America
10 9 8 7 6 5 4 3 2 1
ISBN: 978-1-61740-168-8

Van-Griner Publishing
Cincinnati, Ohio
www.van-griner.com

Breeze 168-8 Su14

Table of Contents

Unit 1 | Media and the New Millennium

Unit 2 | Ethics and Education

Unit 3 | Urban Growth and Renewal

Unit 4 | Cultures and Identities

Unit 5 | Science and Nature

Introduction

> Imagine that you enter a parlor. You come late. When you arrive, others have long preceded you, and they are engaged in a heated discussion, too heated for them to pause and tell you exactly what it is about. In fact, the discussion had already begun long before any of them got there, so that no one present is qualified to retrace for you all the steps that had gone before. You listen for a while, until you decide that you have caught the tenor of the argument; then you put in your oar. Someone answers; you answer him; another comes to your defense; another aligns himself against you, to either the embarrassment or gratification of your opponent, depending on the quality of your ally's assistance. However, the discussion is interminable. The hour grows late, you must depart. And you do depart, with the discussion still vigorously in progress.
>
> —Kenneth Burke, from *The Philosophy of Literary Form: Studies in Symbolic Action*

The text you are now holding in your hands derives from one basic, but important premise: that an educated person must be engaged in the important issues of his or her time. In a world that has become increasingly information-driven, we must take time to consider our lives more closely and with thoughtful scrutiny. In short, our knowledge-seeking selves depend on a willingness to participate in conversations about those topics that most affect us. If you are holding this book, you have already made a choice to undertake the difficult challenge of pursuing a college education. That choice is the beginning of a transformative journey that will see you conversing with classmates, professors and other educators, the authors you read, and even yourself as you grapple with complex issues and ideas.

The time you spend at this university will find you in a great number of conversations on many different subjects. You will be asked to immerse yourself in the disciplinary knowledge of your major, but also in many other fields that make up what we call a "liberal education," defined by the Association of American Colleges and Universities as:

> an approach to learning that empowers individuals and prepares them to deal with complexity, diversity, and change. It provides students with broad knowledge of the wider world (e.g. science, culture, and society) as well as in-depth study in a specific area of interest. A liberal education helps students develop a sense of social responsibility, as well as strong and transferable intellectual and practical skills such as communication, analytical and problem-solving skills, and a demonstrated ability to apply knowledge and skills in real-world settings.

The writing class you are now enrolled in will be one of many classes you take at Cleveland State University that focuses on those intellectual and practical skills, all of which are integral to the academic reading and writing experience. In this class you will read essays on a number of topics, organized in the following units: Media and the New Millennium; Ethics and Education; Urban Growth and Renewal; Cultures and Identities; and Science and Nature. These topics encapsulate a wide range of issues encouraging the kind of academic conversations Kenneth Burke illustrates in the metaphor that begins this introduction. To open this book is to enter a parlor where you will find yourself participating in a number of heated discussions, all of which began before you entered and will continue after you have left. Now, however, it is up to you to help shape the discussion—to listen and to speak. As you read the essays here, as you compose your written assignments, and as you discuss these topics with your teacher and your classmates, you are doing just that: joining the conversation.

What role do we have to play, then, in shaping the world in which we live? That is our guiding question. Joining the conversation is just the first step toward a greater understanding of the world in which we live. We leave traces of ourselves on our world without even trying. Imagine what we might leave if we are motivated to engage fully with the society in which we live and the planet on which we depend.

The many diverse works in this textbook offer a starting point for exploring the place we inhabit as individuals within a population quickly approaching 8 billion people. You are asked here to consider serious and complex questions about how we live and thrive in our community, in our country, and in our world. The essays in Unit 1 of this book ask you to reconsider something very familiar to you: the pervasive role the media plays in our everyday lives. In Unit 2 you will read a range of essays that focus on the ethical dimensions of the place you now inhabit: higher education. Urban life—specifically, life in Cleveland—is the focus of the readings in Unit 3, while Unit 4 asks you to consider how race, class, and gender impact our lives and the roles we must play in society. Finally, Unit 5 explores the connection between science and nature in our quickly-changing world—a world where more and more we must expand our understanding of what is natural, what is human, and what is safe.

In this class you will read and write about, and discuss with diverse classmates, a range of topics that will affect the future of you all. So enter these readings in the spirit that Kenneth Burke invokes—as a participant in a rich, complex (and sometimes heated) conversation. Our hope is that this will be the beginning of a long engagement you have with the issues that are raised here.

Unit 1

Media and the New Millennium

The 21st century has given rise to many astounding changes in the way that we access and utilize media as a culture. As the media landscape has evolved in the new millennium, the confluence of pre-internet industries and digital technologies has resulted in a culture obsessed with—and perplexed by—public media movements and the discourses that stem from them. More than at any previous point in history, common citizens today—students, activists, consumers, artists, workers—can influence not only the information and viewpoints they are exposed to, but also the way in which this information presents itself in their lives.

With these dynamic and groundbreaking changes in technology, access, and even meaning, we find ourselves challenged at every turn to locate and discern new values in both our private and our public lives. In the early 1990s, conversations about the future of media began to turn towards what we now call "the electronic frontier," a digital space both feared and celebrated for allowing an essentially lawless and unrestricted flow of information from and to all corners of civilization.

As the Internet has grown into the ubiquitous cultural force it is today, we have begun to learn to both utilize its benefits and recognize its pitfalls for engaged and conscientious citizens. It is our immense and solemn responsibility, regardless of personal philosophies, political affiliations, or activist impulses, to remain informed and literate as this electronic frontier grows to envelop and encompass more and more moments of our waking, working lives. "Our history," Edward R. Murrow contended in his famous address to the RTNDA in 1958, "will be what we make it." Never before have we had such great power over our media and its reach in our society. Never before has our media had such great power over us. The future of media is up to us, whether it will provide a grand, experimental forum where we can grow, live, and collaborate, or will become a cell in which we entertain, distract, and isolate ourselves.

Wires and Lights in a Box

Edward R. Murrow

On October 15, 1958, veteran broadcaster ***Edward R. Murrow*** *delivered this speech before attendees at the convention of the Radio-Television News Directors Association.*

This just might do nobody any good. At the end of this discourse a few people may accuse this reporter of fouling his own comfortable nest, and your organization may be accused of having given hospitality to heretical and even dangerous thoughts. But the elaborate structure of networks, advertising agencies, and sponsors will not be shaken or altered. It is my desire, if not my duty, to try to talk to you journeymen with some candor about what is happening to radio and television. I have no technical advice or counsel to offer those of you who labor in this vineyard that produces words and pictures. You will forgive me for not telling you that instruments with which you work are miraculous, that your responsibility is unprecedented, or that your aspirations are frequently frustrated. It is not necessary to remind you that the fact that your voice is amplified to the degree where it reaches from one end of the country to the other does not confer upon you greater wisdom or understanding than you possessed when your voice reached only from one end of the bar to the other. All of these things you know.

You should also know at the outset that, in the manner of witnesses before Congressional committees, I appear here voluntarily—by invitation—that I am an employee of the Columbia Broadcasting System, that I am neither an officer nor a director of that corporation, and that these remarks are of a "do-it-yourself" nature. If what I have to say is responsible, then I alone am responsible for the saying of it. Seeking neither approbation from my employers, nor new sponsors, nor acclaim from the critics of radio and television, I cannot well be disappointed. Believing that potentially the commercial system of broadcasting as practiced in this country is the best and freest yet devised, I have decided to express my concern about what I believe to be happening to radio and television. These instruments have been good to me beyond my due. There exists in mind no reasonable grounds for personal complaint.

I have no feud, either with my employers, any sponsors, or with the professional critics of radio and television. But I am seized with an abiding fear regarding what these two instruments are doing to our society, our culture, and our heritage.

Our history will be what we make it. And if there are any historians about fifty or a hundred years from now, and there should be preserved the kinescopes for one week of all three networks, they will there find recorded in black and white, or color, evidence of decadence, escapism, and insulation from the realities of the world in which we live. I invite your attention to the television schedules of all networks between the hours of 8 and 11 p.m., Eastern Time. Here you will find only fleeting and spasmodic reference to the fact that this nation is in mortal danger. There are, it is true, occasional informative programs presented in that intellectual ghetto on Sunday afternoons. But during the daily peak viewing periods, television in the main insulates us from the realities of the world in which we live. If this state of affairs continues, we may alter an advertising slogan to read: LOOK NOW, PAY LATER.

For surely we shall pay for using this most powerful instrument of communication to insulate the citizenry from the hard and demanding realities which must be faced if we are to survive. I mean the word survive literally. If there were to be a competition in indifference, or perhaps in insulation from reality, then Nero and his fiddle, Chamberlain and his umbrella, could not find a place on an early afternoon sustaining show. If Hollywood were to run out of Indians, the program schedules would be mangled beyond all recognition. Then some courageous soul with a small budget might be able to do a documentary telling what, in fact, we have done—and are still doing—to the Indians in this country. But that would be unpleasant. And we must at all costs shield the sensitive citizens from anything that is unpleasant.

I am entirely persuaded that the American public is more reasonable, restrained, and more mature than most of our industry's program planners believe. Their fear of controversy is not warranted by the evidence. I have reason to know, as do many of you, that when the evidence on a controversial subject is fairly and calmly presented, the public recognizes it for what it is—an effort to illuminate rather than to agitate.

Several years ago, when we undertook to do a program on Egypt and Israel, well-meaning, experienced, and intelligent friends shook their heads and said, "This you cannot do—you will be handed your head. It is an emotion-packed controversy, and there is no room for reason in it." We did the program. Zionists, anti-Zionists, the friends of the Middle East, Egyptian and Israeli officials said, with a faint tone of surprise, "It was a fair account. The information was there. We have no complaints."

Our experience was similar with two half-hour programs dealing with cigarette smoking and lung cancer. Both the medical profession and the tobacco industry cooperated in a rather wary fashion. But in the end of the day they were both reasonably content. The subject of radioactive fall-out and the banning of nuclear tests was, and is, highly controversial. But according to what little evidence there is, viewers were prepared to listen to both sides with reason and restraint. This is not said to claim any special or unusual competence in the presentation of controversial subjects, but rather to indicate that timidity in these areas is not warranted by the evidence.

Recently, network spokesmen have been disposed to complain that the professional critics of television have been "rather beastly." There have been hints that somehow competition for the advertising dollar has caused the critics of print to gang up on television and radio. This reporter has no desire to defend the critics. They have space in which to do that on their own behalf. But it remains a fact that the newspapers and magazines are the only instruments of mass communication which remain free from sustained and regular critical comment. If the network spokesmen are so anguished about what appears in print, let them come forth and engage in a little sustained and regular comment regarding newspapers and magazines. It is an ancient and sad fact that most people in network television, and radio, have an exaggerated regard for what appears in print. And there have been cases where executives have refused to make even private comment on a program for which they were responsible until they heard the reviews in print. This is hardly an exhibition of confidence.

The oldest excuse of the networks for their timidity is their youth. Their spokesmen say, "We are young; we have not developed the traditions nor acquired the experience of the older media." If they but knew it, they are building those traditions, creating those precedents everyday. Each time they yield to a voice from Washington or any political pressure, each time they eliminate something that might offend some section of the community, they are creating their own body of precedent and tradition. They are, in fact, not content to be "half safe."

Nowhere is this better illustrated than by the fact that the chairman of the Federal Communications Commission publicly prods broadcasters to engage in their legal right to editorialize. Of course, to undertake an editorial policy, overt and clearly labeled, and obviously unsponsored, requires a station or a network to be responsible. Most stations today probably do not have the manpower to assume this responsibility, but the manpower could be recruited. Editorials would not be profitable; if they had a cutting edge, they might even offend. It is much easier, much less troublesome, to use the money-making machine of television and radio merely as a conduit through which to channel anything that is not libelous, obscene, or defamatory. In that way one has the illusion of power without responsibility.

So far as radio—that most satisfying and rewarding instrument—is concerned, the diagnosis of its difficulties is rather easy. And obviously I speak only of news and information. In order to progress, it need only go backward. To the time when singing commercials were not allowed on news reports, when there was no middle commercial in a 15-minute news report, when radio was rather proud, alert, and fast. I recently asked a network official, "Why this great rash of five-minute news reports (including three commercials) on weekends?" He replied, "Because that seems to be the only thing we can sell."

In this kind of complex and confusing world, you can't tell very much about the why of the news in broadcasts where only three minutes is available for news. The only man who could do that was Elmer Davis, and his kind aren't about any more. If radio news is to be regarded as a commodity, only acceptable when saleable, then I don't care what you call it—I say it isn't news.

My memory also goes back to the time when the fear of a slight reduction in business did not result in an immediate cutback in bodies in the news and public affairs department, at a time when network profits had just reached an all-time high. We would all agree, I think, that whether on a station or a network, the stapling machine is a poor substitute for a newsroom typewriter.

One of the minor tragedies of television news and information is that the networks will not even defend their vital interests. When my employer, CBS, through a combination of enterprise and good luck, did an interview with Nikita Khrushchev, the President uttered a few ill-chosen, uninformed words on the subject, and the network practically apologized. This produced a rarity. Many newspapers defended the CBS right to produce the program and commended it for initiative. But the other networks remained silent.

Likewise, when John Foster Dulles, by personal decree, banned American journalists from going to Communist China, and subsequently offered contradictory explanations, for his fiat the networks entered only a mild protest. Then they apparently forgot the unpleasantness. Can it be that this national industry is content to serve the public interest only with the trickle of news that comes out of Hong Kong, to leave its viewers in ignorance of the cataclysmic changes that are occurring in a nation of six hundred million people? I have no illusions about the difficulties reporting from a dictatorship, but our British and French allies have been better served—in their public interest—with some very useful information from their reporters in Communist China.

One of the basic troubles with radio and television news is that both instruments have grown up as an incompatible combination of show business, advertising, and news. Each of the three is a rather bizarre and demanding profession. And when you get all three under one roof, the dust never settles. The top management of the networks with a few notable exceptions, has been trained in advertising, research, sales, or show business. But by the nature of the corporate structure, they also make the final and crucial decisions having to do with news and public affairs. Frequently they have neither the time nor the competence to do this. It is not easy for the same small group of men to decide whether to buy a new station for millions of dollars, build a new building, alter the rate card, buy a new Western, sell a soap opera, decide what defensive line to take in connection with the latest Congressional inquiry, how much money to spend on promoting a new program, what additions or deletions should be made in the existing covey or clutch of vice-presidents, and at the same time—frequently on the same long day—to give mature, thoughtful consideration to the manifold problems that confront those who are charged with the responsibility for news and public affairs.

Sometimes there is a clash between the public interest and the corporate interest. A telephone call or a letter from the proper quarter in Washington is treated rather more seriously than a communication from an irate but not politically potent viewer. It is tempting enough to give away a little air time for frequently irresponsible and unwarranted utterances in an effort to temper the wind of criticism.

Upon occasion, economics and editorial judgment are in conflict. And there is no law which says that dollars will be defeated by duty. Not so long ago the President of the United States delivered a television address to the nation. He was discoursing on the possibility or probability of war between this nation and the Soviet Union and Communist China—a reasonably compelling subject. Two networks, CBS and NBC, delayed that broadcast for an hour and fifteen minutes. If this decision was dictated by anything other than financial reasons, the networks didn't deign to explain those reasons. That hour-and-fifteen-minute delay, by the way, is about twice the time required for an ICBM to travel from the Soviet Union to major targets in the United States. It is difficult to believe that this decision was made by men who love, respect, and understand news.

So far, I have been dealing largely with the deficit side of the ledger, and the items could be expanded. But I have said, and I believe, that potentially we have in this country a free enterprise system of radio and television which is superior to any other. But to achieve its promise, it must be both free and enterprising. There is no suggestion here that networks or individual stations should operate as philanthropies. But I can find nothing in the Bill of Rights or the Communications Act which says that they must increase their net profits each year, lest the Republic collapse. I do not suggest that news and information should be subsidized by foundations or private subscriptions. I am aware that the networks have expended, and are expending, very considerable sums of money on public affairs programs from which they cannot hope to receive any financial reward. I have had the privilege at CBS of presiding over a considerable number of such programs. I testify, and am able to stand here and say, that I have never had a program turned down by my superiors because of the money it would cost.

But we all know that you cannot reach the potential maximum audience in marginal time with a sustaining program. This is so because so many stations on the network—any network—will decline to carry it. Every licensee who applies for a grant to operate in the public interest, convenience and necessity makes certain promises as to what he will do in terms of program content. Many recipients of licenses have, in blunt language, welshed on those promises. The money-making machine somehow blunts their memories. The only remedy for this is closer inspection and punitive action by the FCC. But in the view of many this would come perilously close to supervision of program content by a federal agency.

So it seems that we cannot rely on philanthropic support or foundation subsidies; we cannot follow the "sustaining route"—the networks cannot pay all the freight—and the FCC cannot or will not discipline those who abuse the facilities that belong to the public. What, then, is the answer? Do we merely stay in our comfortable nests, concluding that the obligation of these instruments has been discharged when we work at the job of informing the public for a minimum of time? Or do we believe that the preservation of the Republic is a seven-day-a-week job, demanding more awareness, better skills, and more perseverance than we have yet contemplated.

I am frightened by the imbalance, the constant striving to reach the largest possible audience for everything: by the absence of a sustained study of the state of the nation. Heywood Broun once said, "No body politic is healthy until it begins to itch." I would like television to produce some itching pills rather than this endless outpouring of tranquilizers. It can be done. Maybe it won't be, but it could. Let us not shoot the wrong piano player. Do not be deluded into believing that the titular heads of the networks control what appears on their networks. They all have better taste. All are responsible to stockholders, and in my experience all are honorable men. But they must schedule what they can sell in the public market.

And this brings us to the nub of the question. In one sense it rather revolves around the phrase heard frequently along Madison Avenue: The Corporate Image. I am not precisely sure what this phrase means, but I would imagine that it reflects a desire on the part of the corporations who pay the advertising bills to have the public image, or believe that they are not merely bodies with no souls, panting in pursuit of elusive dollars. They would like us to believe that they can distinguish between the public good and the private or corporate gain. So the question is this: Are the big corporations who pay the freight for radio and television programs wise to use that time exclusively for the sale of goods and services? Is it in their own interest and that of the stockholders so to do? The sponsor of an hour's television program is not buying merely the six minutes devoted to commercial message. He is determining, within broad limits, the sum total of the impact of the entire hour. If he always, invariably, reaches for the largest possible audience, then this process of insulation, of escape from reality, will continue to be massively financed, and its apologist will continue to make winsome speeches about giving the public what it wants, or "letting the public decide."

I refuse to believe that the presidents and chairmen of the boards of these big corporations want their corporate image to consist exclusively of a solemn voice in an echo chamber, or a pretty girl opening the door of a refrigerator, or a horse that talks. They want something better, and on occasion some of them have demonstrated it. But most of the men whose legal and moral responsibility it is to spend the stockholders' money for advertising are removed from the realities of the mass media by five, six, or a dozen contraceptive layers of vice-presidents, public relations counsel, and advertising agencies. Their business is to sell goods, and the competition is pretty tough.

But this nation is now in competition with malignant forces of evil who are using every instrument at their command to empty the minds of their subjects and fill those minds with slogans, determination and faith in the future. If we go on as we are, we are protecting the mind of the American public from any real contact with the menacing world that squeezes in upon us. We are engaged in a great experiment to discover whether a free public opinion can devise and direct methods of managing the affairs of the nation. We may fail. But we are handicapping ourselves needlessly.

Let us have a little competition. Not only in selling soap, cigarettes, and automobiles, but in informing a troubled, apprehensive, but receptive public. Why should not each of the 20 or 30 big corporations which dominate radio and television decide that they will give up one or two of their regularly scheduled programs each year, turn the time over to the networks and say in effect: "This is a tiny tithe, just a little bit of our profits. On this particular night we aren't going to try to sell cigarettes or automobiles; this is merely a gesture to indicate our belief in the importance of ideas." The networks should, and I think would, pay for the cost of producing the program. The advertiser, the sponsor, would get name credit but would have nothing to do with the content of the program. Would this blemish the corporate image? Would the stockholders object? I think not. For if the premise upon which our pluralistic society rests, which as I understand it is that if the people are given sufficient undiluted information, they will then somehow, even after long, sober second thoughts, reach the right decision—if that premise is wrong, then not only the corporate image but the corporations are done for.

There used to be an old phrase in this country, employed when someone talked too much. It was: "Go hire a hall." Under this proposal the sponsor would have hired the hall; he has bought the time; the local station operator, no matter how indifferent, is going to carry the program—he has to. Then it's up to the networks to fill the hall. I am not here talking about editorializing but about straightaway exposition as direct, unadorned, and impartial as fallible human beings can make it. Just once in a while let us exalt the importance of ideas and information. Let us dream to the extent of saying that on a given Sunday night the time normally occupied by Ed Sullivan is given over to a clinical survey of the state of American education, and a week or two later the time normally used by Steve Allen is devoted to a thorough-going study of American policy in the Middle East. Would the corporate image of their respective sponsors be damaged? Would the stockholders rise up in their wrath and complain? Would anything happen other than that a few million people would have received a little illumination on subjects that may well determine the future of this country, and therefore the future of the corporations? This method would also provide real competition between the networks as to which could outdo the others in the palatable presentation of information. It would provide an outlet for the young men of skill, and there are some even of dedication, who would like to do something other than devise methods of insulating while selling.

There may be other and simpler methods of utilizing these instruments of radio and television in the interests of a free society. But I know of none that could be so easily accomplished inside the framework of the existing commercial system. I don't know how you would measure the success or failure of a given program. And it would be hard to prove the magnitude of the benefit accruing to the corporation which gave up one night of a variety or quiz show in order that the network might marshal its skills to do a thorough-going job on the present status of NATO, or plans for controlling nuclear tests. But I would reckon that the president, and indeed the majority of shareholders of the corporation who sponsored such a venture, would feel just a little bit better about the corporation and the country.

It may be that the present system, with no modifications and no experiments, can survive. Perhaps the money-making machine has some kind of built-in perpetual motion, but I do not think so. To a very considerable extent the media of mass communications in a given country reflect the political, economic, and social climate in which they flourish. That is the reason ours differ from the British and French, or the Russian and Chinese. We are currently wealthy, fat, comfortable, and complacent. We have currently a built-in allergy to unpleasant or disturbing information. Our mass media reflect this. But unless we get up off our fat surpluses and recognize that television in the main is being used to distract, delude, amuse, and insulate us, then television and those who finance it, those who look at it and those who work at it, may see a totally different picture too late.

I do not advocate that we turn television into a 27-inch wailing wall, where longhairs constantly moan about the state of our culture and our defense. But I would just like to see it reflect occasionally the hard, unyielding realities of the world in which we live. I would like to see it done inside the existing framework, and I would like to see the doing of it redound to the credit of those who finance and program it. Measure the results by Nielsen, Trendex, or Silex—it doesn't matter. The main thing is to try. The responsibility can be easily placed, in spite of all the mouthings about giving the public what it wants. It rests on big business and on big television, and it rests at the top. Responsibility is not something that can be assigned or delegated. And it promises its own reward: good business and good television.

Perhaps no one will do anything about it. I have ventured to outline it against a background of criticism that may have been too harsh only because I could think of nothing better. Someone once said—I think it was Max Eastman—that "that publisher serves his advertiser best who best serves his readers." I cannot believe that radio and television, or the corporations that finance the programs, are serving well or truly their viewers or listeners, or themselves.

I began by saying that our history will be what we make it. If we go on as we are, then history will take its revenge, and retribution will not limp in catching up with us.

We are to a large extent an imitative society. If one or two or three corporations would undertake to devote just a small fraction of their advertising appropriation along the lines that I have suggested, the procedure would grow by contagion; the economic burden would be bearable, and there might ensue a most exciting adventure—exposure to ideas and the bringing of reality into the homes of the nation.

To those who say people wouldn't look; they wouldn't be interested; they're too complacent, indifferent, and insulated, I can only reply: There is, in one reporter's opinion, considerable evidence against that contention. But even if they are right, what have they got to lose? Because if they are right, and this instrument is good for nothing but to entertain, amuse, and insulate, then the tube is flickering now and we will soon see that the whole struggle is lost.

This instrument can teach, it can illuminate; yes, and it can even inspire. But it can do so only to the extent that humans are determined to use it to those ends. Otherwise it's nothing but wires and lights in a box. There is a great and perhaps decisive battle to be fought against ignorance, intolerance, and indifference. This weapon of television could be useful.

Stonewall Jackson, who knew something about the use of weapons, is reported to have said, "When war comes, you must draw the sword and throw away the scabbard." The trouble with television is that it is rusting in the scabbard during a battle for survival.

Credit

Speech by Edward R. Murrow to the 1958 Radio Television News Directors Association national convention, Chicago, Ill., October 15, 1958.

The Struggle Over Media Literacy

Justin Lewis and Sut Jhally

The argument we wish to make is, in essence, a simple one: media literacy should be about helping people to become sophisticated citizens rather than sophisticated consumers. The mass media, in other words, should be understood as more than a collection of texts to be deconstructed and analyzed so that we can distinguish or choose among them. They should be analyzed as sets of institutions with particular social and economic structures that are neither inevitable nor irreversible. Media education should certainly teach students to engage media texts, but it should also, in our view, teach them to engage and challenge media institutions.

Although we see textual analysis as an integral part of media education, we suggest that in any media system, the reason why we see some messages and not others raises the question of power and the active construction of the social world. Our arguments here are prompted by comments made by a pioneer in the U.S. media literacy movement, Renée Hobbs, following the National Media Literacy Conference held in Los Angeles in October 1996. Hobbs was concerned that "for some participants, media literacy has been either deliberately or accidentally conflated with activism around media reform issues." In her view, "it is inappropriate to lump media activism together with media literacy." Instead, she argued that "at the heart of the media literacy movement is the open, questioning, reflective, critical stance towards messages." Hobbs (1996) defined *media literacy* as "the process of accessing, critically analyzing media messages, and creating messages using media tools. The goal of media literacy is to promote autonomy through the development of analysis, reasoning, communication, and self-expression skills" (p. iii).

We argue that such avoidance of thorny political territory sidesteps widespread citizen concerns and misses an opportunity to demonstrate the valence and necessity of not merely understanding the world, but of changing it. In making this argument, we take our lead from the work of Len Masterman, for whom

> The democratization of institutions, and the long march toward a truly participatory democracy, will be highly dependent upon the ability of majorities of citizens to take control, become effective change agents, make rational decisions (often on the basis of media evidence), and to communicate effectively perhaps through an active involvement with the media. (Masterman, 1997, p. 60)

This is particularly important in a media system in which most messages are either explicitly or implicitly commercial—either straightforward advertisements or content designed to deliver audience to advertisers in the most efficient and profitable way (see Barnouw, 1978; Jhally 1990). The mass media may be producing art, but they are also producing commerce. We feel that it is impossible to understand one fully without comprehending the other. Unlike some of the more public service-oriented broadcasting systems in Europe and elsewhere, the goals of a loosely regulated, commercial media have no educational, cultural, or informational imperatives. As much of the literature on the political economy of the media suggests, they are there to maximize profits and to serve a set of corporate interests. These imperatives provide a framework that helps to shape both the form and content of media texts (Bagdikian, 1997; Granham, 1990; Herman & Chomsky, 1998; Schiller, 1984, 1989, 1996).

We therefore argue for a contextual approach to media education, one in which the media text is a stage in a process of ideological production. As Richard Johnson (1986–87) suggested in his classic introduction to British cultural studies: Although we may be able to distinguish between a series of analytical moments (i.e., production of text, the text itself, reception of text), we need to be able to understand the determinations and connections between them. Like Johnson, we urge those involved in media education to think of the circuit of cultural production.

In what follows, we first argue, as briefly as we can, for contextual rather than a text-centered approach. Such a perspective allows students to imagine ways of changing media systems and creates the possibility of a more democratic media. We next propose an emphasis on political economy in the face of the current trend towards text-centered approaches. Having stressed the importance of the production end of the circuit, we then consider the role in media education of teaching production skills. We conclude with a more practical consideration of the politics of media literacy, arguing against the pragmatism of text-centered approaches.

Textual Versus Contextual Approaches

The notion of literacy, particularly in relation to forms like television, is a complex one. The call for media education is in response not to a functionally illiterate media public, but to a public who are already voracious readers, viewers, and listeners.

Media literacy is more than a matter of basic comprehension. Few people, after all, need to be taught how to make sense of television or, in most cases, to appreciate its "preferred meanings" (Hall, 1980; Morley, 1980, 1986). On the contrary, the fact that so many have the ability to make sense of a barrage of disconnected, split-second images amidst a sophisticated range of realist conventions implies that—in one, restricted sense at least—a high degree of literacy already exists.

Media literacy is, therefore, more than a question of comprehension: It is concerned with the form and scope of that comprehension. Media literacy is not a simple matter of reading media well, whether in the traditional Leavisite sense (of distinguishing between "good" and "bad" texts, see Leavis, 1950), or in the more deconstructive sense of understanding textual strategies, possibilities, or pleasures (Barthes, 1974, 1975, 1988). There is more to media education than a framework for appreciating the finer nuances of the *Seinfeld* narrative, the montage of the opening credits of *ER*, or ways in which the extreme close-up shot in *60 Minutes* situates the spectator.

The distinction we would like to make is between a text-focused form of media literacy and a contextual approach, in which the unraveling of media texts takes place in the context of their production and reception. This is not to downplay the importance of textual analysis. It is at the level of the text, after all, that vital issues of representation are played out, and a sophisticated textual analysis can tell us something about both encoding and decoding (Hall, 1993). However, a textual analysis that takes place without examining the institutional, cultural, and economic conditions in which texts are produced and understood is necessarily limited.

Media literacy, in short, is about more than the analysis of messages, it is about an awareness of why those messages are there. It is not enough to know that they are produced, or even how, in a technical sense, they are produced. To appreciate the significance of contemporary media, we need to know why they are produced, under what constraints and conditions, and by whom.

Raymond Williams (1977) has documented the way in which early struggles over literacy were bound up with questions of power and control. In the early years of industry, workers were trained to read but not to write. This allowed them to follow orders or read the bible for moral instruction, but not to express their own needs or interests. Although contemporary television audiences are not so consciously deprived, their situation is in many ways analogous. They are expected to consume rather than produce—to pick from the display offered by commercial television rather than debate the terms and conditions in which broadcasting takes place.

We therefore need to differentiate between a text-centered approach that restricts itself to proficiency in reading and Williams' (1974, 1980) more general form of cultural criticism in which both the reading and the production of texts are understood within sets of social relations. So, for example, Janice Radway's (1994) work on romances and the Book of the Month Club engages with determinations at every stage in the circuit of production and reception.

As both Williams' (1974, 1980) and Radway's (1994) work suggests, an analysis of political economy should not be restricted to a narrow set of economic relations. The media are determined by a set of social and economic conditions that involve the key dividing lines of our culture, whether they be race, class, gender, sexuality, age, or mobility. This may be a complex point, but we are concerned that media education in the United States will flounder if it cannot locate media texts in a broad set of social realities.

Roland Barthes' (1977) well-known announcement of the Death of the Author is illustrative here. His argument is, in many ways, a celebration of textual analysis in which a focus on production or reception becomes a constraint on the practice of reading. Barthes' arguments works because he is engaged with a particular site (i.e., traditional literary criticism) in which the politics of production are less central. He is concerned with the way literary texts, many of which have been around for some time, are read and understood, not with the production, marketing, and distribution of contemporary fiction.

Media studies, on the other hand, is forced to deal with limits and constraints to explain absences, such as, for example, the comparative absence of a Black working class on U.S. television (Jhally & Lewis, 1992), and the consequences of those absences. To do so, it is required to go beyond the text.

If this contextual approach makes media literacy less "safe," it also makes it more enticing. So, for example, asking high school students to critique an advertisement by the Campaign for Drug Free America may or may not encourage a vague cynicism about how those in authority view (or attempt to situate) American youth. This kind of cynicism is, on its own, unhelpful to both high school students and their teachers. If the teacher is able to go beyond the text, to point out that the Campaign for Drug Free America is a consortium funded by America's leading alcohol, tobacco, and pharmaceutical companies (Cotts, 1992), the students are confronted with a more concrete political reality. The conclusions they draw may still be cynical but it is likely to be a more directed cynicism, one born of analysis rather than attitude. Students can do more than play textual games: they can question the rules.

Similarly, an analysis of the news should be concerned not only with the way stories are constructed, but also with who is not allowed to speak (Heman & Chomsky, 1998). A purely textual critique of television news is more speculative. For students to evaluate a news story seriously, they need to be able to go beyond the text, to consider the various stories that surround it, and thereby place it within a context that enables them to see the choices ABC or CNN have made.

Political Economy and Citizenship

If the political economy of the media seems a rather dry subject for students to consider, it need not be so. In our experience, students often find this level of analysis easier to grasp than a text-focused analysis. There is, in this respect, a healthy literature on political economy from which to draw (Bagdikian, 1997; Herman & McChesney, 1997; Schiller, 1984, 1989, 1996), much of which is extremely useful in allowing students to appreciate issues raised by a textual analysis. Pedagogically, this is less complex or arduous that it sounds. When automobile ads invariably show cars driving along empty roads, often across pristine landscapes with cloudless skies, we might ask students not only what is being left out of these images (traffic, pollution, smog), but why? In whose interest is it to see the automobile as a symbol of freedom, exploring rather than despoiling the United States landscape? What role do these interests have in media production? What are the consequences of seeing the automobile in only these terms?

Our experience indicates that students find it difficult to make sense of media messages as part of a vast, complex, and contradictory panorama made up of authorless ideologies. The politics of media texts become more tangible if they are seen as produced by real people for specific purposes. If this seems a perilously political approach, it is no less so than allowing students to see the media only on their own terms. It is a little like teaching a literary canon without allowing students to question the limits or foci of the canon. This is all the more troubling, perhaps, when the media canon is a product of purely commercial rationale.

This approach undoubtedly has political consequences. Just as political education allows citizens to think more critically and constructively about politics, media literacy can provide people with the wherewithal for thinking about the limits and possibilities of media systems. This is, needless to say, no small task, particularly in the United States, where exposure to foreign media is as limited as it is anywhere in the world.

U.S. broadcasting is highly distinctive. Unlike the public service models that influence broadcasting in most other industrialized countries, the history of radio and television in the U.S. is one of rampant commercialism (McAllister, 1996). In the United States, media corporations have, since the 1930s, been unusually successful in promoting an idea of broadcasting in economic rather than cultural terms, that is, as a business rather than a public service (McChesney, 1993). Media regulation in the U.S., particularly since the Reagan era, is conspicuous by its absence, yet many Americans find it difficult to imagine how it could be any other way.

This conceptual limitation has little to do with preference. Surveys do not suggest that Americans are especially happy or uncritical about television (Times Mirror, 1993). It is more a matter of education than imagination. It is difficult to propose changes to a system that is regarded as both inevitable and ubiquitous, and when the only alternative ever presented is the dull, propagandist fare of totalitarian regimes. Indeed, it could be argued that one of the successes of commercial broadcasting in the U.S. has been persuading Americans that there is no alternative and that the American system is the only conceivable model in a society that values free speech and free expression. The European concept of public service broadcasting, with its possibilities of public funding, cross subsidy, and regulations to promote education and diversity, remains as well-kept secret. If the British system is capable of offering a wide range of quality programs with a comparatively small number of channels, one can only imagine the breadth and range of a public service system in a country with a media market as large and bountiful as the United States.

As we have suggested, this implicates the notions of citizenship and cultural democracy. When the British government sanctioned a fourth network (Channel Four) at the beginning of the 1980s, it was at the center of a public debate about the funding, remit, regulation, and purpose of a new television network. Although some were critical of the scope of the discussion (Blanchard & Morley, 1982; Lambert, 1982), most recent changes in the North American broadcasting landscape have occurred with little or no public input. The lack of public debate surrounding the passage of the Telecommunications Act of 1996 is a graphic example of how a major restructuring of the media environment disappeared from public view. For us, what is most worrisome about this absence is less the lack of consultation and discussion than an ideological climate in which the public is so accustomed to being interpolated as mere consumers in a corporate world that any notion of democratic input seems difficult to grasp.

A brief anecdote told to us by our colleague, Michael Morgan, suggests the extent of the problem. During an exam students were asked to identify which type of media system was most common in countries worldwide: (a) a government-run or public service model or (b) a commercial model. Before the exam, students were told that when they came to this question, they should not even bother to read it, since the correct answer was "a." Despite this apparently unambiguous advice, half his students proceeded to get the answer wrong. This is not a question of dullness (the students preformed well enough overall), it suggests that the correct answer ran so counter to their own preconceptions that many disregarded not only what they had learned, but an answer they had just been told was correct. They were simply unable to imagine a world in which the U.S. model was atypical.

The blinkered, ideological assumptions behind this premise are fairly deep-rooted, and it will undoubtedly take more than a few media literacy classes to open American minds to other possibilities. Nevertheless, a media literacy curriculum in which issues of representation and content are taught alongside questions of political economy presents a challenge to regulators who have, in recent years, offered little more than the further deregulation of an already lightly regulated system. Debates about the regulation and subsidy of broadcasting can become public debates, rather than esoteric, lopsided discussions among media corporations, legislators, and a few poorly funded pressure groups.

Those currently campaigning for media reform—whether to regulate children's programming so that it is not simply a marketing vehicle for the toy industry, or for a viable public television service, or for restrictions to monopoly ownership—are stymied not because their ideas are unpopular, but because, at a fundamental level, their relevance is not appreciated. Americans have become used to a system of top-down control, where a citizen's input is restricted to being a blip in the Nielsen ratings and where commercial considerations are inexorably paramount. Media literacy is, therefore, a way of extending democracy to the very place where democracy is increasingly scripted and defined.

The Use and Abuse of Technology

If we have focused on political economy, it is because we see a danger of the circuit of cultural production and reception becoming excluded from the discussion. Our argument, nevertheless, it is not about teaching one thing rather than another, but about the integration of these levels of analysis. A focus on media production that excluded textual analysis would, in our view, be as problematic and fragmented as a purely text-centered approach.

In our experience, the way in which high school teachers may, without guidance, interpret the idea of media literacy suggests that this a particular risk when teachers are fortunate enough to have the technology for practical classes in media production. There are instances when the seductive and pseudo-empowering nature of the technology works to exclude both a broad political economy and a critical textual analysis (Frechette, 1997).

For teachers with access to cameras and editing facilities, this technology can be an indispensable component of an education practice that highlights the question of representation. As Stuart Ewen (1996) put it:

> Media literacy cannot simply be seen as a vaccination against PR or other familiar strains of institutionalized guile. It must be understood as an education in techniques that can democratize the realm of public expression and will magnify the possibility of meaningful public interactions. (p. 414)

In this ideal form, teaching production skills can be a vibrant part of a media literacy project. However, we would caution against any unthinking embrace. Although media production offers several pedagogical opportunities, it may close down as many analytical paths as it opens.

It is sometimes assumed, for example, that a practical knowledge of video production will help demystify the world of television and promote a more analytical, critical perspective. There is, however, little evidence to support such an assumption. To the contrary, we have found that students are apt to be seduced by the form, to try to imitate commercial television, and, when their efforts fall short, regard the work of professionals purely in terms of their aesthetic or technical prowess. At best, teaching production as purely a set of technical skills leads to an analytical immersion rather than a critical distance.

Unless the educational limits of teaching production are stressed, well-resourced schools might answer the call for media literacy simply by offering classes in media production. This would, in our view, blunt the critical edge of media literacy and allow it to be co-opted into a system of existing educational inequities. If media education is seen as dependent upon the purchase of video cameras and editing equipment, only those schools with sufficient means will be able to participate. Once media literacy is tied to the size of a school's capital budget, it risks becoming yet another symbol of cultural capital.

This is not to say that teaching production cannot or should not be a component of a media literacy project. It certainly is possible—even desirable—to incorporate production classes into a media literacy context, particularly with groups who already feel marginalized by mainstream media. The Educational Video Center in New York is a good example of such an initiative. Students were encouraged to use video technology to tell stories that are rarely heard on commercial television. This both enhances and develops their senses of critical reflection because they are not so much copying the medium as exploring its potential. This is possible because, at the EVC, production has been integrated into an overall theoretical approach that highlights the question of power.

The Politics of Media Literacy

As we have suggested, this approach to media education inevitably raises challenging political questions that, in some respects, it would be safer to avoid. Yet, we would argue, the feelings of frustration and dissatisfaction that many parents, teachers, and citizens feel is an explicitly political form of discontent—one that gives media literacy its sense of urgency and relevance.

Educators, whether parents or teachers, are tired of competing with television. They are tired of dismissing it as a mere distraction or else resenting it as the "evil twin" of universal education, the proverbial devil with little substance and all the best tunes. They are also tired of being offered the rather smug retort to their complaints that if parents or citizens are unhappy with what's offered, they can always turn it off. Most of us, after all, like watching what we consider to be worthwhile, informative, or entertaining. We don't want it to go away. Most educators are aware that the bumper-sticker invocation to "kill your television" has an ostrich-like impracticality. We want to improve it.

In the current political climate, the political options generally presented to deal with television have been, at best, fairly limited reactions to television's perceived excesses. Calls for censorship, boycotts, or parental control of television viewing via new technologies such as the V-chip all take a fairly negative stance, one in which the basic political economy of loosely regulated commercial television remains intact. If we are to have a television system whose goals have more to do with public service than commerce—whether that means a greater diversity of images and representations, less commercial interruption, more documentary programming, or more educational children's programs—we need to develop a citizenry that appreciates the politics of regulation and funding, to thereby imagine what television might be and how the system might be changed to make it so. The challenge for media literacy, we would argue, is to make this possibility seem less remote.

Conclusion

Whatever this desire for change involves, it will never be fully addressed by a text-centered approach to media education. The demands that give the campaign for media literacy a certain urgency require an approach that addresses questions about social context and social impact. Parents concerned about violence or gender stereotyping in children's programs are unlikely to be mollified by the thought that the Power Rangers can be read on a number of different levels, or even that their children may eventually come to understand the limits of such stereotypes. They want to know what influence such programming may have and how media producers might be persuaded to offer something less pernicious. They are, in short, concerned not just with the nature of the visual environment, but the forces that shape it. A contextual approach to media literacy allows students to see the media within a framework of interests and power relations. If some see a danger here of making media literacy an overtly political project, we take the opposite view. A text-centered approach that fails to address current concerns and dissatisfaction with the media risks losing the political impetus that gives it its current purchase.

For the past four years we have been involved with the Five-College Media Literacy Institute, which introduces teachers to the field of media literacy from the contextual, cultural studies perspective we have briefly outlined. As many in the field are aware, when teachers return to their schools there is little financial, pedagogical, or structural support for the integration of critical questions around media into the existing curriculum. Creating these supportive environments is a political task, one that, as Wally Bowen (1994) argues with unapologetic vigor, needs to

> connect to the interests and concerns of a broad range of scholars, teachers, health educators, parents, and citizens who are seeking ways to critically challenge a media system that exploits children, reduces citizens to consumers, rewards those who poison public discourse, and perpetuates a high-consumption lifestyle that is slowly strangling the planet's life-support systems. (p. 2)

The implementation of media literacy as component of the K–12 curriculum will require enthusiastic community support. If a text-centered approach seems the politically safer option, it is also one, in our view, that is less likely to enthuse teachers and parents.

We acknowledge, however, that a contextual approach with an emphasis on political economy is likely to be less acceptable to some elements within the media literacy coalition than a text-centered approach. Indeed, there is no doubt that advocates for a certain form of text-centered media literacy have been successful in broadening support for media education, and there is certainly an argument that such pragmatism may be more likely to lead to the widespread implementation of media literacy.

As we have stated, this risks diluting the enthusiasm created by the desire for a public voice in decisions about media programming. The rush to embrace media literacy may also lead to its suffocating under the weight of its own incoherence. Even the commercial media industry—perhaps sensing that, in a period of minimal political interference or regulation, the only real danger to its unrestricted growth and profit maximization is a critically informed public—is moving to initiate its own version.

Thus, in the inaugural issue of *Better Viewing* magazine, Continental Cablevision (now MediaOne) invokes media literacy and the general empowerment of its viewers. In this self-serving appropriation, informed citizenship means little more than a weekly perusal of *TV Guide*. It is safe to assume that Continental Cablevision's notion of empowerment does not extend to the regulation of media monopolies or subversive notions about public service broadcasting (Cowie, 1995).

If this attempted colonization is breathtaking in its audacity, it is possible because the phrase itself, with its irresistible invocation of the most basic of skills, is noncommittal on how it applies to the comprehension of mass media. Norman Cowie (1996) described how, in the United States,

> there is an uneasy consensus among media literacy proponents around a definition that was formulated in Canada in 1989, as "the ability to access, analyze, communicate and produce media in a variety of forms." While this definition appears to serve as a rallying point for coalition building, there is a decided lack of consensus around its terms and practices. (p. 1)

In the face attempts to build up a critical mass of reform, it is not surprising that the media literacy movement has avoided hard questions and debate around its core concerns. This avoidance of principle, however, comes at a price. It risks sapping the movement's vitality and replacing it with a vapid ambiguity.

Our advocacy of a contextual approach of media education is influenced by our experience of teaching these issues at the college level, where media analysis thrives in several disciplines in the humanities and liberal arts. The bureaucratic and political contexts of the K–12 situation are very different, and it is easy to see why a more limited, text-based "visual literacy" worked so well in the confines of this environment. As Wally Bowen (1994) put it:

> The inherent conservatism of U.S. public school bureaucracies discourages the broader examination of media culture inherent in a cultural studies approach with its emphasis on questions of political economy, power relations, hegemonic influence. ... The conventional wisdom said that entry into the politically charged minefield of the public school curriculum is achieved by slipping media literacy into the language arts "critical skills" curriculum. (pp. 1–2)

This defensive posture is perfectly understandable in those places where there is little existing institutional support to create an entirely new field. It has also led to the uneasy consensus that Cowie (1996) described among a disparate group of interests. When your numbers are small, why separate over internal doctrinaire disputes? The sheer scale of the U.S. educational system has meant that the focus on diversity of approaches, which Hobbs (1996) argued is the strength of the media literacy, is also our greatest weakness. We would argue with Cowie that "the pluralism that underwrites this diversity has had a depoliticizing effect on the very issues that media literacy seeks to address" and that "when one surveys the work that has been accomplished on the basis of a meaningful consensus in countries such as Canada, Western Europe and Australia, it is difficult to feel that our enduring lack of a consensus is viable" (p. 1).

For us, the risk lies in depriving students of a political education that is essential if they are to be capable of making rational decisions amidst a deluge of media messages. To evaluate those messages, students must learn to see them not simply as true or false, realistic or misleading, stereotypical or positive, but as authored voices with certain interests or assumptions about the world, voices that could be influenced or replaced. As Noam Chomsky (1989) noted: "Citizens of the democratic societies should undertake a course of intellectual self-defense to protect themselves from manipulation and control, and to lay the basis for meaningful democracy" (p. viii). It is important to note that we are not advocating propagandizing in schools for a particular political perspective. We are advocating a view that recognizes that the world is always made by someone, and a decision to tolerate the status quo is as political as a more overtly radical act.

Works Cited

Bagdikian, B. (1997). *The Media Monopoly.* Boston: Beacon Press.

Barnouw, E. (1978). *The Sponsor: Notes on a Modern Potentate.* New York: Oxford University Press.

Barthes, R. (1974). *S/Z.* New York: Hill & Wang.

Barthes, R. (1975). *The Pleasure of the Text.* London: Jonathon Cape.

Barthes, R. (1977). *Image-Music-Text.* Glasgow, Scotland: Fontana.

Barthes, R. (1988). *Mythologies.* New York: Noonday Press.

Blanchard, S., & Morley, D. (1982). *What's this Channel Four?* London: Comedia.

Bowen, W. (1994). "Can U.S. media literacy movement open door to more points of view?" *The New Citizen, 2*(1). (http:/www.main.nc.us/cml/new_citzen/v2n1/win94c.html).

Chomsky, N. (1989). *Necessary Illusions: Thought Control in Democratic Societies.* Boston, MA: South End Press.

Cotts, C. (1992). "Hard sell in the drug war." *The Nation,* 300–303.

Cowie, N. (Summer/Fall, 1995). "The future of media literacy in the age of corporate sponsorship." *Video & Learning,* 5–6.

Cowie, N. (1996, May 9). "Media literacy: From the Creation of 'Critical Consumers' to the Formation of (Radical) Political Subjects." Paper presented at the conference on Alliance for Community Media, Burlington, VT.

Ewen, S. (1996). *PR: A Social History of Spin.* New York: Basic Books.

Frechette, J. (1997). "The Politics of Implementing Media Literacy into the United States: A Look at the Objectives and Obstacles Facing the Massachusetts Public School Teacher." Unpublished master's thesis, Department of Communication, University of Massachusetts at Amherst.

Hall, S. (1980) "Encoding/Decoding." In S. Hall, D. Hobson, A. Lowe, & P. Willis (Eds.). *Culture, Media, Language* (128–138). London: Hutchinson.

Hall, S. (1994). "Reflections upon the encoding/decoding model: An interview with Stuart Hall." In J. Cruz & J. Lewis (Eds.), *Viewing, Reading, Listening: Audiences and Cultural Reception* (253–274). Boulder, CO: Westview.

Herman E., & Chomsky, N. (1988). *Manufacturing Consent: The Political Economy of the Mass Media.* New York: Pantheon.

Herman, E., & McChesney, R. (1997). *The Global Media: The New Missionaries of Corporate Capitalism.* London: Cassell.

Hobbs, R. (1996). "Media literacy, media activism." *Telemedium, The Journal of Media Literacy, 42*(3).

Garnham, N. (1990). *Capitalism and Communication.* London: Sage.

Jhally, S. (1990). *The Codes of Advertising: Fetishism and the Political Economy of Meaning in the Consumer Society.* New York: Routledge.

Jhally, S., & Lewis, J. (1992). *Enlightened Racism: Audiences, the Cosby Show and the Myth of the American Dream.* Boulder, CO: Westview.

Johnson, R. (1986–87). "What is cultural studies anyway?" *Social Text, 16,* 38–80.

Lambert, S. (1982). *Channel 4: Television with a Difference?* London: British Film Institute.

Leavis, R. (1950). *The Great Tradition: George Eliot, Henry James, Joseph Conrad.* London: Chatto & Windus.

Masterman, L. (1997). "A rationale for media education." In R. Kubey (Ed.), *Media Literacy in the Information Age* (15–68). New Brunswick, NJ: Transaction.

McAllister, M. (1996). *The Commercialisation of American Culture: New Advertising, Control and Democracy*. Thousand Oaks, CA: Sage.

McChesney, R. (1993). *Telecommunications, Mass Media and Democracy: The Battle for the Control of U.S. Broadcasting 1928–1935.* New York: Oxford University Press.

Morley, D. (1980). *The Nationwide Audience.* London: British Film Institute.

Morley, D. (1986). *Family Television*. London: Comedia.

Radway, J. (1994). "Romance and the work of fantasy: Struggles over feminine sexuality and subjectivity at century's end." In J. Cruz & J. Lewis (Eds.), *Viewing, Reading, Listening: Audiences and Cultural Reception.* Boulder, CO: Westview.

Schiller, H. (1996). *Information Inequality: The Deepening Social Crisis in America.* New York: Routledge.

Schiller, H. (1984). *Information and the Crisis Economy.* Norwood, NJ: Ablex.

Schiller H. (1989). *Culture Inc.: The Corporate Takeover of Public Expression.* New York: Oxford University Press.

Times Mirror Center for the People and the Press (1993, March 24). Poll.

Williams, R. (1974). *Television, Technology and Cultural Form.* London: Fontana.

Williams, R. (1977). *Marxism and Literature.* New York: Columbia University Press.

Williams, R. (1980). *Problems in Materialism and Culture.* London: New Left Books.

Credit

Lewis, Justin, and Sut Jhally. "The Struggle Over Media Literacy." *Journal of Communication* Dec. 1998: 109 – 20. Print. *Journal of Communication* is published by National Society for the Study of Communication; International Communication Association; Annenberg School of Communications.

The Culture of Shut Up

Jon Lovett

This essay is adapted from a speech given at Loyola Marymount University on February 11, 2014, during its annual First Amendment Week.

Too many debates about important issues degenerate into manufactured and misplaced outrage—and it's chilling free speech.

There once was a remote village deep in the rainforest that had no contact with the outside world. And in this small village there were only three village elders who had the ability to speak. So they were in charge. And they'd have arguments. One would say, "I support a woman's right to choose." Another would say, "I oppose a woman's right to choose." And then the third would say, "A real debate here on a woman's right to choose. When we come back, Justin Bieber arrested!"

Now if you were one of the many villagers who didn't have a way to speak, you just hoped that one of the three elders who could speak would make the argument you wanted to make. Sometimes they did, sometimes they didn't. And it was okay, but it bothered you that these three voices didn't really speak for everybody. They were, after all, pretty rich and all one color. (Green. These were green people.) And they didn't really understand what it was like to be aqua or purple or gay or poor like you were. You're a gay poor purple person. They tried to cover the whole world, but generally they focused on what was on the minds of green people from the big cities who watched *Mad Men* and went to Middlebury.

And even as the elders spoke with confidence and seriousness, it felt like they kept getting it wrong. They invaded neighboring villages, occasionally the wrong village altogether. They trusted the CEOs of the village banks even after they plunged the village into a Great Village Recession and then went right back to village business as usual as if it never happened. They built a massive village prison system that punished non-violent village offenders at higher rates than anywhere else in the rainforest.

They rigged the village economy against the interests of ordinary villagers in favor of those with close ties to the three elders, those who had donated money to their village campaigns, lobbied their village offices.

Then one day you found this rock and you realized that you could use the rock to write on a leaf. And so you developed a written language and taught it to everyone. And at the big village meetings, when the three elders at the front would have their arguments, villagers could participate. People would write things like, "I agree with you and appreciate your position." Or "I hope you get cancer and die." Or "Here's a picture of what I ate for lunch." Or "Please stop drawing pictures of food, no one cares what you ate for lunch." Or "Check out this cat in a shoebox because adorable."

But it turned out by the time we finally had this great way to communicate in our hands, we were already so angry and suspicious that the rock and leaf became a way to vent our frustrations not just at the elders but at each other.

Bill says, "I support single-payer village healthcare."

And then Mary writes, "Bill is a faggot communist."

And then Ted says, "I won't shop at Mary's boutique until Mary apologizes to Bill."

Then Angela says, "Stand with Mary against the assault on her freedom of speech!"

And then Bill says, "Angela is a racist."

And Jeff says, "Anyone who shops at Mary's boutique is a racist."

And Ted says, "Check your privilege."

And Mary says, "I don't remember who I am in this story but I'm furious."

And then someone writes, "FUCKK YOU TED!!1!" in all caps with a bunch of typos.

Soon there were really only two kinds of messages people would write—either vicious personal attacks, or self-righteous calls for apology—until eventually the villagers, angry and exhausted and sick of the noise and rancor just started pelting each other with the rocks until all the rocks were broken and all the leaves were shredded and finally in the silence, after the dust had settled, the villagers shrugged their shoulders, and turned back toward the smug and satisfied village elders who were just waiting for their chance to regain supremacy—just waiting for the moment when the villagers would come crawling back, desperate to be led, desperate for the reassuring simplicity of the old order, of the establishment, of the way things used to be.

ૡ૱ૡ૱ૡ૱

And that's the story of that village.

Anyway, I was thinking about the First Amendment and the freedom of speech, and what lessons I could draw on my time in politics, working for then-Senator Hillary Clinton and our first foreign-born president, Barack Obama, and I kept coming back to a quote by Homer Simpson. Now when I Googled this quote it turned out to be from 1997, which made me realize I am reaching the age when my references stop at a certain year in the culture, and that while you know the *Simpsons*, that episode aired just after today's college freshmen were born and the fact is eventually we all return to the earth.

Anyway, Homer Simpson once said that alcohol is the cause of, and solution to, all of life's problems. And I kept thinking: That's actually a pretty good description of the Internet and how it's changing our discourse. It's basically the cause of, and solution to, everything that plagues our culture.

That's an exaggeration, of course. The Internet didn't cause Donald Trump, and it certainly can't solve Donald Trump. The way you defeat Donald Trump is by getting the ring of power into the hands of a pure soul, a hobbit, say, and that hobbit must journey to Mount Doom and release the ring into its fires. But the Internet: Did you know that every single day, the Internet produces more speech than was created between the dawn of civilization and the year 2006? You didn't know that, because I just made it up. But it feels true. We are all bombarded. We are drowning in information. It's no longer thrown on our doorstep each sunrise, or even just broadcast into our living rooms; it's in our hands every waking hour; the endless stream of talking, as we spend all day moving our eyes from screen to screen to screen; it's the first thing we see each morning and the last thing we see before we go to bed. The shower is the last safe space, which is why it's the only place where we have decent ideas anymore.

In many ways this is good and getting better: We have unlocked the gates and we are removing the gatekeepers. We aren't beholden to the views of the three green elders in the village. (See, I tied it back.) But what happens next—how we face the downside of so much connectedness—will determine whether or not this revolution empowers us, or once again empowers those gatekeepers. And I don't want that to happen, because those gatekeepers suck. They're arrogant and easily swayed by big, nice-sounding dangerous ideas; they're ambitious and careerist and forgetful and unimaginative and shortsighted; they're subject to groupthink, beholden to corporate interests, and enamored of fame and power.

I don't want those voices to drown out the diverse and compelling voices that now have a better chance of making it in front of us than ever before—even as we still have a ways to go. And what I think we have to do, then, to protect this new wonderful thing of "a good idea can come from anyone anywhere"—is we need to stop telling each other to shut up. We need to get comfortable with the reality that no one is going to shut up. You aren't going to shut up. I'm not going to shut up. The idiots aren't going to shut up.

We need to learn to live with the noise and tolerate the noise even when the noise is stupid, even when the noise is offensive, even when the noise is at times dangerous. Because no matter how noble the intent, it's a demand for conformity that encourages people on all sides of a debate to police each other instead of argue and convince each other. And, ultimately, the cycle of attack and apology, of disagreement and boycott, will leave us with fewer and fewer people talking more and more about less and less.

In the past week, the CEO of Mozilla, Brendan Eich, one of the company's co-founders, was forced to resign over his support for Proposition 8, the anti-gay marriage law that passed in a 2008 California referendum before it was later struck down by the courts. But this is only the most recent example.

Here's a list of some other people who were told to shut up, off the top of my head:

The Chick-fil-A guy was told to shut up[1] about gay people.

Martin Bashir was told to shut up about Sarah Palin.

Paula Deen was told to shut up by everyone because her stuff was racist and crazy.

A columnist in the *Guardian* told a woman to shut up[2] about her cancer.

Dylan Farrow was told to shut up about Woody Allen.

Stephen Colbert was told to shut up about satire, I think?

The *Duck Dynasty*[3] guy was told to shut up about gay people.

Alex Wagner was told to shut up about needlepoint[4].

Natasha Legerro[5] was told to shut up about veterans.

Alec Baldwin was also told to shut up about gay people. This one comes up a lot.

Mike Huckabee was told to shut up about women.

The Whole Foods CEO was told to shut up about Obamacare.

Richard Sherman was told to shut up about winning while being black, I guess.

I am not comparing what these people were told to shut up about, or saying some of these examples aren't offensive or stupid or vicious or wrong, often combinations of any or all of those things. And the truth is, these cycles of pearl-clutching followed by either abject sorrow or banishment are of course driven by news outlets looking to score a few hits or viewers by drumming up controversy.

But they're also driven by us, as viewers and readers, all of us part of the culture of shut up. It plays out in the defining down of "hate speech" on liberal college campuses and in the defining down of "anti-American" at conservative conferences. And for every public example there are countless private ones, playing out on Facebook pages and Twitter feeds and I guess Pinterest? I don't get Pinterest.

Yes, it's in some ways a natural response to being more connected to one another; we're just in each other's faces. But it's also dangerous. It narrows the visible spectrum of ideas. It encourages people to be safe and cautious and circumspect when we don't want people to be safe. We don't want people to be afraid of saying something interesting on the off chance it's taken the wrong way.

When the *Duck* person said his crazy thing about the sins of the gays and how nice things were during Jim Crow—which was just wild[6]—Sarah Palin (who maybe didn't know better) and Governor Bobby Jindal (who definitely knew better) said it was a violation of the his First Amendment rights. And it wasn't, obviously. The government wasn't removing anyone from the air. A&E under pressure from GLAAD and others considered removing a reality-show persona from the air. So it wasn't a First Amendment issue and the fact that that has to be said out loud should make all of us sad. But that doesn't mean there aren't speech issues at stake here, which is at the heart of conservatives' complaint.

The right to free speech may begin and end with the First Amendment, but there is a vast middle where our freedom of speech is protected by us—by our capacity to listen and accept that people disagree, often strongly, that there are fools, some of them columnists and elected officials and, yes, even reality-show patriarchs, that there are people who believe stupid, irrational, hateful things about other people and it's okay to let those words in our ears sometimes without rolling out the guillotines.

Look, obviously there's an important counter-argument here. It is natural and healthy that as a society we have deemed certain ideas off-limits. While in this country the government can't stop you from saying these things, or punish you for having said those things, it's often good that the personal, financial, and social costs of saying the unsayable are prohibitively high. We all can name examples: hardcore racism and anti-Semitism and misogyny, *Breaking Bad* spoilers, that kind of thing. And it's also true that hurtful words about, say, gay people have a disproportionate impact on the vulnerable; it's easy for me to say *bring on the homophobia,* but what about the kid in the closet in a conservative neighborhood worried his mom will stumble onto his browser history?

The trouble, I think, is when ostracizing a viewpoint as "beyond the pale" becomes not an end but a means to an end; that by declaring something unsayable, we make it so. It makes me uncomfortable, even as I see the value of it. I for one would love homophobia to fully make it on that list, to get to the point where being against gay marriage is as vulgar and shameful as being against interracial marriage. But it isn't. Maybe it will be. But it isn't. And kicking a reality-show star off his reality show doesn't make that less true. Win the argument; don't declare the argument too offensive to be won. And that's true whether it's GLAAD making demands of A&E or the head of the Republican National Committee making demands of MSNBC.

The bottom line is, you don't beat an idea by beating a person. You beat an idea by beating an idea. Not only is it counter-productive—nobody likes the kid who complains to the teacher even when the kid is right—it replaces a competition of arguments with a competition to delegitimize arguments. And what's left is the pressure to sand down the corners of your speech while looking for the rough edges in the speech of your adversaries. Everyone is offended. Everyone is offensive. Nothing is close to the line because close to the line is over the line because over the line is better for clicks and retweets and fundraising and ad revenue.

It's like a financial bubble. It's a bubble of subprime outrage and subprime apologies. I just hope we can rationalize the market before this chilling effect leaves us with a discourse more boring and monotone than it already is—a discourse that suits the cable networks and the politicians but not the many disparate voices who occasionally need to say outrageous things because there are outrageous things to say.

And there are real consequences to the outrage bubble. When Congress was debating the debt ceiling, one of the sticking points was a set of changes to the military-pension system. You don't even have to take a position on these changes to say that it's a reasonable debate: whether we should save money in the defense budget by reducing the rate of increase in pension benefits received by veterans who are younger than retirement age.

The bottom line is, you don't beat an idea by beating a person. You beat an idea by beating an idea.

Agree, disagree, you're not crossing the line, right? Wrong: Supporting this proposal is described, over and over again, as "sick" and "obscene"[7] and "offensive."[8] Do we really want to make policy this way? Do we want our already timid and craven elected officials to have even more to fear?

I'll be honest: In my own small way I feel the chilling effect. I'm in a fortunate position that nobody really cares what I say, but even so, occasionally I'll make a dumb joke on Twitter and the next thing I know it's on a whole bunch of conservative websites that exist to catch liberals crossing the line. As much as I can pretend otherwise, I'd be lying if I said it didn't make me hold back just a little, doubt myself a little, on occasion. And while it's hard to measure the absence of speech, measure the things unsaid, I have little doubt that others on all sides are feeling the same chilling effect, only more so because people do care what they have to say.

The First Amendment's protections have always put a great deal of responsibility in our hands: not only to respect the power of our own speech, but also to respect that same power in the hands of people we despise. We all have more of that power now. And I for one think that's great. Yes, there are those who would say otherwise. David Brooks says we have a "followership problem,"[9] that our lack of trust in institutions is less caused by their poor performance than by the fact we are "cynical and like to pretend that [we're] better than everything else around [us.]" "Vanity," he says, "has more to do with rising distrust than anything else." Maureen Dowd talks[10] about the "nightmare" of an America that "runs on clicks."

I should go beyond the *New York Times* op-ed page but those were just the most annoying examples I remembered. But there are many others—big platforms all—who would tell us to fear the future, to fear the havoc the Internet is wreaking on journalism, to fear a world in which every event, every public utterance must face the gauntlet of Twitter and Facebook. They'd suggest the cacophony of links and hits and likes and retweets, the triumph of the buzzworthy and the Upworthy, are no replacement for a few trusted outlets—the nightly news, major newspapers, weekly magazines, etc.—that everyone experienced together.

I reject this argument. And I reject it for the simple reason that all the chaos and competition is worth it—for all its many downsides, for all the garbage and gossip—if a few loud voices no longer control the story. But that only works if we don't try to replace one tyranny with another, one narrow band of views with another narrow band of views, if we can live with the noise, even embrace the noise, without trying to drown each other out.

Notes

1 Jonathan Merritt, "In Defense of Eating at Chick-fil-A," *The Atlantic*, July 20, 2012, http://www.theatlantic.com/politics/archive/2012/07/in-defense-of-eating-at-chick-fil-a/260139/

2 Megan Garber, "On Live-Tweeting One's Suffering," *The Atlantic*, January 13, 2014, http://www.theatlantic.com/technology/archive/2014/01/on-live-tweeting-ones-suffering/283013/

3 Conor Friedersdorf, "A *Duck Dynasty* Solution for A&E: Phil Robertson Should Debate Dan Savage," *The Atlantic*, December 27, 2013, http://www.theatlantic.com/politics/archive/2013/12/a-em-duck-dynasty-em-solution-for-a-e-phil-robertson-should-debate-dan-savage/282668/

4 Matt Wilstein, "Megyn Kelly and Guests Go After Alex Wagner's 'Blatantly Sexist' Tweet," *Mediaite*, January 29, 2014, http://www.mediaite.com/tv/megyn-kelly-and-guests-go-after-alex-wagners-blatantly-sexist-tweet/

5 Ashley Lee, "Natasha Leggero 'Not Sorry' for Joke About Pearl Harbor Veterans," *The Hollywood Reporter*, January 3, 2014, http://www.hollywoodreporter.com/live-feed/natasha-leggero-not-sorry-joke-668443

6 Jonathan Merritt, "The Real *Duck Dynasty* Scandal: Phil Robertson's Comments on Race," *The* Atlantic, December 19, 2014, http://www.theatlantic.com/politics/archive/2013/12/the-real-em-duck-dynasty-em-scandal-phil-robertsons-comments-on-race/282538/

7 Wanda Carruthers, "Scarborough: Military Retirement Cuts are 'Sick' and 'Obscene'," *Newsmax*, December 18, 2013, http://www.newsmax.com/Newsfront/obscene-scarborough-budget-military/2013/12/18/id/542534/

8 Patricia Kime, "Pensions Slashed Under Budget Bill Provision," *Army Times*, December 23, 2013, http://www.armytimes.com/article/20131223/BENEFITS/312300001/Pensions-slashed-under-budget-bill-provision

9 David Brooks, "The Follower Problem," *The New York Times*, June 11, 2012, http://www.nytimes.com/2012/06/12/opinion/brooks-the-follower-problem.html?_r=0

10 Maureen Dowd, "Still Mad as Hell," *The New York Times*, February 8, 2014, http://www.nytimes.com/2014/02/09/opinion/sunday/dowd-still-mad-as-hell.html

Credit

The Future of Free Speech

Tim Wu

In 1930, a man named Daniel Lord wrote a Production Code for American motion pictures. He included specific prohibitions: "Dances suggesting indecent passions," he wrote, "are forbidden." But Lord's general point was to ensure that American films didn't glorify that which was morally wrong and that they always had a happy ending. Movies would be a source of uplift. "No picture shall be produced," he wrote, "that will lower the moral standards of those who see it."

Lord wasn't a government censor. Rather, he was a Roman Catholic priest dedicated to the elimination of "filth." Nonetheless, his code—with all of its ambitions of thought control—became one of the most effective regulations on speech in American history, more potent than any law or government program. Lord was successful in large part because the industry imposed his code on itself. The consolidation of the film industry in the 1930s concentrated power in a handful of studios, making them vulnerable to boycotts, ultimately leading to acts of self-censorship.

Americans, who have long mistrusted government, are acutely aware of and sensitive to public censorship—more so, perhaps, than any other nation. There is a strong First Amendment tradition in the courts. But Americans tend to be much less concerned with the danger of private censorship. That's too bad, because the greatest dangers to free speech in the future will come not from government interference but from speech monopolists. That has been true for much of the 20th century, and while it seems hard to imagine now, it could become the fate of the Internet.

Before we get to the future of the Internet, let's go back and see what made Lord's 1930 speech code so effective. Various censors—government and private—had been interested in controlling the content of film since the medium became popular in the 1900s. But the results were mixed. The film industry was disaggregated. There were hundreds of producers and thousands of independent theaters, and men like Lord realized that trying to police so many producers in so many places was futile.

All of that changed in the 1930s. By then, the major studios, which had moved from New York to Hollywood, had integrated production facilities and theater chains, and ruled the once unruly film industry. These studios were vastly more efficient, borrowing methods from Andrew Carnegie and Henry Ford. They produced longer films of better quality, like *King Kong* (1933) and *Gone With the Wind* (1939). The integration of every aspect of film production—from the theaters to the actors and directors—made possible a new era of motion pictures.

Industrial consolidation, in short, gave rise to the classic Hollywood blockbuster. But it also greatly reduced the number of people necessary to control the content of American film. That, in turn, made the industry vulnerable to directed boycotts—which it suffered, at the hands of the "Legion of Decency," a Catholic advocacy group organized to put censorial pressure on the American film industry. The boycotts succeeded, and the studios agreed that every American script would be turned over to a Catholic censor named Joseph Breen for review before production—what the law calls a "prior restraint." As *Liberty* magazine wrote in 1936, this arrangement left Breen with "more influence in standardizing world thinking than Mussolini, Hitler, or Stalin."

The impact of industrial consolidation on speech was not confined to the film industry. In the 1920s, American radio was extraordinarily diverse, a medium, not unlike the early Internet, where it was easy to establish a presence—and hundreds of people did. "A list of all that can be heard with a radio receiver anywhere within 300 miles of greater New York would fill a book," *Radio News* reported in 1922. Amateurs, churches, motorcycle clubs, and universities owned the majority of stations, and radio was how, for example, jazz music first reached white audiences.

By the 1930s, however, most of the nation's radio stations, with the help of the federal government, belonged to one of two networks: NBC or CBS. They delivered higher-quality programming, thanks in part to the advent of advertising. In fact, most radio content was actually produced not by the networks themselves but by advertising firms, who created the concept of "entertainment that sells." The notion of purely public broadcasting would not return to radio until the 1960s.

This may sound like ancient history, but it's very relevant today. We are living in an age where a decreasing number of firms serve as a kind of Master Switch over speech on the Internet—think Google, Facebook, the cable industry, and the major telephone carriers.

These firms are already under strong pressure to censor from powerful governments, religious groups, political parties, and essentially any outfit with a reason to want information suppressed. The Turkish government, for example, demands that Google take down mockery of the nation's founder, not just in Turkey, but everywhere. The Church of Scientology has never stopped demanding of anyone who will listen to remove criticism of its practices from the Internet, usually claiming copyright infringement.

On a daily basis, as we speak, Internet companies are making speech-related decisions more important than those made by any government. YouTube, for instance, has to constantly decide what to censor. Generally, it blocks copyright infringements on request and pornography without request, and it listens to some but not all of the demands of governments. Facebook, for its part, has been tested less, but it has been willing to delete user-generated content at the request of governments, like Pakistan and Bangladesh.

This is what speech management looks like in 2010. No one elected Facebook or YouTube, and neither one is beholden to the First Amendment. Nonetheless, it is their decisions that dictate, effectively, who gets heard. What's the answer? There is no easy answer. Monopolies like Google, Facebook, and Hollywood have certain advantages: That's why they tend to come into existence. That means the American public needs to be aware of the dangers that private censors can pose to free speech. The American Constitution was written to control abuses of power, but it didn't account for the heavy concentration of private power that we see today. And in the end, power is power, whether in private or public hands.

Credit

The Fall and Rise of Partisan Journalism

James L. Baughman

This article is adapted from Prof. Baughman's presentation at the University of Wisconsin-Madison's 3rd annual Journalism Ethics conference in April of 2011.

(ornament)

You don't need to have a degree in history—or even to have paid much attention when you suffered the U.S. history survey course as an undergraduate—to know that American newspapers were very partisan in the 19th century. "Editors," wrote one historian, "unabashedly shaped the news and their editorial comment to partisan purposes. They sought to convert the doubters, recover the wavering, and hold the committed. 'The power of the press,' one journalist candidly explained, 'consists not in its logic or eloquence, but in its ability to *manufacture* facts, or to give coloring to facts that have occurred.'"[1]

Party newspapers gave one-sided versions of the news. Papers in opposition to Andrew Jackson in 1828 attacked him for marrying a woman before her divorce had been finalized. He was the violator of marital virtue, a seducer. Jackson, one paper declared, "tore from a husband the wife of his bosom." Pro-Jackson newspapers insisted on the general's innocence, and accused his critics of violating his privacy. There was no objective, middle ground.[2]

Stories that might flatter the opposition went unreported—or under-reported. As one historian observed, "The truth was not suppressed. It was simply hard to get in any one place."[3] When Democrat Grover Cleveland won the presidency in 1884, the Republican *Los Angeles Times* simply failed to report this unhappy result for several days.[4]

Newspaper economics partly explained why, as one veteran editor observed in 1873, the press "was bound to party."[5] Before the Civil War, parties actually subsidized the operations of many newspapers. Sometimes directly, sometimes through government printing contracts. In many cases, the subsidies were indirect and unknown to readers.

Editors or their reporters worked part time for state legislators or members of Congress. Some of these relationships continued late into the 19th century. Needless to say, they were not terribly ethical.

Journalism historians, including our School's founder, Willard Bleyer, regarded the party press as a bad thing. Bleyer fervently believed newspapers had an obligation to educate the citizenry on matters of public policy. A biased news medium was bad for a self-governing people.

Although Bleyer reflected the views of several generations of journalism historians, more recent work has broken with this consensus. Gerald Baldasty and others argue that the party papers encouraged democratic participation, that they treated readers as citizens and voters, not passive observers. Declared the Worchester (Mass.) *Spy* in 1832, "Go the polls [and] see that your neighbor goes there and vote for the men who have always been faithful to you and your interests."[6] And voter turnouts, especially in the northern states, reached record levels: over 80 per cent in 1856.

The more objective, detached journalists that Bleyer favored may have done their job too well. By examining politicians too closely, Thomas C. Leonard suggests, the press left the voter feeling helpless, even cynical, regarding the electoral process. Why bother? The percentage of voters turning out for elections dropped sharply in the 20th century: that is, once most newspapers ceased being party organs.[7] *An average of about 60 per cent voted in the last three presidential elections.*[8]

At the same time, scholars like Baldasty maintain that the decline of the partisan press is not explained, as Bleyer would have hoped, by a more responsible, professional attitude among journalists and editors, many trained in new schools of journalism at Madison and elsewhere.

Baldasty contends that *commercial* factors encouraged many newspapers to become less partisan. The cost of publishing a daily paper, especially in the largest cities, began growing to the point that party subsidies no longer covered operating costs. Even more, the presence of new revenue sources, specifically department stores and other retailers, more than made up for old party subsidies. Yet these new advertisers all but insisted that editors expand their reach and be less partisan.[9]

Such considerations drove most, though not all, newspapers to present the news more objectively. Newspapers did not march in lock step—especially in the 1930s, when the *Chicago Tribune* made no effort to disguise its distaste for Franklin Roosevelt. There were other holdouts, including, for many years, the *Los Angeles Times*.

Still, I would argue that by the 1950s most newspapers, large and small, as well as the broadcast networks, tried to present the news objectively. What factors, in effect, closed the deal? The relative neutrality of broadcast journalists was explained in large measure by federal regulations that all but mandated fairness. But there are other explanations as to why our national news culture, whether print or broadcast, preferred the middle ground.

The middle ground was more populated. By that I mean that partisanship in the 1950s was less intense. This was in some degree because the Cold War had created a consensus on foreign policy, and much of the Republican party had accepted the outlines of the welfare state created in the 1930s. Even Robert A. Taft, the Republican Senate leader detractors said had the best 19th century mind in the upper chamber, favored federal housing programs.

"Old Party divisions are less meaningful," wrote one *Fortune* magazine writer in 1960. "American political debate is increasingly conducted in a bland, even-tempered atmosphere and extremists of any kind are becoming rare."[10] The differences were often subtle, having less to do with ideology than lifestyle. One journalist told the political scientist Clinton Rossiter that you could tell the Democrats at a Rotary lunch. Their "dress is more casual, salutes are more boisterous, jokes are more earthy."[11] As to Republicans, a friend growing up in suburban Milwaukee in the 1950s recalled, "I was led to understand that the way to tell a Republican household was that it owned a martini pitcher."

In the late 1960s and 1970s we began to see a greater division among our two major political parties. The Vietnam War fractured the Cold War consensus, mainly among more liberal Democrats. We had a much more active debate about fundamentals of U.S. foreign policy.

At the same time, conservatives slowly became *more* conservative, and began to increase their influence within the Republican party. Moderate Republicans as a species all but vanished. A more conservative Republican party challenged some of the premises of the welfare state (and more recently, labor policies), as well as progressive income tax rates.

At the same time, mainstream news media (larger metropolitan daily papers and networks news) lost some if not much of their authority. Part of that loss was due to a change in what constituted objective news presentation. This is something Stephen Ward wrote about so ably in his first book.[12] Reporters were encouraged to add analysis into their stories. Such analytical reporting more often than not, I think, had a liberal centrist slant. Not hard liberal. Not Rachel Maddow liberal. Maybe "neo-liberal." Here, I draw on Herbert Gans's classic study of four major news organizations.[13]

Look at the *The New York Times* in 1960 vs. 2010. The reportage is more interpretive. This is not a problem for me, but it is an issue for my more conservative friends (and I have them). The more analytical journalism could be off-putting for those on the fringes, left and especially on the right. One reader's analysis is another reader's opinion. Sixty per cent of those surveyed by the Pew Research Center in 2009 believed reporting was politically biased.[14]

There is a related problem that editors note and I encountered when I gave public service talks as director of the journalism school. ... a lot of people can't distinguish the editorial page from the rest of the paper. Some assume the worst: that the editorial views of the newspaper inform the rest of the paper.

Various missteps by the mainstream media did not help.

- For many of those opposed to the Iraq war, *New York Times'* mishandling of claims that Hussein had WMD in 2003.
- For Republicans in 2004, the flaws in CBS News's reports about President Bush's military service during the Vietnam war.

News organizations have always made mistakes, but they have greater consequences when the consumers *have somewhere else to go. A safe harbor.*

Safe harbors became visible in 1987, when the end of the FCC's Fairness Doctrine empowered Rush Limbaugh and a much more opinionated talk radio. Then, in 1996, came Fox News, soon followed by the Internet, with websites and blogs. All provided conservatives safe harbors for their world views.

There were safe harbors as well for those holding more liberal views, if we look at Huffington Post a few years ago or substitute MSNBC for Fox.

Has partisan journalism returned? Yes, but only in part. We need to remember that most Americans don't watch Fox News or MSNBC. Limbaugh claims to have the largest audience of any radio host. But most Americans on a given day do not listen to his program or view Glenn Beck. Most Americans are *not* fierce partisans. Independents are the largest block of voters.

Let's look at the numbers. Much has been made of the declining popularity of the network evening newscasts. Katie Couric, anchor of *The CBS Evening News,* has had a particularly rough few years. Her newscast reached what the *New York Times* reported Monday as "a record low" of 4.89 million viewers last August.[15] Well, according to the Pew Research Center, Couric still drew roughly a third more viewers than *The O'Reilly Factor,* and nearly four times what Keith Olbermann's *Countdown* averaged in 2010.

Although the audiences for the new party press should not be exaggerated, we should acknowledge that its fans are more likely to be politically engaged. Or, as Louis Menand wrote in 2009, "people who need an ideological fix."[16] The new partisan media can inspire or simply reassure those resting on the ideological fringes. If you belong to the Tea Party, you have Glenn Beck. If you think the Koch Brothers are trying to purchase the State of Wisconsin, you have Ed Schultz.

You have a safe harbor.

So have we gone full circle? Is it 1850 all over again? I think not. Perhaps not even halfway.

In contrast to the factious newspaper culture of the mid-19th century, today's media culture is in fact divided between the new partisan media of the radio, internet, and cable, and those news outlets that still endeavor to report the news seriously. Serious news services won't, for example, provide platforms for those who insist the President was born in Kenya, or that the Bush administration was behind the destruction of the World Trade Center.

As I noted, the serious or adult journalists still have the larger audience. But can they keep at it? And, more to the point, does that larger audience really pay the freight?

Roger Ailes brilliantly understood this when he founded Fox News in 1996. Ailes anticipated an argument that Joseph Turow[17] made a year later that the media business model was changing. Advertisers, who had once pressed newspaper publishers to covet a mass audience, were now in search of niche audiences. The successful media entrepreneur, whether publishing a magazine or creating a cable channel, went after subgroups of readers or viewers. In the case of Fox News, cultivating a niche audience of 60-something conservatives.

Ailes also recognized that news-gathering is far more expensive than opinion-spouting. It is far cheaper to produce a show from New York than to send reporters, like the Center's very own and gifted Anthony Shadid, into harm's way. And consumers of cable news understand this difference as well; when France, Britain and the United States launched air strikes against Libya several weeks ago, viewers turned to CNN, not Fox. (Alas, we cannot count on new military interventions to prop up CNN's ratings.)

Should everyone remain calm? After all, America survived the fiercely partisan press of the 19th century. But just barely. The robustness of political engagement then could not prevent the Civil War and eliminate slavery peaceably. I am not so sure that Bleyer and others were so wrong to condemn the party press.

As in the 1850s, Americans have to make tough decisions. Not ones, fortunately, involving something as evil as slavery, but still difficult choices about our future. Fiscal crises on the state and national level require some compromise, the finding of common ground. The new partisan press, consumed so lustily by party activists, makes finding that common ground seemingly impossible, or much more difficult than it was a half century ago. And our political culture, as in the 1850s, has become deeply dysfunctional.[18]

Notes

1 William E. Gienapp, "'Politics Seem to Enter into Everything': Political Culture in the North, 1840–1860," in *Essays on Antebellum Politics, 1840–1860*, ed. Gienapp, et al. (College Station, Tex: Texas A & M University Press, 1982), 41.

2 Norma Basch, "Marriage, Morals, and Politics in the Election of 1828," *Journal of American History* 80 (December 1993), 897.

3 Mark Wahlgren Summers, *Press Gang: Newspapers & Politics, 1863–1878* (Chapel Hill: University of North Carolina Press, 1994), 56.

4 Joan Didion, *After Henry* (New York: Vintage, 1993), 227.

5 Frederic Hudson, *Journalism in the United States, from 1690 to 1872* (New York: Harper & Bros., 1873), 414.

6 Gerald J. Baldasty, *The Commercialization of News in the Nineteenth Century* (Madison, Wis.: University of Wisconsin Press, 1992), 28.

7 Leonard, *The Power of the Press: The Birth of American Political Reporting* (New York: Oxford University Press, 1986), ch. 7.

8 David Paul Kuhn, "The Huge Voter Turnout? Didn't Happen," *Politico,* 9 November 2008.

9 Baldasty, 53–54, 56–58, 143.

10 Daniel Seligman, "The New Masses," *in America in the Sixties: The Economy and the Society* (New York: Harper & Row, 1960), 118.

11 Rossiter, *Parties and Politics in America* (New York: New American Library, 1960), 123.

12 Stephen J. A. Ward, *The Invention of Journalism Ethics: The Path to Objectivity and Beyond* (Montreal: McGill-Queen's University Press, 2004), ch. 6.

13 Gans, *Deciding What's News: A Study of CBS Evening News, NBC Nightly News, Newsweek & Time* (New York: Pantheon, 1979).

14 Cited in Louis Menand, "Chin Music," *New Yorker,* 2 November 2009, 40.

15 Bill Carter, "After 5 Years, Couric and CBS Are Said to Seek Exit Strategy," *New York Times,* 11 April 2011.

16 Menand, 40.

17 *Turow, Breaking Up America: Advertisers and the New Media World* (Chicago: University of Chicago Press, 1997).

18 Depressingly suggestive in this regard is David Donald, "An Excess of Democracy: The American Civil Ward and the Social Process," in *Lincoln Reconsidered: Essays on the Civil War Era,* 2nd ed. (New York: Vintage Books, 1961), 209–35.

Credit

Baughman, James L. "The Fall and Rise of Partisan Journalism." University of Wisconsin-Madison Center for Journalistic Ethics (2011): 20 Apr. 2011. Web.

Re-thinking Objectivity: *Columbia Journalism Review*

Brent Cunningham

In a world of spin, our awkward embrace of an ideal can make us passive recipients of the news.

In his March 6 press conference[1], in which he laid out his reasons for the coming war, President Bush mentioned al Qaeda or the attacks of September 11 fourteen times in fifty-two minutes. No one challenged him on it, despite the fact that the CIA had questioned the Iraq-al Qaeda connection, and that there has never been solid evidence marshaled to support the idea that Iraq was involved in the attacks of 9/11.

When Bush proposed his $726 billion tax cut in January, his sales pitch on the plan's centerpiece—undoing the "double-taxation" on dividend earnings—was that "It's unfair to tax money twice." In the next two months, the tax plan was picked over in hundreds of articles and broadcasts, yet a Nexis database search turned up few news stories—notably, one by Donald Barlett and James Steele in *Time* on January 27, and another by Daniel Altman in the business section of *The New York Times* on January 21—that explained in detail what was misleading about the president's pitch: that in fact there is plenty of income that is doubly, triply, or even quadruply taxed, and that those other taxes affect many more people than the sliver who would benefit from the dividend tax cut.

Before the fighting started in Iraq, in the dozens of articles and broadcasts that addressed the potential aftermath of a war, much was written and said about the maneuverings of the Iraqi exile community and the shape of a postwar government, about cost and duration and troop numbers. Important subjects all. But few of those stories, dating from late last summer, delved deeply into the numerous and plausible complications of the aftermath. That all changed on February 26, when President Bush spoke grandly of making Iraq a model for retooling the entire Middle East. After Bush's speech, "aftermath" articles began to flow like the waters of the Tigris—including cover stories in *Time* and *The New York Times* Magazine—culminating in *The Wall Street Journal's* page-one story on March 17, just days before the first cruise missiles rained down on Baghdad, that revealed how the administration planned to hand the multibillion-dollar job of rebuilding Iraq to U.S. corporations. It was as if the subject of the war's aftermath was more or less off the table until the president put it there himself.

There is no single explanation for these holes in the coverage, but I would argue that our devotion to what we call "objectivity" played a role. It's true that the Bush administration is like a clenched fist with information, one that won't hesitate to hit back when pressed. And that reporting on the possible aftermath of a war before the war occurs, in particular, was a difficult and speculative story.

Yet these three examples—which happen to involve the current White House, although every White House spins stories—provide a window into a particular failure of the press: allowing the principle of objectivity to make us passive recipients of news, rather than aggressive analyzers and explainers of it. We all learned about objectivity in school or at our first job. Along with its twin sentries "fairness" and "balance," it defined journalistic standards.

Or did it? Ask ten journalists what objectivity means and you'll get ten different answers. Some, like *The Washington Post's* editor, Leonard Downie, define it so strictly that they refuse to vote lest they be forced to take sides. My favorite definition was from Michael Bugeja, who teaches journalism at Iowa State: "Objectivity is seeing the world as it is, not how you wish it were." In 1996 the Society of Professional Journalists acknowledged this dilemma and dropped "objectivity" from its ethics code. It also changed "the truth" to simply "truth."

Tripping Toward the Truth

As E.J. Dionne wrote in his 1996 book, *They Only Look Dead*, the press operates under a number of conflicting diktats: be neutral yet investigative; be disengaged but have an impact; be fair-minded but have an edge. Therein lies the nut of our tortured relationship with objectivity. Few would argue that complete objectivity is possible, yet we bristle when someone suggests we aren't being objective—or fair, or balanced—as if everyone agrees on what they all mean.

Over the last dozen years, a cottage industry of bias police has sprung up to exploit this fissure in the journalistic psyche, with talk radio leading the way followed by Shout TV and books like Ann Coulter's *Slander* and Bernard Goldberg's *Bias*. Now the left has begun firing back, with Eric Alterman's book *What Liberal Media?* (*CJR*, March/April) and a group of wealthy Democrats' plans for a liberal radio network. James Carey, a journalism scholar at Columbia, points out that we are entering a new age of partisanship. One result is a hypersensitivity among the press to charges of bias, and it shows up everywhere: In October 2001, with the war in Afghanistan under way, then—CNN chairman Walter Isaacson sent a memo to his foreign correspondents telling them to "balance" reports of Afghan "casualties or hardship" with reminders to viewers that this was, after all, in response to the terrorist attacks of September 11. More recently, a *CJR* intern, calling newspaper letters-page editors to learn whether reader letters were running for or against the looming war in Iraq, was told by the letters editor at *The Tennessean* that letters were running 70 per cent against the war, but that the editors were trying to run as many pro-war letters as possible lest they be accused of bias.

Objectivity has persisted for some valid reasons, the most important being that nothing better has replaced it. And plenty of good journalists believe in it, at least as a necessary goal. Objectivity, or the pursuit of it, separates us from the unbridled partisanship found in much of the European press. It helps us make decisions quickly—we are disinterested observers after all—and it protects us from the consequences of what we write. We'd like to think it buoys our embattled credibility, though the deafening silence of many victims of Jayson Blair's fabrications would argue otherwise. And as we descend into this new age of partisanship, our readers need, more than ever, reliable reporting that tells them what is true when that is knowable, and pushes as close to truth as possible when it is not.

But our pursuit of objectivity can trip us up on the way to "truth." Objectivity excuses lazy reporting. If you're on a deadline and all you have is "both sides of the story," that's often good enough. It's not that such stories laying out the parameters of a debate have no value for readers, but too often, in our obsession with, as *The Washington Post's* Bob Woodward puts it, "the latest," we fail to push the story, incrementally, toward a deeper understanding of what is true and what is false. Steven R. Weisman, the chief diplomatic correspondent for *The New York Times* and a believer in the goal of objectivity ("even though we fall short of the ideal every day"), concedes that he felt obliged to dig more when he was an editorial writer, and did not have to be objective. "If you have to decide who is right, then you must do more reporting," he says. "I pressed the reporting further because I didn't have the luxury of saying *X says* this and *Y says this* and you, dear reader, can decide who is right."

It exacerbates our tendency to rely on official sources, which is the easiest, quickest way to get both the "he said" and the "she said," and, thus, "balance." According to numbers from the media analyst Andrew Tyndall, of the 414 stories on Iraq broadcast on NBC, ABC, and CBS from last September to February, all but thirty-four originated at the White House, Pentagon, and State Department. So we end up with too much of the "official" truth.

More important, objectivity makes us wary of seeming to argue with the president—or the governor, or the CEO—and risk losing our access. Jonathan Weisman, an economics reporter for *The Washington Post*, says this about the fear of losing access: "If you are perceived as having a political bias, or a slant, you're screwed."

Finally, objectivity makes reporters hesitant to inject issues into the news that aren't already out there. "News is driven by the zeitgeist," says Jonathan Weisman, "and if an issue isn't part of the current zeitgeist then it will be a tough sell to editors." But who drives the zeitgeist, in Washington at least? The administration. In short, the press's awkward embrace of an impossible ideal limits its ability to help set the agenda.

This is not a call to scrap objectivity, but rather a search for a better way of thinking about it, a way that is less restrictive and more grounded in reality. As Eric Black, a reporter at the *Minneapolis Star Tribune*, says, "We need a way to both do our job and defend it."

An Ideals' Troubled Past

American journalism's honeymoon with objectivity has been brief. The press began to embrace objectivity in the middle of the nineteenth century, as society turned away from religion and toward science and empiricism to explain the world. But in his 1998 book, *Just the Facts*, a history of the origins of objectivity in U.S. journalism, David Mindich argues that by the turn of the twentieth century, the flaws of objective journalism were beginning to show. Mindich shows how "objective" coverage of lynching in the 1890s by *The New York Times* and other papers created a false balance on the issue and failed "to recognize a truth, that African-Americans were being terrorized across the nation."

After World War I, the rise of public relations and the legacy of wartime propaganda—in which journalists such as Walter Lippman had played key roles—began to undermine reporters' faith in facts. The war, the Depression, and Roosevelt's New Deal raised complex issues that defied journalism's attempt to distill them into simple truths. As a result, the use of bylines increased (an early nod to the fact that news is touched by human frailty), the political columnist crawled from the primordial soup, and the idea of "interpretive reporting" emerged. Still, as Michael Schudson argued in his 1978 book *Discovering the News*, journalism clung to objectivity as the faithful cling to religion, for guidance in an uncertain world. He wrote: "From the beginning, then, criticism of the 'myth' of objectivity has accompanied its enunciation. ... Journalists came to believe in objectivity, to the extent that they did, because they wanted to, needed to, were forced by ordinary human aspiration to seek escape from their own deep convictions of doubt and drift."

By the 1960s, objectivity was again under fire, this time to more fundamental and lasting effect. Straight, "objective" coverage of McCarthyism a decade earlier had failed the public, leading Alan Barth, an editorial writer at *The Washington Post*, to tell a 1952 gathering of the Association for Education in Journalism: "There can be little doubt that the way [Senator Joseph McCarthy's charges] have been reported in most papers serves Senator McCarthy's partisan political purposes much more than it serves the purposes of the press, the interest of truth." Government lies about the U2 spy flights, the Cuban missile crisis, and the Vietnam War all cast doubt on the ability of "objective" journalism to get at anything close to the truth. The New Journalism of Tom Wolfe and Norman Mailer was in part a reaction to what many saw as the failings of mainstream reporting. In Vietnam, many of the beat reporters who arrived believing in objectivity eventually realized, if they stayed long enough, that such an approach wasn't sufficient. Says John Laurence, a former CBS News correspondent, about his years covering Vietnam: "Because the war went on for so long and so much evidence accumulated to suggest it was a losing cause, and that in the process we were destroying the Vietnamese and ourselves, I felt I had a moral obligation to report my views as much as the facts."

As a result of all these things, American journalism changed. "Vietnam and Watergate destroyed what I think was a genuine sense that our officials knew more than we did and acted in good faith," says Anthony Lewis, the former *New York Times* reporter and columnist. We became more sophisticated in our understanding of the limits of objectivity. And indeed, the parameters of modern journalistic objectivity allow reporters quite a bit of leeway to analyze, explain, and put news in context, thereby helping guide readers and viewers through the flood of information.

Still, nothing replaced objectivity as journalism's dominant professional norm. Some 75 per cent of journalists and news executives in a 1999 Pew Research Center survey said it was possible to obtain a true, accurate, and widely agreed-upon account of an event. More than two-thirds thought it feasible to develop "a systematic method to cover events in a disinterested and fair way." The survey also offered another glimpse of the objectivity fissure: more than two-thirds of the print press in the Pew survey also said that "providing an interpretation of the news is a core principle," while less than half of those in television news agreed with that.

The More Things Change

If objectivity's philosophical hold on journalism has eased a bit since the 1960s, a number of other developments have bound us more tightly to the objective ideal and simultaneously exacerbated its shortcomings. Not only are journalists operating under conflicting orders, as E.J. Dionne argued, but their corporate owners don't exactly trumpet the need to rankle the status quo. It is perhaps important to note that one of the original forces behind the shift to objectivity in the nineteenth century was economic. To appeal to as broad an audience as possible, first the penny press and later the new wire services gradually stripped news of "partisan" context. Today's owners have squeezed the newshole, leaving less space for context and analysis.

If space is a problem, time is an even greater one. The nonstop news cycle leaves reporters less time to dig, and encourages reliance on official sources who can provide the information quickly and succinctly. "We are slaves to the incremental daily development," says one White House correspondent, "but you are perceived as having a bias if you don't cover it." This lack of time makes a simpleminded and lazy version of objectivity all the more tempting. In *The American Prospect* of November 6, 2000, Chris Mooney wrote about how "e-spin," a relentless diet of canned attacks and counterattacks e-mailed from the Bush and Gore campaigns to reporters, was winding up, virtually unedited, in news stories. "Lazy reporters may be seduced by the ease of readily provided research," Mooney wrote. "That's not a new problem, except that the prevalence of electronic communication has made it easier to be lazy."

Meanwhile, the Internet and cable news' Shout TV, which drive the nonstop news cycle, have also elevated the appeal of "attitude" in the news, making the balanced, measured report seem anachronistic. In the January/February issue of *CJR*, young journalists asked to create their dream newspaper wanted more point-of-view writing in news columns. They got a heavy dose of it during the second gulf war, with news "anchors" like Fox's Neil Cavuto saying of those who opposed the war, "You were sickening then; you are sickening now."

Perhaps most ominous of all, public relations, whose birth early in the twentieth century rattled the world of objective journalism, has matured into a spin monster so ubiquitous that nearly every word a reporter hears from an official source has been shaped and polished to proper effect. Consider the memo from the Republican strategist Frank Luntz, as described in a March 2 *New York Times* story, that urged the party—and President Bush—to soften their language on the environment to appeal to suburban voters. "Climate change" instead of "global warming," "conservationist" rather than "environmentalist." To the extent that the threat of being accused of bias inhibits reporters from cutting through this kind of manipulation, challenging it, and telling readers about it, then journalism's dominant professional norm needs a new set of instructions.

Joan Didion got at this problem while taking Bob Woodward to task in a 1996 piece in *The New York Review of Books* for writing books that she argued were too credulous, that failed to counter the possibility that his sources were spinning him. She wrote:

> The genuflection toward "fairness" is a familiar newsroom piety, in practice the excuse for a good deal of autopilot reporting and lazy thinking but in theory a benign ideal. In Washington, however, a community in which the management of news has become the single overriding preoccupation of the core industry, what "fairness" has often come to mean is a scrupulous passivity, an agreement to cover the story not as it is occurring but as it is presented, which is to say as it is manufactured.

Asked about such criticism, Woodward says that for his books he has the time and the space and the sources to actually uncover what really happened, not some manufactured version of it. "The best testimony to that," he says, "is that the critics never suggest how any of it is manufactured, that any of it is wrong." Then, objectivity rears its head. "What they seem to be saying," Woodward says of his critics, "is that I refuse to use the information I have to make a political argument, and they are right, I won't." Yet some of Woodward's critics do suggest how his material is manufactured. Christopher Hitchens, reviewing Woodward's latest book, *Bush at War*, in the June issue of The *Atlantic Monthly*, argues that, while reporting on a significant foreign-policy debate, Woodward fully presents the point of view of his cooperative sources, but fails to report deeply on the other sides of the argument. Thus he presents an incomplete picture. "Pseudo-objectivity in the nation's capital," Hitchens writes, "is now overripe for regime change."

To Fill the Void

Jason Riley is a young reporter at the *Louisville Courier-Journal*. Along with a fellow reporter, R.G. Dunlop, he won a Polk award this year for a series on dysfunction in the county courts, in which hundreds of felony cases dating back to 1983 were lost and never resolved. Riley and Dunlop's series was a classic example of enterprise reporting: poking around the courthouse, Riley came across one felony case that had been open for several years. That led to more cases, then to a drawer full of open cases. No one was complaining, at least publicly, about this problem. In a first draft, Riley wrote that the system was flawed because it let cases fall of the docket and just disappear for years. "I didn't think it needed attribution because it was the conclusion I had drawn after six months of investigation," he writes in an e-mail. But his editor sent it back with a note: "Says who?"

In a follow-up profile of the county's lead prosecutor, a man Riley has covered for three years, many sources would not criticize the prosecutor on the record. He "knew what people thought of him, knew what his strengths and weaknesses were," Riley says. "Since no one was openly discussing issues surrounding him, I raised many in my profile without attribution." Again his editors hesitated. There were discussions about the need to remain objective. "Some of my conclusions and questions were left out because no one else brought them up on the record," he says.

Riley discovered a problem on his own, reported the hell out of it, developed an understanding of the situation, and reached some conclusions based on that. No official sources were speaking out about it, so he felt obliged to fill that void. Is that bias? Good reporters do it, or attempt to do it, all the time. The strictures of objectivity can make it difficult. "I think most journalists will admit to feeding sources the information we want to hear, for quotes or attribution, just so we can make the crucial point we are not allowed to make ourselves," Riley says. "But why not? As society's watchdogs, I think we should be asking questions, we should be bringing up problems, possible solutions … writing what we know to be true."

Last fall, when America and the world were debating whether to go to war in Iraq, no one in the Washington establishment wanted to talk much about the aftermath of such a war. For the Bush administration, attempting to rally support for a preemptive war, messy discussions about all that could go wrong in the aftermath were unhelpful. Anything is better than Saddam, the argument went. The Democrats, already wary of being labeled unpatriotic, spoke their piece in October when they voted to authorize the use of force in Iraq, essentially putting the country on a war footing. Without the force of a "she said" on the aftermath story, it was largely driven by the administration, which is to say stories were typically framed by what the administration said it planned to do: work with other nations to build democracy. Strike a blow to terrorists. Stay as long as we need to and not a minute longer. Pay for it all with Iraqi oil revenue. There were some notable exceptions—a piece by Anthony Shadid in the October 20 *Boston Globe*, for instance, and another on September 22 by James Dao in *The New York Times*, pushed beyond the administration's broad assumptions about what would happen when Saddam was gone—but most of the coverage included only boilerplate reminders that Iraq is a fractious country and bloody reprisals are likely, that tension between the Kurds and Turks might be a problem, and that Iran has designs on the Shiite region of southern Iraq. David House, the reader advocate for the *Fort Worth Star-Telegram*, wrote a piece on March 23 that got at the press's limitations in setting the agenda. "Curiously, for all the technology the news media have, for all the gifted minds that make it all work … it's a simple thing to stop the media cold. Say nothing, hide documents."

In November, James Fallows wrote a cover story for *The Atlantic Monthly* entitled "The Fifty-First State? The Inevitable Aftermath of Victory in Iraq." In it, with the help of regional experts, historians, and retired military officers, he gamed out just how difficult the aftermath could be. Among the scenarios he explored: the financial and logistical complications caused by the destruction of Baghdad's infrastructure; the possibility that Saddam Hussein would escape and join Osama bin Laden on the Most Wanted list; how the dearth of Arabic speakers in the U.S. government would hinder peacekeeping and other aftermath operations; how the need for the U.S., as the occupying power, to secure Iraq's borders would bring it face to face with Iran, another spoke in the "axis of evil"; the complications of working with the United Nations after it refused to support the war; what to do about the Iraqi debt from, among other things, UN-imposed reparations after the first Gulf War, which some estimates put as high as $400 billion.

Much of this speculation has since come to pass and is bedeviling the U.S.'s attempt to stabilize—let alone democratize—Iraq. So are some other post-war realities that were either too speculative or too hypothetical to be given much air in the pre-war debate. Looting, for instance, and general lawlessness. The fruitless (thus far) search for weapons of mass destruction. The inability to quickly restore power and clean water. A decimated health-care system. The difficulty of establishing an interim Iraqi government, and the confusion over who exactly should run things in the meantime. The understandably shallow reservoir of patience among the long-suffering Iraqis. The hidden clause in Halliburton's contract to repair Iraq's oil wells that also, by the way, granted it control of production and distribution, despite the administration's assurances that the Iraqis would run their own oil industry.

In the rush to war, how many Americans even heard about some of these possibilities? Of the 574 stories about Iraq that aired on NBC, ABC, and CBS evening news broadcasts between September 12 (when Bush addressed the UN) and March 7 (a week and a half before the war began), only twelve dealt primarily with the potential aftermath, according to Andrew Tyndall's numbers.

The Republicans were saying only what was convenient, thus the "he said." The Democratic leadership was saying little, so there was no "she said." "Journalists are never going to fill the vacuum left by a weak political opposition," says *The New York Times*'s Steven R. Weisman. But why not? If something important is being ignored, doesn't the press have an obligation to force our elected officials to address it? We have the ability, even on considerably less important matters than war and nation-building. Think of the dozens of articles *The New York Times* published between July 10, 2002 and March 31 about the Augusta National Country Club's exclusion of women members, including the one from November 25 that carried the headline "CBS Staying Silent in Debate on Women Joining Augusta." Why couldn't there have been headlines last fall that read: "Bush Still Mum on Aftermath," or "Beyond Saddam: What Could Go Right, and What Could Go Wrong?" And while you're at it, consider the criticism the *Times*'s mini-crusade on Augusta engendered in the media world, as though an editor's passion for an issue never drives coverage.

This is not inconsequential nitpicking. *The New Yorker*'s editor, David Remnick, who has written in support of going to war with Iraq, wrote of the aftermath in the March 31 issue: "An American presence in Baghdad will carry with it risks and responsibilities that will shape the future of the United States in the world." The press not only could have prepared the nation and its leadership for the aftermath we are now witnessing, but should have.

The Real Bias

In the early 1990s, I was a statehouse reporter for the *Charleston Daily Mail* in West Virginia. Every time a bill was introduced in the House to restrict access to abortion, the speaker, who was solidly pro-choice, sent the bill to the health committee, which was chaired by a woman who was also pro-choice. Of course, the bills never emerged from that committee. I was green and, yes, pro-choice, so it took a couple of years of witnessing this before it sunk in that—as the anti-abortion activists had been telling me from day one—the committee was stacked with pro-choice votes and that this was how "liberal" leadership killed the abortion bills every year while appearing to let the legislative process run its course. Once I understood, I eagerly wrote that story, not only because I knew it would get me on page one, but also because such political maneuverings offended my reporter's sense of fairness. The bias, ultimately, was toward the story.

Reporters are biased, but not in the oversimplified, left-right way that Ann Coulter and the rest of the bias cops would have everyone believe. As Nicholas Confessore argued in *The American Prospect*, most of the loudest bias-spotters were not reared in a newsroom. They come from politics, where everything is driven by ideology. Voting Democratic and not going to church—two bits of demography often trotted out to show how liberal the press is—certainly have some bearing on one's interpretation of events. But to leap to the conclusion that reporters use their precious column inches to push a left-wing agenda is specious reasoning at its worst. We all have our biases, and they can be particularly pernicious when they are unconscious. Arguably the most damaging bias is rarely discussed—the bias born of class. A number of people interviewed for this story said that the lack of socioeconomic diversity in the newsroom is one of American journalism's biggest blind spots. Most newsroom diversity efforts, though, focus on ethnic, racial, and gender minorities, which can often mean people with different skin color but largely the same middle-class background and aspirations. At a March 13 panel on media bias at Columbia's journalism school, John Leo, a columnist for *U.S. News & World Report*, said, "It used to be that anybody could be a reporter by walking in the door. It's a little harder to do that now, and you don't get the working-class Irish poor like Hamill or Breslin or me. What you get is people from Ivy League colleges with upper-class credentials, what you get is people who more and more tend to be and act alike." That, he says, makes it hard for a newsroom to spot its own biases.

Still, most reporters' real biases are not what political ideologues tend to think. "Politically I'm a reporter," says Eric Nalder, an investigative reporter at the *San Jose Mercury News*. Reporters are biased toward conflict because it is more interesting than stories without conflict; we are biased toward sticking with the pack because it is safe; we are biased toward event-driven coverage because it is easier; we are biased toward existing narratives because they are safe and easy. Consider the story—written by reporters around the country—of how Kenneth L. Lay, the former CEO of Enron, encouraged employees to buy company stock as he was secretly dumping his. It was a conveniently damning narrative, and easy to believe. Only it turned out, some two years later, to be untrue, leading *The New York Times's* Kurt Eichenwald to write a story correcting the record on February 9.

Mostly, though, we are biased in favor of getting the story, regardless of whose ox is being gored. Listen to Daniel Bice, an investigative columnist at the *Milwaukee Journal-Sentinel,* summarize his reporting philosophy: "Try not to be boring, be a reliable source of information, cut through the political, corporate, and bureaucratic bullshit, avoid partisanship, and hold politicians' feet to the fire." It would be tough to find a reporter who disagrees with any of that.

In his 1979 book *Deciding What's News,* the Columbia sociologist Herbert Gans defined what he called the journalist's "paraideology," which, he says, unconsciously forms and strengthens much of what we think of as news judgment. This consists largely of a number of "enduring values"—such as "altruistic democracy" and "responsible capitalism"—that are reformist, not partisan. "In reality," Gans writes, "the news is not so much conservative or liberal as it is reformist; indeed, the enduring values are very much like the values of the Progressive movement of the early twentieth century." My abortion story, then, came from my sense that what was happening violated my understanding of "altruistic democracy." John Laurence distills Gans' paraideology into simpler terms: "We are for honesty, fairness, courage, humility. We are against corruption, exploitation, cruelty, criminal behavior, violence, discrimination, torture, abuse of power, and many other things." Clifford Levy, a reporter for *The New York Times* whose series on abuse in New York's homes for the mentally ill won a Pulitzer this year, says, "Of all the praise I got for the series, the most meaningful was from other reporters at the paper who said it made them proud to work there because it was a classic case of looking out for those who can't look out for themselves."

This "paraideology," James Carey explains, can lead to charges of liberal bias. "There is a bit of the reformer in anyone who enters journalism," he says. "And reformers are always going to make conservatives uncomfortable to an extent because conservatives, by and large, want to preserve the status quo."

Gans, though, notes a key flaw in the journalist's paraideology. "Journalists cannot exercise news judgment," he writes, "without a composite of nation, society, and national and social institutions in their collective heads, and this picture is an aggregate of reality judgments ... In doing so, they cannot leave room for the reality judgments that, for example, poor people have about America; nor do they ask, or even think of asking, the kinds of questions about the country that radicals, ultraconservatives, the religiously orthodox, or social scientists ask as a result of their reality judgments."

This understanding of "the other" has always been—and will always be—a central challenge of journalism. No individual embodies all the perspectives of a society. But we are not served in this effort by a paralyzing fear of being accused of bias. In their recent book *The Press Effect*, Kathleen Hall Jamieson and Paul Waldman make a strong case that this fear was a major factor in the coverage of the Florida recount of the 2000 presidential election, and its influence on journalists was borne out in my reporting for this piece. "Our paper is under constant criticism by people alleging various forms of bias," says the *Star-Tribune's* Eric Black. "And there is a daily effort to perform in ways that will make it harder to criticize. Some are reasonable, but there is a line you can cross after which you are avoiding your duties to truth-telling." In a March 10 piece critical of the press's performance at Bush's pre-war press conference, *USA Today*'s Peter Johnson quoted Sam Donaldson as saying that it is difficult for the media—especially during war—"to press very hard when they know that a large segment of the population doesn't want to see a president whom they have anointed having to squirm." If we're about to go to war—especially one that is controversial—shouldn't the president squirm?

It is important, always, for reporters to understand their biases, to understand what the accepted narratives are, and to work against them as much as possible. This might be less of a problem if our newsrooms were more diverse—intellectually and socioeconomically as well as in gender, race, and ethnicity—but it would still be a struggle. There is too much easy opinion passing for journalism these days, and this is in no way an attempt to justify that. Quite the opposite. We need deep reporting and real understanding, but we also need reporters to acknowledge all that they don't know, and not try to mask that shortcoming behind a gloss of attitude, or drown it in a roar of oversimplified assertions.

Toward a Better Definition of Objectivity

In the last two years, Archbishop Desmond Tutu has been mentioned in more than 3,000 articles on the Nexis database, and at least 388 (11 percent) included in the same breath the fact that he was a Nobel Peace Prize winner. The same search criteria found that Yasser Arafat turned up in almost 96,000 articles, but only 177 (less than .2 percent) mentioned that he won the Nobel prize. When we move beyond stenography, reporters make a million choices, each one subjective. When, for example, is it relevant to point out, in a story about Iraq's weapons of mass destruction, that the U.S. may have helped Saddam Hussein build those weapons in the 1980s? Every time? Never?

The rules of objectivity don't help us answer such questions. But there are some steps we can take to clarify what we do and help us move forward with confidence. A couple of modest proposals:

Journalists (and journalism) must acknowledge, humbly and publicly, that what we do is far more subjective and far less detached than the aura of objectivity implies—and the public wants to believe. If we stop claiming to be mere objective observers, it will not end the charges of bias but will allow us to defend what we do from a more realistic, less hypocritical position.

Secondly, we need to free (and encourage) reporters to develop expertise and to use it to sort through competing claims, identify and explain the underlying assumptions of those claims, and make judgments about what readers and viewers need to know to understand what is happening. In short, we need them to be more willing to "adjudicate factual disputes," as Kathleen Hall Jamieson and Paul Waldman argue in *The Press Effect*. Bill Marimow, the editor of the *Baltimore Sun,* talks of reporters "mastering" their beats. "We want our reporters to be analysts," he told a class at Columbia in March. "Becoming an expert, and mastering the whole range of truth about issues will give you the ability to make independent judgments."

Timothy Noah, writing in *The Washington Monthly* for a 1999 symposium on objectivity, put it this way: "A good reporter who is well-steeped in his subject matter and who isn't out to prove his cleverness, but rather is sweating out a detailed understanding of a topic worth exploring, will probably develop intelligent opinions that will inform and perhaps be expressed in his journalism." This happens every day in ways large and small, but it still happens too rarely. In a March 18 piece headlined "Bush Clings to Dubious Allegations About Iraq," *The Washington Post*'s Walter Pincus and Dana Milbank laid out all of Bush's "allegations" about Saddam Hussein "that have been challenged—and in some cases disproved—by the United Nations, European governments, and even U.S. intelligence." It was noteworthy for its bluntness, and for its lack of an "analysis" tag. In commenting on that story, Steven Weisman of *The New York Times* illustrates how conflicted journalism is over whether such a piece belongs in the news columns: "It's a very good piece, but it is very tendentious," he says. "It's interesting that the editors didn't put it on page one, because it would look like they are calling Bush a liar. Maybe we should do more pieces like it, but you must be careful not to be argumentative."

Some reporters work hard to get these same "argumentative" ideas into their stories in more subtle ways. Think of Jason Riley's comment about "feeding information" to sources. Steven Weisman calls it making it part of the "tissue" of the story. For example, in a March 17 report on the diplomatic failures of the Bush administration, Weisman worked in the idea that the CIA was questioning the Iraq-al Qaeda connection by attributing it to European officials as one explanation for why the U.S. *casus belli* never took hold in the UN.

The test, though, should not be whether it is tendentious, but whether it is true.

There are those who will argue that if you start fooling around with the standard of objectivity you open the door to partisanship. But mainstream reporters by and large are not ideological warriors. They are imperfect people performing a difficult job that is crucial to society. Letting them write what they know and encouraging them to dig toward some deeper understanding of things is not biased, it is essential. Reporters should feel free, as Daniel Bice says, to "call it as we see it, but not be committed to one side or the other." Their professional values make them, Herbert Gans argues, akin to reformers, and they should embrace that aspect of what they do, not hide it for fear of being slapped with a bias charge. And when actual bias seeps in—as it surely will—the self-policing in the newsroom must be vigorous. Witness the memo John Carroll, editor of the *Los Angeles Times,* wrote last month to his staff after a front-page piece on a new Texas abortion law veered left of center: "I want everyone to understand how serious I am about purging all political bias from our coverage."

Journalists have more tools today than ever to help them "adjudicate factual disputes." In 1993, before the computer-age version of "precision journalism" had taken root in the newsroom, Steve Doig helped *The Miami Herald* win a Pulitzer with his computer-assisted stories that traced damage done by Hurricane Andrew to shoddy home construction and failed governmental oversight of builders. "Precision journalism is arguably activist, but it helps us approach the unobtainable goal of objectivity more than traditional reporting strategies," says Doig, who now teaches computer-assisted reporting at Arizona State University. "It allows you to measure a problem, gives you facts that are less controvertible. Without the computer power, our Hurricane Andrew stories would have essentially been finger-pointing stories, balanced with builders saying there is no way any structure could have withstood such winds."

On April 1, Ron Martz, a reporter from the *Atlanta Journal-Constitution* embedded with the Army in Iraq, delivered a "war diary" entry on National Public Radio in which he defended his battlefield decision to drop his reporter's detachment and take a soldier's place holding an intravenous drip bag and comforting a wounded Iraqi civilian. The "ethicists," Martz said on NPR, tell us this is murky territory. That Martz, an accomplished reporter, should worry at all that his reputation could suffer from something like this says much about journalism's relationship with objectivity. Martz concluded that he is a human being first and a reporter second, and was comfortable with that. Despite all our important and necessary attempts to minimize our humanity, it can't be any other way.

Note

1 Press conference was held on March 6, 2003.

Credit

Cunningham, Brent. "Re-thinking Objectivity." *Columbia Journalism Review* 11 July 2003. Web.

Liberation vs. Control: The Future of Cyberspace

Ronal Deibert and Rafal Rohozinski

Every day there seems to be a new example of the ways in which human ingenuity combines with technology to further social change. For the Green Movement in Iran, it was Twitter; for the Saffron Revolution in Burma, it was YouTube; for the "color revolutions" of the former Soviet Union, it was mobile phones. No matter how restrictive the regulations or how severe the repercussions, communities around the world have exhibited enormous creativity in sidestepping constraints on technology in order to exercise their freedoms.

Looking at the seemingly endless examples of social innovation, one might easily assume that cyber-technologies possess a special power, that they are "technologies of liberation."[1] No other mode of communication in human history has facilitated the democratization of communication to the same degree. No other technology in history has grown with such speed and spread so far geographically in such a short period of time. Twitter, to take just the latest cyber-application as an example, has grown from an average of 500,000 tweets a quarter in 2007 to more than four billion tweets in the first quarter alone of 2010. The continual innovations in electronic communications have had unprecedented and far-reaching effects.

Yet some observers have noted that the very same technologies which give voice to democratic activists living under authoritarian rule can also be harnessed by their oppressors.[2] Cyber-communication has made possible some very extensive and efficient forms of social control. Even in democratic countries, surveillance systems penetrate every aspect of life, as people implicitly (and perhaps unwittingly) consent to the greatest invasion of personal privacy in history. Digital information can be easily tracked and traced, and then tied to specific individuals who themselves can be mapped in space and time with a degree of sophistication that would make the greatest tyrants of days past envious. So, are these technologies of freedom or are they technologies of control?

This dichotomy is itself misleading, however, as it suggests a clearcut opposition between the forces of light and the forces of darkness. In fact, the picture is far more nuanced and must be qualified in several ways. Communications technologies are neither empty vessels to be filled with products of human intent nor forces unto themselves, imbued with some kind of irresistible agency. They are complicated and continuously evolving manifestations of social forces at a particular time and place. Once created, technologies in turn shape and limit the prospects for human communication and interaction in a constantly iterative manner. Complicating matters further is the inescapable presence of contingency. Technical innovations may be designed for specific purposes but often end up having wildly different social uses and effects than those intended by their creators. Yet these "alternative rationalities"—systems of use based on local culture and norms, particularly those that originate outside the developed world—often become the prevailing paradigm around which technologies evolve, until they in turn are disrupted by unanticipated uses or new innovations.[3]

The concepts of "liberation" and "control" also require qualification. Both are socially constructed ideas whose meaning and thus application can vary widely depending on the context in which they appear. Different communities work to be free (or "liberated") from different things—for example, colonial rule or gender or religious discrimination. Likewise, social control can take many forms, and these will depend both on the values driving them as well as what are perceived to be the objects of control. Countless liberation movements and mechanisms of social control coexist within a shared but constantly evolving communications space at any one time. This makes any portrayal of technology that highlights a single overarching characteristic biased toward either liberation or control seem fanciful.

This social complexity is a universal characteristic of all technological systems, but it is especially marked in the communications arena for several reasons. Processes of globalization, which are both products of and contributors to cyberspace, intensify the mix of actors, cultures, interests, and ideas in the increasingly dense pool of communications. Although it may seem clichéd to note that events on one side of the planet can ripple back at the speed of light to affect what happens on the other side, we must not underestimate the proliferation of players whose actions help to shape cyberspace and who in turn are shaped by their own interactions within cyberspace. This "dynamic density" also accelerates the pace of change inherent in cyberspace, making it a moving target.[4] Innovations, which potentially may come from any of the millions of actors in cyberspace, can occur daily. This means that rather than being a static artifact, cyberspace is better conceptualized as a constantly evolving domain—a multilevel ecosystem of physical infrastructure, software, regulations, and ideas.

The social complexity of cyberspace is compounded by the fact that much of it is owned and operated by thousands of private actors, and some of their operations cross national jurisdictions. Guided by commercial principles, these enterprises often make decisions that end up having significant political consequences. For example, an online chat service may handle or share user data in ways that put users in jeopardy, depending on the jurisdiction in which the service is offered. Such considerations are especially relevant given the current evolution toward "cloud computing" and software-as-a-service business models. In these models, information and the software through which users interact are not physically located on their own computers but are instead hosted by private companies, often located in faraway jurisdictions. As a result, we have the curious situation in which individuals' data are ultimately governed according to laws and regulations over which they themselves have no say as citizens. This also accelerates existing trends toward the privatization of authority.[5]

Although the decisions taken by businesses—the frontline operators in cyberspace—play a critical role, cyberspace is also shaped by the actions of governments, civil society, and even individuals. Because corporations are subject to the laws of the land in which they operate, the rules and regulations imposed by national governments may inadvertently serve to carve up the global commons of information. According to the OpenNet Initiative research consortium, more than forty countries, including many democracies, now engage in Internet-content filtering.[6] The actions of civil society matter as well. Individuals, working alone or collectively through networks, can create software, tools, or forms of mobilization that have systemwide implications—not all of them necessarily benign. In fact, there is a hidden subsystem of cyberspace made up of crime and espionage.

In short, the actions of businesses, governments, civil society, criminal organizations, and millions of individuals affect and in turn are affected by the domain of cyberspace. Rather than being an ungoverned realm, cyberspace is perhaps best likened to a gangster-dominated version of New York: a tangled web of rival public and private authorities, civic associations, criminal networks, and underground economies. Such a complex network cannot be accurately described in the one-dimensional terms of "liberation" or "control" any more than the domains of land, sea, air, or space can be. Rather, it is composed of a constantly pulsing and at times erratic mix of competing forces and constraints.

Liberation: From What and for Whom?

Much of the popular reporting about cyberspace and social mobilization is biased toward liberal-democratic values. If a social movement in Africa, Burma, or Iran employs a software tool or digital technology to mobilize supporters, the stories appear throughout the global media and are championed by rights activists.[7] Not surprisingly then, these examples tend to be generalized as the norm and repeated without careful scrutiny. But social mobilization can take various forms motivated by many possible rationales, some of which may not be particularly "progressive."[8] Due to both media bias and the difficulties of conducting primary research in certain contexts, these alternative rationalities tend to be obscured from popular view by the media and underexplored by academics.[9] Yet they are no less important than their seemingly more benign counterparts, both for the innovations that they produce and the reactions that they generate.

Consider, for example, the enormous criminal underworld in cyberspace. Arguably at the cutting edge of online innovation, cybercriminals have occupied a largely hidden, parasitic ecosystem within cyberspace, attacking the insecure fissures that open up within this constantly morphing domain. Although most cyber-crime takes the form of petty spam (the electronic distribution of unsolicited bulk messages), the sophistication and reach of cyber-criminals today are startling. The production of "malware"—malicious software—is now estimated to exceed that of legitimate software, although no one really knows its full extent. About a million new malware samples a month are discovered by security engineers, with the rate of growth increasing at a frightening pace.

One of the more ingenious and widespread forms of cyber-crime is "click fraud," whereby victims' computers are infected with malicious software and redirected to make visits to online pay-per-click ads operated by the attackers. Although each click typically generates income on the order of fractions of a penny, a "botnet" (a group of thousands of infected computers referred to as "zombies") can bring in millions of dollars for the criminals.

One such cyber-criminal enterprise called Koobface (an anagram of Facebook) exploits security vulnerabilities in users' machines while also harvesting personal information from Facebook and other social-networking services. It creates thousands of malicious Facebook accounts every day, each of which is then directed toward click fraud or malicious websites that prompt the download of Trojan horses (malware downloads that appear legitimate). With the latter, Koobface can extract sensitive and confidential information such as credit-card account numbers from the infected computers of unwitting users, or deploy the computers as zombies in botnets for purposes of distributed computer-network attacks. Like the mirror universe on the television series *Star Trek,* in which parallel Captain Kirks and Spocks were identical to the originals except for their more malicious personalities, these phony accounts are virtually indistinguishable from the real ones. The Koobface enterprise demonstrates extraordinary ingenuity in social networking, but directed entirely toward fraudulent ends.

Just as software, social-networking platforms, and other digital media originally designed for consumer applications may be redeployed for political mobilization, innovations developed for cyber-crime are often used for malicious political activity. Our research reveals the deeply troubling trend of cyber-crime tools being employed for espionage and other political purposes.

Twice in the last two years, the Information Warfare Monitor has uncovered major global cyber-espionage networks infiltrating dozens of high-level political targets, including foreign ministries, embassies, international organizations, financial institutions, and media outlets. These investigations, documented in the reports "Tracking *GhostNet*" and "Shadows in the Clouds," unearthed the theft of highly sensitive documents and the extensive infiltration of targets ranging from the offices of the Dalai Lama to India's National Security Council. The tools and methods used by the attackers had their origins in cyber-crime and are widely available on the Internet black market.[10] Indeed, "Ghost Rat," the main device employed by the cyber-espionage network, is available for free download and has been translated into multiple languages. Moreover, although the networks examined in both studies are almost certainly committing politically motivated espionage rather than crime per se, our research suggests that the attackers were not direct agents of government but were probably part of the Chinese criminal underworld, either contracted or tolerated by Chinese officials.

Likewise, the OpenNet Initiative analyzed the cyber-attacks waged against Georgian government websites during the August 2008 war with Russia over South Ossetia. The computers that were harvested together to mount distributed denial-of-service attacks were actually botnets already well known to researchers studying cyber-crime and fraud, and had been used earlier to attack pornography and gambling sites for purposes of extortion.[11]

The most consistent demonstrations of digital ingenuity can be found in the dark worlds of pornography, militancy, extremism, and hate. Forced to operate in the shadows and constantly maneuvering to stay ahead of their pursuers while attempting to bring more people into their folds, these dark networks adapt and innovate far more rapidly and with greater agility than their more progressive counterparts. Al Qaeda persists today, in part, because of the influence of jihadist websites, YouTube channels, and social-networking groups, all of which have taken the place of physical meeting spaces. Just as disparate human-rights groups identify with various umbrella causes to which they belong through their immersion in social-networking services and chat platforms, so too do jihadists and militants mobilize around a common "imagined community" that is nurtured online.

Perhaps even more challenging to the liberal-democratic vision of liberation technology is that much of what is considered criminal and antisocial behavior online increasingly originates from the young online populations in developing and postcommunist countries, many of whom live under authoritarianism and suffer from structural economic inequalities. For these young "digital natives," operating an email scam or writing code for botnets, viruses, and malware represents an opportunity for economic advancement. It is an avenue for tapping into global supply chains and breaking out of conditions of local poverty and political inequality—itself a form of liberation.

In other words, regardless of whatever specific characteristics observers attribute to certain technologies, human beings are unpredictable and innovative creatures. Just because a technology has been invented for one purpose does not mean that it will not find other uses unforeseen by its creators. This is especially true in the domains of crime, espionage, and civil conflict, where innovation is not encumbered by formal operating procedures or respect for the rule of law.

Enclosing the Commons: Next-Generation Controls

Arguments linking new technologies to "liberation" must also be qualified due to the ongoing development of more sophisticated cyberspace controls. Whereas it was once considered impossible for governments to control cyberspace, there are now a wide variety of technical and nontechnical means at their disposal to shape and limit the online flow of information. Like the alternative rationalities described above, these can often escape the attention of the media and other observers. But these control mechanisms are growing in scope and sophistication as part of a general paradigm shift in cyberspace governance and an escalating arms race in cyberspace.

To understand cyberspace controls, it is important first to consider a sea-change in the ways in which governments approach the domain. During the "dot-com" boom of the 1990s, governments generally took a hands-off approach to the Internet by adhering to a *laissez-faire* economic paradigm, but a gradual shift has since occurred. While market ideas still predominate, there has been a growing recognition of serious risks in cyberspace.

The need to manage these risks has led to a wave of securitization efforts that have potentially serious implications for basic freedoms.[12] For example, certain security measures and regulations have been put in place for purposes of copyright and intellectual-property protection. Although introduced as safeguards, these regulations help to legitimize government intervention in cyberspace more generally—including in countries whose regimes may be more interested in self-preservation than in property protections. If Canada, Germany, Ireland, or another industrialized democracy can justifiably regulate behavior in cyberspace in conformity with its own national laws, who is to say that Belarus, Burma, Tunisia, or Uzbekistan cannot do the same in order to protect state security or other national values?

The securitization of cyberspace has been driven mainly by a "defensive" agenda—to protect against threats to critical infrastructures and to enable law enforcement to monitor and fight cyber-crime more effectively. There are, however, those who argue that "offensive" capabilities are equally important. In order to best defend key infrastructures, the argument goes, governments must also understand how to wage attacks, and that requires a formal offensive posture. Most of the world's armed forces have established, or are in the process of establishing, cybercommands or cyberwarfare units. The most ambitious is the U.S. Cyber Command, which unifies U.S. cyber-capabilities under a separate command led by General Keith Alexander of the National Security Agency. Such an institutional innovation in the armed forces of the world's leading superpower provides a model for similar developments in other states' armed forces, who feel the need to adapt or risk being left behind.

Not surprisingly, there have been a growing number of incidents of computer-network attacks for political ends in recent years, including those against Burmese, Chinese, and Tibetan human-rights organizations, as well as political-opposition groups in the countries of the former Soviet Union. It would be disingenuous to draw a direct line between the establishment of the U.S. Cyber Command and these incidents, especially since many of these practices have been pioneered through innovative and undeclared public-private partnerships between intelligence services in countries such as Burma, China, and Russia and their emergent cyber-criminal underclasses. Yet it is fair to argue that the former sets a normative standard that allows such activities to be tolerated and even encouraged. We should expect these kinds of attacks to grow as governments explore overt and declared strategies of offensive action in cyberspace.

Further driving the trend toward securitization is the fact that private-sector actors, who bear the brunt (and costs) of defending cyberspace's critical infrastructures against a growing number of daily attacks, are increasingly looking to their own governments to carry this burden as a public good. Moreover, a huge market for cyber-security services has emerged, estimated to generate between U.S. $40 and $60 billion annually in the United States alone. Many of the companies that now fill this space stand to gain by fanning the flames of cyberwar. A few observers have questioned the motivations driving the self-serving assessments that these companies make about the nature and severity of various threats.[13] Those criticisms are rare, however, and have done little to stem fear-mongering about cyber-security.

This momentum toward securitization is helping to legitimize and pave the way for greater government involvement in cyberspace. Elsewhere, we have discussed "next generation" controls—interventions that go beyond mere filtering, such as those associated with the Great Firewall of China.[14] Many of these controls have little to do with technology and more to do with inculcating norms, inducing compliant behavior, and imposing rules of the road, and they stem from a multitude of motivations and concerns. Any argument for the liberating role of new technologies needs to be evaluated in the wider context of these next-generation controls.

Legal measures. At the most basic level, government interventions in cyberspace have come through the introduction of slander, libel, copyright-infringement, and other laws to restrict communications and online activities.[15] In part, the passage of such laws reflects a natural maturation process, as authorities seek to bring rules to cyberspace through regulatory oversight. Sometimes, however, it also reflects a deliberate tactic of strangulation, since threats of legal action can do more to prevent damaging information from surfacing than can passive filtering methods implemented defensively to block websites. Such laws can create a climate of fear, intimidation, and ultimately self-censorship.

Although new laws are being drafted to create a regulatory framework for cyberspace, in some cases old, obscure, or rarely enforced regulations are cited *ex post facto* to justify acts of Internet censorship, surveillance, or silencing. In Pakistan, for example, old laws concerning "blasphemy" have been used to ban access to Facebook, ostensibly because there are Facebook groups that are centered around cartoons of Muhammad.[16] Governments have also shown a willingness to invoke national-security laws to justify broad acts of censorship. In Bangladesh, for example, the government blocked access to all of YouTube because of videos clips showing Prime Minister Sheikh Hasina defending her decision to negotiate with mutinous army guards.

The Bangladesh Telecommunications Commission chairman, Zia Ahmed, justified the decision by saying: "[T]he government can take any decision to stop any activity that threatens national unity and integrity."[17] In Lebanon, infrequently used defamation laws were invoked to arrest three Facebook users for posting criticisms of the Lebanese president, in spite of constitutional protections of freedom of speech.[18] In Venezuela, several people were arrested recently after posting comments on Twitter about the country's banking system. The arrests were made based on a provision in the country's banking laws that prohibits the dissemination of "false information."[19] Numerous other examples could be cited that together paint a picture of growing regulatory intervention into cyberspace by governments, shaping and controlling the domain in ways that go beyond technical blocking. Whereas at one time such regulatory interventions would have been considered exceptional and misguided, today they are increasingly becoming the norm.

Informal requests. While legal measures create the regulatory context for denial, for more immediate needs, authorities can make informal "requests" of private companies. Most often such requests come in the form of pressure on Internet service providers (ISPs) and online hosting services to remove offensive posts or information that supposedly threatens "national security" or "cultural sensitivities." Google's recent decision to reconsider its service offerings in China reflects, in part, that company's frustration with having to deal with such informal removal requests from Chinese authorities on a regular basis. Some governments have gone so far as to pressure the companies that run the infrastructure, such as ISPs and mobile phone operators, to render services inoperative in order to prevent their exploitation by activists and opposition groups.

In Iran, for example, the Internet and other telecommunications services have slowed down during public demonstrations and in some instances have been entirely inaccessible for long periods of time or in certain regions, cities, and even neighborhoods. While there is no official acknowledgement that service is being curtailed, it is noteworthy that the Iranian Revolutionary Guard owns the main ISP in Iran—the Telecommunication Company of Iran (TCI).[20] Some reports indicate that officials from the Revolutionary Guard have pressured TCI to tamper with Internet connections during the recent crises. In authoritarian countries, where the lines between public and private authorities are often blurred or organized crime and government authority mingle in a dark underworld, such informal requests and pressures can be particularly effective and nearly impossible to bring to public account.

Outsourcing. It is important to emphasize that cyberspace is owned and operated primarily by private companies. The decisions taken by those companies about content controls can be as important as those taken by governments. Private companies often are compelled in some manner to censor and surveil Internet activity in order to operate in a particular jurisdiction, as evidenced most prominently by the collusion of Google (up until January 2010), Microsoft, and Yahoo in China's Internet censorship practices. Microsoft's Bing, which tailors its search engine to serve different countries and regions and offers its services in 41 languages, has an information-filtering system at the keyword level for users in several countries. According to research by the OpenNet Initiative's Helmi Noman, users located in the Arab countries where he tested are prevented from conducting Internet searches relating to sex and other cultural norms in both Arabic and English. Microsoft's explanation as to why some search keywords return few or no results states, "Sometimes websites are deliberately excluded from the results page to remove inappropriate content as determined by local practice, law, or regulation." It is unclear, however, whether Bing's keyword filtering in the Arab world is an initiative of Microsoft or whether any or all of the Arab states have asked Microsoft to comply with local censorship practices and laws.[21]

In some of the most egregious cases, outsourced censorship and monitoring controls have taken the form either of illegal acts or of actions contrary to publicly stated operating procedures and privacy protections. This was dramatically illustrated in the case of Tom-Skype, in which the Chinese partner of Skype put in place a covert surveillance system to track and monitor prodemocracy activists who were using Skype's chat function as a form of outreach. The system was discovered only because of faulty security on the servers operated by Tom Online. In May 2009, the Chinese government introduced new laws that required personal-computer manufacturers to bundle a filtering software with all of the computers sold in the country. Although this was strongly resisted by many companies, others willingly complied. While this requirement seems to have faded over time, it is nonetheless indicative of the types of actions that governments can take to control access points to cyberspace via private companies.

Access points such as Internet cafes are becoming a favorite regulatory target for authoritarian governments. In Belarus, ISPs and Internet cafes are required by law to keep lists of all users and turn them over to state security services.[22] Many other governments have similar requirements. In light of such regulations, it is instructive to note that many private companies collect user data as a matter of course and reserve the right in their end-user license agreement to share such information with any third party of their choosing.

Presumably, there are many still undiscovered acts of collusion between companies and governments. For governments in both the developed and developing worlds, delegating censorship and surveillance to private companies keeps these controls on the "frontlines" of the networks and coopts the actors who manage the key access points and hosting platforms. If this trend continues, we can expect more censorship and surveillance responsibilities to be carried out by private companies, carrier hotels (ISP co-location centers), cloud-computing services, Internet exchanges, and telecommunications companies. Such a shift in the locus of controls raises serious issues of public accountability and transparency for citizens of all countries. It is in this context that Google's dramatic announcement to end censorship of its Chinese search engine should be considered a watershed moment. Whether other companies follow Google's lead, and how China, other countries, and the international community as a whole will respond, are critical open questions that may help to shape the public accountability of private actors in this domain.

"Just-in-time blocking." Disabling or attacking critical information assets at key moments in time—during elections or public demonstrations, for example—may be the most effective tool for influencing political outcomes in cyberspace. Today, computer-network attacks, including the use of distributed denial-of-service attacks, can be easily marshaled and targeted against key sources of information, especially in the developing world, where networks and infrastructure tend to be fragile and prone to disruption. The tools used to mount botnet attacks are now thriving like parasites in the peer-to-peer architectures of insecure servers, personal computers, and social-networking platforms. Botnets can be activated against any target by anyone willing to pay a fee. There are cruder methods of just-in-time blocking as well, such as shutting off power in the buildings where servers are located or tampering with domain-name registration so that information is not routed to its proper destination. This kind of just-in-time blocking has been empirically documented by the OpenNet Initiative in Belarus, Kyrgyzstan, and Tajikistan, as well in numerous other countries.

The attraction of just-in-time blocking is that information is disabled only at key moments, thus avoiding charges of Internet censorship and allowing for plausible denial by the perpetrators. In regions where Internet connectivity can be spotty, just-in-time blocking can be easily passed off as just another technical glitch with the Internet. When such attacks are contracted out to criminal organizations, determining attribution of those responsible is nearly impossible.

Patriotic hacking. One unusual and important characteristic of cyberspace is that individuals can take creative actions—sometimes against perceived threats to their country's national interest—that have systemwide effects. Citizens may bristle at outside interference in their country's internal affairs or take offense at criticism directed at their governments, however illegitimate those governments may appear to outsiders. Those individuals who possess the necessary technical skills have at times taken it upon themselves to attack adversarial sources of information, often leaving provocative messages and warnings behind. Such actions make it difficult to determine the provenance of the attacks: Are they the work of the government or of citizens acting independently? Or are they perhaps some combination of the two? Muddying the waters further, some government security services informally encourage or tacitly approve of the actions of patriotic groups. In China, for example, the Wu Mao Dang, or 50 Cent Party (so named for the amount of money its members are supposedly paid for each Internet post), patrol chatrooms and online forums, posting information favorable to the regime and chastising its critics. In Russia, it is widely believed that the security services regularly coax hacker groups to fight for the motherland in cyberspace and may "seed" instructions on prominent nationalist websites and forums for hacking attacks. In late 2009 in Iran, a shadowy group known as the Iranian Cyber Army took over Twitter and some key opposition websites, defacing the home pages with their own messages. Although no formal connection to the Iranian authorities has been established, the groups responsible for the attacks posted pro-regime messages on the hacked websites and services.

Targeted surveillance and social-malware attacks. Accessing sensitive information about adversaries is one of the most important tools for shaping political outcomes, and so it should come as no surprise that great effort has been devoted to targeted espionage. The Tom-Skype example is only one of many such next-generation methods now becoming common in the cyber-ecosystem. Infiltration of adversarial networks through targeted "social malware" (software designed to infiltrate an unsuspecting user's computer) and "drive-by" Web exploits (websites infected with viruses that target insecure browsers) is exploding throughout the dark underbelly of the Internet. Among the most prominent examples of this type of infiltration was a targeted espionage attack on Google's infrastructure, which the company made public in January 2010.

These types of attacks are facilitated by the careless practices of civil society and human-rights organizations themselves. As Nart Villeneuve and Greg Walton have shown in a recent Information Warfare Monitor report, many civil society organizations lack simple training and resources, leaving them vulnerable to even the most basic Internet attacks.[23] Moreover, because such organizations generally thrive on awareness-raising and advocacy through social networking and email lists, they often unwittingly become compromised as vectors of attacks, even by those whose motivations are not political per se. In one particularly egregious example, the advocacy group Reporters Without Borders unknowingly propagated a link to a malicious website posing as a Facebook petition to release the Tibetan activist Dhondup Wangchen. As with computer network attacks, targeted espionage and social-malware attacks are being developed not just by criminal groups and rogue actors, but also at the highest levels of government. Dennis Blair, the former U.S. director of national intelligence, recently remarked that the United States must be "aggressive" in the cyber-domain in terms of "both protecting our own secrets and stealing those of others."[24]

A Nuanced Understanding

There are several theoretical and policy implications to be drawn from the issues we raise. First, there needs to be a much more nuanced understanding of the complexity of the communications space in which we operate. We should be skeptical of one-dimensional or ahistorical depictions of technologies that paint them with a single brush. Cyberspace is a domain of intense competition, one that creates an ever changing matrix of opportunities and constraints for social forces and ideas. These social forces and ideas, in turn, are imbued with alternative rationalities that collide with one another and affect the structure of the communications environment. Unless the characteristics of cyberspace change radically in the near future and global culture becomes monolithic, linking technological properties to a single social outcome such as liberation or control is a highly dubious exercise.

Second, we must be cautious about promoting policies that support "freedom" software or other technologies presented as magic solutions to thorny political problems. Early on, the Internet was thought to be a truly democratic arena beyond the reach of government control. Typically, the examples used to illustrate this point related to heavy-handed attempts to filter access to information, which are relatively easy to bypass. This conventional wisdom has, in turn, led to efforts on the part of governments to sponsor "firewall-busting" programs and to encourage technological "silver bullets" that will supposedly end Internet censorship once and for all. This viewpoint is simplistic, as it overlooks some of the more important and powerful next-generation controls that are being employed to shape the global commons. Liberation, freedom, and democracy are all socially contested concepts, and thus must be secured by social and political means. Although the prudent support of technological projects may be warranted in specific circumstances, they should be considered as adjuncts to comprehensive strategies rather than as solutions in and of themselves. The struggles over freedom of speech, access to information, privacy protections, and other human-rights issues that now plague cyberspace ultimately pose political problems that are grounded in deeply rooted differences. A new software application, no matter how ingenious, will not solve these problems.

Third, we need to move beyond the idea that cyberspace is not regulated or is somehow immune to regulation. Nothing could be further from the truth. If anything, cyberspace is overregulated by the multitude of actors whose decisions shape its character, often in ways that lack transparency and public accountability. The question is not *whether* to regulate cyberspace, but rather *how* to do so—within which forum, involving which actors, and according to which of many competing values. The regulation of cyberspace tends to take place in the shadows, based on decisions taken by private actors rather than as a result of public deliberation. As the trend toward the securitization and privatization of cyberspace continues, these problems are likely to become more, rather than less, acute.

Finally, for the governance of cyberspace to be effective, it must uncover what is going on "below the surface" of the Internet, largely invisible to the average user. It is there that most of the meaningful limits on action and choice now operate, and they must be unearthed if basic human rights are to be protected online. These subterranean controls have little to do with technology itself and more to do with the complex nature of the communications space in which we find ourselves as we enter the second decade of the twenty-first century. Meaningful change will not come overnight with the invention of some new technology. Instead, it will require a slow process of awareness-raising, the channeling of ingenuity into productive avenues, and the implementation of liberal-democratic restraints.

Notes

1 Larry Diamond, "Liberation Technology," *Journal of Democracy 21* (July 2010): 70–84.

2 Elia Zureik et al., *eds., Surveillance, Privacy, and the Globalization of Personal Information* (McQuill-Queen's University Press, 2010).

3 Our conception of "alternative rationalities" is inspired by Ulrich Beck et al., *Reflexive Modernization* (Cambridge: Polity, 1994). The concept of alternative rationalities has its origins in Max Weber's work and is further developed in critical and postmodern theories.

4 For the concept of "dynamic density," see John Gerard Ruggie, "Continuity and Transformation in the World Polity: Toward a Neorealist Synthesis," *World Politics* 35 (January 1983): 261–85.

5 A. Claire Cutler, Virginia Haufler, and Tony Porter, *Private Authority and International Affairs* (New York: SUNY Press, 1999).

6 Ronald J. Deibert, Rafal Rohozinski, John Palfrey, and Jonathan Zittrain, eds., *Access Controlled: The Shaping of Power, Rights and Rule in Cyberspace* (Cambridge: MIT Press, 2010).

7 See, for example, "Iran's Twitter Revolution," *Washington Times,* 16 June 2009; available at *www.washingtontimes.com/news/2009/jun/16/irans-twitter-revolution.*

8 Chrisanthi Avgerou, "Recognising Alternative Rationalities in the Deployment of Information Systems," *Electronic Journal of Information Systems in Developing Countries 3 (2000); available at www.ejisdc.org/ojs2/index.php/ejisdc/article/view/19.*

9 Rafal Rohozinski, "Bullets to Bytes: Reflections on ICTs and 'Local' Conflict," in Robert Latham, ed., *Bombs and Bandwidth: The Emerging Relationship between Information Technology and Security* (New York: New Press, 2003), 222.

10 Information Warfare Monitor and Shadowserver Foundation, *Shadows in the Cloud: Investigating Cyber Espionage 2.0,* JR03-2010, 6 April 2010; Information Warfare Monitor, *Tracking GhostNet: Investigating a Cyber Espionage Network,* JR02-2009, 29 March 2009.

11 Ronald Deibert, Rafal Rohozinski, and Masashi Crete-Nishihata, "Cyclones in Cyberspace: Information Shaping and Denial in the 2008 South Ossetia War," ms. forthcoming.

12 Ronald Deibert and Rafal Rohozinski, "Risking Security: The Policies and Paradoxes of Cyberspace Security," *International Political Sociology* 4 (March 2010): 15–32.

13 Stephen Walt, "Is the Cyber Threat Overblown?" *Foreign Policy*, 3 March 2010; available at *http://walt.foreignpolicy.com/posts/2010/03/30/is_the_cyber_threat_overblown.*

14 Deibert et al., *Access Controlled.*

15 The following section draws from an earlier article of ours: "Cyber Wars," Index on Censorship, March 2010; available at *www.indexoncensorship.org/2010/03/cyberwars-technology-deiber.*

16 See *http://en.rsf.org/pakistan-court-orders-facebook-blocked-19-05-2010,37524. htm.*

17 See *www.telegraph.co.uk/news/worldnews/asia/bangladesh/4963823/YouTube-blocked-in-Bangladesh-after-guard-mutiny.html.*

18 *See www.guardian.co.uk/commentisfree/libertycentral/2010/jul/03/lebanon-facebook-president-insult.*

19 *See www.latimes.com/technology/sns-ap-lt-venezuela-twitter,0,6311483.story.*

20 "IRGC Consortium Takes Majority Equity in Iran's Telecoms," 5 October 2009, *www.zawya.com/story.cfm/sidv52n40-3NC06/IRGC%20Consortium%20Takes%20Majority%20Equity%20In%20Iran%26rsquo%3Bs%20Telecoms.*

21 See *http://opennet.net/sex-social-mores-and-keyword-filtering-microsoft-bingarabian-countries.*

22 See *http://technology.timesonline.co.uk/tol/news/tech_and_web/the_web/article1391469.ece.*

23 See *www.infowar-monitor.net/2009/10/0day-civil-society-and-cyber-security.*

24 See *www.govinfosecurity.com/p_print.php?t=a&id=1786.*

Credit

Deibert, Ronald, and Rafal Rohozinski. "Liberation vs. Control: The Future of Cyberspace" *Journal of Democracy* 21.4 (2010): 43–57. Print.

Good News for the Future? Young People, Internet Use, and Political Participation

Tom P. Baker and Claes H. de Vreese

Introduction

Much research on youth and politics from the last decade shows increasing detachment of younger people from politics. Most discussions revolve around declining political interest, dropping participation, and low turnout at elections (e.g., Delli Carpini, 2000; Phelps, 2004; Pirie & Worcester, 2000). Although the assumption that political participation among the young has been low for a long time is generally accepted, the role of the media in affecting (non)participatory behavior has become particularly interesting with the ever-growing popularity of the Internet among younger people and the possible effects of the new medium. The use of new media for political ends in the United States was visible during the 2008 U.S. presidential elections. President Obama actively and successfully employed social media like Facebook, Twitter, and YouTube as communication tools, capitalizing on the heavy use of the Internet for political activities by younger people (Smith & Rainie, 2008). Also, in most Western European countries there seems high potential for the Internet, considering the high usage levels over the last few years (Eurostat, 2009) and the continuing debates on decreasing participation levels among youth.

A considerable amount of research is already available on the ways the Internet affects civic or political involvement. Although findings have sometimes been inconclusive, recent studies acknowledge that Internet use is not a unidimensional concept and thus does not—if at all—affect all groups in society similarly; rather, its effects depend on a complex combination of personal and social characteristics, usage patterns, and the specific content and context of the medium. More specifically, Shah, Kwak, and Holbert (2001) have shown that modeling specified Internet use (as opposed to "overall Internet use") as a predictor of social capital worked best for younger generations (people under 35 in this case). Similar arguments about differential effects have earlier been made concerning the effects of watching television (McLeod & McDonald, 1985; Norris, 1996).

A plethora of both specific and generic terms have been used to cover diverging forms of civic and political involvement, ranging from *social capital* (e.g., Putnam, 2000), *civic literacy* (Milner, 2002), and *political* and *civic engagement* to more concrete terms like *membership, political knowledge,* and *turnout.* In this article, we focus on *political participation.* In a comprehensive overview, Delli Carpini (2004, p. 396) defines political participation as part of a wider notion of "democratic engagement" which includes most of the terms mentioned above. While confining ourselves to politics, we claim that the understanding of political participation should not be limited to institutional and traditional ways. The definitions and boundaries of political participation have been subjects of discussion for decades (for an early overview and discussion, see Conge, 1988), but contemporary research simply cannot ignore online ways of participation. This article focuses on offline and online political participation in the Netherlands. Just like in the United States and many other Western European countries, Internet usage among Dutch youth is very high, while at the same time there are debates about declines in participation. Our study finally aims to generate general insights into the role of specific uses of the Internet in affecting participatory behavior among the so-called Internet generation.

A Closer Look at Decline in Participation

Historically, the participation of citizens in the political process has been considered a crucial element for a functioning and healthy democracy. Irrespective of the various changes in the social and political landscape on both international and national levels during the last decades, the significance of participatory behavior of citizens is at the core in several key works on democracy (e.g., Held, 2006). In the light of this alleged importance, serious concerns have been raised over the rate of political participation among young and future generations. Recent reports from western countries show low or decreasing levels of participation. However, questions arise if *all* forms of political participation are declining or if the existing literature is biased by a disproportional focus on institutional and limited measures of participatory behavior. As—among others—Verba, Schlozman, and Brady (1995) have made clear, political participation has several dimensions, is changing over time, and requires different levels of input of time, money, and skills. It may well be that participatory acts that require a substantial amount of input in offline settings are more accessible and attractive for some people when they can be carried out in an online context (e.g., sending an e-mail to a politician is faster, cheaper, and easier than sending a letter).

Some suggest that it is not so much the levels of interest or participation that are being challenged but rather the attitudes toward politics that are changing. For example, younger people are thought to be more skeptical and to show more political apathy (e.g., Henn, Weinstein, & Wring, 2002), something that should not be equated with nonparticipation or disengagement. Younger people may form a new generation that is less attracted by traditional forms of political engagement (Phelps, 2004; Zukin,

Keeter, Andolina, Jenkins, & Delli Carpini, 2006). Such assertions have led to a call for a broader and more contemporary notion of political or civic participation (Dahlgren, 2000; de Vreese, 2006; Dunleavy, 1996; Livingstone, Bober, & Helsper, 2005; O'Toole, Lister, Marsh, Jones, & McDonagh, 2003; Phelps, 2005; Russell, 2004; Verba et al., 1995) and to look beyond established and institutional measures of participation like party membership, attendance at political meetings, or voter turnout. Taking a broader approach, Zukin et al. (2006) concluded that "simple claims that today's youth (...) are apathetic and disengaged from *civic* life are simply wrong" (pp. 188–189).

The Internet is a natural medium for alternative and digital ways of political participation. It offers—potentially—new modes of easily accessible, low-cost forms of participation. The web and all other online applications are heavily used by younger people. For example, in 2007, the average level of Internet use[1] in the 27 European Union member states was 60%, whereas this was 88% for the age group of 16 to 24, peaking at 99% in the Netherlands and 100% in Denmark, Finland, and Iceland (Eurostat, 2007). In the United States, younger people also belong to the group of heaviest Internet users. While in May 2008 the overall percentage of Internet users[2] among the adult American population was 73%, this percentage was 90% for the age group 18 to 29 (Pew Internet & American Life Project, 2008). The Internet offers a wide scope of possibilities to engage in political activities like visiting political blogs, researching political information, following online news, participating in forums, discussing politics by e-mail, or organizing electronic petitions.

There have been divergent expectations about the development of the Internet and how it may affect certain aspects of civic and political life. Supporters of a so-called utopian view not only praise the wide-ranging technical possibilities but also commend the social potential of the Internet to increase political engagement and participation. Followers of a more dystopian view consider the Internet more as a social threat, disconnecting people from "real" life (Kraut et al., 1998; Nie & Erbring, 2002) or even endangering key elements of a healthy democracy (Sunstein, 2001). Many empirical studies from recent years, however, have not found evidence for either strong positive or negative effects of Internet use on (offline forms of) political engagement (see Boulianne, 2009). Nevertheless, as we shall see, studies that have included more specified forms of Internet use in their model were able to shed more light under what circumstances, or for which audience, effects actually *do* appear.

Media and Politics: An Unclear Relationship

The notion that media, including the Internet, serve multiple functions and lead to different effects is commonly adopted in the field of political communication. A range of studies—usually employing multivariate analyses—have addressed the relationships between particular uses of the Internet and forms of political and civic engagement (e.g., Quintelier & Vissers, 2008; Scheufele & Nisbet, 2002; Shah, McLeod, & Yoon, 2001). Tolbert and McNeal (2003), for example, found that being exposed to election news on the Internet increased the probability that people would vote during the 1996 and 2000 U.S. presidential elections, leading to the idea that the Internet has a mobilizing potential. Focusing on civic engagement, Shah et al. (2001) showed that "information exchange" on the Internet was a better predictor than "overall Internet use." Xenos and Moy (2007), however, show that positive effects of online news on engagement are higher for people with more political interest, and, also, Bimber (2003) argues that mainly already politically engaged citizens benefit from the Internet's potential.

The rapid growth of Internet use and the alleged declining levels of political involvement of younger people have made the relationship between these two a popular and much debated issue. New media may well challenge the role or fill some of the gap left by traditionally strong socializers such as family, church, and school. Especially, the role played by parents for their children as key socializers with regard to politics is changing. In the past decades, trends of increasing individualization and volatile electoral behavior are observed (Dalton, 2002). Although traditionally parents were stable voters and played an important role, they are now increasingly becoming floating voters and losing ground as political socializers. Taking this development into account, media in general, and the Internet in particular, are becoming more central in the process of affecting participatory behavior. As Delli Carpini (2004) notes, "As one of several socializing agents, the media provide much of the 'raw material' that make up social and political beliefs, attitudes, and schema" (p. 408).

Looking first at the role of "traditional" news media, newspaper use repeatedly proved to be positively related to various forms of civic and political engagement. Eveland and Scheufele (2000) showed that reading newspapers positively impacted political participation and voting, and Weaver and Drew (2001) found positive relationships between paying attention to campaign news in newspapers and voting (see also McLeod, Scheufele, & Moy, 1999; Scheufele, 2002). Jeffres, Lee, Neuendorf, and Atkin (2007) showed that readership of newspapers was positively related with different forms of community activities and social capital. Also, television news use, although less consistently, has been found to—directly (Norris, 1996) or indirectly (Shah, Cho, Eveland, & Kwak, 2005)—impact political participation in a positive direction.

The impact of news consumption has also been tested in online contexts and showed similar positive relationships. Tolbert and McNeal (2003) showed that using online news increased voting probability, and Quintelier and Vissers (2008) found that consuming online news positively related to political participation among teenagers, while both studies included a large set of control variables (see also Esser & de Vreese, 2007; Kenski & Stroud, 2006; Shah et al., 2005) We therefore hypothesize, *ceteris paribus,* the following:

> *Hypothesis 1 (H1):* News consumption via newspapers, television, and the Internet is positively related to political participation.

Besides news use, discussing politics with family or friends is considered an important factor as regard to political participation. Various studies have convincingly linked political discussion with participatory behavior (Kim, Wyatt, & Katz, 1999; McLeod et al., 1999; Wyatt, Katz, & Kim, 2000) and knowledge (Eveland, 2004; Eveland & Thomson, 2006). Parallel to the relationships between *offline* discussion and participation, positive associations have been suggested between *online* discussion and political knowledge and participation (Hardy & Scheufele, 2005; Price & Cappella, 2002). This leads us to our second hypothesis:

> *Hypothesis 2 (H2):* Interactive online communication is positively related to political participation.

Although there seems to be wide agreement on the potential benefits of Internet use, some have argued that time spent on the Internet (or watching television) reduces the available time to engage in meaningful civic and political activities (Nie & Erbring, 2002; Putnam, 1995, 2000), a process that is generally referred to as *time displacement.* These assertions, however, have been countered in other research (e.g., Shah, Schmierbach, Hawkins, Espino, & Donavan, 2002).

Because of the high development pace of the Internet and the phenomenon's relative newness in social science, research approaches and findings vary widely and theories on the potential effects of the new medium are neither too stable nor convincing. Although scholars agree on the assumption that the Internet leads to differential effects for different types of users, recent research on the relationship between media use and politics is still very limited in the examination of the multidimensional relationship between Internet use and political participation. Previous research (Pasek, Kenski, Romer, & Jamieson, 2006) acknowledges the varied functions media can serve, but the multidimensional character of the Internet in analyses is often overlooked. Although most researchers aim at determining the role that media play in younger people's lives with regard to political participation, for the most part solely informational uses or general indicators (e.g., web use, e-mail) are taken into consideration with regard to the Internet. Limited specification of Internet use in survey research may lead to scholars to underestimate the actual magnitude of Internet effects (see also Boulianne, 2009). We argue that given the high level of Internet use among younger people along with their diverging usage patterns, the multidimensional character of the new medium deserves greater attention. Following this need to specify the type of use and online activity, we hypothesize the following:

> *Hypothesis 3 (H3):* Specified media usage is a stronger predictor of political participation than time spent with a medium.

Another often overlooked but important aspect when tapping political or civic participation is the various digital possibilities the Internet offers to engage in political activities, which then leads to the expectation that intensive use of the Internet does not *necessarily* lead to decreased participation. As noted earlier, the Internet can be used to be politically active in various ways (visiting political websites, discussing politics in discussion forums, signing online petitions) and requires different levels of skills or energy. Moreover, many online activities, like signing petitions or sending political messages, have also been measured in an offline form (e.g., McLeod et al., 1999; Putnam, 2000; Verba et al., 1995). Given the popularity and relative ease of online political participation, such activities should not be neglected when measuring participatory behavior. However, taking into account the theory of time displacement, increased online participatory behavior may lead to lower levels of offline participation. Given the centrality of the Internet among younger people, we therefore hypothesize the following:

> *Hypothesis 4 (H4):* Internet use is a stronger predictor for newer forms of political participation than traditional forms.

Our last expectation relates to intrinsic preferences toward specific media content. Prior (2005) proposes a measure of relative entertainment preference (REP), which is aimed at understanding the political implications of people's preference for news or entertainment content. Prior's results point at a negative relationship between REP and political knowledge and voter turnout. For this research, we will focus on the potential link between REP and political participation, to see if this proposition can be extended. We do so—in analogy to our Internet use measures—also to acknowledge that it is the type of use of a medium that matters and not the duration of the use. Our last hypothesis therefore reads as follows:

> *Hypothesis 5 (H5):* There is a negative relationship between REP and political participation.

Method

We designed an online survey in the Netherlands to explore the possible relationships between different media uses and political participation. Ten thousand people in the age group of 16 to 24 were sampled by the marketing company TAPPS. These people were invited by e-mail to fill in the questionnaire. The sampling frame consists of a selection of databases that are composed of different modes of recruitment including both offline and online modes. The survey was administered by the Amsterdam School of Communication Research (ASCoR) in the spring of 2006. To maximize the response rate, the survey was kept relatively short (average response time was less than 10 minutes) and incentives were raffled off among the participants.

An online survey design was chosen, given our key interest in the relationship between different forms of political participation and Internet use patterns. Although online surveys are critiqued for their skewed distributions (i.e., only Internet users), in the Netherlands, Internet access among 16 to 24 years is almost 100%, and our interest is not a comparison between online and offline users. The questionnaire was successfully completed by 2,409 respondents (M = 19.2 years, SD = 2.29), resulting in a response rate of 24% (AAPOR RR1).[3]

Dependent Variables

Given the high Internet usage among younger people, we tapped two discrete forms of participatory behavior, labeled *traditional participation* and *digital participation*. A factor analysis (principal component analysis with Varimax rotation) yielded two factors for both forms of participation, which we tagged *passive* and *active participation*.

Digital participation was measured by asking people about the frequency they participated in online political activities, ranging on a 5-point scale from *never* to *very often*. Following the factor analysis, the variables *digital passive participation* and *digital active participation* were created, respectively explaining 42% (eigenvalue 3.82) and 12% (eigenvalue 1.07) of the variance.[4] Digital passive participation (M = 1.70, SD = 0.69) was measured by asking respondents to indicate how often they, in relation to politics, (1) visited websites of the municipality, (2) visited websites of the government and public administration, and (3) visited websites with political content. The three items showed to be internally consistent (α = .77). Digital active participation (M = 2.05, SD = 0.69) involved more active forms of participation and was gauged by asking how often the respondent in relation to politics (1) reacted online to a message or article on the Internet, (2) signed online petitions, and (3) participated in online polls. The items formed an acceptable internally consistent scale (α = .59).

A similar approach was used to tap traditional participation. For this measure, people again were asked with what frequency (5-point scale, *never* to *very often*) they participated in political activities, but this time in an offline setting. Factor analysis led to the creation of traditional passive participation (explained variance 15%, eigenvalue 1.02) and traditional active participation (explained variance 45%, eigenvalue 3.16). Respondents' traditional passive participation (M = 1.80, SD = 0.73) was made up of three items (α = .63), asking people how often they (1) retrieved books or information about political or social issues, (2) signed petitions, and (3) followed newspapers and television in election times to learn about politics and political parties. Traditional active participation (M = 1.21, SD = 0.41) consisted of four items (α = .75), asking how often the respondents (1) sent letters to newspapers or magazines to comment on articles, (2) protested or complained by mail or telephone about decisions taken by the government or public administration, (3) participated in demonstrations, and (4) actively engaged in discussions during debates or lectures.

Independent Variables

Media variables. To assess the types of media and media content that respondents usually consume, a set of detailed questions was asked, following Slater's argument (2004, p. 169) that a lack of specified measures of media use could, among others, lead to underestimates of its possible effects. In this article, specificity of media exposure measures is taken into account by assessing uses of newspaper, television, and Internet.

Newspapers. Respondents were asked to indicate how much time they spent reading paid and free newspapers on an average day (in 10-minute intervals), leading to *reading time paid dailies* (M = 2.66, SD = 1.03) and *reading time free dailies* (M = 2.67, SD = 0.84). Participants were also asked how often (in days) during an average week they read the following newspapers: *AD/Algemeen Dagblad, Metro, NRC Handelsblad, NRC.next, Het Parool, Spits, De Telegraaf, Trouw, de Volkskrant,* and a regional daily. Additive index scores were created for quality newspapers *(NRC Handelsblad, NRC. next, Het Parool, Trouw,* and *de Volkskrant;* M = 1.10, SD = 0.24), popular newspapers *(AD/Algemeen Dagblad* and *De Telegraaf;* M = 1.40, SD = 0.57), and free newspapers *(Metro and Spits;* M = 2.05, SD = 0.90).

Television. The setup for the television questions corresponded with the design of the newspaper section. First the respondents were asked how long (in 0.5-hour intervals) they watched television on an average day, leading to creation of the variable *viewing time television* (M = 6.97, SD = 2.30). The respondents then were asked how often (in days) they tuned into different national, regional, international, and thematic channels. A factor analysis revealed two forms of viewing behavior: *public television viewing* (eigenvalue 1.85, explained variance 14.3%) and *commercial television viewing* (eigenvalue 3.98, explained variance 30.6%). Public television viewing (M = 1.83, SD = 0.73) consisted of the channels Nederland 1, Nederland 2, and Nederland 3, and commercial television viewing (M = 2.41, SD = 0.66) was formed by RTL4, RTL5, RTL7, SBS6, Net5, and Veronica/JETIX. Both the public and the commercials channels formed reliable scales (Cronbach's α = .78).

An additional measure was used to tap the respondents' relative preference for entertainment- or news-related content on television. The REP is based on Prior's REP (Prior, 2005) and was measured by letting the respondents choose, in five rounds, between their preference for an entertainment program or a news/current affairs program. Consequently, the total amount of choices (five) was divided by the amount of choices for entertainment programs (ranging between 0 and 5) and a REP ratio was computed between 0 and 1 (M = 0.73, SD = 0.24).

Internet. First, respondents were asked how much time they spent online on an average day (15 minutes or less, 30 minutes, 45 minutes, 1 hour, 1.5 hours, 2 hours, 2.5 hours, 3 hours, 3.5 hours, 4 hours, or 4.5 hours or more), resulting in the variable time spent online (M = 6.88, SD = 2.64).

As noted earlier, it is considered relevant to examine not only informational or overall use of media types but rather include detailed measures of media use (Slater, 2004). For example, taking into account the large battery of possible Internet activities, Norris and Jones (1998) distinguish between four different types of Internet users, labeled *researchers, home consumers, political expressives,* and *party animals.* Shah et al. (2001) discriminated between using the Internet for social recreation, product consumption, financial management, or information exchange (see also Quintelier & Vissers, 2008). In our survey, we presented our respondents with a list of 16 surfing activities and 4 communication activities and asked to indicate how often (5-point scale, ranging between *never* and *very often*) they took part in those activities. After factor analysis, four categories were determined: Internet news use (eigenvalue 1.37, explained variance 8.65%), services (eigenvalue 2.91, explained variance 18.2%), music (eigenvalue 1.99, explained variance 12.4%), and club/organization (eigenvalue 1.10, explained variance 6.9%). Internet news use (M = 2.05, SD = 0.83) is the combined measure of visiting newspaper websites, visiting news sites and news blogs, and visiting showbizz news sites (α = .59). Services (M = 2.39, SD = 0.68) is formed by online banking, job searching, housing sites, looking for product information, holiday bookings, and online shopping (α = .65). Music (M = 3.59, SD = 1.11) is a two-item measure of downloading music and software and listening music on your PC (α = .69). Club/organization (M = 2.46, SD = 1.31) is created by asking people how often they visited the website of an organization or club they were a member of. Respondents were also asked how often (5-point scale, between *never* and *very often)* they participated in online communication activities. The three variables were e-mail (M = 4.25, SD = 0.77), social networking (chat and online communities; eigenvalue = 1.54, explained variance = 38.5%; M = 3.33, SD = 0.98), and forum (M = 2.29, SD = 1.24).

Control variables. Respondents were asked to indicate their gender (1 = *male*, 2 = *female)* and level of education. A dummy variable was used to check for differences between respondents below and above legal voting age, which is 18 in the Netherlands ($1 \geq 18$). Political talk (M = 2.28, SD = 1.11) was measured by asking on a 5-point scale, ranging between *never* and *very often*, how often the respondent talked with friends about local or national political issues. Political interest (M = 2.85, SD = 1.12) was tapped by asking to what extent people agreed with the statement "Politics is interesting" (5-point scale, ranging between *totally disagree* and *totally agree*). Although both political talk and political interest are generally used as dependent variables, here they were purposefully implemented as control variables in order to provide a conservative test of the four main dependent political participation variables. Political talk and political interest can be expected to account for a considerable amount of the variance in the dependent variables, but inserting both variables in the early stage as control variables can assist in clarifying whether particular media use explains forms of political participation, while both political talk and interest are controlled for.

Analysis

To test our hypotheses, hierarchical multiple regressions analyses were run for the four forms of participation. The independent variables were grouped into four blocks that were consecutively taken into the regression. The variables in the first block were used as control variables, consisting of gender, legal voting age, education, political interest, and political talk. The second block was formed by measures of *duration* of newspaper, television, and Internet use. The third and fourth blocks were formed by respectively traditional media variables (newspapers and television) and Internet variables.

As already indicated earlier, by using political interest and political talk as control variables, a conservative test could be conducted of the participation measures. Also, entering media duration variables at an early stage allowed us to both test for main effects of media duration use and differential effects based on specified use of newspapers, television, and Internet, helping us to address the expectation (H3) that specified media usage (block 3 and 4) would be a stronger predictor of political participation than time spent with a medium (block 2), with possible effects weakening or diminishing when participation forms are regressed on all variable blocks in the final model.

Results

When looking at the results of all four regression analyses (Tables 1 to 4), we find support for our hypothesis that specified media usage is a stronger predictor of political participation than time spent with a medium (H3). Almost all initial significant beta coefficients in block 2 (time spent with a medium) vanish when the remaining blocks (block 3 and 4, specified media use) are entered in the third and fourth step of the analysis. Only in the regression model for traditional passive participation, a significant positive association remains for *reading time paid dailies* (Table 1). No significant effects are found for gender and education, except for modest negative significant associations in the model for traditional active participation (Table 2). In the models for active participation (both online and offline), a negative effect was found for legal voting age.[5]

Examining both the traditional media block and the Internet block, we find that using the Internet for news is a positive predictor for all four forms of participation. However, quality newspaper reading only shows significant positive associations with traditional forms of participation (Tables 1 and 2). No negative effects are found for reading popular or free newspapers (with one exception). Public television viewing (often seen as strongly correlated with news viewing) only proves to be a positive predictor of passive forms of participation, while commercial viewing is not a significant predictor for any type of participatory behavior. Given the systematic positive associations of news use on the Internet and the mixed results of newspaper reading and watching (public) television, we can partially confirm H1 that news consumption via newspapers, television, and the Internet is positively related to political participation. As expected, respondents' entertainment preference was negatively related to political participation, so H5 can be confirmed.

Looking at the Internet block, a considerable amount of variables are (modest) positive predictors of participation. Concerning surfing activities, particularly news, service, and club/organization are significantly and positively related to most forms of participation. The same tendency is found for online forms of communication. Predominantly significant positive relationships were found between online forms of communication (mainly e-mail and forum use) and participation, supporting our expectation that interactive online communication is positively related to participation (H2).

Comparing the predictive power of the Internet block on the four dependent variables, higher amounts of explained variance were found for digital forms of participation (passive 8.6%, active 20.2%) than for traditional participation, supporting H4 (Internet use is a stronger predictor for newer forms of political participation than for traditional forms). However, several Internet variables are also significant positive predictors for traditional ways of participation.[6]

Table 1. Predicting Traditional Passive Participation

	M1	M2	M3	M4	M5
Control Variables					
Gender	.00	.00	.02	.02	.03
Education	.01	.01	.00	.00	.00
Legal voting age	.04**	.04*	.03	.01	.03
Political talk	.55***	.55***	.51***	.48***	.01
Political interest	.24***	.23***	.19***	.18***	.01
Duration					
Reading time paid dailies		.07***	.06***	.04**	.01
Reading time free dailies		–.01	–.01	–.02	.01
Viewing time television		–.01	–.01	.00	.01
Time spent online		.01	.01	–.03	.00
Traditional media					
Quality newspaper reading			.04*	.03*	.05
Popular newspaper reading			–.02	–.03*	.02
Free daily reading			.00	–.02	.01
Public television viewing			.08***	.06***	.02
Commercial television viewing			.00	–.02	.02
Relative entertainment preference			–.09***	–.10***	.05
Internet					
Internet new use				.10***	.01
Services				.06***	.02
Music				.00	.01
Club/organization				.02	.01
E-mail				.05***	.01
Social networking				.01	.01
Forum				.04*	.01
N				2,409	
R^2 change		.004	.017	.021	
Total R^2 (adjusted)	.502	.506	.523	.544	

Note: Entries are standardized beta coefficients and standard errors.

$^*p \leq .05$. $^{**}p \leq .01$. $^{***}p \leq .001$.

Table 2. Predicting Traditional Active Participation

	M1	M2	M3	M4	SE
Control Variables					
Gender	–.09***	–.08***	–.06**	–.06**	.02
Education	–.04*	–.04	–.03	–.04*	.00
Legal voting age	–.01	–.02	–.04	–.05*	.02
Political talk	.26***	.26***	.23***	.19***	.01
Political interest	.13***	.12***	.08***	.07***	.01
Duration					
Reading time paid dailies		.06**	.03	.01	.01
Reading time free dailies		.03	.00	–.01	.01
Viewing time television		–.01	–.04*	–.03	.00
Time spent online		.06**	.06**	.01	.00
Traditional media					
Quality newspaper reading			.11***	.12***	.03
Popular newspaper reading			.01	–.01	.01
Free daily reading			.08***	.07***	.01
Public telvision viewing			.06*	.03	.01
Commercial television viewing			.06**	.04	.01
Relative entertainment preference			–.03	–.04	.04
Internet					
Internet new use				.09***	.01
Services				.09***	.01
Music				–.04*	.01
Club/organization				.03	.01
E-mail				–.03	.01
Social networking				.06**	.01
Forum				.10***	.01
N				2,409	
R^2 change		.007	.026	.034	
Total R^2 (adjusted)	.130	.137	.163	.197	

Note: Entries are standardized beta coefficients and standard errors.

*p ≤ .05. **p ≤ .01. *** p ≤ .001.

Table 3. Predicting Digital Passive Participation

	M1	M2	M3	M4	SE
Control Variables					
Gender	–.06***	–.05**	–.02	–.03	.03
Education	.02	.02	.01	.01	.01
Legal voting age	.09***	.09***	.08***	.00	.03
Political talk	.31***	.31***	.27***	.20***	.01
Political interest	.27***	.26***	.21***	.19***	.01
Duration					
Reading time paid dailies		.05**	.02	–.01	.01
Reading time free dailies		.02	.02	.00	.02
Viewing time television		.01	–.01	.02	.01
Time spent online		.07***	.07***	.01	.00
Traditional media					
Quality newspaper reading			.02	.02	.05
Popular newspaper reading			.00	–.02	.02
Free daily reading			.01	–.02	.01
Public telvision viewing			.13***	.09***	.02
Commercial television viewing			.02	–.01	.02
Relative entertainment preference			–.10***	–.10***	.06
Internet					
Internet new use				.18***	.02
Services				.18***	.02
Music				–.04*	.01
Club/organization				.05**	.01
E-mail				.07***	.02
Social networking				–.01	.01
Forum				.06***	.01
N				2,409	
R^2 change		.007	.029	.086	
Total R^2 (adjusted)	.282	.289	.318	.404	

Note: Entries are standardized beta coefficients and standard errors.

*$p \leq .05$. **$p \leq .01$. *** $p \leq .001$.

Table 4. Predicting Digital Active Participation

	M1	M2	M3	M4	SE
Control Variables					
Gender	–.07***	–.05**	–.04	–.01	.03
Education	–.02	.00	–.01	–.01	.01
Legal voting age	–.12***	–.14***	.15***	–.13***	.03
Political talk	.31***	.32***	.29***	.22***	.01
Political interest	.03	.03	.01	.01	.01
Duration					
Reading time paid dailies		.03	.02	–.02	.01
Reading time free dailies		.06	.05*	.03	.02
Viewing time television		.03	–.01	.03	.01
Time spent online		.13***	.13***	–.01	.00
Traditional media					
Quality newspaper reading			.02	.01	.05
Popular newspaper reading			.00	–.03	.02
Free daily reading			.04	.00	.01
Public telvision viewing			.07**	.02	.02
Commercial television viewing			.07**	.03	.02
Relative entertainment preference			–.05*	–.05**	.06
Internet					
Internet new use				.18***	.02
Services				.07***	.02
Music				.05*	.01
Club/organization				.04*	.01
E-mail				.05**	.02
Social networking				.03	.01
Forum				.36***	.01
N				2,409	
R^2 change		.023	.012	.202	
Total R^2 (adjusted)	.123	.146	.158	.360	

Note: Entries are standardized beta coefficients and standard errors.

*p ≤ .05. **p ≤ .01. *** p ≤ .001.

Discussion

The shortcomings in the communication environment are often highlighted when the shortcomings of today's democratic practices are discussed. The empirical evidence for the negative effects of suboptimal communications is at best mixed and more complex than most assumed relationships (see also Shah, McLeod, & Yoon, 2001; Tolbert & McNeal, 2003). This study particularly tackled the relationships between various types of media use and various forms of political participation for the citizens of tomorrow, young people aged 16 to 24. We found that various types of media use are positively linked to measures of political participation. In addition to all kinds of informational uses, noninformational uses of the web (e.g., online communication and visiting nonnews websites) also had positive relationships with diverse forms of participation. With conventional wisdom and much extant research focusing on the *negative* role played by the media in understanding younger people's political participation, this article has shown otherwise. Although high usage of particular (entertainment) media or a total detachment from any news media may indeed be disadvantageous for participatory behavior, a broader look at the use of media is unarguably relevant.

The findings of this study support our expectation that tapping specific uses of newspapers, television, and Internet improves our understanding of the relationships between media use and participatory behavior. Reversely, overall *duration* of specific media use proves to have weak predictive power. This finding is supported in related studies (e.g., Shah et al., 2001). While established positive effects of news use are indeed found in this article, the inclusion of other online activities, like using digital services and engaging in online communication and discussion, also shows positive relationships with most forms of political participation. This augments our argument that most effects of media use on political participation are *positive* in nature.

Moreover, this study extends Putnam's view (2000) that social networks are beneficial to participatory behavior. However, while Putnam, in his work on the building of social capital, stresses the importance of physical presence and reality, we extend this argument to also show that "being connected" online is positively related to both on and offline forms of participation. Although results for the four different forms of participation pointed in the same direction, the strength of associations differed. Forum use, for example, proved to be a much stronger predictor of digital active participation than of other forms, while traditional media use proved to be a (slightly) better predictor of traditional forms of participation than digital forms. Overall, however, several positive associations have been found between use of the Internet and both (digital and traditional) forms of participation, corroborating our expectation that online activities may be equally important measures in research on younger people's participatory behavior.

Although we have found associations between media use and participatory behavior of youth, the cross-sectional setup of the analysis does not permit us to make firm assertions about the causal direction of the relationship. It may very well be that specific media use drives on the intrinsic motivation of people to be politically active. This potentially reverse, reciprocal, or maybe even reinforcing process of media selection deserves special attention in current and future media effects research, using more complex combinations of both cross-sectional and overtime analysis of panel data (Slater, 2007). Longitudinal analysis could also be very useful in revealing cohort effects for different (media) generations. Although an online survey is a very useful instrument regarding our sample (young people) and the subject of this study (Internet use), the online invitations and surveys may have led to a somewhat skewed distribution of our sample. Hence, we are unable to make comparisons with youth that are not online or hardly use the Internet and might be active newspaper readers.

While the current study has limitations that should be considered and explored in future research, we have tried to improve the understanding of the varied functions of Internet use and to determine certain online usage patterns of younger people (e.g., consumer-related use, communication, online networking) as potential predictors of political participation (see also Quintelier & Vissers, 2008; Shah et al., 2001). The article demonstrates the limitations of research designs that are heavily focused on overall measures of (news) media use, passing over the wide-ranging and diverging uses and usage patterns of active online citizens. In a research field where Internet and younger generations are of key interest, scholars should not limit their approach to only the established offline and institutional ways of participation and media use. When research takes into account both offline and online political participation, including institutional and alternative ways of participatory behavior, a better understanding can be developed of the challenges and changes political participation is really facing in the current millennium.

Notes

1 Internet use is defined as the percentage of individuals who used the Internet in the last year.

2 An Internet user is defined as someone who at least occasionally uses the Internet or sends and receives e-mail.

3 While this response rate may seem low, it should be noted that random digit dialing (RDD) samples in the Netherlands typically yield response rates around 30%. Moreover, Krosnick (1999) shows that low a response rate is not per se an issue if the sample is not too far off the targeted population.

4 Our original factor analysis included three additional items, but these were removed because they suffered from extreme positive skewness or did not load clearly on one of the two extracted components.

5 Additional analyses suggest that the negative coefficients appear because of the negative associations with participation for respondents between 22 and 24 years old. Although we are not sure about the cause of this finding, it may be that the participatory acts that were measured become less relevant, interesting or accessible for this group, for example because of life changes such as working and thus having less free time to engage in participatory acts.

6 We emphasize that our test is rather conservative, given the controls for not only demographics but also for political talk and political interest which account for a large share of the explained variance. The robustness of our findings is augmented by this conservative estimate.

Works Cited

Bimber, B. (2003). *Information and American Democracy: Technology in the Evolution of Political Power.* Cambridge, UK: Cambridge University Press.

Boulianne, S. (2009). "Does Internet Use Affect Engagement? A Meta-Analysis of Research." *Political Communication, 26,* 193–211.

Conge, P. J. (1988). "The Concept of Political Participation: Toward a Definition." *Comparative Politics, 20,* 241–249.

Dahlgren, P. (2000). "The Internet and the Democratization of Civic Culture." *Political Communication, 17,* 335–340.

Dalton, R. J. (2002). *Citizen Politics: Public Opinion and Political Parties in Advanced Industrial Democracies* (3rd ed.). New York: Chatham House.

de Vreese, C. H. (2006). "10 Observations About the Past, Present, and Future of Political Communication. Inaugural Lecture Delivered at the University of Amsterdam, Chair in Political Communication." Amsterdam: Amsterdam University Press.

Delli Carpini, M. X. (2000). "Gen.com: Youth, Civic Engagement, and the New Information Environment." *Political Communication, 17,* 341–349.

Delli Carpini, M. X. (2004). "Mediating Democratic Engagement: The Impact of Communications on Citizens' Involvement in Political and Civic Life." In L. L. Kaid (Ed.), *Handbook of Political Communication* (395–434). Mahwah, NJ: Lawrence Erlbaum.

Dunleavy, P. (1996). "Political Behavior: Institutional and Experiential Approaches." In R. Goodin & H.-D. Klingemann (Eds.), *A New Handbook of Political Science* (276–294). Oxford, UK: Oxford University Press.

Esser, F., & de Vreese, C. H. (2007). "Comparing Young Voters' Political Engagement in the United States and Europe." *American Behavioral Scientist, 50,* 1195–1213.

Eurostat. (2007). *Individuals—Internet use 2007.* Retrieved April 3, 2008, from http://epp.eurostat.ec.europa.eu/.

Eurostat. (2009). *Data in Focus 46/2009, Internet Usage in 2009, Households and Individuals.* Retrieved December 22, 2009, from http://epp.eurostat.ec.europa.eu/cache/ITY_PUBLIC/4-08122009-BP/EN/4-08122009-BP-EN.PDF.

Eveland, W. P., Jr. (2004). "The Effect of Political Discussion in Producing Informed Citizens: The Roles of Information, Motivation, and Elaboration." *Political Communication, 21,* 177–193.

Eveland, W. P., Jr., & Scheufele, D. A. (2000). "Connecting News Media Use With Gaps in Knowledge and Participation." *Political Communication, 17,* 215–237.

Eveland, W. P., Jr., & Thomson, T. (2006). "Is It Talking, Thinking, or Both? A Lagged Dependent Variable Model of Discussion Effects on Political Knowledge." *Journal of Communication, 56,* 523–542.

Hardy, B. W., & Scheufele, D. A. (2005). "Examining Differential Gains From Internet Use: Comparing the Moderating Role of Talk and Online Interactions." *Journal of Communication, 55*(1), 71–84.

Held, D. (2006). *Models of democracy*. Cambridge, UK: Polity.

Henn, M., Weinstein, M., & Wring, D. (2002). "A Generation Apart? Youth and Political Participation in Britain." *British Journal of Politics and International Relations, 4,* 167–192.

Jeffres, L. W., Lee, J.-W., Neuendorf, K., & Atkin, D. (2007). "Newspaper Reading Supports Community Involvement." *Newspaper Research Journal,* 28(1), 6–23.

Kenski, K., & Stroud, N. J. (2006). Connections Between Internet Use and Political Efficacy, Knowledge, and Participation." *Journal of Broadcasting & Electronic Media, 50,* 173–192.

Kim, J., Wyatt, R. O., & Katz, E. (1999). "News, Talk, Opinion, Participation: The Part Played by Conversation in Deliberative Democracy." *Political Communication, 16*, 361–385.

Kraut, R., Patterson, M., Lundmark, V., Kiesler, S., Mukopadhyay, T., & Scherlis, W. (1998). "Internet Paradox: A Social Technology that Reduces Social Involvement and Psychological Well-Being?" *American Psychologist, 53,* 1017–1031.

Krosnick, J. A. (1999). "Survey Research." *Annual Review of Psychology, 50*, 537–567.

Livingstone, S., Bober, M., & Helsper, E. J. (2005). "Active Participation or Just More Information? Young People's Take-Up of Opportunities to Act and Interact on the Internet." *Information, Communication & Society, 8*, 287–314.

McLeod, J. M., & McDonald, D. G. (1985). "Beyond Simple Exposure: Media Orientations and Their Impact on Political Processes." *Communication Research, 12*(1), 3–33.

McLeod, J. M., Scheufele, D. A., & Moy, P. (1999). "Community, Communication, and Participation: The Role of Mass Media and Interpersonal Discussion in Local Political Participation." *Political Communication, 16*, 315–336.

Milner, H. (2002). *Civic Literacy: How Informed Citizens Make Democracy Work.* Hanover, NH: University Press of New England.

Nie, N. H., & Erbring, L. (2002). "Internet and Mass Media: A Preliminary Report." *IT & Society, 1*(2), 134–141.

Norris, P. (1996). "Does Television Erode Social Capital? A Reply to Putnam." *PS: Political Science and Politics, 29*, 474–480.

Norris, P., & Jones, D. (1998). "Editorial: Virtual Democracy." *International Journal of Press/Politics, 3*(2), 1–4.

O'Toole, T., Lister, M., Marsh, D., Jones, S., & McDonagh, A. (2003). "Tuning Out or Left Out? Participation and Nonparticipation Among Young People." *Contemporary Politics, 9*(1), 45–61.

Pasek, J., Kenski, K., Romer, D., & Jamieson, K. H. (2006). "America's Youth and Community Engagement: How Use of Mass Media is Related to Civic Activity and Political Awareness in 14- to 22-Year-Olds." *Communication Research, 33*(3), 115–135.

Pew Internet & American Life Project. (2008). *Pew Internet & American Life Survey, May 2008.* Retrieved December 22, 2009, from http://www.pewinternet.org/Static-Pages/Trend-Data/Usage-Over-Time.aspx/.

Phelps, E. (2004). "Young Citizens and Changing Electoral Turnout, 1964–2001." *Political Quarterly, 75*, 238–248.

Phelps, E. (2005). "Young Voters at the 2005 Britain General Election." *Political Quarterly, 76*, 482–487.

Pirie, M., & Worcester, R. (2000). *The Big Turn-Off: Attitudes of Young People to Government, Citizenship and Community*. London: Adam Smith Institute.

Price, V., & Cappella, J. N. (2002). "Online Deliberation and its Influence: The Electronic Dialogue Project in Campaign 2000." *IT & Society, 1*, 303–329.

Prior, M. (2005). "News vs. Entertainment: How Increasing Media Choice Widens Gaps in Political Knowledge and Turnout." *American Journal of Political Science, 49*, 577–592.

Putnam, R. D. (1995). "Tuning In, Tuning Out: The Strange Disappearance pf Social Capital in America." *PS: Political Science and Politics, 28*, 664–683.

Putnam, R. D. (2000). *Bowling Alone: The Collapse and Revival of American Community.* New York: Simon & Schuster.

Quintelier, E., & Vissers, S. (2008). "The Effect of Internet Use on Political Participation: An Analysis of Survey Results for 16-Year-Olds in Belgium." *Social Science Computer Review, 26*, 411–427.

Russell, A. (2004). "The Truth About Youth? Media Portrayals of Young People and Politics in Britain." *Journal of Public Affairs, 4*, 347–354.

Scheufele, D. A. (2002). "Examining Differential Gains From Mass Media and Their Implications for Participatory Behavior." *Communication Research, 29*(1), 46–65.

Scheufele, D. A., & Nisbet, M. C. (2002). "Being a Citizen Online: New Opportunities and Dead Ends." *Harvard International Journal of Press/Politics, 7*(3), 55–75.

Shah, D. V., Cho, J., Eveland, W. P., Jr., & Kwak, N. (2005). "Information and Expression in a Digital Age: Modeling Internet Effects on Civic Participation." *Communication Research, 32*, 531–565.

Shah, D. V., Kwak, N., & Holbert, R. L. (2001). "'Connecting' and 'Disconnecting' With Civic Life: Patterns of Internet Use and the Production of Social Capital." *Political Communication, 18*, 141–162.

Shah, D. V., McLeod, J. M., & Yoon, S. (2001). "Communication, Context, and Community: An Exploration of Print, Broadcast and Internet Influences." *Communication Research, 28*, 464–506.

Shah, D. V., Schmierbach, M., Hawkins, J., Espino, R., & Donavan, J. (2002). "Nonrecursive Models of Internet Use and Community Engagement: Questioning Whether Time Spent Online Erodes Social Capital." *Journalism & Mass Communication Quarterly, 79*, 964–987.

Slater, M. D. (2004). "Operational and Analyzing Exposure: The Foundation of Media Effects Research." *Journalism & Mass Communication Quarterly, 81*, 168–183.

Slater, M. D. (2007). "Reinforcing Spirals: The Mutual Influence of Media Selectivity and Media Effects and Their Impact on Individual Behavior and Social Identity." *Communication Theory, 17*, 281–303.

Smith, A., & Rainie, L. (2008). *The Internet and the 2008 election. Washington, DC: Pew Internet & American Life Project.*

Sunstein, C. (2001). *Republic.com*. Princeton, NJ: Princeton University Press.

Tolbert, C. J., & McNeal, R. S. (2003). "Unraveling the Effects of the Internet on Political Participation?" *Political Research Quarterly, 56*, 175–185.

Verba, S., Schlozman, K. L., & Brady, H. E. (1995). *Voice and Equality: Civic Voluntarism in American Politics. Cambridge*, MA: Harvard University Press.

Weaver, D., & Drew, D. (2001). "Voter Learning and Interest in the 2000 Presidential Election: Did the Media Matter?" *Journalism & Mass Communication Quarterly, 78*, 787–798.

Wyatt, R. O., Katz, E., & Kim, J. (2000). "Bridging the Spheres: Political and Personal Conversation in Public and Private Spaces." *Journal of Communication, 50*(1), 71–92.

Xenos, M., & Moy, P. (2007). "Direct and Differential Effects of the Internet on Political and Civic Engagement." *Journal of Communication, 57*, 704–718.

Zukin, C., Keeter, S., Andolina, M., Jenkins, K., & Delli Carpini, M. X. (2006). *A New Engagement? Political Participation, Civic Life, and the Changing American Citizen.* New York: Oxford University Press.

Credit

What is a 'Hackivist'?

Peter Ludlow

The untimely death of the young Internet activist Aaron Swartz, apparently by suicide, has prompted an outpouring of reaction in the digital world. Foremost among the debates being reheated—one which had already grown in the wake of larger and more daring data breaches in the past few years—is whether Swartz's activities as a "hacktivist" were being unfairly defined as malicious or criminal. In particular, critics (as well as Swartz's family in a formal statement[1]) have focused on the federal government's indictment of Swartz for downloading millions of documents from the scholarly database JSTOR, an action which JSTOR itself had declined to prosecute.

I believe the debate itself is far broader than the specifics of this unhappy case, for if there was prosecutorial overreach it raises the question of whether we as a society created the enabling condition for this sort of overreach by letting the demonization of hacktivists go unanswered. Prosecutors do not work in a vacuum, after all; they are more apt to pursue cases where public discourse supports their actions. The debate thus raises an issue that, as philosopher of language, I have spent time considering: the impact of how words and terms are defined in the public sphere.

"Lexical Warfare" is a phrase that I like to use for battles over how a term is to be understood. Our political discourse is full of such battles; it is pretty routine to find discussions of who gets to be called "Republican" (as opposed to RINO—Republican in Name Only), what "freedom" should mean, what legitimately gets to be called "rape"—and the list goes on.

Lexical warfare is important because it can be a device to marginalize individuals within their self-identified political affiliation (for example, branding RINO's defines them as something other than true Republicans), or it can beguile us into ignoring true threats to freedom (focusing on threats from government while being blind to threats from corporations, religion and custom), and in cases in which the word in question is "rape," the definition can have far reaching consequences for the rights of women and social policy.

Lexical warfare is not exclusively concerned with changing the definitions of words and terms—it can also work to attach either a negative or positive affect to a term. Ronald Reagan and other conservatives successfully loaded the word "liberal" with negative connotations, while enhancing the positive aura of terms like "patriot" (few today would reject the label "patriotic," but rather argue for why they are entitled to it).

Over the past few years, we've watched a lexical warfare battle slowly unfold in the treatment of the term "hacktivism." There has been an effort to redefine what the word means and what kinds of activities it describes; at the same time there has been an effort to tarnish the hacktivist label so that anyone who chooses to label themselves as such does so at their peril.

In the simplest and broadest sense, a hacktivist is someone who uses technology hacking to effect social change. The conflict now is between those who want to change the meaning of the word to denote immoral, sinister activities and those who want to defend the broader, more inclusive understanding of hacktivist. Let's start with those who are trying to change the meaning so that it denotes sinister activities.

Over the past year, several newspapers and blogs have cited Verizon's 2012 Data Breach Investigations Report,[2] which claimed that 58 per cent of all data leaked in 2011 was owing to the actions of "ideologically motivated hacktivists." An example of the concern was an article[3] in Infosecurity Magazine:

> The year 2011 is renowned for being the year that hacktivists out-stole cybercriminals to take top honors according to the Verizon data breach report. Of the 174 million stolen records it tracked in 2011, 100 million were taken by hacktivist groups.
>
> Suddenly, things are looking black and white again. Regardless of political motivation or intent, if there are victims of the attacks they perpetrate, then hacktivism has crossed the line. Not OK.

Meanwhile an article[4] in ThreatPost proclaimed "Anonymous: Hacktivists Steal Most Data in 2011."

The first thing to note is that both of these media sources are written by and for members of the information security business—it is in their interest to manufacture a threat, for the simple reason that threats mean business for these groups. But is it fair to say that the threat is being "manufactured"? What of the Verizon report that they cite?

The problem is that the headlines and articles, designed to tar hacktivists and make us fear them, did not reflect what the Verizon report actually said. According to page 19 of the report, only 3 per cent of the data breaches in the survey were by hacktivists—the bulk of them were by routine cybercriminals, disgruntled employees and nation states (83 per cent were by organized criminals).

The "most data" claim, while accurate, gives a skewed picture. According to Chris Novak, the Managing Principal of Investigative Response on Verizon's RISK Team, interviewed in ThreatPost, 2 per cent of the 90 actions analyzed in the report accounted for 58 per cent of the data released. The interview with Novak suggests that this data loss came from precisely two hacktivist actions—both by spin-offs of the well-known hacktivist group Anonymous—and that these large data dumps stemmed from the actions against the security firm HB Gary Federal, which had publicly announced their efforts to expose Anonymous, and a computer security firm called Stratfor). That means that in 2011 if you were worried about an intrusion into your system it was 33 times more likely that the perpetrator would be a criminal, nation state or disgruntled employee than a hacktivist. If you weren't picking fights with Anonymous the chances would have dropped to zero—at least according to the cases analyzed in the report.

In effect, these infosecurity media outlets cited two actions by Anonymous spin-offs, implicated that actions like this were a principle project of hacktivism, and thereby implicated a larger, imminent threat of hacktivism. Meanwhile, the meaning of hacktivist was being narrowed from people who use technology in support of social causes to meaning individuals principally concerned with infiltrating and releasing the data of almost anyone.

Now let's turn to an attempt to maintain the broader understanding of hacktivism. Several months ago I attended a birthday party in Germany for Daniel Domscheit-Berg, who was turning 34. As it happened, Domscheit-Berg had also been the spokesperson for Wikileaks and, after Julian Assange, the group's most visible person. He had left the organization in 2010, and now he had a new venture, OpenLeaks. The party was also meant to be a coming out party for OpenLeaks.

The party was to be held in the new headquarters and training center for OpenLeaks—a large house in a small town about an hour outside of Berlin. I was half-expecting to find a bunker full of hackers probing websites with SQL injections and sifting through State Department cables, but what I found was something else altogether.

When I arrived at the house the first thing I noticed was a large vegetable garden outside. The second thing I noticed was that a tree out front had been fitted out with a colorful knit wool sweater. This was the effort of Daniel's wife Anke—"knit hacking," she called it. And around the small town I saw evidence of her guerilla knit hacking. The steel poles of nearby street signs had also been fitted with woolen sweaters. Most impressively, though, a World War II tank, sitting outside a nearby former Nazi concentration camp for women had also been knit-hacked; the entire barrel of the tank's gun had been fit with a tight colorful wool sweater and adorned with some woolen flowers for good measure. I interpreted these knit-hackings as counteractions to the attempts to define hacktivist as something sinister; they serve as ostensive definitions of what hacktivism is and what hacktivists do.

Of course the birthday party had elements of hackerdom understood more narrowly. There were some members of the Chaos Computer Club (a legendary hacker group), and there was a healthy supply of Club Mate—the energy drink of choice of European hackers, but the main message being delivered was something else: a do-it-yourself aesthetic—planting your own garden, knitting your own sweaters, foraging for mushrooms and counting on a local friend to bag you some venison. What part of this lifestyle was the hacktivism part? Daniel and his friends would like to say that all of it is.

The intention here was clear: an attempt to defend the traditional, less sinister understanding of hacktivism and perhaps broaden it a bit, adding some positive affect to boot; more specifically, that hacking is fundamentally about refusing to be intimidated or cowed into submission by any technology, about understanding the technology and acquiring the power to repurpose it to our individual needs, and for the good of the many. Moreover, they were saying that a true hacktivist doesn't favor new technology over old—what is critical is that the technologies be in our hands rather than out of our control. This ideal, theoretically, should extend to beyond computer use, to technologies for food production, shelter and clothing, and of course, to all the means we use to communicate with one another. It would also, of course, extend to access to knowledge more generally—a value that was inherent in Aaron Swartz's hacking of the JSTOR data base.

Our responsibility in this particular episode of lexical warfare is to be critical and aware of the public uses of language, and to be alert to what is at stake—whether the claims made by the infosecurity industry or the government, or the gestures by the hacktivists, are genuine, misleading or correct. We are not passive observers in this dispute. The meaning of words is determined by those of us who use language, and it has consequences. Whether or not Aaron Swartz suffered because of the manipulation of the public discourse surrounding hacking, his case is a reminder that it is important that we be attuned to attempts to change the meanings of words in consequential ways. It is important because we are the ones who will decide who will win.

Notes

1. Cory Doctorow, "Aaron Swartz's Memorial Service," *Boingboing*, January 12, 2013, http://boingboing.net/2013/01/12/aaron-swartzs-memorial-servi.html
2. Download: "2012 Data Breach Investigations Report," http://www.verizonbusiness.com/resources/reports/rp_data-breach-investigations-report-2012_en_xg.pdf
3. Eleanor Dallaway, "Hacktivism: Shades of Gray," *Infosecurity* Magazine, July 6, 2012, http://www.infosecurity-magazine.com/blog/2012/6/7/hacktivism-shades-of-gray-/559.aspx
4. Paul Roberts, "Verizon: Hacktivists Steal Most Data in 2011," *Threat Post,* March 22, 2012, http://threatpost.com/verizon-hacktivists-steal-most-data-2011-032112/76350

Credit

How Connective Tech Boosts Political Change

Alec Ross

The 21st century is a terrible time to be a control freak. When I speak with leaders around the world and ask them what one thing has most changed for them over the last 15 years, they almost always cite the perceived loss of control. The thing they cite as the major reason? "Connection technologies"—technologies like the internet and mobile phone networks that connect people to information and each other.

Media and information environments, political agendas, social movements, governmental decision-making processes and control over corporate brands have all been disrupted by citizens using what are now billions of devices and billions of internet connections. Information no longer flows exclusively from mainstream media and government out to society. It flows in a vast network of citizens and consumers interacting with once-dominant information sources. This network of people is constantly reading, writing, and evaluating everything, shaping the ideas that guide society and politics. In a groundbreaking speech on internet freedom given by Secretary of State Hillary Clinton in January 2010, she described this by saying that the "spread of information networks is forming a new nervous system for our planet." A little bit of hindsight shows that this disruption has come to the foreign policy domain.

We can draw at least three early conclusions about the impact of these connection technologies on the development of political movements:

Conclusion #1: These technologies accelerate the growth of social and political movements.

Distance and time no longer limit access to real-time information. Movements that would have once taken years to develop and relied on strong ties between people well-known to each other now can be built in days or weeks, leveraging the relatively open platforms that social media provide. This phenomenon is plain to see in world events as diverse as the Arab Spring, political protests in Russia, disaster response in Japan, and the populist online movements supporting open internet policies in Europe and the United States.

Conclusion #2: Connection technologies have enriched the information environment, changing our ability to share and receive information.

Many people know the story of Mohamed Bouazizi, a fruit vendor from the small town of Sidi Bouzid in Tunisia whose self-immolation on December 17, 2010, catalyzed what became the Arab Spring. On December 18, his mother and other family members began a protest that spread to the rest of Tunisia. What most people don't know, though, is that just two years earlier there were protests in Tunisia that started off far larger but failed to spread beyond the confines of the Gafsa mining basin where they began.

What changed in those two years? During the initial protests in Sidi Bouzid, acts of protest were documented on video-enabled mobile phones and posted to social media sites. Activists in the Tunisian Diaspora curated and distributed this content, leading to its pick-up by pan-Arab satellite television networks including Al-Jazeera. This allowed students with a few dozen friends and followers on social media to become eyewitness sources for satellite TV networks that broadcast their stories to hundreds of millions of viewers. The Tunisian government of president Zine el-Abidine Ben Ali was unable to contain this flow of media and information. This combination of new and traditional media can amplify the voices of citizen-centered movements into potent political forces and demonstrate how governments lose control over their information environments.

Conclusion #3: New information networks have disrupted leadership structures.

Internet-enabled movements tend to lack the traditional single charismatic leader, inspiring and organizing the masses from on high. Rather, movements that rely heavily on the internet tend to have leadership structures that look like the internet itself—a distributed web of nodes and connections, rather than a pyramidal, top-down structure. This enables a decentralized form of organization bringing together unlikely combinations of people into rapidly formed movements. While this has the virtue of making movements more citizen-centered and less bound to the cults of personality one often finds in and around protest movements, it also makes these movements more ephemeral and less sustainable. A lack of real structure and widely-accepted leaders has limited the sustainability of many movements, both political and issue-oriented.

More than anything else, we can draw the early conclusion that connection technologies redistribute power from hierarchies to citizens and networks of citizens. These technologies are changing the entire political ecosystem. They are changing the nature of who is participating, who has power and how that power is exercised.

Most of the time, this is a good thing. It allows for more open, transparent and participatory government. It allows citizens to make their voices heard and participate in the political process.

However, the same power given to people seeking to connect the governing to the governed also gives the world's criminals and terrorists powerful tools to build sophisticated networks through which to perpetuate fraud, graft, and violence. In this respect, Secretary Clinton has likened our information networks to nuclear power, which can either fuel a city or destroy it, and to steel, which can be used to build a hospital or a machine gun.

It is difficult to imagine how connection technologies will shape political movements and systems over the next decade, but we can anticipate more empowerment of the citizen and more disruption, for both good and ill. How political leaders respond to this connectivity and its power will be a test of values, open versus closed. Closure strictly constrains the benefits technology can bring and separates the aspirations of the governed from the governing. Openness brings transparency, democratizes information, and empowers people to achieve things together that none could attain by themselves.

Credit

Ross, Alec. "How Connective Tech Boosts Political Change." CNN. 20 June 2012. Web.

Notes

Notes

Notes

Unit 2

Ethics and Education

Based on current trends, the average bachelor's student entering college this year will graduate with over $30,000 worth of debt. Sixty percent of all undergraduates will graduate with unpaid loans, which is only shocking until one considers that the cost of their college experience, including tuition, fees, books, and housing, will be well over $100,000 by the end of four years of degree courses at most public universities. At the same time, the advent of distance learning technologies, Massive Open Online Courses (MOOCs), diversity and disability initiatives, and open admissions over recent decades has made the university experience more accessible than ever. The great paradox of the modern academy is that it must be both celebrated for its progress and condemned for failing to meet the financial and professional needs of its students.

At the same time, the role of students themselves is changing. Involved, engaged scholarship demands more of students than ever before in terms of personal, moral, and scholastic development. Students of the 21st century are expected to involve themselves in the contemporary issues of their time, hold themselves to a higher standard of academic honesty and excellence, respect and endeavor to integrate experiences and views opposite their own, to be—at the most fundamental level—members not only of an institution, but of a supportive and productive community of scholars who aim to shape and change the world around them.

Education in America is at a crossroads. Changes in focus, funding, and mission have redefined the university and its relationships within the community in ways that will have uncertain and long-lasting consequences. It is not, however, the responsibility of the institution alone to address these issues—active and mindful students must also recognize their role in defining their educations and the spaces in which they find meaning and engage with the ideas, technologies, and demographics that will shape the next century.

Who Are You and What Are You Doing Here?

Mark Edmundson

A message in a bottle to the incoming class.

ଔଔଔ

Welcome and congratulations: Getting to the first day of college is a major achievement. You're to be commended, and not just you, but the parents, grandparents, uncles, and aunts who helped get you here.

It's been said that raising a child effectively takes a village: Well, as you may have noticed, our American village is not in very good shape. We've got guns, drugs, two wars, fanatical religions, a slime-based popular culture, and some politicians who—a little restraint here—aren't what they might be. To merely survive in this American village and to win a place in the entering class has taken a lot of grit on your part. So, yes, congratulations to all.

You now may think that you've about got it made. Amidst the impressive college buildings, in company with a high-powered faculty, surrounded by the best of your generation, all you need is to keep doing what you've done before: Work hard, get good grades, listen to your teachers, get along with the people around you, and you'll emerge in four years as an educated young man or woman. Ready for life.

Do not believe it. It is not true. If you want to get a real education in America you're going to have to fight—and I don't mean just fight against the drugs and the violence and against the slime-based culture that is still going to surround you. I mean something a little more disturbing. To get an education, you're probably going to have to fight against the institution that you find yourself in—no matter how prestigious it may be. (In fact, the more prestigious the school, the more you'll probably have to push.) You can get a terrific education in America now—there are astonishing opportunities at almost every college—but the education will not be presented to you wrapped and bowed. To get it, you'll need to struggle and strive, to be strong, and occasionally even to piss off some admirable people.

I came to college with few resources, but one of them was an understanding, however crude, of how I might use my opportunities there. This I began to develop because of my father, who had never been to college—in fact, he'd barely gotten out of high school. One night after dinner, he and I were sitting in our kitchen at 58 Clewley Road in Medford, Massachusetts, hatching plans about the rest of my life. I was about to go off to college, a feat no one in my family had accomplished in living memory. "I think I might want to be pre-law," I told my father. I had no idea what being pre-law was. My father compressed his brow and blew twin streams of smoke, dragon-like, from his magnificent nose. "Do you want to be a lawyer?" he asked. My father had some experience with lawyers, and with policemen, too; he was not well-disposed toward either. "I'm not really sure," I told him, "but lawyers make pretty good money, right?"

My father detonated. (That was not uncommon. My father detonated a lot.) He told me that I was going to go to college only once, and that while I was there I had better study what I wanted. He said that when rich kids went to school, they majored in the subjects that interested them, and that my younger brother Philip and I were as good as any rich kids. (We were rich kids minus the money.) Wasn't I interested in literature? I confessed that I was. Then I had better study literature, unless I had inside information to the effect that reincarnation wasn't just hype, and I'd be able to attend college thirty or forty times. If I had such info, pre-law would be fine, and maybe even a tour through invertebrate biology could also be tossed in. But until I had the reincarnation stuff from a solid source, I better get to work and pick out some English classes from the course catalog. "How about the science requirements?"

"Take 'em later," he said, "you never know."

My father, Wright Aukenhead Edmundson, Malden High School Class of 1948 (by a hair), knew the score. What he told me that evening at the Clewley Road kitchen table was true in itself, and it also contains the germ of an idea about what a university education should be. But apparently almost everyone else—students, teachers, and trustees and parents—sees the matter much differently. They have it wrong.

Education has one salient enemy in present-day America, and that enemy is education—university education in particular. To almost everyone, university education is a means to an end. For students, that end is a good job. Students want the credentials that will help them get ahead. They want the certificate that will give them access to Wall Street, or entrance into law or medical or business school. And how can we blame them? America values power and money, big players with big bucks.

When we raise our children, we tell them in multiple ways that what we want most for them is success—material success. To be poor in America is to be a failure—it's to be without decent health care, without basic necessities, often without dignity. Then there are those back-breaking student loans—people leave school as servants, indentured to pay massive bills, so that first job better be a good one. Students come to college with the goal of a diploma in mind—what happens in between, especially in classrooms, is often of no deep and determining interest to them.

In college, life is elsewhere. Life is at parties, at clubs, in music, with friends, in sports. Life is what celebrities have. The idea that the courses you take should be the primary objective of going to college is tacitly considered absurd. In terms of their work, students live in the future and not the present; they live with their prospects for success. If universities stopped issuing credentials, half of the clients would be gone by tomorrow morning, with the remainder following fast behind.

The faculty, too, is often absent: Their real lives are also elsewhere. Like most of their students, they aim to get on. The work they are compelled to do to advance—get tenure, promotion, raises, outside offers—is, broadly speaking, scholarly work. No matter what anyone says, this work has precious little to do with the fundamentals of teaching. The proof is that virtually no undergraduate students can read and understand their professors' scholarly publications. The public senses this disparity and so thinks of the professors' work as being silly or beside the point. Some of it is. But the public also senses that because professors don't pay full-bore attention to teaching they don't have to work very hard—they've created a massive feather bed for themselves and called it a university.

This is radically false. Ambitious professors, the ones who, like their students, want to get ahead in America, work furiously. Scholarship, even if pretentious and almost unreadable, is nonetheless labor-intense. One can slave for a year or two on a single article for publication in this or that refereed journal. These essays are honest: Their footnotes reflect real reading, real assimilation, and real dedication. Shoddy work—in which the author cheats, cuts corners, copies from others—is quickly detected. The people who do this work have highly developed intellectual powers, and they push themselves hard to reach a certain standard: That the results have almost no practical relevance to the students, the public, or even, frequently, to other scholars is a central element in the tragicomedy that is often academia.

The students and the professors have made a deal: Neither of them has to throw himself heart and soul into what happens in the classroom. The students write their abstract, over-intellectualized essays; the professors grade the students for their capacity to be abstract and over-intellectual—and often genuinely smart. For their essays can be brilliant, in a chilly way; they can also be clipped off the Internet, and often are. Whatever the case, no one wants to invest too much in them—for life is elsewhere. The professor saves his energies for the profession, while the student saves his for friends, social life, volunteer work, making connections, and getting in position to clasp hands on the true grail, the first job.

No one in this picture is evil; no one is criminally irresponsible. It's just that smart people are prone to look into matters to see how they might go about buttering their toast. Then they butter their toast.

As for the administrators, their relation to the students often seems based not on love but fear. Administrators fear bad publicity, scandal, and dissatisfaction on the part of their customers. More than anything else, though, they fear lawsuits. Throwing a student out of college, for this or that piece of bad behavior, is very difficult, almost impossible. The student will sue your eyes out. One kid I knew (and rather liked) threatened on his blog to mince his dear and esteemed professor (me) with a samurai sword for the crime of having taught a boring class. (The class was a *little* boring—I had a damned cold—but the punishment seemed a bit severe.) The dean of students laughed lightly when I suggested that this behavior might be grounds for sending the student on a brief vacation. I was, you might say, discomfited, and showed up to class for a while with my cellphone jiggered to dial 911 with one touch.

Still, this was small potatoes. Colleges are even leery of disciplining guys who have committed sexual assault, or assault plain and simple. Instead of being punished, these guys frequently stay around, strolling the quad and swilling the libations, an affront (and sometimes a terror) to their victims.

You'll find that cheating is common as well. As far as I can discern, the student ethos goes like this: If the professor is so lazy that he gives the same test every year, it's okay to go ahead and take advantage—you've both got better things to do. The Internet is amok with services selling term papers and those services exist, capitalism being what it is, because people purchase the papers—lots of them. Fraternity files bulge with old tests from a variety of courses.

Periodically the public gets exercised about this situation, and there are articles in the national news. But then interest dwindles and matters go back to normal.

One of the reasons professors sometimes look the other way when they sense cheating is that it sends them into a world of sorrow. A friend of mine had the temerity to detect cheating on the part of a kid who was the nephew of a well-placed official in an Arab government complexly aligned with the U.S. Black limousines pulled up in front of his office and disgorged decorously suited negotiators. Did my pal fold? Nope, he's not the type. But he did not enjoy the process.

What colleges generally want are well-rounded students, civic leaders, people who know what the system demands, how to keep matters light, not push too hard for an education or anything else; people who get their credentials and leave the professors alone to do their brilliant work, so they may rise and enhance the rankings of the university. Such students leave and become donors and so, in their own turn, contribute immeasurably to the university's standing. They've done a fine job skating on surfaces in high school—the best way to get an across-the-board outstanding record—and now they're on campus to cut a few more figure eights.

In a culture where the major and determining values are monetary, what else could you do? How else would you live if not by getting all you can, succeeding all you can, making all you can?

The idea that a university education really should have no substantial content, should not be about what John Keats was disposed to call Soul-making, is one that you might think professors and university presidents would be discreet about. Not so. This view informed an address that Richard Brodhead gave to the senior class at Yale before he departed to become president of Duke. Brodhead, an impressive, articulate man, seems to take as his educational touchstone the Duke of Wellington's precept that the Battle of Waterloo was won on the playing fields of Eton. Brodhead suggests that the content of the courses isn't really what matters. In five years (or five months, or minutes), the student is likely to have forgotten how to do the problem sets and will only hazily recollect what happens in the ninth book of *Paradise Lost.* The legacy of their college years will be a legacy of difficulties overcome. When they face equally arduous tasks later in life, students will tap their old resources of determination, and they'll win.

All right, there's nothing wrong with this as far as it goes—after all, the student who writes a brilliant forty-page thesis in a hard week has learned more than a little about her inner resources. Maybe it will give her needed confidence in the future. But doesn't the content of the courses matter at all?

On the evidence of this talk, no. Trying to figure out whether the stuff you're reading is true or false and being open to having your life changed is a fraught, controversial activity. Doing so requires energy from the professor—which is better spent on other matters. This kind of perspective-altering teaching and learning can cause the things which administrators fear above all else: trouble, arguments, bad press, etc.

After the kid-samurai episode, the chair of my department not unsympathetically suggested that this was the sort of incident that could happen when you brought a certain intensity to teaching. At the time I found his remark a tad detached, but maybe he was right.

So, if you want an education, the odds aren't with you: The professors are off doing what they call their own work; the other students, who've doped out the way the place runs, are busy leaving the professors alone and getting themselves in position for bright and shining futures; the student-services people are trying to keep everyone content, offering plenty of entertainment and building another state-of-the-art workout facility every few months. The development office is already scanning you for future donations. The primary function of Yale University, it's recently been said, is to create prosperous alumni so as to enrich Yale University.

So why make trouble? Why not just go along? Let the profs roam free in the realms of pure thought, let yourselves party in the realms of impure pleasure, and let the student-services gang assert fewer prohibitions and newer delights for you. You'll get a good job, you'll have plenty of friends, you'll have a driveway of your own.

You'll also, if my father and I are right, be truly and righteously screwed. The reason for this is simple. The quest at the center of a liberal-arts education is not a luxury quest; it's a necessity quest. If you do not undertake it, you risk leading a life of desperation—maybe quiet, maybe, in time, very loud—and I am not exaggerating. For you risk trying to be someone other than who you are, which, in the long run, is killing.

By the time you come to college, you will have been told who you are numberless times. Your parents and friends, your teachers, your counselors, your priests and rabbis and ministers and imams have all had their say. They've let you know how they size you up, and they've let you know what they think you should value. They've given you a sharp and protracted taste of what they feel is good and bad, right and wrong. Much is on their side. They have confronted you with scriptures—holy books that, whatever their actual provenance, have given people what they feel to be wisdom for thousands of years. They've given you family traditions—you've learned the ways of your tribe and your community. And, too, you've been tested, probed, looked at up and down and through. The coach knows what your athletic prospects are, the guidance office has a sheaf of test scores that relegate you to this or that ability quadrant, and your teachers have got you pegged. You are, as Foucault might say, the intersection of many evaluative and potentially determining discourses: you boy, you girl, have been made.

And—contra Foucault—that's not so bad. Embedded in all of the major religions are profound truths. Schopenhauer, who despised belief in transcendent things, nonetheless thought Christianity to be of inexpressible worth. He couldn't believe in the divinity of Jesus, or in the afterlife, but to Schopenhauer, a deep pessimist, a religion that had as its central emblem the figure of a man being tortured on a cross couldn't be entirely misleading. To the Christian, Schopenhauer said, pain was at the center of the understanding of life, and that was just as it should be.

One does not need to be as harsh as Schopenhauer to understand the use of religion, even if one does not believe in an otherworldly god. And all of those teachers and counselors and friends—and the prognosticating uncles, the dithering aunts, the fathers and mothers with their hopes for your fulfillment—or their fulfillment in you—should not necessarily be cast aside or ignored. Families have their wisdom. The question "Who do they think you are at home?" is never an idle one.

The major conservative thinkers have always been very serious about what goes by the name of common sense. Edmund Burke saw common sense as a loosely made, but often profound, collective work, in which humanity has deposited its hard-earned wisdom—the precipitate of joy and tears—over time. You have been raised in proximity to common sense, if you've been raised at all, and common sense is something to respect, though not quite—peace unto the formidable Burke—to revere.

You may be all that the good people who raised you say you are; you may want all they have shown you is worth wanting; you may be someone who is truly your father's son or your mother's daughter. But then again, you may not be.

For the power that is in you, as Emerson suggested, may be new in nature. You may not be the person that your parents take you to be. And—this thought is both more exciting and more dangerous—you may not be the person that you take yourself to be, either. You may not have read yourself aright, and college is the place where you can find out whether you have or not. The reason to read Blake and Dickinson and Freud and Dickens is not to become more cultivated, or more articulate, or to be someone who, at a cocktail party, is never embarrassed (or who can embarrass others). The best reason to read them is to see if they may know you better than you know yourself. You may find your own suppressed and rejected thoughts flowing back to you with an "alienated majesty." Reading the great writers, you may have the experience that Longinus associated with the sublime: You feel that you have actually created the text yourself. For somehow your predecessors are more yourself than you are.

This was my own experience reading the two writers who have influenced me the most, Sigmund Freud and Ralph Waldo Emerson. They gave words to thoughts and feelings that I had never been able to render myself. They shone a light onto the world and what they saw, suddenly I saw, too. From Emerson I learned to trust my own thoughts, to trust them even when every voice seems to be on the other side. I need the wherewithal, as Emerson did, to say what's on my mind and to take the inevitable hits. Much more I learned from the sage—about character, about loss, about joy, about writing and its secret sources, but Emerson most centrally preaches the gospel of self-reliance and that is what I have tried most to take from him. I continue to hold in mind one of Emerson's most memorable passages: "Society is a joint-stock company, in which the members agree, for the better securing of his bread to each shareholder, to surrender the liberty and culture of the eater. The virtue in most request is conformity. Self-reliance is its aversion. It loves not realities and creators, but names and customs."

Emerson's greatness lies not only in showing you how powerful names and customs can be, but also in demonstrating how exhilarating it is to buck them. When he came to Harvard to talk about religion, he shocked the professors and students by challenging the divinity of Jesus and the truth of his miracles. He wasn't invited back for decades.

From Freud I found a great deal to ponder as well. I don't mean Freud the aspiring scientist, but the Freud who was a speculative essayist and interpreter of the human condition like Emerson. Freud challenges nearly every significant human ideal. He goes after religion. He says that it comes down to the longing for the father. He goes after love. He calls it "the overestimation of the erotic object." He attacks our desire for charismatic popular leaders. We're drawn to them because we hunger for absolute authority. He declares that dreams don't predict the future and that there's nothing benevolent about them. They're disguised fulfillments of repressed wishes.

Freud has something challenging and provoking to say about virtually every human aspiration. I learned that if I wanted to affirm any consequential ideal, I had to talk my way past Freud. He was—and is—a perpetual challenge and goad.

Never has there been a more shrewd and imaginative cartographer of the psyche. His separation of the self into three parts, and his sense of the fraught, anxious, but often negotiable relations among them (negotiable when you come to the game with a Freudian knowledge), does a great deal to help one navigate experience. (Though sometimes—and this I owe to Emerson—it seems right to let the psyche fall into civil war, accepting barrages of anxiety and grief for this or that good reason.)

The battle is to make such writers one's own, to winnow them out and to find their essential truths. We need to see where they fall short and where they exceed the mark, and then to develop them a little, as the ideas themselves, one comes to see, actually developed others. (Both Emerson and Freud live out of Shakespeare—but only a giant can be truly influenced by Shakespeare.) In reading, I continue to look for one thing—to be influenced, to learn something new, to be thrown off my course and onto another, better way.

My father knew that he was dissatisfied with life. He knew that none of the descriptions people had for him quite fit. He understood that he was always out-of-joint with life as it was. He had talent: My brother and I each got about half the raw ability he possessed and that's taken us through life well enough. But what to do with that talent—there was the rub for my father. He used to stroll through the house intoning his favorite line from Groucho Marx's ditty "Whatever it is, I'm against it." (I recently asked my son, now twenty-one, if he thought I was mistaken in teaching him this particular song when he was six years old. "No!" he said, filling the air with an invisible forest of exclamation points.) But what my father never managed to get was a sense of who he might become. He never had a world of possibilities spread before him, never made sustained contact with the best that had been thought and said. He didn't get to revise his understanding of himself, figure out what he'd do best that might give the world some profit.

My father was a gruff man, but also a generous one, so that night at the kitchen table at 58 Clewley Road he made an effort to let me have the chance that had been denied to him by both fate and character. He gave me the chance to see what I was all about, and if it proved to be different from him, proved even to be something he didn't like or entirely comprehend, then he'd deal with it.

Right now, if you're going to get a real education, you may have to be aggressive and assertive.

Your professors will give you some fine books to read, and they'll probably help you understand them. What they won't do, for reasons that perplex me, is to ask you if the books contain truths you could live your lives by. When you read Plato, you'll probably learn about his metaphysics and his politics and his way of conceiving the soul. But no one will ask you if his ideas are good enough to believe in. No one will ask you, in the words of Emerson's disciple William James, what their "cash value" might be. No one will suggest that you might use Plato as your bible for a week or a year or longer. No one, in short, will ask you to use Plato to help you change your life.

That will be up to you. You must put the question of Plato to yourself. You must ask whether reason should always rule the passions, philosophers should always rule the state, and poets should inevitably be banished from a just commonwealth. You have to ask yourself if wildly expressive music (rock and rap and the rest) deranges the soul in ways that are destructive to its health. You must inquire of yourself if balanced calm is the most desirable human state.

Occasionally—for you will need some help in fleshing-out the answers—you may have to prod your professors to see if they take the text at hand—in this case the divine and disturbing Plato—to be true. And you will have to be tough if the professor mocks you for uttering a sincere question instead of keeping matters easy for all concerned by staying detached and analytical. (Detached analysis has a place—but, in the end, you've got to speak from the heart and pose the question of truth.) You'll be the one who pesters his teachers. You'll ask your history teacher about whether there is a design to our history, whether we're progressing or declining, or whether, in the words of a fine recent play, *The History Boys*, history's "just one fuckin' thing after another." You'll be the one who challenges your biology teacher about the intellectual conflict between evolution and creationist thinking. You'll not only question the statistics teacher about what *numbers* can explain but what they can't.

Because every subject you study is a language and since you may adopt one of these languages as your own, you'll want to know how to speak it expertly and also how it fails to deal with those concerns for which it has no adequate words. You'll be looking into the reach of every metaphor that every discipline offers, and you'll be trying to see around their corners.

The whole business is scary, of course. What if you arrive at college devoted to pre-med, sure that nothing will make you and your family happier than a life as a physician, only to discover that elementary-school teaching is where your heart is?

You might learn that you're not meant to be a doctor at all. Of course, given your intellect and discipline, you can still probably be one. You can pound your round peg through the very square hole of medical school, then go off into the profession. And society will help you. Society has a cornucopia of resources to encourage you in doing what society needs done but that you don't much like doing and are not cut out to do. To ease your grief, society offers alcohol, television, drugs, divorce, and buying, buying, buying what you don't need. But all those too have their costs.

Education is about finding out what form of work for you is close to being play—work you do so easily that it restores you as you go. Randall Jarrell once said that if he were a rich man, he would pay money to teach poetry to students. (I would, too, for what it's worth.) In saying that, he (like my father) hinted in the direction of a profound and true theory of learning.

Having found what's best for you to do, you may be surprised how far you rise, how prosperous, even against your own projections, you become. The student who eschews medical school to follow his gift for teaching small children spends his twenties in low-paying but pleasurable and soul-rewarding toil. He's always behind on his student-loan payments; he still lives in a house with four other guys (not all of whom got proper instructions on how to clean a bathroom). He buys shirts from the Salvation Army, has intermittent Internet, and vacations where he can. But lo—he has a gift for teaching. He writes an essay about how to teach, then a book—which no one buys. But he writes another—in part out of a feeling of injured merit, maybe—and that one they do buy.

Money is still a problem, but in a new sense. The world wants him to write more, lecture, travel more, and will pay him for his efforts, and he likes this a good deal. But he also likes staying around and showing up at school and figuring out how to get this or that little runny-nosed specimen to begin learning how to read. These are the kinds of problems that are worth having and if you advance, as Thoreau said, in the general direction of your dreams, you may have them. If you advance in the direction of someone else's dreams—if you want to live someone else's life rather than yours—then get a TV for every room, buy yourself a lifetime supply of your favorite quaff, crank up the porn channel, and groove away. But when we expend our energies in rightful ways, Robert Frost observed, we stay whole and vigorous and we don't weary. "Strongly spent," the poet says, "is synonymous with kept."

Credit

Edmundson, Mark. "Who Are You and What Are You Doing Here?" *Oxford American* 74. 22 Aug. 2011. Print.

Global Imperatives of the 21st Century: The Academy's Response

Nels H. Granholm

Introduction

Our twenty-first century world is rapidly declining while we in the Ivory Tower bury our collective ostrich heads in the sand while continuing to pursue our disciplinary truths. The purpose of this article is to make the case that we in the Academy have to "step up," become authentic members of our proud tradition and profession in the Academy, and take an active role in resolving global problems. We need to "get out of our parent's basements," "smell the coffee," and get a life—a real twenty-first century life. It is both reckless and unethical for us to ignore the world around us. We would prefer not to leave our comfortable disciplinary homes; we are warm and secure. Or, so we think. Perhaps we are paralyzed in academia because we do not know "how to get out," how to grapple with twenty-first century global imperatives. The parakeet when liberated from its cage flies back to the security of its "home." We academic parakeets need to break out, engage the world, and make a difference. We need to lead by example! Hopefully this article will provide some of that impetus.

"The sky is falling" opined Chicken Little in the traditional fairy tale. Well, the sky is not falling, but it is accumulating CO_2 at the highest concentrations (reaching 400 ppm) known to science over the last 800,000 years as revealed in deep drilled Antarctic ice cores (Pachauri and Reisinger 2007).

In addition to atmospheric CO_2 our Eden, our home, our world has other problems as well—social, biological, and physical—unprecedented natural resource depletion; stark evidence of incipient global environmental change disasters (flooding of coastal cities, displacement of agricultural zones, melting of Himalayan glaciers that provide significant annual flows to major rivers in China, India, and southeast Asia), pollution and dead zones in our oceans; crashing losses of biodiversity affecting the health of global ecosystems, food insecurity for millions of people; serious poverty and lack of fundamental resources (a.k.a. Maslow's hierarchy) for one to two billion people; political unrest, terrorism, war, WikiLeaks, and various conflicts; failing, and failed states like Somalia and DRC; absence of decent schooling for millions of children; child soldiers, violations of basic women's rights, abhorrent health conditions in developing countries, and others. I have dubbed these horrendously comprehensive problems our twenty-first century global imperatives.

Academia's Responsibility

Are we in the Academy responding in any way to these global challenges? For the most part, no. Most of the time we academics act as if we have no clue. We, the time-honored and cherished professoriate, are doing virtually nothing in the way of addressing and resolving global problems. However, as members of one of society's "special institutions," the Academy, we should. After all we, at least in principle, represent society's intellectual vanguard, a cadre presumably of public intellectuals. Because of academic freedom, our presumed desire to seek myths, and our unconstrained ability to probe deeply into all manner of societal activity, we have the power to expose wrongs, injustices, and damaging human behaviors no matter how well-concealed, shielded, and protected they may be. Collectively, we are one of society's most valuable and capable institutional means to seek the truth, to engage the world, and ultimately to redress the wrongs of the world. I would like to argue that in this early twenty-first century, the Academy's primary and most essential responsibility entails informing our students, colleagues, administrators, and others about our global crises in compelling ways. But most importantly, our job largely involves instilling a sense of passion and desire to work in teams to provide solutions to resolve these seemingly intractable global issues.

In short, what the world needs most is a cadre of authentic global citizens who communicate well, have a passion for solving problems, and are willing and able to work in teams. We desperately need lawyers, businesspeople, CEOs, CFOs, global financiers, governmental agencies at all levels, NGOs, supra-national groups (like UN, IMF, WTO, WLO, WB, and others) who dedicate a good part of their time and efforts to effective global problem solving. What we no longer need is university graduates, socially blasé egomaniacal hyper-individuals, and others hell-bent on a materially-addicted, self-centered, and highly resource-extractive Western lifestyle and who show little regard for community interests and the public good. We in the professoriate have an iron-clad responsibility, a duty or obligation, to produce globally competent student-citizens, i.e., passionate and competent authentic global citizens who just happen to be majoring in electrical engineering, dairy science, nursing, agriculture, business, accounting, marketing, advertising, modern languages, global studies, biology, sociology, history, political science, and others and who just happen to have a passion to remedy the wrongs of this seriously-troubled and severely-compromised twenty-first century Earth.

"OK," you say. "This is classic 'pie in the sky Pollyannaish stuff'!" And I can hear you say, "All of this is probably impossible." However, there really is no alternative. Given the present state of our Earth, we have no other rational choice. In the end, it is "the only game in town." And, should we not "give it our best shot"? Perhaps "for openers," we could remember the lines of the Edgar Albert Guest poem of 1916 entitled "It Couldn't Be Done"—"He started to sing as he tackled the thing that couldn't be done and he did it" (Guest 1916).

Ignorance of the World is No Excuse

We in the Academy can no longer afford to ignore twenty-first century global realities. Because of our economically integrated, highly interdependent, profoundly troubled, resource depleted, conflict-ridden, and thoroughly interconnected twenty-first century world, we in the Academy can ill afford the luxury of exclusively pursuing our own individual disciplines, our own careers, and our own personal interests while ignoring pervasive global resource problems and fundamental social inequities. We cannot, in good faith, stand by and passively watch the slow disintegration of our physical, biological, and social world. Somehow, we need to act. And, somehow, we need to get this action message across to not only our students, our hope for tomorrow, but also to our faculty colleagues and our university administrators, our hope for today. Neglecting our twenty-first century global imperatives is simply not a choice—not for our professoriate, one of society's presumed intellectual elites.

Neglecting global imperatives presents two fundamental problems: 1) Quite simply, as ethical human beings, it is incumbent upon us to engage with and attempt to resolve global imperatives—to do the right thing! We ought to act for our fellow human beings (as well as the rest of the global biota) from a Rawlsian ("Justice as Fairness") and Kantian (each and every person has equal worth) kind of universally-accepted principled approach and 2) If we are ill-inclined to "buy" the purely ethical approach, then perhaps the brutally pragmatic approach may "cut the mustard," i.e., unless there is at least a basal level of social, political, biological, and environmental stability in the world, those of us with wealth (members of the G20, OECD, rapidly-developing countries, and others) may be unable to enjoy a high quality of life. In the absence of global stability, our lives may be greatly diminished, perhaps even impoverished. Thus, for purely selfish, egoistic reasons we ought to have the good sense to promote fairness, justice, and freedom for all people of the world. Also, we should be clever enough to understand that our well being on planet Earth is a direct reflection of the overall health and welfare of our biotic brethren. Accordingly, a rational species would work to ensure the bounty and flourishing of the global biota. I prefer the principled Kantian approach as opposed to the starkly practical and utilitarian modus, but we can and should do both!

My Hope for this Article

It is my fervent hope that you will gain an understanding of why it is incumbent upon those of us in Academia to respond in highly active and significant measure to current global imperatives. And hopefully, I can convince you that we in the Academy have a special role to play in this process. By introducing ourselves, our students, colleagues and administrators to these twenty-first century global dilemmas in our various course curricula and other academic forums (faculty senate; all-campus colloquia; year of the book (read Lester Brown or Bill McKibben); distinguished lecture series; department/college meetings; community-university programs; and others) we can become major change agents in this process. The situation is so dire that we really have no alternative. I wish I could convince you of this. Academia must "get on board!" This is one train the professoriate cannot afford to miss. Let us begin.

Section One—Framing the Problem: Institutional Indifference to Global Imperatives

Colleges, universities, related institutions, and other professional organizations have been, at best, unresponsive and, at worst, derelict in their societal obligations to confront and resolve global imperatives.

Our college and university education, although highly specialized, rigorous, and of excellent academic quality has been fragmented, overly discipline-specific, and has generally "missed the mark" of a comprehensive global education. Our graduating seniors are simply not globally competent. They possess little "worldliness." *It is not their fault, it is ours!* Our colleges and universities have failed to deliver the necessary strategies, methodologies, and requisite information for students "to connect the interdisciplinary dots" in ways that address fundamental global problems.

In defense of our current system of higher education, the quality of the overall system should not be faulted. It is simply "misguided." In a sense, we may have done it right over the course of human history or at least until the twentieth century. But in the last century the world has changed; we have drastically altered our Earth biologically, physically, socially, and politically. Because of our incredible "Earth extraction efficiencies," we have laid bare the mantel of the Earth. As Aldo Leopold (1949) stated in his essay "The Land Ethic," "We are remolding the Alhambra with a steam-shovel, and we are proud of our yardage." Because of our greatly increasing human social problems as well as our drastic global extirpation of our natural resource base, our current Earth is qualitatively distinctive from our early twentieth century Earth (McKibben 2010). Accordingly, we desperately require fresh ways to view our Earth as well as new global regulatory and governing paradigms if we are to, and I would rather not say this, survive in some kind of stable and peaceful twenty-first century world.

Academic Deception?

Because of the devastating effects of our disruptive activities on the surface of the Earth, especially the biosphere, the twenty-first century is qualitatively different from all previous centuries. It is hard to imagine that one species could have such a devastating effect. But we have! *Homo sapiens* is such an enigma—so creative, imaginative, sublime on one hand and so uninformed, violent, destructive, unthinking, blasé, and devastating on the other. We in the Academy need to address what we, as a global community, have done to our Earth, attempt to rectify, and to the maximum extent possible, work to remediate our past actions. But this is a tall order. How should we go about this?

Quite simply, we in the twenty-first century professoriate are called not only to teach disciplinary myths, but also international and global studies truths. Students desperately need to know what is truly going on in our world. The Academy's twenty-first century primary responsibility is to provide students with real and ongoing global truth, the authentic global situation, and then to provide the tools and training to engage productively with that world. It is deceptive if not dishonest for the professoriate not to inform students about our twenty-first century world. Such behavior is akin to our physician telling us that everything is fine when, in reality, we are suffering from a serious and life-threatening systemic disorder.

We possess scientific clarity regarding phenomena like global environmental change, impact of the global population on the world's natural resources (horrendously detrimental collective ecological footprint), pervasive social problems of poverty, poor health, food insecurity, failed/fragile states, global terrorism, and others; we now (twenty-first century) live in a drastically and qualitatively different world than humans have heretofore experienced. Bill McKibben (2010) has dubbed this qualitatively different, ecologically compromised world *Eaarth*—the title of his new book. And yes, Earth with a new spelling to signify a new, significantly degraded earth, not the Eden we inherited. This is a sad business indeed.

To continue with academic business as usual in the twenty-first century would deceive ourselves, our stakeholders, and compromise our academic mission. We need to address ourselves to the critical business at hand—the clear understanding and then, resolution of global imperatives. Accordingly, we ought to devote a significant portion of the academic enterprise to analyzing and developing methodologies for resolving global imperatives. In short, we ought to keep our focus on academic excellence, but shift the subject from disciplinary pursuit to interdisciplinary, international endeavors, i.e., pursuit of interdisciplinary problem-solving including service learning—especially in the resolution of global dilemmas. In short, to be effective, we need to work at all institutional levels. An institution's mission statement is a good place to begin; we might as well start at the top!

If You Know You Are in Trouble, it is Generally a Good Idea to Take Corrective Action

We know in our bones that our world is hurting. If we know we are in global jeopardy, it would seem that the proper role for the Academy would be to "take action." It seems we should, as a globally informed academic community, take corrective action. We have no other reasonable alternative than to attend to these global challenges. Could we not vigorously embrace a new and heightened urgency leading to action on behalf of the world's deteriorating sociopolitical, as well as physical and biological conditions, including devastating poverty of the world's poor and disenfranchised peoples? Philosophically, academia's response to twenty-first century global imperatives is nothing less than a bona fide categorical imperative in and of itself.

Yet, for a number of very curious reasons, we continue to be "held hostage" (an extraordinary self-imposed hostage) in our Ivory Towers (disciplinary specialties). We academics just do not seem to get it! We do not seem to recognize that the world's plight is our plight. We are all in this together. And for those who may recognize the future consequences of our twenty-first century global imperatives, they cannot seem to muster the energy, motivation, or persuasive and compelling arguments to convince others (or ourselves) to embrace the kinds of significant academic adjustments and incentives to address these global realities. It is a most curious business, but all so human!

Moot at Best

The Academy needs to act. It is our societal obligation. We need to clearly, graphically, and starkly outline the undeniable and pervasive global challenges we face in the twenty-first century. We need to "grab" ourselves and our students. Our college and university colleagues do not truly sense the precariousness of our current global status. Unless we can bring them "on board," the whole idea of energizing colleges and universities to engage productively in twenty-first century global imperatives will be moot at best!

Section Two—Principles, Tools, and Modus Operandi to Address the Problem

University courses that focus on interdisciplinary global interrelationships and global interdependence, the kinds of education we require in the twenty-first century, are simply not being taught. Few if any university courses allow students to connect the dots between what goes on in one country and how those apparently isolated national events can drastically affect millions of people in scores of other countries around the world. University students receiving training in global citizenship and intercultural competence may be equipped to connect the dots. We must work to train students in all disciplines to become authentic global citizens. Our world needs civil engineers trained in global studies as well as in the design of sewage treatment plants, highways, and bridges. We need nursing majors who advocate for global health, and education majors willing to go abroad and teach in developing countries. In short, we need students of all disciplines who, by virtue of their specialty training (economics, history, pharmacy, English, dairy science, theatre, speech, etc.) as well as their education in global citizenry and intercultural competence, will engage and inform the world in the twenty-first century.

The World Needs Legions of Authentic Global Citizens

By definition, well-trained global citizens possess the wherewithal to understand the complex relationships between the events of one country and the consequences of those events on others. This ability to draw compelling connections, sometimes referred to as "connecting the dots," remains the *sine qua non* of true global citizens. Let me provide two examples to affirm the power of connecting the dots—the phenomenon of quantitative easing and underground water supplies (aquifers) in fertile agricultural zones.

Take the concept of "quantitative easing" as a case in point. In November 2010, the U.S. Federal Reserve ("The Fed") decided to conduct an experiment called "quantitative easing" to stimulate the American economy. It purchased six billion dollars worth of U.S. bonds to increase the supply of money, lower long-term interest rates, and hopefully, stimulate the economy by expanding businesses and creating new jobs. However, what may be good for the American economy may not be advantageous for other countries. In short, the U.S.' attempts to improve our economy could have negative effects in the global economy. Quantitative easing could also cause inflation, lowering the value of the dollar causing serious ripple effects throughout the global economy. Did decision-makers at the Fed carefully consider the potential global consequences of quantitative easing? Did they connect the dots between U.S. quantitative easing and the possibility of currency devaluation, inflation, and potentially drastic economic dislocations in the global economy? The upshot—a holistic understanding of the global economy, the motivation of individual countries, a true conversation between representatives of many countries, transparency, and an ability to connect the fiscal and monetary dots represent the *sine qua non* of an educated, interculturally competent, global citizen. In our twenty-first century world we need legions of such authentic global citizens. Let us look next at agricultural aquifers.

We excel at collecting data, but lack the political will to connect the dots and formulate beneficial policy based on those data. With respect to aquifers (underground water supplies under prime agricultural land), we acquire data describing in comprehensive, "excruciatingly quantitative" detail how we are drawing down or depleting the world's most critical aquifers beneath fertile agricultural land (i.e., data galore on annual drawdown levels, recharge rates, number of years until depletion, liters per day of drawdown, and so on *ad nauseam*). Armed with knowledge of sociology (human nature), economics, soils/geology, agriculture, history, local culture, and others, global citizens may be able to connect all of these dots. Following this analysis, we may recognize that specific incentives must be provided for people in order to: 1) Increase efficiency of irrigation via new methods like drip irrigation; 2) Create private watershed or irrigation districts where local people with vested interests have pricing control of the water rather than larger, indifferent governmental or distant private agencies; 3) Devise pricing incentives—by charging more for each unit of water, the total water usage will decline; and 4) Other creative and highly sustainable incentives that embrace the aboriginal "Seventh Generation" principle, i.e., act in such a way that the resource will be available seven generations into the future (140–175 years hence).

Intercultural Competence and Global Citizenship

Two critically fundamental foci for engaging in twenty-first century dilemmas include intercultural competence—seeing the world through the eyes of "the other" and authentic global citizenship—connecting the dots and devising policies most optimal for multiple nations or the global community rather than simply one nation (Adams and Carfagna 2006; Tetreault and Lipschutz 2009). One could say that intercultural competence and global citizenship are fundamental if not the *sine qua non* for engagement with and resolution of twenty-first century global imperatives. But there are others.

Other intellectual tools and educational approaches for productive twenty-first century engagement include: (a) intercultural communication; (b) language training; (c) knowledge of global governance (e.g., role of the United Nations and other governing structures like the World Trade Association, World Bank, International Monetary Fund, and others); (d) knowledge of the physical and biological conditions of our world; (e) critical need for education of young women in developing Sub-Saharan and other desperately poor countries: (f) how the global economy really works along with basic training in international economics (e.g., role of subsidies and trade barriers, structural adjustment programs of the IMF and WB, economic factors hostile to developing countries like escalating tariffs, and others); (g) role of international treaties like human rights treaties, the International Campaign to Ban Landmines, the International Criminal Court, the Kyoto Protocol; (h) why the number of "failed" and "fragile" States is increasing (Brown 2009) and (i) others deemed to be central to the discussion.

In essence, faculty colleagues and students alike need to learn "how the world works" and how to connect the dots. Such training requires multidisciplinary approaches; serious, deliberate, and exhaustive case study analyses; rigorous service work abroad; learning of foreign languages; knowledge of international governing agencies, and many others. Because of our traditional and ingrained disciplinary bias, we have failed to create the kinds of interdisciplinary international studies and other globally-defined interdisciplinary programs to provide that critical background sorely needed to productively engage in the analysis and resolution of global imperatives. But, the good news—we still have time. Not much, but enough if we can get on board.

Lessons from Aldo Leopold

During his early forestry career, Aldo Leopold (1887–1948) was an unabashed advocate for intense utilization of forestry and agricultural resources of America's vast and rich lands. However, as he observed the devastating ecological effects of such all encompassing utilitarian practices on the health and vigor of the land, he underwent a profound sea change as comprehensively described in his seminal work, *A Sand County Almanac* (Leopold 1949). In short, Leopold evolved from a strictly utilitarian, economic approach (harvest lumber and trees at all costs) to a profoundly deep and rational ecological approach (preserve forest ecosystems well into the future via strict adherence to ecological principles including sustainable harvests). The simple but profound lesson that Leopold learned is that the economy is a subset of the ecology and not, as most of us assume, the other way around. In short, ecology is primary while economy is secondary! In order to sustainably maintain reasonable yields of lumber, agricultural products, oceanic fisheries, and other natural resources over time, one must be attuned to and operate in concert with the ecology of the various resources.

Leopold could not understand why professionals in resource management did not share this fundamental view of the necessity to operate by the basic ecological rules. He reasoned that part of the problem lies in the absence of holistic ecological training in our universities and professional schools. Leopold wrote about the "fragmentation" that occurs within the university. The quote below provides striking and thoughtful metaphors (a single *"instrument of the great orchestra"* for each discipline, research as *"dismemberment,"* and the concept of *"the place for dismemberment"* as the university):

> There are men charged with the duty of examining the construction of plants, animals, and soils which are the instruments of the great orchestra. Each selects one instrument and spends his life taking it apart and describing its strings and sounding boards. This process of dismemberment is called research. The place for dismemberment is called a university. A professor may pluck the strings of his own instrument, but never that of another, and if he listens for music he must never admit it to his fellows or his students. For all are restrained by an iron-bound taboo which decrees that the construction of instruments is the domain of science while the detection of harmony is the domain of poets. (Leopold 1949)

Somehow, we in the Academy must get to the point where we can simultaneously "construct the instruments of the great orchestra and listen to the harmony" with our peers in a truly collective enterprise. We are in need of Leopold's message. If somehow we could get on board with a truly holistic education at our universities, one which unifies disciplines as opposed to our current pattern of fragmentation, then we may possess not only the basic understanding, but also the mental courage and the political backbone to engage with twenty-first century global imperatives.

A Paradigm Shift: New Programs, Majors, Courses—Our Academic Imperative

Addressing twenty-first century global imperatives will require higher education to shift or refocus the fundamental role of the Academy and of its practitioners—the professoriate to one of interdisciplinarity and global focus as opposed to single discipline study and local or national focus. Creation of a new model, a new paradigm in academia—one that is fundamentally interdisciplinary and one that is capable of rigorous and enthusiastic engagement in our twenty-first century world is fundamental. We have very little to lose and everything to gain from this paradigm shift. We need this large-scale restructuring in order to act and make progress on behalf of the world's basic social restoration goals and earth restoration goals clearly delineated by Lester Brown (2009). Essential tools include the overarching fundamental principles of global citizenship, intercultural competence, and fundamental knowledge of how the world really works politically, economically, socially, biologically, and others. Along with these tools, we in the professoriate need somehow to gain the desire and confidence to engage in the twenty-first century world—to have the courage to make a difference.

One approach may be to develop a number of uniquely new and comprehensively structured interdisciplinary university programs. Examples of such new programs include: Global Ethics; Global Studies; Political History of Global Resources; Global Languages; International Development; Global Agriculture; Global Governance; Global Regulatory and Governing Paradigms; Global Resource Sustainabihty; National Sovereignty, Global Literature (Literature of Humanity); or how about just plain Sustainability; and others. Think of the fun and reinvigoration we could have developing these novel, overlapping, interdisciplinary, and fascinating programs! Think of the new, productive, and exciting contacts we could make with our university colleagues in different departments, maybe even different colleges no less! And think of the wonderful opportunities to work abroad!

Another approach could be development of new interdisciplinary courses that stress international themes and concepts in each of our current academic majors. For example, math majors could enroll in a course on "Global Mathematicians: How Language and Culture Shape Mathematics." Biology majors could analyze "Indigenous Biology: Lessons from the Oral Tradition," and others. Failing this, at the very least, each of us can introduce themes and texts of internationalization in our ongoing courses; this individual course development stressing broader international concepts and views should become another one of our academic imperatives.

Interdisciplinary Course Content and Twenty-First Century Global Imperatives: The Case for Great Literature

To achieve an international understanding, there is simply no substitute for living abroad and working with the people. However, the critical analysis of great books that comprehensively, with great sensitivity, depict the very soul of humanity from different cultural perspectives may also be constructive. Fundamentals of the human condition including human rights issues can be productively evaluated by deliberative and serious analysis of fiction as well as nonfiction. For example, poignant and compelling texts include: (a) Wangari Maathai's *Unbowed*. As a Nobel Peace Prize recipient, Parliamentarian, and human rights advocate of Kenya (Dr. Maathai died in December 2011), Dr. Maathai's life represents an exquisite model of the profound value of one individual in improving the world; (b) Ellen Johnson Sirleaf, now in her second term as head of state of Liberia in West Africa. Her autobiography, *This Child will be Great: Memoir of a Remarkable Life by Africa's First Woman President,* is a serious and honest recounting of her life and times in Liberia, a stunningly magnificent life. Can you imagine what it must have been like for Ms. Sirleaf to deal with the likes of Samuel Doe and Charles Taylor?; (c) Chinua Achebe's *Things Fall Apart*—all was well and in balance in this nineteenth century Nigerian community until the British colonized the Ibo; then, things degenerated and fell totally apart; (d) Alan Paton's *Cry the Beloved Country*. One of the few white citizens of South Africa attempting to help the Blacks during apartheid was ruthlessly murdered in a random act of violence by a gang of Black youths (total irony); (e) Kamala Markandaya's *Nectar in a Sieve*. A poor Indian woman overcomes insurmountable odds of poverty, political adversity, rapidly changing societal rules, and disaster testifying to the unyielding "fiber of the human spirit"; (f) Amndhati Roy's *God of Small Things*. "History's Henchmen," or the established order, come and "clean things up" no matter how insidiously heinous the social disruption; (g) Louis DeBernieres' *Birds Without Wings* is a text of extraordinary depth and feeling allowing the reader to gain an appreciation of how the plight of Turkey itself and the destinies of many of Turkey's ethnic groups were tragically controlled by the Great Powers and other forces external to Turkey; and (h) Readings by and of Mohandas K. Gandhi (Mahatma Gandhi) and other models, heroes, or exemplars. Who are your heroes? "Be the change"—Mahatma Gandhi.

Finally, Antoine de Saint-Exuper's *The Little Prince* is nothing short of a beautiful, lyrical text embedded within a simple story with a huge message. Not unlike the characters in Voltaire's *Micromegas*, the Little Prince wanders around the earth and solar system looking for "truths" of one sort or another. The desert fox explains two truths to the Little Prince: (a) When you "tame" something like getting married, having children, or living in and reaping the benefits of a globalized world, you have a responsibility to the things you tame! The fox laments that we may have forgotten that fundamental lesson and (b) If you succumb to living in our current era of "numbers envy," hyper-individualistic lifestyles, material addiction, and pursuit of numerous false gods without concern for community and the public good, you too may also have forgotten the desert fox's "lesson of responsibility."

Productive Models and Issues to Address Twenty-First Century Global Imperatives

Our global population could be around nine billion people by 2050; unfortunately the collective "global footprint" of nine billion people requires vast global resource requirements and, at the same time, inhibits resolution of global problems like poverty, hunger, illiteracy, health, and many others. Lester Brown (2009) quotes economist Gene Sperling who states, "Expansion of female secondary education may be the single best lever for achieving reductions in fertility." Young girls in developing countries who stay in school marry later, have fewer children, and because of their education, are better able to care for their children nutritionally and with respect to health. Connecting these dots should be highly instructive for our students. We would also learn the value in taking positive action to keep young women in school. A university course entitled "Keeping Girls In School" could become a national and international model—one in which virtually all concerned global citizens could participate. Would that our higher education institutions could offer an exciting course entitled "Keeping Girls in School"; it could be offered as an optional institutional requirement. By exploring the many dimensions of education, poverty, malnutrition, adverse health conditions, and diminishment of human dignity suffered by one to two billion poor people daily, such a course could serve as a unique frame of reference comparing our world of plenty and opportunity versus their world of abject poverty. It may even encourage us to act.

Promotion and Tenure Requirements at the University

As outlined in Childress (2010), there exist ways to incentivize universities to encourage faculty members to address global imperatives and a range of other international issues in their respective courses. Tenure and promotion criteria could reward faculty who: (a) serve as members of cross-disciplinary campus internationalization committees; (b) internationalize their individual courses; (c) develop foreign language proficiency (seems like an ideal win-win situation for nine-month faculty to receive pay for learning a foreign language during the summer); (d) take students abroad; (e) conduct service work either abroad or at home as one component of course requirements; (f) join and participate in international organizations; (g) serve on various departmental or college internationalization committees; (h) publish papers on international themes; (i) develop interdisciplinary research and teaching teams with foreign faculty members across departments and colleges, and others.

The Direct Approach: Changing the Mission of the University to Address Twenty-First Century Global Imperatives

Those of us concerned with addressing global problems studies including issues of global justice should all be proud of Fairleigh Dickenson University (FDU). The FDU mission statement is presented below:

> Fairleigh Dickinson University is a center of academic excellence dedicated to the preparation of world citizens through global education. The University strives to provide students with the multi-disciplinary, intercultural, and ethical understandings necessary to participate, lead, and prosper in the global marketplace of ideas, commerce, and culture. (Adams and Carfagna 2006)

This mission statement sets the tone for an extensive reorganization and restructuring of academic programs at FDU. Fortunately, we have a wonderful opportunity, in fact a detailed "Operator's Manual," to evaluate philosophical rationale and practical aspects of this FDU global competency initiative in the published book of FDU President, Dr. J. Michael Adams (Adams and Carfagna 2006). This text details the kinds of academic experiences and training at FDU that led to the fulfillment of the goals and objectives in the mission statement above. An excellent source of fundamental principles, tools, and recipes for reshaping one's institution, this text provides the necessary tools and rationale to enable us to engage productively in the resolution of our twenty-first century global imperatives.

A second compelling text (Tetreault and Lipschutz 2009) provides additional "hands on" approaches to tackle global problems; the last chapter (Chapter 10: People Matter) provides a superb analysis of how everyday people like you, me, our faculty colleagues, and our college and university students can "get into the action" in highly productive ways to become agents of change for global imperatives. Finally, Lisa K. Childress (2010) has recently published *The Twenty-First Century University: Developing Faculty Engagement in Internationalization*. This excellent "nuts and bolts" text delineates both historical contexts and critical analyses of "how-to-do-it" internationalization instructions plus compelling descriptions of heuristic models of internationalization employed at Duke University and the University of Richmond. In short, these three above-mentioned texts provide bedrock directions and highly practical methods of strategically organizing our universities to enable us to get on with the business of confronting and engaging productively with our twenty-first century global imperatives.

Summary

We (our world and its people) find ourselves at a critical turning point, perhaps even a "point of no return"; we can continue on with business as usual (Plan A) or we can accept the fact that our twentieth century global modus operandi will simply not work in the twenty-first century and therefore adopt Plan B (Brown 2009). With "business as usual," we have little to gain and much to lose including our credibility as academics, not to mention the inexorable degradation and decline of our social, political, biological, and physical worlds.

Recognizing the precariousness of our current situation, we are then required to act. How then can we carry out "Plan B"? As academics, we return to our base, our foundation, our well of pure "truth-pursuit"—our research, curricula, academic programs, instructors, and our entire academic armamentarium—the panoply of the noble Academy going back to one of our very first Western mentors—Socrates and his analysis of fundamental truths. We have all the necessary tools; we simply need the political will to get into the thick of the action.

We have sufficient human energy, intellectual curiosity, academic zeal, and history of learning communities of the ages dating back to Plato's noble academy. We even have Socrates' admonition in Plato's *Apology*: "The unexamined life is not worth living." We simply need to redirect that academic zeal from our individual disciplinary pursuits to the collective, frightful, and horrific imperatives of the twenty-first century—to very real and sobering global imperatives instead of our individual academic domains, however exciting, compelling, and rewarding our disciplinary academic truths may be.

We need to recognize anew that we are all in the global business (life on this planet) together. We will survive together or perish together. Just as all nations of the world need to shift from carbon-based energy to renewable energy, we in higher education need to redirect our energies from pure disciplinary pursuit to interdisciplinary, connect-the-dots-type projects directed toward the understanding and resolution of specific global imperatives.

We can, like Fairieigh Dickenson University, revamp our institutional missions, either comprehensively all at once or in a non-threatening, incremental fashion while creating the kinds of academic programs to productively and successfully confront our twenty-first century demons. We just need some boldness and daring. We may need a little old-fashioned 'backbone.' We can do this. We just need some impetus. This "academic redirection" could tum out to be one of the most significant turning points in the history of higher education and the noble Academy. I am convinced this redirection is going to happen sooner or later (if and when global conditions become so apparently dire that we will be forced to finally acknowledge our grim situation and the need for action). We would all be better off if the Academy could act now. And our initiatives might as well occur at any one of a number of private universities (like Fairleigh Dickenson University) as well as public institutions including our noble Land-Grant Institutions.

Conclusion: Lewis Thomas' Admonition

In his classic text *Late Night Thoughts on Listening to Mahler's Ninth Symphony*, mid-twentieth century physician/scientist Lewis Thomas (1983) asserted that our species *Homo sapiens* is an immature species. The late Dr. Thomas worried that we, by virtue of our immaturity, would blow ourselves to smithereens in a nuclear holocaust. He hoped that our immature species could survive for a couple more millennia, or at least for a sufficient duration of time for us to become a mature species. Then *H. sapiens*, along with non-human biota of the world's global ecosystems as well as our physical global environment would have a real chance at longevity.

We are now confronted with a series of profoundly serious, unprecedented, and life-threatening global problems—our twenty-first century global imperatives. Can we mature as a species and confront our ominous global imperatives? We are a highly resilient species. That is proven. We can rise to the occasion, engage the world, design new curricula, programs, majors, colleges, endowed chairs, get excited, and have a lot of fun in this energizing process. We have the tools to understand how we arrived at this precipice of global jeopardy. And the good news—we possess the creativity, artistry, sufficient cerebral "gray cells," and resilience to work together to resolve our current twenty-first century global dilemmas. Our future's in the balance!

Works Cited

Achebe, Chinua. 1994. *Things Fall Apart*. New York. Knoph Doubleday Publishers.

Adams, J. Michael and Angelo Carfagna. 2006. *Coming of Age in a Globalized World: The Next Generation*. Bloomfield, CT. Kumarian Press, Inc.

Brown, Lester. 2009. *Plan B 4.0: Mobilizing to Save Civilization*. Earth Policy Institute. New York. W.W. Norton & Company.

Childress, Lisa K. 2010. *The Twenty-First Century University: Developing Faculty Engagement in Internationalization*. New York. Peter Lang Publishing Inc.

DeBernieres, Louis. 2007. *Birds Without Wings*. New York. Knoph Doubleday Publishers.

De Saint-Exupery, Antoine. 2000. *The Little Prince*. New York. Houghton Mifflin Harcourt.

Guest, Edgar A. 2007. *Collected Works of Edgar A. Guest*. Charleston, South Carolina. BiblioBazar Press.

Leopold, Aldo. 1949. *A Sand County Almanac: Sketches Here and There*. New York. Oxford University Press.

Maathai, Wangari. 2007. *Unbowed: A Memoir*. New York. Anchor Books.

Markandaya, Kamala. 2010. *Nectar in a Sieve*. New York. Penguin Group.

McKibben, Bill. 2010. *Eaarth: Making a Life on a Tough New Planet*. New York. Times Books.

Pachauri, R.K. and A. Reisinger. (Eds). 2007. Intergovernmental Panel on Climate Change (IPCC) Fourth Assessment Report. Geneva, Switzerland. Climate Change 2007: Synthesis Report. IPCC.

Paton, Alan. 1996. *Cry, The Beloved Country*. New York. Scribner Publishing.

Roy, Arundhati. 1998. *The God of Small Things*. New York. Random House.

Sirleaf, Ellen Johnson. 2009. *This Child Will Be Great: Memoir of a Remarkable Life by Africa's First Woman President*. New York. Harper Collins Publishers.

letreault, Mary Ann and Ronnie D. Lipschutz. 2009. *Global Politics as if People Mattered*. New York. Rowman & Littlefield Publishers, Inc.

Thomas, Lewis. 1983. *Late Night Thoughts on Listening to Mahler's Ninth Symphony*. New York. Bantam Books.

Credit

Marketization of Education: An Ethical Dilemma

Samuel M. Natale and Caroline Doran

> It is still a rather common misconception that marketing should be primarily focused on admissions. Such a mindset fails to consider that students will often have much greater value to the institution as alumni. Thus, it is important to establish strong relationships with students before they even arrive at the college, continue to build upon those relationships while they are attending college, and ideally extend the value of those relationships across a lifetime. If IHEs do not consider the entire lifetime value chain of a student and connect the links in the chain with concepts such as IMC, they will undoubtedly lose considerable opportunities to advance their institutions. (Edmiston 2009, p. 173)

Education considered in such a context reduces students to a revenue stream and colleges to businesses; this is the contemporary face of education.

As educational leaders seek solutions to the complex problems facing their institutions, including rapidly shifting mission and changes which perhaps capture fewer and fewer qualified students, many perceive the marketization of education as a viable answer. Although the adoption of business practices may initially benefit universities, it remains questionable whether these new approaches benefit students and faculty. Focusing resources to elevate university rankings and to drive student enrollment may improve the institution's revenues; however, is it wise to redirect the efforts of faculty from their core responsibility as educators?

Shifting Priorities and How They Affect Universities and Faculty

The University Within the Context of the State's and Society's Goals

In recent years, the dwindling supply of federal funds coupled with the growth of consumer culture and growing fervor for corporate capitalism have done much to transform higher education (Molesworth et al. 2009). In such a society, students seek to secure a degree, rather than experience an education, with their goals limited to the acquisition of skills needed for employment and maximizing income. Within this context, universities are being pushed to produce knowledgeable students that society and employers deem valuable—not knowledge for its own sake or classical approaches that focus more on the process and ability to think. Additionally, higher learning institutions are being asked to graduate more students while maintaining the same standards of quality, closing achievements gaps, and becoming more efficient and productive organizations (Lingenfelter 2006).

The issue of accountability and the measurement of outcomes is now commonplace in education (Sigler 2007). Such accountability is usually couched in the language of accounting. The kinds of questions advanced by such a discourse include: Does the academy provide good value for money? Is money being spent wisely and well? Is there an appropriate social return on the billions of dollars that are invested in higher education, both directly and indirectly, by students and their parents, the state and corporations? In such a discourse, "wisely and well" are redefined by an increasing concern with the economic and vocational relevance of what is taught rather than by an older set of more liberal concerns. Do students have the requisite knowledge and skills to make them employable in a modern economy? Students may well be versed in the details of medieval history or the poetry of William Blake, but what can they *do*? Are they able to communicate and work in teams? Do they understand business? Do they have the key or core skills necessary for work?

Furthermore, newer economic and cultural imperatives mean that the state's interest in the university is considerably more intrusive and less benign. Concerns with economic competitiveness, for example, mean that the state's interests in the university are vested along new lines and dimensions. Because the state encourages or coerces universities to produce graduates who have more useful knowledge and who have developed the right kind of core generic skills, the modern university is at increasing risk of losing its distinctive and balanced character by emphasizing, for example, newer business values rather than the older academic ones.

Society's relationship with knowledge is also changing: it is shifting to one where society is increasingly concerned with the utility of knowledge. A new model of higher education appears to be developing in which the pursuit of knowledge related to the "practical" rather than the pursuit of knowledge related to what is "true" or "good" has become the dominant goal. The knowledge society is interested only in *certain kinds* of knowledge and values only *certain kinds* of learning. Therefore, students are torn between self-development and the need to have marketable skills. More so than in the past, students are focused on preparation for the workplace and are overly concentrated on content related only to the job (Molesworth et al. 2009). Such a new discourse potentially rips the roots of the university from its time-honored position.

Universities were once thought of as institutions for the public good, serving the interests of the community and the citizens of the world. A question central to the education debate, with the growing proportion of education being provided by non-traditional sources, is whether education is still a public good or whether it contributes to the development of society as opposed to the development of individuals (Knight 2006). Today education is largely viewed as a marketable commodity. Education, once seen as a process, has been reduced to job preparation, making higher education a product in which one invests for the purpose of one's future employment opportunities in business and technology. Of the more than 1.5 million degrees that were granted in 2007–2008, the most common degrees were: 21% in business, 10.5% in the social sciences and history, 7% in health science, and 6.5% in education (IES 2009). Furthermore, rather than guiding and supporting the student in becoming more intellectually complex, universities and colleges that are highly commercialized serve to prepare the student to become a participant in the consumer culture and no longer strive to encourage the student's reflection and critical thinking.

The University Within the Context of Financial Goals

The concern of any institution with a strong corporate orientation is to meet the demands of the student (consumer) in the most efficient (cost-effective) manner. Adoption of business practices by educational institutions is transforming the educational landscape. As business practices are accepted in education, students have been transformed into consumers, and, in some institutions, programs are deemed successful only when they drive revenue production or support the acquisition of corporate funding. Many institutions are headed by presidents who are paid like corporate executives, and recruitment of university leaders often focuses on the business acumen of candidates, rather than their expertise as educators or their commitment to learning (Marris 2005).

The changes in higher education reach far beyond vocabulary and run deeply into the heart of institutions. In an environment of academic production, courses that do not garner interest from large numbers of students may be eliminated. To improve the efficiency of faculty, universities may seek to reduce the hours that academics spend in discussions with students, creating an atmosphere of passive, reproductive learning that does not encourage critical thinking and reflection by the student (Molesworth et al. 2009).

The University Within the Context of Other Organizations' Goals

Corporations that desire greater tailoring of information fund universities to serve their own needs. But corporate sponsorship of research may be placing faculty members in a position where they face conflicts of interest and commitment. Faculty may be diverted from teaching to financially productive research and become preoccupied with producing research for corporations, securing grants from businesses, and engaging in consultant assignments with corporate clients (Kaplan 1996).

In the past, research largely consisted of individual scholars engaged in a quest for new knowledge in their fields of study. Today there are research programs, collective projects with multiple researchers, consisting of individuals who are expendable and interchangeable. Some of today's research programs may no longer represent a search for knowledge; instead, they have become structured programs controlled by management with clearly defined business goals heavily influenced by corporations. Research is expensive and only certain disciplines generate funding. As corporate dollars pour in to support pharmaceutical, technology, and biomedical research, research in other disciplines is no longer attractive because it cannot secure funding.

The ethical concern with this research focus, as posed by Yassi et al. (2010), is that the more universities come to depend on research funding from businesses, the more researchers are compelled not to deviate in their findings from the interests of those who fund them. Should their findings be incongruent with their funders, they risk their careers, which raises the question, or at least *should* raise the question, regarding the integrity of contemporary university research.

Training and the Contemporary Model of Education

Historically, the university was seen as a community that nurtured ideas and innovations, built the morals of its students, and contributed to democracy through producing political and social leaders (Tilak 2009). This is no longer the case. Concerns with accountability, knowledge, and student abilities pave the way for new forms of assessment, monitoring, and surveillance, where supposedly liberal processes are valued less than the measurable outcomes of higher education. Given the new grounding in absolute pragmatism, the university is pressured to produce graduates who are ready to blend into the workforce or into those agencies of society responsible for social change. Curriculum that has been distorted to focus heavily on technology and business has undermined the core values of higher education. The earlier commitment of higher education institutions to a core curriculum is being eroded as they become training centers for industry (Miscamble 2006). The former distinction between education and training has collapsed here into a new hybrid.

The study of the humanities may no longer be valued in this new environment. One wonders why though, when the actual outcomes of an effective liberal education involve, "the ability to listen carefully, to read critically, to write accurately and persuasively, and to analyze exactly" (Ryan 1999, p. 17). There is now so much focus on workplace skills, that there is little value to knowing anything that cannot help students become more "marketable" in the workforce, garner a raise, or advance a career. Having read the *Iliad* is not likely to help in any of these respects.

Faculty and the Contemporary Model of Education: The Teacherpreneur

While universities become increasingly focused on the application of business practices, one might question whether this new paradigm of higher education dismisses what was once thought to be the role of faculty members. In the new corporate model of higher education, faculty members are seen as providers of customer service and transmitters of industry-relevant skills. Professors are often no longer seen as scholars; rather they are viewed as employees with publications (Molesworth et al. 2009).

The new vision of higher education as an economic institution and knowledge as a product is likely to not be aligned with the fundamental values of many faculty members. Some claim higher education has been transformed, while many other and more seasoned academics see it as the death of the university as they have known it. As leaders of higher education institutions grow obsessed with the corporate vision of profit, faculty members are relegated to positions where they are less involved in the mission of their institutions (Thacker 2005). The role of faculty is changing dramatically.

Schools are commonly recruiting faculty from industry and now focus on their industry skills as opposed to their critical thinking skills (Molesworth et al. 2009). In fact, scholarship may no longer be a requisite skill for teaching in higher education. Even though business is the most commonly pursued undergraduate degree, the most common degree at the master's level is education, followed by business. The greatest number of degrees granted in 2009 at the doctorate level were related to health and clinical sciences, followed by education, engineering, biological and biomedical sciences, psychology, and physical sciences (IES 2009). Therefore, what is emerging is a trend whereby pursuing a terminal degree in business is less common than in other fields, perhaps because so much focus is now placed on field experience among new business faculty. In an effort to satisfy the consumers' demand for preparation for the workplace, colleges and universities seek to maximize their connection with corporations, which may mean recruiting faculty from industry, drawing into question the qualifications of such individuals to be mentors in a deep and meaningful learning process. Moreover, the new financial demands lead to hiring more adjuncts (Meyerson 2005).

In earlier times, faculty members enjoyed significant autonomy over their teaching and research, but with the new emphasis on corporate management, this too has changed. Furthermore, the move to external accountability driven by financial rather than intellectual goals transforms faculty into employees through competence-based audits and assessments, and changes a community of scholars into a training ground for corporate workers with too much emphasis on finances and too little focus on the education of students (Gibbs 2006). More important, professors often feel compelled to focus on what will allow students to pass as opposed to focusing on critical thinking and reflection. Furthermore, because students are so focused on the post-graduation job hunt, they are overly focused on the outcomes of assessments (Molesworth et al. 2009). Combined, these relegate professors' role to one concentrated on grade-related outcomes, rather than on the process of learning.

Moreover, in an environment where higher education institutions have become research centers for corporations, the qualifications for faculty members, which were once thought to be scholarship and the ability to mentor students, are being replaced by the candidate's skill as an entrepreneur. Corporate influence is particularly widespread in the fields of medicine, biotechnology, and pharmacology. The media has exposed numerous tales of corporate funding by the tobacco, energy, and pharmaceutical industries where university-based researchers received millions of dollars to produce research in support of their corporate benefactors (Bridenthal 2005). Humanities, however, are less able to create marketable products for industry and attract less corporate funding, which has resulted in a trend toward higher salaries for top researchers who garner major corporate funding while adjuncts are teaching at barely livable salaries. Moral and civic-focused courses are often offered only at the introductory level, and some senior faculty members are unwilling to teach these lower level courses because they value their research activities over teaching.

Faculty members are often faced with balancing professionalism and commercialism in today's higher education environment. While institutions may no longer hire faculty to be active members of a rigorous intellectual community, faculty members may now see their positions in the university as mere platforms for moving forward entrepreneurial agendas. And, every faculty member must have such an agenda or feel at risk. As objectivity of university-based research is questioned, the integrity of higher education is also questioned. This issue of teacher as entrepreneur (teacherpreneur) is exacerbated by disparity in pay. While salaries for university and college presidents may approach the levels of corporate executives, compensation for professors has barely increased (Marris 2005). The average salary for male professors in 2009 was $79,706 and $65,638 for females (IES 2009).

Statistics indicate a steady increase in part-time faculty positions and a reduction in tenure-track positions (Altbach 2009). Only 49% of full-time professors had tenure in 2008 compared to 56% in 1994 (IES 2009). There were 0.7 million full-time and 0.7 million part-time faculty in 2007, and the rate of part-time to full-time staff in education has also been growing. Between 1997 and 2007, part-time staff increased by 39%, whereas full-time staff rose by only 25%. Much of the growth in part-time staff can be attributed to the hiring of part-time faculty (IES 2009). For those teachers who are not fully employed outside of the school, they are likely teaching at multiple institutions to make a living. This should pose an ethical quandary for institutions and students: in many cases, these teachers are not making an acceptable living as they do not have a permanent full-time job. This impacts commitment to an institution and its students; professors who teach at multiple institutions at one time teach well beyond what is considered a full-time load for full-time professors.

Furthermore, in recent years, many not-for-profit universities have launched for-profit online and other degree-granting programs in which faculty members are expected to teach. With this additional workload, professors may find it difficult to be committed to the responsibilities once thought to be the essence of academic life: teaching, research, participation in the academic community, and governance of their institutions. Again, the ethical dilemma is whether the issue of fairness or reasonableness has been taken off the table for a cadre of employees that is seeing the core of their work changing like a daily menu. This surely impacts morale, which has a negative effect on schools and students.

Shifting Priorities and How They Affect Learning, Students, and Society

Between 1988 and 1998, enrollment in colleges grew by 11% but, between 1998 and 2008, enrollment grew by 32% (IES 2009). In sync with the public's growing interest in acquiring a college education, this era has seen great changes in the *modus operandi* on the supply side. What has emerged in the last 20 years, therefore, is an increasing focus on the marketization of education (Newman and Jahdi 2009).

The economic strife and reduced availability of federal funds for higher education in the 1990s created an atmosphere ripe for the leaders of America's colleges and universities to find the marketing strategies of the business community appealing, as they pursued their quest for new sources of funds with the added rivalry of the "for profit" sector. History indicates that securing funding has long been a challenge for American colleges and universities. Many of the private higher education institutions were funded through donations from nineteenth century industrialists, who later turned their attention to philanthropic activities. Following World War II, the GI Bill provided funding for the expansion of many colleges and universities, but a decline in the population in the 1970s and 1980s drove institutions to seek new methods of financial support (Hossler 2004). In these years, new trends such as federal funding for science and engineering research, as well as a growing application of aggressive marketing practices, including the use of financial aid for student recruitment, began to emerge (Miscamble 2006).

One of the problems imposed by the state on higher education is that state leaders view schools as having an independent income stream in the form of tuition and consequently, expect students to pay an increasingly larger proportion for the cost of their education (Sigler 2007). Tuition as a percentage of college's revenue has increased 10 points over the last 25 years. Tuition now comprises 36.3% of school revenues (SHEEO 2009). Student-derived revenue is now more important than ever, making student satisfaction more important than ever. Consequently, parents have become customers, students are now consumers, and education and research, once believed to be processes, are now seen as products (Miscamble 2006). Terms of the managerial vocabulary, such as performance assessment, quality control, and competitive edge, are also now commonplace in discussions of higher education. It is not difficult to understand how this new vocabulary has been so readily adopted, when one considers that corporate lawyers and business leaders hold the majority of positions on the governing boards of most universities and colleges in America (Miscamble 2006).

Colleges now operate as bottom line-oriented organizations and the marketization of higher education has been accompanied by the adoption of a managerialist ideology and a new drive for quality and efficiency, which has resulted in increased bureaucracy in many institutions (Lock and Lorenz 2007). Consequently, the composition of the varying employment classifications in educational institutions has also changed considerably, directly reflecting a shift in the importance of the administrative function of education. For example, the percentage of non-teaching professionals has risen from 10 to 20% between 1979 and 2007 (IES 2009). From the perspective of an institution with a strong corporate focus, these changes may appear to be process improvements in that universities may be more cost-efficient and able to produce more graduates at a lower per capita cost, but this type of administrative approach to education is unrealistic (Goldspink 2007).

Enrollment Management and Student Aid

There are now more students (consumers) than ever interested in pursuing a college degree, and these consumers are paying a higher percentage of their education—schools are relying more heavily than ever on tuition dollars. Therefore, the contemporary face of education is extremely competitive. Schools have developed enrollment management strategies to allow them to be competitive and to influence whom and how many students they matriculate. Some of the practices employed in enrollment management are not without controversy, however, and they largely center on institutions' use of campus-based financial aid to attract preferential students. The use of needbased financial assistance has long been seen as an appropriate method of promoting diversity and inclusion of less affluent students in the college community, but merit awards, which have become increasingly popular both in private and public institutions, serve a different end.

Colleges offer merit-based aid to high scoring students to improve their rankings, elevate their prestige, and support their brand image. As the focus has shifted away from promoting the promise of social justice, access to quality education for low income students is being pushed aside in the pursuit of a corporate vision. One reason is that merit-based aid is instrumental in increasing the cost of getting an education (Lingenfelter 2006). Students from middle or higher income families are more likely than students from lower income families to receive merit-based aid (IES 2009). Also, with limited financial aid resources available, merit-based awards have resulted in fewer students receiving need-based aid (Ehrenberg 2005). Merit-based aid increased 212%, while needs-based aid increased only 47% between 1996 and 2004 (Marklein 2007). Moreover, while colleges are using merit-based aid to woo students they deem as most desirable, they are also spending more money on recruiting, leaving fewer resources available for faculty salaries and the education of students.

Enrollment Management and Rankings

Furthermore, rankings have taken on greater meaning in an environment where colleges are actively competing for students' tuition dollars. Students frequently turn to the rankings of universities when formulating their application decisions (Thacker 2005). Playing the rankings game has undoubtedly contributed to the marketization of higher education. Because students and their families are paying a larger proportion of students' education, they are demanding information on retention rate, graduation rates, and job prospects—information that will indicate their return on investment (Sigler 2007). The down side to this is that, over the past decade, rankings have become increasingly important, causing educational institutions to redirect funds to improving their rankings in such publications as *U.S. News and World Report* (Lingenfelter 2006).

The rankings game is not always played fairly either. It is possible to improve a college's rankings in terms of 6-year graduation rates by relaxing standards, admitting highly qualified students, or throwing a lot of money at support services. Colleges can also improve their rankings by improving their spend-per-student, which discourages schools from being financially prudent. This increases the need for tuition or forces faculty to look for research funds (Ehrenberg 2005). Furthermore, schools are pressuring faculty into helping improve rankings (Hossler 2000). Diver (2005) highlights other practices, such as:

> failing to report low SAT scores from foreign students, "legacies," recruited athletes, or members of other 'special admission' categories; exaggerating per capita instructional expenditures by misclassifying expenses for athletics, faculty research, and auxiliary enterprises; artificially driving up the number of applicants by counting as a completed application the first step of a 'two-part' application process; and inflating the yield rate by rejecting or wait-listing the highest achievers in the applicant pool (who are least likely to come if admitted). (p. 137)

There is an ethical issue with chasing ranking status. Playing the rankings game has refocused colleges on recruiting high potential students and persuading students who will likely have better grades from leaving for out-of-state schools through discounting tuition (Lingenfelter 2006). Also, the number of students receiving Pell grants in the top ranks seems to decrease as ranks improve, pointing to the use of the adjustment of tuition to influence rankings (Meredith 2004). An incidental outcome of this is that access to college for the financially disadvantaged would intuitively have to be more difficult. The ethical concern with rankings should be the emphasis it puts on seeking highly qualified students, deflecting attention from the tradition of wanting to make access to higher education equitable (Ehrenberg 2005).

Enrollment management has become a critical tool in playing the rankings game, and enrollment management in most public and private higher education institutions has gained increased importance. Enrollment management offices are concerned with the positioning of the university's brand in the marketplace and are often leaders in designing marketing, pricing, and financial aid strategies employed to attract the institution's target consumer. A commonly used tool used to deploy information regarding a school's message is the college view book (Klassen 2000). In a study examining the content of view books, Klassen (2000) found universities communicate what they are about to prospective students through their view books. As an example of how view books are used as marketing tools, schools ranked in the top 15 of the *U.S. News and World Report* ranking of U.S. colleges and universities primarily employ imagery in their view books of engagement between students and professors, cultural events, and artistic activities. On the other hand, imagery used by tier four schools focuses on graduation, alumni events, and posteducational endeavors. According to Klassen (2000), the message sent by each type of university is that graduation can be achieved with little disruption in terms of jobs, relationship, children, etc. Schools are creating a vision of Utopia … degrees without any hassles.

> By excising the disagreeable but common routines of ordinary life, all of the view books examined here have unwittingly sidestepped the very longings that have compelled young people for centuries to seek a higher education: service to humanity and their fellow citizens, commitment to family and work, and the search for higher meaning. (p. 21)

Ethically, these types of enrollment management/marketing practices are questionable. From the student's perspective, it is difficult to evaluate higher education as a consumer product and, for many students, the brand image of the institution as presented in such materials as the view books becomes the deciding factor. Studies indicate that students are influenced by effective advertising campaigns that begin to blur the lines between marketing a school and selling it (Nicholls et al. 1995).

Issues of Rigor and Utility of Learning

Colleges and universities are in threat of becoming institutions whose primary service is to prepare the student for lifelong consumerism rather than a "better life." People must remain more important than the acquisition of things. Student consumerism is pervasive in the U.S., where they believe that, regardless of effort, students deserve the degree they pay for and, should they not feel satisfied with the services rendered, they are justified in challenging the provider of that service—the teacher—about the perceived weakness of the teacher's performance. In addition, students are lazier, harder to motivate, and bored; they do not want to be there; they want to get to work (Ng and Forbes 2009). There is no room for rigor or meaningful journeys in such an environment, and the marketization of education is largely to blame. When students are not happy, they can threaten to take their needed tuition dollars elsewhere, just as they would change car insurance to obtain a policy with better value. The problem is that these students are not forced to see that they are an integral part of the process and not just an addendum by administrators vying for rankings and tuition dollars.

Furthermore, obtaining a degree solely focused on employment denies students the opportunity to transform themselves on a personal level. The problem with this focus on content at the expense of critical thinking is that society no longer has the large number of creative critical thinkers required in a capitalist society (Raduntz 2007, p. 242). Moreover, the ethical issue posed by this orientation to please and not engage the student is that, for all the heartache evoked, the new model of business is not serving the universities any more adequately, as we hear from Arum and Roska in *Academically Adrift: Limited Learning on College Campuses*—at least 45% of undergraduates demonstrated "no improvement in critical thinking, complex reasoning, and writing skills in the first two years of college, and 36 per cent showed no progress in four years" (Benton 2011). According to Benton, this is "just the beginning of the bad news" (para 1). Professors often feel compelled to focus on what will allow students to pass as opposed to focusing on critical thinking and reflection (Molesworth et al. 2009). In the long term, this can only spell demise on a personal and societal level, and teachers and schools, rather than improving society, are adding to its burden. Again, the marketization of education plays no small part in schools' failure to improve the future of society.

Problems and Solutions

What to do About Rankings?

The marketing of colleges in the U.S. is now more prevalent than at any other time in history (Klassen 2000), and this calls for an urgent conversation on the commercialization of education. First and foremost, the issue of rankings needs to be addressed. According to Lingenfelter (2006, p. 6)

> In the past dozen years both state governments and institutions have spent increasing amounts of money for what amounts to expensive efforts to improve their rankings in *U.S. News and World Report.* Institutions are discounting tuition to attract more students with better grades and test scores, and some of our states have been discounting tuition to keep better students at home.

Recommendations have been made that institutions should no longer cooperate with organizations that issue rankings. In fact, this is just what some schools have chosen to do. Colin Diver, president of Reed College, describes the school's lack of cooperation with *U.S. News & World Report* ranking system as follows:

> By far the most important consequence of sitting out the rankings game, however, is the freedom to pursue our own educational philosophy, not that of some news magazine. ... We are free to admit the students we think will thrive at Reed and contribute to its intellectual atmosphere, rather than those we think will elevate our standing on *U.S. News's* list. ... Pleasing students *can* mean superb educational programs precisely tailored to their needs; but it can also mean dumbing down graduation requirements, lessening educational rigor, inflating grades, and emphasizing nonacademic amenities. At Reed we have felt free to pursue an educational philosophy that maintains rigor and structure—including a strong core curriculum in the humanities,

> extensive distribution requirements, a junior qualifying examination in one's major, a required senior thesis, uninflated grades (not reported to students unless they request them), heavy workloads, and graduate-level standards in many courses. We have also felt free to resist pressure to provide an expensive and highly selective program of varsity athletics and other nonacademic enticements simply for their marketing advantages. ... Unlike many of our rankings-sensitive peers, we feel no pressure to use part-time adjunct faculty or teaching assistants as an inexpensive but educationally dubious technique for even further increasing the percentage of small classes. (pp. 137–139)

What to do About Branding?

The financial feasibility of many colleges is now dependent on marketing and maintaining market share (Edirisooriya 2009). Because the competitive landscape in education is now so competitive, schools feel they have no alternative but to differentiate themselves through branding. No person could argue for complete removal of a business model as it seems critical in these difficult economic times and, while one may question the appropriateness of marketing an institution, marketing in higher education is now a global phenomenon. Many in higher education are not pleased with their new roles as marketing representatives, and many members of the higher education community do not have the experience to be skillful marketers. Furthermore, there is a degree of whitewashing enveloping the educational landscape as a result of this branding effort that might be considered misleading and unethical that needs to be addressed. Obtaining a degree should be hard work, it should require personal sacrifice, it should require personal accountability, and students who are not capable should be allowed to fail. Society should not be burdened with graduates who are not up to par and schools need to accept their responsibility in this regard by not attempting to sell utopia. Then, when students enroll, they are prepared to work hard for their degrees and will not expect to sail through the process simply because they are paying. Perhaps, institutions might then consider transforming their marketing-focused enrollment management offices into counseling services that encourage students to become participants in learning rather than consumers of education.

What to do About Faculty Morale?

Faculty spend 58% of their time teaching, 20% of the balance in research and scholarship, and 22% on issues, such as administration and professional development (IES 2009). With so many part-time and adjunct faculty, there is considerable pressure on full-time faculty to publish to meet standards for accreditations, such as AACSB, to serve on committees, and to engage in administrative effort. This is deeply problematic in an entrepreneurial environment. According to Goldspink

(2007), faculty morale is low because so much focus is being placed on additional administrative responsibilities in an effort to achieve operational efficiencies. This also detracts from learning outcomes. Furthermore, Benton (2011, para 17) writes:

> Students may be enjoying high self-esteem, but college teachers seem to be suffering from a lack of self-confidence. It starts in graduate school, when we begin to fear we are destined for unemployment, when we compare our pay with that of comparably educated professionals, and when we realize that—for all the sacrifices that we've made, often with idealistic motives—we are held in slight regard. Many people even think of us as subversives who 'hate America.' During the latest economic crisis—perhaps the endpoint of a 40-year slide—many of us have felt as if we've become expendable, if we are employed at all. That makes it hard for us to make strong demands on our students, or, perhaps more important, to stand up for any kind of change in our institutions.

A holistic approach is necessary to address the problem of low faculty morale, which has become epidemic. This issue is a broad social one. Educators are no longer valued as they once were. A good place to start addressing this issue is to support a return of academic power to the faculty in the teacher-student dyad. Administrators need to examine the efficacy of anonymous student evaluations in determining teaching quality as it gives no voice to faculty. Administrators need to reevaluate the level of administrative burden placed on faculty when the ranks of full-time faculty are falling. These are becoming embedded ethical issues.

What to do About Critical Thinking and Dumbing Down?

The university was once seen as the center for investigation and critical thinking, and it would be a tremendous loss to society if higher education became an activity solely driven by the demands of a capitalist culture. Higher education has now come to be a means of securing material affluence, and education may no longer be viewed as a potentially transformative experience able to affect the student's intellectual perspective of the world.

The student as consumer perspective causes harm. It has the propensity to lower quality and promote a passive, disengaged student body. Because the consumer is always right, implicit in the student as consumer model is that students must be happy with the services rendered. When the consumer is an integral part of the delivery of education, one would have to question this consumer satisfaction orientation. Further, when the outcome of learning is reduced to a grade, with the student as a consumer and the teacher as the provider, the faculty is perceived as solely responsible for learning. This is problematic. According to Rojstaczer and Healy (2010), grade inflation has been on an upward trajectory since the 1980s, and it is very probable that this is as a result of student-based teacher evaluation. According to Benton (2011), it has become difficult to give students honest feedback as teachers must now envelop students with praise and encouragement to avoid student disappointment, thus retarding student growth. This new form of higher education is not likely to prepare students for corporate careers because it does not provide them with the opportunity to become critical thinkers, who are able to innovate and cope with change. Compounding this is the growing number of adjunct or part-time faculty whose performance is measured in large part by student evaluations and who are not always in sync with the institution's mission (Benton 2011).

Contemporary education is currently situated uneasily between "traditional" and "relevant." Teachers must once again emphasize supporting personal student transformation, even if they are under pressure from management and students to focus on the skills that support a job search (Molesworth et al. 2009). Faculty must concur on this.

What to do About Ethical Issues in Research?

Externally funded research raises a host of ethical concerns. Yassi et al. (2010) call on universities to address the ethical issues posed by non-university funded research rather than jeopardize the integrity of research and scholarship. They also call for schools to deal swiftly with researchers who subordinate research integrity to their career goals and the demands of those funding their research.

What to do About the Export Market?

Higher education, which was once viewed as contributing to the social and moral well-being of society, is now viewed through the lens of neoliberalism (Gibbs 2001), and we are also exporting this viewpoint. Education is now a highly exported product and its commodification in an international context raises the ethical urgency to act immediately to ensure that the standard of education that is being exported is up to par.

The commercialization of education in a cross-border context calls for vigilant oversight in the provision of education and the portability of qualifications (Matsuura 2006). By 2025, there will be 7.2 million students worldwide (Bohm et al. 2002). The international market in higher education is valued in excess of $30 billion with the U.S. ranking as the leading player. Exporting higher education programs to less developed countries has become big business. Non-traditional schools use virtual universities, branch campuses, and corporate universities and are creating a "new paradigm" of higher education (Matsuura 2006). This engages directly with the contemporary debate as to whether this increase in cross-border education undermines the traditional values of education in terms of the relevance of service, research, and learning/teaching (Knight 2006). Furthermore, according to Daniel (2006):

> Cross-border provision without concern for equity and social justice has generated a backlash that manifests itself as restrictive regulations and punitive measures. This clearly indicates that the providers from the developed world must instill confidence and trust within the developing world by forging partnerships, facilitating the development of quality assurance mechanisms, and building indigenous human resource capacity.

Final Thoughts

Issues such as academic freedom are becoming less important than accountability; truth is deemed less important than utility; performance is to be valued over thoughtfulness. The system of higher education that has worked for centuries was founded on the belief that education was a process. Today's system cannot work because it views higher education as a product from a perspective of economic value. If a university in a consumer-driven culture is to educate students to participate as informed purchasers in the market economy, then the institution must prepare students by doing more than developing their sense of economic self-interest; it requires a university that mentors students in developing a moral understanding of humanity (Gibbs 2001).

In this belief system, the values of free-market policies, entrepreneurship, deregulation, and reduced government funding have replaced the commitment to social outcomes. With this major revision of higher education, universities are no longer seen as centers for intellectual activity. If the marketization of higher education continues, there may come a time when academics will become skills trainers with the sole purpose of transmitting knowledge to prepare students for employment—already, educators have taken a back seat to trainers and business managers (Raduntz 2007, p. 242)—and they will bear little resemblance to the scholars who once filled the halls of the universities and filled the minds of their students with ideas, questions, and visions.

Works Cited

Altbach, P. G. (2009, April 30). "It's the Faculty, Stupid!" *The Times Higher Education Supplement, 1894*, 40.

Benton, T. H. (2011, February). "A Perfect Storm in Undergraduate Education, Part I." *The Chronicle of Higher Education.* Retrieved from http://chronicle.com/article/A-Perfect-Storm-in/126451/.

Bohm, A., Davis, D., Meares, D., & Pearce, D. (2002). *The Global Student Mobility 2025 Report: Forecasts of the Global Demand for International Education.* Canberra: IDP.

Bridenthal, R. (2005, August). Review of the book *University, Inc: The Corporate Corruption of Higher Education*, by J. Washburn. *Radical Teacher, 73*, 35–37.

Daniel, J. (2006). Preface. In J. Knight (Ed.), *Higher Education Crossing Borders: A Guide to the Implications of the General Agreement on Trade in Services (GATS) for Cross-Border Education.* Commonwealth of Learning and UNESCO.

Diver, C. (2005, November). "Is There Life After Rankings?" *The Atlantic.* Retrieved from http://www.reed.edu/president/speeches/atlantic_ monthly05Diver.pdf.

Edirisooriya, G. (2009). "A Market Analysis of the Latter Half of the Nineteenth-Century American Higher Education Sector." *History of Education, 38*(1), 115–132.

Edmiston, D. (2009). "An Examination of Integrated Marketing Communication in U.S. Public Institutions of Higher Education." *International Journal of Educational Advancement, 8*(3), 152–175.

Ehrenberg, R. C. (2005). "Method or Madness? Inside the *U.S. News & World Report* College Rankings." *Journal of College Admission, 189,* 29–35.

Gibbs, P. (2001). "Higher Education as a Market: A Problem or Solution?" *Studies in Higher Education, 26*(1), 85–94.

Goldspink, C. (2007). "Rethinking Educational Reform." *Educational Management Administration & Leadership, 35*(1), 27–50.

Hossler, D. (2000). "The Problem with College Rankings." *About Campus, 5,* 20–24.

Hossler, D. R. (2004). "How Enrollment Management has Transformed—or Ruined—Higher Education." *Chronicle of Higher Education, 34,* B3.

IES (2009). "*Digest of Education Statistics:* Chapter 3 Post Secondary Education." Retrieved from http://nces.ed.gov/programs/digest/ d09/ch_3.asp.

Kaplan, G. R. (1996). "Profits R Us: Notes on the Commercialization of America's Schools." *Phi Delta Kappan, 78*(3), 1–12. Retrieved March 17, 2011, from EBSCO*host*.

Klassen, M. L. (2000). "Lots of Fun, Not Much Work, and No Hassles: Marketing Images of Higher Education." *Journal of Marketing for Higher Education, 10*(2), 11–26.

Knight, J. (2006). *Higher Education Crossing Borders: A Guide to the Implications of the General Agreement on Trade in Services (GATS) for Cross-Border Education*. Commonwealth of Learning and UNESCO.

Lingenfelter, P. E. (2006). "The Unfunding of Public Education." Presented at the Public Affairs Week, Baruch College, City College of New York. Retrieved from http://www.sheeo.org/ about/paulpres/baruch%20college.pdf.

Lock, G., & Lorenz, C. (2007). "Revisiting the University Front." *Studies in Philosophy and Education, 26,* 405–418.

Marklein, M. B. (2007). "Colleges Taking Another Look at Value of Merit-Based Aid." *USA Today.* Retrieved from http://www.usa today.com/news/education/2007-03-14-merit-aid_N.htm.

Marris, E. (2005). "Corporate Culture Nets Big Bucks for University Heads." *Nature, 434,* 1059.

Matsuura, K. (2006). Foreword. In J. Knight (Ed.), *Higher Education Crossing Borders: A Guide to the Implications of the General Agreement on Trade in Services (GATS) for Cross-Border Education.* Commonwealth of Learning and UNESCO.

Meredith, M. (2004). "Why Do Universities Compete in the Ratings Game? An Empirical Analysis of the Effects of the *U.S. News and World Report* College Rankings." *Research in Higher Education, 45*(5), *443*–461.

Meyerson, G. (2005, August). Review of the book *Universities in the Marketplace: The Commercialization of Higher Education*, by D. Bok. *Radical Teacher, 73,* 33–35.

Miscamble, W. D. (2006). "The Corporate University: A Catholic Response." *America,* 14–17.

Molesworth, M., Nixon, E., & Scullion, R. (2009). "Having, Being and Higher Education: The Marketisation of the University and the Transformation of the Student into Consumer." *Teaching in Higher Education, 14*(3), 277–287.

Newman, S., & Jahdi, K. (2009). "Marketisation of Education: Marketing, Rhetoric and Reality." *Journal of Further and Higher Education, 33*(1), 1–11.

Ng, I. C. L., & Forbes, J. (2009). Education as Service: The Understanding of University Experience Through the Service Logic. *Journal of Marketing for Higher Education, 19*(1), 38–64.

Nicholls, J., Harris, J., Morgan, E., Clarke, K., & Sims, D. (1995). "Marketing Higher Education: The MBA Experience." *International Journal of Educational Management, 9*(2), 31–38.

Raduntz, H. (2007). Chapter 13: "The Marketization of Education within the Global Capitalist Economy." In *Globalizing Education: Policies, Pedagogies, & Politics* (pp. 231–245). New York: Peter Lang Publishing, Inc.

Rojstaczer, S., & Healy, C. (2010). "Grading in American Colleges and Universities." Retrieved from http://gradeinflation.com/tcr2010 grading.pdf.

SHEEO. (2009). *State Higher Education Finance FY 2008*. Retrieved from www.sheeo.org/finance/shef_fy08.pdf.

Sigler, W. (2007). "The Age of Outcomes." *College and University, 83*(2), 53–56, 58–60.

Thacker, L. (2005). "Confronting the Commercialization of Admissions." *Chronicle of Higher Education, 51*(25), B26. Retrieved March 17, 2011, from EBSCO*host*.

Tilak, J. B. G. (2009). "Higher Education: A Public Good or a Commodity for Trade?" *Prospects, 38*, 449–466.

Yassi, A., Dharamsi, S., Speigel, J., Rojas, A., Dean, E., & Woolard, R. (2010). "The Good, the Bad, and the Ugly of Partnered Research: Revisiting the Sequestration Thesis and the Role of Universities in Promoting Social Justice." *International Journal of Health Services, 40*(3), 485–505.

Credit

Slip-Sliding Away, Down the Ethical Slope

Robert J. Sternberg

The consequences of cheating, for the individual and society too, must be incorporated into the curriculum.

"You see your roommate at his computer, writing a paper. You notice him transferring text from an online document to the paper he is writing without attribution. He changes a few words here and there so he cannot be accused of plagiarism. Is there a problem here? What, if anything, should you do?"

"Professor Johnson is known for not giving back exams because he uses pretty much the same questions from year to year. Your roommate comes back to your room with a big smile. A fraternity brother has managed to slip out a copy of last year's exam and has given it to him. Your roommate figures he can get an edge on this year's exam by studying last year's. 'Not my fault,' he says, 'that Professor Johnson reuses his test questions.' Is there a problem here? What, if anything, should you do?"

In presenting problems such as these to various student groups, I have been taken aback by the number of those who either do not see an ethical breach or, if they have, feel that it is minor or not of concern to them. It's a problem that goes much deeper than the occasional incident—we find cheating on the rise even before students get to college, and many cheaters more concerned with getting caught than with actually committing the act.

When it comes to unethical behavior such as cheating, our society has, I believe, engaged in a fundamental misperception. It derives from our conviction that, through religious training or other ethical training—at home, for example—students have been brought up to know right from wrong and thus to behave ethically. The misperception is that it is easy to do the right thing, and that doing the wrong thing requires extra mental or other effort. In fact, the opposite is true: It is often hard to do the right thing, which is why there is cheating.

To behave ethically is not a one-step process: Do the right thing. It is a sometimes arduous eight-step process. To behave ethically, you must:

1. Recognize that there is a situation that deserves to be noticed and reflected upon.
2. Define the situation as having an ethical component.
3. Decide that the ethical component is important enough to deserve attention.
4. View the ethical component as relevant to you personally.
5. Ascertain what ethical rule applies to the situation.
6. Figure out how to apply the ethical rule.
7. Prepare for possible adverse consequences, such as retaliation, if you should act ethically.
8. Act.

All of those steps can be relatively difficult to execute, and, unfortunately, behaving ethically can be as challenging for parents as it is for students. Parents may cross the line by going from helping their children with homework, papers, science projects, and writing college-application essays to essentially doing the work. It then is little wonder that students reach college and hire others to do their work for them. This point came home in a *Chronicle Review* article, "The Shadow Scholar," by an individual who anonymously writes student papers for pay. Of course, it is not clear that professors are immune: Just as students are outsourcing the writing of papers, so are some professors now outsourcing the grading of papers. One wonders whether our society will eventually eliminate the middlemen—college students and faculty—and simply have the outsourced writers and the outsourced graders work together directly.

More realistically, educators need to stop assuming that ethical behavior is the normal course of action for a well-educated individual, and that cheating and other forms of unethical behavior are not the norm. Rather, they have to assume that behaving ethically is often challenging, as any fired whistle-blower can tell you.

Schools need to teach students the steps involved in ethical behavior and the challenges of executing them. And they need to do so with real-life case studies relevant to the students' lives. The steps toward ethical behavior are not ones that students can internalize by memorization, but only through active experiential learning with personally relevant examples.

There is a larger question our society must face: Have we abrogated what should be a fundamental responsibility of higher education? The financiers who helped to create the financial meltdown of 2008 were, for the most part, bright and well educated. Many were graduates of this country's finest colleges and universities. Is it possible that, in placing so much emphasis on grades and test scores, we are failing to select for and teach the qualities that will produce not just ethical individuals but also ethical leaders?

We have come, in large part, to use standardized-test scores and other objective measurements to provide opportunities to students who score well—opportunities that are much scarcer for others. But is it enough to look for such narrowly defined academic skills? Is it not time to search for and develop the wisdom and positive ethical skills that we need in order to steer this country up the slippery slope rather than down?

Once started on that slide, it is hard to stop before the crash at the bottom. Just ask any disgraced politician, executive, clergyman, or educator. While unethical behavior may start in schools with plagiarism or stolen exams, we know all too sadly, and all too well, that it doesn't end there.

A Question of Honor

Cheating on Campus Undermines the Reputation of Our Universities and the Value of their Degrees. Now is the Time for Students Themselves to Stop it.

William M. Chace

One of the gloomiest recent reports about the nation's colleges and universities reinforces the suspicion that students are studying less, reading less, and learning less all the time: "American higher education is characterized," sociologists Richard Arum and Josipa Roksa said last year, "by limited or no learning for a large proportion of students." Their book, *Academically Adrift*, joins a widening, and often negative, reassessment of what universities contribute to American life. Even President Obama has gotten into the act, turning one problem with higher education into an applause line in his latest State of the Union address. "So let me put colleges and universities on notice," he said: "If you can't stop tuition from going up, the funding you get from taxpayers will go down. Higher education can't be a luxury—it is an economic imperative that every family in America should be able to afford."

Where should we lay the blame for the worsening state of one of the foundations of American civilization, one that has long filled us with justifiable pride? The big public universities are already bogged down by diminishing financial support from the states; private education is imperiled by tuition costs that discourage hundreds of thousands of middle-class and poorer students from applying. Some schools have made heroic attempts to diversify their student bodies, but too little financial aid is available to make access possible for all the applicants with academic promise.

What is happening inside the classroom for those who do get in? Who is teaching the students? Less and less often it is a member of an institution's permanent faculty, and rarer still one of its distinguished professors. More and more of the teaching has been parceled out to part-time instructors who have no hope of landing a full-time position. Because of this, their loyalty to the school that hired them, and to the students they will probably meet in just one course and never again, has diminished.

Amid such melancholy reports from the front, campus amusements that have nothing to do with education—intercollegiate athletics leads the festivities—sop up money, keep coaches in the headlines, and divert public attention from the essential mission of education: to strengthen the minds of young people and to prepare them to cope with the demands of life.

Perhaps that is why, when the public is asked about colleges and universities, the response is increasingly negative with each passing year. According to the Pew Research Center, most American citizens (57 percent) say that higher education "fails to provide good value for the money students and their families spend." Within the innermost sanctum of the academy the view is almost the same: "About four-in-ten college presidents say the system is headed in the wrong direction," according to Pew. If university presidents, who by profession and temperament routinely find every glass more than half-full, are so disconsolate, the public can't be expected to be optimistic.

Were this situation to get any worse, it could legitimately be called a crisis. But American colleges and universities are not going under anytime soon. Despite their problems, they employ hundreds of thousands of people, keep towns and even cities financially afloat, and offer cultural resources and, yes, athletic and other entertainments. They adorn the nation with their well-kept campuses. The research done on those campuses makes us safer, improves our health, and inspires our nobler human impulses. Along the way, colleges and universities provide multiyear habitat for millions of postadolescents who, more often than not, are bewilderingly short of ideas about what to do after leaving secondary school. And they continue to offer a haven to those who finish their undergraduate years and do not or cannot enter the present bleak job market. Most of these students are happy to find themselves—for four, five, or even six years—with other people their age, with whom they can develop social skills while entertaining each other and themselves and exposing their minds to selected academic topics. For all these reasons, the college experience in this country long ago became one of its most acceptable rites of passage. The schools are there because they serve a variety of needs. The challenge is to make them better.

But now they are up against a spectrum of problems whose magnitude they have never faced before. What can they do—amid financial pressures, dwindling public esteem, pre-professional anxieties on the part of their students, and eroded faculty loyalty—to recover the prestige they once enjoyed?

One answer, I believe, rests in what they can do, and must do, about a large and ugly presence on almost every campus: academic dishonesty. Cheating now hurts American higher education; it might well be cheating that can begin to save it.

ଔଓ୦ଓଚ୦ଓଃ୦

In college and university classrooms across the country, every student sooner or later faces the apparently simple task of writing an essay. The essay might focus on a philosophical topic (the argumentative structure of John Stuart Mill's *On Liberty*, for example), or the student's interpretation of a play (Harold Pinter's *The Homecoming*, say), or a political issue (the likely shape of demographic changes in the United States in the next 20 years). The topics are endless, but the ground rules are not: be clear, employ the rules of logic, and most pointedly, be original.

The last requirement is where the system gets confused. No teacher really expects any student essay to revolutionize our understanding of the world, to be so original that the firmament begins to wobble. The opportunity to be truly original has gotten rarer through the eons. As Mark Twain put it, "What a good thing Adam had. When he said a good thing he knew nobody had said it before." No, originality means something more modest: that the student, after much reflection and weighing of the assembled evidence, has written in a way that reflects the particular contours of his or her thinking. The turns and twists of the prose, the things emphasized and the things neglected, the way the essay opens and closes, and how errors, some small and some large, inevitably infiltrate the prose—these features, constituting the essay's fingerprint, are evidence that the student has written something original. But truth to tell, it's not working that way. Today, lots of students cheat. They use the work of others. They buy essays. They plagiarize. Still, even though the Web makes cheating easier than ever before, and thus more prevalent, the phenomenon of cheating is nothing new. Students have been at it for a long time.

Eighty years ago, Dean Clarence W. Mendell of Yale University declared that the problem of cheating at his school was widespread enough to require instant reform: "It is altogether imperative that the growing disregard of this traditional standard on the part of many unthinking undergraduates should be wiped out." He sternly added, "the faculty has but one attitude toward cheating, an attitude shared, we believe, by the undergraduate body." But 45 years later, in 1976, another Yale dean, Eva Balogh, described cheating at the school as "rampant." New Haven hadn't changed much, and Yale was no isolated case. That same year, on the other side of the country, the student newspaper at the University of Southern California reported that as many as 40 per cent of students there were plagiarizing their written work.

The first comprehensive study of cheating at colleges and universities (5,000 students at almost 100 institutions) was completed in 1964. It found that 75 per cent of the students had engaged in one form or another of academic dishonesty. A generation later, in 2001, an authoritative survey conducted by Donald L. McCabe of Rutgers and his colleagues concluded that cheating was now "prevalent" across the country and that "some forms of cheating have increased dramatically in the last 30 years."

Indeed, every study over the decades has concluded that cheating at American colleges and universities is rampant. Despite Dean Mendell's desire long ago to wipe it out, grim admonitions from college presidents year after year, and any number of cheating eruptions around the nation, dishonesty, indigenous to almost every campus, flourishes. A recent survey by the online journal *Inside Higher Ed* of more than a thousand chief academic officers at schools nationwide revealed that more than two-thirds of them believe that cheating has become a much worse problem than it once was. But, interestingly enough, fewer than a quarter of them thought it was on the rise on their own campuses.

Students cheat for many reasons, some of them even doing so without malign intent, either because they don't understand the rules of academic honesty or are confused about the assignment. Some students cheat because of pressures to succeed in a competitive world. Some cheat because they are lazy, tired, or indifferent. Some, overwhelmed by the oceanic wash of information pouring in upon them as they open their computers to the Web, conclude that there is nothing new to say. And some cheat because they look at all academic tasks as exciting opportunities to fool the system as well as the teacher.

They learn early. The Josephson Institute of Ethics sampled more than 40,000 public and private high school students and found that three-fifths of them admitted to having cheated on a test. Nearly half of these were honors students; a third had cheated twice or more in the previous year. In high school, every applicant to college is given an open invitation to cheat—the personal essay that college admissions offices require. How many students write these essays without help? How many parents write them? How many friends, counselors, and commercial agencies write them? No one knows, but the pressure to get such help must be precisely as strong as the pressure to write the kind of essay that will win respect from an admissions dean. The temptation to cross the line shows up early in a young person's life.

As with any transgressive cultural activity both scorned and widespread (running red lights, using recreational drugs, evading taxes), some cheaters are exposed while others go untouched. For every cheating student who is nabbed, another slips under the radar. Nor is the radar kept in good working order. Some teachers know when a student's work is fraudulent but elect to do nothing. It takes time, and time is expensive; bringing a student before a campus judicial council is also labor intensive, and the outcome is unpredictable; students or their parents can retain attorneys to fight the charges and endlessly complicate the procedure; administrators cannot be counted on to back up professors making accusations. Professors like the elevation of teaching but not the grubby business of prosecuting. For the increasing number of adjunct instructors, vigilance about cheating could put their professional futures at risk. They could earn an unappealing tag: "high maintenance." And some teachers have concluded that the only person hurt by cheating is the cheater, and so they wash their hands of the entire business.

On many campuses, dishonesty is simply accepted as an unwelcome but ubiquitous feature of teaching and learning, the equivalent of friction in the pedagogical machine. Reflect on what Dean Mendell said, but perhaps only dimly understood, all those decades ago. The "unthinking undergraduates" at Yale who were cheating made up part of the undergraduate body at Yale as a whole that presumably shared the faculty's revulsion toward cheating. Denouncing a wrong does not necessarily mean being innocent of committing it. Most students know that cheating surrounds them, but few see ways to do anything about it, even when they hold it in contempt. Some of those who cheat are morally offended by others who cheat, but they too are, for obvious reasons, disinclined to complain. In every cultural domain, we grow accustomed to breaches that, with time and repetition, we wind up believing are normal.

But how does cheating become tolerated, assimilated, and ultimately absorbed into our understanding of normality? The answer partly resides in the peculiar kind of wrong it is. Compared with the violation of copyright, a crime punishable in a court of law, cheating at school is "only" a moral and ethical wrong. Plagiarism, one of the most common forms of cheating, often leaves behind no apparent victim; the author from whose body of work the plagiarist extracts a useful portion might never know anything has happened; and the work, despite the theft, remains in the author's possession (lawyers call this "usufruct"). The downloading without attribution of finished essays from the Internet, another immensely popular way of completing classroom assignments, harms no honest author, as copying them for publication would. And if several students conspire to compose an essay in the name of one, who is the exploited party? Any outrage can seem tolerable if it looks victimless.

Consider, moreover, with what emollients any feeling of guilt about cheating can be soothed in a student's mind. To begin, the culture outside the campus gates seems long ago to have accepted dishonesty when it comes to the writings of certain important people. Just how much of *Profiles in Courage* did John F. Kennedy write and how much did Theodore Sorensen write? How strongly do we care? What should we say about the Rev. Martin Luther King Jr.'s doctoral dissertation at Boston University, once we know that it is filled with the writings of others, copied down paragraph after paragraph, in vast profusion? Think also of Roger Clemens, Barry Bonds, and almost everyone involved in international cycling—sports figures about whom allegations of cheating are now featured in every newspaper in the land. What of the plagiarism of prize-winning historians Doris Kearns Goodwin and Stephen E. Ambrose, not to mention the elaborate transfer, generations ago, of the ideas of German philosophers into the "philosophy" of Samuel Taylor Coleridge? Don't we just note such derelictions and then generously move on to matters more pressing?

The much-quoted aphorism by T. S. Eliot that "immature poets imitate; mature poets steal" can give license enough to a student faced with the chore of writing an original senior thesis on, say, Eliot himself. That immature student, emboldened by fantasies, can think himself into maturity by doing no more than what Eliot said the great customarily do: steal.

Yet another social reality erodes the moral offensiveness of cheating, a reality that universities and colleges find themselves ill equipped to cope with. Given that so much professional life—the legal and medical systems, entrepreneurial capitalism, the operations of established companies and the public sector, the very working life that many college graduates will enter—is based on the pooling of ideas and the energy of teamwork, how is it that the academic world can demand wholly independent work and originality? Indeed, students can wonder why colleges observe the principles of solitary labor when they will soon work in offices where ideas are meant to be merged and where the inspiration of one person achieves value only when coupled with the inspiration of many others.

Nowhere is this tension between the ethical code of the campus and that of the working world more awkwardly felt than in the discipline of computer science. On campuses, students taking courses in this fertile area of study are urged to work independently to develop their skills, but if they are fortunate enough upon graduation to get a job with a firm making use of such skills, they will join highly ambitious teams of men and women who, to succeed, will merge their talent and their scientific knowledge to create something—a new piece of money-making software, for instance—that not one of them, working alone, could have come up with.

On campus, solitary independence; off campus, collective energy. The contradiction between these two methods partially explains why the greatest incidence of cheating at high-powered universities like Stanford and others occurs among students enrolled in computer science courses. Those students must hold in their minds that a wrong in one place is highly prized in another. Nor is it irrelevant, as one imagines the incentives to cheat, to consider the attractive beginning salaries offered to successful computer-science graduates of schools such as Stanford. The urge to succeed can yield to the temptation to cheat if a good job awaits just beyond the campus gates.

Few students are ignorant of the prevailing ethical standards of their home institutions. Should those standards be strong and consistently enforced, and should those institutions provide example after example of moral courage, students who cheat do so with the knowledge that they are violating a code of honor that has substance. But if the institutions themselves exhibit questionable ethical standards—leaving a trail of shoddy compromise, corner cutting, and breaches of trust—those students come to understand that honor is only a word and not a practice. Since nothing more quickly leaps into a young person's mind than the recognition of hypocrisy, cheating becomes easier once institutional duplicity is detected.

In colleges and universities, then, where primary teaching duties are given over to part-time instructors so that well-paid professors can devote themselves to research projects; where tuition is very high but certain classes are large and crowded; where extra tutorial help is lavishly provided to students on athletic scholarships (many of whom never would be admitted on academic grounds) and only rarely to students who play no intercollegiate sports; where the values seem to be corporate rather than academic; where, as at Claremont McKenna College, an administrator submits false SAT scores to publications like *U.S. News & World Report* in order to boost the school's "selective" reputation; and where, as a consequence, campus morale is low, some students can and will respond as one would to any organization proclaiming one set of values while practicing another. Students entering colleges and universities are told that these places are, and have been, "special." When they turn out to be commonplace, standards will triumph.

Students are under personal, parental, and pre-professional pressures that have never been more intense. Getting into the right school, and achieving in such a way that one can then proceed to the next right station in life, makes the college experience for many young people more a matter of getting ahead—acquiring the proper credential—than undergoing a unique ritual devoted to self-knowledge and meeting intellectual growth. If resources beyond oneself are needed to get ahead—even illicit resources such as the writings of others, all easily acquired by a few keyboard strokes in the privacy of one's room, and all gained with no apparent sense of injury to anyone else—so be it. Nothing seems lost; forward motion has been sustained.

The most appalling aspect of the rise of cheating on campus in recent times is that some professors themselves have offered sophisticated defenses of plagiarism. An ambitious student can now turn to the writings of teachers who have made ingenious theoretical defenses for the very cheating practices proscribed by the universities at which they teach. If a student faces the accusation that his work is not original, that student can respond: Don't you know that the idea of "originality" has been hammered into nothingness by thinkers such as Michel Foucault? After all, he proclaimed four decades ago that the very idea of an author, any author, is dead, and hence there is no one around to claim originality. Instead, wrote Foucault, in *What Is an Author?*, we should welcome a new world in which the inhibiting codes of authorship have been cast to the winds:

> All discourses, whatever their status, form, value, and whatever the treatment to which they will be subjected, would then develop in the anonymity of a murmur. We would no longer hear the questions that have been rehashed for so long: Who really spoke? Is it really he and not someone else? With what authenticity or originality? ... And behind all these questions, we would hear hardly anything but the stirring of an indifference: What difference does it make who is speaking?

Once a student adopts, under so impressive an aegis as Foucault, an indifference about authorship, the coast is clear and all noisome ethical restrictions can be jettisoned. *Perspectives on Plagiarism* (1999), edited by Lise Buranen and Alice Myers Roy, brings together essays demonstrating the problem. Gilbert Larochelle, who teaches political philosophy at the University of Quebec and who is a professorial devotee of the celebrated philosopher, puts it this way: "Can plagiarism still exist in an intellectual universe where it has become impossible to differentiate the representation from the referent, the copy from the original, and the copyist from the author?" Another teacher, Debora Halbert of Otterbein College, inspired by both Foucault and feminism, ups the ante and provides students who might be thinking of plagiarizing with dreams of anti-establishment revolution: "Appropriation or plagiarism are acts of sedition against an already established mode of knowing, a way of knowing indebted to male creation and property rights. … No concept of intellectual property should exist in a feminist future." Yet another professor, Marilyn Randall of the University of Western Ontario, writes that "later critical discourse whole-heartedly adopts the notion of plagiarism as an intentional political act" and, perhaps sensitive to the unattractive connotations of the word itself, repackages plagiarism as "discursive repetition." Buoyed up by such sophisticated arguments, and keen to be part of a bright new future, students might well be ashamed if they did *not* cheat.

A less theoretical defense of cheating comes by way of something called "patchwriting." It combines low-level Foucauldian thinking ("no such thing as originality") with American confessionalism ("folks, let's be honest, everybody cheats all the time"). It argues that whatever we write is no more than proof that we are forever standing on the shoulders of giants. We're fooling ourselves if we believe that we are writing something that has not, in so many words, been written before. Human beings can't be original. As a species, we endlessly use and reuse what has been used and reused before, forever recycling the logic, the words, the turns of phrase, and all the rest. So why not, says a chief apologist for patchwriting, go easy on the students? Teach them, says Rebecca Moore Howard of Syracuse University, that it's okay to download essays from the Internet, to pluck useful phrases or even paragraphs from Wikipedia, and to cobble whatever seems to fit together into the semblance of an essay ready for grading. "[Patchwriting] is a form of verbal sculpture, molding new shapes from preexisting materials, Howard writes. "It is something that all academic writers do. Patchwriting belongs not in a category with cheating on exams and purchasing term papers but in a category with the ancient tradition of learning through apprenticeship and mimicry." It's really how we all write anyway, if only we had the courage as patchwriters to say so.

What explains this peculiar defense of plagiarism? Pedagogical and professional anxiety may be one cause: if we go after cheaters, pursuing them all the way to the judicial councils, we will have done nothing, say the defenders, but reinforce the barriers between teachers and students, the invidious social hierarchies separating those possessing the standards (even if they are ill-paid teachers of composition) and those supplying the tuition (even if they are freshmen and sophomores). In the interests of both candor and classroom egalitarianism, why not let everyone in on the secret about writing: plagiarism is at the heart of prose; it's how it gets done. Once that forbidden truth is out in the open, genuine teaching can begin. Neither students nor teacher will feel inferior any longer. They will hold in common the abiding truth of writing: it's all patched together.

And yet. As I have written these words, one by one, knowing all the while that none of them is original with me, all of them (except "usufruct") drawn from the common well of English diction, and recognizing that neither my sentence construction nor my way of organizing paragraphs is unique to me, and while I have gone to many sources to find the information I've needed to write, I believe this essay is mine, mine alone, and would not exist had I not written it. I don't believe I have patched, or that I've plagiarized. As it is with me, so it has always been with writers, and so it will always be. The arguments protecting or even championing plagiarism fall before the palpable evidence of originality, modest and grand, ephemeral and enduring, as it has existed in writing everywhere.

ଔଔଔ

Almost every reader of this essay began, I assume, with the presumption that plagiarism is a serious wrong. Most readers will find its assorted defenders more ridiculous than credible, whether they are disciples of postmodern theory or teachers warning students away from the allegedly phony attractions of originality. Such readers can find kinship, then, with the students who do not cheat. To them we must turn our attention. Both groups have a stake in a clean system. For the students, it means grades honestly earned; for the readers, it means the hope that this country's educational enterprise is ethically sound. Together the two groups can find much to respect in what another kind of composition teacher, Augustus M. Kolich, expressed a generation ago:

> [P]lagiarism cuts deeply into the integrity and morality of what I teach my students, and it sullies my notions about the sanctity of my relationship to students. It is a lie, and although lies are often private matters between two people, plagiarism is never merely private because it breaches a code of behavior that encompasses my classroom, my teaching, my university, and my society.

Here, then, is the situation: abundant evidence that something is wrong, coupled with an abiding sense that the wrong is pernicious and widespread, and highly resistant to remedies. So, to quote Vladimir Lenin's famous pamphlet (whose title was plagiarized from a novel by Nikolai Chernyshevsky): *What Is to Be Done?*

Assuming that something should be done, one response could be to stiffen the apparatus of policing. Internet sites such as "Turnitin," to which students and teachers can submit student work to see if it contains material from essays already on electronic file, could be employed by more and more teachers to track down those who misuse the material. Penalties could be increased; the pursuers could try to become more clever than the pursued; teaching could take on an even more suspicious and hostile attitude. But this plan of attack might well underestimate the resourceful talents of young people—versed as they are in every aspect of the digital world—to outwit even vigilant professorial hawks.

But another strategy already exists. Some institutions, rare but sturdily resolute in spirit, have fought the infection of cheating for decades. Many of them, but hardly all, are small liberal arts colleges. They have had history and tradition at their back. All of them have expended both time and social capital in encouraging honesty and trust. Instead of a campus culture in which adversarial tensions between administrators and students are a given and where cheating is presumed, these institutions convey to the students themselves the authority to monitor the ethical behavior of their classmates. Every student on these campuses is informed, directly and formally, what honor means and why it is important. Every student is presumed to want every classmate to observe the principles of honor. This puts everyone at the same moral starting line. Then students are expected to act as if the work of one is in fact the responsibility of all. Nothing about this is perfunctory. Indeed, at these schools, academic honor is a dominating concern.

Which are these colleges and universities, few in number and proud of their traditions? Washington and Lee, Haverford, Rice, Cal Tech, and the University of Virginia are among them. At some of them, the students themselves hear cases of alleged honor violations and render the judgments with no members of the faculty joining them. Professors note the violation; students then take charge. At such schools, when students cheat, students mete out the justice, which can be swift and uncompromising. At a few of these schools, there exists what is called the "single sanction": any violation of the honor code means permanent expulsion. At all these places, honor has been enshrined as fundamental to the history and the life of the institution. Known to every student who enrolls, the code of honor is already in practice while they matriculate; it is remembered with respect after they graduate. By maintaining such systems, these campuses are less likely to be collections of individuals than, at their best, small societies of truthful men and women. They see the dangers of cheating for what they are: practices in which many students can be hurt by the dishonesty of a few. And not just students but, in the words of Professor Kolich, the university as a whole, and the larger society beyond the gates.

Can the number of such campuses increase? More than 100 American campuses have some form of honor code already, even if many of them give only lip service to the concept. What would it take to transform classrooms throughout the United States into arenas of moral practice? How would American higher education look then? Might it have in hand one small but powerful argument to turn aside the criticisms hurled against it by those who think that it has lost its ethical bearings and who see it as given over to misplaced values such as pre-professional practicalities or simple-minded political correctness? Such critics—noisy and passionate—might be brought to attention with the news that moral instruction, at the foundation of some of the nation's best schools, had been given a central position at other schools across the country.

If such a reconsideration of one of the essential purposes of higher education were to take place, things on American campuses could begin to seem quite different. Instead of training a suspicious eye on students, professors could turn to them with an understanding of how much they have at stake, and how much they fear they can lose, as long as cheating thrives. In those students who do not cheat resides a core of strength, a habit of mind and morality, thus far employed at too few schools. Those schools should remind themselves of one central fact: at their best, students are dedicated to learning. Students who cheat undermine who they are. At its core, cheating is self-destructive.

The lesson is about students and what they alone can do, not about schools and what they have failed to do. The institutions, after all, can always find ways to walk away from the problem. Although no school welcomes negative publicity about academic dishonesty, administrators can always point the finger downward at those who break the rules. And professors can always distance themselves in the same way. So it is the students who stand at the center of this drama.

Doubters might say that what works at small schools couldn't work at larger ones. Big universities, sprawling with students, promote anonymity, and with anonymity comes blamelessness. At such places, no one is responsible for anything and honor codes are bound to fail. But even big places are composed of individual classes, each taught by one teacher, often in small rooms where, once again, principles of individual honor and personal responsibility can be secured and, once again, those with the most to lose can act to bring honesty to bear. Keep in mind that though universities might be large or small, the average student-teacher ratio today is excellent, according to a 2010 survey by *U.S. News & World Report*: slightly less than 15-to-one, with liberal arts colleges averaging 12.2 students per faculty member, and national universities averaging 15.5 students per faculty member. The numbers are small enough to permit, if not to encourage, local and intimate moral responsibility.

To do nothing is not an answer. Once the emptiness of such a response to so serious a problem is recognized, a form of education beneficial to all can come. To encourage moral awareness is to appreciate what rests at the heart of what it means to teach. In the end, it also rests at the heart of what it means to learn.

Should such a pattern of student responsibility spread more widely across the nation, classroom after classroom will benefit. Students will more fully understand how legitimate societies are established and how they survive—by a consensual agreement that they will govern themselves by rule, by mutual respect, and by vigilance. At that point, universities and colleges will be able to recover some of the trust and respect they have lost. They will be able to say, with authority, that the essential virtue of honorable behavior is both promoted and protected on campus.

Credit

Chace, William M. "A Question of Honor: Cheating on Campus Undermines the Reputation of Our Universities and Their Degrees. Now Is the Time for Students Themselves to Stop It." Copyright of *American Scholar* is the property of Phi Beta Kappa Society, Spring 2012: 20–32. Print.

MOOCs of Hazard

Andrew Delbanco

Will online education dampen the college experience? Yes. Will it be worth it? Well …

In the spring of 2011, Sebastian Thrun was having doubts about whether the classroom was really the right place to teach his course on artificial intelligence. Thrun, a computer-science professor at Stanford, had been inspired by Salman Khan, the founder of the online Khan Academy, whose videos and discussion groups have been used by millions to learn about everything from arithmetic to history. And so that summer, Thrun announced he would offer his fall course on Stanford's website for free. He reorganized it into short segments rather than hour-long lectures, included problem sets and quizzes, and added a virtual office hour via Google Hangout. Enrollment jumped from 200 Stanford undergraduates to 160,000 students around the world (only 30 remained in the classroom). A few months later, he founded an online for-profit company called Udacity; his course, along with many others, is now available to anyone with a fast Internet connection.

Meanwhile, two of Thrun's Stanford colleagues, Daphne Koller and Andrew Ng, founded another for-profit company, Coursera, that posts courses taught by faculty from leading universities such as Princeton, Michigan, Duke, and Penn. Three million students have signed on. Not to be outdone, Harvard and MIT announced last spring their own online partnership, edX, a nonprofit with an initial investment of $60 million. A new phenomenon requires a new name, and so MOOC—massive open online course—has now entered the lexicon. So far, MOOCs have been true to the first "o" in the acronym: Anyone can take these courses for free.

Many people outside academia—including *New York Times* columnists David Brooks and Thomas L. Friedman—are gushing that MOOCs are the best thing to happen to learning since movable type. Inside academia, however, they have been met with widespread skepticism. As Joseph Harris, a writing professor at Duke, recently remarked in *The Chronicle of Higher Education,* "I don't see how a MOOC can be much more than a digitized textbook."

In fact, MOOCs are the latest in a long series of efforts to use technology to make education more accessible. Sixty years ago, the Ford Foundation funded a group of academics to study what was then a cutting-edge technology: television. In language almost identical to that used today, a report on the project announced that television had the power to drive down costs, enable the collection of data on how students learn, and extend "the reach of the superior teacher to greater numbers of students." From 1957 to 1982, the local CBS channel in New York City broadcast a morning program of college lectures called "Sunrise Semester." But the sun never rose on television as an educational "delivery system."

In the 1990s, my own university, Columbia, started a venture called Fathom, using the relatively new technology of the Web. The idea was to sell online courses taught by star faculty such as Simon Schama and Brian Greene to throngs of supposedly eager customers. But the paying consumers never showed up in the anticipated numbers, and by the time it was shut down, Fathom had cost Columbia, according to some estimates, at least $20 million. Looking back, the project's director, Ann Kirschner, concluded that she and her colleagues had arrived too soon—"pre-broadband, pre-videocasting and iPods, and all the rest."

Of course, we will always be pre-something. Former University of Michigan President James Duderstadt foresees a technology that will be "totally immersive in all our senses"—something like the "feelies" that Aldous Huxley, in *Brave New World,* imagined would render the "talkies" obsolete. The MIT Media Lab has already developed a vest that gives you a hug when a friend "likes" something you have posted on Facebook. It may not be long before we can log onto a Shakespeare course taught by, say, Stephen Greenblatt and feel the spray of his saliva as he recites "tomorrow and tomorrow and tomorrow." Such technologies will likely find their biggest market through the pornography industry, but there's no reason to doubt that academia will adopt and adapt them.

The Luddite in me is inclined to think that the techno-dreamers are headed for another disappointment. But this time around, something does seem different—and it's not just that the MOOC pioneers have an infectious excitement rarely found in a typical faculty meeting. They also have a striking public-spiritedness. Koller sees a future in which a math prodigy in a developing country might nurture his or her gifts online and then, having been identified by a leading university, enroll in person—on a scholarship, one might imagine, funded by income derived from Coursera. This idea of using online courses as a detection tool is a reprise (on a much larger scale) of the one that spurred the development of standardized tests in the mid-twentieth century, such as the SAT, which was originally envisioned as a means for finding gifted students outside the usual Ivy League "feeder" schools.

Koller speaks with genuine passion about the universal human craving for learning and sees in Internet education a social good that reminds me of Thomas Jefferson's dream of geniuses being "raked from the rubbish"—by which he meant to affirm the existence of a "natural aristocracy" to be nurtured for the sake of humankind. No one knows whether the MOOCs will achieve any of these things, but many academic leaders are certain that, as Stanford President John Hennessy predicts, higher education is about to be hit by a "tsunami."

What's driving all this risk-taking and excitement? Many people are convinced that the MOOCs can rein in the rising costs of colleges and universities. For decades, the price of tuition has outstripped the pace of inflation. Over the past ten years, the average sticker price at private colleges has increased by almost 30 per cent (though net tuition has risen less because financial aid has grown even faster). At state universities, the problem has been exacerbated by public disinvestment. For example, less than 6 per cent of the annual budget of the University of Virginia is covered by state funds. Last fall, I heard the chief financial officer of an urban public university put the matter succinctly: The difficulty, he said, is not so much the cost of college, but the shift of the financial burden from the state to the student.

There are many reasons why college costs continue to soar: the expense of outfitting high-tech science labs, the premium placed on research that lures faculty out of the classroom (and, in turn, requires hiring more faculty to teach classes), the proliferation of staff for everything from handling government regulation to counseling increasingly stressed students. At some institutions, there are also less defensible reasons, such as wasteful duplication, lavish amenities, and excessive pay and perks for top administrators and faculty.

But the most persuasive account of the relentless rise in cost was made nearly 50 years ago by the economist William Baumol and his student William Bowen, who later became president of Princeton. A few months ago, Bowen delivered two lectures in which he revisited his theory of the "cost disease." "In labor-intensive industries," he explained, "such as the performing arts and education, there is less opportunity than in other sectors to increase productivity by, for example, substituting capital for labor." Technological advances have allowed the auto industry, for instance, to produce more cars while using fewer workers. Professors, meanwhile, still do things more or less as they have for centuries: talking to, questioning, and evaluating students (ideally in relatively small groups). As the Ohio University economist Richard Vedder likes to joke, "With the possible exception of prostitution … teaching is the only profession that has had no productivity advance in the 2,400 years since Socrates."

This is a true statement—but it unwittingly undercuts its own point: Most people, I suspect, would agree that there are some activities—teaching and prostitution among them—in which improved productivity and economies of scale are not desirable, at least not from the point of view of the consumer.

True believers think that the new digital technologies will finally enable educators to increase productivity by allowing a smaller number of teachers to produce a larger number of "learning outcomes" (today's term for educated students) than ever before. But it's too soon to say whether MOOCs will really help cure the cost disease. Their own financial viability is by no means certain. The for-profits must make money for their investors, and the non-profits must return revenue to the universities that give them start-up funds.

Coursera has begun to try out a number of different strategies. It provides a matchmaking service for employers looking to hire people with certain demonstrable skills—a logical extension of a role that colleges already play. When a company expresses interest in a top-performing student, Coursera e-mails the student, offering an introduction, and receives a finder's fee from the prospective employer. The college that developed the course also receives a cut. As for Udacity, Thrun says only that it charges companies looking for talent "significantly less than you'd pay for a headhunter, but significantly more than what you'd pay for access to LinkedIn."

A few months ago, Coursera also announced a licensing arrangement with Antioch University, which agreed to pay a fee in return for incorporating selected Coursera offerings into its curriculum. The idea is for students to supplement their online experience by working with on-campus faculty—a practice known as "hybrid" or "blended" learning. The college can expand its course offerings without hiring new faculty, and Coursera can earn income that will be shared by the institutions and professors who develop the courses. So far, however, student interest has been low.

Other possible sources of revenue include selling expertise to universities that want to set up their own MOOCs or partnering with textbook publishers willing to share revenue in exchange for selling to online students. Some MOOCs are also beginning to charge fees for proctored exams (in person or by webcam) for students seeking a certificate marking their successful completion of a course.

If new technologies can cure, or even slow down, the cost disease before it kills the patient, that would be a great public service. The dark side of this bright dream is the fear that online education could burst what appears to be a higher education bubble. Consumers, the argument goes, are already waking up to the fact that they're paying too much for too little. If they are priced out of, or flee from, the market, they will find new ways to learn outside the brick-and-mortar institutions that, until now, have held a monopoly on providing credentials that certify what graduates have supposedly learned. If that happens, it would be a classic case of "disruptive innovation"—a term popularized by Harvard Business School Professor Clayton Christensen, who argues that, "in industries from computers to cars to steel those entrants that start at the bottom of their markets, selling simple products to less demanding customers and then improving from that foothold, drive the prior leaders into a disruptive demise."

We've already witnessed the first phase of this process. Early consumers of online courses tended to be students with families or jobs for whom full-time attendance at a residential or even a commuter college was out of the question. As underfunded public colleges struggled to meet the needs of such students, private for-profit "universities" such as Phoenix, Kaplan, DeVry, and Strayer emerged. They offer mainly online courses that serve—some would say exploit—an expanding population of consumers (a word increasingly used as a synonym for students). The first time I heard someone commend for-profit universities was five or six years ago, when a savvy investor said to me, "Look at California—the public system can't meet the demand, so we will step in." He was making the safe, and sad, assumption that public reinvestment is unlikely to restore what was once an unrivaled system of public higher education. Last August, nearly half a million students found themselves on waiting lists for oversubscribed courses at California's community colleges.

Many online students meet the low-income eligibility threshold for federal Pell grants—a ripe market for the for-profit universities. These institutions offer cheaper courses than traditional private colleges, usually in practical or technical subjects such as cosmetology or computer programming. Their business model depends heavily on faculty who receive low compensation and on students with high loan obligations. It's a system that works well for investors. (In 2009, the CEO of Strayer University collected a cool $42 million, mainly in stock options.) How well it works for students is another question. Last summer, a U.S. Senate committee noted that for-profit universities spend more on advertising and recruiting than on instruction and that, without significant reform, they "will continue to turn out hundreds of thousands of students with debt but no degree."

So far, the for-profit sector has been regarded with disdain or indifference by established universities. This fits the Christensen theory of "disruptive innovation": The leap by low-end products into higher-end markets is sudden and surprising because the higher-ups have been lulled into thinking their place in the pecking order is unassailable. What has happened to newspapers and publishing are obvious examples. Suddenly everything changes, and the old is swept away by the new.

Because of the durable value of prestige, it will be a long time before Harvard has to fear for its existence. But one reason to think we're on the cusp of major change is that online courses are particularly well-suited to the new rhythms of student life. On traditional campuses, many students already regard time offline as a form of solitary confinement. Classrooms have become battlegrounds where professors struggle to distract students from their smartphones and laptops. Office hours are giving way to e-mail. To the millions who have used sites such as the Khan Academy, the idea of hour-long lectures spread out over 15-week semesters is already anachronistic. "Disruptive innovation" is a variant of Joseph Schumpeter's famous declaration that capitalism works by "creative destruction." What will be innovated and created in our colleges and universities, and what will be disrupted and destroyed?

One vulnerable structure is the faculty itself, which is already in a fragile state. This is especially true of those who teach subjects such as literature, history, and the arts. The humanities account for a static or declining percentage of all degrees conferred, partly because students often doubt their real-world value. And as humanities departments shrink, some institutions are collaborating to shrink them faster (or close them altogether) in order to avoid duplicative hiring in subjects with low student demand. For example, Columbia, Yale, and Cornell have announced a collaboration whereby certain languages—such as Romanian, Tamil, or Yoruba—will be taught via teleconferencing. This is good for students, since the subjects will still be available. But it's bad for aspiring faculty—as the number of positions dwindles, research and scholarship in these fields will dry up.

MOOCs also seem likely to spur more demand for celebrity professors in a teaching system that is already highly stratified. Among tenured faculty, there is currently a small cadre of stars and a smaller one of superstars—and the MOOCs are creating megastars. Michael Sandel, for example, who teaches a famous course on justice at Harvard, has become a global figure with millions of followers, notably in Asia, since his lectures became available online through Harvard's website and at a site called Academic Earth. A few months ago, Harvard announced that Sandel had signed up with edX. Sandel is an exceptional educator, but as master-teachers go global, lesser-known colleagues fear being relegated to a supporting role as glorified teaching assistants.

In some respects, this is the latest chapter in an old story of faculty entrepreneurship. By the mid-twentieth century, the president of the University of California, Clark Kerr, was already describing the Berkeley faculty as "individual entrepreneurs held together by a common grievance over parking." Today, as star professors increasingly work for themselves, more faculty members at less prestigious institutions face low wages, meager benefits, and—since many lack tenure—minimal job security. But if the new technology threatens some professors with obscurity, others face obsolescence. Language instructors may someday be replaced by multilingual versions of Siri on your iPhone. One of my colleagues speaks of the imminent "evisceration" of graduate study, once young people who might have pursued an academic career are deterred as it becomes harder and harder to find a dignified job after years of training.

These prospects raise many pressing questions—not just speculative ones about the future, but actionable ones about the present. What, if anything, can universities do to formulate new rules governing conflicts of interest? As faculty stars relocate to cyberspace, how can institutions sustain the community of teachers and students that has been the essence of the university for a thousand years? (The pacesetting Thrun, who is a vice president of Google, resigned from his tenured teaching post at Stanford, though he remains a "research professor.") In this brave new world, how can the teaching profession, already well on its way to "adjunctification," attract young people with a pastoral impulse to awaken and encourage students one by one?

There are also unanswered questions about how much students actually learn from MOOCs. Coursera recently withdrew one course at Georgia Tech because of student discontent and another, at the University of California, Irvine, because the professor disputed how much students were really learning.

So far, most testimonials to the value of online learning come from motivated students, often adults, who seek to build on what they have already learned in traditional educational settings. These are people with clear goals and confidence in their abilities. Stanford has even established an online high school "for gifted students" from around the world (a residential program brings them together in the summers). Its medical school has introduced "lecture halls without lectures," whereby students use short videos to master the material on their own, then converge in class for discussion of clinical applications of what they've learned.

And yet it's one thing to expect brilliant teens or medical students to be self-starters. It's another to teach students who are in need of close guidance. A recent report from the Community College Research Center at Columbia finds that underprepared students taking online courses are, according to one of the authors, "falling farther behind than if they were taking face-to-face courses." Michael Crow, one of the architects of Fathom and now president of Arizona State University and certainly no traditionalist, warns against a future in which "rich kids get taught by professors and poor kids get taught by computer."

Back in the mid-twentieth century, the Ford Foundation report on "telecourses" asked the key question about technology and education: "How effective is this instruction?" When I came upon that sentence, it put me in mind of something Ralph Waldo Emerson wrote a long time ago. "Truly speaking," he said, "it is not instruction, but provocation, that I can receive from another soul." I first understood this distinction during my own student days, while struggling with the theologian Jonathan Edwards's predestinarian view of life. Toward the end of the course, my teacher, the scholar of American religion Alan Heimert, looked me in the eye and asked: "What is it that bothers you about Edwards? Is it that he's so hard on self-deception?" This was more than instruction; it was a true provocation. It came from a teacher who listened closely to his students and tried to grasp who they were and who they were trying to become. He knew the difference between knowledge and information. He understood education in the Socratic sense, as a quest for self-knowledge.

Nearly 40 years later, in my own course on American literature, one of my gifted teaching assistants received an e-mail from a student after a discussion on Emerson:

> Hi, I just wanted to let you know that our section meeting tonight had a really profound effect on me. ... [T]he way you spoke and the energy our class had really moved me. ... I walked the whole way home staring at the sky, a probably unsafe decision, but a worthwhile one nonetheless. I actually cannot wait for next week's class just so I can dive even further into this. So I just wanted to send you a quick message thanking you, letting you know that this fifty minutes of class has undeniably affected the rest of my life. ... [S]ome fire was lit within me tonight, and I guess I'm blowing the smoke towards you a little bit.

No matter how anxious today's students may be about gaining this or that competence in a ferociously competitive world, many still crave the enlargement of heart as well as mind that is the gift of true education. It's hard for me to believe that this kind of experience can happen without face-to-face teaching and the physical presence of other students.

Yet I'm convinced that those leading us into the digital future truly want to dispense the gift of learning more widely than ever before. Currently, the six-year graduation rate at America's public four-year colleges is approximately 58 percent. It would be a great benefit to society if online education can improve on that record—although it should be noted that, so far, the completion rate by students who sign up for MOOCs is even worse—barely 10 percent.

In one experiment, Udacity is providing remedial courses to students at San Jose State for a much lower price than in-person courses. A bill is now under discussion in the California legislature that would require public colleges to offer online courses to students whom they can't accommodate in their classrooms. If the new technology can bring great teaching to students who would otherwise never encounter it, that could lessen inequities between the haves and have-nots, just as digital technologies now give students and scholars worldwide access to previously locked-up books and documents. But so far, there is scant evidence on which to base these hopes.

Quite apart from the MOOCs, there's an impressive array of new efforts to serve low-income students—including the online public Western Governors University, which charges around $6,000 in tuition and awards reputable degrees in such fields as information technology and business. Southern New Hampshire University—also a nonprofit—has moved aggressively into online learning, which it combines with on-campus programs; and Carnegie Mellon University has launched an "open learning initiative" that offers non-credit free courses, with substantial interactive capabilities, and seems to be working well in science, math, and introductory languages.

The best of the new education pioneers have a truly Emersonian passion for remaking the world, for rejecting the stale conviction that change always means degradation. I sense in them a fervent concurrence with Emerson's refusal to believe "that the world was finished a long time ago" and with his insistence that, "as the world was plastic and fluid in the hands of God, so it is ever to so much of his attributes as we bring to it."

In the face of such exuberance, it feels foolish and futile to demur. In one form or another, the online future is already here. But unless we are uncommonly wise about how we use this new power, we will find ourselves saying, as Emerson's friend Henry David Thoreau said about an earlier technological revolution, "We do not ride the railroad; it rides upon us."

Credit

Delbanco, Andrew. "MOOCs of Hazard." *The New Republic* 8 Apr. 2013. Print.

Educating the Future: The End of Mediocrity

Rob Bencini

On May 18, 2012, the president of Chester College in Chester, New Hampshire, announced that the small, arts-oriented college was going to close for good at the end of the semester. Last-ditch fundraising efforts and finger-pointing at the school's administration were natural parts of the school's final days as the reality of poor finances and low enrollment finally took its toll. Nearby colleges of similar educational types graciously (but eagerly) welcomed Chester's student transfers, generously offering the same tuition, board, and fees as the closing college.

I do not intend to cast aspersions toward the academic quality of Chester. It would take more than some second-guessing to properly assess all the factors that led to the closing. However, in most cases (and it appears to be the case with Chester College), the biggest obstacle to overcome is financial. Being cash-poor and deep in debt is harder to cure than creating an academic revival.

The lack of both short-term and long-term financial sustainability has become pervasive in the ranks of small colleges. Mediocrity that is related to poor finances is very difficult to overcome. In many other situations, the mediocrity is truly academic, and that aspect puts those schools at a competitive disadvantage in the current environment. Either or both types of mediocrity threaten the existence of hundreds of private colleges across the United States. But since the onset of the economic slowdown five years ago, the weak signals that were emerging have become full-blown trends that will soon have huge ramifications for higher education throughout the country.

Mobilizing Growth Through Education

America found its growth hormone after the Second World War in the incredible educational success of the GI Bill. Young men (mostly) who, prior to the war, would have had little interest in or ability to go to college now were given the opportunity. Colleges swelled with millions of new students—and college graduates.

Throughout the heyday of the industrial growth from the end of World War II until about the year 2000, young people were admonished to earn the highest possible diploma commensurate with their standing in life. And somehow it all seemed to work. Companies could rely on the abilities of sharp high-school grads to fulfill most industrial functions. Those who needed technical training to perform a task went to the local technical institute or community college. Those who wanted to climb the ladder of success went to night school. As the United States was in an ascending mode of perceived eternal growth, there seemed to be plenty of room for any college graduate to enter the workforce—the type of degree of little consequence—and do no worse than become a management trainee or sales trainee as the economy boomed. The world made sense. All was well.

The notion that a college degree affords its possessor a great future, "the good life," thus became institutionalized. Potential workers have been told for generations: "You must get a college degree to succeed." So that is what they have done. The college degree was the universally accepted clear path to success.

Then, around 2000, several trends came together to give us the situation we have today.

The first trend is generalized and somewhat anecdotal. A common refrain among many employers is that they are frustrated with the college graduates they hire not having the exact pool of knowledge to contribute immediately. The quality of the applicants just doesn't seem to measure up to their existing personnel—or at least not up to the companies' expectations. The "quality" of the education must not be as good, they argue; the colleges are out of touch with the marketplace.

The second trend that has emerged is the proliferation of online college education. Phoenix University, DeVry, Capella University, and others have taken advantage of the convenience of online learning and, again, the institutionalized thinking that a college degree—any college degree—is the ticket to prosperity.

However, the recent extension of this development has a new component that may threaten the business model of the for-profit online university, as well. MIT, Stanford, Harvard, and other highly regarded universities are offering standard courses online for free, but without the course credit. Now, more than 40 top-flight U.S. colleges and universities are participating in one of at least five different free (or nearly free) online non-course-credit educational systems: Khan Academy, Udacity, edX (MITX), Coursera, and TED ED, collectively known as *massive open online courses* (MOOCs).

The onset of the MOOCs shows no sign of slowing down. In fact, it is escalating at an astounding pace, and most colleges and universities don't seem to know what to do about it. So far, only the most secure institutions—both in their academic standing and financially—are participating. The development of the free MOOCs democratizes knowledge to such an extent that it is only eclipsed by the advent of free public education more than a century ago.

The third trend is the rapidly escalating cost of a college education. By now you've surely seen the hyperinflation related to the costs of a college education, particularly for private institutions. The price increases for this brand of education far overshot the paltry growth in incomes of most American families. Still, very few families seemed to flinch at the cost (for the bright future that education promised was worth the price), and private college and university enrollment kept climbing.

The fourth trend is a continuation of the third: massive student debt, which in the United States now exceeds all auto loans and credit-card debt, with twice the level of delinquency. The Federal Reserve Bank of New York released a report in March 2012 stating that 30% of the 37 million Americans who have student debt are behind at least 30 days on their payments and that 70% of the debtors are 30 years old or older; 17% are older than 50. According to a September 2012 article in the *New York Times*: "The amount of defaulted loans—$76 billion—is greater than the yearly tuition bill of all students at public two- and four-year colleges and universities, according to a survey of state education officials."

Connection with the Workplace: Degree or Knowledge?

All it took to unravel the great education growth machine was the economic slowdown. The four trends have now hit a fifth: Even with this expensive, debt-creating education, many graduates simply can't find a job in the careers for which they have prepared. And the ranks of young, well-educated restaurant workers and janitors jumped between 2000 and 2010, 81% and 87% respectively, according to Census Bureau figures.

On the demand side, meeting the skills needs of the workplace will still be a central issue, whether it's companies with full-time jobs to fill, those providing contract work, or entrepreneurial efforts.

But changes in the workplace, where companies no longer really want employees (as evidenced by position cuts at many of America's largest companies in the name of "increased profitability"), have been more abrupt than those in the higher educational system. The workplace cuts—both those caused by a depressed economy and those undertaken as restructuring efficiency—have happened faster than any educational workplace preparation or retraining could ever do. And that is a large part of the problem.

So if colleges and universities aren't providing the right skills, how are potential employers (who are averse to hiring in the first place) solving their true hiring needs? In fact, there very well may be another way to finding qualified contributors to such businesses. Some employers are already doing it. And it's not what colleges and universities want to hear.

Some early-adopter employers are looking more closely at uncredentialed savants—that is, knowledgeable, creative, and driven workers without diplomas, who may turn out to be the next Bill Gates or Steve Jobs. Apple even allowed application developers as young as 13 years old into its prestigious Worldwide Developer Conference. Clearly, a college degree is no longer an absolute necessity to make intellectual contributions to the economy.

The sources of education, learning, and training utilized by this new breed of applicant will likely be a combination of many traditional experiences: formal postsecondary education, internships, summer jobs, and life experiences (e.g., armed services, Peace Corps, AmeriCorps). But increasingly, the MOOC will be the route they will take. When Stanford University computer scientist Sebastian Thrun (who led the development of the DARPA challenge winning Stanley robotic vehicle) offered his first free online course in artificial intelligence, 160,000 people around the world signed up. The students knew they were not getting Stanford course credit; they were taking the course to gain the knowledge. And it was free.

Employers now face the challenge of assessing an applicant's knowledge of a subject coming from MOOCs. But this is no different from the challenge of assessing a college graduate's ability to contribute immediately. Some companies are already testing applicants for knowledge beyond educational prowess, and this is a huge development. This is the first signal that it will be knowledge—not necessarily a degree—that companies will be pursuing. Successful connection between course completion and assessment of course content application to the workplace will go through some growing pains in this process. Mozilla Badges and *smarterer* are two current assessing systems: Mozilla is the more standard gauge, and *smarterer,* more personalized to the company.

Late adopters (government and higher education, in particular) will still insist on the degree credential. (Government is the last to respond to any significant trend, and higher education is in the business of granting degrees!) The same is likely to hold true in older mainline, hierarchical companies, and even more so in those businesses located in less connected areas of the United States, because they tend to be later in becoming aware of most new trends of all types. This disparity in time frame of adoption will cause major confusion in the education and business marketplaces.

The private sector's acceptance of online, nondegree education will happen unevenly, starting with the high technology, social media, and communication services industries. The trend will then find some acceptance in the next 10 years in manufacturing and sales-dominated organizations, and, in another 10–20 years, in government and education.

A number of crucial questions will naturally arise: How will professional organizations, such as the American Bar Association, the American Medical Association, and so on, respond to this trend? And how will consumers of professional services respond? Despite evidence of competence (and even excellence), at what point would you accept and pay for legal advice from a legal "layman"? Or accept and pay for architectural plans from a "draftsman"? And what new words must we come up with to designate all of these work roles (compared with the existing meaning) during the transition period? What would be the process for their work becoming "insured," "bonded," or even "legal"?

Impacts of Increased Educational Choices

As the knowledge base, rather than the academic degree, becomes the preferred credential among employers, and as the idea of taking on exorbitant student debt becomes more inhibiting in a deflating wage market, high-school graduates will be creating a slightly different priority list for their next step. Many will still follow the more traditional path by seeking some sort of degree, but those who are worried about potential debt load will increasingly apply to the cheaper, state-supported institutions first, rather than private colleges.

Imagine the dilemma faced by a recent high-school graduate. She has been indoctrinated with a base understanding that becoming more educated will likely provide opportunities for her to have a better life. No one is disputing that. Like most students, she will likely not qualify academically for admission to the elite schools in America. But with her 3.5 GPA, two passing scores on AP exams, and 1120 on the (old) SAT—plus a healthy number of extracurricular activities—she is a viable candidate for more than 70% of college admission slots in America.

This new grad's family finances have eroded in the past four years; her college fund has been raided to make ends meet. She has been accepted to a state-supported university two hours away, as well as to the nice, small, but expensive local college that is the pride of the community. There is a community college near her home with course offerings that interest her and would allow for transferability.

She hangs out with some friends who have had some success writing apps—they regard themselves as cool hackers who are on to something really great. They can pick up on the Internet whatever knowledge they don't nurture organically among themselves. Most are serious about taking online courses to engage with outside thinking. The group has invited her to join their merry band. They even have a friend who will give her a job waiting tables to make ends meet, as they are doing.

What does she do?

A decision made now versus 20 years ago, 10 years ago, or even five years ago may be different—as will a decision five, 10, or 20 years from now. Whatever generation of thinking is dominant when she does make her decision may direct her path.

Since it is the college education that is creating the debt, perhaps it is worth looking at the breadth of college education options. *Kiplinger's Personal Finance's* 2012 Top 100 "Best Values in Public Colleges" includes colleges and universities from more than 35 states. Every state represented has at least one public university that admits more than 50% of all applicants, meaning that a reasonably good student could qualify for the less-expensive in-state tuition available for at least one college in his or her home state.

So the final choice among these affordable, in-state colleges may increasingly be for the more prestigious, well-connected, and unique ones—not the mediocre. It is thus likely that more and more 18-year-olds will experiment with the benefits of starting their higher education process in the community college system.

This shift toward state-supported universities and community colleges will have several downstream effects. The state-supported colleges and universities will have a much higher number of applicants. At some point, the stress of growth limits the numbers of enrollees that each campus can accommodate, and even strains the capacity of online and virtual courses within a mainstream curriculum. With a higher number of applicants (many of whom represent those deciding not to pursue a college education at a private school), public colleges and universities will undoubtedly raise admission standards such as GPA and SAT scores.

This will simply make the schools harder to get into than in the past. In addition, schools such as North Carolina State University have announced that they are slowing the growth of undergraduate enrollment to focus more on postgraduate offerings. The old C-average, 800-SAT applicant may no longer find room at the less expensive state-supported institutions. And if the four-year institutions aren't available, the next best solution is increasingly becoming the community college.

State legislatures are also easing students' entry into higher education by allowing credits earned at community colleges to count toward degrees at state-supported four-year institutions. Though easing transferable credits may cheapen the value of the degree from a four-year school (which needs to be monitored diligently), the move to starting higher education at the community college level lowers students' cost and debt risks and provides more educational flexibility.

From the perspective of institutions, the trend is already bringing challenges. The *Los Angeles Times* reported in October 2012 that California, the largest community college system in the United States, is having huge student capacity problems. Part of the issue is funding, where the state has cut nearly a third of its financial support for the community college system in the last five years.

An equally troublesome issue is the heavy demand for student enrollment and course offerings among the 2.4 million students in the system. Students trying to go full time are finding that they can only get into one or two courses per semester. According to the *Times*: "Without enough money, course offerings have dropped almost a quarter since 2008. In a survey, 78 of the system's 112 colleges reported that more than 472,300 students are on waiting lists for classes this fall semester—an average of about 7,150 a campus."

The heavy demand for community college courses is the result of several factors coming together: a retraining opportunity for many who have lost their jobs, a lack of job opportunities in the first place (making any education the next best option), low cost in absolute terms, very low cost in comparative terms with public universities, and dramatically lower cost compared with private colleges.

That's why private colleges and universities are at risk in the current economy: high prices in a deflating wage market that offers little guarantee of a job after graduation, combined with a new work paradigm that is beginning to demand demonstrated knowledge rather than a degree from any college or university.

The institutions most at risk are not the elite private schools: the MITs, the Ivies, Stanfords, Vanderbilts, Dukes, and Davidsons. Nor the schools with unique curricula, geographic identity, heavy endowments, or sustained religious organization backing. The institutions at risk are the private colleges with no discernible academic advantage over public schools—and perhaps little over community colleges—at two to four times the cost (and present cost likely means future debt).

Though the cheaper alternatives discussed still do not guarantee subsequent workplace benefits, current trends portend a devastating effect on small, mediocre private colleges. They will certainly be tested moving forward.

Most likely, we will hear the death knell ring for scores if not hundreds of marginal colleges throughout the United States. Some will be absorbed into state university systems or community colleges; some will merge with larger, healthier schools. Others will transition to become part of online universities as a first step before closing the campus in its existing state.

The closure of perhaps hundreds of college campuses will have a wide range of impacts, starting with the unemployment of tens of thousands of college instructors, administrators, and support personnel. Many will retire, but the majority will still need to produce income. Their reinsertion into the job market will provide a further glut of college and university personnel, providing more downward pressure on wages.

Abandoned Campuses?

Yet, the bigger question is what to do with an empty college campus—a hundred acres of classrooms and administration buildings and dormitories, perhaps a gymnasium, cafeteria, and auditorium, most built to standards of efficiency set in the 1950s. The schools that will be closing will probably not be in areas of high growth, and they will probably be redundant of other higher education opportunities in the area. They will likely reemerge as some sort of public school or community college campus, or, as said before, merged into another entity. Shuttering these assets will not be an attractive option, since in most cases it would have quite a chilling effect on the community.

So what happens with other schools like Chester College? What happens when parents no longer agree to pay $30,000 to $60,000 per year for the uncertain outcome at a school carrying little prestige and even marginal academic standing? Or when students no longer take out loans of such magnitude that repayment may horribly impact their economic future?

The bottom line is that businesses now are not getting what they expect in terms of skills and talents that can immediately contribute to their success. Higher education is starting to get blamed for being out of touch with the marketplace. And the education consumer is wary of creating huge debt for an education that may not apply to the job marketplace.

So a new educational paradigm—free, high-quality online education offered by MOOCs—has emerged that may better serve the business community. It threatens to undermine a huge part of the education sector.

This washout will be painful. Higher education will go through a metamorphosis in the next 20 years that leaves the landscape looking much different from today's. The first casualty will be the most expensive and least effective private colleges. But the ultimate casualty will be mediocrity.

Credit

Bencini, Rob. "Educating the Future: The End of Mediocrity." *The Futurist* March–April 2013: 40–44. Print.

The End is Not Nigh for Colleges

Robert J. Sternberg

Doomsayers are predicting that MOOCs, for-profit colleges, or other forces will soon put many colleges out of business. Here's why they're wrong.

The sky is not falling on higher education. Doomsayers believe that purveyors of massive open online courses, or for-profit companies, or shadowy entrepreneurs will make higher education so cheap that any number of existing colleges and universities soon may find themselves out of business.

Those arguments are off track because they make two false assumptions: that participants in higher education have homogeneous goals, and that students are consumers and not producers, or constructors, of their own personalized product of higher education.

First, the doomsayers assume that every potential college student is looking for more or less the same thing in a college education. This means that if push comes to shove, the student will choose the cheapest version of higher education that provides a degree employers will accept. But when students are looked at as consumers, the marketplace of consumers of higher education is no more undifferentiated than any other marketplace.

If you want lip moisturizer, you can go online and buy it for $2 or $22. Both products moisturize lips. Some people pay more than $400,000 for a new car; others, less than $10,000. Both cars get you from one point to another. Watches range in price from a few dollars to over a million. They all tell time.

The higher-education marketplace, like the marketplaces for lip moisturizers, cars, and watches, is differentiated. Some people want the cheapest education possible that will get them the job they want. Others want much more: nice dormitories, diverse student activities, world-famous professors, top-flight institutional reputation—and are willing to pay for it. An advantage of the higher-education market is that financial aid is often available to help students reach beyond what they normally could afford.

Second, students are not merely consumers of higher education; they also actively construct their college careers. They develop a plan for their coursework, their project work, their extracurricular activities, and their social network.

Two consumers buying a particular model of car get essentially the same car (except perhaps for unfortunate production errors). But two students going to the same college may produce entirely different educations. Indeed, students may choose their college in large part on the basis of their projection as to whether they can construct the entire educational experience they wish to create. So there is great variation in students not only as consumers but also as producers of an educational product—their college careers.

This is important because those two roles interact with costs. For example, a degree from a top-rated German university costs a small fraction of what a comparable degree would cost in the United States. But typically the German institution would have no university-sponsored athletic teams or facilities, fraternities, sororities, student clubs, dormitories, meal plans, or other accouterments that many students take for granted in the United States.

If students in Germany want activities, they organize them and bear the costs themselves. More of the burden of students as producers is placed on them—for better or worse. As producers they are basically on their own, without the supports that most American colleges provide.

American universities can reduce costs by greatly lowering their overhead, as do the German universities, or by having professors do some or even all of their teaching online. What students may lose, however, is much, or even most, of the informal curriculum of college—the networking and the face-to-face personal interactions that many people feel are so important to the college experience.

So less-expensive degrees can be had. The only question is: What does one want to give up to reduce costs? This question is playing itself out on a much larger stage in the United States, as local, state, and federal levels of government struggle to balance services and costs.

The problem with the Chicken Little view of higher education is that it can create self-fulfilling prophecies. If decision makers in higher education believe the sky is falling, they may find themselves taking actions that are value-destroying rather than value-enhancing. For example, institutions may start to teach courses online not because that is the optimal way to teach them (and there may be some courses that optimally are taught online) but merely to cut costs; or valuable student activities may be discontinued in order to anticipate the falling of the sky.

Framing the debate about the costs of higher education solely in terms of what it costs students to go to college is the wrong way to go about fixing the problem. The debate instead should be framed in terms of value received. How much value do students, as producers and as consumers, receive for the dollars spent? Is education at a prestigious private college worth several times the cost of education at a not-very-prestigious public college? Let the student (and his or her parents) decide the costs and benefits, much as they do with lip balm, cars, and watches. As long as an institution appeals to some marketplace segment, provides value, and watches its finances, it will do just fine.

Credit

Taking the Measure of Graduation Rates in Big-Time College Sports

Richard M. Southall

Popular-press headlines touting the academic strides of athletes in higher education seem encouraging. "Six-Year Grad Rate at All-time High," proclaims one.[1] But the real story about this demographic is less simplistic and more problematic. Numerous other sources, from sports conferences to schools themselves, document much lower graduation rates for college football and men's basketball and baseball players than for general students.[2] Compounding matters is that only about 57 per cent of all college students complete a bachelor's degree in six years.[3]

In addition, a large segment of the public remains uneasy about big-time athletic programs that generate many millions of dollars in net revenues apiece—via amateur players enrolled on nonprofit campuses.[4] And college football and men's basketball coaches' salaries dwarf those of faculty members; by the end of 2011, 32 National Collegiate Athletic Association (NCAA) Football Bowl Subdivision (FBS) coaches and 11 NCAA Division I men's basketball coaches earned more than $2 million annually, with Texas' Mack Brown the highest paid in football at $5.19 million and Louisville's Rick Pitino the highest paid in basketball at $8.93 million.[5] (Not for nothing has Wake Forest University sociologist Earl Smith called big-time college sport an "athletic industrial complex."[6])

Some college sport fans and school personnel might be aware the uneasy relationship between athletics and higher education dates back generations. For instance, University of Chicago was a football powerhouse at the turn of the 20th century, and its senior halfback Jay Berwanger won the first Heisman Trophy, awarded to the nation's outstanding college football player, in 1935. But four years later, university president Robert Maynard Hutchins, concerned about an "overemphasis on athletics" on the field, in the classroom, throughout the stadium and beyond it, abolished the football program essentially because, as he remarked, "apologists of athleticism have created a collection of myths to convince the public that biceps are a substitute for brains."[7] (Varsity football—albeit NCAA Division III, in which athletic scholarships are not awarded—was reinstated there in 1969.)

Perhaps less apparent to mainstream society is how 266 NCAA major infractions in the 1980s and '90s (including 57 of the 106 major universities competing in the NCAA's top competitive level being censured, sanctioned, or put on probation during the 1980s) resulted in inquiries and reports by the Knight Commission on Intercollegiate Athletics in 1991, '92 and '93 and Congressional action.[8] The NCAA and its members accordingly enacted a series of reforms, including Proposition 48, which mandated prospective college athletes must earn at least a 2.0 grade point average, score a minimum of 700 on the SAT (since recalibrated to reflect revisions to the SAT) and complete no less than 11 core courses, and Proposition 16, which established an "initial eligibility index based on standardized test scores and grade-point averages."[9] But a real or perceived athletic-academic divide has persisted, and more high-profile academic scandals involving cheating, plagiarism, clustering of athletes in certain majors, and excessive use of independent study or interdisciplinary study programs have continued (e.g., University of Tennessee, 1991–2001; University of Minnesota, 1999; Auburn University, 2006; University of Michigan, 2008; Florida State University, 2008–10; University of North Carolina at Chapel Hill currently). Further correctives ensued, including FBS universities increasing their annual budget for tutoring and academic services substantially. More than half of the nation's 73 biggest athletics programs at least doubled it between 1997 and 2007, and the average at FBS schools topped $1 million.[10]

Simultaneously, new methods arose to measure graduation rates of college athletes. Not surprisingly, having a variety of metrics complicates things. The Graduation Success Rate, Federal Graduation Rate, and Adjusted Graduation Gap chart their academic progress. All of these tabulations are useful, but none of them is perfect, as each employs different sampling and analysis based on distinct principles and assumptions. Parsing these factors gives interested parties essential information from which best practices may be developed—and helps ensure more college athletes make the grade.

Background and Context

American intercollegiate athletics began in the 1850s. Today, college sport is synonymous with the NCAA, a 501(c)(3) organization founded in 1906 that governs programs at more than 1,000 colleges and universities in three divisions (I, II, and III), oversees 89 championships in 23 sports, and assists schools in monitoring upwards of 400,000 athletes.[11] The NCAA attempts to uphold, among other precepts, its "principle of amateurism": college athletes pursuing sport in their unobligated time.

"Amateur sport, as the term has been defined historically and as it is currently defined in the *NCAA Manual,* is an 'avocation,' meaning that it is a form of leisure activity," note Allen L. Sack, director of the Institute for Sports Management at University of New Haven, and Ellen J. Staurowsky, professor of sport management and media at Drexel University, in their seminal 1998 book, *College Athletes for Hire: The Evolution and Legacy of the NCAA's Amateur Myth.*[12] "This does not mean that amateur sport is taken less seriously than professional sport," the authors continue. "What separates the amateur from the professional is the absence of remunerative, or instrumental, constraint, not the absence of desire." In other words, college athletes are not paid. "Critical for the future of intercollegiate athletics will likely be a better understood definition of amateurism," the NCAA acknowledges, "that isolates the principle to the way in which student-athletes are viewed without imposing its avocational nature on revenue-producing opportunities."[13]

The late NCAA president and Phi Kappa Phi member Myles Brand knew that "[a]s the scale of both revenue generation and spending has grown over the last few decades, there is a general sense that 'bigtime' athletics is in conflict with the principle of amateurism."[14] Therefore, he established the Collegiate Model of Athletics in 2003. Brand envisioned it as "a surrogate for—but not a replacement for—the concept of amateurism" and as a means to demarcate college sports from professional sports and "change the way people talked about intercollegiate athletics."[15] The Collegiate Model of Athletics is

> intended to impart two principles: (1) Those who participate in college sports are students, and (2) intercollegiate athletics is embedded in the values and mission of higher education. A comparison of the collegiate model vs. the professional model runs like this: In the professional model, the athletes are a work force, a commodity that can be traded from team to team. In the collegiate model, the athlete is a student. In the professional model, the goal is to generate revenue through entertainment. In the collegiate model, the goal is to acquire an education, including learning the value of hard work and teamwork, self-sacrifice and self-discipline, resilience and persistence, and the pursuit of excellence. In the professional model, the team is connected to a community only so long as the community supports the franchise through the building and maintenance of facilities and the purchase of tickets. In the collegiate model, the team is enduringly connected to a community through the sponsoring college or university.[16]

Graduation Success Rate

As part of this strategy, the NCAA strives "to ensure the academic commitment of student-athletes and to increase the likelihood that they will earn degrees."[17] Along these lines, in 2005 the NCAA formulated a tool called the Graduation Success Rate (GSR) for Division I schools.[18] GSR basically removes athletes who leave an institution in good academic standing from the denominator and adds those who transfer in and eventually graduate to the sample. Thus, GSR recognizes that college athletes (based at least partly on their interests and abilities) may take a different path to graduation than other full-time students and in some aspects is an accurate yardstick. The latest single-year GSR for all NCAA Division I athletes (who began college in 2004) was 82 percent. GSR for Division I FBS football was 67 percent, for men's basketball 66 percent, for women's basketball 84 percent, and for baseball 72 percent.[19]

However, GSR fails to take stock of a number of things. For instance, including and excluding various students necessarily yields different graduation rates. Also, GSR does not differentiate between athletes who leave early for a professional sport, transfer schools for more playing time, or drop out but would be eligible to play and study the following semester. (A record 65 underclassmen entered the 2012 National Football League draft and 18 of the 33 players selected in the first round of the 2011 Major League Baseball draft were juniors.[20] Forty per cent of NCAA Division I men's basketball players transfer before their junior year, in search of more playing time, to be closer to family, or because they are unhappy.[21] The number who drop out but would be eligible to play and study the following semester is not known.) The crucial liability to GSR is that it cannot line up against the earning of degrees by the general student body because it's apples to oranges for reasons discussed below. But the NCAA intermingles both sets of figures, and, as a result, the public may have a more favorable impression of college athletes' graduation success than warranted.

Federal Graduation Rate

The Federal Graduation Rate (FGR), which came earlier, was set up by the Department of Education through the 1990 Student Right-to-Know and Campus Security Act. The law requires schools to release graduation and retention rates in addition to other institutional information such as cost of attendance, accreditation and academic program data, services available to disabled students, security reports, and financial aid. Compiling college athletes' graduation rates stemmed partly from press coverage that 76 to 92 per cent of professional athletes lacked college degrees[22] and from revelations that some were functionally illiterate, like Dexter Manley, an All-American defensive lineman at Oklahoma State and winner of two Super Bowls with the Washington Redskins, who tearfully testified as much before Congress.[23]

FGR straightforwardly calculates how many students earn degrees within six years. It determines the extent to which colleges and universities retain and graduate students who begin as full-time pupils. FGR is the only easily available survey based on longitudinal student experience. And it's one way to ascertain if NCAA schools fulfill the organization's mission of maintaining college athletes as part of the entire full-time campus community. This is germane because research shows that retention rates increase the more academics and extracurricular activities like sports are integrated.[24] The latest single-year FGR (for those who began college in 2004) was 63 per cent for all students and 65 per cent for all NCAA Division I athletes. Corresponding FGR rates for various Division I sports were FBS football at 56 percent, men's basketball at 45 percent, women's basketball at 63 percent, and baseball at 48 percent.[25]

But FGR, like GSR, doesn't paint the whole picture. The NCAA concedes that FGR sampling and methodology exclude athletes who transfer in or out. Additionally, as E. Woodrow Eckard, professor of economics at University of Colorado Denver, observes, FGR is biased because it doesn't account for the reality that students included in the initial FGR cohort can change from full- to part-time status.[26] These part-time students graduate at significantly lower rates, therefore pulling down the all-student FGR average. Also, the NCAA intended to supplement FGR with GSR since there was no comparable way to track general student body transfer or retention rates, but over time, the NCAA has increasingly highlighted GSR and referred to it as "a more accurate measure of graduation."[27] Because of differing methodology, GSR is almost always higher than FGR. (In the four sports discussed in this article, GSR is, on average, 18.7 per cent higher.)[28]

Adjusted Graduation Gap

For another perspective, the College Sport Research Institute at University of North Carolina at Chapel Hill, for which I serve as director, in 2010 began publishing a graduation-rate analysis that has become known as the Adjusted Graduation Gap (AGG). Based on a regression model developed by Eckard, which accounts for part-time students included in FGR samples, AGG reports, as its name suggests, graduation gaps between full-time students and athletes in several sports on NCAA Division I campuses.

Here's why this matters. First, other gauges juxtapose college athletes with counterparts presumed to be full-time students. However, as mentioned above, at many schools, the general student body includes a significant number of part-time students. In fact, according to one source, nationally only four in 10 students at public campuses and only 25 per cent of college students across the board go to school full time.[29] And part-time students' graduation rates are much worse than those of full-time students:

24 percent, even when taking eight years to finish.[30] Second, because college athletes must enroll full time to maintain their eligibility, it is legitimate to compare their FGR with the FGR of full-time peers in the general population, yet some of the latter switch to part time. AGG compensates for this downward bias through regression-based adjustments utilizing data from the National Center for Education Statistics and compiled in the Integrated Postsecondary Education Data System. The latest single-year AGG for NCAA Division I sports (for academic year 2011–12) include FBS football at –19.7 percent, men's basketball at –20.6 percent, women's basketball at –9.4 percent, and baseball at –18.8 per cent vis-àvis FGR samples.[31]

As with the other two appraisals, AGG cannot incorporate everything. It tallies only NCAA Division I football, men's and women's basketball, softball, and baseball because of inherent restrictions in how the NCAA goes about its reckoning and because of finite manpower at the College Sport Research Institute.

Applications and Connotations

None of these benchmarks for college athletes' graduation rates is foolproof, not to mention better or fairer, than another. Each quantifies different things. Use should be guided by such parameters. FGR concentrates on an institution's ability to retain and graduate students within six years, including athletes, who initially enroll full time. GSR, recognizing that this subset transfers a great deal, removes those who leave a school and totals those who stay and subsequently graduate. AGG's fundamental premise is that because athletes attend school full time (and "work" at their sport full time), it makes sense to compare their FGR to a graduation rate of other full-time students (who may or may not hold an additional job) and account for part-timers.

Why should anyone care about all this? According to one investigation, Division I FBS athletes are up to 10 times more likely to benefit from "special admissions" programs than other students. And 77 of 92 FBS schools participating in the study granted them "special admissions waivers," which the NCAA defines "as those designed for students who don't meet 'standard or normal entrance requirements.'"[32] So a sizeable portion of male high school athletes may enter higher education with different academic preparation, abilities, or interests. Plus, the long hours, grueling regimen, and exhausting travel necessary for sport often result in missed classes and inconsistent academics. No wonder college athletes often struggle to make the grade (even as their game exploits fuel the ESPNification of big-time college sport). No wonder many depart early for professional sport opportunities, or transfer in search of more playing time, even though only a small per cent make it to the professional level (1.2 per cent in men's basketball, 1.7 per cent in football, and 11.6 per cent in baseball).[33]

If big-time college sport serves as a de facto pre-professional or minor league in the U.S. and abroad, accepting this outright might be a step in reintegrating these athletes into the classroom after the end of their usually short professional sport careers (3.5 years in the National Football League, 5.6 years in Major League Baseball, and 4.8 years in the National Basketball Association).[34] And it could reinforce the importance of the learning process from the get-go. Everyone involved in college sport—administrators, coaches, athletes, faculty, watchdogs, researchers, sponsors, and fans—has a moral obligation to ask some difficult questions about intercollegiate athletics' relationship to higher education. Ignoring any metric, or promoting one over another, will not help college athletes make the grade.

Notes

1 "Six-Year Grad Rate at All-time High." (2011, October 25). ESPN College Sports.

2 "The Bootleg's 2011 Graduation Rate Analysis." [Supplemental material]. (2011, April 22). *The Bootleg.* Southall, R. M., Eckard, E. W., and Nagel, M. S. (2011–2012). "2011–2012 Adjusted Graduation Gap Reports." College Sport Research Institute, Chapel Hill, N.C.

3 Rotherham, A. J. (2011, April 7). "Low Graduation Rates: It's Not Just Student-Athletes." *Time.*

4 Jessop, A. (2011, March 21). "Highest Net Income Among Athletic Departments." *The Business of College Sports.*

5 "*USA Today* College Football Coach Salary Database, 2006–2011." *USA Today.* "*USA Today*—NSLI Coaches' Salary Database Salaries." *USA Today.*

6 Smith, E. (2009). *Race, Sport and the American Dream* (2nd ed.). Durham, N.C.: Carolina Academic Press.

7 Quoted from Hutchins, R. M. (1938 December 3). "Gate Receipts and Glory." *Saturday Evening Post*, pp. 23, 73–74, 76–77. In the article, Hutchins laid out what would become his reasons for subsequently shutting down the football program at University of Chicago.

8 "Matching Major Infractions Cases—241 Cases." (2012). Retrieved using the NCAA Legislative Services Database—LSDBi. "Reports of the Knight Commission on Intercollegiate Athletics." (1999), p. 4. Retrieved from the Knight Commission on Intercollegiate Athletics website. The Library of Congress. (n.d.). "Bill Summary and Status: 101st Congress (1989–1990) S.580."

9 "History of Academic Reform." (2011). Retrieved from National Collegiate Athletic Association website.

10 "Growth in Academic Support for Athletes." (2008, September 5). [Supplemental material]. *The Chronicle of Higher Education.*

11 "About the NCAA." (2011). Retrieved from National Collegiate Athletic Association website.

12 Allen L. Sack and Ellen J. Staurowsky, *College Athletes for Hire: The Evolution and Legacy of the NCAA's Amateur Myth*, Westport, Conn.: Praeger, 1998, page 4.

13 "Amateurism." (2010). (NCAA President's Briefing Document). Retrieved Sept. 17, 2011, from National Collegiate Athletic Association website.

14 Ibid.

15 "Protecting the Collegiate Model." (2010). (NCAA President's Briefing Document). Retrieved Sept. 17, 2011, from National Collegiate Athletic Association website.

16 Ibid.

17 For instance, click on the "Academics" tab of the NCAA website and the landing page "NCAA's Commitment to Academics" opens up. Retrieved from NCAA website.

18 "NCAA Graduation Success Rates Point to Increased Academic Success for Most Division I Student-Athletes, Teams." (2005, December 19). [Archived NCAA News Release]. Retrieved from National Collegiate Athletic Association website.

19 "NCAA Grad Rates Hit All-Time High: Single-Year Graduation Success Rate Reaches 82 Percent." (2011, October 25). [Archived NCAA News Release]. Retrieved from National Collegiate Athletic Association website.

20 *The Associated Press*. (2012, January 19). "Record 65 Underclassmen in NFL Draft: Despite New Rookie Wage Scale, Previous High of 56 Easily Topped." Retrieved from NCAA/Turner Interactive website. "2011 Draft Tracker." (2011–2012). [Supplemental material]. MLB.com.

21 Goodman, J. (2012, April 10). "2012 End-of-Year Updated Transfer List: 425-Plus and Growing." [Supplemental material]. CBSSPORTS.com. *The Associated Press*. (2012, May 17). "Transfer Rules Won't Be Easily Lifted." ESPN.com.

22 Nyad, D. (1989, May 28). "View of Sport; How Illiteracy Makes Athletes Run." *The New York Times*.

23 Dexter Manley played football for four years at Oklahoma State. He did not graduate, being 50 credits short of fulfilling requirements.

24 Nora, A., and Cabrera, A. F. (1993). "The Construct Validity of Institutional Commitment: A Confirmatory Factor Analysis." *Research in Higher Education, 34*, 243–251. Tinto, V. A. (1997). "Classrooms as Communities: Exploring the Educational Characteristics of Student Persistence." *Journal of Higher Education,* 20, 65–72.

25 National Collegiate Athletic Association. (2012). "Aggregate Federal Graduation Rate Data Report."

26 Eckard, E. W. (2010). "NCAA Athlete Graduation Rates: Less Than Meets the Eye." *Journal of Sport Management*, 24(1), 45–58.

27 Hosick, M. B. (2010, October 12). "NCAA Grad Rate a Success by Any Measure." [NCAA Resources-Latest News Archive]. Retrieved from National Collegiate Athletic Association website.

28 Ibid at 24.

29 Complete College America. (2011, September). "Time Is the Enemy: The Surprising Truth about Why Today's College Students Aren't Graduating ... and What Needs to Change." p. 2.

30 de Vise, D. (2011, September 27). "Report Exposes Hidden Failure of Part-Time Students." College Inc. [Web log post]. *The Washington Post.*

31 Southall, R. M., Eckard, E. W., and Nagel, M. S. (2010–2012). "Adjusted Graduation Gap Reports." Reports are available on the College Sport Research Institute website.

32 Zagier, A. (2009, December 30). "College Admissions Exceptions Benefit Athletes." *The Huffington Post.*

33 National Collegiate Athletic Association. (2012). "Estimated Probability of Competing in Athletics beyond the High School Interscholastic Level."

34 Information regarding average length of professional sport careers was retrieved from the NFL; *Science Daily*; and RAM Financial Group.

Credit

NCAA Athlete Graduation Rates: Less Than Meets the Eye

E. Woodrow Eckard

The standard evaluations of NCAA student-athlete graduation rates involve comparisons with rates for the general student body. The latter rates as actually calculated, however, include a significant number of part-time students at many schools. This is problematic because athletes must be full-time, and should be compared with other full-time students. The downward "part-timer bias" in the student body rate distorts the comparison, making the relative graduation rates for athletes appear more favorable. Example calculations demonstrate that *relative* rates for major college football and men's basketball players are substantially worse when the bias is removed.

A common misperception is that student-athletes perform poorly in the classroom. The evidence is quite the contrary. NCAA student-athletes [all sports] are completing their bachelor's degrees at rates *higher* [italics added] than the American college student population at large. ... "The academic achievement of our student-athletes continues to improve," said NCAA President Myles Brand. "It is becoming one of our greatest success stories." (NCAA, 2006b).

Graduation rates are central to the controversy regarding the National Collegiate Athletic Association's requirement that college athletes be amateurs. Critics argue that the NCAA is a cartel whose regulations constitute, in effect, monopsonistic collusion by member universities designed to minimize the price paid for sports team labor inputs.[1] Compensation is essentially limited to payment in kind: room, board, and tuition. Other forms of compensation, monetary or otherwise, are prohibited. The result is exploitation of athletes with related rents transferred to the universities and their athletic departments. This pertains mainly to the top revenue-generating sports, football and men's basketball, where the marginal revenue product of many athletes can be substantial. For example, Brown and Jewell (2004) estimated that premium Division IA football players generate more than $400,000 for their school and basketball players more than $1 million.

The NCAA counters by arguing that athletes are students first, hence the term "student-athlete."[2] They are not exploited because their scholarships (not "athleticships") provide the opportunity to earn a college degree. Success in graduating athletes then constitutes supporting evidence. This success, or lack thereof, is universally measured by comparing athlete graduation rates to general student body rates, as in Dr. Brand's quotation (see above) and in various academic studies of the issue, such as Matheson (2006), Rishe (2003), and DeBrock, Hendricks, and Koenker (1996).

There is, however, a fundamental problem with this comparison, given the way graduation rates are actually computed. In particular, the student body rate, although generally presumed to pertain to full-time students, includes a significant number of part-time students at many institutions. In contrast, athletes must be full-time. Because part-timers take longer to graduate, this significantly reduces the measured general student-body graduation rates, and makes the *relative* rate of athletes at many schools appear more favorable.

The present article attempts to correct this problem, using major college football and men's basketball as examples. The approach is to estimate full-time student-body rates for individual schools using regression-based adjustments for the percentage of part-timers. These estimates then become the basis for comparison. The bottom-line: football and basketball players graduate at rates significantly lower, relative to the general *full-time* student body, than commonly believed.

In promoting comparisons with the general student body, the NCAA in effect assumes that athletes on average have the same interest in and/or aptitude for academics as do their fellow students. Of course, a principal criticism of "big time" college sports is precisely that schools select athletes mainly for their athletic, not academic, interests and abilities, and that once on campus they are de facto regarded primarily as "athlete-students" rather than "student-athletes."[3] If this is true, as seems likely, then there is no reason to expect equivalent performance. But, at the same time, it undermines the rationale for (NCAA-enforced) "amateur" status, i.e., limitations on compensation.

The paper proceeds as follows. The first two sections describe the graduation rate data and samples, respectively. The third section presents the standard student body-athlete comparisons. The next section explains the full-time versus part-time issue. The fifth section presents the graduation rate comparisons for football and basketball corrected for the "part-time bias." The last section concludes the paper.

Graduation Rate Data

The NCAA prepares a Graduation Rate Report for each member institution, available on the NCAA website (www.NCAA.org), based on data supplied by the institution. The Reports include rates for the general undergraduate student body and for student-athletes. The underlying data are from the IPEDS Graduation Rate Surveys that virtually all colleges and universities are required to file with the U.S. Department of Education.[4] Student-athletes are defined as students who receive financial aid because of their participation in an athletic program. This may be a scholarship, grant, tuition waiver, or other similar form of assistance.

The graduation rate is calculated as the percentage of "first-time full-time freshmen" who graduate within six years of their initial enrollment. Rates are published for the most recent cohort for which the calculation is possible, and a "4-class" average for that cohort and the three previous ones. For example, the 2006 Graduation Rate Reports, used in the current study, contain the percentage of freshmen who enrolled in the fall of 1999 and graduated by August 2005, and the average rate for cohorts who entered in the fall of 1996, 1997, 1998, and 1999 and who had graduated within six years of their entry. The 4-class averages are used in the analysis below to reduce the influence of "random" annual fluctuations.

Graduation rates are reported for all students, with gender breakdowns, and for student-athletes. Athlete rates are available for all sports combined, and separately for major sports including football and men's basketball. The NCAA calls these "federal rates," hereafter referred to as Fed Rates, so called because of their derivation from the above mentioned IPEDS data.

In addition to the Fed Rate, the NCAA independently calculates another graduation rate for student-athletes only, called the Graduation Success Rate (GSR). It is designed primarily to adjust the Fed Rates for transfer students. The NCAA prefers the GSR, but acknowledges that there is no directly comparable number for the general student body.[5] The GSR can be calculated for athletes because the NCAA tracks transfers to police its eligibility limits. No such tracking occurs for the general student body, presumably because of the high cost involved. Therefore, to allow comparisons, the analysis that follows relies on the Fed Rates.

The Samples

The part-time student bias is illustrated using the two main revenue-generating sports: "major college" football and men's basketball.[6] The first sample includes NCAA Division IA schools in football and the second, members of the major Division I conferences in basketball.[7] Separate samples for the two sports are necessary because the qualifying schools differ. Some have major basketball programs, but in football compete below Division IA or not at all. Other schools have Division IA football programs, but are considered second-tier in basketball. Since the 4-class Fed Rates of 2006 cover the period 1996–2005, the samples contain only those schools where sports qualify as majors for the entire period. In addition, the military service academies are excluded because their graduation data are not comparable to "civilian" universities.

For football, sample selection starts with the 2006–07 list of 119 Division IA schools, i.e., the "top-tier" programs.[8] Eliminating those not classified in Division IA throughout 1996–2005 and the service academies leaves a sample of 106. For basketball, selection starts with the 2006–07 list of *all* Division I schools, 327 in total. While the major Division I football programs are classified in Division IA, there is no corresponding subdivision for basketball. To objectively identify second-tier programs for exclusion from the sample, Collegeinsider.com's list of 22 "mid-major" Division I conferences is used. Members of these conferences are eligible for ranking in the Mid-Major Basketball Poll conducted by Collegeinsider.com. Members of the ten Division I conferences *ineligible* for this poll are defined as "major."[9] For inclusion in the basketball sample, a school must have been a member of a major conference (i.e., not midmajor) for all of 1996–2005.[10] A total of 102 schools meet these criteria. The football and basketball samples together contain 126 different schools, with 82 common to both. The Appendix lists the schools in each sample.

The Standard Comparisons

The academic performance of student-athletes is usually evaluated by comparing their mean graduation rate to that of the general student body at their school. For male sport comparisons, however, the male-only student body rate is more appropriate because male college graduation rates are generally about 6 percentage points less than female rates.[11] A similar male-female difference is present in our samples.[12]

The standard comparison between the student body and student-athlete 4-class average Fed Rates is presented in Table 1. The upper panel shows the athlete Rates for the two samples. The football Rate is 54.9% and the basketball Rate is 40.6%. The lower panel of Table 1 presents paired difference-between-means tests that compare each sport's rate to the all-male student body rate, school by school. At this point, no adjustment is made for the presence of part-time students. For the football sample, the mean all-male student-body Rate is 58.1%, 3.2 percentage points more than for football players. The difference, while small, is statistically significant at the 5% level ($t = 2.00$). For the basketball sample, the mean all-male Fed Rate is 62.9%, 22.3 percentage points more than the athlete Rate. The difference is large and has a high degree of statistical significance ($t = 11.9$).

Football and basketball graduation rates also are lower than those for male athletes in other sports, i.e., those that do not generate significant revenues. The rates cannot be directly compared, however, because the Graduation Rate Reports for individual institutions do not include the *number* of athletes by sport. However, the NCAA published a Graduation Rate Report for Division IA in 2006 that includes these numbers aggregated for all Division IA schools. Thus, average rates can be computed for football and basketball combined and all other male sports combined, for the 1996–1999 cohorts. First, football and basketball account for almost half (49.2%) of all male athletes at Division IA schools, with football alone accounting for 42.4%. The combined 4-class Fed Rate for football and basketball is 52.9%, over five percentage points less than the 58.0% Rate for other male sports combined. The latter in turn is three percentage points less than the Division IA male student body mean of 61%.

Table 1. Paired Differences-Between-Means Test: Unadjusted All-Male Federal Graduation Rate vs. Football and Men's Basketball Graduation Rates

	Football Sample	Basketball Sample
Number of Schools	106	102
Athlete Fed Rate Means	54.9%	40.6%
Unadjusted Fed Rate Comparison		
Mean—All Male Students	58.1%	62.9%
Mean Difference	3.2 points	22.3 points
t-statistic	2.00**	11.9***

Note: Graduation rates are the 4-class average rates for freshman cohorts entering Fall 1996, 1997, 1998, and 1999.

*p < .10. **p < .05. *** p < .01.

Part-Time Students in the Fed Rates

A fundamental problem with the standard comparison is that part-time students comprise an often significant, albeit uncertain, portion of the student-body Fed Rate cohorts. In contrast, *all* student-athletes are required to be full-time students. The difficulty arises, of course, because part-time students take longer to get through school. Their graduation rates consequently are lower for fixed time periods, such as the six years stipulated for the Fed Rates. Therefore, the difference between athlete and student-body graduation rates is biased downward to the extent that the latter includes schools with a significant number of part-time students.

General student body Fed Rates appear to include full-time students only, but at most institutions this is not the case. The Rates are based on cohorts comprised of what are commonly called "first-time, full-time freshmen." The Institute of Education Sciences (2006) described these as "freshmen who enroll in the fall of a specified year… , who have never attended college before, who attend full time *when they begin,* and who intend to earn a degree" (p. v, italics added). But the assessment regarding "full-time" (at least 12 credit hours) is made only once, at initial enrollment. Students who later switch to part-time remain in the cohort.[13] While the precise number of "switchers" cannot be determined from available data, it could be significant at many schools. For example, O'Toole, Stratton, and Wetzel (2003) analyzed enrollment behavior in a sample of about 5,000 first-time college students over a period of five years after initial enrollment. They found that "15%–30% … enrolled part time during their first nonsummer term [but] over the 5-year period, no less than 40% and possibly as many as 52% of the sample enrolled part time" (p. 526). These results imply that roughly 30% of sample students who initially enrolled full-time later switched to part-time during the five-year study period, a figure that would be higher for six years.[14]

In contrast to the Fed Rate cohort, athletes must maintain full-time enrollment to be eligible for sport competition. In particular, Article 14 of the NCAA Bylaws states, "a student-athlete [must] be enrolled in at least a minimum *full-time* program of studies, be in good academic standing, and maintain progress toward a baccalaureate or equivalent degree" (NCAA, 2006e, p. 131, italics added). The terms "full-time," "good standing" (including academic performance), and "progress toward degree" are defined by each institution according to the same standards applied to all its students. In addition, "full-time" means enrollment in all terms during the regular academic year, excluding summer (NCAA, 2006e, p. 155). Thus, athletes are required to be full-time students throughout their academic careers.

The presence of part-timers in the general student body Fed Rate reduces reported graduation rates. The impact can be estimated by using as a proxy the available data on the proportion of part-timers among all undergraduates. The assumption is that the characteristics of a school and its student body that generally are associated with a relatively high part-time population would also increase the likelihood that students originally in the Fed Rate full-time cohort would later switch to part-time. The characteristics include location in a metropolitan area where jobs, including part-time, are more plentiful and where the socioeconomic characteristics of the student body make continuous full-time study less likely. In addition, schools with significant part-time populations usually offer a variety of evening courses that would facilitate a switch from full-time to part-time.

Data on part-time enrollment by school for 2006 are reported by IPEDS, in addition to its standard graduation rates.[15] For the sample of football schools, the mean percentage of part-time students is 12.1 and for the basketball sample the mean is 11.3%. Both samples range from 0.2% part-timers (Notre Dame) to 36.7% (Utah). There is a significant difference between private and public schools. Pooling the football and basketball samples (126 schools), the mean part-time rate for the 31 private schools is 8.5% and that for the 95 public schools is 13.6%. A difference between-means-test is significant at the one per cent level ($t = 3.16$).

Evidence that the Fed Rate "full-time" cohorts for many schools contain a significant proportion of part-timers is presented in Figures 1 and 2. The figures plot the all-male student-body Fed Rates versus the percentage of part-time students for public and private schools, respectively, again pooling the football and basketball samples. Public and private are separated because the relation is different for the two groups (see below). For public schools the simple correlation between the two variables is –0.81 and for private it is –0.45. Clearly, higher percentages of part-time students are associated with lower "full-time" graduation rates.

Full-Time to Full-Time Comparisons

As noted above, graduation rates for student-athletes should be compared with other students who are similarly full-time. The all-student rate can be adjusted for the possible presence of part-timers by using the relations evident in Figures 1 and 2 to estimate each school's (hypothetical) full-time all-male Fed Rate. The estimated full-time Rates can then be compared with the actual Rates for student-athletes, all of whom are full-time. Other variables may contribute to explaining the gap between athlete and male student body Rates, but the requisite data are not available for athletes.[16] For example, DeBrock et al. (1996) and Rishe (2003) found that lower SAT scores help explain the football/basketball graduation gap, based on data formerly included in the NCAA Graduation Rate Reports. However, these data have not been published since 1998 and are no longer available. In any event, the NCAA apparently believes that college athletes should be held to the same academic standards as the general student body.

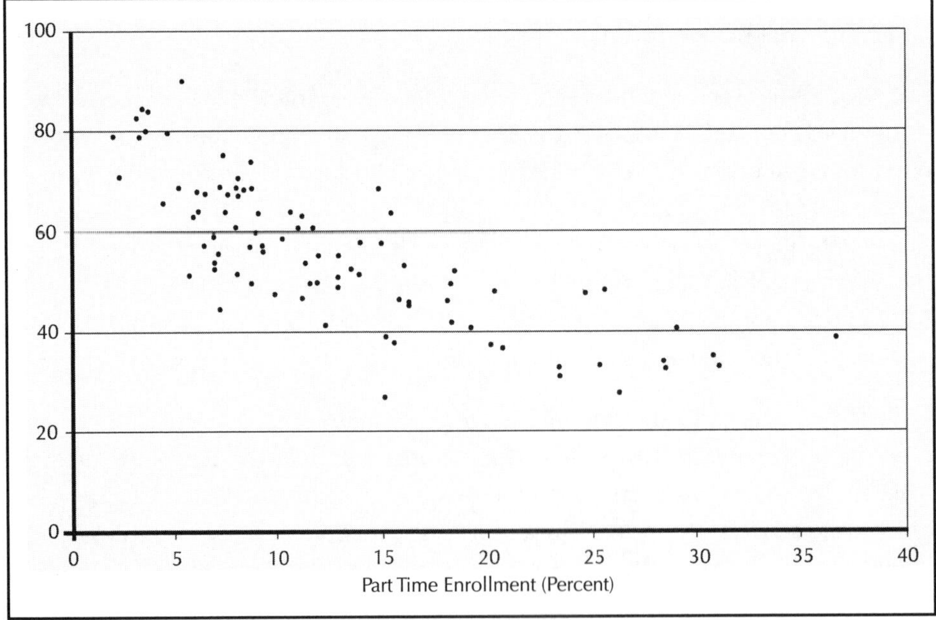

Figure 1. Private school all-male federal graduation rate vs. part-time enrollment: Pooled sample (N = 95). Vertical axis indicates graduation rate percent.

The first step in the adjustment process is to regress the all-male student body Fed Rates on the percentage of part-time students. The relations are different for public and private schools, requiring separate regressions. The football and basketball samples are pooled in each case, assuring that the full-time all-male estimate for a particular school is the same for both sports. Both linear and quadratic models are estimated, the latter accounting for possible nonlinearities.

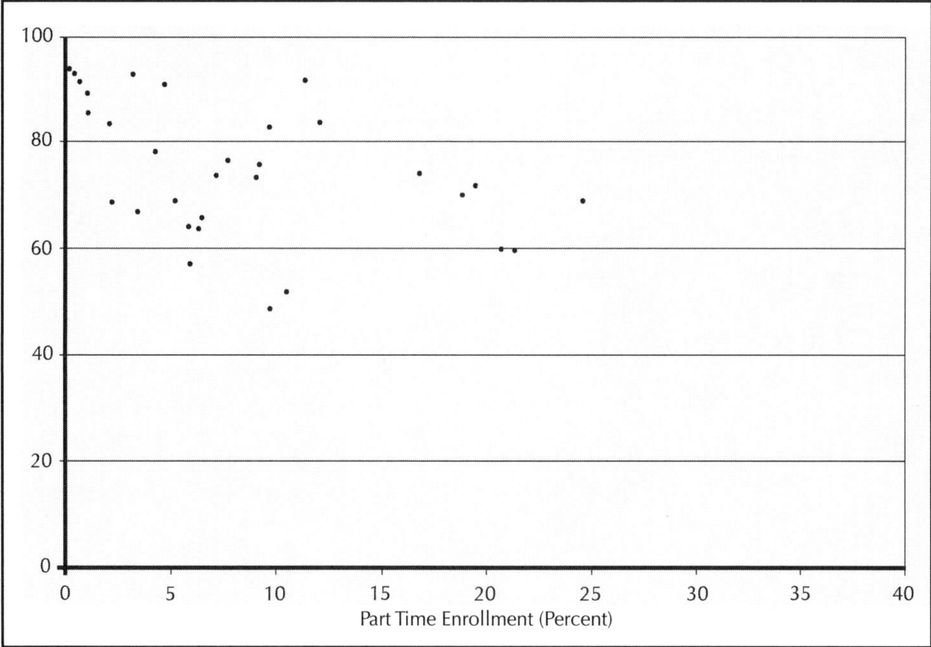

Figure 2. Private school all-male federal graduation rate vs. part-time enrollment: Pooled sample (N = 31). Vertical axis indicates graduation rate percent.

The results are shown in Table 2. For public schools (N = 95), both specifications indicate a relatively strong relation. The quadratic form has an adjusted R-squared of 0.702, with a high degree of statistical significance (F = 111.7). Both the linear and squared terms show appropriate signs and are significant at better than the 0.1% level. For the much smaller sample of private schools (N = 31), a relation also exists between the Fed Rate and the percentage of part-time students, albeit weaker. In the quadratic form, both terms have appropriate signs, but the adjusted R-squared of 0.231 is substantially lower than for public schools. The model is nevertheless significant at the one per cent level (F = 5.51). The linear term is significant at the two per cent level, although the squared term is only marginally significant (10% level). A Chow test performed on the quadratic specifications indicates that the public and private schools should not be pooled (F = 19.0).[17] The smaller (absolute) slope coefficients for private schools suggest that their first-time full-time freshmen are less likely to switch to part-time. The estimates below are based on the quadratic specifications.

Table 2. Regression of All-Male Federal Graduation Rates on the Percentage of Part-time Students, Public and Private Schools

	Public		Private	
Variable	(1)	(2)	(3)	(4)
Intercept	74.9***	85.5***	82.0***	87.9***
	(41.0)	(28.0)	(24.5)	(18.9)
%Part-time	−1.53***	−3.17***	−0.843**	−2.60**
	(−13.3)	(−7.72)	(−2.73)	(−2.48)
Part-time^2		0.0472***		0.0773*
		(4.14)		(1.75)
Adj. R^2	0.650	0.702	0.177	0.231
F-statistic	175.8***	111.7***	7.44**	5.51***
Number of Schools	95	95	31	31

Note: *t*-statistics in parentheses

*p < .10. **p < .05. *** p < .01.

The second step in the adjustment process is to estimate the expected value for the all-male Fed Rate associated with each school's part-time percentage, based on the above regressions.[18] The residual for each school, the difference between its actual all-male Rate and the expected value, provides a (noisy) measure of the influence of characteristics other than the percentage of part-time students.[19] For example, a positive residual indicates that these other characteristics allow a school to do better in terms of graduating students than the average for schools with the same part-time percentage.

The last step is to estimate each school's all-male Fed Rate as though it were a full-time institution. "Full-time" is arbitrarily defined to include five per cent part-timers. Twenty sample schools have part-time percentages less than five, nine of them public. For these schools no adjustment is made. The calculation of the estimated full-time Rate has two components. The first is the (quadratic) regression-based male student-body Fed Rate prediction (expected value) for a five per cent part-time school. This expected rate is 70.8% for public schools and 76.8% for private schools. Next, for each school the above-mentioned residual is added to account for school characteristics other than part-time percentage that may affect the graduation rate.

Table 3 reports difference-between-means tests for the *adjusted* all-male Fed Rates and the student-athlete Rates for our two samples. For the football sample, the adjusted mean all-male Rate is 72.6%, 17.7 percentage points above the athlete Rate of 54.9%. The difference is both large and highly significant (t = 12.5). For basketball, the adjusted mean all-male Rate of 74.9% is 34.3 points more than the mean athlete Rate of 40.6%, a difference that is very large and also highly significant (t = 19.0).[20] The adjusted differences between the athlete and all-male Rates are much higher than the unadjusted differences (Table 1). For the football sample, the adjusted difference of 17.7 points is more than five times larger than the unadjusted difference of 3.2 points, whereas for basketball the adjusted difference is over 50% larger (34.3 vs. 22.3).

Table 3. Paired Differences-Between-Means Test: Adjusted All-Male Federal Graduation Rate vs. Football and Men's Basketball Graduation Rates

	Football Sample	Basketball Sample
Number of Schools	106	102
Athlete Fed Rate Means	54.9%	40.6%
Unadjusted Fed Rate Comparison		
Mean—All Male Students	72.6%	74.9%
Mean Difference	17.7 points	34.3 points
t-statistic	12.5***	19.0***

Note: Graduation rates are the 4-class average rates for freshman cohorts entering Fall 1996, 1997, 1998, and 1999.

*p < .10. **p < .05. *** p < .01.

Conclusions and Discussion

The NCAA touts its success at graduating student-athletes based on the standard comparison of athlete graduation rates with those of the general student body. The latter rates as actually calculated, however, involve a significant number of part-time students at many schools. Because part-timers take longer to graduate, their graduation rates are lower for fixed periods like the six years used in the standard data. This is problematic because athletes must be full-time, and should be compared with other full-time students. The downward "part-timer bias" in the student body rate distorts the comparison, making the *relative* graduation rates for athletes appear more favorable.

Example calculations demonstrate that relative rates for football and men's basketball players are substantially worse when the bias is removed. In a sample of 106 major football schools, uncorrected football player graduation rates are on average a relatively small 3.2 percentage points less than the general all-male student body rates. However, when the effect of part-timers is removed from the student body rates using regression analysis, the average difference is 17.7 percentage points, over five times larger. The results are similar for a sample of 102 major men's basketball programs. Without the correction, basketball player graduation rates are an already sizable 22.3 percentage points less than the all-male general student body rate. With the correction the difference is 34.3 percentage points, more than 50% larger.

A subject for future research is the investigation of the part-timer bias in other collegiate sports, both male and female. The nonrevenue sports, in fact, comprise the majority of student-athletes. The necessary corrections, however, would likely be smaller in these sports since their graduation rates are generally higher than the rates for football and men's basketball (see above). For women's sports, the general student body data should be gender-matched, as is done for the male sports in the current study. Failure to account for gender differences, of course, creates an additional favorable bias in the *relative* graduation rates for women.

The large graduation rate differences in the two principal men's sports are not going to disappear any time soon. They are likely explained to a significant degree by corresponding differences between college athletes and the general student body regarding their interest in and/or aptitude for academic study. For example, many athletes in "big time" programs, in reality, may view themselves as "majoring" in their sport in preparation for (an often improbable) career as a professional athlete. And it is likely that a much larger proportion of athletes is at, or close to, their school's minimum academic entrance requirements, compared with the general student body. Another factor is the time commitment required by participation in big-time athletics that inevitably reduces study time, akin to part-time jobs held by nonathlete students. Recognizing all this, however, would require that the NCAA admit that "student-athletes" are really "athlete-students," which in turn would undermine the rationale for its cartel-like enforcement of compensation restrictions. The NCAA must therefore persist in generating unrealistic expectations and performing comparisons in which athletes, particularly in revenue-generating sports, will inevitably come up short.

Notes

1 The NCAA is a private not-for-profit organization that regulates most intercollegiate athletics in the United States. It is organized and managed by member colleges and universities. Many observers view the NCAA as a cartel, e.g., Fleischer, Goff, and Tollison (1992), DeShriver and Stotlar (1996), Eckard (1998), and Zimbalist (1999).

2 For example, NCAA spokesman Erik Christianson recently asserted, "We educate student-athletes; they are students first," as quoted in Southall, Nagel, Amis, and Southall (2008, p. 3). The NCAA created the term "student-athlete" in the 1950s to promote the perception that college athletes are primarily students; e.g., see Staurowsky and Sack (2005) and references cited therein.

3 For example, commenting on a player during spring training, University of Florida football coach Urban Meyer recently stated, "For a year and a half here, he was just a guy that ate up a scholarship. He was not serious about his profession, and his profession is football." ("A Professional Student-Athlete?" 2007). DeBrock et al. (1996) provided empirical evidence that many football and basketball players at major schools see themselves as primarily involved in "minor league" preparation for professional sport careers.

4 IPEDS is the Integrated Postsecondary Education Data System, a data collection program of the National Center for Education Statistics at the U.S. Department of Education.

5 See NCAA (2006a). The NCAA notes therein that if a proposed new record system is adopted by the Department of Education, "comparable data to the GSR will be available through the federal rate."

6 For Division IA in 2002–03, revenue from football and men's basketball combined accounted for about 84% of all athletic program revenues (men and women), with football alone accounting for about 64%. These are the author's calculations based on revenue data in Fulks (2005), Tables 3.2a and 3.2b (pp. 32–33).

7 Lower-tier Division I football programs are classified in Division IAA. Divisions IA and IAA recently have been renamed the Football Bowl Subdivision and the Football Championship Subdivision, respectively. The designations IA and IAA are retained herein because they were in use during our study period. The NCAA also has Divisions II and III whose members are involved in lower levels of athletic competition across all sports.

8 Identification of Division IA status is from NCAA (2006c), Major-College Alignment History (pp. 518–519).

9 The major basketball conferences thus defined are the Atlantic Coast, Atlantic 10, Big Ten, Big 12, Big East, Conference-USA, Mountain West, Pacific-10, Southeastern, and Western Athletic.

10 Identification of Division I status and conference membership are from NCAA (2006d), Division I Conference Alignment History (pp. 271–274) and Division I Alignment History (pp. 274–276). Marquette (Big East) and Xavier (Atlantic10), otherwise eligible for the basketball sample, are excluded because of missing data on graduation rates by sport.

11 For example, see Institute of Education Sciences (2006, p. 25) and Goldin, Katz, and Kuziemko (2006).

12 In the pooled sample ($N = 126$), the mean male Rate is 6.4 percentage points less than the female Rate (59.2% vs. 65.6%), a difference that is highly significant based on a paired difference-between-means test (t-statistic = 21.3).

13 This is implied in the published cohort description, and confirmed by IPEDS staffer Brittany Herman via an e-mail query, May 29, 2007. Ignoring students who switch is understandable given the high cost of tracking cohort members throughout their academic careers.

14 Research in this issue is sparse. Stratton, O'Toole, and Wetzel (2004) analyzed the socioeconomic determinants of students' decisions to *initially* attend college on a part-time basis, but did not analyze first-time full-time students who later switch. They noted that "relatively little is known about the factors associated with … the decision to enroll part-time" (p. 167) and regarded their paper as "a first step to examine the enrollment intensity decision" (p. 174).

15 The part-time data are available on http://nces.ed.gov/ipeds (College Navigator).

16 The NCAA Graduation Reports include ethnicity for all athletes combined, but not for individual sports. No other data on relevant athlete characteristics are available.

17 Scott, Bailey, and Kienzl (2006) obtained similar results: "In the past, institutional analyses have included public/private indicator variables. This approach assumes that all of the other variables in the model have the same influence in public and private institutions [i.e., identical slope coefficients]. We test this assumption, and find strong evidence that it is false" (pp. 256–257).

18 The quadratic specification has a minimum where d*Rate*/d%*PT* = Among public schools, this occurs at %*PT* = 32.3, yielding a minimum expected Fed Rate of 32.3. For the two schools with a higher %*PT* (Boise State and Utah), the expected value is set equal to the 32.3% minimum. Among private schools, the minimum occurs at %*PT* = 16.8, yielding a minimum expected Fed Rate of 66.0. For the five schools with higher %*PT* (DePaul, La Salle, St. John's, St. Louis, and Tulane), the expected values are set equal to the 66.0 minimum.

19 The assumption is that the residual or error term in the regression equation has two components. The first is the net effect of excluded variables that affect a particular school's graduation rate. The second is a purely random component (i.e., mean zero). The use of the 4-class average reduces the variance of the random component.

20 The adjusted all-male student body rate is somewhat higher for the basketball sample because it contains a larger proportion of private schools. The large gap for basketball is particularly troublesome because the NCAA derives the bulk of its own revenue from the annual "March Madness" Division I men's basketball tournament (e.g., see Southall et al., 2008).

Acknowledgments

Valuable assistance was provided by Dr. Christine Stroup-Benham of Institutional Research, Planning, and Analysis at UC-Denver. In addition, helpful comments were provided by seminar participants at the Business School, UC-Denver.

Works Cited

Brown, R.W., & Jewell, R.T. (2004). "Measuring Marginal Revenue Product in College Athletics: Updated Estimates." In J. Fizel & R. Fort (Eds.), *Economics of College Sports* (pp. 153–162). Westport, CT: Praeger.

DeBrock, L., Hendricks, W., & Koenker, R. (1996). "The Economics of Persistence: Graduation Rates of Athletes as Labor Market Choice." *The Journal of Human Resources, 31*, 513–539.

DeShriver, T.D., & Stotlar, D.K. (1996). "An Economic Analysis Of Cartel Behavior Within the NCAA." *Journal of Sport Management, 10*, 388–400.

Eckard, E.W. (1998). "The NCAA Cartel and Competitive Balance in College Football." *Review of Industrial Organization, 13*, 347–369.

Fleisher, A.A., Goff, B.L., & Tollison, R.D. (1992). *The National Collegiate Athletic Association: A Study in Cartel Behavior.* Chicago: University of Chicago Press.

Fulks, D. L. (2005, February). 2002–03 *NCAA Revenues and Expenses of Division I and II Intercollegiate Athletics Programs Report.* Indianapolis, IN: National Collegiate Athletic Association.

Goldin, C., Katz, L.F., & Kuziemko, I. (2006, March). *The Homecoming of American College Women: The Reversal of the College Gender Gap.* NBER Working Paper No. 12139. Cambridge, MA: National Bureau of Economic Research.

Institute of Education Sciences. (2006, October). *Placing College Graduation Rates in Context: How 4-Year College Graduation Rates Vary With Selectivity and the Size of Low-Income Enrollment.* National Center for Education Statistics, U.S. Department of Education. Washington, DC: U.S. Department of Education.

Matheson, V.A. (2006). Research note: "Athletic Graduation Rates and Simpson's Paradox." *Economics of Education Review, 26*, 516–520.

National Collegiate Athletic Association. (2006a, September 27). "Division I Graduation Success Rate Climbs to 77 Percent." Press release. Retrieved March 28, 2009, from http://www.ncaa.org/wps/ncaa?ContentID=4307.

National Collegiate Athletic Association. (2006b, November 9). "Division I Student-Athletes Excel in Classroom, Exceed Student Body Graduation Rates." Press release. Retrieved March 27, 2009, from http://www.ncaa.org/wps/ncaa?ContentID=4308.

National Collegiate Athletic Association. (2006c). *Official 2006 NCAA Divisions I-A and I-AA Football Records Book.* Indianapolis, IN: National Collegiate Athletic Association.

National Collegiate Athletic Association. (2006d). *Official 2007 NCAA Men's Basketball Records Book.* Indianapolis, IN: National Collegiate Athletic Association.

National Collegiate Athletic Association. (2006e). *2006–07 NCAA Division I Manual.* Indianapolis, IN: National Collegiate Athletic Association.

O'Toole, D.M., Stratton, L.S., & Wetzel, J.N. (2003). "A Longitudinal Analysis of the Frequency of Part-Time Enrollment and the Persistence of Students Who Enroll Part Time." *Research in Higher Education, 44*, 519–537.

"A Professional Student-Athlete?" (2007, April 15). *The Denver Post,* p. 2B.

Rishe, P.J. (2003). "A Reexamination of How Athletic Success Impacts Graduation Rates: Comparing Student Athletes to All Other Undergraduates." *American Journal of Economics and Sociology, 62*, 407–427.

Scott, M., Bailey, T., & Kienzl, G. (2006). "Relative Success? Determinants of College Graduation Rates in Public and Private Colleges in the U.S." *Research in Higher Education, 47*, 249–279.

Southall, R.M., Nagel, M.S., Amis, J., & Southall, C. (2008). "A Method to March Madness? Institutional Logics and the 2006 National Collegiate Athletic Association Division I Men's Basketball Tournament." *Journal of Sport Management, 22*, 677–700.

Staurowsky, E.J., & Sack, A.L. (2005). "Reconsidering the Use of the Term *Student-Athlete* in Academic Research." *Journal of Sport Management, 19*, 103–116.

Stratton, L.S., O'Toole, D.M., & Wetzel, J.N. (2004). "Factors Affecting Initial Enrollment Intensity: Part-Time Versus Full-Time Enrollment." *Economics of Education Review, 23*, 167–175.

Zimbalist, A. (1999). *Unpaid professionals*. Princeton, NJ: Princeton University Press.

Appendix

Sample Schools by Sport and Conference

Football

Atlantic Coast Conference: Boston College, Clemson, Duke, Florida State, Georgia Tech, Maryland, Miami (FL), North Carolina, N.C. State, Virginia, Virginia Tech, Wake Forest

Big 12 Conference: Baylor, Colorado, Iowa State, Kansas, Kansas State, Missouri, Nebraska, Oklahoma, Oklahoma State, Texas, Texas A&M, Texas Tech

Big East Conference: Cincinnati, Louisville, Pittsburgh, Rutgers, Syracuse, West Virginia

Big Ten Conference: Illinois, Indiana, Iowa, Michigan, Michigan State, Minnesota, Northwestern, Ohio State, Penn State, Purdue, Wisconsin

Conference-USA: Central Florida, East Carolina, Houston, Memphis, Rice, Southern Methodist, Southern Mississippi, Texas-El Paso, Tulane, Tulsa

Independents[1]: Notre Dame, Temple

Mid-American Conference: Akron, Ball State, Bowling Green, Central Michigan, Eastern Michigan, Kent State, Miami (OH), Northern Illinois, Ohio, Toledo, Western Michigan

Mountain West Conference: Brigham Young, Colorado State, Nevada-Las Vegas, New Mexico, San Diego State, Texas Christian, Utah, Wyoming

Pacific-10 Conference: Arizona, Arizona State, California, Oregon, Oregon State, Southern California, Stanford, UCLA, Washington, Washington State

Southeastern Conference: Alabama, Arkansas, Auburn, Florida, Georgia, Kentucky, Louisiana State, Mississippi, Mississippi State, South Carolina, Tennessee, Vanderbilt

Sun Belt Conference: Arkansas State, Louisiana-Lafayette, Louisiana-Monroe, North Texas

Western Athletic Conference: Boise State, Fresno State, Hawaii, Louisiana Tech, Nevada, New Mexico State, San Jose State, Utah State

Basketball

Atlantic Coast Conference: Boston College, Clemson, Duke, Florida State, Georgia Tech, Maryland, Miami (FL), North Carolina, N.C. State, Virginia, Virginia Tech, Wake Forest

Atlantic 10 Conference: Charlotte, Dayton, Duquesne, Fordham, George Washington, La Salle, Massachusetts, Rhode Island, St. Bonaventure, St. Joseph's, St. Louis, Temple

Big 12 Conference: Baylor, Colorado, Iowa State, Kansas, Kansas State, Missouri, Nebraska, Oklahoma, Oklahoma State, Texas, Texas A&M, Texas Tech

Big East Conference: Cincinnati, Connecticut, DePaul, Georgetown, Louisville, Notre Dame, Pittsburgh, Providence, Rutgers, Seton Hall, South Florida, St. John's, Syracuse, Villanova, West Virginia

Big Ten Conference: Illinois, Indiana, Iowa, Michigan, Michigan State, Minnesota, Northwestern, Ohio State, Penn State, Purdue, Wisconsin

Conference-USA: Alabama-Birmingham, Houston, Memphis, Rice, Southern Methodist, Southern Mississippi, Texas-El Paso, Tulane

Mountain West Conference: Brigham Young, Colorado State, New Mexico, San Diego State, Texas Christian, Utah, Wyoming

Pacific-10 Conference: Arizona, Arizona State, California, Oregon, Oregon State, Southern California, Stanford, UCLA, Washington, Washington State

Southeastern Conference: Alabama, Arkansas, Auburn, Florida, Georgia, Kentucky, Louisiana State, Mississippi, Mississippi State, South Carolina, Tennessee, Vanderbilt

Western Athletic Conference: Fresno State, Hawaii, San Jose State

Footnote

1 Temple was a football independent in 2006. For basketball, Notre Dame is in the Big East and Temple is in the Atlantic 10.

Credit

Eckard, E. Woodrow. "NCAA Athlete Graduation Rates: Less Than Meets the Eye." Reprinted, by permission, from *Journal of Sport Management,* 2010, 24(1): 45–59. © Human Kinetics, Inc.

The Shame of College Sports

Taylor Branch

"I'm not hiding," Sonny Vaccaro told a closed hearing at the Willard Hotel in Washington, D.C., in 2001. "We want to put our materials on the bodies of your athletes, and the best way to do that is buy your school. Or buy your coach."

Vaccaro's audience, the members of the Knight Commission on Intercollegiate Athletics, bristled. These were eminent reformers—among them the president of the National Collegiate Athletic Association, two former heads of the U.S. Olympic Committee, and several university presidents and chancellors. The Knight Foundation, a nonprofit that takes an interest in college athletics as part of its concern with civic life, had tasked them with saving college sports from runaway commercialism as embodied by the likes of Vaccaro, who, since signing his pioneering shoe contract with Michael Jordan in 1984, had built sponsorship empires successively at Nike, Adidas, and Reebok. Not all the members could hide their scorn for the "sneaker pimp" of schoolyard hustle, who boasted of writing checks for millions to everybody in higher education.

"Why," asked Bryce Jordan, the president emeritus of Penn State, "should a university be an advertising medium for your industry?"

Vaccaro did not blink. "They shouldn't, sir," he replied. "You sold your souls, and you're going to continue selling them. You can be very moral and righteous in asking me that question, sir," Vaccaro added with irrepressible good cheer, "but there's not one of you in this room that's going to turn down any of our money. You're going to take it. I can only offer it."

William Friday, a former president of North Carolina's university system, still winces at the memory. "Boy, the silence that fell in that room," he recalled recently. "I never will forget it." Friday, who founded and co-chaired two of the three Knight Foundation sports initiatives over the past 20 years, called Vaccaro "the worst of all" the witnesses ever to come before the panel.

But what Vaccaro said in 2001 was true then, and it's true now: corporations offer money so they can profit from the glory of college athletes, and the universities grab it. In 2010, despite the faltering economy, a single college athletic league, the football-crazed Southeastern Conference (SEC), became the first to crack the billion-dollar barrier in athletic receipts. The Big Ten pursued closely at $905 million. That money comes from a combination of ticket sales, concession sales, merchandise, licensing fees, and other sources—but the great bulk of it comes from television contracts.

Educators are in thrall to their athletic departments because of these television riches and because they respect the political furies that can burst from a locker room. "There's fear," Friday told me when I visited him on the University of North Carolina campus in Chapel Hill last fall. As we spoke, two giant construction cranes towered nearby over the university's Kenan Stadium, working on the latest $77 million renovation. (The University of Michigan spent almost four times that much to expand its Big House.) Friday insisted that for the networks, paying huge sums to universities was a bargain. "We do every little thing for them," he said. "We furnish the theater, the actors, the lights, the music, and the audience for a drama measured neatly in time slots. They bring the camera and turn it on." Friday, a weathered idealist at 91, laments the control universities have ceded in pursuit of this money. If television wants to broadcast football from here on a Thursday night, he said, "we shut down the university at 3 o'clock to accommodate the crowds." He longed for a campus identity more centered in an academic mission.

The United States is the only country in the world that hosts big-time sports at institutions of higher learning. This should not, in and of itself, be controversial. College athletics are rooted in the classical ideal of *Mens sana in corpore sano*—a sound mind in a sound body—and who would argue with that? College sports are deeply inscribed in the culture of our nation. Half a million young men and women play competitive intercollegiate sports each year. Millions of spectators flock into football stadiums each Saturday in the fall, and tens of millions more watch on television. The March Madness basketball tournament each spring has become a major national event, with upwards of 80 million watching it on television and talking about the games around the office water cooler. ESPN has spawned ESPNU, a channel dedicated to college sports, and Fox Sports and other cable outlets are developing channels exclusively to cover sports from specific regions or divisions.

With so many people paying for tickets and watching on television, college sports has become Very Big Business. According to various reports, the football teams at Texas, Florida, Georgia, Michigan, and Penn State—to name just a few big-revenue football schools—each earn between $40 million and $80 million in profits a year, even after paying coaches multimillion-dollar salaries. When you combine so much money with such high, almost tribal, stakes—football boosters are famously rabid in their zeal to have their alma mater win—corruption is likely to follow.

Scandal after scandal has rocked college sports. In 2010, the NCAA sanctioned the University of Southern California after determining that star running back Reggie Bush and his family had received "improper benefits" while he played for the Trojans. (Among other charges, Bush and members of his family were alleged to have received free airfare and limousine rides, a car, and a rent-free home in San Diego, from sports agents who wanted Bush as a client.) The Bowl Championship Series stripped USC of its 2004 national title, and Bush returned the Heisman Trophy he had won in 2005. Last fall, as Auburn University football stormed its way to an undefeated season and a national championship, the team's star quarterback, Cam Newton, was dogged by allegations that his father had used a recruiter to solicit up to $180,000 from Mississippi State in exchange for his son's matriculation there after junior college in 2010. Jim Tressel, the highly successful head football coach of the Ohio State Buckeyes, resigned last spring after the NCAA alleged he had feigned ignorance of rules violations by players on his team. At least 28 players over the course of the previous nine seasons, according to *Sports Illustrated*, had traded autographs, jerseys, and other team memorabilia in exchange for tattoos or cash at a tattoo parlor in Columbus, in violation of NCAA rules. Late this summer, Yahoo Sports reported that the NCAA was investigating allegations that a University of Miami booster had given millions of dollars in illicit cash and services to more than 70 Hurricanes football players over eight years.

The list of scandals goes on. With each revelation, there is much wringing of hands. Critics scold schools for breaking faith with their educational mission, and for failing to enforce the sanctity of "amateurism." Sportswriters denounce the NCAA for both tyranny and impotence in its quest to "clean up" college sports. Observers on all sides express jumbled emotions about youth and innocence, venting against professional mores or greedy amateurs.

For all the outrage, the real scandal is not that students are getting illegally paid or recruited, it's that two of the noble principles on which the NCAA justifies its existence—"amateurism" and the "student-athlete"—are cynical hoaxes, legalistic confections propagated by the universities so they can exploit the skills and fame of young athletes. The tragedy at the heart of college sports is not that some college athletes are getting paid, but that more of them are not.

Don Curtis, a UNC trustee, told me that impoverished football players cannot afford movie tickets or bus fare home. Curtis is a rarity among those in higher education today, in that he dares to violate the signal taboo: "I think we should pay these guys something."

Fans and educators alike recoil from this proposal as though from original sin. Amateurism is the whole point, they say. Paid athletes would destroy the integrity and appeal of college sports. Many former college athletes object that money would have spoiled the sanctity of the bond they enjoyed with their teammates. I, too, once shuddered instinctively at the notion of paid college athletes.

But after an inquiry that took me into locker rooms and ivory towers across the country, I have come to believe that sentiment blinds us to what's before our eyes. Big-time college sports are fully commercialized. Billions of dollars flow through them each year. The NCAA makes money, and enables universities and corporations to make money, from the unpaid labor of young athletes.

Slavery analogies should be used carefully. College athletes are not slaves. Yet to survey the scene—corporations and universities enriching themselves on the backs of uncompensated young men, whose status as "student-athletes" deprives them of the right to due process guaranteed by the Constitution—is to catch an unmistakable whiff of the plantation. Perhaps a more apt metaphor is colonialism: college sports, as overseen by the NCAA, is a system imposed by well-meaning paternalists and rationalized with hoary sentiments about caring for the well-being of the colonized. But it is, nonetheless, unjust. The NCAA, in its zealous defense of bogus principles, sometimes destroys the dreams of innocent young athletes.

The NCAA today is in many ways a classic cartel. Efforts to reform it—most notably by the three Knight Commissions over the course of 20 years—have, while making changes around the edges, been largely fruitless. The time has come for a major overhaul. And whether the powers that be like it or not, big changes are coming. Threats loom on multiple fronts: in Congress, the courts, breakaway athletic conferences, student rebellion, and public disgust. Swaddled in gauzy clichés, the NCAA presides over a vast, teetering glory.

Founding Myths

From the start, amateurism in college sports bas been honored more often in principle than in fact; the NCAA was built of a mixture of noble and venal impulses. In the late 19th century, intellectuals believed that the sporting arena simulated an impending age of Darwinian struggle. Because the United States did not hold a global empire like England's, leaders warned of national softness once railroads conquered the last continental frontier. As though heeding this warning, ingenious students turned variations on rugby into a toughening agent. Today a plaque in New Brunswick, New Jersey, commemorates the first college game, on November 6, 1869, when Rutgers beat Princeton 6–4.

Walter Camp graduated from Yale in 1880 so intoxicated by the sport that he devoted his life to it without pay, becoming "the father of American football." He persuaded other schools to reduce the chaos on the field by trimming each side from 15 players to 11, and it was his idea to paint measuring lines on the field. He conceived functional designations for players, coining terms such as *quarterback*. His game remained violent by design. Crawlers could push the ball forward beneath piles of flying elbows without pause until they cried "Down!" in submission.

In an 1892 game against its archrival, Yale, the Harvard football team was the first to deploy a "flying wedge," based on Napoleon's surprise concentrations of military force. In an editorial calling for the abolition of the play, *The New York Times* described it as "half a ton of bone and muscle coming into collision with a man weighing 160 or 170 pounds," noting that surgeons often had to be called onto the field. Three years later, the continuing mayhem prompted the Harvard faculty to take the first of two votes to abolish football. Charles Eliot, the university's president, brought up other concerns. "Deaths and injuries are not the strongest argument against football," declared Eliot. "That cheating and brutality are profitable is the main evil." Still, Harvard football persisted. In 1903, fervent alumni built Harvard Stadium with zero college funds. The team's first paid head coach, Bill Reid, started in 1905 at nearly twice the average salary for a full professor.

A newspaper story from that year, illustrated with the Grim Reaper laughing on a goalpost, counted 25 college players killed during football season. A fairy-tale version of the founding of the NCAA holds that President Theodore Roosevelt, upset by a photograph of a bloodied Swarthmore College player, vowed to civilize or destroy football. The real story is that Roosevelt maneuvered shrewdly to preserve the sport—and give a boost to his beloved Harvard. After *McClure's* magazine published a story on corrupt teams with phantom students, a muckraker exposed Walter Camp's $100,000 slush fund at Yale. In response to mounting outrage, Roosevelt summoned leaders from Harvard, Princeton, and Yale to the White House, where Camp parried mounting criticism and conceded nothing irresponsible in the college football rules he'd established. At Roosevelt's behest, the three schools issued a public statement that college sports must reform to survive, and representatives from 68 colleges founded a new organization that would soon be called the National Collegiate Athletic Association. A Haverford College official was confirmed as secretary but then promptly resigned in favor of Bill Reid, the new Harvard coach, who instituted new rules that benefited Harvard's playing style at the expense of Yale's. At a stroke, Roosevelt saved football and dethroned Yale.

For nearly 50 years, the NCAA, with no real authority and no staff to speak of, enshrined amateur ideals that it was helpless to enforce. (Not until 1939 did it gain the power even to mandate helmets.) In 1929, the Carnegie Foundation made headlines with a report, "American College Athletics," which concluded that the scramble for players had "reached the proportions of nationwide commerce." Of the 112 schools surveyed, 81 flouted NCAA recommendations with inducements to students ranging from open payrolls and disguised booster funds to no-show jobs at movie studios. Fans ignored the uproar, and two-thirds of the colleges mentioned told *The New York Times* that they planned no changes.

Embarrassed, the NCAA in 1948 enacted a "Sanity Code," which was supposed to prohibit all concealed and indirect benefits for college athletes; any money for athletes was to be limited to transparent scholarships awarded solely on financial need. Schools that violated this code would be expelled from NCAA membership and thus exiled from competitive sports.

This bold effort flopped. Colleges balked at imposing such a drastic penalty on each other, and the Sanity Code was repealed within a few years. The University of Virginia went so far as to call a press conference to say that if its athletes were ever accused of being paid, they should be forgiven, because their studies at Thomas Jefferson's university were so rigorous.

The Big Bluff

In 1951, the NCAA seized upon a serendipitous set of events to gain control of intercollegiate sports. First, the organization hired a young college dropout named Walter Byers as executive director. A journalist who was not yet 30 years old, he was an appropriately inauspicious choice for the vaguely defined new post. He wore cowboy boots and a toupee. He shunned personal contact, obsessed over details, and proved himself a bureaucratic master of pervasive, anonymous intimidation. Although discharged from the Army during World War II for defective vision, Byers was able to see an opportunity in two contemporaneous scandals. In one, the tiny College of William and Mary, aspiring to challenge football powers Oklahoma and Ohio State, was found to be counterfeiting grades to keep conspicuously pampered players eligible. In the other, a basketball point-shaving conspiracy (in which gamblers paid players to perform poorly) had spread from five New York colleges to the University of Kentucky, the reigning national champion, generating tabloid "perp" photos of gangsters and handcuffed basketball players. The scandals posed a crisis of credibility for collegiate athletics, and nothing in the NCAA's feeble record would have led anyone to expect real reform.

But Byers managed to impanel a small infractions board to set penalties without waiting for a full convention of NCAA schools, which would have been inclined toward forgiveness. Then he lobbied a University of Kentucky dean—A. D. Kirwan, a former football coach and future university president—not to contest the NCAA's dubious legal position (the association had no actual authority to penalize the university), pleading that college sports must do something to restore public support. His gambit succeeded when Kirwan reluctantly accepted a landmark precedent: the Kentucky basketball team would be suspended for the entire 1952–53 season. Its legendary coach, Adolph Rupp, fumed for a year in limbo.

The Kentucky case created an aura of centralized command for an NCAA office that barely existed. At the same time, a colossal misperception gave Byers leverage to mine gold. Amazingly in retrospect, most colleges and marketing experts considered the advent of television a dire threat to sports. Studies found that broadcasts reduced live attendance, and therefore gate receipts, because some customers preferred to watch at home for free. Nobody could yet imagine the revenue bonanza that television represented. With clunky new TV sets proliferating, the 1951 NCAA convention voted 161–7 to outlaw televised games except for a specific few licensed by the NCAA staff.

All but two schools quickly complied. The University of Pennsylvania and Notre Dame protested the order to break contracts for home-game television broadcasts, claiming the right to make their own decisions. Byers objected that such exceptions would invite disaster. The conflict escalated. Byers brandished penalties for games televised without approval. Penn contemplated seeking antitrust protection through the courts. Byers issued a contamination notice, informing any opponent scheduled to play Penn that it would be punished for showing up to compete. In effect, Byers mobilized the college world to isolate the two holdouts in what one sportswriter later called "the Big Bluff."

Byers won. Penn folded in part because its president, the perennial White House contender Harold Stassen, wanted to mend relations with fellow schools in the emerging Ivy League, which would be formalized in 1954. When Notre Dame also surrendered, Byers conducted exclusive negotiations with the new television networks on behalf of every college team. Joe Rauh Jr., a prominent civil-rights attorney, helped him devise a rationing system to permit only 11 broadcasts a year—the fabled *Game of the Week*. Byers and Rauh selected a few teams for television exposure, excluding the rest. On June 6, 1952, NBC signed a one-year deal to pay the NCAA $1.14 million for a carefully restricted football package. Byers routed all contractual proceeds through his office. He floated the idea that, to fund an NCAA infrastructure, his organization should take a 60 per cent cut; he accepted 12 per cent that season. (For later contracts, as the size of television revenues grew exponentially, he backed down to 5 percent.) Proceeds from the first NBC contract were enough to rent an NCAA headquarters, in Kansas City.

Only one year into his job, Byers had secured enough power and money to regulate all of college sports. Over the next decade, the NCAA's power grew along with television revenues. Through the efforts of Byers's deputy and chief lobbyist. Chuck Neinas, the NCAA won an important concession in the Sports Broadcasting Act of 1961, in which Congress made its granting of a precious antitrust exemption to the National Football League contingent upon the blackout of professional football on Saturdays. Deftly, without even mentioning the NCAA, a rider on the bill carved each weekend into protected broadcast markets: Saturday for college, Sunday for the NFL. The NFL got its antitrust exemption. Byers, having negotiated the NCAA's television package up to $3.1 million per football season—which was higher than the NFL's figure in those early years—had made the NCAA into a spectacularly profitable cartel.

"We Eat What We Kill"

The NCAA's control of college sports still rested on a fragile base, however: the consent of the colleges and universities it governed. For a time, the vast sums of television money delivered to these institutions through Byers's deals made them willing to submit. But the big football powers grumbled about the portion of the television revenue diverted to nearly a thousand NCAA member schools that lacked major athletic programs. They chafed against cost-cutting measures—such as restrictions on team size—designed to help smaller schools. "I don't want Hofstra telling Texas how to play football," Darrell Royal, the Longhorns coach, griped. By the 1970s and '80s, as college football games delivered bonanza ratings—and advertising revenue—to the networks, some of the big football schools began to wonder: Why do we need to have our television coverage brokered through the NCAA? Couldn't we get a bigger cut of that TV money by dealing directly with the networks?

Byers faced a rude internal revolt. The NCAA's strongest legions, its big football schools, defected en masse. Calling the NCAA a price-fixing cartel that siphoned every television dollar through its coffers, in 1981 a rogue consortium of 61 major football schools threatened to sign an independent contract with NBC for $180 million over four years.

With a huge chunk of the NCAA's treasury walking out the door, Byers threatened sanctions, as he had against Penn and Notre Dame three decades earlier. But this time the universities of Georgia and Oklahoma responded with an antitrust suit. "It is virtually impossible to overstate the degree of our resentment … of the NCAA," said William Banowsky, the president of the University of Oklahoma. In the landmark

1984 *NCAA v. Board of Regents of the University of Oklahoma* decision, the U.S. Supreme Court struck down the NCAA's latest football contracts with television—and any future ones—as an illegal restraint of trade that harmed colleges and viewers. Overnight, the NCAA's control of the television market for football vanished. Upholding Banowsky's challenge to the NCAA's authority, the *Regents* decision freed the football schools to sell any and all games the markets would bear. Coaches and administrators no longer had to share the revenue generated by their athletes with smaller schools outside the football consortium. "We eat what we kill," one official at the University of Texas bragged.

A few years earlier, this blow might have financially crippled the NCAA—but a rising tide of money from basketball concealed the structural damage of the *Regents* decision. During the 1980s, income from the March Madness college basketball tournament, paid directly by the television networks to the NCAA, grew tenfold. The windfall covered and then far exceeded—what the organization had lost from football.

Still, Byers never forgave his former deputy Chuck Neinas for leading the rebel consortium. He knew that Neinas had seen from the inside how tenuous the NCAA's control really was, and how diligently Byers had worked to prop up its Oz-like façade. During Byers's tenure, the rule book for Division I athletes grew to 427 pages of scholastic detail. His NCAA personnel manual banned conversations around water coolers, and coffee cups on desks, while specifying exactly when drapes must be drawn at the NCAA's 27,000-square-foot headquarters near Kansas City (built in 1973 from the proceeds of a 1 per cent surtax on football contracts). It was as though, having lost control where it mattered, Byers pedantically exerted more control where it didn't.

After retiring in 1987, Byers let slip his suppressed fury that the ingrate football conferences, having robbed the NCAA of television revenue, still expected it to enforce amateurism rules and police every leak of funds to college players. A lethal greed was "gnawing at the innards of college athletics," he wrote in his memoir. When Byers renounced the NCAA's pretense of amateurism, his former colleagues would stare blankly, as though he had gone senile or, as he wrote, "desecrated my sacred vows." But Byers was better positioned than anyone else to argue that college football's claim to amateurism was unfounded. Years later, as we will see, lawyers would seize upon his words to do battle with the NCAA.

Meanwhile, reformers fretted that commercialism was hurting college sports, and that higher education's historical balance between academics and athletics had been distorted by all the money sloshing around. News stories revealed that schools went to extraordinary measures to keep academically incompetent athletes eligible for competition, and would vie for the most-sought-after high-school players by proffering under-the-table payments. In 1991, the first Knight Commission report, "Keeping Faith With the Student Athlete," was published; the commission's "bedrock conviction" was that university presidents must seize control of the NCAA from athletic directors in order to restore the preeminence of academic values over athletic or commercial ones. In response, college presidents did take over the NCAA's governance. But by 2001, when the second Knight Commission report ("A Call to Action: Reconnecting College Sports and Higher Education") was issued, a new generation of reformers was admitting that problems of corruption and commercialism had "grown rather than diminished" since the first report. Meanwhile the NCAA itself, revenues rising, had moved into a $50 million, 116,000-square-foot headquarters in Indianapolis. By 2010, as the size of NCAA headquarters increased yet again with a 130,000-square-foot expansion, a third Knight Commission was groping blindly for a hold on independent college-athletic conferences that were behaving more like sovereign pro leagues than confederations of universities. And still more money continued to flow into NCAA coffers. With the basketball tournament's 2011 television deal, annual March Madness broadcast revenues had skyrocketed 50-fold in less than 30 years.

The Myth of the "Student-Athlete"

Today, much of the NCAA's moral authority—indeed much of the justification for its existence—is vested in its claim to protect what it calls the "student-athlete." The term is meant to conjure the nobility of amateurism, and the precedence of scholarship over athletic endeavor. But the origins of the "student-athlete" lie not in a disinterested ideal but in a sophistic formulation designed, as the sports economist Andrew Zimbalist has written, to help the NCAA in its "fight against workmen's compensation insurance claims for injured football players."

"We crafted the term *student-athlete*," Walter Byers himself wrote, "and soon it was embedded in all NCAA rules and interpretations." The term came into play in the 1950s, when the widow of Ray Dennison, who had died from a head injury received while playing football in Colorado for the Fort Lewis A&M Aggies, filed for workmen's-compensation death benefits. Did his football scholarship make the fatal collision a "work-related" accident? Was he a school employee, like his peers who worked part-time as teaching assistants and bookstore cashiers? Or was he a fluke victim of extracurricular pursuits? Given the hundreds of incapacitating injuries to college athletes each year, the answers to these questions had enormous consequences. The Colorado Supreme Court ultimately agreed with the school's contention that he was not eligible for benefits, since the college was "not in the football business."

The term *student-athlete* was deliberately ambiguous. College players were not students at play (which might understate their athletic obligations), nor were they just athletes in college (which might imply they were professionals). That they were high-performance athletes meant they could be forgiven for not meeting the academic standards of their peers; that they were students meant they did not have to be compensated, ever, for anything more than the cost of their studies. *Student-athlete* became the NCAA's signature term, repeated constantly in and out of courtrooms.

Using the "student-athlete" defense, colleges have compiled a string of victories in liability cases. On the afternoon of October 26, 1974, the Texas Christian University Horned Frogs were playing the Alabama Crimson Tide in Birmingham, Alabama. Kent Waldrep, a TCU running back, carried the ball on a "Red Right 28" sweep toward the Crimson Tide's sideline, where he was met by a swarm of tacklers. When Waldrep regained consciousness. Bear Bryant, the storied Crimson Tide coach, was standing over his hospital bed. "It was like talking to God, if you're a young football player," Waldrep recalled.

Waldrep was paralyzed: he had lost all movement and feeling below his neck. After nine months of paying his medical bills, Texas Christian refused to pay any more, so the Waldrep family coped for years on dwindling charity.

Through the 1990s, from his wheelchair, Waldrep pressed a lawsuit for workers' compensation. (He also, through heroic rehabilitation efforts, recovered feeling in his arms, and eventually learned to drive a specially rigged van. "I can brush my teeth," he told me last year, "but I still need help to bathe and dress.") His attorneys haggled with TCU and the state worker-compensation fund over what constituted employment. Clearly, TCU had provided football players with equipment for the job, as a typical employer would—but did the university pay wages, withhold income taxes on his financial aid, or control work conditions and performance? The appeals court finally rejected Waldrep's claim in June of 2000, ruling that he was not an employee because he had not paid taxes on financial aid that he could have kept even if he quit football. (Waldrep told me school officials "said they recruited me as a student, not an athlete," which he says was absurd.)

The long saga vindicated the power of the NCAA's "student athlete" formulation as a shield, and the organization continues to invoke it as both a legalistic defense and a noble ideal. Indeed, such is the term's rhetorical power that it is increasingly used as a sort of reflexive mantra against charges of rabid hypocrisy.

Last Thanksgiving weekend, with both the FBI and the NCAA investigating whether Cam Newton had been lured onto his team with illegal payments, Newton's Auburn Tigers and the Alabama Crimson Tide came together for their annual game, known as the Iron Bowl, before 101,821 fans at Bryant-Denny Stadium. This game is always a highlight of the football season because of the historic rivalry between the two schools, and the 2010 edition had enormous significance, pitting the defending national champion Crimson Tide against the undefeated Tigers, who were aiming for their first championship since 1957. I expected excited fans; what I encountered was the throbbing heart of college sports. As I drove before daybreak toward the stadium, a sleepless caller babbled over WJOX, the local fan radio station, that he "couldn't stop thinking about the coin toss." In the parking lot, ticketless fans were puzzled that anyone need ask why they had tailgated for days just to watch their satellite-fed flat screens within earshot of the roar. All that morning, pilgrims packed the Bear Bryant museum, where displays elaborated the misery of Alabama's 4–24 run before the glorious Bryant era dawned in 1958.

Finally, as Auburn took the field for warm-ups, one of Alabama's public-address-system operators played "Take the Money and Run" (an act for which he would be fired). A sea of signs reading $CAM taunted Newton. The game, perhaps the most exciting of the season, was unbearably tense, with Auburn coming from way behind to win 28–27, all but assuring that it would go on to play for the national championship. Days later, Auburn suspended Newton after the NCAA found that a rules violation had occurred: his father was alleged to have marketed his son in a pay-for-play scheme; a day after that, the NCAA reinstated Newton's eligibility because investigators had not found evidence that Newton or Auburn officials had known of his father's actions. This left Newton conveniently eligible for the Southeastern Conference championship game and for the postseason BCS championship bowl. For the NCAA, prudence meant honoring public demand.

"Our championships," NCAA President Mark Emmert has declared, "are one of the primary tools we have to enhance the student-athlete experience."

"Whoremasters"

NCAA V. Regents left the NCAA devoid of television football revenue and almost wholly dependent on March Madness basketball. It is rich but insecure. Last year, CBS Sports and Turner Broadcasting paid $771 million to the NCAA for television rights to the 2011 men's basketball tournament alone. That's three-quarters of a billion dollars built on the backs of amateurs—on unpaid labor. The whole edifice depends on the players' willingness to perform what is effectively volunteer work. The athletes, and the league officials, are acutely aware of this extraordinary arrangement. William Friday, the former North Carolina president, recalls being yanked from one Knight Commission meeting and sworn to secrecy about what might happen if a certain team made the NCAA championship basketball game. "They were going to dress and go out on the floor," Friday told me, "but refuse to play," in a wildcat student strike. Skeptics doubted such a diabolical plot. These were college kids—unlikely to second-guess their coaches, let alone forfeit the dream of a championship. Still, it was unnerving to contemplate what hung on the consent of a few young volunteers: several hundred million dollars in television revenue, countless livelihoods, the NCAA budget, and subsidies for sports at more than 1,000 schools. Friday's informants exhaled when the suspect team lost before the finals.

Cognizant of its precarious financial base, the NCAA has in recent years begun to pursue new sources of revenue. Taking its cue from member schools such as Ohio State (which in 2009 bundled all its promotional rights—souvenirs, stadium ads, shoe deals—and outsourced them to the international sports marketer IMG College for a guaranteed $11 million a year), the NCAA began to exploit its vault of college sports on film. For $29.99 apiece, NCAA On Demand offers DVDs of more than 200 memorable contests in men's ice hockey alone. Video-game technology also allows nostalgic fans to relive and even participate in classic moments of NCAA Basketball. NCAA Football, licensed by the NCAA through IMG College to Electronic Arts, one of the world's largest video-game manufacturers, reportedly sold 2.5 million copies in 2008. Brit Kirwan, the chancellor of the Maryland university system and a former president at Ohio State, says there were "terrible fights" between the third Knight Commission and the NCAA over the ethics of generating this revenue.

All of this money ultimately derives from the college athletes whose likenesses are shown in the films or video games. But none of the profits go to them. Last year. Electronic Arts paid more than $35 million in royalties to the NFL players union for the underlying value of names and images in its pro football series—but neither the NCAA nor its affiliated companies paid former college players a nickel. Naturally, as they have become more of a profit center for the NCAA, some of the vaunted "student-athletes" have begun to clamor that they deserve a share of those profits. You "see everybody getting richer and richer," Desmond Howard, who won the 1991 Heisman Trophy while playing for the Michigan Wolverines, told *USA Today* recently. "And you walk around and you can't put gas in your car? You can't even fly home to see your parents?"

Some athletes have gone beyond talk. A series of lawsuits quietly making their way through the courts cast a harsh light on the absurdity of the system—and threaten to dislodge the foundations on which the NCAA rests. On July 21, 2009, lawyers for Ed O'Bannon filed a class-action antitrust suit against the NCAA at the U.S. District Court in San Francisco. "Once you leave your university," says O'Bannon, who won the John Wooden Award for player of the year in 1995 on UCLA's national-championship basketball team, "one would think your likeness belongs to you." The NCAA and UCLA continue to collect money from the sales of videos of him playing. But by NCAA rules, O'Bannon, who today works at a Toyota dealership near Las Vegas, alleges he is still not allowed to share the revenue the NCAA generates from his own image as a college athlete. His suit quickly gathered co-plaintiffs from basketball and football, ex-players featured in NCAA videos and other products. "The NCAA does not license student-athlete likenesses," NCAA spokesperson Erik Christianson told *The New York Times* in response to the suit, "or prevent former student-athletes from attempting to do so. Likewise, to claim the NCAA profits off student-athlete likenesses is also pure fiction."

The legal contention centers on Part IV of the NCAA's "Student-Athlete Statement" for Division I, which requires every athlete to authorize use of "your name or picture ... to promote NCAA championships or other NCAA events, activities or programs." Does this clause mean that athletes clearly renounce personal interest forever? If so, does it actually undermine the NCAA by implicitly recognizing that athletes have a property right in their own performance? Jon King, a lawyer for the plaintiffs, expects the NCAA's core mission of amateurism to be its "last defense standing."

In theory, the NCAA's passion to protect the noble amateurism of college athletes should prompt it to focus on head coaches in the high-revenue sports—basketball and football—since holding the top official accountable should most efficiently discourage corruption. The problem is that the coaches' growing power has rendered them, unlike their players, ever more immune to oversight. According to research by Charles Clotfelter, an economist at Duke, the average compensation for head football coaches at public universities, now more than $2 million, has grown 750 per cent (adjusted for inflation) since the *Regents* decision in 1984; that's more than 20 times the cumulative 32 per cent raise for college professors. For top basketball coaches, annual contracts now exceed $4 million, augmented by assorted bonuses, endorsements, country-club memberships, the occasional private plane, and in some cases a negotiated percentage of ticket receipts. (Oregon's ticket concessions netted former football coach Mike Bellotti an additional $631,000 in 2005.)

The NCAA rarely tangles with such people, who are apt to fight back and win. When Rick Neuheisel, the head football coach of the Washington Huskies, was punished for petty gambling (in a March Madness pool, as it happened), he sued the NCAA and the university for wrongful termination, collected $4.5 million, and later moved on to UCLA. When the NCAA tried to cap assistant coaches' entering salary at a mere $16,000, nearly 2,000 of them brought an antitrust suit, *Law V. NCAA,* and in 1999 settled for $54.5 million. Since then, salaries for assistant coaches have commonly exceeded $200,000, with the top assistants in the SEC averaging $700,000. In 2009, Monte Kiffin, then at the University of Tennessee, became the first assistant coach to reach $1 million, plus benefits.

The late Myles Brand, who led the NCAA from 2003 to 2009, defended the economics of college sports by claiming that they were simply the result of a smoothly functioning free market. He and his colleagues deflected criticism about the money saturating big-time college sports by focusing attention on scapegoats; in 2010, outrage targeted sports agents. Last year *Sports Illustrated* published "Confessions of an Agent," a firsthand account of dealing with high-strung future pros whom the agent and his peers courted with flattery, cash, and tawdry favors. Nick Saban, Alabama's head football coach, mobilized his peers to denounce agents as a public scourge. "I hate to say this," he said, "but how are they any better than a pimp? I have no respect for people who do that to young people. None."

Saban's raw condescension contrasts sharply with the lonely penitence from Dale Brown, the retired longtime basketball coach at LSU. "Look at the money we make off predominantly poor black kids," Brown once reflected. "We're the whoremasters."

"Picayune Rules"

NCAA officials have tried to assert their dominion—and distract attention from the larger issues—by chasing frantically after petty violations. Tom McMillen, a former member of the Knight Commission who was an All-American basketball player at the University of Maryland, likens these officials to traffic cops in a speed trap, who could flag down almost any passing motorist for prosecution in kangaroo court under a "maze of picayune rules." The publicized cases have become convoluted soap operas. At the start of the 2010 football season, A. J. Green, a wide receiver at Georgia, confessed that he'd sold his own jersey from the Independence Bowl the year before, to raise cash for a spring-break vacation. The NCAA sentenced Green to a four-game suspension for violating his amateur status with the illicit profit generated by selling the shirt off his own back. While he served the suspension, the Georgia Bulldogs store continued legally selling replicas of Green's No. 8 jersey for $39.95 and up.

A few months later, the NCAA investigated rumors that Ohio State football players had benefited from "hook-ups on tatts"—that is, that they'd gotten free or underpriced tattoos at an Ohio tattoo parlor in exchange for autographs and memorabilia—a violation of the NCAA's rule against discounts linked to athletic personae. The NCAA Committee on Infractions imposed five-game suspensions on Terrelle Pryor, Ohio State's tattooed quarterback, and four other players (some of whom had been found to have sold their Big Ten championship rings and other gear), but did permit them to finish the season and play in the Sugar Bowl. (This summer, in an attempt to satisfy NCAA investigators, Ohio State voluntarily vacated its football wins from last season, as well as its Sugar Bowl victory.) A different NCAA committee promulgated a rule banning symbols and messages in players' eye black—reportedly aimed at Pryor's controversial gesture of support for the pro quarterback Michael Vick, and at Bible verses inscribed in the eye black of the former Florida quarterback Tim Tebow.

The moral logic is hard to fathom: the NCAA bans personal messages on the bodies of the players, and penalizes players for trading their celebrity status for discounted tattoos—but it codifies precisely how and where commercial insignia from multinational corporations can be displayed on college players, for the financial benefit of the colleges. Last season, while the NCAA investigated him and his father for the recruiting fees they'd allegedly sought, Cam Newton compliantly wore at least 15 corporate logos—one on his jersey, four on his helmet visor, one on each wristband, one on his pants, six on his shoes, and one on the headband he wears under his helmet—as part of Auburn's $10.6 million deal with Under Armour.

"Resitution"

Obscure NCAA rules have bedeviled Scott Boras, the preeminent sports agent for Major League Baseball stars, in cases that may ultimately prove more threatening to the NCAA than Ed O'Bannon's antitrust suit. In 2008, Andrew Oliver, a sophomore pitcher for the Oklahoma State Cowboys, had been listed as the 12th-best professional prospect among sophomore players nationally. He decided to dismiss the two attorneys who had represented him out of high school, Robert and Tim Baratta, and retain Boras instead. Infuriated, the Barattas sent a spiteful letter to the NCAA. Oliver didn't learn about this until the night before he was scheduled to pitch in the regional final for a place in the College World Series, when an NCAA investigator showed up to question him in the presence of lawyers for Oklahoma State. The investigator also questioned his father, Dave, a truck driver.

Had Tim Baratta been present in their home when the Minnesota Twins offered $390,000 for Oliver to sign out of high school? A *yes* would mean trouble. While the NCAA did not forbid all professional advice—indeed, *Baseball America* used to publish the names of agents representing draft-likely underclassmen—NCAA Bylaw 12.3.2.1 prohibited actual negotiation with any professional team by an adviser, on pain of disqualification for the college athlete. The questioning lasted past midnight.

Just hours before the game was to start the next day, Oklahoma State officials summoned Oliver to tell him he would not be pitching. Only later did he learn that the university feared that by letting him play while the NCAA adjudicated his case, the university would open not only the baseball team but all other Oklahoma State teams to broad punishment under the NCAA's "restitution rule" (Bylaw 19.7), under which the NCAA threatens schools with sanctions if they obey any temporary court order benefiting a college athlete, should that order eventually be modified or removed. The baseball coach did not even let his ace tell his teammates the sad news in person. "He said, 'It's probably not a good idea for you to be at the game,'" Oliver recalls.

The Olivers went home to Ohio to find a lawyer. Rick Johnson, a solo practitioner specializing in legal ethics, was aghast that the Baratta brothers had turned in their own client to the NCAA, divulging attorney-client details likely to invite wrath upon Oliver. But for the next 15 months, Johnson directed his litigation against the two NCAA bylaws at issue. Judge Tygh M. Tone, of Erie County, came to share his outrage. On February 12, 2009, Tone struck down the ban on lawyers negotiating for student-athletes as a capricious, exploitative attempt by a private association to "dictate to an attorney where, what, how, or when he should represent his client," violating accepted legal practice in every state. He also struck down the NCAA's restitution rule as an intimidation that attempted to supersede the judicial system. Finally, Judge Tone ordered the NCAA to reinstate Oliver's eligibility at Oklahoma State for his junior season, which started several days later.

The NCAA sought to disqualify Oliver again, with several appellate motions to stay "an unprecedented Order purporting to void a fundamental Bylaw." Oliver did get to pitch that season, but he dropped into the second round of the June 2009 draft, signing for considerably less than if he'd been picked earlier. Now 23, Oliver says sadly that the whole experience "made me grow up a little quicker." His lawyer claimed victory. "Andy Oliver is the first college athlete ever to win against the NCAA in court," said Rick Johnson.

Yet the victory was only temporary. Wounded, the NCAA fought back with a vengeance. Its battery of lawyers prepared for a damages trial, ultimately overwhelming Oliver's side eight months later with an offer to resolve the dispute for $750,000. When Oliver and Johnson accepted, to extricate themselves ahead of burgeoning legal costs. Judge Tone was compelled to vacate his orders as part of the final settlement. This freed NCAA officials to reassert the two bylaws that Judge Tone had so forcefully overturned, and they moved swiftly to ramp up rather than curtail enforcement. First, the NCAA's Eligibility Center devised a survey for every drafted undergraduate athlete who sought to stay in college another year. The survey asked whether an agent had conducted negotiations. It also requested a signed release waiving privacy rights and authorizing professional teams to disclose details of any interaction to the NCAA Eligibility Center. Second, NCAA enforcement officials went after another Scott Boras client.

The Toronto Blue Jays had made the left handed pitcher James Paxton, of the University of Kentucky, the 37th pick in the 2009 draft. Paxton decided to reject a reported $1 million offer and return to school for his senior year, pursuing a dream to pitch for his team in the College World Series. But then he ran into the new NCAA survey. Had Boras negotiated with the Blue Jays? Boras has denied that he did, but it would have made sense that he had—that was his job, to test the market for his client. But saying so would get Paxton banished under the same NCAA bylaw that had derailed Andrew Oliver's career. Since Paxton was planning to go back to school and not accept their draft offer, the Blue Jays no longer had any incentive to protect him—indeed, they had every incentive to turn him in. The Blue Jays' president, by telling reporters that Boras had negotiated on Paxton's behalf, demonstrated to future recruits and other teams that they could use the NCAA's rules to punish college players who wasted their draft picks by returning to college. The NCAA's enforcement staff raised the pressure by requesting to interview Paxton.

Though Paxton had no legal obligation to talk to an investigator, NCAA Bylaw 10.1(j) specified that anything short of complete cooperation could be interpreted as unethical conduct, affecting his amateur status. Under its restitution rule, the NCAA had leverage to compel the University of Kentucky to ensure obedience.

As the 2010 season approached, Gary Henderson, the Kentucky coach, sorely wanted Paxton, one of *Baseball America's* top-ranked players, to return. Rick Johnson, Andrew Oliver's lawyer, filed for a declaratory judgment on Paxton's behalf, arguing that the state constitution—plus the university's code of student conduct—barred arbitrary discipline at the request of a third party. Kentucky courts deferred to the university, however, and Paxton was suspended from the team. "Due to the possibility of future penalties, including forfeiture of games," the university stated, it "could not put the other 32 players of the team and the entire UK 22-sport intercollegiate athletics department at risk by having James compete." The NCAA appraised the result with satisfaction. "When negotiations occur on behalf of student-athletes," Erik Christianson, the NCAA spokesperson, told *The New York Times* in reference to the Oliver case, "those negotiations indicate that the student-athlete intends to become a professional athlete and no longer remain an amateur."

Paxton was stranded. Not only could he not play for Kentucky, but his draft rights with the Blue Jays had lapsed for the year, meaning he could not play for any minor-league affiliate of Major League Baseball. Boras wrangled a holdover job for him in Texas with the independent Grand Prairie Air-Hogs, pitching against the Pensacola Pelicans and Wichita Wingnuts. Once projected to be a first-round draft pick, Paxton saw his stock plummet into the fourth round. He remained unsigned until late in spring training, when he signed with the Seattle Mariners and reported to their minor-league camp in Peoria, Arizona.

"You Might as Well Shoot Them in the Head"

"When you dream about playing in college," Joseph Agnew told me not long ago, "you don't ever think about being in a lawsuit." Agnew, a student at Rice University in Houston, had been cut from the football team and had his scholarship revoked by Rice before his senior year, meaning that he faced at least $35,000 in tuition and other bills if he wanted to complete his degree in sociology. Bereft of his scholarship, he was flailing about for help when he discovered the National College Players Association, which claims 7,000 active members and seeks modest reforms such as safety guidelines and better death benefits for college athletes. Agnew was struck by the NCPA scholarship data on players from top Division I basketball teams, which showed that 22 per cent were not renewed from 2008 to 2009—the same fate he had suffered.

In October 2010, Agnew filed a class action antitrust suit over the cancellation of his scholarship and to remove the cap on the total number of scholarships that can be awarded by NCAA schools. In his suit, Agnew did not claim the right to free tuition. He merely asked the federal court to strike down an NCAA rule, dating to 1973, that prohibited colleges and universities from offering any athletic scholarship longer than a one-year commitment, to be renewed or not, unilaterally, by the school—which in practice means that coaches get to decide each year whose scholarships to renew or cancel. (After the coach who had recruited Agnew had moved on to Tulsa, the new Rice coach switched Agnew's scholarship to a recruit of his own.) Agnew argued that without the one year rule, he would have been free to bargain with all eight colleges that had recruited him, and each college could have decided how long to guarantee his scholarship.

Agnew's suit rested on a claim of an NCAA antitrust violation combined with a laudable academic goal—making it possible for students to finish their educations. Around the same time, lawyers from President Obama's Justice Department initiated a series of meetings with NCAA officials and universities in which they asked what possible educational rationale there was for allowing the NCAA—an organization that did not itself pay for scholarships—to impose a blanket restriction on the length of scholarships offered by colleges. Tidbits leaked into the press. In response, the NCAA contended that an athletic scholarship was a "merit award" that should be reviewed annually, presumably because the degree of "merit" could change. Justice Department lawyers reportedly suggested that a free market in scholarships would expand learning opportunities in accord with the stated rationale for the NCAA's tax-exempt status—that it promotes education through athletics. The one-year rule effectively allows colleges to cut underperforming "student-athletes," just as pro sports teams cut their players. "Plenty of them don't stay in school," said one of Agnew's lawyers, Stuart Paynter. "They're just gone. You might as well shoot them in the head."

Agnew's lawsuit has made him a pariah to former friends in the athletic department at Rice, where everyone identified so thoroughly with the NCAA that they seemed to feel he was attacking them personally. But if the premise of Agnew's case is upheld by the courts, it will make a sham of the NCAA's claim that its highest priority is protecting education.

"The Want to Crush These Kids"

Academic performance has always been difficult for the NCAA to address. Any detailed regulation would intrude upon the free choice of widely varying schools, and any academic standard broad enough to fit both MIT and Ole Miss would have little force. From time to time, a scandal will expose extreme lapses. In 1989, Dexter Manley, by then the famous "Secretary of Defense" for the NFL's Washington Redskins, teared up before the U.S. Senate Subcommittee on Education, Arts, and Humanities, when admitting that he had been functionally illiterate in college.

Within big-time college athletic departments, the financial pressure to disregard obvious academic shortcomings and shortcuts is just too strong. In the 1980s, Jan Kemp, an English instructor at the University of Georgia, publicly alleged that university officials had demoted and then fired her because she refused to inflate grades in her remedial English courses. Documents showed that administrators replaced the grades she'd given athletes with higher ones, providing fake passing grades on one notable occasion to nine Bulldog football players who otherwise would have been ineligible to compete in the 1982 Sugar Bowl. (Georgia lost anyway, 24–20, to a University of Pittsburgh team led by the future Hall of Fame quarterback Dan Marino.) When Kemp filed a lawsuit against the university, she was publicly vilified as a troublemaker, but she persisted bravely in her testimony. Once, Kemp said, a supervisor demanding that she fix a grade had bellowed, "Who do you think is more important to this university, you or Dominique Wilkins?" (Wilkins was a star on the basketball team.) Traumatized, Kemp twice attempted suicide.

In trying to defend themselves, Georgia officials portrayed Kemp as naive about sports. "We have to compete on a level playing field," said Fred Davison, the university president. During the Kemp civil trial, in 1986, Hale Almand, Georgia's defense lawyer, explained the university's patronizing aspirations for its typical less-than-scholarly athlete. "We may not make a university student out of him," Almand told the court, "but if we can teach him to read and write, maybe he can work at the post office rather than as a garbage man when he gets through with his athletic career." This argument backfired with the jurors: finding in favor of Kemp, they rejected her polite request for $100,000, and awarded her $2.6 million in damages instead. (This was later reduced to $1.08 million.) Jan Kemp embodied what is ostensibly the NCAA's reason for being—to enforce standards fairly and put studies above sports—but no one from the organization ever spoke up on her behalf.

ঌঌঌ

The NCAA body charged with identifying violations of any of the Division I league rules, the Committee on Infractions, operates in the shadows. Josephine Potuto, a professor of law at the University of Nebraska and a longtime committee member who was then serving as its vice chair, told Congress in 2004 that one reason her group worked in secret was that it hoped to avoid a "media circus." The committee preferred to deliberate in private, she said, guiding member schools to punish themselves. "The enforcement process is cooperative, not adversarial," Potuto testified. The committee consisted of an elite coterie of judges, athletic directors, and authors of legal treatises. "The committee also is savvy about intercollegiate athletics," she added. "They cannot be conned."

In 2009, a series of unlikely circumstances peeled back the veil of secrecy to reveal NCAA procedures so contorted that even victims marveled at their comical wonder. The saga began in March of 2007, shortly after the Florida State Seminoles basketball team was knocked out of the NIT basketball tournament, which each spring invites the best teams not selected for the March Madness tournament. At an athletic-department study hall, Al Thornton, a star forward for the team, completed a sports-psychology quiz but then abandoned it without posting his written answers electronically by computer. Brenda Monk, an academic tutor for the Seminoles, says she noticed the error and asked a teammate to finish entering Thornton's answers onscreen and hit "submit," as required for credit. The teammate complied, steaming silently, and then complained at the athletic office about getting stuck with clean-up chores for the superstar Thornton (who was soon to be selected by the Los Angeles Clippers in the first round of the NBA draft). Monk promptly resigned when questioned by FSU officials, saying her fatigue at the time could not excuse her asking the teammate to submit the answers to another student's completed test.

Monk's act of guileless responsibility set off a chain reaction. First, FSU had to give the NCAA preliminary notice of a confessed academic fraud. Second, because this would be its seventh major infraction case since 1968, FSU mounted a vigorous self-investigation to demonstrate compliance with NCAA academic rules. Third, interviews with 129 Seminoles athletes unleashed a nightmare of matter-of-fact replies about absentee professors who allowed group consultations and unlimited retakes of open-computer assignments and tests. Fourth, FSU suspended 61 of its athletes in 10 sports. Fifth, the infractions committee applied the byzantine NCAA bylaws to FSU's violations. Sixth, one of the penalties announced in March of 2009 caused a howl of protest across the sports universe.

Twenty-seven news organizations filed a lawsuit in hopes of finding out how and why the NCAA proposed to invalidate 14 prior victories in FSU football. Such a penalty, if upheld, would doom coach Bobby Bowden's chance of overtaking Joe Paterno of Penn State for the most football wins in Division I history. This was sacrosanct territory. Sports reporters followed the litigation for six months, reporting that 25 of the 61 suspended FSU athletes were football players, some of whom were ruled ineligible retroactively from the time they had heard or yelled out answers to online test questions in, of all things, a music-appreciation course.

When reporters sought access to the transcript of the infractions committee's hearing in Indianapolis, NCAA lawyers said the 695-page document was private. (The NCAA claimed it was entitled to keep all such records secret because of a landmark Supreme Court ruling that it had won in 1988, in *NCAA V. Tarkanian,* which exempted the organization from any due-process obligations because it was not a government organization.) Media outlets pressed the judge to let Florida State share its own copy of the hearing transcript, whereupon NCAA lawyers objected that the school had never actually "possessed" the document; it had only seen the transcript via a defendant's guest access to the carefully restricted NCAA website. This claim, in turn, prompted intercession on the side of the media by Florida's attorney general, arguing that letting the NCAA use a technical loophole like this would undermine the state's sunshine law mandating open public records. After tumultuous appeals, the Florida courts agreed and ordered the NCAA transcript released in October of 2009.

News interest quickly evaporated when the sports media found nothing in the record about Coach Bowden or the canceled football victories. But the transcript revealed plenty about the NCAA. On page 37, T. K. Wetherell, the bewildered Florida State president, lamented that his university had hurt itself by cooperating with the investigation. "We self-reported this case," he said during the hearing, and he later complained that the most ingenuous athletes—those who asked "What's the big deal, this happens all the time?"—received the harshest suspensions, while those who clammed up on the advice of lawyers went free. The music-appreciation professor was apparently never questioned. Brenda Monk, the only instructor who consistently cooperated with the investigation, appeared voluntarily to explain her work with learning-disabled athletes, only to be grilled about her credentials by Potuto in a pettifogging inquisition of remarkable stamina.

In January of last year, the NCAA's Infractions Appeals Committee sustained all the sanctions imposed on FSU except the number of vacated football victories, which it dropped, ex cathedra, from 14 to 12. The final penalty locked Bobby Bowden's official win total on retirement at 377 instead of 389, behind Joe Paterno's 401 (and counting). This carried stinging symbolism for fans, without bringing down on the NCAA the harsh repercussions it would have risked if it had issued a television ban or substantial fine.

Cruelly, but typically, the NCAA concentrated public censure on powerless scapegoats. A dreaded "show cause" order rendered Brenda Monk, the tutor, effectively unhirable at any college in the United States. Cloaking an old-fashioned blackball in the stately language of law, the order gave notice that any school hiring Monk before a specified date in 2013 "shall, pursuant to the provisions of Bylaw 19.5.2.2(1), show cause why it should not be penalized if it does not restrict the former learning specialist [Monk] from having any contact with student-athletes." Today she works as an education supervisor at a prison in Florida.

❧❧❧

The Florida State verdict hardly surprised Rick Johnson, the lawyer who had represented the college pitchers Andrew Oliver and James Paxton. "All the NCAA's enforcements are random and selective," he told me, calling the organization's appeals process a travesty. (Johnson says the NCAA has never admitted to having wrongly suspended an athlete.) Johnson's scalding experience prompted him to undertake a law-review article on the subject, which in turn sent him trawling through NCAA archives. From the summary tax forms required of nonprofits, he found out that the NCAA had spent nearly $1 million chartering private jets in 2006. "What kind of nonprofit organization leases private jets?," Johnson asks. It's hard to determine from tax returns what money goes where, but it looks as if the NCAA spent less than 1 per cent of its budget on enforcement that year. Even after its plump cut for its own overhead, the NCAA dispersed huge sums to its 1,200 member schools, in the manner of a professional sports league. These annual payments are universal—every college gets something—but widely uneven. They keep the disparate shareholders (barely) united and speaking for all of college sports. The payments coerce unity within the structure of a private association that is unincorporated and unregulated, exercising amorphous powers not delegated by any government.

Searching through the archives, Johnson came across a 1973 memo from the NCAA general counsel recommending the adoption of a due-process procedure for athletes in disciplinary cases. Without it, warned the organization's lawyer, the association risked big liability claims for deprivation of rights. His proposal went nowhere. Instead, apparently to limit costs to the universities, Walter Byers had implemented the year-by-year scholarship rule that Joseph Agnew would challenge in court 37 years later. Moreover, the NCAA's 1975 convention adopted a second recommendation "to discourage legal actions against the NCAA," according to the minutes. The members voted to create Bylaw 19.7, Restitution, to intimidate college athletes in disputes with the NCAA. Johnson recognized this provision all too well, having won the temporary court judgment that the rule was illegal if not downright despotic. It made him nearly apoplectic to learn that the NCAA had deliberately drawn up the restitution rule as an obstacle to due process, contrary to the recommendation of its own lawyer. "They want to crush these kids," he says.

The NCAA, of course, has never expressed such a desire, and its public comments on due process tend to be anodyne. At a congressional hearing in 2004, the infractions committee vice chair, Josephine Potuto, repeatedly argued that although the NCAA is "not bound by any judicial due process standards," its enforcement, infractions, and hearing procedures meet and "very likely exceed" those of other public institutions. Yet when pressed, Potuto declared that athletes would have no standing for due process even if the Supreme Court had not exempted the NCAA in the 1988 *Tarkanian* decision. "In order to reach due-process issues as a legal Constitutional principle, the individual challenging has to have a substantive property or liberty interest," she testified. "The opportunity to play intercollegiate athletics does not rise to that level."

To translate this from the legal jargon, Potuto used a circular argument to confine college athletes beneath any right to freedom or property in their own athletic effort. They have no stake to seek their rights, she claimed, because they have no rights at stake.

Potuto's assertion might be judged preposterous, an heir of the *Dred Scott* dictum that slaves possessed no rights a white person was bound to respect. But she was merely being honest, articulating assumptions almost everyone shares without question. Whether motivated by hostility for students (as critics like Johnson allege), or by noble and paternalistic tough love (as the NCAA professes), the denial of fundamental due process for college athletes has stood unchallenged in public discourse. Like other NCAA rules, it emanates naturally from the premise that college athletes own no interest in sports beyond exercise, character-building, and good fun. Who represents these young men and women? No one asks. The debates and commissions about reforming college sports nibble around the edges—trying to reduce corruption, to prevent the "contamination" of athletes by lucre, and to maintain at least a pretense of concern for academic integrity. Everything stands on the implicit presumption that preserving amateurism is necessary for the well-being of college athletes. But while amateurism—and the free labor it provides—may be necessary to the preservation of the NCAA, and perhaps to the profit margins of various interested corporations and educational institutions, what if it doesn't benefit the athletes? What if it hurts them?

"The Plantation Mentality"

"Ninety per cent of the NCAA revenue is produced by 1 per cent of the athletes," Sonny Vaccaro says. "Go to the skill positions"—the stars. "Ninety per cent African Americans." The NCAA made its money off those kids, and so did he. They were not all bad people, the NCAA officials, but they were blind, Vaccaro believes. "Their organization is a fraud."

Vaccaro retired from Reebok in 2007 to make a clean break for a crusade. "The kids and their parents gave me a good life," he says in his peppery staccato. "I want to give something back." Call it redemption, he told me. Call it education or a good cause. "Here's what I preach," said Vaccaro. "This goes beyond race, to human rights. The least educated are the most exploited. I'm probably closer to the kids than anyone else, and I'm 71 years old."

Vaccaro is officially an unpaid consultant to the plaintiffs in *O'Bannon v. NCAA*. He connected Ed O'Bannon with the attorneys who now represent him, and he talked to some of the additional co-plaintiffs who have joined the suit, among them Oscar Robertson, a basketball Hall of Famer who was incensed that the NCAA was still selling his image on playing cards 50 years after be left the University of Cincinnati.

Jon King, an antitrust lawyer at Hausfeld LLP in San Francisco, told me that Vaccaro "opened our eyes to massive revenue streams hidden in college sports." King and his colleagues have drawn on Vaccaro's vast knowledge of athletic-department finances, which include off-budget accounts for shoe contracts. Sonny Vaccaro and his wife, Pam, "had a mountain of documents," he said. The outcome of the 1984 *Regents* decision validated an antitrust approach for O'Bannon, King argues, as well as for Joseph Agnew in his continuing case against the one-year scholarship rule. Lawyers for Sam Keller—a former quarterback for the University of Nebraska who is featured in video games—are pursuing a parallel "right of publicity" track based on the First Amendment. Still other lawyers could revive Rick Johnson's case against NCAA bylaws on a larger scale, and King thinks claims for the rights of college players may be viable also under laws pertaining to contracts, employment, and civil rights.

Vaccaro had sought a law firm for O'Bannon with pockets deep enough to withstand an expensive war of attrition, fearing that NCAA officials would fight discovery to the end. So far, though, they have been forthcoming. "The numbers are off the wall," Vaccaro says. "The public will see for the first time how all the money is distributed."

Vaccaro has been traveling the after-dinner circuit, proselytizing against what he sees as the NCAA's exploitation of young athletes. Late in 2008, someone who heard his stump speech at Howard University mentioned it to Michael Hausfeld, a prominent antitrust and human-rights lawyer, whose firm had won suits against Exxon for Native Alaskans and against Union Bank of Switzerland for Holocaust victims' families. Someone tracked down Vaccaro on vacation in Athens, Greece, and he flew back directly to meet Hausfeld. The shoe salesman and the white-shoe lawyer made common cause.

Hausfeld LLP has offices in San Francisco, Philadelphia, and London. Its headquarters are on K Street in Washington, D.C., about three blocks from the White House. When I talked with Hausfeld there not long ago, he sat in a cavernous conference room, tidy in pinstripes, hands folded on a spotless table that reflected the skyline. He spoke softly, without pause, condensing the complex fugue of antitrust litigation into simple sentences. "Let's start with the basic question," he said, noting that the NCAA claims that student-athletes have no property rights in their own athletic accomplishments. Yet, in order to be eligible to play, college athletes have to waive their rights to proceeds from any sales based on their athletic performance.

"What right is it that they're waiving?," Hausfeld asked. "You can't waive something you don't have. So they had a right that they gave up in consideration to the principle of amateurism, if there be such." (At an April hearing in a U.S. District Court in California, Gregory Curtner, a representative for the NCAA, stunned O'Bannon's lawyers by saying: "There is no document, there is no substance, that the NCAA ever takes from the student-athletes their rights of publicity or their rights of likeness. They are at all times owned by the student-athlete." Jon King says this is "like telling someone they have the winning lottery ticket, but by the way, it can only be cashed in on Mars." The court denied for a second time an NCAA motion to dismiss the O'Bannon complaint.)

The waiver clause is nestled among the paragraphs of the "Student-Athlete Statement" that NCAA rules require be collected yearly from every college athlete. In signing the statement, the athletes attest that they have amateur status, that their stated SAT scores are valid, that they are willing to disclose any educational documents requested, and so forth. Already, Hausfeld said, the defendants in the Ed O'Bannon case have said in court filings that college athletes thereby transferred their promotional rights forever.

He paused. "That's ludicrous," he said. "Nobody assigns rights like that. Nobody can assert rights like that." He said the pattern demonstrated clear abuse by the collective power of the schools and all their conferences under the NCAA umbrella—"a most effective cartel."

The faux ideal of amateurism is "the elephant in the room," Hausfeld said, sending for a book. "You can't get to the bottom of our case without exposing the hypocrisy of amateurism, and Walter Byers says it eloquently." An assistant brought in Byers's memoir. It looked garish on the shiny table because dozens of pink Post-its protruded from the text. Hausfeld read to me from page 390:

> The college player cannot sell his own feet (the coach does that) nor can he sell his own name (the college will do that). This is the plantation mentality resurrected and blessed by today's campus executives.

He looked up. "That wasn't me," he said. "That was the NCAA's architect." He found a key recommendation on page 388:

> Prosecutors and the courts, with the support of the public, should use antitrust laws to break up the collegiate cartel—not just in athletics but possibly in other aspects of collegiate life as well.

Could the book become evidence? Might the aged Byers testify? (He is now 89.) Was that part of the plaintiffs' strategy for the O'Bannon trial? Hausfeld smiled faintly. "I'd rather the NCAA lawyers not fully understand the strategy," he said.

He put the spiny book away and previewed what lies ahead. The court soon would qualify his clients as a class. Then the Sherman Antitrust Act would provide for thorough discovery to break down exactly what the NCAA receives on everything from video clips to jerseys, contract by contract. "And we want to know what they're carrying on their books as the value of their archival footage," he concluded. "They say it's a lot of money. We agree. How much?"

The work will be hard, but Hausfeld said he will win in the courts, unless the NCAA folds first. "Why?" Hausfeld asked rhetorically. "We know our clients are foreclosed: neither the NCAA nor its members will permit them to participate in any of that licensing revenue. Under the law, it's up to them [the defendants] to give a precompetitive justification. They can't. End of story."

In 2010 the third Knight Commission, complementing a previous commission's recommendation for published reports on academic progress, called for the finances of college sports to be made transparent and public—television contracts, conference budgets, shoe deals, coaches' salaries, stadium bonds, everything. The recommendation was based on the worthy truism that sunlight is a proven disinfectant. But in practice, it has not been applied at all. Conferences, coaches, and other stakeholders resisted disclosure; college players still have no way of determining their value to the university.

"Money surrounds college sports," says Domonique Foxworth, who is a cornerback for the NFL's Baltimore Ravens and an executive-committee member for the NFL Players Association, and played for the University of Maryland. "And every player knows those millions are floating around only because of the 18-to-22-year-olds." Yes, he told me, even the second-string punter believes a miracle might lift him into the NFL, and why not? In all the many pages of the three voluminous Knight Commission reports, there is but one paragraph that addresses the real-life choices for college athletes. "Approximately 1 per cent of NCAA men's basketball players and 2 per cent of NCAA football players are drafted by NBA or NFL teams," stated the 2001 report, basing its figures on a review of the previous 10 years, "and just being drafted is no assurance of a successful professional career." Warning that the odds against professional athletic success are "astronomically high," the Knight Commission counsels college athletes to avoid a "rude surprise" and to stick to regular studies. This is sound advice as far as it goes, but it's a bromide that pinches off discussion. Nothing in the typical college curriculum teaches a sweat-stained guard at Clemson or Purdue what his monetary value to the university is. Nothing prods students to think independently about amateurism—because the universities themselves have too much invested in its preservation. Stifling thought, the universities, in league with the NCAA, have failed their own primary mission by providing an empty, cynical education on college sports.

The most basic reform would treat the students as what they are—adults, with rights and reason of their own—and grant them a meaningful voice in NCAA deliberations. A restoration of full citizenship to "student-athletes" would facilitate open governance, making it possible to enforce pledges of transparency in both academic standards and athletic finances. Without that, the NCAA has no effective checks and balances, no way for the students to provide informed consent regarding the way they are governed. A thousand questions lie willfully silenced because the NCAA is naturally afraid of giving "student-athletes" a true voice. Would college players be content with the augmented scholarship or allowance now requested by the National College

Players Association? If a player's worth to the university is greater than the value of his scholarship (as it clearly is in some cases), should he be paid a salary? If so, would teammates in revenue sports want to be paid equally, or in salaries stratified according to talent or value on the field? What would the athletes want in Division III, where athletic budgets keep rising without scholarships or substantial sports revenue? Would athletes seek more or less variance in admissions standards? Should non-athletes also have a voice, especially where involuntary student fees support more and more of college sports? Might some schools choose to specialize, paying players only in elite leagues for football, or lacrosse? In athletic councils, how much would high-revenue athletes value a simple *thank you* from the tennis or field-hockey players for the newly specified subsidies to their facilities?

University administrators, already besieged from all sides, do not want to even think about such questions. Most cringe at the thought of bargaining with athletes as a general manager does in professional sports, with untold effects on the budgets for coaches and every other sports item. "I would not want to be part of it," North Carolina Athletic Director Dick Baddour told me flatly. After 44 years at UNC, he could scarcely contemplate a world without amateur rules. "We would have to think long and hard," Baddour added gravely, "about whether this university would continue those sports at all."

I, too, once reflexively recoiled at the idea of paying college athletes and treating them like employees or professionals. It feels abhorrent—but for reasons having to do more with sentiment than with practicality or law. Not just fans and university presidents but judges have often found cursory, non-statutory excuses to leave amateur traditions intact. "Even in the increasingly commercial modern world," said a federal-court judge in *Gaines v. NCAA* in 1990, "this Court believes there is still validity to the Athenian concept of a complete education derived from fostering the full growth of both mind and body." The fact that "the NCAA has not distilled amateurism to its purest form," said the Fifth Circuit Court of Appeals in 1988, "does not mean its attempts to maintain a mixture containing some amateur elements are unreasonable."

But one way or another, the smokescreen of amateurism may soon be swept away. For one thing, a victory by the plaintiffs in O'Bannon's case would radically transform college sports. Colleges would likely have to either stop profiting from students or start paying them. The NCAA could also be forced to pay tens, if not hundreds, of millions of dollars in damages. If O'Bannon and Vaccaro and company win, "it will turn college sports on its ear," said Richard Lapchick, the president of the National Consortium for Academics and Sports, in a recent interview with *The New York Times*.

Though the O'Bannon case may take several years yet to reach resolution, developments on other fronts are chipping away at amateurism, and at the NCAA. This past summer, *Sports Illustrated* editorialized in favor of allowing college athletes to be paid by non-university sources without jeopardizing their eligibility. At a press conference last June, Steve Spurrier, the coach of the South Carolina Gamecocks football team (and the winner of the 1966 Heisman Trophy as a Florida Gator), proposed that coaches start paying players $300 a game out of their own pockets. The coaches at six other SEC schools (Alabama, Florida, Ole Miss, Mississippi State, LSU, and Tennessee) all endorsed Spurrier's proposal. And Mark Emmert, the NCAA president, recently conceded that big changes must come. "The integrity of collegiate athletics is seriously challenged today by rapidly growing pressures coming from many directions," Emmert said in July. "We have reached a point where incremental change is not sufficient to meet these challenges. I want us to act more aggressively and in a more comprehensive way than we have in the past. A few new tweaks of the rules won't get the job done."

Threats to NCAA dominion also percolate in Congress. Aggrieved legislators have sponsored numerous bills. Senator Orrin Hatch, citing mistreatment of his Utah Utes, has called witnesses to discuss possible antitrust remedies for the Bowl Championship Series. Congressional committees have already held hearings critical of the NCAA's refusal to follow due process in disciplinary matters; other committees have explored a rise in football concussions. Last January, calls went up to investigate "informal" football workouts at the University of Iowa just after the season-ending bowl games—workouts so grueling that 41 of the 56 amateur student-athletes collapsed, and 13 were hospitalized with rhabdomyolysis, a life-threatening kidney condition often caused by excessive exercise.

The greatest threat to the viability of the NCAA may come from its member universities. Many experts believe that the churning instability within college football will drive the next major change. President Obama himself has endorsed the drumbeat cry for a national playoff in college football. This past spring, the Justice Department questioned the BCS about its adherence to antitrust standards. Jim Delany, the commissioner of the Big Ten, has estimated that a national playoff system could produce three or four times as much money as the existing bowl system does. If a significant band of football schools were to demonstrate that they could orchestrate a true national playoff, without the NCAA's assistance, the association would be terrified—and with good reason. Because if the big sports colleges don't need the NCAA to administer a national playoff in football, then they don't need it to do so in basketball. In which case, they could cut out the middleman in March Madness and run the tournament themselves. Which would deprive the NCAA of close to $1 billion a year, more than 95 per cent of its revenue. The organization would be reduced to a rule book without money—an organization aspiring to enforce its rules but without the financial authority to enforce anything.

Thus the playoff dreamed of and hankered for by millions of football fans haunts the NCAA. "There will be some kind of playoff in college football, and it will not be run by the NCAA," says Todd Turner, a former athletic director in four conferences (Big East, ACC, SEC, and Pac-10). "If I'm at the NCAA, I have to worry that the playoff group can get basketball to break away, too."

This danger helps explain why the NCAA steps gingerly in enforcements against powerful colleges. To alienate member colleges would be to jeopardize its own existence. Long gone are television bans and the "death penalty" sentences (commanding season-long shutdowns of offending teams) once meted out to Kentucky (1952), Southwestern Louisiana (1973), and Southern Methodist University (1987). Institutions receive mostly symbolic slaps nowadays. Real punishments fall heavily on players and on scapegoats like literacy tutors.

A deeper reason explains why, in its predicament, the NCAA has no recourse to any principle or law that can justify amateurism. There is no such thing. Scholars and sportswriters yearn for grand juries to ferret out every forbidden bauble that reaches a college athlete, but the NCAA's ersatz courts can only masquerade as public authority. How could any statute impose *amateur* status on college athletes, or on anyone else? No legal definition of amateur exists, and any attempt to create one in enforceable law would expose its repulsive and unconstitutional nature—a bill of attainder, stripping from college athletes the rights of American citizenship.

❧❧❧

For all our queasiness about what would happen if some athletes were to get paid, there is a successful precedent for the professionalization of an amateur sports system: the Olympics. For years, Walter Byers waged war with the NCAA's older and more powerful nemesis, the Amateur Athletic Union, which since 1894 had overseen U.S. Olympic athletes. Run in high-handed fashion, the AAU had infamously banned Jesse Owens for life in 1936—weeks after his four heroic gold medals punctured the Nazi claim of Aryan supremacy—because instead of using his sudden fame to tour and make money for the AAU at track meets across Europe, he came home early. In the early 1960s, the fights between the NCAA and the AAU over who should manage Olympic athletes become so bitter that President Kennedy called in General Douglas MacArthur to try to mediate a truce before the Tokyo Olympic Games.

Ultimately, Byers prevailed and effectively neutered the AAU. In November 1978, President Jimmy Carter signed the bipartisan Amateur Sports Act. Amateurism in the Olympics soon dissolved—and the world did not end. Athletes, granted a 20 per cent voting stake on every Olympic sport's governing body, tipped balances in the United States and then inexorably around the world. First in marathon races, then in tennis tournaments, players soon were allowed to accept prize money and keep their Olympic eligibility. Athletes profited from sponsorships and endorsements. The International Olympic Committee expunged the word *amateur* from its charter in 1986. Olympic officials, who had once disdained the NCAA for offering scholarships in exchange for athletic performance, came to welcome millionaire athletes from every quarter, while the NCAA still refused to let the pro Olympian Michael Phelps swim for his college team at Michigan.

This sweeping shift left the Olympic reputation intact, and perhaps improved. Only hardened romantics mourned the amateur code. "Hey, come on," said Anne Audain, a track-and-field star who once held the world record for the 5,000 meters. "It's like losing your virginity. You're a little misty for awhile, but then you realize. *Wow, there's a whole new world out there!"*

Without logic or practicality or fairness to support amateurism, the NCAA's final retreat is to sentiment. The Knight Commission endorsed its heartfelt cry that to pay college athletes would be "an unacceptable surrender to despair." Many of the people I spoke with while reporting this article felt the same way. "I don't want to pay college players," said Wade Smith, a tough criminal lawyer and former star running back at North Carolina. "I just don't want to do it. We'd lose something precious."

"Scholarship athletes are already paid," declared the Knight Commission members, "in the most meaningful way possible: with a free education." This evasion by prominent educators severed my last reluctant, emotional tie with imposed amateurism. I found it worse than self-serving. It echoes masters who once claimed that heavenly salvation would outweigh earthly injustice to slaves. In the era when our college sports first arose, colonial powers were turning the whole world upside down to define their own interests as all-inclusive and benevolent. Just so, the NCAA calls it heinous exploitation to pay college athletes a fair portion of what they earn.

Credit

Branch, Taylor. "The Shame of College Sports." *The Atlantic*, Oct 2011:80–110.

Bad Sports

The Fake Classes Scandal at Chapel Hill and the $16 Billion Business of College Athletics

Paul M. Barrett

Sitting in Memorial Hall at the heart of the Chapel Hill campus of the University of North Carolina, Mary Willingham wondered what William Friday would want her to do. Friday's memorial service in October 2012 drew a large and reverent audience: scholars of the humanities and sciences, national political figures, and university staff members such as Willingham, who'd spent the previous decade tutoring athletes and other undergraduates in need of remedial reading help. The tribute to Friday, president of the state university system from 1956 to 1986, reflected the accomplishments and contradictions of the institution he embodied. Slaves helped build UNC, the nation's first public university, which opened in 1795. The original Memorial Hall, dedicated in 1885, honored students and faculty who'd died defending the Confederacy. Taking office only two years after the Supreme Court ordered an end to "separate but equal" in *Brown v. Board of Education*, Friday pushed for desegregation in the face of sometimes-violent opposition. Under his stewardship, Chapel Hill earned a reputation for excellence and became a powerhouse in the National Collegiate Athletic Association.

As she listened to the eulogies, Willingham pondered another aspect of Friday's legacy. In his last decades he'd tried to stir discussion about whether commercialized intercollegiate athletics was distorting higher education. That's why Willingham had approached Friday in his 92nd and final year. In private conversations, she'd told him about her mounting anxiety that rather than educating its recruited athletes, UNC was playing a shell game to keep them from needing to study at all. She'd told him about basketball and football stars who read at grade school level. She confessed that she'd helped steer some of these young men—many of them black—into lecture classes that never met. Worst of all, given Carolina's racial history, the phony courses were offered in the black studies department.

Acting as an unnamed source, Willingham had been feeding information since 2011 about academic fraud to a reporter with the *News & Observer* in Raleigh. The coverage had put UNC on the defensive. But rather than seriously investigate the connection between sports and classroom corruption, top university administrators used vague committee reports to obfuscate the issue. Willingham's conversations with the elderly Friday hadn't addressed the tradecraft of whistle-blowing. Still, he'd encouraged her to act on her concerns. "At his memorial," she says, "I realized I had to speak up." In November 2012, she went public with what she knew.

College sports is a $16 billion business, and it coexists uneasily with its host—nonprofit, tax-exempt institutions dedicated to education and research. The tension has become acute at UNC, in large part because of Willingham's decision at Friday's memorial service. What she disclosed has devastated UNC's image of itself and may potentially hobble its athletic program. Beginning in the 1990s and continuing at least through 2011, UNC's Department of African, African American, and Diaspora Studies offered more than 200 lecture courses that never met. The department also sponsored hundreds of independent study classes of equally dubious value. Internal reviews have identified forged faculty signatures and more than 500 grades changed without authorization. The students affected were disproportionately football and basketball players.

"I was part of something that I came to be ashamed of," says Willingham. "We weren't serving the kids. We weren't educating them properly. We were pushing them toward graduation, and that's not the same as giving them an education." Last summer she was stripped of her supervisory title—an action she's appealing as retaliatory. In January senior UNC officials took the further step of publicly condemning her for suggesting that some football and basketball stars couldn't read well enough to get through college classes honestly.

While her outspokenness and the vilification it brought make Willingham unique, her role as a secret enabler of NCAA Inc. is hardly unusual. Every Division I sports power employs low-profile advisers like Willingham without whom the facade of academic eligibility would swiftly collapse, says Richard Southall, director of the College Sport Research Institute at the University of South Carolina.

"We pretend," he says, "that it's feasible to recruit high school graduates with minimal academic qualifications, give them a full-time job as a football or basketball player at a Division I NCAA school, and somehow have them get up to college-level reading and writing skills at the same time that they're enrolled in college level classes." Willingham's experience, Southall adds, shows how "we're all kidding ourselves."

What's more, in response to escalating demands that undergraduate athletes deserve pay for their services, the NCAA argues that a scholarship and degree are sufficient compensation. The NCAA position crumbles, however, if the parchment represents little or no real education.

ઌ ઌ ઌ

Mary and Chuck Willingham didn't have ties to Chapel Hill when they arrived in 1999. "We just thought this was a great place to raise a family," Mary, now 52, says. "I love being around smart people, and there are a ton of them in Chapel Hill."

The Willinghams met in the late 1980s at Amgen, the California biotech company. Chuck worked in finance, Mary in human resources. She'd gone into HR straight out of Loyola University Chicago, a Jesuit school in her hometown. She worked at Mobil and the Arthur Young accounting firm before landing at Amgen. "We were lucky," she says. "We got together just as the biotech boom took off. There were stock options. We did well."

Once they'd settled in Chapel Hill, some of the Amgen windfall went into a small chain of restaurants Chuck opened. Mary earned a teaching degree and became a reading tutor in the public schools A few years later, on a lark, she applied for a job at UNC. To her delight, the university hired her in 2003 as a $33,000-a-year staff member in the athletics department. "Everyone in Chapel Hill wants to work at UNC," she says. "The benefits are great, and you're part of the in-club."

Soon she was dressing her three children—two sons and a daughter—in Carolina blue for Christmas card photographs. Chuck and the kids became loyal Tar Heels fans. (The nickname refers to the tar and pitch extracted since Colonial times from Carolina pine trees. During the Civil War, the state's troops were called "tar heels.") A dedicated runner with a lean physique, Mary didn't relish football or basketball, but she loved the gracious red-brick campus and the solidarity that bound her family to the place where they lived.

"The Carolina Way," an ethos of pride, achievement, and integrity, is taken quite seriously in Chapel Hill. UNC counts among its alumni James Polk, U.S. president from 1845 to 1849; novelists Thomas Wolfe and Russell Banks; and such business leaders as Hugh McColl, retired chairman and chief executive officer of Bank of America, and Peter Grauer, chairman of Bloomberg LP, owner of *Bloomberg Businessweek*. Today the school enrolls 18,000 undergraduates and an additional 11,000 graduate and professional school students.

What most people know about Carolina, though, is basketball. The 36-year reign of coach Dean Smith, from 1961 to 1997, is legendary. Michael Jordan led the team to an NCAA title in March 1982 and went on to win six NBA championships with the Chicago Bulls. All told, UNC has won five NCAA tournaments, most recently in 2005 and 2009 under current coach Roy Williams.

"I grew up in Los Angeles a total nut for sports," says Chuck. "It's different here. The intensity in a small town like Chapel Hill when you get 60,000 people in for a football game or 22,000 in the Dean Dome for basketball—it's like something I'd never seen before."

Conditioned by her HR training, Mary quickly assessed the 800 varsity athletes she was hired to assist. "Four hundred of them at any given time are on the [Atlantic Coast Conference] honor roll or the UNC dean's list," she says. "They're doing great." Most of these play "nonrevenue sports," such as soccer, tennis, or field hockey. In NCAA lingo, revenue sports are men's football and basketball—the ones that generate lucrative TV and licensing fees and ticket sales. Of the remaining 400 UNC athletes, Willingham continues, "another 200 are doing OK, and about 150 to 200 are underperforming—some of them badly underperforming. Most of the last group are playing football or men's or women's basketball."

This distribution shouldn't surprise anyone. UNC officials acknowledge that historically they've enrolled 160 athletes a year based partly on their "special talent." The highest priorities are football and basketball recruits. An additional 40 special-talent slots are allotted for music and drama.

In 2012, UNC reported total sports revenue of $82.4 million, offset by expenses of $81.9 million. According to NCAA figures analyzed by Indiana University's National Sports Journalism Center and *USA Today*, UNC ranked 25th on a revenue list headed by the University of Texas at Austin, with $163.3 million.

During the seven years Willingham counseled athletes, UNC's Academic Support Program for Student-Athletes reported to the athletic director. The program's dozen advisers divide up the 28 varsity teams, with the lion's share of attention going to football and men's basketball. A couple of "learning specialists," including Willingham, serve as floating tutors, focusing on the players most in need. A separate academic support program handles all other undergraduates.

In the mornings, Willingham met one-on-one with basketball and football players. "We would work together on reading or writing skills" usually related to class assignments, she says. "It was spoon-feeding the information in, or getting the information out." After the athletes spent the afternoon lifting weights and practicing, Willingham supervised evening study halls. On game days and during road trips, tutoring ground to a halt.

Willingham noticed that some highly recruited revenue-sport athletes lacked basic literacy skills. She won't discuss individuals by name but will say that beginning in 2003, she taught members of the football and basketball team to sound out multisyllable words and piece together simple sentences. Other athletes who could read somewhat better wanted her help so they could more easily follow sports news online. Willingham says that of undergraduate sports stars who accepted tutoring—not all did—a number made substantial progress. But the notion that athletes with elementary school skills "would be able to write papers for college classes," she says, "just made no sense."

A female varsity basketball player showed her a class paper that "was obviously a cut-and-paste job she's copied from somewhere," Willingham says. A colleague advised Willingham to allow the young woman to submit the paper for credit, and it received a B. "I came home and told Chuck, but I didn't stop it," she says.

When she asked more experienced colleagues how to handle their lagging charges, she was told not to lose any sleep. Willingham became, in effect, "an eligibility specialist," she says, "knowing just how much I could get away with in helping these guys, without actually doing the work for them."

Football players whispered to her about a computer hard drive maintained by the team that contained a bank of term papers. Athletes slightly altered and submitted the inventoried papers for course credit. "There's no way the professors could not have noticed the same papers coming in from athletes," she says.

By 2005 she'd learned something was seriously awry in the black studies department. Julius Nyang'oro, a native of Tanzania who chaired the department until 2011, offered lecture courses on topics such as Swahili and black history, but the lectures never happened. Athletes and their academic advisers referred to the no-show classes as "paper classes" because all that was required was a single 20-page paper. "We put athletes in the paper classes specifically because they didn't meet," Willingham says. "Any kind of paper got an A or a B grade. It wasn't clear whether anyone was even reading the papers."

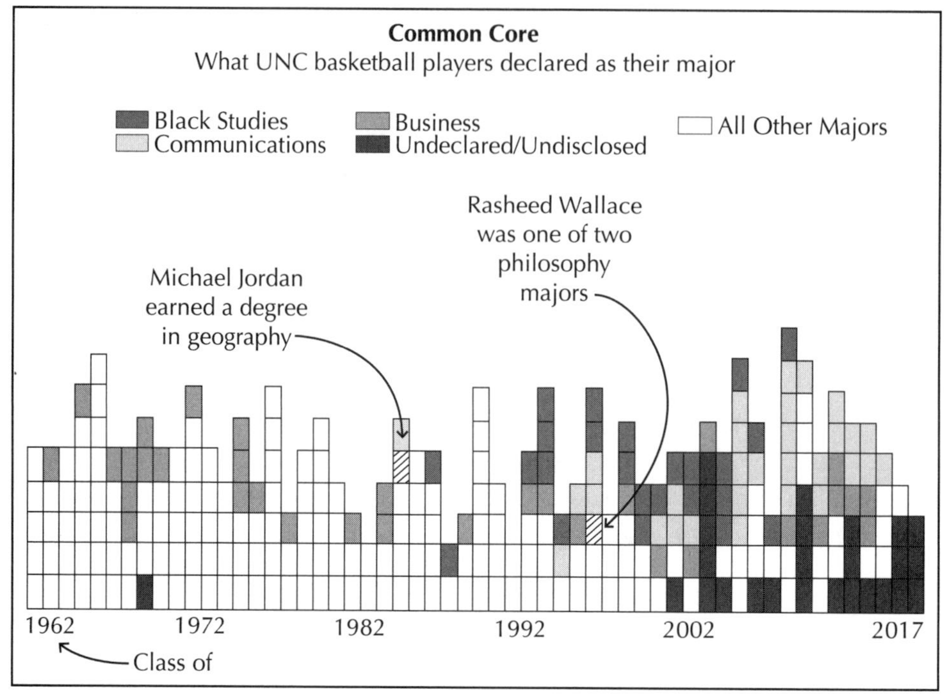

A related phenomenon was the profusion of independent study classes that were supposedly tailored to individual students. Nyang'oro supervised hundreds of independent studies, even though he spent extended periods traveling abroad, Willingham says. In 2004–05 alone, members of UNC's NCAA championship men's basketball team enrolled in 15 independent studies. Of the 15 players on the squad who declared a major, six listed black studies. Five majored in communication studies.

In 2006, UNC announced a major push to improve its football program, including the hiring of former NFL coach Paul "Butch" Davis Jr. "I knew what that meant," Willingham says. "Recruiting would get more aggressive under Butch Davis, and we'd see more top players who couldn't do college class work." Feeling as if she were "drowning," Willingham confronted Dick Baddour, then the university's athletic director, at a department meeting. She asked him whether he recognized that making football more competitive would result in graduation rates declining. "He just said yes," she recalls. Baddour says he doesn't recall the exchange. Because of his concern for academics, he adds, "I am confident I did not respond as she indicated."

In the summer of 2009, after the men's basketball team won another NCAA championship, a new adviser took charge of the squad's academic affairs. In the fall, basketball player enrollments in paper courses and independent studies declined drastically. "That was encouraging," says Willingham. The adviser to the basketball team, Jenn Townsend, still works at UNC but didn't respond to interview requests.

In contrast, Willingham says, football players were continuing to sign up in large numbers for paper classes. Moreover, in connection with a master's degree in liberal studies she earned in 2009 from the Greensboro branch of UNC, Willingham had begun analyzing diagnostic tests of incoming athletes. The statistics, she says, confirmed her impression that some football and basketball recruits had the literacy skills of grade school students. "How could we in good conscience place them in no-show classes with a 20-page paper?" she recalls asking herself. "And how could they get Bs and As?" In 2010 she transferred to the general undergrad academic counseling program.

The same year Willingham stepped away from athletics tutoring, the UNC football program erupted in scandal. Most of the initial headlines concerned NCAA inquires into improper financial benefits provided to players There were also academic violations. A defensive star named Michael McAdoo got pulled from competition because an undergraduate tutor had provided him with excessive help on term papers. The McAdoo case was the first public hint of widespread academic fraud.

McAdoo had taken an intermediate Swahili class offered by Nyang'oro. As part of a lawsuit McAdoo filed in 2011 seeking reinstatement to the football team, his Swahili paper—written in English—became public. Fans of North Carolina State, a bitter UNC rival, noted online that McAdoo seemed to have plagiarized much of his work. (McAdoo, through a spokesman, declined to comment.) This caught the attention of *News & Observer* reporter Dan Kane, whose inquiries revealed that lectures supposedly offered for the Swahili class never happened. Kane began investigating rumors of other no-show classes. He interviewed Willingham, who insisted at first on anonymity because she wanted to keep her job. That changed after William Friday's October 2012 memorial service.

By the time Willingham went public, UNC had organized a series of committees to review the black studies department. She, however, saw the overlapping inquires as a shield and not a serious investigation. The reputational bleeding had already been heavy: In 2011, UNC Chancellor Holden Thorp fired Davis as football coach and accepted the early retirement of athletic director Baddour, who says he wanted his replacement to select the new football coach. Thorp then announced that in penance for the football debacle, he would step down, too.

In December 2012, former North Carolina Governor James Martin announced the results of an internal investigation the university had asked him to oversee and which he touted as conclusive. Looking back to the mid-1990s, Martin found 216 corrupted courses, up from an earlier estimate of 54. He also identified 560 grade changes he suspected were unauthorized. A former chemistry professor at Davidson College, Martin acknowledged that athletes were enrolled disproportionately in UNC's problematic classes. He stressed, though, that he found more nonathletes than athletes in the phony classes. This led to his main finding: "This was not an athletic scandal," he said. "It was an academic scandal."

Martin also emphasized that the corruption was limited to the black studies department, although it wasn't clear how he'd reached that particular conclusion. Nyang'oro, who hadn't explained himself publicly, had resigned. Martin said the corruption began and ended with the mysterious ex-professor and a department aide, who'd also left the university.

Jay Smith, a professor of early-modern French history at UNC, studied each university-sponsored report as it appeared. A rare academic in Chapel Hill who openly expresses unease about the influence of revenue sports, he publicly supported Willingham. "The obvious question raised by all the so-called investigations was why [the university was] so determined to exonerate the athletic department when Mary was providing first-person evidence that athletic eligibility was the motive behind the academic fraud," he says. "The answer, I'm afraid, is that we're terrified at the prospect of having to go back and look" at whether members of the 2005 and 2009 championship basketball teams were eligible only because they took bogus classes.

Incomplete Passes

Academic Irregularities related to athletic eligibility have haunted several U.S. colleges

Auburn (2006)	**Georgia (2003)**	**Standford (2011)**
Helped by academic advisers, football players padded their grade-point averages in "direct reading" classes.	The university withdrew from postseason play after basketball players received inflated grades in a coaching class.	Academic advisers discontinued a list of classes recommended for years because they were easy and/or convenient.
Florida (2008)	**Memphis (2008)**	**Tennessee (2000)**
Cam Newton, now quarterback of the NFL's Carolina Panthers, left Florida after facing potential expulsion for cheating, Fox Sports reported.	The NCAA stripped the basketball team of its run to the finals after Derrick Rose's SAT scores were ruled invalid.	ESPN profiled an English professor whose objections led the university to acknowledge that, on average, athletes recieved twice as many grade changes as other students.
Florida State (2009)	**Michigan (2008)**	**USC (2001)**
Academic advisers participated in taking tests and in writing papers for basketball and football players.	The *Ann Arbor News* reported that from 2004 to 2007, 251 athletes took independent study classes with the same professor and received suspiciously high grades.	The NCAA issued sanctions against the football and women's swimming teams after tutors were found to have written papers for athletes.
Fresno State (2003)	**Minnesota (1999)**	
The men's basketball statistician and academic adviser were caught in a paper-writing-for-athletes scheme.	The basketball team had tournament victories erased after hundreds of assignments were completed for players.	

That's not an idle anxiety. In 2009 the NCAA retroactively vacated 12 victories by the Florida State Seminoles as punishment for the ghostwriting of term papers and tests for football team members. The NCAA stripped the University of Memphis of its entire 2007–08 season, including a run to the NCAA men's basketball finals, because of academic fraud: Memphis star Derrick Rose, now with the NBA's Chicago Bulls, had his SAT scores retroactively invalidated after allegations that someone else had taken the entrance exam for him.

So far the NCAA has refrained from investigating the black studies fraud, apparently accepting UNC's contention that the problem had nothing to do with athletics. The fear in Chapel Hill that the NCAA might change its mind is normally discussed in hushed tones. Last May, though, former Chancellor James Moeser didn't restrain himself in an interview with *Chapel Hill Magazine*. Condemning media coverage of the scandal he said of journalists: "I think they target people, and they take pleasure in bringing people down. I think their real goal here was to remove banners from the Smith Center," UNC's basketball arena.

ઉજીઉજીઉજી

In the summer of 2013, a few months after Moeser's comments, Carol Folt, a top official at Dartmouth College, took over as UNC's chancellor. She brought with her Jim Dean, the onetime head of UNC's highly regarded business school, who became executive vice chancellor and provost. Willingham decided to warn the administration that in addition to the black studies debacle, it needed to address the problem of highly recruited football and basketball players arriving without the tools to do college class work.

By this time, she had extended her master's research and amassed data on a selection of 183 academically "at-risk" UNC athletes from 2004 to 2012. Eighty-five per cent were football and basketball players. In an e-mail in July, she told Dean that 60 per cent of the athletes she had studied had from fourth- to eighth-grade reading levels. About 10 per cent read below a third-grade level. Willingham added: "Of the 183 students, 45 (about 24 percent) had UNC GPAs under 2.0, thus putting them at risk of academic disqualification. Ninety-four of the 183 students, over half, had GPAs under 2.3. Keep in mind that the bogus system of eligibility—UNC's paper class system—was assisting these players to stay on the court/field." So far as she knew, the flagrant paper classes had ended with Nyang'oro's departure, but she wasn't in a position to know what went on in other departments at the sprawling university.

Coincidentally, and without Willingham's knowledge, Bradley Bethel, a reading and writing specialist with the Academics Support Program for Student-Athletes, sent a similar e-mail to Chancellor Folt in July. "There have been many student-athletes who were specially admitted whose academic preparedness is so low they cannot succeed" at UNC, Bethel wrote.

Dean asked Willingham to provide raw test data supporting her analysis. She declined, explaining that she'd obtained the confidential information that by promising the university's Institutional Review Board not to share it with anyone. She told Dean he could obtain the data directly from the athletic department, which gathered it in the first place. He declined to do as she suggested. "If she had the proof," Dean says, "why wouldn't she share the proof?"

Willingham had good reason to be wary. After a performance review last spring (a process that preceded Folt's and Dean's assuming their posts), she was demoted from her position as assistant director of UNC's Center for Student Success and Academic Counseling. She was moved to a basement office and consigned to the paperwork-intensive task of advising students on graduation requirements. Alleging that she was punished for speaking out, she has filed an internal grievance, which is pending.

In December the criminal indictment of Nyang'oro, whom the university has cast as a rogue, brought Chapel Hill to a boil. An Orange County (NC) grand jury accused the 59-year-old scholar of fraudulently accepting payment for a class he did not teach in the summer of 2011. Eighteen of the 19 students enrolled in AFAM 280: Blacks in North Carolina were members of the Tar Heel football team; the 19th was a former player.

Nyang'oro faces as many as 30 months in prison on the charge of obtaining property by false pretenses. His attorney, Bill Thomas, of Durham, NC, told reporters that Nyang'oro is innocent and has no intention of taking the fall. "There's been one side of this story that has been put forth in the press," Thomas declined to comment for this article, but his meaning was clear: Nyang'oro is threatening to identify others at UNC who knew about his paper courses.

In January, CNN broadcast a national investigation entitled "Some College Athletes Play Like Adults, Read Like 5th-Graders." Among its findings, CNN featured Willingham and her 183-athlete study. In the glare of the media spotlight, she got carried away, saying at one point: "I mean, we may as well just go over to Glenwood Elementary up the street and just let all the fourth graders in here." Stephen Colbert amplified the furor when he satirized athlete education in a segment on his Comedy Central show. After playing a clip of Willingham's quip about admitting fourth graders, the comedian asked: "Why? How fast can they run the 40? Can they really take a hit?"

Many in Chapel Hill took offense. Tar Heel basketball coach Roy Williams suggested at a press conference that Willingham had impugned the moral character of his players. "Every one of the kids that we've recruited in 10 years you'd take home and let guard your grandchildren," he said. Smith, the French history scholar, observes that "getting criticized by the basketball coach in Chapel Hill is a scary thing." The wave of hostile e-mail Willingham has received included several death threats.

In this volatile atmosphere, Folt convened her faculty on Jan. 17 to hear what amounted to an indictment of Willingham led by Dean. The defendant was tried in absentia for defaming the university. Pointing to slides projected on a large screen, Dean, a scholar of organizational behavior, accused Willingham of making slanderous statements about the academic abilities of Carolina football and basketball players. Her assessments "are virtually meaningless and grossly unfair to our students and the university that admitted them," he said. "Using this data set to say that our students can't read is a travesty and unworthy of this university." The verdict, recorded on videotape, was swift: The assembled scholars erupted in applause.

"In 25 years of faculty meetings, I've never seen anything like it," Smith said later. "It was a public conviction and an intellectual execution."

At Dean's order, Willingham turned over her data on the 183 athletes to him. He declared that the diagnostic test she used, the Scholastic Abilities Test for Adults (SATA), assesses vocabulary and isn't recommended for judging literacy levels. She further muddled her results, he added, by miscalculating grade-equivalent levels.

After Dean's presentation elicited applause, Frank Baumgartner, a political science professor, got to his feet. He mused aloud about the university's focusing on Willingham as a form of coverup. "President Nixon went down for denial," he told his colleagues. In an interview later, he elaborated: "What I heard was stonewalling," he said. "The university is trying to distract us by going after Mary Willingham when there are much bigger issues here about sports and academics, and they're not unique to North Carolina."

For reasons she didn't explain, Folt softened UNC's message when she addressed her board of trustees six days later. She admitted publicly for the first time "a failure in academic oversight for years." Two days after that, Dean traveled to New York on a Saturday to clarify Folt's point. "Horrible things happened that I'm ashamed of," he said, although he noted this was all before he and Folt took over.

He outlined a range of nascent reforms: new leadership for a tighter supervision of the athlete-advising office, fewer "special talent" admits who fail to meet academic standards, a fresh "strategic plan" to keep UNC among the top Division I schools academically, and an administrative overhaul of the black studies department. On Feb. 21, Folt announced yet another investigation of the scandal, but this time UNC has hired Kenneth Wainstein, a former U.S. Department of Justice official, to undertake what is billed as an entirely independent probe.

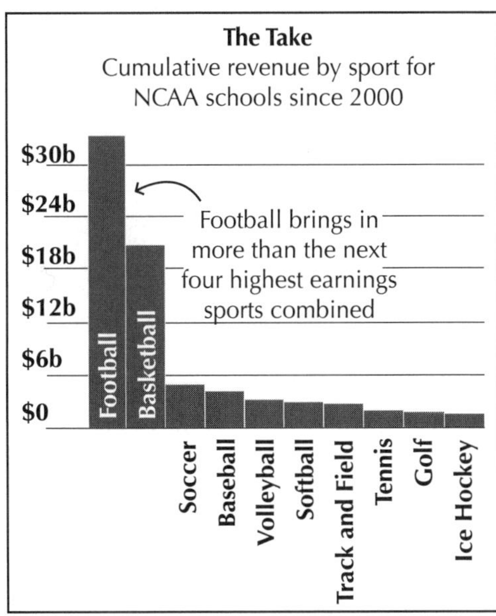

Bethel, the reading specialist who warned Folt last July about unprepared athletes, told me via e-mail the latest reforms seem meaningful, adding: "I am confident UNC's integrity will be restored." And Lawrence "Bubba" Cunningham, the university's current athletic director, said in a separate e-mail exchange: "The NCAA scholarship that students have been awarded for the past 50 years are the best scholarship program ever created with the possible exception of the GI Bill. While they're not perfect, sports scholarships certainly provide great opportunities for an awful lot of students."

The impulse to kill the messenger hasn't receded, however. During his visit to New York, Dean said of Willingham: "She's said our students can't read, our athletes can't read, and that's a lie."

Dean grossly distorted Willingham's statements. What she's said is that 18 out of the 183 special admit athletes whose records she assessed read at roughly a third-grade level. An additional 110 of the athletes, she said, read at between fourth- and eighth-grade levels. She never said that most, let alone all, of the 800 athletes at UNC are illiterate, and she said nothing at all about the other 18,000 undergraduates.

When challenged, Dean conceded he'd misspoken. He also admitted that he doesn't really think Willingham is a liar and assumes she means well. But would he similarly qualify his assault on Willingham back in Chapel Hill?

Willingham stands behind her work and says Dean has mischaracterized it. The SATA diagnostic test on which she relied was administered by a UNC-hired Ph.D. psychologist, she says. It included a writing portion in addition to vocabulary questions. And her assessment wasn't based solely on the SATA; she also looked at results from athletes' SAT and ACT entrance exams. UNC has referred her unpublished research to outside experts for analysis. Such a review seems appropriate.

Willingham isn't a professional statistician. She's an HR exec-turned-reading teacher. That she loves helping students seems beyond dispute. When I walked with her on the Chapel Hill campus in February, undergraduates approached her unbidden to say hello. She knew them by name. She inquired whether they'd followed through on registering for a class or on finishing the work for another one.

"Let's say my data are off a little bit," she said. "I don't think they are, but let's say they are. Set aside the data. Forget about it. The paper classes were still fake, and they existed to keep athletes eligible."

"I've sat with these kids," Willingham continued, referring to heavily recruited athletes. "Some of them can barely read. We have to meet them where they're at and teach them to read." That'll be tough to do, however, while they're also attending college classes and playing Division I basketball or football.

Credit

Barrett, Paul M. "Bad Sport: The Fake Classes Scandal at Chapel Hill and the $16 Billion Business of College Athletics." *Bloomberg Businessweek* 27 Feb. 2014: 50–55. Print.

Notes

Notes

Notes

Notes

Unit 3

Urban Growth and Renewal

As Cleveland evolves to accommodate new industries, social realities, and challenges, our conceptualization of both our community and its people must similarly evolve to incorporate these and other developments. Discussions of how the new millennium will change our understanding of the American city must include myriad questions of race, class, policy, sustainability, history, logistics, and economics. The modern perception of America's urban centers is constantly shifting, and yet it is eternally bound to dichotomies between economy and creativity, between personal security and public prosperity, between a philosophy of comfort at any cost and a celebration of diversity, equality, and opportunity for all.

More now than ever before, the role of the citizen is key in shaping the image and forms of city life. Even as Cleveland and other cities have been forced to either advance new policies or be relegated to a long, painful decline into poverty and obsolescence, the rise of "engaged" residents has birthed some of the most influential, significant changes to our city and our way of life. The past organic, industrial growth of downtown Cleveland and its outlying communities has given way to a structured, neighborhood-centric model, and we as engaged members of the public must understand that old models based on the manufacturing boomtowns of the 19th century and the unfettered economic growth of the 20th must give way to novel ideas, new opportunities, and updated definitions of civic responsibility.

In its time, our city has been known by many names—"The Sixth City," "The Mistake on the Lake," "The Comeback City"—yet however one views Cleveland's role in America's past and future, one thing is clear: it is a space, both physical and philosophical, that is always changing, under construction, moving. In order to move through a discourse on the challenges facing urban development both in Northeast Ohio and around the world, together we must redefine metropolitan landscapes and populations to reflect these ever-changing dynamics in innovative and exciting ways.

Engaging the City: Civic Participation and Teaching Urban History

Amy L. Howard

In the last several years, "civic engagement" has become one of the buzzwords of American higher education, yet the notion that U.S. colleges and universities have an obligation to prepare students for lives of active citizenship and to produce knowledge that addresses societal needs is as old as the American academy itself.[1] Colonial colleges were created in part to educate "learned men" to bolster a fledging society. Religiously affiliated colleges worked to provide moral instruction for young citizens. Land-grant universities were founded to improve farming and instruct engineers. "Normal schools" opened their doors to train teachers to staff a growing public education system. Statewide extension services emerged after World War II, linking universities to the social and economic issues facing their states. As the Cold War intensified, universities used federal funds to support research on defense, health, and the sciences. Growing student activism in the 1960s, spurred by the civil rights movement, galvanized college students across the nation to tackle social problems.[2] Two decades later, faculty responded to community needs by starting to incorporate service-learning and community-based research into the curriculum. The quest for higher education institutions to realize their potential for the public good continues. Through working in a campus-based center focused on local social issues and teaching an urban history course tied to a living-learning community, I have gained insight into the academy's ability to impact social change.

Urban colleges and universities with their proximity to social, cultural, political, economic, and health networks have established a wide range of outreach programs over the years. From the University of Chicago's School of Social Service Administration's work in local neighborhoods in the early twentieth century to Indiana University-Purdue University Indianapolis' creation in 1969 and subsequent outreach efforts, urban higher education institutions have trained professionals, provided applied research, and developed public service opportunities for local communities.[3] In recent years, urban colleges and universities have begun to promote community engagement more intentionally. Building on a history of outreach and student participation, institutions have embraced engaged citizenship—broadly defined—in mission statements, strategic plans, and resource allocation. A number of urban universities have expanded their work into community development. A prominent example of this trend was the University of Pennsylvania's partnership with the neighboring West Philadelphia district beginning in the late 1990s to rebuild the area's "social and economic capacity" by addressing housing, public education, safety, and economic development through research and financial commitment. A showcase of the partnership, a university-assisted public elementary school, opened in 2001.[4] Other colleges and universities have deepened their commitment to their local communities through the creation of new schools and centers. Tufts University launched an interdisciplinary College of Citizenship and Public Service to empower students, faculty, and alumni to be active leaders in their communities in 2000.[5] In 2005, Bates opened the Harward Center for Community Partnership's to support "teaching, research, artistic creation, environmental stewardship and volunteer service—that enrich community life."[6] The Carnegie Foundation for the Advancement of Teaching's addition, in 2006, of community engagement as a category in their elective classification system for higher education institutions registers this growing interest in civic engagement in the academy.[7]

As the emphasis on civic engagement in higher education continues, urban history courses have a central role to play in providing context, creating new knowledge, strengthening campus–community partnerships, and supporting student engagement. Urban historians teaching in or near city settings have myriad opportunities to connect their courses with their institution's local engagement efforts. Courses in urban history linking local and national trends provide an opportunity to leverage student learning and interest in the history of the city students call home for a few years as a means of generating research with impact and educating engaged citizens for the twenty-first century. Student (and faculty) research on the historical context and contours of the local area equips university and community leaders with important knowledge for making informed decisions about community and economic development and public service opportunities. With community-based courses, activities, and programs on the rise, urban historians and other educators have a range of tools to draw from, including literature on community-based research and service-learning, research funds targeted at those projects addressing local issues, and a growing national network of faculty, staff, and administrators committed to blending theory and practice through community-based learning.[8] New scholarship and networks have emerged along with a number of positions within higher education to coordinate and support the myriad ways individuals and campuses are engaging in local, national, and international communities.

Centering Engagement

Five years ago I stumbled into this world by accident. With my dissertation nearing completion, I began looking for positions. For personal reasons related to my family, I confined my job search to central Virginia.[9] After extensive research I applied for a position that stood out for me: working at the newly created Bonner Center for Civic Engagement (CCE) at the University of Richmond. Situated within the university's academic affairs division, and with a mission of connecting faculty, staff, and students to the metropolitan Richmond community to address social issues through action, reflection, and research, the center appealed to me. I was hired and soon jumped into a broad range of activities, including program planning, fellowship creation, and even looking at carpet samples for the center's new space. The collaborative experience of shaping the CCE from the ground up with the founding director has been incredibly rewarding. In this position I have combined my research and teaching interests in the history of cities and civic participation by low-income Americans with administrative duties focused on building sustained campus-community partnerships and educating students to, in the words of the university's mission statement, "live lives of purpose, thoughtful inquiry, and responsible leadership in a global and pluralistic society."[10] In my position I get to think about social change, to learn about the local community, and to work with students inside and outside the classroom. Serendipity landed me a great job.

The CCE grew out of a long tradition of student service at the University of Richmond. Building on community service days and the Bonner Scholars Program, started at the university in 1993 to fund one hundred students to engage in service and related educational and developmental experiences for ten hours a week, the university began talks with the Bonner Foundation about starting a center in 2002.[11] With the support of the president, provost, the Board of Trustees, and the Bonner Foundation, the university allocated a portion of Bonner Foundation endowment funds to support a new center dedicated to integrating civic engagement into a University of Richmond education.

As urban historians have demonstrated, location and design can influence perceptions of people and places.[12] The University of Richmond, located in the tony west end of Richmond with gothic-style buildings surrounded by lush green space and a lake, is fifteen minutes and a world away from the center city, which has a 20 per cent poverty rate. A large endowment, high tuition rate, and proximity to a country club have contributed to the perception that the school is divorced from the city and focused on perpetuating class privilege by educating students from wealthy families.[13] While located within the city of Richmond, the university is associated with the upper-class neighborhoods of Henrico County near the campus.[14] In Virginia, state laws prevent annexation and call for separate city and county governments. As a result, regional silos have exacerbated disparities in public schools, housing, and wealth between Richmond and the surrounding counties.[15] Battling community misperceptions that the University of Richmond is insular and isolated, as well as challenging some of our students' assumptions that the city of Richmond is dangerous, impoverished, and uninteresting, comprises a key aspect of the CCE's work. We aim to combat stereotypes with substantive, meaningful, educationally grounded programs. With an urban historical frame undergirding many of our efforts, we have taken on the challenge of bursting the University of Richmond "bubble" by making the city an extension of the classroom.

The CCE has created a number of programs to connect the university with the city, to stimulate engagement, and to address community-identified needs while deepening connections with curricular and cocurricular learning. We have established numerous pathways to cultivate civic involvement. Each fall during orientation, 150 first-year students participate in UniverCity Day. This half-day program includes a bus tour of Richmond that introduces students to the city, past and present. As part of the tour, students stop at a nonprofit agency to hear about a social issue and ways to address it through research, internships, and service. Local leaders and faculty present on major issues facing the region. The discussions that UniverCity Day initiates continue throughout the year at weekly CCE brown bags where students, faculty, staff, and community leaders discuss local, national, and international social issues.

Other students take another step out of the "bubble" by signing on to join Build It, the university's largest community engagement initiative focused on sustained partnerships. The four-year-old program is designed to connect students, staff, and faculty to each other and to the residents of metropolitan Richmond through "community-based experiences that support both students' broad learning goals and local efforts to meet pressing social needs."[16] Participants, a number coming from community-based learning courses with a required service component, commit to work weekly at one of six partner sites in Richmond's Highland Park district as part of a sustained partnership with the community.[17] Other students join because they want to volunteer as part of their college experience, and the program provides a structured way for them to serve. Students in the Build It program attend an orientation session where they learn about the neighborhood's history as a middle-class street car suburb in the late nineteenth century, a white middle-class city district in the early 1940s, an African American middle-class district in the wake of white flight by mid-century, an increasingly poor African American neighborhood neglected by the city in the 1970s and 1980s, and, in recent decades, a community fighting crime, class divisions, and creeping gentrification.[18] The session also addresses issues of privilege, reciprocity, responsibility, and partnership. Throughout the school year, the CCE invites Build It participants (and the university community) to attend educational programs on topics such as public schools in Richmond, affordable housing, and payday lending, all to provide further context for their work and to make intentional links with coursework. During the past two years, the CCE has collaborated with our Build It community partners and other nonprofits on two large-scale projects: a campus-community fair held in Highland Park in 2007 and a four-way partnership to construct a historically accurate Habitat for Humanity house in the neighborhood in 2008.[19] As we continue our relationship with Highland Park, we strive to educate students about the need for building sustained, reciprocal partnerships to work for social change.

In connecting with students interested in "change," the CCE staff stresses the importance of research and understanding social problems in context. We have incentivized the process as well. The CCE offers paid summer fellowships that support independent student research and faculty–student collaborative research projects that address ways to "effect change in social, cultural, legal, environmental or political spheres" with dedicated funding for projects focusing on Richmond.[20] Past fellows have examined gentrification in Richmond, the history of community-building in Highland Park, voting technology and its impact on local elections, global warming in Richmond, and other related topics. Fellows are required to share their work in both academic and community forums for broad impact.

Support for faculty is also a critical component of the CCE's work. In May 2008 we piloted a community-based learning faculty fellows program. Thirteen faculty members from four schools and a wide array of disciplines, including business management, English, political science, and law, were selected to transform or create a new course with a rigorous community-based learning—including service-learning or community-based research—component.[21] Faculty fellows participated in a two-day workshop and continued to work with the CCE community-based learning program manager throughout the school year to connect their courses and pedagogical aims to community needs. The faculty cohort will also participate in a faculty learning community throughout the academic year as part of their fellowship.

In spring 2009, in partnership with the University of Richmond's School of Law, the CCE launched the Richmond Families Initiative (RFI) out of the newly opened University of Richmond Downtown, located in the heart of the city. Equipped with a classroom, community room, and multipurpose gallery, UR Downtown houses the Harry L. Carrico Center for Pro Bono Service, and the Jeanette Lipman Family Law Clinic. The latter partners with Virginia Commonwealth University's psychology and social work graduate programs to provide wraparound programs for clients working with the law clinic. The University of Richmond Downtown also serves as the headquarters for the RFI program aimed at promoting healthy, stable families through undergraduate engagement in research, community-based learning, and service in collaboration with nonprofits and city agencies addressing family needs.[22] The RFI provides another outlet for faculty to connect their courses and research while the University of Richmond Downtown serves as a visual and spatial marker of the university's growing commitment to live up to its name.

Civic Engagement House

The line between the CCE's commitment to Richmond and my own is blurred. My partner and I choose to live in the city rather than the surrounding counties that boast lower property taxes and better schools. I am a resident, student, and teacher of the city. A colleague and I are working on a book proposal on leadership, racial politics, and the city's development since 1970 that will follow on Christopher Silver's *Twentieth-Century Richmond: Planning, Politics, and Race*.[23] In the first history course that I taught at the university, "The American City, 1880-Present," I devoted three weeks to a case study on the city. We read Elsa Barkley Brown and Gregg D. Kimball's article on "Mapping the Terrain of Black Richmond" and took a walking tour of Jackson Ward.[24] The executive director of the Richmond's Valentine History Center spoke eloquently on the city's role in our national history when he visited the class. Students wrote their final papers on a Richmond subject, and I learned more about such topics as the baseball stadium, the history of the Churchill neighborhood, gentrification in the Fan District, and the history and spatial impact of the Medical College of Virginia through their work.

Despite the success of these assignments and the course overall, the students had not really engaged the city where they lived in meaningful ways. Many students in class confessed that their trips off campus were confined to nearby suburban malls and restaurants. The parts of the city I assumed would beckon to students, Carytown with its funky shops and cafes and Shockoe Bottom with its cobblestone streets, restaurants, and bars, were not frequented by the young people in my class, a number of whom felt these areas might be "dangerous." Students were not only socially isolated but intellectually adrift from the city as well: few had knowledge of the city's assets, problems, or political landscape. My course had provided research opportunities and a field trip in the city, but it did not do enough to burst the University of Richmond "bubble."

Around the time I fully began to realize my students' disconnection from the city, I was invited to participate in a pilot living-learning community with a focus on civic engagement. Living-learning communities tied to an academic course had been selected by the university community (through an open voting process) as the Quality Enhancement Plan (QEP) portion of our Southern Association of Colleges and Schools (SACS) reaccreditation review in March 2006. Course-based living-learning communities holistically bring together residence life with coursework in an effort to link curricular and cocurricular learning. Participants sign on to live together in a dormitory, to take a course, and to join in cocurricular programs related to the course content. Because civic engagement was deemed a popular topic by students, I was asked to pilot a course-based living-learning community.[25] The opportunity to create a new urban history course with ties to cocurricular programs sparked my interest. Perhaps I could devise a way to structure the living-learning community to combat student apathy, address the historical roots of urban social issues, and activate students. I signed on to pilot a new living-learning initiative called the Civic Engagement House, a coed residential program supported by student development and the CCE. I sought to better integrate urban history, current urban problems, and community engagement on campus.

In the fall of 2006, I began the pilot year of the Civic Engagement House. Thirteen students were selected through an application process in the spring of 2006 to participate in the program. Students signed on to live together for the year, take my one-unit history course in the fall semester, and participate when they could in related cocurricular activities throughout the academic year. These students, representing a variety of majors, moved into the on-campus house and registered for my history course, "The Urban Crisis in America."[26] The course examines the roots and impact of the urban crisis on metropolitan areas from 1945 to the present. Throughout the semester we investigated racial segregation, poverty, demographic shifts, public housing, urban renewal, deindustrialization, and suburbanization. At different points in the course, I brought in Richmond as a case study to illustrate both the specific challenges the region faced as well as to represent problems that impacted metropolitan regions nationally. Texts included Thomas Sugrue's *The Origins of the Urban Crisis: Race and Inequality in Postwar Detroit*, Peter Medoff and Holly Sklar's *Streets of Hope*, Dolores Hayden's *Building Suburbia: Green Fields and Urban Growth, 1820-2000,* Philippe Bourgois's *In Search of Respect: Selling Crack in El Barrio*, essays from Raymond Mohl and Arnold Hirsch's *Urban Policy in Twentieth-Century America*, and a range of primary documents, essays, and films.[27]

The difference between this course and others I had designed and taught came in the assignments. [28] My aim was for students to understand urban social problems in historical context, to examine an issue nationally and locally, and to produce knowledge that could stimulate others to think about and possibly take action for social change. I explained this process to my students as "learning out," and

I used technology at different times to support the process.[29] Students drew on and connected lectures, readings, class discussion, current events, and Civic Engagement House cocurricular activities to write seven blog entries and three comments on their peers' entries. Called the Urban Issues and Action blog, the site described our quest to examine the history of urban policies, problems, and the possibilities for social change. The postings increased in sophistication over the semester as students gained knowledge, and posts and comments from bloggers inside and outside the class fueled their motivation to continue the dialogue. The blog, as a virtual venue, encouraged discussion outside the classroom and provided an alternate format to classroom dialogue for student participation. The assignment also reinforced the concept that students could engage other people at the university and elsewhere in discussing and thinking about urban history, policies, and activism.

The concept of "learning out" played a larger role in the multifaceted individual and group assignment described as an "urban issues and action portfolio." The language from the syllabus sums up my intent:

> Students will form groups to study particular aspects of cities and suburbs after World War II at the beginning of the semester. Each group will work with me to study the historical and current parameters of an urban problem, to account for past attempts to solve the problem, and to pose recommendations for a course of action. Topics for study might include transportation, downtown redevelopment, affordable housing, or the impact of racial segregation on metropolitan regions. This assignment is designed to help you understand urban policy and problems both nationally and locally and *to share what you are learning with others on campus* and in the community. You will have the opportunity to disseminate information on your selected issue and to suggest actions that will affect change.[30]

The portfolio included three different parts designed to build on one another, depending on students' effort and engagement with the assignments. During the second week of class, students formed groups around shared interests they identified. Topics ranged from homelessness to gang violence. Over the next week each group put together a one-page description of the issue they intended to study and an annotated bibliography of sources illuminating the history of the issue. Students met with me to go over their bibliographies and to discuss sources and local resources for them to consider as they moved forward. Students used these shared sources as they began work on their individual research papers related to the group's chosen issue. Due before fall break, these research papers provided an important foundation, along with class materials, for the groups to draw on as they moved forward with the final portfolio assignment: creating a ten- to fifteen-minute documentary film on an urban issue in Richmond.

The preparation for making documentary films, I learned after my pilot year, needs to begin on the first day of the course. My students have had mixed emotions—some excited, some scared—about the prospect the two times I have taught the course. The University of Richmond's Center for Teaching, Learning, and Technology (CTLT) has been a key partner in my efforts to teach students visual literacy skills and the possibilities and limits of historical storytelling through documentary filmmaking. These lessons have come at some cost: I give over two full days of class during the semester so my coeducator from the CTLT can train the students to use the cameras and editing software.[31] I also wrestle with what some of my students call the "beast" of the Institutional Review Board (IRB) requiring each student group, with my assistance, to receive IRB approval before starting their interviews. Receiving IRB approval protects interviewees and allows the students to screen their documentaries widely.[32]

Over the past two years, the benefits of the assignment have outweighed these costs. The documentary has proved to be a powerful engagement tool. Students have toured the city, met and interviewed nonprofit and governmental leaders, and began reading multiple local publications to seek out different perspectives on an issue. They have connected in clear ways urban history to Richmond's present state. They have developed a keener sense of visual literacy. They have started to see themselves as citizens of the city of Richmond, not just as students at the University of Richmond. The range of topics as well as the quality of the documentaries produced over the past two years varies. Film titles include "Homelessness: It Could Be You," "Latinos in Richmond," "Urban Environmental Justice: A Case Study of Battery Park," and "Not Just Sticks and Bricks: Affordable Housing in Richmond." Each film focuses on a social issue in Richmond, within a national historical context, and provides suggestions for change. Public screenings of the films on campus have brought in over one hundred people and students, and I have distributed copies to nonprofits and other citizens to share what we have learned and to galvanize others to think about pressing problems in the city, their historical origins, and possible solutions. The documentaries, as the students, have noted, can continue to interest and educate others after the course ends and even after they graduate: these are intellectual artifacts created for—and often reaching—a larger audience than just me, their professor.

Connecting with the City

In addition to the filmmaking assignment, the "learning" part of the Civic Engagement House living-learning community occurred through the portfolio project and other readings and assignments but also through the cocurricular activities connected to the course. Removed from the traditional classroom setting during Civic Engagement House activities, students loosened up and began asking me and each other questions about life, career choices, city politics, pop culture, and even urban history. The "living" part of the Civic Engagement House created a quick familiarity between the students, a shared purpose, and an ease with one another that yielded great gains in and outside the classroom. Students felt a sense of community early on because of their living arrangements and seemed willing and able to tackle difficult issues such as race, class, and inequality, to disagree with one another respectfully, and to challenge one another to think through their opinions and assumptions.

Cocurricular activities for the living-learning community dovetailed with my work at the CCE. In early September, students took part in a Community Action Poverty Simulation with seventy other participants.[33] Many students wrote insightful and reflective blog postings on their experience at the simulation while critiquing their peers, and, at the time, the simulation itself. Later in the month students joined another class in taking a four-hour bus tour of Richmond neighborhoods with local expert Dr. John Moeser. Equipped with census data on twelve Richmond neighborhoods, the students learned about the history of the city and current challenges facing several districts. Stops included a meeting with a city council member to learn more about her district and a tour of a new real estate project with the developer. This Saturday tour, which I required students to attend, provided important context for the course and their portfolio projects. It also generated more interest in Richmond and sparked new answers to the question I posed the first day of class: "What activities do you all want to do this year?"

Building on student interest, with feedback from the resident assistant, I planned other programs, casting a wide net for "engagement." Many students wanted to volunteer for a day, so we spent a Saturday in Highland Park working on a house rehab project with our Build It community partners. Others asked for social outings into the city, which included dining at independently-owned restaurants and introducing students to the best local ice cream shop in town (Bev's). We also went as a group to hear speakers on and off campus and met up for discussion afterwards. My aim in scheduling these activities was to balance what I thought the students should do with what they wanted to do. When green architecture emerged as a popular discussion topic, I brought in a Leadership in Energy and Environmental Design (LEED)-certified architect to discuss the process and to talk about the LEED buildings on campus at students' request. During exam time I coordinated with the resident assistant to host a study break. Funding from the student development division paid for these activities as well as the programs in the spring. Without the class, there were fewer cocurricular programs during the spring semester. The upside for me was to see continued interest in and discussion about the themes we had covered in the fall. The major spring semester program was the premier of the documentary films. Students, faculty, staff, interviewees, nonprofit leaders, and interested citizens turned out to view and discuss the films with the student filmmakers. A culmination of a semester's work, the films impressed the audience and left me scrambling to order more copies from the CTLT. The assignment, and the course, seemed successful, at least to me.

Evaluation

What about the students? How did they evaluate the documentary film project, the course, and the living-learning experience? At the end of the fall semester, I asked the students to write short reflection papers on the process of completing their group documentary film. The paper provided a chance for each student to assess his or her work and to comment on the amount of effort put in by group members. A constant refrain in the papers was that the assignment, on top of the reading load, was "too much work." These comments were not news to me: I had received similar responses in all of my teaching evaluations in past courses. What surprised me was the impact the process of making the documentaries had on students, only one of whom had any experience with a camera and editing software. A star biology student, taking the course as an elective, reflected on her group's project in a paper entitled "Homelessness: Behind the Scenes."

> In retrospect, this project was the most difficult task I have ever tackled simply because it was completely out of my element and because of the sheer amount of work. In spite of that, I will never regret taking this class and making this documentary because the point of it was bigger than just doing an assignment. It was, finally, the kind of class I came to college for.[34]

A student in a group examining youth gang violence in Richmond characterized the documentary filmmaking process as a struggle. "We struggled to meet as a group, we struggled to find relevant information, we struggled to schedule interviews, and we struggled in editing our documentary." Because of, rather than despite, these challenges, she claimed to have "learned more from it than I have from any other school assignment."[35] Other reflection papers included similar comments about frustration with different members of the group, scheduling issues, and the amount of work involved in film production. Overall, though, students indicated that they had a deeper knowledge of the issue they studied and a sense of responsibility toward the city. They also expressed pride in their films and excitement that the documentaries could reach a broad audience.

The course evaluations bear out the themes in the response papers on the documentaries. With a 100 per cent response rate, I have strong data to draw from. I learned that the course was hard, there was too much reading, and I had set very high expectations. Good, good, and good. Despite complaints about the intense work load, the evaluations were quite positive. One student noted that the course

> … was one of the most rigorous yet rewarding courses I have taken. … I really enjoyed the integration of activism and engagement with developing a working knowledge of the subject areas over the course of the semester. It really allowed us to apply what we learned in real, meaningful context.

In my estimation, because of the living-learning component, students had a richer learning experience, which they reflected in their evaluations. "This course has been a great eye-opener for me in terms of specific historical decisions and trends that create our urban landscape. I feel more empowered and knowledgeable about how to function within American cities," commented an anonymous student. Another student directly addressed the benefits of living with classmates: "As part of a living and learning community, I think its design aids in the community effect. I also think it incorporates innovative ways to get students involved in the community, making change, and connecting those things to the classroom."[36]

While the strong evaluations reflected well on the course and the living-learning community, it was the comments that came from students after the school year ended that point to the value of engaging the city in different ways as part of an urban history course. In July 2007, a rising senior took time away from her summer internship to write me a two-page email to illuminate the connections she was making between her work and the course. As an intern for the local government in her hometown of Orlando, Florida, the student had the opportunity to work on homeless outreach (after making the documentary on homelessness) and downtown revitalization. The course, she explained, had prepared her well for her work:

> So when I hear about HOPE VI or listen in on a community discussion about the need, lack, or growing partnership and input of citizens, businesses, and the government, I think, "Hey! I already know this!" Pretty much everything from green buildings, transportation, affordable housing, etc., is coming into play in my experience as a summer intern, which has been really neat to see.[37]

In 2007, as the second year of the Civic Engagement House was gearing up, a junior from the pilot year wrote an email with a subject line I smiled to read: "The Urban Crisis applies to everything." The student had worked at Camp Bob, an outreach camp for low-income kids in North Carolina, and she found the course materials provided important context for her duties. She continued:

> [T]he knowledge that I gained in Urban Crisis really added a lot to what I experienced working with the kids. The kids who attended Camp Bob faced issues that we studied every single day. A lot of them lived in housing projects, were homeless, or were in (or had brother and sisters in) gangs. If I had not taken your class and done the documentary on gangs or studied

> homelessness, I would not have been as well equipped to work with these kids, because I would have had almost no understanding of the situations that they are in. It was so awesome to apply everything that I had learned in class to something practical—helping kids.[38]

These emails, along with conversations with returning students in the hallways and the dining hall and their zeal to recruit more students to participate in the Civic Engagement House, have proved rewarding. I am now a convert to course-based living-learning communities. The pilot year and my second year with the Civic Engagement House in 2007–2008 have been highlights in my teaching career. Students stop me to talk about sprawl; to express frustration about the history of redlining; to discuss local politics; and to complain that they can not drive on the interstate without thinking of transportation technologies and policy. Spending the year together in and outside the classroom created tight bonds between the students and shaped their shared interest in engaging the city.

Next Steps

The future of living-learning programs at the University of Richmond looks bright. In fall 2008 seventeen students participated in the Civic Engagement House. They lived in a new dorm (nicknamed the "the hotel" by students on campus because it is so plush) and take my course in a classroom located on the ground floor of the building. Over thirty students applied to join the community. I applied what I had learned over the past two years as I continued to improve my syllabus. Four other faculty members also taught courses tied to a living-learning community, and all the students in these courses lived together in the new dorm. Themes included Literature of the Heart, Election 2008, the Earth Lodge, and Spanish in the Community. These programs generated more interest in living-learning communities and provided a basis of support for the development of the university's new Sophomore Scholars in Residence Program (SSIR), the final evolution of the QEP tied to reaccreditation.

Four faculty members, selected through an application process to serve as the first cohort for the SSRI, designed or revised their courses as living-learning communities with a one-unit (four-credit) class in the fall and a half-unit in the spring, plus cocurricular programs for the 2009–2010 school year. After the initial year the number of programs will grow to ten over five years. Targeted at sophomores in an effort to provide a variety of communities for students to join and to improve retention, the four programs have substantial budgets to engage students in a range of educational experiences. As a faculty participant, I revised my course based on past lessons. The biggest changes have come with the addition of a half-unit in the spring and a large budget to spend. I envision adding a comparative element during the spring semester.

My aim is to take the students to New York, Philadelphia, and Washington D.C. during spring break. I hope to tap (and pay) colleagues who teach urban history in these cities to provide educational tours with a focus on the main themes studied in the fall including urban renewal, public housing, poverty, transportation, and downtown development. Along with the tours and discussions with local faculty members, students will meet with political and nonprofit leaders to discuss the topics they covered in their documentary films in the fall. They may consider the following questions: How did the issue play out historically in New York, Philadelphia, and Washington, D.C.? What is the current state of affairs? What steps have leaders and citizens taken to address these issues? Students will also share what they have learned about Richmond, including their documentaries. After the trip, students will write a comparative paper integrating their historical knowledge with the information they learned during the fall and the spring semesters. The comparative framework and spring break trip provide new opportunities for examining urban history, engaging students in active learning, and building community among participants.

As colleges and universities continue to prioritize civic engagement, urban historians are poised to become leaders in thoughtful, rigorous, place-based, community-based learning courses. The elements are in place, including excellent secondary and primary sources to lay out the context for how and why cities and suburbs look and function as they do; eager community partners waiting to build or strengthen relationships with university faculty to foster student learning; seemingly endless research questions; and a growing number of students asking for "real world" experiences as part of their college education. Whether through an individual class, administrative work focused on community engagement, or the further development of informal networks of urbanists committed to creative, meaningful campus-community partnerships, we have untold possibilities to leverage our intellectual and institutional resources for engaged student learning and the slow process of social change.

Acknowledgments

Special thanks to Lisa Krissoff Boehm, Jennifer Blanchard, and Robert K. Nelson for their comments and suggestions on this article.

Notes

1 Kenneth P. Gonzalez and Raymond V. Padilla, "Latina/o Faculty Perspectives on Higher Education for the Public Good," in *Doing the Public Good: Latina/o Scholars Engage Civic Participation* (Sterling, VA: Stylus, 2008), 1.

2 Tony C. Chambers, "The Special Role of Higher Education in Society: As a Public Good for the Public Good," in *Higher Education for the Public Good*, ed. Adrianna J. Kezar, Tony C. Chambers, John C. Burkhardt, and Associates (San Francisco: Jossey-Bass, 2005).

3 The University of Chicago School of Social Service Administration was called the Chicago School of Civics and Philanthropy when it started in 1908. See http://ssacentennial.uchicago.edu/history/ for more information on the history of the school. In "The Impact of an Urban University on Community Development," George Hampton and David Higham outline the categories of contributions urban universities have made to local communities and discuss the emerging role of urban higher education institutions in community development. See www.umdnj.edu/comreweb/pdf/The_Impact_of_an_Urban%20University.PDF (accessed June 24, 2008). For information on IUPUI, see Ralph D Gray, *IUPUI: The Making of an Urban University* (Bloomington and Indianapolis: Indiana University Press, 2003).

4 From http://www.upen.edu/campus/westphilly/index.html (accessed on May 15, 2008). The Penn Alexander School, a collaboration between parents, neighborhood organizations, and the university, opened for kindergarteners and first-graders in 2001. In September 2002, the new building for students in grades K–8 opened. For more information on the history behind the Penn-West Philadelphia partnership, see David J. Maurrasse, *Beyond the Campus: How Colleges and Universities Form Partnerships with Their Communities* (Routledge: New York, 2001), 29–64.

5 The University College of Citizenship and Public Service launched in 2000. The school became the Jonathan M. Tisch College of Citizenship and Public Service after Tisch gave a $40 million gift to endow the school in 2006. See http://www.tufts.edu/home/feature/?p=tisch_gift (accessed May 2, 2008) for information on the gift and http://activecitizen.tufts.edu/?pid=1 for information on the college.

6 Bates announced a $1.7 million endowment to fund the center named in honor of former president Donald Harward and his wife, Ann. David Scobey, the former director of the Arts of Citizenship Program and associate professor of architecture and urban planning at the University of Michigan, was named as the first director of the Harward Center in 2005. See http://www.bates.edu/x166253.xml accessed on May 2, 2008.

7 Schools are selected for the elective classification through a competitive application process. Audrey Williams June, "Carnegie Foundation Offers Community–Engagement Classification," *Chronicle of Higher Education*, April 2006, http://chronicle.com/weekly/v52/i32/32a03003.htm (accessed on May 2, 2008), and Amy Driscoll, "Carnegie's Community–Engagement Classification: Intentions and Insights," *Change*, January/February 2008, http://www.carnegiefoundation.org/files/elibrary/Driscoll.pdf (accessed on May 2, 2008). For more information on the classification and application process, see http://www.carnegiefoundation.org/classifications/index.asp?key=1213.

8 There are a range of networks including the National Service-Learning Clearinghouse (http://www.servicelearning.org/), Campus Compact (http://www.compact.org/), Project Pericles (http://www.projectpericles.org/), Imagining America (http://www.imaginingamerica.org/), and others. Colleges and universities with Bonner Scholars and Bonner Leader programs connect through the Bonner Foundation network (http://www.bonner.org/).

9 I earned my PhD in American studies from the College of William and Mary, where I focused on twentieth-century cultural, social, and urban history, and film.

10 From the University of Richmond mission statement; see http://provost.richmond.edu/.

11 The founding director of the CCE, Dr. Douglas A. Hicks, ably led the center until August 2009 when he returned to full-time teaching in the Jepson School of Leadership Studies. The Bonner Foundation in Princeton University supports the Bonner Scholars Program at twenty-seven colleges and universities across the country. The Foundation seeks to "transform the lives of students... campuses, local communities, and the nation by providing access to education and opportunities to serve." To this end, the Foundation provides four-year scholarships to 1,500 students—Bonner Scholars—annually who have "high financial need and a commitment to service." For more information, see http://www.bonner.org/campus/bsp/ home.htm.

12 See, for example, Thomas J. Sugrue, *The Origins of the Urban Crisis: Race and Inequality in Postwar Detroit* (Princeton, NJ: Princeton University Press, 1996).

13 In 2007, the University of Richmond had over $1 billon in endowment funds. In 2007–2008, tuition, room, board, and fees totaled $44,810. The university uses a need-blind admission process for applicants and has a program that offers full tuition, room, and board to admitted Virginia applicants whose parents earn less than $40,000 a year. The new strategic plan focuses on access and affordability, integrated academic and student experiences, community engagement, and diversity and inclusion.

14 The University of Richmond apartments are located in Henrico County. The rest of the campus is in the city of Richmond. Chesterfield County also abuts the city.

15 The former capital of the Confederacy with a high poverty rate and a majority African American population, Richmond's political landscape has been further complicated by a unique trio of Virginia state laws. Cities in Virginia are independent from counties, forbidden to annex, and constrained by the Dillon Rule that mandates that all local charter changes must be approved by the General Assembly.

16 From http://buildit.richmond.edu/ (accessed May 5, 2008). Text written by Betsy Kelly.

17 The CCE has partnered with the Highland Park community and the following partners since 2005: Overby-Sheppard Elementary School, Chandler Middle School, Hotchkiss Field Community Center, Reach Out and Read Virginia, Boaz and Ruth (a nonprofit dedicated to successful prisoner reentry), and the William Byrd Community House's youth program in Highland Park. These partnerships were established through asset-mapping, dialogue, and relationship building with the goal of forming sustained partnerships to address community-identified needs while educating students. In 2005–2006 approximately eighty students participated in ongoing service, many through service-learning courses. The numbers increased to 150 participants in 2006–2007. During the 2007–2008 school year, one hundred students participated in the program.

18 See Christopher Silver, *Twentieth-Century Richmond: Planning, Politics, and Race* (Knoxville: University of Tennessee Press, 1984), and Danielle Amarant, "The Redevelopment of Highland Park and the Role of the Residents," undergraduate research paper, http://research.richmond.edu/students/Dani_Amarant.htm, for more information on Highland Park's history.

19 The campus-community fair was held at the Hotchkiss Community Field in April 2007. Over three hundred neighbors came out to the event that included a number of booths with social and legal services information, college admissions information, and other services requested by community members, as well as music, food, games, and readings circles for kids. In 2008, the collaborative efforts of four community partners made possible the building of an affordable house in Highland Park. Richmond Redevelopment and Housing Authority donated the land for the project; Richmond Metropolitan Habitat for Humanity offered supplemental funding and logistical support; Boaz and Ruth catered the lunches for the volunteers and provided some volunteers; and University of Richmond provided significant funding and many volunteers, drawn from the ranks of students, faculty, staff, alumni, and friends of the university, for the eight-week build. Two graduates of the Boaz and Ruth program are the owners of the Habitat house.

20 For more information on these ten-week fellowships, see http://engage.richmond.edu/programs/fellowships/research.html.

21 The University of Richmond has five schools: the School of Arts and Sciences, the Jepson School of Leadership Studies, the T. C. Williams School of Law, the Robins School of Business, and the School of Continuing Studies. Selected faculty fellows receive $1,800 to transform a course and $3,000 to create a new course with a community-based learning component. They also receive a stipend for participating in the faculty learning community during the academic year. Faculty fellows, with the support of their department chair or dean, commit to teach the course within three semesters.

22 For more information on the RFI program and the University of Richmond Downtown see http://downtown.richmond.edu/.

23 Thad Williamson, assistant professor of leadership studies, and I have recently begun working on this project. We presented a conference paper at the Urban Affairs Association entitled "Richmond, Doug Wilder, and the Move to a Strong Mayor System: A Report on a Political Experiment in Progress" in April 2008. An excerpt from this paper appeared in the May 14, 2008 edition of *Style Weekly*, Richmond, Virginia. Christopher Silver, *Twentieth-Century Richmond: Planning, Politics, and Race* (Knoxville: University of Tennessee Press, 1984).

24 Elsa Barkley Brown and Gregg D. Kimball, "Mapping the Terrain of Black Richmond," *Journal of Urban History* (March 1995): 296–345. Thanks to Kelly Quinn for recommending this article.

25 My colleague Lee Carlton piloted the first course-based learning community in 2006–2007 called the Outdoor House. Students enrolled in the program lived together, took a course on the environment in literature, and participated in a range of outdoor offerings.

26 My course draws from a rich syllabus put together by Joseph Heathcott. Joseph is currently an associate professor of urban studies at the New School and a leader of the school's civic engagement efforts.

27 Readers interested in a copy of the syllabus can email the author at ahoward3@richmond.edu.

28 I have now taught the course three times and I have included the changes I have made—through trial and error—in this article. I would be remiss not to offer special thanks to Andy Gurka and the Richmond College Dean's Office staff for their support of the Civic Engagement House.

29 "Learning out" is a phrase I came up with in talking with my students.

30 Amy L. Howard, Syllabus, "The Urban Crisis in America," University of Richmond, Fall 2006.

31 Special thanks to Hil Scott in the CTLT.

32 Over the past two years I have developed a template for students to work off of as they put together their IRB forms. The first year, my students' requests were expedited. Last year, with a new person running IRB, the students' requests went to the full committee. I put the IRB deadline on the syllabus and worked with students to submit their forms on time. For an engaging discussion on the debates around IRB in the social sciences and humanities see Zachary Schrag's blog at http://www.institutionalreviewblog. com. While students have learned about the importance of protecting vulnerable populations through the IRB process, they complain and question it.

33 See http://www.communityaction.org/Poverty%20Simulation.htm for more information on the simulation.

34 Kay Holstein, "Homelessness: Behind the Scenes," reflection paper submitted on December 8, 2006.

35 Lindsey Foss, "Youth, Gangs, and Violence Reflection," reflection paper submitted on December 8, 2006.

36 Comments from course evaluations, December 2007.

37 Dominique Thomas, email to author, July 24, 2007.

38 Lindsey Foss, email to author, September 18, 2007. Lindsey went on to say that her experience working at Camp Bob combined with what she learned in the Civic Engagement House led her to "completely change her career path. ... from international work, to work with at-risk kids."

Credit

Urban Renewal

"We Must Start All Over from the Ground Up"

John Rennie Short

In the first part of the postwar era, from 1945 to 1970, the federal government, in alliance with municipal authorities and various business interests, declared war on the central cities. The government spent money and marshaled resources to destroy much of the urban fabric, forcibly relocating central-city inhabitants and aiding the outward movement of jobs and people.

The battle plan was unveiled at the World's Fair in 1939 in New York. An exhibit, funded by General Motors, showed a city of high-rise towers and fast, free-flowing motorways; it was a tantalizing vision presented to almost five million visitors. And in large measure, this vision brutally reshaped central-city America.

The plan drew upon a number of foreign and domestic inspirations. Earlier in the twentieth century, futurist Filippo Marinetti preached the physical annihilation of the traditional city and said, "We must invent and rebuild *ex novo* our Modern City." In Germany Walter Gropius of the early Bauhaus School wanted to replace the shabby irregularity of the slums with giant blocks of straight lines. Other architectural modernists were equally enthusiastic for a clean, new beginning. Le Corbusier's Radiant City plans of the 1920s, for example, envisioned three million people living in giant skyscrapers surrounded by motorways. These visions of modernity involved the destruction of the past. They transcended political ideology and found a home in Mussolini's Rome, Hitler's Berlin, and Stalin's Moscow. Even the liberal critic and public-housing advocate Catherine Bauer, who expounded the value of urban planning for use rather than profit, wrote in a 1934 essay, "If we are to build houses and cities adequate to the needs of the twentieth century, we must start all over again from the ground up."[1] And there were also the business interests, such as General Motors, eager to profit in the proposed transformation; their corporate success was tied to the successful incorporation of this future vision. Various downtown business interests also bought into the vision because they believed, wrongly as it turned out, that redevelopment would halt decentralization and save their investments.

The bright new future merely implicit in the interwar period was developed fully in the immediate postwar period, supported by revolutionaries and corporate executives alike, liberals as well as conservatives. The demand for a new modernist city decreed a massive transformation of the existing city, effacing its past to make room for its future. The future depended upon the destruction of the past. The construction of the modern was the annihilation of history; a forward march of progress held aloft a banner of urban renewal. Old housing, now called slums, was seen as the main problem of urban decline. A special report in *Business Week* in 1940 spoke of the "dry rot" at the core of all American cities.[2] The metaphor provided its own solution: dry rot had to be hacked away.

Urban Renewal

It began with noble aims. The major goals of the Housing Act of 1949 were to eliminate substandard housing and construct good housing. Its main goal was to provide a decent built environment. The act wended a contentious path through Congress. Senators Robert Taft, Robert Wagner, and Allen Ellender first put a housing bill before Congress in 1945. Reformers wanted provisions for low-income housing; business interests wanted urban renewal. The act passed by six votes, and it was the only part of Truman's Fair Deal legislation that was enacted by Congress.

Under Title I of the 1949 act, the federal government would pay for two-thirds of the cost of purchasing and clearing blighted houses. It remains the single largest federal urban program. By 1973, when the program officially ended, two thousand individual projects had been undertaken, covering one thousand square miles of urban land. In total six hundred thousand units were demolished, and two million people were displaced. It ranks with the removal of Native Americans as one of the largest and saddest forced migrations in the history of the nation. It involved thirteen billion dollars in federal spending (in 1973 dollars) and probably closer to almost twenty billion dollars when local-authority spending is included. In today's dollars, it amounts to almost one hundred billion dollars. The program that began with so much hope, the elimination of substandard housing, ended up destroying communities, increasing segregation, and laying the basis for subsequent central-city decline.

Assembling land for major developments in central cities is a costly and complicated process. Urban land is expensive, and landholdings are often fragmented among a variety of owners. These difficulties stymied prewar New Deal goals for major public works in central-city areas. The Housing Act overcame these difficulties by creating local public agencies (LPAs) with the power of eminent domain to acquire sites. The LPAs would acquire land, primarily through federal subsidies but with some municipal dollars, then sell or lease to private developers. Eminent domain had been used in the past to acquire land for public use, such as the construction of a transport route or a school. This new scheme involved the compulsory purchase of private land by a public agency and its transfer to a private corporation. A property owner took the Urban Renewal Agency to court, but in the 1954 ruling *Berman v. Parker*, the Supreme Court ruled in favor of the agency.[3] The legal door was now open.

The initial plan was to demolish substandard housing. The legislation stipulated that for each unit of housing torn down, one should be built. In practice, local authorities and local redevelopment agencies packed with bankers and downtown business interests implemented the plans in favor of replacing low-income housing with tax-generating commercial property. Thus the plan emanating from Washington with concern to eliminate substandard housing soon became compromised at the local level by municipalities and redevelopment agencies following their own definition of urban renewal. Under the Housing Act, agencies were not required to construct housing—the legislation required only "predominantly residential" developments, but even this vague directive was seldom followed. There was no requirement to build low-income housing, and the directive to rehouse displaced families was widely ignored. The initial housing program soon became an urban-renewal program.

The election of Dwight Eisenhower in 1952 produced a further shift away from public housing. A presidential advisory committee on housing inserted changes into the 1954 Housing Act that effectively turned the housing policy into a renewal policy. When implemented on the ground, the program involved a net loss of housing: four dwellings were demolished for every one built, and a tightened housing market emerged for low-income families as low-rent homes were demolished and replaced by more expensive housing and by commercial developments such as parking garages, hospitals, shopping centers, luxury housing, and office blocks. The 1954 Housing Act resulted in one of the largest, most regressive policies ever funded by the federal government. Housing-market conditions were worst for the poorest, whereas business interests received massive federal subsidization.

The use of Title I varied. Table 2.1 lists all those cities receiving more than one million dollars up to 1958. The geographical distribution is clearly related to big cities in the Northeast and Midwest. By 1958 New York City had received thirty-four million dollars, followed by Chicago at nearly fourteen million dollars and Baltimore at almost five million dollars. When we factor in population, Baltimore, New York, and Pittsburgh were in the lead.

Table 2.1. Urban renewal grants, 1949–1958

City	Total ($ million)	Amount ($) per 1,000 of 1950 population	Rank of amount ($) per 1,000 of 1950 population
New York	34.064	4,570	2
Chicago	13.723	3,790	4
Baltimore	4.825	5,084	1
Philadelphia	3.468	1,674	9
Detroit	2.809	1,519	10
Pittsburgh	2.704	4,000	3
Cleveland	2.314	2,531	7
Cincinnati	1.895	3,767	5
Boston	1.808	2,257	8
Minneapolis	1.516	2,909	6

Urban renewal was not restricted to Title I legislation. In many cities urban renewal was undertaken by various combinations of municipal authorities and private developers, with very little federal assistance. In Pittsburgh, for example, federal urban-renewal funds were involved in only one out of the ten projects before 1958. By the late 1950s and 1960s, however, federal funds were being used more, as the 1954 act made it easier to use them for redevelopment rather than rehousing.

The effects were dramatic. Take the case of Detroit. The postwar master plan for the city, devised before the federal legislation, was for the destruction of low-income "blighted" housing and the construction of middle-class housing. Slum clearance, it was hoped, would revitalize the urban core and hence increase the tax-revenue base. The 1949 Housing Act gave federal assistance to these plans. The bulldozer and the wrecking ball were used to knock down densely populated black neighborhoods. In one of the six schemes, the Gratiot redevelopment site on the city's Lower East Side, 129 acres of land were condemned, and almost 2,000 families were evicted. The initial plans called for 3,600 units of public housing on the site, but by 1958 no public housing was built. A twenty-two-story apartment building with expensive rents was the end result of this particular urban-renewal scheme.

The original housing in Gratiot was poor quality. It was the lowest-rent area of the city. Half of the houses did not have indoor plumbing. Slums may have been demolished, but there was no effective rehousing of the low-income residents. When the area residents began to be evicted in 1950, the most vulnerable households were displaced onto a tight housing market. Many households simply moved to nearby areas. With little assistance in getting alternative housing, displaced families simply doubled up and made marginal areas even more marginal through overcrowding. Only about one-third of the residents in Gratiot were rehoused in high-rise blocks; fully one-third could not be traced. City officials estimated that they moved less than one mile to marginal areas of the city. The end result was the "confinement of blacks to densely packed, run-down, and over priced housing."[4]

The most dramatic effect of the war on the central cities was the increasing concentration of the disadvantaged. One example is the Hough (pronounced "Huff") neighborhood, a two-square-mile tract on Cleveland's East Side. In 1900 it was a fashionable neighborhood, with large single-family dwellings housing some of the city's wealthiest residents. In 1950 it was a solid white working-class area. In 1950 only 3.9 per cent of the area's population was African American, and the median family income was almost 90 per cent of the county average. Hough was affected by the urban-renewal project in a neighboring area, the St. Vincent project in the Central District, which began in 1955. This neighborhood was razed to the ground, and almost 1,780 families, most of them black, were displaced. With nowhere else to go, the pressure built. In the late 1950s many white households left, and landlords subdivided dwellings. An owner of two houses and a barn converted them into thirty-three dwelling units. By 1960 the African American population had increased to 73 percent, and the median family income had fallen to 66 per cent of the county average. By 2000 the total population had declined, median income had fallen, and poverty rates were very high (Table 2.2).

Table 2.2. Characteristics of Hough in 1950, 1960, and 1990

Census Variables	1950	1960	1990
Total population	65.424	71,575	19,715
Total housing units	23,118	22,954	9,383
Median family income			
as % of county median	90.9	66.6	30.7
% of families below poverty level	—	—	50.6
% African American	3.9	73.6	97.4

Note: See Norman Krumholz, "Cleveland," 91.

The case of Hough is emblematic of what happened to many of the neighborhoods of central-city America since 1950. From 1950 to 1960 there was increased overcrowding of poor households, creating a time bomb; Hough was the site of a riot in 1966 that lasted for seven days. And since the 1960s there has been a further deterioration, as areas have lost both housing units and population. In many cities the residual population is now overwhelmingly poor and black.

The Federal Bulldozer

Urban-renewal programs not only demolished substandard housing but also destroyed sound housing and functioning neighborhoods. Almost 40 per cent of the dwellings that were demolished were classified as sound. As the program geared up, especially after 1954, little consideration was given to individual families or to the fate of the neighborhoods. Only one-half of 1 per cent of the total budget was spent on relocation. Studies of relocated families paint a depressing picture. One study, for example, examined the fate of families relocated from Boston's West End (Figure 2.1). This thirty-eight-block, forty-one-acre neighborhood of some eighty-five hundred persons was demolished in 1958–1959. Luxury apartments were built on the demolished ruins of the low-rent, low-rise Italian neighborhood, and it was a similar pattern across the country as predominantly low-income housing was destroyed for predominantly upper-income and luxury housing. The study showed that for most of those individuals relocated, housing costs had increased whereas their housing quality was often only marginally improved.[5]

Urban sociologist Herbert Gans lived in the area for eight months in 1957–1958, using local services, attending meetings, and interviewing and socializing with local people. The result is a classic of urban sociology: a sympathetic yet not uncritical account of a working-class Italian neighborhood. Gans did not romanticize the place; he described it as "a run-down area of people struggling with the problems of low-income, poor education and related difficulties." But he could also see that "it was by and large a good place to live." He painted a picture of a vibrant community where life in the neighborhood revolved around family connections more than educational attainment or career aspirations. A tightly demarcated peer-group society was making a life in difficult circumstances. It was less a "*slum*" and more a low-rent area. But the term slum was the designation used to justify its destruction. Only 10 per cent of the residents were rehoused in public housing."[6]

Highway Construction

The postwar highway-building program exacerbated urban clearance. At the end of World War II use of public transportation was at an all-time high: 19 billion trips were made in 1945. By 1975 the number of trips made by public transportation, despite the population doubling in size, fell to 5.6 billion. Cars became the preferred mode of transportation. It was not only a change in the mode of transportation; it was also the creation of a whole new culture as more people saw the world through the windshield of their private automobiles. Car ownership exploded from 25 million cars, or 1 car for every 5.3 people in 1945, to 134 million cars, 1 car for every 1.9 people, in 2000. It was not only that there were more cars but also more car movement as people used them to go to work, go shopping, drop off their kids at school, and go to the movies. The U.S. became a car culture, and U.S. cities transformed to accommodate the private auto. In comparison with other rich countries, public transportation received little government encouragement, and the urban structure evolved to fit the car rather than the car to fit the city.

In 1944 Congress earmarked 25 per cent of all federal highway funds for road construction in urban areas. Half the cost of urban highways was to be paid by the federal government—a generous subsidy—but building new roads in urban areas was still expensive and difficult. Land-assembly and construction costs were huge. With the Federal-Aid Highway Act of 1956, however, the federal government now agreed to pay 90 per cent of the costs of interstate-highway construction. The highway system eventually consisted of more than forty-one thousand miles in one of the biggest construction projects in the history of the world. The concrete motorway became so pervasive that Lewis Mumford suggested that the national flower should be the concrete cloverleaf in honor of the ubiquitous interchanges sprouting across the American landscape.

Road construction became a self-generating system. Roads and highways are still paid for by charges and taxes on automobile use. License and registration fees and federal excise taxes on gasoline go into the Highway Trust Fund that pays for road construction. Road construction generates more traffic, which in turn creates more revenue for road construction.

By 1960 the states were receiving one billion dollars a year for these expressways. Of the twenty-seven billion dollars that was spent on highways between 1956 and 1966, fifteen billion was spent on urban roadways. The construction of these motorways reshaped the city to suit the car and the commuter. The city was remade as a place of automobile flows and traffic movement, a vision of infinite mobility. But at a tremendous cost. Almost fifty-three hundred miles of urban expressways were blasted through cities. Neighborhoods were torn down and people evicted in order to make room for the expressways. Slum housing, substandard housing, and even adequate housing were pulled down to remake the city as a place of endless automotive movement. Between 1957 and 1968 alone, approximately 330,000 housing units were demolished in the federal highway program.

In Detroit the Oakland-Hastings Freeway (later the Chrysler Freeway) went right through the heart of the black Lower West Side, and the Edsel Ford Freeway bisected the black West Side. Neighborhoods were destroyed, and, in their wake, abandoned, depressing wastelands remained. To make way for the Lodge Freeway in Detroit, 109 businesses, 22 manufacturing plants, and 423 residences were condemned for a three-mile stretch, and for its total seven-mile stretch, 2,800 buildings were removed. Families received thirty days' notice and no help in relocation. Throughout the 1950s and 1960s the heart of much of metropolitan America received such treatment. The worst hit were the inner-city, low-income, minority neighborhoods where housing stock was torn down and communities were riven by noisy, polluting motorways that created destruction in order to provide suburbanites with easy and quick journeys to work. The inner city became less a living neighborhood and more a deadened setting for concrete expressways. The highway program benefited the middle- and upper-income commuters; its negative costs were most severely visited upon the inner-city poor.

Housing demolition was not an incidental, unintended consequence of urban highway construction; it was planned. The director of the Bureau of Public Roads, Thomas McDonald, explicitly saw inner-city expressways as eliminating "blighted" districts. The Urban Land Institute, a think tank for downtown property owners and developers founded in 1936, produced a series of pamphlets in the 1950s that promoted expressways as solutions to "blighted" neighborhoods and central-city decline. Expressways cut through the blighted neighborhoods to increase the accessibility of the downtown. Highway construction was explicitly promoted and used to demolish low-income neighborhoods. Expressways were used as blight busters to remove "slums" surgically and to remove from the central city the "dry rot of low-income neighborhoods."[7]

Urban expressways were routed through low-income minority communities: Interstate 95 in Miami plowed through the black community of Overtown; in Nashville Interstate 40 kinked so that it went through the black community of North Nashville; Interstate 81 in Syracuse cut a swath through the city's black inner-city community. Across the country urban highways smashed through low-income, and especially low-income minority, communities: Interstate 10 in New Orleans; Interstate 85 in Montgomery and Interstate 59 in Birmingham, Alabama; Interstate 95 in Camden, New Jersey; and Interstate 77 in Charlotte, North Carolina. In most cities of the country urban highway construction blighted low-income neighborhoods and reduced housing opportunities for the poorest. Highways did not even have the desired effect of bringing people back to the city. Rather than bringing middle-class people back, the new roads made it easier for them to escape. An unmitigated disaster, they blighted much of the central areas of U.S. cities, destroyed communities, and were completely regressive in their distribution of costs and benefits.

The urban-renewal programs and associated highway-construction programs constituted a form of high-intensity warfare against the inner city. Sound housing was demolished, neighborhoods were destroyed, and communities were broken by the bulldozer and the wrecking ball in a concentrated federal program that recast the city in the image of the futurist city first outlined in the 1939 World's Fair in New York. The future had arrived on the broken back of the historic inner city.

Notes

1 Catherine Bauer, "House and Cities," 79–80.

2 A full discussion of the discourse of urban decline is available in Robert A. Beauregard's *Voices of Decline: The Postwar Fate of U.S. Cities*.

3 The case arose from an urban-renewal project in Washington D.C.'s Southwest neighborhood. The area contained many small businesses and homes for African Americans. Sam Berman was the executor of an estate that contained a small department store in the area. When the store was condemned under eminent domain by the public agency responsible for the project, he took the issue to court. It ended up in the Supreme Court that ruled in favor of the public agency and the subsequent urban renewal that demolished the homes and business and replaced them with offices and residential and hotel complexes. For years afterward Southwest had the dismal, antiseptic feeling of poor architecture and even worse urban design that marked so many of the urban-renewal schemes. Lacking restaurants, shopping, and entertainment the area was a sterile barren, monotonous district. Since the early 2000s there are signs of revival, almost fifty years after the Supreme Court ruled in favor of its destruction.

4 Thomas J. Sugrue, *The Origins of the Urban Crisis*, 55. Sugrue's careful analysis of Detroit suggest that concentrated racialized poverty owes its roots to the urban policies pursued in the 1940s and 1950s.

5 See Chester Hartman, "The Housing of Relocated Families."

6 Herbet Gans, *The Urban Villagers*, 315.

7 Raymond A. Mohl, "Planned Destruction: The Interstates and Central City Housing," 227.

Works Cited

Bauer, Catherine. "House and Cities." In *Art in America in Modern Times,* edited by Holger Cahill and Alfred Barr Jr. New York: Reynal and Hitchcock, 1934.

Beauregard, Robert A. *Voices of Decline: The Postwar Fate of U.S. Cities*. 2d ed. Malden, Mass: Blackwell, 2003.

Gans, Herbert. *The Urban Villagers*. New York: Free Press, 1962.

Hartman, Chester. "The Housing of Relocated Families." *Journal of the American Institute of Planners* 30 (1964): 266–86.

Mohl, Raymond A. "Planned Destruction: The Interstates and Central City Housing." *In From Tenements to the Taylor Homes*, edited by J.F. Bauman, R. Biles, and K.M. Szylvian. University Park: Pennsylvania State Univ. Press, 2000.

Sugrue, Thomas J. *The Orgins of the Urban Crisis*. Princeton: Princeton Univ. Press, 1996.

Credit

Short, John Rennie. "Urban Renewal: 'We Must Start All Over from the Ground Up." *Alabaster Cities: Urban U.S. Since 1950* (Syracuse: Syracuse University Press, 2006. 19–29. Print. Reprinted with permission.

Doing a Florida Thing: The Creative Class Thesis and Cultural Policy

Jim McGuigan

The work of Richard Florida has proven extremely influential in cultural policy circles in recent years. His arguments concerning 'the rise of the creative class' and the concentration of 'technology, talent and tolerance' in successful cities are grounded in certain theoretical assumptions and supported by specific kinds of evidence that should be submitted to critical interrogation in order to test their robustness. This paper addresses the following questions: What are the theoretical assumptions underpinning Florida's arguments? Is the evidence upon which these arguments are substantiated sound? What are the implications of Florida's thesis for cultural policy? A critical reading of Florida's key writings is presented. The paper also comments on the impact of Florida's work around the world and focuses upon a particularly significant policy document in Britain, the Work Foundation's *Staying Ahead—The Economic Performance of the UK's Creative Industries.* It is necessary to trace the intellectual framework of 'post-industrial' thinking about contemporary capitalism, the incorporation of bohemianism into business and aspirations for urban regeneration and competitive advantage in a global economy with local and regional peculiarities in order to evaluate the 'Florida thing.' The paper reflects upon the synthesis of cultural policy with economic policy and argues that this is not the best way forward for the politics of art and culture in the twenty-first century.

Introduction

A few years ago, on a lecture tour of Australia and New Zealand, whilst at Canberra, I received an email from a colleague who was organizing a couple of lectures for me in Wellington, New Zealand. He told me that the city of Wellington was "doing a Florida thing." At first, I misunderstood his meaning. I thought by "Florida" he was referring to a state in the south-eastern United States and, straight away, I wondered what Wellington might have in common with Miami and what exactly it was that the capital of New Zealand might be learning from the capital of Florida. Immediately, it occurred to me that there was something distinctly Floridian lacking in Wellington, to whit, Hispanic gangsters. Perhaps they needed to bring in a few such folk in order to liven up the place and recruit some coppers from the Miami Vice department too. Of course, I was soon disabused of my error. Shortly afterwards, I spoke at a seminar in Wellington that was chaired by the mayor. Apparently, Richard Florida, the American management guru, had been there some time earlier doing something similar to myself but, as it transpired, with greater impact than my miserable discourse. They were following his precepts for urban development. I realised that I needed to read Florida seriously in order to grasp the appeal of his magical advice, which was not about attracting Hispanic gangsters after all but, instead, about capitalising not "the rise of the creative class."

On reading his work, I realised that Richard Florida's thesis was less impressive than it might appear at first sight to readers without an academic background in the social sciences. It was evident that Florida's discourse is characterised by a typically managerialist rhetoric that over-simplifies and, to an extent, bowdlerises social-scientific reasoning and research. To demystify his work, it is necessary, then, to interrogate Florida's pronouncements with regard to their theoretical assumptions, empirical evidence, and implications for cultural policy.

It is perhaps surprising that Florida's work should have been taken so seriously by some cultural policy scholars (e.g. Billie 2008), especially considering the fact that he is not much if at all interested in cultural policy itself. Florida's theorising is derivative of post-industrial theory, which is at least 50 years old and was given its fullest enunciation in Daniel Bell's (1976 [1973]) *The Coming of Post-Industrial Society: A Venture in Social Forecasting* and acknowledged by Florida himself:

> We've effectively become the "post-industrial society" that Harvard sociologist Daniel Bell predicted in the 1970s, hinging our prosperity on the growth of a knowledge class, reliant on science to bring forth innovation and social change, and more dependent on services than goods. (2008, p. 103)

Florida's ideas—or, rather, buzzwords—make little in the way of an original contribution to such questionable thought, and the specious arguments he repeats constantly are either seriously flawed or merely trite. Although Florida combines ideas from the sociology of culture with post-industrial theory, in fact, his work is not so much that of a social theorist or a cultural researcher as a knowledge entrepreneur, skilled at combining the ideas of others and artful at drawing attention to his not entirely original insights and marketing them as consultancy. He is currently a professor at the Rotman School of Management, University of Toronto, having moved there from George Mason University in Washington in 2007. His principal source of income, however, probably derives from his consultancy firm, the Creative Class Group, where his many clients range from Absolut Vodka through BBC Creativity and Audiences, Citigroup Investment Inc., *Esquire* Magazine, Goldman Sachs, IBM, and

Microsoft to a number of city and indeed national governments, including Dublin, San Diego, Seattle, Toronto, Washington, and, of course, New Zealand. Whatever we might wish to say for and against the relation between research and consultancy, it is evident that Florida's work is driven by consultancy rather than by research as such; and, indeed, consultancy of a rather promiscuous kind. According to its website, the Creative Class Group: "offers regions, companies and associations the customized information, analysis, tools and research necessary for competitiveness and greater economic prosperity" (Creative Class Group 2008). It is not surprising that some are inclined to view Florida as a busy, globetrotting trader in a good old American product, snake oil, instead of a serious scholar with some genuine wisdom to impart for cultural policy.

The Creative Class

Florida's (2003 [2002]) main thesis—stated in his book, *The Rise of the Creative Class*—is a familiar iteration of a longstanding tradition of "new class" theorising, going back at least to the communist dissident, Milovan Djilas (1966 [1957]) in the 1950s. Class formations are complex and they change over time, particularly due to shifting occupational structures and the habitus of different socio-economic groups. In Djilas's thesis, a new class was identified as a power bloc, the party *nomenklatura*. Florida discerns the emergence of a specifically middle-class formation (a power bloc?), rather more reminiscent, however, of Pierre Bourdieu's (1984 [1979]) "new *petite bourgeoisie*," the significance of which Florida both oversimplifies and exaggerates. Bourdieu's new *petite bourgeoisie* was famously characterised by him as consisting of "all the occupations involving presentation and representation" (1984, p. 359). They include "the cultural intermediaries" of advertising, journalism, marketing, public relations, and the modern—or rather, postmodern—media and culture generally. Their numbers have increased dramatically since the Second World War, and these people are, in Bourdieu's terms, engaged in a struggle for distinction. Their strategy tends to blur the boundaries between and diminish the hierarchical structure of, on the one hand, the arts and high culture and, on the other hand, commerce and mass-popular culture.

What we find, however, is that Florida's "creative class" is a much broader formation than even Bourdieu's new *petite bourgeoisie*, making up an astonishingly high proportion of the population in the USA—for, after all, it is with the USA that he is principally concerned despite his influence on the rest of the world. Florida (2003, p. 74) makes the startling claim that the Creative Class constitutes 38.3 million Americans and 30% of the U.S. workforce. Yet, it transpires that this claim is not quite so startling as it appears at first sight because the Creative Class is divided into two segments: the Super Creative Class and Creative Professionals. The Super Creatives, in fact, are made up of 11.7% of the U.S. workforce. Super Creatives range from artists and educators through—somewhat less obviously "super creative" in an artistic sense—librarians, scientists, engineers and computer and mathematical occupations (Florida 2003, p. 330). So, even the 11% calculation might be considered a little exaggerated. The rest—the Creative Professionals, making up 18.3% of the U.S. workforce—include lawyers, managers, technicians and what Florida calls "high-end" sales personnel.

So, the Creative Class, then, is largely what would otherwise be called routinely "the professional-managerial class," which also includes artistic occupations. Florida (2003, p. 68) says that the "distinguishing characteristic of the Creative Class is that its members engage in work whose function is to 'create meaningful new forms.'" It is reasonable to ask, exactly how many of those formally listed in the category of Creative Class would this actually apply to?

The American Working Class consists of 33 million workers (26.1% of the workforce), according to Florida, whereas there are 55.3 million Service Class workers, 43% of the workforce, which is a much more meaningful indication of "post-industrialism" than a dubiously calculated Creative Class. And, as Florida (2003, p. 74) says, the Service Class "includes workers in low-wage, low-autonomy service occupations such as health care, food preparation, personal care, clerical work and other low-end office work."

What is the social character of this putatively new Creative Class (which is not quite so prominent, we learn on close inspection, as we might initially have supposed)? In depicting their habitus, Florida follows David Brooks's typification of the bobo—the bourgeois bohemian—and calls it "the Big Morph" whereby there is "a new resolution of the centuries-old tension between two value systems: the Protestant work ethic and the bohemian ethic" (Florida 2003, p. 192). Brooks provided a superstructural description of how the differences between business people and bohemian rebels have dissolved so that each side of the divide co-opts the other side's *modus operandi* and only noted in passing that this represented "a cultural consequence of the information age" (Brooks 2000, p. 10). Florida went further in supplying a deeper, infrastructural account of the socio-economic foundation of the bobo lifestyle. These people, he says, are on "a passionate quest for experience" (Florida 2003, p. 166), but they are not against working hard and making money. Their creative energy, apparently, is the driving force of wealth creation in the world today, not the people who actually make things. Florida disputes Robert Putnam's (2000) concern with social capital. Creative people are individualistic and expressive. They like "cool" scenes in which to hang out and where they can interact with other similarly go-getting bobos without having to go the whole hog by actually reinventing the intimate communal ties of a *passé* small-town America.

The Creative City

This characterisation of the Creative Class is at the crux of Florida's arguments concerning the success of certain kinds of city, which is where a fascination with his work amongst cultural-policy professionals comes into the picture. In this sense, Florida's work is readily taken to resonate with that of Charles Landry and Franco Bianchini (1995) on "the creative city," which has been especially influential in Europe. However, as has already been suggested, a principal concern with cultural policy, which certainly characterises Bianchini's work, is not actually a motivating factor shared by Florida, who is much more concerned, in effect, with economic policy and how it may be enhanced by cultural means, thus reducing culture to economics. Place, it seems, matters today for economic development—though it is hard to imagine that was ever in doubt—in spite of the speed and convenience of remote communications across vast tracts of space facilitated by the Internet in a global world. It is on this basis that Florida's work can be connected to a cultural-policy discourse of culture-led urban regeneration, though, when looked at closely, the good sense of that connection tends to diminish in plausibility.

Florida, it is necessary to stress yet again, is not so much concerned with cultural development as with economic development. According to Florida, "economic growth" derives from a felicitous combination of three factors, "the three Ts": Technology, Talent and Tolerance (Florida 2005, p. 6). As post-industrial/information-society theorists all argue, high-tech is at the heart of post-industrial prosperity (Webster 2007). This tends to be closely correlated, according to the Creative Class thesis, with the attraction of talented people to particular places, Silicon Valley in California being an obvious example. For Florida, talent is defined simply by the possession of a bachelor's degree, which is a rather crude calculator of talent, to say the least, in the era of massified higher education.

Tolerance is also crucial to economic success in his scheme of things, though it is not quite clear why; and it tends to be found in cities like New York and Seattle. These are places that welcome diverse groups of people in terms of ethnic mix and lifestyle preferences. Especially notable in this respect is that they are Gay-friendly places.

Florida produces indexes that demonstrate the concentration of Technology, Talent and Tolerance in particular city locations. For instance, he has, to quote him, "a Bohemian Index … a measure of the concentration of working artists, musicians and the like in given areas" (Florida 2005, p. 19). To illustrate the point, he says, "Seattle, New York and Los Angeles top the list with more than nine bohemians per thousand people" (2005, p. 122). Moreover, Florida even has what he calls a "Coolness Index" that correlates with all the other factors that make for successful places: "high-human capital individuals, particularly young ones, are drawn to places with vibrant music scenes, street-level culture, active nightlife and other sources of 'coolness'" (2005, p. 101). In sum, then, making a not entirely logical connection from this kind of data, "ideas and intellectual capital have replaced natural resources and mechanical innovation as the raw material of economic growth [in] the age of creative capital" (2005, p. 144).

Florida is a writer who misses no tricks in the literary marketplace of knowledge. He is adept at popularising his ideas, down to writing advice books for go-getting bobos about the virtues of personal mobility. His latest book, *Who's Your City? How the Creative Economy is Making Where to Live the Most Important Decision in Your Life* (Florida 2008), largely repeats, like all his books, what he has said *ad infinitum* elsewhere but with an added spin. This particular text reads like a meta-estate agent's guide for bobos. The use of "You" is very significant. It is an advice book, indicating where it would be lucrative and comforting to live. In order to get on it might be best to move, to go where the networking is better and the amusements are to your taste; somewhere like Toronto. Such advice resonates with Luc Boltanski and Eve Chiapello's ideal figure of "the new spirit of capitalism," "the *network-extender*" (Boltanski and Chiapello 2005 [1999], p. 390). As Boltanski and Chiapello remark, "Great men do not stand still. Little men remain rooted to the spot" (p. 361). This "mobile/immobile differential" is relational in Boltanski and Chiapello's account: the mobility of some is facilitated by the immobility of others.

It is important to emphasise that Florida is not really motivated at all by the usual concerns of cultural policy or at least the normative concerns of agents of cultural policy hitherto—to list some obvious ones, such as the preservation of heritage, wider social access to cultural resources, opportunities for cultural production, and the like—as with accounting for why some places are economically successful in an era of de-industrialisation in what were hitherto the leading centres of industrial production in the sense of making things, especially in the USA. And, he finds that certain kinds of lifestyle culture—what I have elsewhere called the culture of cool capitalism (McGuigan 2009)—contribute to economic success by attracting the agents of post-industrial wealth creation to particular places. Florida's thinking, it is worth noting in passing, also resonates with Jeremy Rifkin's (2000) notion of "cultural capitalism"? This is a way of thinking that also characterises Bill Gates's latest pronouncements. In his speech at the 2008 World Economic Forum, the founder of Microsoft spoke of "creative capitalism," though he was anxious, as well, to stress the nodal importance of self-interest and the magic wand of finalisation as the driving forces of wealth creation today (Gates 2008). This is not the place to discuss the downside of finalisation, which is something that we have all experienced rather dramatically in the recent period. More germane here, with regard to cultural policy, is the buzzword, "creativity."

The Creative Economy

Florida's ideas are not so much an original contribution to cultural policy as consistent with certain questionable assumptions and conventional wisdoms on economic policy that come together around a notion of "the creative economy." Take New Labour Britain, for example, where the government has enshrined this notion of "creative economy" as a key plank of economic policy. Since this seems to enhance the role of cultural policy in governmental strategy, it has been seized upon enthusiastically as the leading justification—wealth creation—for subsidising culture. Thus, cultural-policy discourse has, in effect, been infected by economistic reasoning and, indeed, turns into a branch—and a weak branch at that—of economic policy.

Key here, of course, is the notion of "creative industries," a term which seems first to have been used to widespread attention around the world in a British Department for Culture, Media and Sport (DCMS) document of 1998, *Creative Industries—Mapping Document*. The very notion of "creative industries" used by that document covered an expansive range of practices, from advertising to software in general, not just practices like the arts, film and television. It was estimated in 1998 that the creative industries contributed £60 billion a year to the British economy and employed something in the region of one-and-a half million people. Prophetically, the document claimed that: "The value of the creative industries to the UK domestic product is ... greater than the contribution of any of the UK's manufacturing industry" (Creative Industries Task Force 1998, p. 8), though it did not cite comparative figures for either armaments or pharmaceuticals. This was an extraordinary declaration for the historical "workshop of the world" and was part of a short-lived rhetoric of "Cool Britannia" during New Labour's first term of office.

A couple of years later, the mapping document was revised and updated. The original definition of creative industries was retained—"those industries which have their origin in individual creativity, skill and talent and which have a potential for wealth and job creation through the generation and exploitation of intellectual property"—whilst also adding "the close economic relationships with sectors such as tourism, hospitality, museums and galleries, heritage and sport" (Ministerial Creative Industries Mapping Group 2001, p. 00.05).

Recently, the DCMS commissioned the Work Foundation to further develop the government's "Creative Economy Programme." The Work Foundation report, *Staying Ahead*, which was published in 2007, cites Richard Florida as an inspiration. His imprimatur was hardly necessary, however, since the reduction of culture to economics, which is hardly a rhetorical overstatement in the circumstances, has been such a deeply rooted feature of hegemonic neoliberalism since the 1970s.

The Work Foundation report observed that the UK—or what Raymond Williams (1983) was apt to call "Yookay PLC" in his more facetious moments several years ago—has the largest creative industries sector in the European Union (EU) and is arguably the largest proportionately in relation to the Gross Domestic Product (GDP) in the whole wide world; second only to the USA in range, yet much smaller in size (and hegemonic reach), of course. The creative industries are calculated to account for 7.3% of "gross value added (GVA)," twice that of the tourist industry's contribution to the British economy and 2.7% of total employment, though the percentage is higher if jobs linked but not directly involved in creative work are included, giving a grand yet vaguely computed total of 1.8 million. In actual fact, such figures are not anything like so impressive as the report makes out. Nevertheless, it might be argued, the calculated growth rate of 14.9% in the late 1990s, led especially by software development, gives rather more convincing support to the claim that the creative industries are at the cutting edge of the economy as a whole. Still, a certain measure of scepticism is called for, especially considering that the largest industrial sectors in Britain include armaments, finance and pharmaceuticals, making up a much larger part of the economy than the creative industries; and of which none were noticeably in decline until the cataclysm of 2008 when the sub-prime spark of the previous year in the USA finally blew up the tinder box of the international financial system, impacting hugely on places like the City of London, not to mention the rest of us wherever we are.

In addition to establishing the quantifiable facts, the Work Foundation report is devoted to identifying what it calls the "drivers" of "the creative economy"—such as stimulating demand and providing education and skills—and what the government can do to oil these drivers. According to the report, "Creativity and innovation are overlapping concepts" (Work Foundation 2007, p. 6). Also, the creative industries are integral to "a paradigm shift" towards "the knowledge economy" and the development of a "new class of consumers" (p. 117). Typical of the Work Foundation's rhetoric is the following claim: "Creative origination is sparked by challenges to existing routines, lifestyles, protocols and ways of doing things and where societies want to experiment with the new" (p. 18). Furthermore, "expressive value" is said to be the fundamental source of value in the world. The purpose of cultural industries—and, more broadly, creative industries—is to commercialise expressive value; hence the importance of exploiting intellectual property rights in order to "grow" the business of a country: "The business model of the creative industries depends significantly on their capacity to copyright expressive value" (p. 23).

Staying Ahead addresses the thorny problem of definition and explains why it is necessary to expand the definition of cultural industries into the all-encompassing idea of creative industries in spite of the fact that advertising and art are not necessarily the same kind of thing. A diagram to illustrate what is at stake is helpfully provided (p. 103):

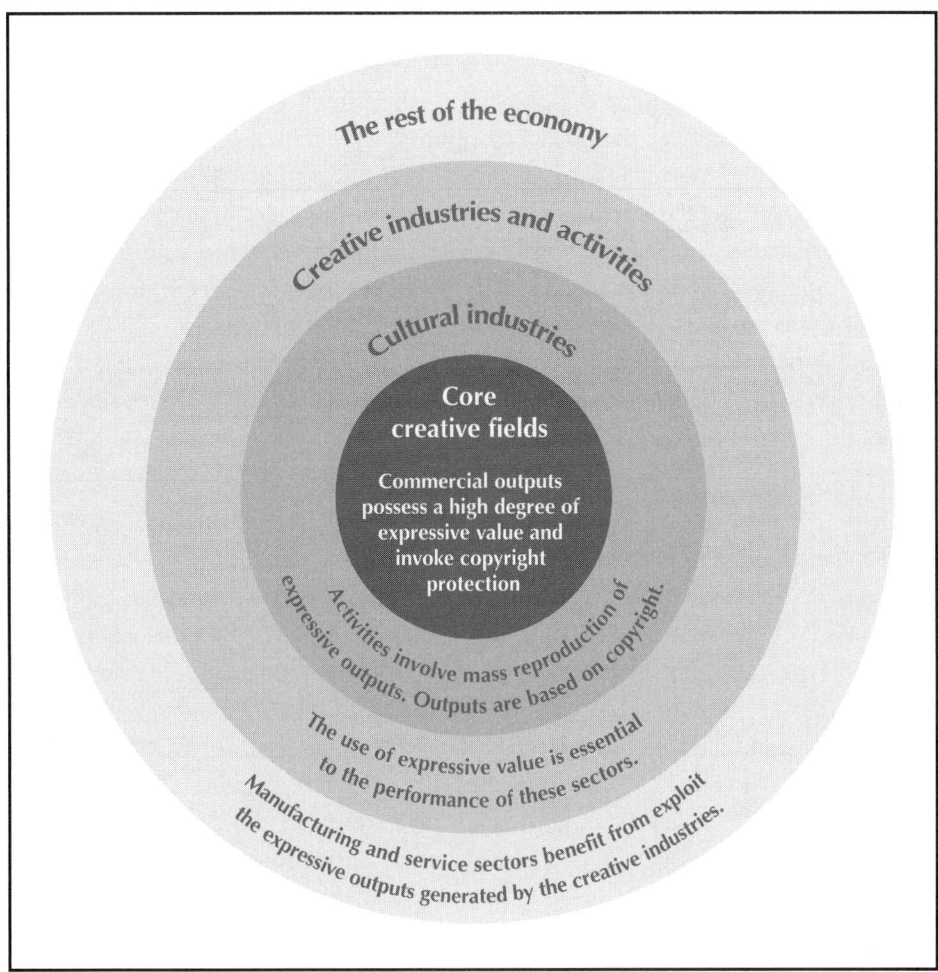

The creative industries: A stylised typology.

At the centre—or "core"—of the diagram, copyrightable expressive value, the object of "cultural industries," is illustrated with a list of typical examples, including quite reasonably, no doubt, video games. Circling further out are the "creative industries," including design and software other than video games, that is, rather more "functional" entities; and constituting "an important bridge to the wider economy" (p. 106). This circle represents the mediation between "cultural industries" and "the rest of the economy," illustrated by "the emotional ergonomics of the Apple iPod and Dyson's vacuum cleaner or the 'retailment' of service, e.g. Virgin Atlantic and BA." Quite apart from the questionable choice of examples and infelicitous use of language, as the modelling of an economy, it is rather hard to take such an implausible scheme seriously.

Are the creative industries—not to mention the cultural industries—being asked to do too much here? There is a pervasive blurring of categories—indeed, a category error—going on and excessive fuzzy reasoning in the construction of this model. Another currently fashionable example of such confusion is the argument that "creativity" in artistic practice and business management are roughly the same kind of thing (Bilton 2007). Moreover, in "the creative economy," seems to be swallowing up creativity whole rather like a Pac-Man on the loose. It is tempting to agree with Larry Elliott and Dan Atkinson's (2007, p. 92) summary judgment on creative economy rhetoric: "Bullshit Britain reaches its apotheosis in the lionization of the cultural industries." "Bullshit" is not an unknown phenomenon in academic discourse (see Belfiore 2008) and especially in its degenerate branch of knowledge entrepreneurship that so infects the field of cultural-policy research.

The Fallacies of Economistic Cultural Policy

To reiterate, Florida's principal concerns are not to do with cultural policy as such but instead are about the articulation of neoliberal economics with cool culture. This is also true of the Work Foundation's 2007 report and the discourse of the creative economy promoted by the British government in the mid-2000s. That chain of reasoning, which I have traced here, is only apparently and, indeed, tangentially a matter of specifically *cultural* policy. In consequence, I would argue, it is a fatal error on the part of agents of cultural policy in Britain—and elsewhere—to align themselves uncritically with this discourse of the creative economy, which I have sought to show is associated with the thesis of a Creative Class and, by implication, a particular set of class interests and a reading of the world which has long been questionable and especially so since the crisis of virtual capitalism in the sense of the ruses of finance capital—and hence of "real," that is, neoliberal capitalism—in the recent period.

Economistic cultural policy, then, is connected to a dubious set of political and, indeed, sociological assumptions that can be questioned on many different grounds. The context that has fertilised this set of assumptions is that of de-industrialisation in the formerly "industrial" societies and a neoliberal regeneration strategy that is represented by an ideological rhetoric that is variously named, "post-industrialism," "information society," "knowledge society" and, fairly recently, "cultural capitalism." Like all powerful ideological forces, this complex of ideas has not been entirely false. It relates to certain realities, most notably the transfer of certain kinds of work from high-wage to low-wage economies and the globalisation of economic process, informational and cultural exchange. Putting it crudely, stuff is designed and marketed in what are still comparatively high-wage parts of the world and made in low-wage parts of the world where the conditions of work are appalling. It is all coordinated by fast communications. The general process has already been named in the field of cultural-policy studies by Toby Miller and George Yudice (2002) as "the new international division of cultural labour" (NICL), a sub-category of the new international division of labour in general. The effects of the NICL have been traced by them in several cases around the world. Uncritical acceptance of this state of affairs anywhere, which can be extremely exploitative, is ethically questionable and—more consequential—politically unstable. Students of cultural policy should instead of succumbing to reductively economistic discourse be concerned not only with the conditions of labour in general throughout the world, like any responsible citizen, but also quite particularly, for this field of enquiry, with the actual conditions of cultural labour that have suffered likewise from what may become, perhaps over the next few years, an increasingly delegitimised way of running the world (see McGuigan, forthcoming).

It is quite reasonable that socially and culturally responsible people, wherever they are, may be keen to ameliorate the situation for their own people with, say, vocational training for the newer economic realities, strategies for reviving run-down places and staking claims on resources for making life pleasurable and meaningful. Urban regeneration strategies are typical manifestations of this reasonableness. And, it is not unusual for culture to be latched onto as the panacea for a whole plethora of woes in particular places. It is extremely doubtful, however, that culture can solve deep-seated economic and political problems in places suffering from routine forms of creative destruction. Unfortunately, this mistaken assumption has distracted exponents of cultural policy from their principal concerns, which are probably best summed up as attempts to facilitate something differently pleasurable and meaningfully better for most people than the usual produce of cool capitalism.

Acknowledgments

I should like to thank Michael Volkerling for alerting me to the Florida craze and Jen Webb for correcting my initial mistake concerning it. I should also like to thank Kevin Mulcahy for his constructive and helpful remarks on my paper at the International Conference on Cultural Policy Research at Istanbul in August 2008 and for his more generally entertaining contribution to that conference.

Works Cited

Belfiore, E., 2008. "On Bullshit in Cultural Policy Practice and Research—Notes From the British Case." *5th international conference on Cultural Policy Research*, 20–24 August, Istanbul: Yeditepe University.

Bell, D., 1976 [1973]. *The Coming of Post-Industrial Society: A Venture in Social Forecasting.* Penguin: Harmondsworth.

Billie, T., 2008. "The Creative Class and Preferences for Culture." *5th International Conference on Cultural Policy Research*, 20–24 August, Istanbul: Yeditepe University.

Bilton, C., 2007. *Management and Creativity: From Creative Industries to Creative Management*. Oxford: Blackwell.

Boltanski, L. and Chiapello, E., 2005 [1999]. *The New Spirit of Capitalism*. G. Elliott, trans. London: Verso.

Bourdieu, P., 1984 [1979]. *Distinction: A Social Critique of the Judgement of Taste*. London: Routledge.

Brooks, D., 2000. *Bobos In Paradise: The New Upper Class and How They Got There*. New York: Simon & Schuster.

Creative Class Group, 2008. Clients and workshops & services. Available from: http:// www.creativeclass.com [Accessed 16 November 2008].

Creative Industries Task Force, 1998. *Creative Industries: Mapping Document*. London: Department for Culture, Media and Sport.

Djilas, M., 1966 [1957]. *The New Class: An Analysis of the Communist System*. London: Unwyn.

Elliott, L. and Atkinson, D., 2007. *Fantasy Island: Waking Up to the Incredible Economic, Political and Social Illusions of the Blair Legacy*. London: Constable.

Florida, R., 2003 [2002]. *The Rise of the Creative Class: And How it's Transforming Work, Leisure, Community and Everyday Life*. Melbourne: Pluto.

Florida, R., 2005. *Cities and the Creative Class*. London: Routledge.

Florida, R., 2008. *Who's Your City? How the Creative Economy is Aking Where to Live the Most Important Decision of Your Life*. New York: Basic Books.

Gates, B., 2008. "Remarks on a New Approach to Capitalism in the 21st Century." World Economic Forum, 24 January, Davos, Switzerland.

Landry, C. and Bianchini, F., 1995. *The Creative City*. London: Demos.

McGuigan, J., 2009. *Cool Capitalism*. London: Pluto.

McGuigan, J., forthcoming. "Creative Labour, Cultural Work and Individualisation." *International journal of cultural policy* [special issue on creativity].

Miller, T. and Yudice, G., 2002. *Cultural Policy*. London: Sage.

Ministerial Creative Industries Mapping Group, 2001. *Creative Industries: Mapping Document*. London: Department for Culture, Media and Sport.

Putnam, R., 2000. *Bowling Alone: The Collapse and Revival of American Community*. New York: Simon & Schuster.

Rifkin, J., 2000. *The Age of Access: How the Shift From Ownership to Access is Transforming Capitalism*. London: Penguin.

Webster, F., 2007. *Theories of the Information Society*. 3rd ed. London: Routledge.

Williams, R., 1983. *Towards 2000*. London: Chatto & Windus.

Work Foundation, 2007. *Staying Ahead: The Economic Performance of the UK's Creative Industries*. London: Work Foundation/DCMS.

Credit

McGuigan, Jim. "Doing a Florida Thing: The Creative Class Thesis and Cultural Policy." *International Journal of Cultural Policy*, 15.3 (Aug. 2009): 291–300. Print.

Neoliberals Dressed in Black; or, the Traffic in Creativity[1]

Imre Szeman

In communist society, where nobody has one exclusive sphere of activity but each can become accomplished in any branch he wishes, society regulates the general production and thus makes it possible for me to do one thing today and another tomorrow, to hunt in the morning, fish in the afternoon, rear cattle in the evening, criticize after dinner, just as I have a mind, without ever becoming hunter, fisherman, herdsman, or critic.

Karl Marx
The German Ideology

It is now impossible to tell an espresso-sipping artist from a cappuccino-gulping banker.

David Brooks
Bobos in Paradise

With the publication of *The Rise of the Creative Class (RCC)* in 2002, Richard Florida became almost instantly an influential figure across a range of fields and disciplines. An academic by training, over the past decade Florida has advanced ideas that have shaped discussions of current affairs and the decisions made by businesses and governments. Although he did not invent the term "Creative Class," his thorough analysis and description of the characteristics and function of what he sees as this newly hegemonic socio-economic group guaranteed that he would be identified as its progenitor and primary spokesperson. Florida has remained a staunch defender and advocate of the Creative Class and its related concepts (creative cities and creative economies) over a series of follow-up books that answer criticisms and provide further nuance to the central ideas developed in *RCC*[2]; for him, the financial crash only further confirms the need to place creativity at the center of how we imagine the economy.[3] Nevertheless, it is the first book that remains the most significant, in terms of the articulation of the concepts and ideas he continues to advance, the attention and criticism it has generated, and its lasting impact on the language in which contemporary economic and urban planning decisions are framed.

In Canada, Florida's ideas have generated more praise than criticism, more acceptance than dismissal. His appointment in 2007 at the University of Toronto's Rotman School of Management as Professor of Business and Creativity, and as Academic Director of the newly established Prosperity Institute, was celebrated by local and national media alike. Here was an example of just the kind of Creative Class migration that Florida himself wrote about, with the bonus being that his move from Washington DC to Toronto seemed to confirm the latter's growing importance as a creative city. Even before his physical arrival in Canada, the discourse of creative cities had been taken up fervently by city governments anxious to find an urban planning narrative to match the challenges and expectations of a neoliberal age. If organizations such as the Creative City Network of Canada (CCNC) or the series of Creative Places + Spaces conferences organized by the non-profit group Artscape are any indication, the idea that creativity is essential to economic growth has been swallowed whole by urban governments across Canada—in big cities such as Vancouver and Montreal, but also in smaller places from Moncton, New Brunswick, to Moose Jaw, Saskatchewan[4]; the Canada Excellence Research Chairs program to bring highly coveted scientific and medical researchers to Canada suggests that the federal government also believes in the economic impact of innovation and creativity. For artists and arts and cultural groups, this attention to the material conditions of creativity might not seem to be a problem. In an effort to create urban environs attractive to members of the Creative Class, local, regional, and national governments have created new programs to support and encourage culture. Instead of being a drain on economies, around the world the arts and culture sector is now seen as a potential financial boon: a segment of the economy in which it is necessary to invest given its overall fiscal impact.[5]

Is there anything wrong with this interest in the economic spinoffs of creativity? Even if only strategically—focusing on the outcome as opposed to the concepts, arguments, and theories employed by Florida and others championing creativity today—doesn't this development represent a productive and positive situation for the arts and culture in Canada (and everywhere else)? If the language of creative cities and the creative class generates more money for museums, increases in grants for artists, expansion of government sponsorship of festivals, support for humanities research on campuses, and so on, what could possibly be wrong with it? I want to argue that the redefinition of culture as an economic resource and as one creative practice amongst many making up the twenty-first century economy is a problem. It is not a gain for arts and culture; as recent (2009) cuts to arts and culture funding in both Alberta and British Columbia suggest, the arts continue to be seen as (unfortunately) amongst the least essential elements of public and social life. But beyond such facts, the expansion of discourses of creativity into the economy at large represents a loss in how we understand the politics of culture—a shift from a practice with a certain degree of autonomy (however questionable, however problematic at a theoretical level) to one without any. In what follows, I offer a detailed analysis of Florida's *RCC* to show what work his discourse of creativity does in relation to the arts and culture. There have now been numerous criticisms made of Florida's ideas, primarily by urban geographers and economists who question his claims about the precise character of Creative Class and the spaces they inhabit. What has not been addressed directly is the very idea of "creativity" on which it all hinges—a concept that has been increasingly called upon to do important conceptual and political work on both right and left.

As is to be expected from a contemporary popular non-fiction text addressing social issues (indeed, it is fundamental to the genre), the core promise and attraction of Florida's *RCC* is its presentation of a new social phenomenon that its author has uncovered; the significance of this phenomenon is figured as being essential to an understanding of the nature of contemporary society, as well as its coming future. The rhetorical form of the book is that of the explorer's tale—the breathless recounting of the discovery of a paradigm shift that reorganizes our very sense of the operations of the social world. Though few others may have grasped it, Florida aims to convince us that the Creative Class is the one primarily responsible for the bulk of economic development today and that its influence on and importance for the economy will only grow in the coming decades. The emphasis on a specific class in relation to its economic function is significant. While Florida presumes to offer a wide-ranging analysis of contemporary society—he positions himself as heir to the work of sociologists such as William H. Whyte, C. Wright Mills, and Jane Jacobs—at its heart this is a labour management book. In the context of a variety of social changes and developments, especially the coming-to-be of the technological society, *RCC* analyzes the characteristics of the Creative Class—their motivations, pleasures, habits, tendencies, goals, likes, and dislikes—in order to give companies the conceptual tools with which they might better capture the fruits of their employees' creativity. It is also a book designed to offer economic advice to city councils and urban planners.[6] Florida makes it abundantly clear that it is not enough to change the work environment of the Creative Class to improve the bottom line. The energies of the Creative Class can be harnessed only in urban environments in which this class finds it appealing to live. The book offers guidelines for the character and nature of the cultural amenities and urban characteristics that provide the preconditions for the creativity so essential to economies today.

It is this aspect of the book that has received most of the critical and media attention directed Florida's way. The long fourth section, "Community," offers an account of what constitutes Creative Centers ("the economic winners of our age" [p. 218]) and an overview of the various statistical procedures he and his colleagues have used to map out the new urban geography of class in the United States.[7] Florida explores the logic of the growing gap between those cities with large numbers of the Creative Class and those without; this division correlates directly with the current financial status of the cities in question. The main question that organizes his examination of urban economics is why members of the Creative Class choose to live in some cities more than in others. A clarification of which characteristics make those cities high on the creative cities index—San Francisco, Austin, Seattle, Boston—so attractive to the Creative Class is intended to assist those at the bottom of the list—Memphis, Norfolk, Buffalo, Louisville—to develop programs and policies to improve their economies.

One can understand why criticism might be directed here. First, local media seized on Florida's book to either trumpet the standing of their cities or dispute it. (Are Buffalo or Memphis really such terrible places to live? Can such places really make themselves attractive to software engineers and financiers?) Second, challenges were made to veracity and utility of the new indices Florida used to generate his rankings. In addition to indices such as innovation (measured by patents per capita) and high-tech ranking (the Milken Institute's Tech Pole Index), he also made use of two even more controversial measurements: the Gay index and the Bohemian index. It is the politics many felt to be hidden in these measures that produced controversy. For Florida, the Gay index—the number of gay people in a city or a region—indicates a region's tolerance, while the Bohemian index—"the number of writers, designers, musicians, actors and directors, painters and sculptors, photographers and dancers" (p. 260)—identifies the cultural amenities in a region—less such things, it should be noted, as symphonies and concert halls (for which there are other indices) and more the cutting-edge, indie vibe of a place.[8] What do these factors have to do with urban economies? Florida claims that "artists, musicians, gay people and the members of the Creative Class in general prefer places that are open and diverse" (p. 250). He identifies a high correlation between these various indexes, the numbers of Creative Class in an area, and economic success. For reasons that will become clear momentarily, members of the Creative Class are thought to value lifestyle, social interaction, diversity, authenticity, identity. Florida proposes the theory that "regional economic growth is powered by creative people, who prefer places that are diverse, tolerant and open to ideas" (p. 249). Cities didn't like being deemed uncool (Memphis, Detroit) or intolerant (St Louis and poor Memphis again); further, the breakdown of creative cities as opposed to uncreative ones along party lines—with creative cities tending to be blue (Democrat) and uncreative ones red (Republican)—made many on the U.S. right suspicious of the real intentions of Florida's study.

The claims and arguments made in the latter part of Florida's book about the relationship between cities and creativity have generated criticism; the earlier, more substantive part far less so. The first three sections—"The Creative Age," "Work," and "Life and Leisure"—offer a detailed examination of the character of the Creative Class. It is here, in other words, that he identifies what makes this class meaningfully a class at all. As the preferences for tolerance, diversity, and openness to ideas already named above might suggest, this is not a class in any objective sense of the term, whether understood in the terms of classical economics (the division of the social world into quartiles or quintiles based on income) or in the Marxist sense of those who sell their labour as opposed to those who purchase it. The Creative Class is first and foremost treated as an economic class. It is an economic class that is brought together, however, not just by the fact that its members occupy certain professions but because they adopt a common *style de vie*, an outlook on life that cuts across and ties together the different registers of work, leisure, self-actualization, and social goods. If one had to capture this mode of being in a word, it is in the adjective that Florida gives to this class: creative. One might then expect a clear definition—even an attempt at one—given the very looseness and indefiniteness of the social meaning of the term, which can at times act as little more than an empty approbative: to label something creative is to offer approval or praise. Startlingly, none is given. Nevertheless, there *is* a core significance and function for "creative" (adjective) and "creativity" (noun) that emerges in Florida's book. To understand the work that the concept of creativity does for his understanding of the social—and indeed, the work it does more generally today, outside of Florida's book as much as within it—one has to consider the significance of the multiple identifications and associations he proposes for the term throughout the book.

Even though many of Florida's descriptions of creativity appear to operate in the same register (that is, they point to the same noun, the same thing, even if they do so with slight variations), looking at the claims and assumptions made in each case is essential. There are (at least) *seven* forms or modes of creativity identified in *RCC*:

(a) Creativity is an innate characteristic of the human mind or brain. "The creative impulse—the attribute that distinguishes us as humans from other species" (p. 4). It is an attribute that distinguishes the human *as such*, although it is also described as "a capacity inherent to varying degrees in virtually all people" (p. 31).

(b) It is a cultural or social characteristic and/or good. Just as with individuals, societies can be more or less creative or can be organized to be conducive to creativity or to limit or prohibit it. The text stands as a warning to the U.S. to be careful about losing its creative edge to countries such as the UK, Germany, and the Netherlands, which are doing a better job of being creative.

(c) Creativity is the subversion or breaking of rules: "It disrupts existing patterns of thought and life. It can feel subversive and unsettling even to the creator. One famous definition of creativity is 'the process of destroying one's gestalt in favor of a better one'" (p. 32).[9] Creativity as subversion is especially important in Florida's reparation of the social drama of the 1960s and its central place in the constitution of the ethos of Silicon Valley (pp. 190–211, especially pp. 202–10) and in technological industries more generally.

(d) It constitutes the key element of certain kinds of work, which cuts across the spectrum of previous definitions and distinctions of labour, that is, white collar, blue collar, executive class, working class. There can be white-collar creative jobs just as there can be blue-collar ones, which is why for Florida it is better to speak of a Creative Class instead of depending on these older, Fordist categories. Creative jobs are challenging and involve problem solving. There is an innate pleasure to this kind of work—it wouldn't even be work except for the fact that you are paid (bonus!). Creative people are attracted to their jobs because of "intrinsic rewards … tied to the very creative content of their work" (p. 87). Such work allows one to exercise the innate impulse identified in (a).

(e) Creativity is used as a stand-in term for acts that produce the "new": new ideas, new concepts, or new products. In other words, novelty is creativity (and vice versa).

(f) Creativity is strongly linked to technology. One measure of creativity is the number of patents issued per capita; another is the amount of spending on research and development. Florida identifies Nokia cellphones and the film series *The Lord of the Rings* as "creative products." Although he identifies other fields of endeavor and other products as "creative," there is no doubt that he sees the field of contemporary high technology as a place where it is especially in force.

(g) Finally, creativity is repeatedly identified as a characteristic of work in the arts—work done by those whose activities are named by the Bohemian index. This is an element of the arts that has now expanded to cover other forms of human endeavor as a result of social change, technological development, or simply insight into the productive process: in hindsight, many forms of work were always already creative: "Writing a book, producing a work of art or developing new software requires long periods of concentration" (p. 14). When creativity is described by Florida, the arts are always in the pole position: "[Prosperity] requires increasing investments in the multidimensional and varied forms of creativity—arts, music, culture, design and related fields—because all are linked and flourish together" (p. 320).

At times these varied appeals to creativity stand alone; more often, creativity is described and discussed by linking two or more of these different ideas of creativity together. The chain of associations through which Florida runs these works something like this:

> technology *(f)* is creative because
>
> it is full of people who are allowed to be subversive *(c)* and so
>
> create new things *(e)*,
>
> all as a result of a new social setting *(b)*
>
> that enables companies to *(d)* create working conditions to permit this to happen.

Working in a high-tech company and being able to be creative in this fashion is the best of all possible worlds but is nonetheless at heart: *(a)* an expression of an innate human impulse which the economic world has hitherto squashed underfoot.

Unsurprisingly, the circulation of these multiple ideas of creativity generates an increasing number of tautologies and inconsistencies as the book progresses. "Creativity … is an essential part of everyone's humanity that needs to be cultivated" (p. 317), and yet we are also repeatedly told that there are "creative people" (and so presumably less creative ones, too) and a distinct class whose creativity must therefore be the function of something other than simply being human.

The seventh definition of creativity (g) is without question the most important one in Florida's view. His most substantive definition of the Creative Class identifies its key characteristic to be "that its members engage in work whose function is to 'create meaningful new forms'" (p. 68).[10] A broad definition, to be sure; the nature of these forms and their function is clarified in his elaboration of the kinds of work that constitute the Creative Class. Drawing on categories from the Occupational Employment Survey of the U.S. Bureau of Labor Statistics, he divides the Creative Class into two component elements: the Super-Creative Core and the Creative Class more generally. The first group includes workers across a wide field of employment categories:

> scientists and engineers, university professors, poets and novelists, artists, entertainers, actors, designers and architects, as well as the thought leadership of modern society: nonfiction writers, editors, cultural figures, think-tank researchers, analysts and other opinion-makers. Whether they are software programmers or engineers, architects or filmmakers, they fully engage in the creative process. I define the highest order of creative work as producing new forms or designs that are readily transferable and widely useful—such as designing a product that can be widely made, sold and used. (p. 69)

The Super-Creative Core is paid to engage in the production of new forms that are transferable and useful. By contrast, while the rest of the Creative Class might at times produce new forms, it is "not part of the basic job description. What they *are* required to do regularly is think on their own" (p. 69). The second group is just as broad and includes knowledge-intensive workers such as legal and health professionals, financial services workers, lawyers, and those who work in the high-tech industry. Should any of these workers have the opportunity to engage in the creation of new forms in their jobs—everything from new products to new job opportunities—they have the chance to move up to the Super-Creative level, "producing transferable, widely usable new forms" (p. 69) as the main purpose of their professions.

Like commodities, such as oil or coal, or the work of labourers in taxfree zones or *maquiladoras*, for Florida creativity is an economic good. Indeed, it is not just one good amongst many. As he states directly in the preface to the paperback edition and repeats throughout the book: "Human creativity is the ultimate economic resource" (p. xiii).[11] Many might imagine creativity to be a quality or characteristic with intrinsic value—a value which isn't established by markets or through its utility or transferability. Florida sees things differently. For him, "creativity has come to be valued—and systems have evolved to encourage and harness it—because new technologies, new industries, new wealth and all other good economic things flow from it" (p. 21). The contribution made by *The Rise of the Creative Class* is thus twofold. First, Florida plays the role of a lobbyist on behalf of creativity to government, business, and the general public, working tirelessly to get these sectors to recognize the importance of creativity to the economy. And second, in his role as a social scientist, he develops numerous theoretical and empirical schemes to understand better the creative-economic systems that have up until now evolved on their own. His aim is to help encourage and harness creativity, so that with the knowledge provided by social science these systems can operate even better, which will equally benefit nation-states and the lives of those workers whose creativity is currently being wasted in jobs that fall outside of the Creative Class.

A utopian vision, is it not? Who could be against more creativity in the world? And the outcomes that creativity seems to produce: more diverse and tolerant societies, better jobs and wealth for all.[12] Florida's view of the significance of the Creative Class for our collective futures in unambiguous: "We have evolved economic and social systems that tap human creativity and make use of it as never before. This in turn creates an unparalleled opportunity to raise our living standards, build a more humane and sustainable economy, and make our lives more complete" (p. xiii). This opportunity has not yet been taken up. Luckily, for this extraordinary future to be realized all that is needed is a completion of the "transformation to a society that taps and rewards our full creative potential" (p. xiii). A proud member of the thought leadership of "our" society, Florida is prepared to help light the path and to make a fortune (through his consultancy firm) along the way.

Despite his enthusiasm for the project of rendering the world safer for creativity, Florida's view of a social and economic system nearing perfection functions only to the degree that it fails to address or account for a number of issues that—given his subject matter and the concepts he employs—he cannot leave by the wayside. We can get a sense of these gaps and elisions by looking at the few moments in which he raises concerns or questions about the picture he paints. In a four-hundred page book that sometimes seems intent on addressing almost everything (Jimi Hendrix and the rise of agriculture, Thomas Frank and the Frankfurt School, Silicon Valley and Florida's own childhood skill at building wooden cars), there are only *three* moments of doubt or hesitation about the views for which he argues. These are worth citing in full:

> [The creative economy] is not a panacea for the myriad social and economic ills that confront modern society. It will not somehow magically alleviate poverty, eliminate unemployment, overcome the business cycle and lead to greater happiness and harmony for all. In some respects, left unchecked and without appropriate forms of human intervention, this creativity-based system may well make some of our problems worse. (p. 23)

> My statistical research identifies a troubling negative statistical correlation between concentrations of high-tech firms and the percentage of the non-white population—a finding that is particularly disturbing in light of our findings on other dimensions of diversity. It appears that the Creative Economy does little to ameliorate the traditional divide between the white and nonwhite segments of the population. It may even make things worse. (pp. 262–63)

> Creativity is not an unmitigated good but a human capacity that can be applied toward many different ends. The scientific and technical creativity of the last century gave us wonderful new inventions, but also terrible new weapons. Massive, centralized experiments in new forms of economic and social life led to fiascos like the Soviet Union, while here in the United States, free-market creativity has turned out a great deal that is trivial, vulgar and wasteful. (p. 325)

There is no comment offered following the first two quotations; they come at the end of sections, after which Florida's cheerleading enthusiasm resumes unabated. The third warning about the potential dangers of creativity comes in the book's conclusion, in which he directs his energies toward convincing the U.S. public and their governments to recognize and support the Creative Class. There is a meek defense offered concerning the potential for creativity to be put toward totalitarian uses or result in the detritus of consumer culture. Put simply, since creativity is now at the core of the economy, and since it is only an increase in resources that will enable the potential to do "good in the world" (p. 325), creativity remains essential, no matter that its results include everything from the atomic bomb to the doodads lining the shelves of dollar stores around the world.

What emerges in these three passages is what is almost entirely absent in the rest of the book: the *political*. Why a creativity-based system might make our problems worse is never specified; it also comes as somewhat of a surprise, given the tone and triumphalism of the book, to learn that it is *not* a panacea. One realizes in reading these passages that little or no mention has been made of poverty, unemployment, or the business cycle—or race and ethnicity, for that matter. Yet these are all crucial factors in shaping the experience of work and one's degree of economic participation. There are other ways to make sense of Florida's list of cities and their existing levels of Creative Class workers, which correlate *precisely* with poverty, unemployment, race, lack of access to education (required for Creative Class jobs), lack of mobility, and lack of opportunity.[13] These are deeply political issues, not mere externalities or afterthoughts to the system he describes. When ethnicity or immigration is discussed, it is framed by Florida as context or backdrop in an urban setting—urban coloring, in other words, much the same as a good alternative music scene: part of the necessary makeup of a city that allows white Creative Class members to feel good about themselves and the place they live. One of the reasons the political is missing—beyond, that is, that its inclusion would spoil the elegance of Florida's system and its apparently strong correlations between job type and so-called tolerance and diversity—is announced in his response to the problem introduced in the last passage above. When it comes right down to it, the logic of the economy trumps everything, even the possibility of the terrible new weapons that some members of the Creative Class are (without doubt) commissioned to design.

At one level, it would not be going too far to see the absence of the political as the absence of the world in general: the contingencies and challenges that shape economic decisions, civic policies, and urban planning are nowhere to be found. This is one of the reasons, perhaps, that there seems to be a fundamental confusion in Florida's work between cause and effect in imagining how urban spaces operate: nowhere does one have the production of creative city spaces that *then* attract creative workers (away from other creative cities, one can only imagine), but more the reverse is true, with certain kinds of cities emerging out of historically contingent processes of industry and labour. But it is perhaps more productive to focus on a smaller element of the book that nevertheless captures some of its wider absences; this attention will also bring us back around to the function of creativity in relation to culture. The limits of Florida's construction of the Creative Class and its future promise can be seen in the fact that in a book whose fundamental theme is labour, a real discussion of work is entirely absent. The Creative Class engages in the creation of meaningful new forms. It does so, however, as *work*, as an activity within corporations and institutions familiar to all of us (the ones that capture Florida's interest are high-tech giants such as Dell, Microsoft, and Apple). Work has a number of social and economic functions. One of the most important of these, the reason why a corporation or institution might hire a member of the Creative Class, is to generate a product or offer a service (transferable and useful, whether material or immaterial). This process is not carried out for the good of humanity but to generate profit. As any fourth grader knows, profit can only be realized if the amount one pays the creative staff (and the rest of the workers) is less than the income that can be generated by means of the product. This sense of work—as part of a system of profit, work as something necessary for life—never appears in *The Rise of the Creative Class*. Instead, it is essential for Florida to make the point that members of the Creative Class *aren't* motivated by money and that the Super-Creative Core makes even less than their Creative peers (p. 77). In surveys which he cites, IT workers indicate that work challenge, flexibility, and stability all come before base pay as reasons why they choose their jobs, with many other values (vacations, opinions being valued, etc.) standing only a few percentage points behind (88–101). For Florida, this interest in factors other than salary is viewed as a defining element of the Creative Class. Their desire for flexible and open forms of work, which allows them to avoid wearing a tie, to come late to work, or, better yet, to continue to work wherever and whenever (at home, on the subway, while shopping, while reading messages on their Blackberries, etc.) is seen as a sign not just of a new mode of labour freedom but a form of social freedom more generally.

Numerous social and cultural critics have drawn attention to the ways in which this apparent new-found freedom in fact covers up an expansion of the work day from nine to five to every aspect of one's life.[14] For those with a more systemic understanding of the economy and the changes it has undergone over the past two decades in particular, this liberalization of the work environment can be understood as little more than a new mode of labour management, whose overall aim remains that of generating as much profit as possible for companies and shareholders. If workers see their jobs as sites of self-definition, challenge, and freedom instead of the opposite, so much the better for the bottom line! The training of bodies willing to work at any time of the day—and to do so not due to exterior compulsion but because of some imagined, self-defining innate drive—is an easy way of increasing productivity without having to increase pay. Many critics and social commentators have expressed deep worries about the ways in which work in the new economy has come to entirely consume life; Florida expresses no such anxieties and even argues that such worries are overstated and beside the point.[15]

At its core, what is expressed in Florida's book is a fantasy of labour under capitalism: the possibility *within* capitalism of work without exploitation, of work as equivalent to play. What might give those of us who study the arts and culture pause here is how closely this vision approximates that of the ideal social function and purpose of culture—if in reverse. The aim of the historical avant-garde was to reject the deadened rationality of capitalist society through the creation of "a new life praxis from a basis in art" (Bürger p. 49). Florida's characterization of the Creative Class suggests that this new life has in fact been achieved. The passage to the utopia of a new life praxis was supposed to occur via the transformation of life and work by art, such that art as a separate, autonomous sphere of life was no longer necessary. The division of art and life that first made the autonomous activity called art what it is would be undone through the critical activity of art itself. In Florida's vision of our creative present, work tends toward art by means of changes to the character of labour, partly as a result of technological developments and partly due to what can only be described as new-found enlightenment about the way in which the work-place should be configured. Equating the Creative Class with the activity of the avant-garde might seem far-fetched. It is, however, the fundamental way in which Florida envisions the social function of the Creative Class: as having collapsed different spheres of life together in such a way that what is now finally expressed socially is that innate element of creativity that makes us human and distinguishes us from the beasts. He writes, "we are impatient with the strict separations that previously demarcated work, home and leisure" (*RCC* p. 13). Luckily, we live at a time when these separations have become undone: "The rise of the Creative Economy is drawing the spheres of innovation (technological creativity), business (economic creativity) and culture (artistic and cultural creativity) into one another, in more intimate and more powerful combinations than ever" (201). And again: "Highbrow and lowbrow, alternative and mainstream, work and play, CEO and hipster are all morphing together today" (p. 191).

This is, of course, more wish fulfillment than actually realized utopia. Florida imagines capitalism to have achieved what the avant-garde had wished to bring about as a means of *undoing* capitalism. How can this be? What enables and sustains the fantasy of capitalism as an avant-garde—capitalism as having gone beyond itself in the way art once imagined it could—is the concept of creativity itself. The history of the concept of creativity and the changes it has undergone over the centuries is enormously complicated. Suffice it to say that in terms of its recent history, creativity is most commonly associated with the act of generation in the fine arts. The idea that the production of a painting or musical score involves generation *ex nihilo*—the emergence of the new out of nothingness—sprang in part from the individualization of the artistic endeavor at the beginning of the nineteenth century and in part from the break with strictly determined formal categories within which artistic activities were supposed to be carried out. Artists are the model for the creative individual; they are also a model of a kind of labour done for intrinsic purposes and outside of the formal institutions of work.

Over the course of the twentieth century, creativity has come to be associated with all manner of activities: scientific discovery, mathematics, economics, business activity, and so on—anything thought to involve the production of newness of any sort. Despite its residual Romantic humanism, one effect of the expansion of uses of the term is to have rendered creativity into a synonym for originality or innovation. In Florida's use of the term, creativity becomes an act with even less specificity, being understood at times as little more than "problem-solving" of a kind that takes place all the time in work and daily life. Yet it is also essential that in virtually every one of its invocations in his work creativity retain its link to the arts and to (the imagined) freedoms and autonomy connected with such work. This is reinforced by the equivalences Florida repeatedly draws between the work of artists and engineers, musicians and computer scientists. There would be something critical missing in Florida's account if he was to champion the work not of the Creative Class but of "knowledge workers," the "postindustrial class," the "professional-managerial class," "symbolic analysts," or even "cognitive labourers." "Creative" obscures the work function of this class, transforming it into something much grander and more ideal than just a label for a new category of work in late capitalism. The genius of making use of "creative" and "creativity" in the way that Florida does is to render the world into something comprised—if not today, then just over the horizon—of *nothing but artistic activity* carried out through different forms of labour (not with paint, but XML; not by videos intended for the artist-run space, but for clients on the internet) and with different ends in mind. The distinctions between engineer, computer scientist, and lawyer thus become something akin to those between painter, sculptor, and filmmaker—variants of the same fundamental creative impulse.

The group that most fascinates Florida are workers in the high-tech industry in places such as Silicon Valley and Austin, Texas. His understanding of the nature of technological innovation, the creation of wondrous new hardware and software, shapes his sense of what constitutes creativity. Although he does not say as much, if artistic work stands as the model of what constitutes creative labour in general, new technology is the mechanism by which it is imagined that creativity can form the life activity of more and more people: innovation can eliminate tedious work, leaving only challenging work behind (the dream of a world without work, returned a half century later in a new form). There is, however, another level at which artistic labour and that of technological industries in which Florida is so interested can be seen as connected. At one point in *RCC*, Florida boasts that the number of people who identify themselves as artists and cultural workers expanded dramatically over the past half century in the United States, from 525,000 in 1950 to 2.5 million in 1999, "an increase of more than 375 percent" (p. 46). He declines, however, to consider how such workers actually make a living, which is understandable since, for him, artists and cultural workers value the opportunity to enact their creative freedom much more than they worry about how they might eat.

Florida may be correct in identifying a connection between artists and workers in the knowledge industries of the "new economy." Where he is mistaken is the precise nature of this relationship. What is being carried over from artist to IT worker through the medium of creativity is the "cultural discount" that has long accompanied artistic labour of all kinds. One of the reasons why most artists aren't able to survive on the fruits of their labour is that it is assumed that they are "willing to accept non-monetary rewards—the gratification of producing art—as compensation for their work, thereby discounting the cash price of their labour" (Ross 6). Although IT workers are far better compensated for their work than artists, the adoption of an artistic relation to their work effects a similar labour discount that benefits their employer—even if they believe that the primary benefits are theirs. The characteristics of the postindustrial knowledge worker exemplary of Florida's Creative Class entail being "comfortable in an ever-changing environment that demands creative shifts in communication with different kinds of clients and partners; attitudinally geared toward production that requires long, and often unsocial, hours; and accustomed, in the sundry exercises of their mental labour, to a contingent, rather than a fixed, routine of self-application" (Ross 11). We are all artists now, which doesn't mean a life of unfettered freedom and creativity. Rather, it means that if we're, lucky the labour of crunching code for long hours can be offset by no longer having to wear a tie to work and by getting to play with your colleagues at the corner foosball table once in awhile.

There is much more that one could criticize about Florida's vision of our collective futures. There is the fact, for instance, that despite the link he wishes to make between art and the Creative Class, in the end artists and musicians don't really get to play with the big boys of the IT world. The Bohemian index confirms that they are simply the humus out of which the creativity of technological types grows: just like ethnic diversity, they give a place its colour and maybe provide an occasional evening's entertainment. The limited vision Florida has of creativity—the almost complete crowding out, say, of any sense of the intrinsic value, or political or social function, of certain kinds of human activity—is indicated by his use of patents as a means to measure it and the unembarrassed description of creativity as pure utility, transferability, and economic functionality. Florida imagines the gradual expansion of the Creative Class so that it would one day encompass *everyone*. Who would be left to pull the espressos and cappuccinos so beloved by professors and bankers is unclear. What is clear, however, is that even amidst all the creativity in which the Creative Class and Florida himself engages, there is one "new" thing ruled out from the beginning: an entirely new economic system, one in which work would have a very different social character than liberal capitalism even at its most utopic might be able to provide.

Some concluding words are necessary to bring this back around to how we think about art and culture in Canada today. To be clear: Florida's views on creativity are less idiosyncratic than symptomatic. One finds these ideas circulating widely in the culture at large. It is endemic in the language of business and economics. As Paul Krugman writes (to take but one example), "in the 1990s the old idea that wealth is the product of virtue, or at least of creativity, made a comeback" (24). The redefinition of business as art via the concept of creativity might not seem to be an especially worrisome problem for the study of culture. Creativity was never really a feature of older conceptual vocabularies of cultural study (from Winckelmann to Kant to Lessing), and it is certainly not important in more recent ones. My criticisms of Florida might have pertinence to the ongoing ideological redefinition of work and even of social experience and expectation under neoliberalism yet only be of minor relevance to the practice of contemporary literary criticism, which has never needed creativity, even if creativity has been tied to the activity of art, literature, and culture in the quotidian vocabulary of the social.

But to this I want to sound two warnings. The first has to do precisely with the significance of these shifts in our social understanding of art and culture. In Florida's worldview, what was once dangerous or revolutionary about art has been fully domesticated. The freedom of the artist with respect to some aspects of the organization of their work has, as I argued above, become a model for work in general. As a result, it is thus only the social or political content and not its social form (as work) that might be threatening or dangerous. But once art becomes universalized through the spread of the discourse of creativity, this political challenge, too, is diluted. It is in the adventurous radicality of the artists exhibited in independent galleries and contemporary art museums that Florida locates the kindred spirits of creative workers in other parts of the economy; established museums that display the classics of Western art don't interest him or the Creative Class in the least. If everyone is participating in the same narrative of social development through creativity—artists and IT workers, professors and bankers—what remains of art is to furnish the capitalist economy with ideas indirectly, through the spark or flash of a new concept that might emerge when a software designer is standing in front of a canvas denouncing technological capitalism. The reign of creativity thus poses challenges for the way in which theory and criticism operate today, even if creativity as such may not be a concept with particular theoretical salience within literary or cultural criticism.

But the challenge or threat goes beyond this. I suggested at the outset that creativity was a concept that was being used by both left and right. This essay has focused on the right's use of creativity, identifying Florida as the chief theorist and champion of an idea of creativity that transforms capitalism from a machine of exploitation into something that enables people to fully employ their innate capacities. But what about the left? On the left, too, the principle of creativity has come to form an important part of how the present social context is conceptualized. Especially in the work of writers associated with Italian autonomist thought, from Paolo Virno to Michael Hardt and Antonio Negri, the current hegemony of post-Fordist, cognitive or affective labour is seen as making evident what was always already true about work but which has become structurally impossible to ignore today. Social prosperity is dependent on language, communication, knowledge, and creativity—that is, on the "general intellect" that Marx describes in a passage in the *Grundrisse* that has become a key part of contemporary left political philosophy. Although it might seem surprising to say so, the difference between right and left, between Florida and Virno, is not in their analysis of the structure of contemporary capitalism and the social and political developments that have accompanied it so much as the lessons that each draws from it. The post-Fordist labour utopia imagined by Florida is for left thinkers anything but the realization of a world without work; instead, it constitutes a new form of exploitation and perhaps an even more dangerous one given the ideological power of accounts of contemporary work such as that of Florida's. Creativity *does* flourish in contemporary capitalism, but insofar as it is put to use to generate profit, the potential political implications of this new situation are defused, at least temporarily. For the left, the increasing dependence of contemporary societies on forms of creative labour constitutes a political and imaginative opening—recognition (at long last) that capitalism needs labour far more than labour needs capitalism and that the sovereignty of the state can be replaced by a new society founded on the general intellect.

Yet despite the different lesson left and right draw from the social and political implications of post-Fordist work, they share a surprisingly common view of what constitutes creativity and its links to art, culture, and the aesthetic. In recent social and political thought, creativity seems to have become nothing short of the defining element of human being: we are no longer *homo faber* but *homo genero*. As in the case of Florida, creativity on the left finds its referent in an idealized vision of artistic labour and a skewed view of the character of classical aesthetics and is also imagined as what needs to be enabled and set loose in order for there to be genuine social freedom. In a recent interview, Virno points to the troubling integration of aesthetics into production but in so doing affirms a view of aesthetics that is reminiscent of Florida's own claims about the place of creativity in human nature.[16] While admitting at the outset of this long interview that his knowledge of modern art "is actually very limited," Virno is fearless in extending several of his key concepts to discussions of art and aesthetics, such as "virtuosity," one of many names for the innate productive capacity of human beings, which in the work of Antonio Negri goes by the name "constituent power." If left discourses are attuned to the blind spots that exist in Florida's celebration of the conditions of work under contemporary capital, they nevertheless enact the same rhetorical and conceptual gesture of transforming human activity (or at least its potential) *as such* into art—and an idea of art taken not from sociology but from fantasies about its ideal relationship to something called creativity.

The effect once again is to render mute the critical capacities and political function of art and culture, even as it becomes coterminous with human life activity as such. Contemporary left theoretical discourse might not result in increased funding for the arts, but its temptations for cultural theory can be just as great—and just as problematic. It places art at the center of politics but only by doing away with the significance of art *as* art. Contemporary art and cultural production have a social specificity that plays an essential role in their political function. They don't need to think of themselves as creative or as the exemplar of creative acts. Indeed, it would seem that the farther they stay away from the intellectual and political traffic in creativity, the greater suspicion with which they treat this mobile and uncritically accepted discourse, the more likely they are able to continue to challenge the limits of our ways of thinking, seeing, being, and believing.

Notes

1 I take the first phrase in title from Jamie Peck's excellent "The Creativity Fix."

2 See *The Flight of the Creative Class*, in which he examines the global competition of states and cities to attract members of this class; *Cities and the Creative Class*, which constitutes an elaboration of his description of the communities creative workers are attracted to and in which they flourish; and *Who's Your City?*, which puts his analysis to use in the form of a city guide for members of the creative class.

3 See Florida's *The Great Reset* and his article "How the Crash Will Reshape America."

4 Although the CCNC predates Florida's books, its growth and expansion since becoming a not-for-profit organization in 2002 has been enabled by the spread of the idea that city spending on culture supports economic development. The CCNC acts as advocate of and clearinghouse for ideas linking culture and economic development. For example, the January 2010 *Creative City News* reports on the investment of $5 million by the City of Woodstock in the creation of a new art gallery; the December 2009 newsletter includes stories on urban investments in culture in places such as Barrie and Collingwood, Ontario, and Halifax, Nova Scotia.

5 Governments across the world have in recent years produced planning strategies for their cultural sector in relation to its economic impact or have developed new departments of government to manage the economics of culture. To give a few examples: Winnipeg is concluding its year as Cultural Capital of Canada with the production of an arts and culture strategy document, "Ticket to the Future: The Economic Impact of the Arts and Creative Industries in Winnipeg." In the United Kingdom, the Creative and Cultural Skills unit of the national government announced £1.3 million to create two hundred culture jobs for young people claiming unemployment benefits, including positions "such as theatre technician, costume and wardrobe assistant, community arts officer and business administrator."

The action is just as great on the international level. Numerous international conferences focus on culture and economics, such as the annual Culturelink Conference (the third meeting of which was held in Zagreb, Croatia, in 2009) and the World Summit on the Arts (the fourth meeting held in Johannesburg in 2009). The recently released report of the Commonwealth Group on Culture and Development, a body established in 2009, links the achievement of development goals with the support of culture. And UNESCO's November 2009 World Report, "Investing in Cultural Diversity and Intercultural Dialogue," warns governments against cutting funding to culture during the current financial crisis, not just because it will impact on the issues contained in the report's title but because such fiscal cost saving will have a deep impact on any possible financial recovery.

6 Less so for state or national governments: just as for thinkers such as Saskia Sassen, for Florida the city is the primary political and economic unit of the contemporary era. See, for example, his review of Thomas Friedman's *The World is Flat*, "The World is Spiky."

7 The Canadian edition of *Who's Your City?* extends this analysis to Canada, if in a more limited way.

8 "This milieu provides the underlying eco-system or habitat in which the multidimensional forms of creativity take root and flourish. By supporting lifestyle and cultural institutions like a cutting-edge music scene or vibrant artistic community, for instance, it helps to attract and stimulate those who create in business and technology" (*RCC* 55).

9 This quotation is unattributed by Florida, as are a number of others in the book. The likely source for the quotation is Max Wertheimer, one of the founders of Gestalt theory.

10 The quotation Florida includes here is unattributed.

11 The number of times this claim is asserted is too numerous to cite, but take for instance statements such as these at opposite ends of the book: "Today's economy is fundamentally a Creative Economy" (*RCC* 44) and "Creativity is the fundamental source of economic growth" (*RCC* 317).

12 The critical importance of tolerance to manage the perpetuation of hegemony appears in numerous works in the genre of the popular books on current affairs. See, for example, Amy Chua, *Day of Empire: How Hyperpowers Rise to Global Dominace—and Why They Fall.*

13 Mobility is presumed to be a central characteristic of the Creative Class. They can go wherever they want, which is why cities have to make certain that they have the appropriate environs to attract them. Yet even in the case of certain members of the Super-Creative Core, this mobility is close to a fiction. For example, academics find it extremely difficult to move; the nature of their work means that they have to participate in specific kinds of institutions (universities and colleges) that aren't found in the same proportion as institutions of private industry and many of which are located in smaller cities and towns. There's a reason why Durham, NC, and State College, PA, rank highly on his rankings of creative cities: it's not because they have a huge number of amenities (art, coffee houses, alternative music, etc.) that exist outside of work but because the nature of the institutions that exist there render large number of PHDs (especially relative to population) immobile.

14 There are a number of texts that examine the causes and consequences of the production of "'free labor' of users, i.e., of a labor that is not paid and not supervised, but is nonetheless controlled" (Terranova). See, for instance, Jill Andresky Fraser, *White Collar Sweatshop*; Christian Marazzi, *The Violence of Financial Capitalism*; Andrew Ross, *Nice Work If You Can Get It: Life and Labor in Precarious Times;* Juliet Schor, *The Overworked American: The Unexpected Decline of Leisure*; and Tiziana Terranova, "Free Labor: Producing Culture for the Digital Economy."

15 "The no-collar workplace is not being imposed on us from above; we are bringing it on ourselves ... We do it because we long to work on exciting projects with exciting people. We do it because as creative people, it is a central part of who we are or want to be" (*RCC* 134).

16 "There is an aesthetic base component in human nature." Paolo Virno.

Works Cited

Brooks, David. *Bobos in Paradise*: *The New Upper Class and How They Got There*. New York: Simon and Schuster, 2001.

Bürger, Peter. *Theory of the Avant-garde*. Trans. Michael Shaw. Minneapolis: University of Minnesota Press, 1985.

Chua, Amy. *Day of Empire: How Hyperpowers Rise to Global Dominance—and Why They Fall*. New York: Doubleday, 2007.

Florida, Richard. *Cities and the Creative Class*. New York: Routledge, 2004.

———. *The Flight of the Creative Class*. New York: Harper Business, 2005.

———. *The Great Reset: How New Ways of Living and Working Drive Post-Crash Prosperity*. Toronto: Random House, 2010.

———. "How the Crash Will Reshape America." *Atlantic Monthly*, March 2009. Web. 3 August 2010.

———. *The Rise of the Creative Class*. New York: Basic Books, 2003.

———. *Who's Your City?: How the Creative Economy Is Making Where to Live the Most Important Decision of Your Life* . New York: Basic Books, 2008.

———. "The World is Spiky." *Atlantic Monthly*. October 2005: 48–51.

Fraser, Jill Andresky. *White Collar Sweatshop*. New York: W.W. Norton, 2002.

Krugman, Paul. *The Return of Depression Economics and the Crisis of 2008*. New York: W. W. Norton, 2009.

Marazzi, Christian. *The Violence of Financial Capitalism*. Los Angeles: Semiotext(e), 2010.

Marx, Karl. "The German Ideology: Part 1." *The Marx-Engels Reader*. Ed. Robert C. Tucker. New York: W. W. Norton, 1978. 146–75.

———. *Grundrisse*. Trans. Martin Nicolaus. Harmondsworth: Penguin, 1973.

Negri, Antonio. *Insurgencies: Constituent Power and the Modern State*. Trans. Maurizia Boscagli. Minneapolis: University of Minnesota Press, 2005.

Peck, Jamie. "The Creativity Fix." *Eurozine*, 28 June 2007. Web. 18 January 2010.

Ross, Andrew. "The Mental Labor Problem." *Social Text* 63 (2000): 1–31.

———. *Nice Work If You Can Get It: Life and Labor in Precarious Times* . New York: New York UP, 2009.

Schor, Juliet. *The Overworked American: The Unexpected Decline of Leisure*. New York: Basic Books, 1993.

Terranova, Tiziana. "Free Labor: Producing Culture for the Digital Economy." *Social Text 18.2* (2000): 33–58.

Virno, Paolo. "The Dismeasure of Art. An Interview with Paolo Virno." *Open 17* (2009). Web. 22 February 2010.

Credit

Szeman, Imre. "Neoliberals Dressed in Black: Or, the Traffic in Creativity." *University of Alberta English Studies in Canada* ESC 36.1 (March 2010): 15–36. Print.

Gentrification and its Discontents: Cleveland Needs to Go Beyond Being Creatively Classes

Richey Piiparinen

"Indeed, we have the know-how, but we do not have the know-why, nor the know-what-for"—Erich Fromm, social psychologist.

The question of how you "become" as a city has been weighing on me lately. Is it enough to get people back into the emptiness? Is it enough to pretty the derelict? I mean, is the trajectory of Cleveland's success simply a collection of micro-everythings, start-ups, and occupancy rates? That is, is Cleveland's reward simply the benefit of being creatively classed?

I hope not. It won't work. Here is why.

The problem with most city revitalization these days relates to its playbook: there are the investors who have the capital, and then the political power from which finance flows. Here, money not only talks, it builds, with investors' wishes transcribed in how a city looks, feels, and functions. That said, the main interest of the investors is to make money, and so people are seen as consumers as opposed to citizens. Consumers that fill up real estate space. Consumers that salivate over tastes. Consumers of art and design, with the attraction to beauty meant to establish a "vibrancy for profit" mindset as opposed to experiencing beauty for the value of beauty's sake. Come to think of it, the creative class is really just the consumer class, just like the rest of us. Yet they are anointed in status by city makers because they are thought to have more spending power than their working- and service-class counterparts.

"Follow the creative community, and property values will rise," states one recent article in a real estate publication. "You have given real estate developers the playbook," echoes Albert Ratner, head of Cleveland-based Forest City, on his reading of "The Rise of the Creative Class." The motivations, as such, are quite blatant.

Now, why is this a problem?

Because developers have extraordinary amounts of pull in directing where finances go (this is particularly true in Cleveland), which means investment can get skewed to a select demographic. As such, the gap between the haves and have nots grows, and the geographic disparities begin to cement social inequities into the city's fabric. Cracks then show: drug use, murders, alienation and disenfranchisement, growing pockets of continued disinvestment, and it won't stop because research has consistently shown that inequity is an endless source of social ills. The only thing left to do is to compartmentalize our shadows, with "bad" kept in places away from the spots of our "hope." This is not unique to Cleveland or to this era. It is just the way things have been, which leads me to wonder if Cleveland's recent comeback is just a carousel in which progress is simply rearranging the broken deckchairs.

But while the future is uncertain, failure need not be inevitable. Yet what can be done in Cleveland and other Rust Belt cities to ensure we don't waste our opportunity? Unfortunately, little outside of a radical shift in how cities think about themselves, particularly as it relates to the notion of "revitalization."

This is where the concept of "Rust Belt Chic" comes in, which—when it is boiled down—is really just a process of collectively "knowing thyself" (an in-depth description of Rust Belt Chic economic development will be delineated in a subsequent post). Specifically, by becoming aware of who we are as "Cleveland," we know who we are not, or more exactly: what we don't need to be. This is important as it relieves the temptation of Cleveland trying to copy some other city's so-called success which, in the end, is counterproductive, as such efforts—like the historic Columbia Building demolition for a Vegas-style "look"—ultimately eliminate those things like history and architecture which tie us together.

This is all to say that Cleveland need not be "brochured" for the so-called creative class. That is simply objectifying your city as a product as opposed to *a people*, which is crude, and such posturing and posing is hardly Cleveland, besides.

Instead, a hammering down of who we are in our process of becoming is needed. We are Clevelanders. We care and fight for this city, endlessly. We swear, shake hands, bleed, heal, work, fight, and pray—all in an environment molded more so by the reality of Mickey Rourke than the donning of Ashton Kutcher. And so while repopulating the core is needed, we also must engage in building the productive capacity of people as opposed to simply relying on a capacity to spend. Specifically, squeezing out price per sq. feet at the expense of community fabric is not true economic growth. It is mountains turned to coal.

I cannot emphasize enough how important community development is to Cleveland's future. For as creative classification goes main stream, more and more cities will begin looking and feeling the same, and more and more cities will be turned to products to be gobbled up by those with stars in their eyes. But this kind of thing is not for everyone, or even for most. It is for a slice, a finicky slice. And so I gather creative classification will go the way of the fad, like all styles do. Some cities will be stuck left to look at the cartoon tattoos that dot their body, while the people left longing will decompress to find something a little more real.

Then—if we do it right—people will turn to Cleveland not because we faked the place as attractive, but because Cleveland made an effort to turn to its people.

Credit

Piiparinen, Richey. "Gentrification and Its Discontents: Cleveland Needs to Go Beyond Being Creatively Classes." newgeography.com. 28 Feb. 2013: Web.

Cities Mobilize to Help Those Threatened by Gentrification

Timothy Williams

Cities that have worked for years to attract young professionals who might have once moved to the suburbs are now experimenting with ways to protect a group long deemed expendable—working- and lower-middle class homeowners threatened by gentrification.

The initiatives, planned or underway in Boston, Philadelphia, Washington, Pittsburgh and other cities, are centered on reducing or freezing property taxes for such homeowners in an effort to promote neighborhood stability, preserve character, and provide a dividend of sorts to those who have stayed through years of high crime, population loss, and declining property values, officials say.

Newcomers, whose vitality is critical to cities, are hardly being turned away. But officials say a balance is needed, given the attention and government funding being spent to draw young professionals—from tax breaks for luxury condominium buildings to new bike lanes, dog parks, and athletic fields.

"We feel the people who toughed it out should be rewarded," said Darrell L. Clarke, president of the Philadelphia City Council, which last year approved legislation to limit property tax increases for longtime residents. "And we feel it is incumbent upon us to protect them."

In doing so, cities are turning urban redevelopment policy on its head and shunning millions in property tax revenue that could be used to restore municipal services that were trimmed during the recession because of budget cuts, including rehiring police officers.

A decision to reduce property taxes can be risky because such levies account for at least 50 per cent of operating budgets in most American cities and sometimes provide as much as 80 per cent of a city's revenue.

But even Detroit, where a declining tax base has been at the core of the bankrupt city's troubles, recently announced plans to cut property tax rates.

Last month, Mike Duggan, Detroit's new mayor, said property taxes would be cut by up to 20 per cent to levels that more accurately represent the value of homes in the city. The reduction could cost Detroit as much as $15 million annually in revenue.

The tax adjustments are part of a broader strategy by cities to aid homeowners—who continue to struggle financially since the home mortgage crisis. In Richmond, Calif., lawmakers are attempting to use eminent domain to seize underwater mortgages to try to help homeowners keep their houses.

Housing experts say the arrival of newcomers to formerly working-class areas—from the Mission District in San Francisco to the Shaw neighborhood in Washington—is distinct from previous influxes over the past 30 years because new residents are now far more likely to choose to move into new condominiums or lofts instead of into existing housing, making the changes more disruptive.

"This latest wave of gentrification has happened very quickly, and cities are cognizant to keep from turning over entirely," said Lisa Sturtevant, executive director of the Center for Housing Policy, a nonprofit research group. "And cities where property values are up and budgets are generally more stable have the wherewithal to provide tax breaks."

Ms. Sturtevant said that given that many of the younger, newer arrivals do not necessarily plan to stay for long, cities are making a sensible economic choice.

"There's less personal investment and less incentive to stay, so cities are saying, 'Let's invest in the stayers,' " she said.

In Boston, which an analysis by the Federal Reserve Bank of Cleveland last year found had the highest gentrifying pressure in the nation—followed by Seattle, New York, San Francisco, Washington and Atlanta—concluded that about one-fourth the city's population lived in gentrifying neighborhoods.

"Property values are increasing exponentially, and longtime homeowners are victims of the success story," said Stephen J. Murphy, a city councilor in Boston who co-introduced legislation allowing residents who have owned homes for more than 10 years and whose property taxes have increased by 10 per cent or more to defer property tax payments until they sell their home. The bill, approved by the City Council, is pending the approval of the state legislature.

But Philadelphia, undergoing a resurgence during which the city has had its first population increase since the 1950s, appears to have enacted the most comprehensive measures to safeguard longtime homeowners.

The first, the Homestead Exemption, allows most homeowners to reduce the assessed value of their house by $30,000 for tax purposes, while a second law, called Gentrification Protection or LOOP, short for Longtime Owner Occupants Program, is more narrowly focused on protecting homeowners from increases to their property tax bills because of gentrification.

The program generally allows homeowners who have lived in homes for 10 years or more and whose household income is less than about $110,000 annually to cap and freeze their assessments for 10 years if the assessments increased by 300 per cent or more as part of the city's new property tax formula.

"Philadelphia is a city of neighborhoods, and the reason people want to move to our neighborhoods is because of the character they have," said Mark Squilla, a council member who said it had been common in his district for home assessments to surge by as much as 10 times in a single year. "Gentrification is a great thing. But we have to keep a handle on it."

Rene Goodwin, who lives in the same South Philadelphia neighborhood her grandparents lived in during the 1920s, has seen the value of her home rise to $281,000 from $90,000 in a single year.

"To keep an urban area vital, there has to be an infusion of new people and buildings, but that doesn't mean you destroy people who have kept up the neighborhood, who've swept the sidewalk," she said. "It's that commitment that has made developers interested in the neighborhood—and then you're going to penalize the people who've stayed?"

Jacy Webster, 56, who lives on what had until recently been an Italian-American block in South Philadelphia, said he had come to feel like a stranger.

The new arrivals, mostly young families, seem to move a step faster than he does or to not see him. Old courtesies like waving hello and casual chats have become rare.

"I don't belong anymore," he said.

The changes have meant that the assessment on his house has more than quintupled during the past year—to $250,000 from $45,000—which he said might force him to move and perhaps rent his home out if he does not qualify for LOOP. The Feb. 17 deadline to apply has passed, and he is waiting to hear from the city.

Mr. Webster said, however, that there was at least one advantage to being surrounded by wealthier neighbors: "It's actually safer than it's ever been."

Credit

Is Gentrification All Bad?

Justin Davidson

Gentrification: New Yorkers can sense it immediately. It plumes out of Darling Coffee, on Broadway and 207th Street, and mingles with the live jazz coming from the Garden Café next door. Down the block, at Dichter Pharmacy, it's visible on the shelf of Melissa & Doug toys. An algae bloom of affluence is spreading across the city, invading the turf of artists and ironworkers, forming new habitats for wealthy vegans.

It's an ugly word, a term of outrage. Public Advocate Letitia James sounded the bugle against it in her inauguration speech on New Year's Day: "We live in a gilded age of inequality where decrepit homeless shelters and housing developments stand in the neglected shadow of gleaming multimillion-dollar condos," she cried, making it clear that she would love to fix up the first two and slam the brakes on the third. In this moral universe, gentrification is the social equivalent of secondhand smoke, drifting across class lines.

Yet gentrification can be either a toxin or a balm. There's the fast-moving, invasive variety nourished by ever-rising prices per square foot; then there's a more natural, humane kind that takes decades to mature and lives on a diet of optimism and local pride. It can be difficult to tell the two apart. "The things that low-income people think are nice are the same as what wealthy people want," says Nancy Biberman, who runs the Women's Housing and Economic Development Corporation in the Bronx. Communities fight for basic upgrades in quality of life, and when they're successful, their food options and well-kept streets attract neighbors (and developers). It also works the other way: Richer, more entitled parents can lift up weak schools, says Biberman. "They're more aggressive, and they empower other parents."

Gentrification doesn't need to be something that one group inflicts on another; often it's the result of aspirations everybody shares. All over the city, a small army of the earnest toils away, patiently trying to sluice some of the elitist taint off neighborhoods as they grow richer. When you're trying to make a poor neighborhood into a nicer place to live, the prospect of turning it into a racially and economically mixed area with thriving stores is not a threat but a fantasy. As the cost of basic city life keeps rising, it's more important than ever to reclaim a form of urban improvement from its malignant off shoots. A nice neighborhood should be not a luxury but an urban right.

Somewhere, a mournful bugle sounds for every old shoe-repair place that shutters to make way for a gleaming cookie boutique. And yet some old-school businesses, if they're flexible enough, can do more than survive: They can help nudge a neighborhood into the right kind of change.

"I'm a corner druggist," says Manny Ramirez, the stocky, genial owner of Dichter Pharmacy. You can feel the pleasure he gets from pronouncing the phrase—the same retro jolt he gets from saying *stickball, soda shop,* and *candy store.* But he is hardly living in the past. He's a canny businessman, Inwood-born, and bilingual in English and Spanish, who has known some of his customers from his own childhood and keeps his antennae tuned to the tastes of those he hasn't even met. Keenly conscious of his low-income neighborhood, he undersells the chain stores on basics like Tylenol and keeps the prices of most items at his lunch counter below $5. But he also stocks expensive lotions, organic moisturizers, and those Melissa & Doug toys. "Now we have people who will buy that stuff," he says, sounding a little amused. "The idea of a new group of people with disposable income is excellent."

The drugstore doubles as an ad hoc performance center, where Ramirez hosts chamber-music concerts, "Shakespeare Saturdays," and poetry slams. "I'm big on social media, and I read the comments," he says. "Among the people who have migrated here, there's a large vegetarian and vegan group, so we have veggie chili on Wednesdays and Sundays. If you're listening, however the neighborhood changes, that's how you stay in business."

Ramirez's optimistic realism contrasts with a common perception of neighborhoods that remain unchanged for generations—at least until the gentrifiers roar in. A few areas where the change is that stark do exist, but far more typical are enclaves that each dominant ethnic group cedes to the next. Of course Inwood is changing; it always was. Right now, it's a neighborhood of immigrants. Nearly half of its residents were born abroad, most in the Dominican Republic. Yet that "old Inwood" isn't the one Ramirez grew up in. The year he was born, 1968, a TV station in Ireland aired a documentary, *Goodbye to Glocamorra,* which chronicled a neighborhood that could have passed for a city in County Mayo. "Five years ago, these apartment buildings were Irish to the last man, woman, and child," the narrator says mournfully. "Today, their defenses have begun to crumble. The first Puerto Ricans have moved in. The first Negroes have moved in. And more will certainly follow."

Ramirez was one of those Puerto Ricans, and he grew up acutely conscious of his bifurcated world. "I was too Spanish for the white community and too white for the Spanish community," he recalls. When he was 10, his family moved from the mostly

Hispanic east side of Broadway to the still whitish west side. In the early nineties, he moved to a New Jersey suburb. But Ramirez kept roots in the neighborhood, commuting to work for the district Rite Aid office and attending Good Shepherd. One day, he heard the checkout girls at a Dominican bakery grumbling in Spanish about how the neighborhood was changing. "I remembered when I was a kid and the white people were talking about the neighborhood changing—only they were speaking English." Same complaint, different language.

Ramirez detected an opening. "I saw that there was an antiques store now, and a Moroccan restaurant, and I thought, *This is something I need to jump on.*" He bought the 100-year-old Dichter Pharmacy, where he had worked as a teenager. At times, it looked like a bad call. The recession hit the neighborhood hard. The Moroccan restaurant and the antiques store closed. In 2012, a fire destroyed the block. But Ramirez moved the business a few dozen yards up the street. Soon, the Badger Balm and apple-crumb muffins started to sell, and his poetry slams built a following—mostly from the west side of Broadway, though he's trying to recruit some Dominican bards too.

With strong feelings about the past and an eye on the future, Ramirez is a one-man neighborhood-improvement center. He knows that the change he's helping to nurture could one day turn on him, though he draws comfort from the fact that his lease won't expire (so his rent can't soar) for another twenty years. He keeps a fatherly eye on local kids and notes the low-margin stores that close and the new bars that force up rents. It pains him to see how few Latinos from the east side of Broadway welcome the new stores, and he knows that goodwill extends only so far. "If they're a low-income family and they're walking up the hill, past three or four other pharmacies, to buy Tylenol from me, are they going to go next door to Darling for a $4 cup of coffee? Probably not." That doesn't stop Ramirez from steering occasional customers there—until the day when he can feed their soy-latte cravings himself.

Nothing symbolizes the abyss between plenty and deprivation more than their physical proximity. The rapid gilding of Brooklyn has, in places, produced a grotesque companionship of vintage-clothing boutiques and Goodwill stores. Even as Bedford-Stuyvesant real estate approaches Manhattan prices, nearly a third of its residents—47 per cent of its children—live below the poverty line. The neighborhood remains a bastion of unemployment, public assistance, and crime, moated by great ramparts of public housing. The old inner-city anxieties—that poor people who know only other poor people are more likely to remain that way—have not disappeared. Only now, instead of being stranded in sprawling ghettos, the poor are confined to islands of deprivation, encircled by oceans of prosperity.

Yet those Dickensian juxtapositions are actually a sign of a city that is doing something right. Subsidized housing helps preserve neighborhoods from a uniform wash of affluence. Chelsea and the Upper West Side—two of the wealthiest districts in the nation—still make room for low-income residents in nycha projects. "Those are neighborhoods where gentrification has been meaningfully tempered," says Brooklyn city councilman Brad Lander, a staunchly progressive ally of Bill de Blasio's. And all over the city, developers reap tax benefits by erecting luxury buildings and earmarking 20 per cent of the apartments for renters who pay far less than their neighbors. A group of visiting developers from Mumbai was thunderstruck by that custom: They couldn't imagine why well-off New Yorkers would voluntarily share their enclaves with the poor.

The fact that single-family townhouses and public housing often share the same few blocks gives community organizers a versatile set of tools. Colvin Grannum, the president of the Bedford-Stuyvesant Restoration Corporation, arrives at his offices the morning after the city has announced a $50,000 grant to help restore a small ice rink that's been sitting idle for years near the corner of Fulton and Marcy Streets. He had been hoping for a more robust infusion; now he has to raise nine times as much as he's getting. A staffer greets him with a shot of ambivalence: "Congratulations, I guess."

Robert F. Kennedy's children went skating on the Bed-Stuy rink in the seventies, when the area was an encyclopedia of urban decline. "It looked like a war zone," Grannum says—"a desolate and blighted community." In the summer of 1964, riots fared at the corner of Fulton Street and Nostrand Avenue, and mounted police shot at looters. Three years later, RFK and Senator Jacob Javits founded Restoration, the country's first comprehensive community-development organization. Kennedy envisioned a fusion of public funds and private investment that would nurture local, self-reliant businesses: "What is given or granted can be taken away," he said. "What you do for yourselves and for your children can never be taken away ... We must combine the best of community action with the best of the private-enterprise system."

That principle forms the foundation of nonprofit community-building groups all over the country and motivates private do-gooder developers like Jonathan Rose. "Can you create models of gentrification in which the benefits are spread out through the community?" Rose asks. The key, he says, is to make sure that residents and shopkeepers in low-income neighborhoods have equity and a political voice—before a real-estate surge. African-American residents of Bed-Stuy who managed to cling to their brownstones through the misery of the sixties, the heroin and crack years, and the devastating epidemic of foreclosures can finally reap the benefit that any longtime homeowner takes for granted: selling the house for a profit. "Development can be a positive force," Rose says.

Today, Grannum has inherited the dream of healing through business. "I see our job as trying to create a healthy commercial corridor and capture as many retail dollars as we can," he says. It's not as if he's got his eye on Tiffany and Per Se, but he would like the dollar stores and pawnbrokers to be joined by some slightly more genteel options. He mentions Island Salad, a Caribbean-themed place just across Fulton Street from his office, where $6.99 will buy an Asian Rasta (romaine, roasted teriyaki chicken, mandarin oranges, cucumbers, sliced almonds, crispy chow mein noodles, and "island sesame ginger"). It's the sort of place a couple of young Park Slopers in search of an extra bedroom might wander into and think: *Yes! I could live here.*

Grannum is unapologetic about trying to bring a better life to Bed-Stuy's poor by attracting the very outsiders who are supposedly making things worse. "We need affluent and middle-income people," he insists. "We need a healthy community, and we need services that are first-rate. I just came from a meeting, and someone said, 'Go to Seventh Avenue in Park Slope and recruit some of those stores!' And I tell them: Businesses don't bring affluence; they follow affluence."

To the residents of East Harlem, a neighborhood ribbed with nycha towers and dotted with new condos, almost any change seems ominous. Andrew Padilla's 2012 documentary *El Barrio Tours: Gentrification in East Harlem* ends with a group of conga players on a patch of sidewalk at Lexington Avenue and East 108th Street, with a tenement building on one corner and the DeWitt Clinton Houses on the other. Padilla's film traces the creep of generic luxury and residents' tenacious desire to hang on. The conga players' impromptu jam session encapsulates both the history and the fragility of East Harlem's identity: All it takes for it to vaporize is for the musicians to pick up their drums and walk away. And they have. According to the Center for Urban Research, Hispanics made up 52.9 per cent of southeastern Harlem's population in 2000; a decade later, that figure had fallen to 47.5. Whites took their place (11.5 per cent before, 17.5 per cent after).

But trend lines are not destiny. Who does the gentrifying, how, and how quickly—these variables separate an organically evolving neighborhood from one that is ruthlessly replaced. A trickle of impecunious artists hungry for space and light is one thing; a flood of lawyers with a hankering to renovate is quite another. The difference may be just a matter of time—but when it comes to gentrification, time is all.

Gus Rosado, a deceptively mild-mannered activist with a brush cut and a graying Clark Gable mustache, runs El Barrio's Operation Fightback, which rehabs vacant buildings for affordable housing, and his latest undertaking is a huge gothic hulk at the far end of East 99th Street. Surrounded by public housing and the Metropolitan Hospital, it used to be P.S. 109, closed by the Department of Education in 1995 and badly decayed since then. After years of scrounging for some way to convert the school into living space, Rosado teamed up with the nationwide organization Artspace for a $52 million overhaul that will yield PS109 Artspace, 90 affordable live work studios, half of them set aside for artists who live nearby. "The only way we were able to get this done was because of the arts," Rosado recently said. "Suddenly, there was a whole other set of funding sources."

Leveraging the moneyed art world to provide low-cost housing in a creative community seems like the perfect revitalization project. It promotes stability, fosters local culture, recycles unused real estate, and brings in philanthropic dollars rather than predatory investors. Artspace's website makes the link between creativity and urban improvements plain: "Artists are good for communities. The arts create jobs and draw tourists and visitors. Arts activities make neighborhoods livelier, safer, and more attractive."

At the same time, Rosado's P.S. 109 project triggers a spray of explosive hypotheticals. Who should get preference: a white filmmaker from Yale who moved to East Harlem a few years ago and therefore qualifies as a resident, or a Dominican-born muralist who grew up in El Barrio but has since left for cheaper quarters in the South Bronx? Or: If East Harlem's new Artspace incubates a nascent gallery scene, will its cash and snobbery help the neighborhood or ruin it? Will the Lexington Avenue conga players find a place in the neighborhood's new arts hub?

Artists are like most people: They think gentrification is fine so long as it stops with them. They are pioneers, all-accepting enthusiasts, and they wish to change nothing about their new home turf (although a halfway decent tapas place would be nice). The next arrivals, though, will be numerous and crass. Interlopers will ruin everything. As artists migrate across the boroughs, from the East Village to Williamsburg, Red Hook, Bushwick, and Mott Haven, surfing a wave of rising rents, they are simultaneously victims and perpetrators of gentrification.

Rosado understands these dynamics well, but he believes that a little local involvement can go a long way toward shaping the subtleties of neighborhood change. "You can't stop development and growth, but we'd like to have a say in how that transition takes place." Lurking in that plain statement is the belief that gentrification happens not because a few developers or politicians foist it on an unwilling city but because it's a medicine most people want to take. The trick is to minimize the harmful side effects.

In the popular imagination, gentrification and displacement are virtually synonymous, the input and output of a zero-sum game. One professional couple's $2 million brownstone renovation in Bedford-Stuyvesant equals three families drifting toward Bayonne in search of barely adequate shelter. And so a sense of grievance and shame permeates virtually all discussions of neighborhood change. Even gentrifiers themselves are convinced they are doing something terrible. Young professionals whose moving trucks keep pulling up to curbs in Bushwick and Astoria carry with them trunkfuls of guilt.

The link between a neighborhood's economic fortunes and the number of people being forced to move away, while anecdotally obvious, is difficult to document. Everyone's heard stories of brutally coercive landlords forcing low-income tenants out of rent-controlled apartments in order to renovate them and triple the rent. But it's difficult to know how often that takes place. Between 2009 and 2011, about 7 per cent of New York households—around 200,000 of them—moved within the city in each year. Others left town altogether. Yet we know little about where they went, or why, or whether their decisions were made under duress.

Among experts, a furor continues to swirl over whether gentrification and displacement are conjoined. What qualifies as displacement, anyway? Forcible eviction by a rapacious landlord, obviously, but what about a rent that creeps up while a household's income doesn't? How about the intangible, dispiriting feeling of being out of place, or a young person's knowledge that leaving the family home means living in another borough? Or the dislocation that comes when an industry flees, taking its jobs along?

These pressures can affect investment bankers and nurses, as well as busboys and the unemployed, and it's not always easy to distinguish coerced departure from a fresh opportunity, or gentrifies from the displaced.

In 2005, Lance Freeman, a professor of urban planning at Columbia, examined national housing statistics to see whether low-income residents move more often once their neighborhoods start to gentrify. His conclusion was that they don't. Mobility, he suggested, is a fact of American life, and he could find no evidence to suggest that gentrification intensifies it. Instead, it appears that many low-income renters stay put even as their rents go up. "It may be that households are choosing to stay in these neighborhoods because quality of life is improving: They're more satisfied, but they're dedicating a larger slice of their income to housing," says Ingrid Gould Ellen, co-director of NYU's Furman Center for Real Estate and Urban Policy. There is an exception: Poor homeowners who see the value of their properties skyrocket often do cash out. Freeman garnished his findings with caveats and qualifications, but his charged conclusion fueled an outbreak of headlines that have dogged him ever since.

Eight years after he lit the gentrification-is-good-for-everyone match, Freeman sits in his office at Columbia, more resigned than rah-rah about the implications of his work. He doesn't doubt that displacement occurs, but he describes it as an inevitable consequence of capitalism. "If we are going to allow housing to be a market commodity, then we have to live with the downsides, even though we can blunt the negative effects to some extent. It's pretty hard to get around that."

That infuriates the British scholar Tom Slater, who sees Freeman's data studies as largely irrelevant because, he has written, they "cannot capture the struggles low-income and working-class people endure *to remain where they are*." Freeman waves away the binary rhetoric. "You can't boil gentrification down to good-guy-versus-bad-guy. That makes a good morality play, but life is a lot messier than that." In the days when RFK was helping to launch Restoration, an ideological split divided those who wrote cities off as unlivable relics from those who believed they must be saved. Today, a similar gulf separates those who fear an excess of prosperity from those who worry about the return of blight. Economic flows can be reversed with stunning speed: Gentrification can nudge a neighborhood up the slope; decline can roll it off a cliff. Somewhere along that trajectory of change is a sweet spot, a mixed and humming street that is not quite settled or sanitized, where Old Guard and new arrivals coexist in equilibrium. The game is to make it last.

Credit

Davidson, Justin. "Is Gentrification All Bad?" *New York Magazine* 2 Feb. 2014. Print.

Gentrification's Insidious Violence: The Truth about American Cities

Daniel José Older

Too many claim white people are at risk in communities of color. Really, it's those communities that are threatened.

ശ്ശ്ശ

A few years back, when I was still a paramedic, we picked up a white guy who had been pistol whipped during a home invasion in Williamsburg. "I can't believe this happened to me," he moaned, applying the ice pack I'd given him to a small laceration on his temple. "It's like a movie!"

Indeed.

While film narratives of white folks in low-income neighborhoods tend to focus on how endangered they are by a gangland black or brown menace, this patient was singular in that he was literally the only victim of black on white violence I encountered in my entire 10-year career as a medic.

"What is distinctively 'American' is not necessarily the amount or kind of violence that characterizes our history," Richard Slotkin writes, "but the mythic significance we have assigned to the kinds of violence we have actually experienced, the forms of symbolic violence we imagine or invent, and the political uses to which we put that symbolism." Slotkin was talking about the American frontier as a symbolic reference point for justifying expansionist violence throughout history. Today, we can see the mytho-political uses of symbolic violence in mainstream media portrayals of the "hood."

It's easy to fixate on physical violence. Movies sexualize it, broadcasters shake their heads as another fancy graphic whirs past sensationalizing it, politicians build careers decrying it with one side of their mouths and justifying it with the other. But institutionalized violence moves in far more insidious and wide-reaching patterns. "Gentrification," Suey Park and Dr. David J. Leonard wrote in a recent post at Model View Culture, "represents a socio-historic process where rising housing costs, public policy, persistent segregation, and racial animus facilitates the influx of wealthier, mostly white, residents into a particular neighborhood. Celebrated as 'renewal' and an effort to 'beautify' these communities, gentrification results in the displacement of residents."

Gentrification is violence. Couched in white supremacy, it is a systemic, intentional process of uprooting communities. It's been on the rise, increasing at a frantic rate in the last 20 years, but the roots stretch back to the disenfranchisement that resulted from white flight and segregationist policies. Real estate agents dub changing neighborhoods with new, gentrifier-friendly titles that designate their proximity to even safer areas: Bushwick becomes East Williamsburg, parts of Flatbush are now Prospect Park South. Politicians manipulate zoning laws to allow massive developments with only token nods at mixed-income housing.

Beyond these political and economic maneuvers, though, the thrust of gentrification takes place in our mythologies of the hood. It is a result, as Park and Leonard explain, of a "discourse that imagines neighborhoods of color as pathological and criminal, necessitating outside intervention for the good of all." Here's where my pistol-whipped patient's revelation about his cinematic experience kicks in. The dominant narrative of the endangered white person barely making it out of the hood alive is, of course, a myth. No one is safer in communities of color than white folks. White privilege provides an invisible force field around them, powered by the historically grounded assurance that the state and media will prosecute any untoward event they may face.

With gentrification, the central act of violence is one of erasure. Accordingly, when the discourse of gentrification isn't pathologizing communities of color, it's erasing them. *Girls*, for example, reimagines today's Brooklyn as an entirely white community. Here's a show that places itself in the epicenter of a gentrifying city with gentrifiers for characters—it is essentially a show about gentrification that refuses to address gentrification. After critics lambasted Season 1 for its lack of diversity, the show brought in Donald Glover to play a black Republican and still managed to avoid the more pressing and relevant question of displacement and racial disparity that the characters are, despite their self-absorption, deeply complicit with. What's especially frustrating about *Girls* not only dodging the topic entirely but pushing back—often with snark and defensiveness against calls for more diversity—is that it's a show that seems to want to bring a more nuanced take on the complexities of modern life.

In an appallingly overwritten New York magazine article with the (I guess) provocative title "Is Gentrification All Bad?," Justin Davidson imagines a first wave of gentrifiers much the way I've heard it described again and again: "A trickle of impecunious artists hungry for space and light." This is the standard, "first it was the artists" narrative of gentrification, albeit a little spruced up, and the unspoken but the understood word here is "white." Because, really, there have always been artists in the hood. They aren't necessarily recognized by the academy or using trust funds supplementing coffee shop tips to fund their artistic careers, but they are still, in fact, artists. The presumptive, unspoken "white" in the first round of artists gentrification narrative is itself an erasure of these artists of color.

"In the popular imagination, gentrification and displacement are virtually synonymous," Davidson writes without giving any actual data to back up his claim. And, he adds, "a sense of grievance and shame permeates virtually all discussions of neighborhood change." Davidson's euphemistic, maybe-it's-this-but-probably-it's-that take on gentrification is precisely the type of reporting we hear on WNYC and other media outlets on a regular basis. The standard frame for a story on gentrification pits the upside of "urban renewal" against what's painted as a necessary byproduct of this renewal: some folks have to move out. The underlying premise is, are these bakeries and coffee shops worth a few people having to move? And the underlying answer is, of course! The entirety of Bloomberg's tenure as mayor was a continuous stream of bring-in-the-rich schemes, openly flaunted and always at the cost of New York's poor. What's missing from this analysis is that the forced displacement of peoples and dispersal of communities, whether through economic, political or cultural policies, is a long-term human rights violation.

For groups facing economic and cultural marginalization in the U.S., community means much more than just a residential area. In a country whose institutions historically fail or deliberately erase us, community constitutes a central pillar in surviving hetero-patriarchal white supremacy. Technology has brought new possibilities for collective action and resistance, but the centrality of physical community remains crucial. What becomes of community organizing, which is responsible for our continued survival here, when communities are increasingly uprooted and scattered?

The shifting power dynamics of today's urban neighborhoods are reflected even in issues of food and nutrition. "Once-affordable ingredients have been discovered by trendy chefs," cultural critic Mikki Kendall writes, "and have been transformed into haute cuisine. Food is facing gentrification that may well put traditional meals out of reach for those who created the recipes. Despite the hype, these ingredients have always been delicious, nutritious and no less healthy than other sources of protein." Writing about this phenomenon at Bitch Media, Soleil Ho stated that food gentrification takes "the form of a curious kind of reacharound logic wherein economic and racial minorities are castigated for eating 'primitively' and 'unhealthily' while their traditional foods are cherry picked for use by the upper class as 'exotic' delicacies."

"Even gentrifiers themselves are convinced they are doing something terrible," Davidson continues. "Young professionals whose moving trucks keep pulling up to curbs in Bushwick and Astoria carry with them trunkfuls of guilt." It's an odd and eloquent assumption about the mind of a gentrifier, but really, it's irrelevant what they think or what Davidson thinks they think. The gears are all already in place, the mechanisms of white supremacy and capitalism poised to make their moves. Davidson talks of a "sweet spot": some mythical moment of racial, economic harmony where the neighborhood stays perfectly diverse and balanced. There is no "sweet spot," as Andrew Padilla at El Barrio Tours points out in his excellent point-by-point takedown, just fleeting moments of harmony in the midst of an ongoing legacy of forced displacement.

Here's a refrain you'll hear a lot in conversations about gentrifications: "Well, it's really a class issue." Davidson's piece manages to avoid any race analysis whatsoever. Of course economics plays a huge role in this. But race and class are inseparably entwined. Rising rents, along with institutionally racist policies like stop-and-frisk, have forced black people to leave New York and urban areas around the country at historic rates. And yes, there are many layers at play: When non-black people of color with class privilege, like myself, move into a historically black and lower-income neighborhood, the white imagination reads our presence as making the area a notch safer for them. The mythology of safety and racial coding regards our presence as a marker of change; the white imagination places higher value on anything it perceives as closer to itself, further from blackness. We become complicit in the scam; the cycle continues.

These power plays—cultural, political, economic, racial—are the mechanics of a city at war with itself. It is a slow, dirty war, steeped in American traditions of racism and capitalism. The participants are often wary, confused, doubtful. Macklemore summarized the attitudes of many young white wealthy newcomers in his fateful text to Kendrick Lamar on Grammy night: "It's weird and sucks that I robbed you." But as with Macklemore, being surprised about a system that has been in place for generations is useless. White supremacy is nothing if not predictable. To forge ahead, we require an outrageousness that sees beyond the tired tropes and easy outs that mass media provides. This path demands we organize with clarity about privilege and the shifting power dynamics of community. It requires foresight, discomfort and risk-taking. It will be on the Web and in the streets, in conversations, rants and marches.

We need a new mythology.

Credit

Older, Daniel José. "Gentrification's Insidious Violence: The Truth about American Cities." This article first appeared in Salon.com, at *http://www.Salon.com*. An online version remains in the Salon archives. Reprinted with permission.

Go Forth and Gentrify?

Dashka Slater

Eighteen years ago my husband and I bought our first house in what real estate agents termed an "up and coming" neighborhood in Oakland, California. We didn't think of ourselves as gentrifiers. We were paying more than we could afford, hoping that someday our neighborhood would have more cafés and fewer car thefts. We eventually bailed, but today the pawnshops and porn theater have indeed been replaced by boutiques and bakeries, and the house we sold at a loss has tripled in value.

So are "transitional" homebuyers guilty of class warfare? It's easy to talk about the downside of gentrification—high housing prices, evictions, and a creeping nimbyism that elbows out social services. But there are benefits, too. When the white middle class left America's cities in the 1950s and '60s, they took the tax base with them, leaving behind concentrated pockets of poverty and powerlessness. Upscale newcomers bring investment, jobs, and tax revenue to neighborhoods that desperately need them, as well as intangibles like the political know-how required to extract money and services from urban bureaucracies.

There's also the environmental benefit. Renovating a house in the urban core is far more sustainable than commuting to a newly built subdivision. A University of Toronto study found that residents of low-density suburbs consumed twice as much energy and produced twice as much greenhouse gases as those living in the city centers.

Whether the costs outweigh the benefits is a tough call, partly because some of what we think we know about gentrification isn't exactly right. Take displacement. A 2005 study by Lance Freeman, a professor of urban planning at Columbia University, found the chances that a poor resident of a gentrifying neighborhood would be forced to move were only 1.5 percent—compared to a 1 per cent chance of that same resident being displaced in a nongentrifying neighborhood. This is partly because poor people tend to be transient anyway, and partly because poor neighborhoods tend to have high vacancy rates. Maureen Kennedy, a Clinton administration housing official who coauthored a study of gentrification for the Brookings Institution, found that in one Cleveland neighborhood, city residents believed there had been an enormous displacement of blacks by whites, although census data revealed that there had been only a "modest inflow" of white residents. But, she adds, "perception becomes reality."

That's in part because blacks are moving to the suburbs at twice the rate of whites, an exodus driven as much by high crime as it is by high housing prices. "At least 50 per cent have left because of poor education and poor public safety," says housing activist Charlene Overshown, who two years ago moved back into the West Oakland neighborhood where she grew up and has been astonished by the rise in rents and the increase in white residents.

It's true, though, that gentrifiers often exist in a kind of parallel universe. They live behind locked gates, send their kids to private schools, shop outside the neighborhood, and avoid the parks. As Freeman observes, their only interaction with the neighbors may come when they call the cops because the music's too loud.

The problem, says John A. Powell, a leading scholar of race at Ohio State University, stems from making choices based solely on your own costs and benefits. For example, should you send your kid to the local public school? "If I decide to send my kid to a school that's dysfunctional, I feel bad. If I decide not to send my kid to a school that's dysfunctional, I also feel bad. Regardless of my choice, the school remains the same. The question is, how can I transform the system not just for me but for the people who don't have the choices?"

Get involved, suggests Nancy Gapasin Gnass, a high school history teacher who bought into San Francisco's Mission district during the final days of the dot-com boom. She sends her daughter to a local school where 79 per cent of the students receive free or subsidized lunches and 80 per cent are Latino or black; she volunteers at the school, sits on the PTA and the school site council, and has organized a group that revitalized the local park. When Gnass' daughter turned six this year, she invited the entire class. Eighteen out of twenty children came to the party and brought their families. "We all walk to school together," says Gnass, who is Filipina. "My Spanish is horrible, but I try."

Newcomers elsewhere have helped their neighbors fight evictions, taught at the local school, and started businesses that hired locals. Make sure to patronize local businesses and help the owners figure out how to "ride the wave" of new customers, adds Kennedy. Most important, urges Overshown, "Help us fight for more affordable housing. If you say this is the only place you can afford to live, well, let's all fight so that at least some of the folks, the folks who *want* to stay, can stay here."

Credit

Slater, Dashka. "Go Forth and Gentrify?" *Mother Jones* 1 July 2007: Web.

Before Downtown

Cleveland, Ohio, and Urban Renewal, 1949–1958

William D. Jenkins

Cleveland residents were in a quandary over their city. A civic booster, Frank Ryan of the Cleveland Electric Illuminating Company, had launched an advertising campaign in 1946 depicting Cleveland as "the best location in the nation." The victory of the Cleveland Indians in the 1948 World Series and the Cleveland Browns' domination of the All-American Conference prior to joining and winning the National Football League in 1950 seemed to confirm that status. But the signs of deterioration and decentralization present within the city put a damper on this enthusiasm. In 1950, Cleveland—like other industrial cities whose population plateaued around 1930—was losing its middleclass base to the suburbs; retail stores and other businesses were to follow. To reverse the decline, city leaders latched onto the federal urban renewal legislation of 1949.

The housing act of 1949 (the Wagner-Ellender-Taft [WET] Act) was designed to revive declining cities. Title I encouraged private enterprise to redevelop slums and blighted areas by providing federal funds to support the cost of buying, clearing, and preparing land in such areas. Local urban renewal authorities, under the control of city government, would superintend the process, and then sell the land to private developers with federal funds absorbing two-thirds of the difference between the cost and the selling price. Federal regulations restricted funding to projects that were primarily residential either before or after the development, thus enabling the land to be used for residential, commercial, or industrial development. The legislation also required the rehousing of displaced families in livable quarters. Recognizing the inability of private enterprise to provide affordable, decent housing for those displaced, the bill, under Title I, provided for the building of 810,000 units of public housing over a six-year period.

This legislation was a compromise between competing visions of urban redevelopment. The National Association of Real Estate Brokers, through its subsidiary, the Urban Land Institute, wanted to create a developmental partnership between private enterprise and government for the rebuilding of cities and the preservation of urban real estate values. They opposed public housing as socialistic and wanted as few federal strings attached as possible. Their version of the bill would have permitted the redevelopment of any section of the city for residential, commercial, or industrial purposes. Liberals, in particular public housers, were more concerned about the provision of proper housing for the poor and the elimination of slums as a cause of social problems. They managed to create a compromise measure that restricted the bill to the clearance of slum or blighted areas, required the relocation of displaced families to livable quarters, and provided for the building of public housing. Although the bill offered something for each side, it did not settle the underlying philosophical and political issues, nor had it really tested how the provisions would work, given the inevitable disturbance of urban living patterns caused by the clearance of slums and blighted areas.[1] This article will examine Cleveland's failed attempt to make the 1949 housing act work to halt its downward spiral.

Cleveland and Urban Planning

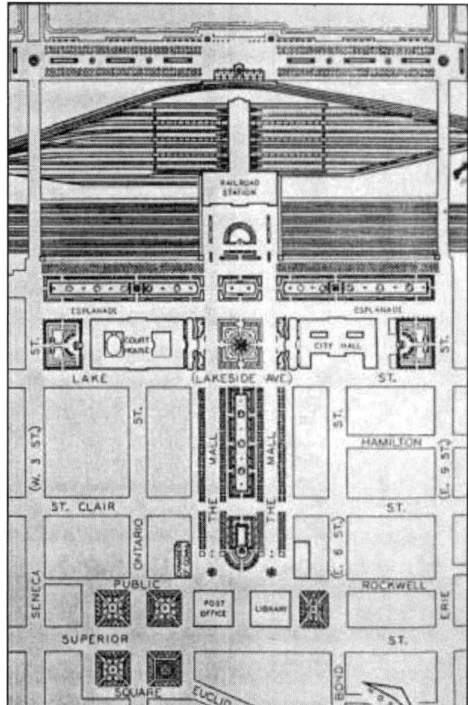

Figure 1. An Early Rendition of the Group Plan (Source: The Kelvin Library, Case Western Reserve University).

Cleveland was well prepared to take advantage of this legislation. It had a long history of cooperation between its business leaders, politicians, and newspapers centered around the planning and development of a better Cleveland. Through organizations such as the Chamber of Commerce, the American Institute of Architects, and the Citizens League, business leaders had concentrated their efforts in the 1890s on the development of the Group Plan, designed by Daniel Burnham, John Carrere, and Arnold W. Brunner to place a coterie of government buildings around a mall extending from Public Square to the lakefront (see Figure 1). This project marked the initiation of a movement from the personal, piecemeal, and privately funded planning of a nineteenth-century city to the public, comprehensive, and government-funded planning of a mid-twentieth-century city.[2] In between these end points, Cleveland established a City Plan Commission in 1913 to oversee the development of the Group Plan. Although the commission finished the Group Plan in 1930 (without a railway station as the gateway), a lack of funds and staffing stymied the production of a comprehensive city plan, which it was also called on to prepare. The Chamber of Commerce tried to fill in the gap by underwriting studies on transportation, zoning, and smoke abatement. It also recommended in 1923 the creation of a privately run organization to generate money and staffing for the production of a city plan (see Figure 2).[3] But the creation of an effective planning infrastructure awaited the Depression.

The Cleveland Chamber of Commerce
Founded in 1848

A City Plan
for
Greater Cleveland

Bohn Library CWRU

Report of the Committee on City Plan
The Cleveland Chamber of Commerce
Submitted to the Board of Directors
September 19, 1923

Figure 2. The Cleveland Chamber of Commerce Was an Important Advocate of City Planning (Source: The Kelvin Library, Case Western Reserve University).

These business organizations also united to promote good government and the defeat of political bosses. From Mayor Tom Johnson in 1901, when Cleveland identified itself as a "city upon a hill," through Thomas Burke in 1950, Cleveland's mayors were generally known for independence from their parties and freedom from corruption. This good government tradition had spawned a climate receptive to using planning initiatives to stem the decline of the city.[4]

The onset of the Depression in 1930 provided much needed federal assistance for the rehabilitation of cities like Cleveland. When citizens and politicians throughout the United States became interested in federal planning—whether industrial, agricultural, or regional—as a means of ending the depression, social reformers used the opportunity to interest the federal government in clearing slums and providing housing for the poor because such programs promoted recovery by putting construction personnel back to work.[5] Cleveland's response to these developments included slum clearance, public housing, and postwar planning, as well as the creation of a powerful City Planning Commission and a comprehensive plan for the city.

A key figure in observing the prevailing pattern of urban decentralization; in devising strategies to channel civic energies toward the rebuilding of Cleveland; and in pulling together the business, political, and social forces already interested in attacking the problem was Ernest J. Bohn. An emigre from Rumania at the age of eleven, Bohn had attended Western Reserve University and then its law school. A liberal Republican, he ran successfully in the late 1920s for a seat on the city council from the relatively affluent Hough area. The advent of the Depression introduced him to the problems of the slums and ultimately into his career as a houser and a planner. Because of Bohn's thoroughness in investigating the causes of slums, his ability to educate and to organize, and his political intuition, city officials appointed him as the director of the Cuyahoga Metropolitan Housing Authority in 1933 and the chairman of the City Planning Commission in 1943. Bohn also commanded national attention because of his many contacts with federal officials, his founding of the National Association of Housing and Rehabilitation Officials, and his association with the passage of federal legislation. Bohn's stature in Cleveland was apparent in the drive to have him run for mayor in the immediate postwar years. Bohn refused to run, however, contending that housing needed him.[6]

Bohn was a critical, but not singular, factor in preparing Cleveland for urban renewal. From the very beginning of his career, he had linked public housing and the control of slums with planning. In 1930, he had acquired financial support for the Regional Association of Cleveland (RAC), a private planning society similar to the one proposed by the Chamber of Commerce in 1923. Bohn used this organization to study the needs of the area, to educate the public about the benefits of planning, and to launch a campaign to create a powerful City Planning Commission. Supported with monies provided by the Works Progress Administration, RAC gathered numerous databases about housing, population densities, recreation, transportation, land utilization, and other features of the urban landscape that would be available for postwar planning.[7] The work of the RAC culminated in 1943 with the creation of a powerful City Planning Commission—its decisions required a two-thirds override by City Council to veto—with Ernest Bohn as its chair. Bohn orchestrated the appointment of John T. Howard, a graduate of the Massachusetts Institute of Technology's planning program, as planning director. Howard prepared a comprehensive plan for the city of Cleveland, which was finished and adopted in 1949.[8] With its passage, the city of Cleveland had the key elements in place to begin urban renewal.

Other Cities and Urban Renewal

Cleveland was but one of many cities interested in urban renewal. In recent years, historical investigation of urban renewal, its successes and failures, has proceeded along two lines. Some historians have studied individual cities, such as Philadelphia,

Chicago, Cincinnati, and Detroit. These research projects are demanding, and time-consuming, but they do not satisfy the historian's need for a broad sweeping assessment of national patterns. And so, Jon Teaford, in spite of the even greater demands and consumption of time involved in the study of multiple cities, has undertaken an assessment of urban renewal programs in twelve cities, primarily in the northern and eastern United States. His book *The Rough Road to Renaissance: Urban Revitalization in America, 1940–1985* offers an interpretive framework that allegedly fits all twelve cities, including Cleveland, Ohio. It is the purpose of this article to demonstrate, however, that Cleveland, in the period between 1945 and 1960, deviates in significant ways from that pattern.

Teaford argues convincingly that continuing decentralization of these cities in the post–World War II era threatened business leaders and municipal officials. A declining central business district, the loss of middle- and upper-class residents to suburban living, a lowered tax base, and the spread of slums and blight provoked them to attack the signs of physical deterioration and thereby reverse the trend toward decentralization. "During the first decade after World War II," according to Teaford, "these aging cities optimistically planned for a better future, assuming that a physical renovation of the city could erase the existing flaws in urban life."[9] For Teaford, the primary emphasis of these leaders was on physical, rather than social, renewal. Thus, highways, airports, new houses, open spaces, and the elimination of air and water pollution garnered the largest allocations of money. According to Teaford, "The engineer, architect, and contractor and not the social worker or agitator were to cure the city's ills. They were to mix the elixir that would bring new life to Boston, Buffalo, Cleveland and Chicago."[10] Because the emphasis was on brick, mortar, and asphalt and not social restructuring or the redistribution of wealth or power, neighborhood clubs, labor unions, and progressive political clubs were usually on the periphery of urban renewal efforts. Yet, urban leaders, according to Teaford, saw the need "to unite the diverse elements of the city behind the program of physical amelioration, patching over social and political divisions with a booster rhetoric promising a better life for all."[11]

Teaford also suggests that political change, especially in the type of mayor, accompanied and reinforced physical redevelopment. "In the minds of major metropolitan newspapers, prominent business figures, leaders of civic organizations, and even many politicians," according to Teaford, "the central cities had to have a new leadership projecting a fresh image that proclaimed to the nation the revitalization of the shabby, tired urban hubs of the past."[12] These leaders rejected "portly, cigar-smoking bosses," "shortsighted hacks," and "ethnic politicians" for a new breed of mayors who would appeal to businessmen and to bureaucrats in Washington with their dedication to efficient government. Such mayors, who usually won landslide victories, appealed to voters from the middle class and more substantial members of the working class living in the outer rings of the city. They favored incorruptible and less expensive government, as well as efforts to enhance the tax base by attracting investors back into the city. Teaford cites the election of Anthony Celebrezze in 1953 as mayor of Cleveland as an example of this pattern.[13]

Last, Teaford portrays the actual removal of slums and blight in these twelve cities as meager. Although admitting that "the ultimate dream of planners, public officials, and civic leaders was the eradication of slums,"[14] Teaford deprecates the small sum of federal money offered these cities as inadequate. He also correctly blames local planning delays, bureaucratic roadblocks in Washington, and the lack of investor interest for the inadequate results. In contrast to federal efforts, Teaford contends that "the most highly publicized and widely admired redevelopment schemes of the late 1940s and the 1950s were the product of cooperation between local authorities and private enterprise with the federal government playing no role." Pittsburgh's Allegheny Conference constitutes his major example.[15]

There is much to acknowledge as insightful within the Teaford analysis. The fright of decline and further decentralization was affecting Cleveland's leadership at midcentury. Also, more money was spent in Cleveland on physical aspects, and, consequently, little was accomplished in the elimination of slums and blight. But much of that failure has to be attributed to funding priorities affected by the Korean War and conservative control of Congress in the 1950s, not to local leadership's emphasis on physical rather than social renaissance as the key to urban renaissance. Moreover, Teaford's reliance on data about money spent as an indicator of priorities does not tell us why such choices were made. His underlying assumption that urban leadership did not consider social reform important was not the case in Cleveland.

Teaford has left out the story of how a coalition of newspaper editors, leading businessmen, major political figures, and social reformers in Cleveland attempted to revivify the slums and induce social reform before thinking of downtown renaissance as the key to urban renewal. Social reform was indeed at the center, not the periphery, of early urban renewal efforts in Cleveland. Union leaders and welfare groups served on urban renewal committees and organized political support on its behalf. A sampling of newspaper editors, leading businessmen, and major political figures agreed with the vision of social reformers and participated in development of plans only to suffer frustration when opposition generated by racial and class differences proved intractable. Teaford has produced, at least as far as Cleveland is concerned, a sanitized history of its efforts at urban renewal.

Ernest J. Bohn

Although downtown merchants, real estate brokers, and leading politicians played essential roles in the efforts to renew Cleveland, it is important to examine the thrust toward planning and renewal that came from Ernest Bohn who, because of expertise and the positions he held, controlled the design of the plans. A technocrat trained in the Progressive tradition, Bohn was a reformer determined to make social changes part of the program to renew Cleveland. He believed, for instance, that society had a responsibility to provide decent housing for all its citizens. Although a member for a short duration of the very conservative National Association of Real Estate Brokers (NAREB) subsidiary organization, the Urban Land Institute, he disagreed sharply with its president, Seward H. Mott, and his attitude that public housing represented a socialistic experiment.[16] Bohn considered public housing "not socialism, but a necessary support for capitalism,"[17] and challenged opponents of public housing to explain the difference between federal credit extended to middle class home buyers and direct appropriations to provide public housing to the poor. He characterized NAREB's promotion of programs to assist the building industry as hypocritical and self-serving.[18] Because of his concerns after World War II that urban renewal legislation might support housing built by private developers only, Bohn had worked to assure the inclusion of public housing in the Ohio Urban Redevelopment Act (he served as an advisor to the state legislature's urban redevelopment committee) and the federal Wagner-Ellender-Taft Housing Act, both of which passed in 1949. Much to Bohn's satisfaction, both acts provided for public housing and required that the demolition of slum properties could not occur if it displaced slum dwellers and their families, as had happened with federal slum clearance programs during the Depression.[19]

Bohn's thinking in regard to public housing is best characterized as capitalistic and Christian, not socialistic. As a lifelong Republican, he accepted private enterprise as the basis of the economic system. Even before the start of World War II, Bohn had identified the belt around the central business district north of Woodland Avenue from East 22nd to East 79th streets as an area that "must be redeveloped for middle- and low-income housing" and with private enterprise stepping in and doing "the same sort of large-scale reconstruction, as the federal government had done with public housing."[20] Bohn willingly conceded that private enterprise would provide most of the new housing after World War II and even supported granting federal subsidies to private developers in the clearance of slums. As a practicing Roman Catholic who had read and imbibed the social principles embodied in papal encyclicals, such as

Rerum Novarum and *Castii Canubi*, Bohn assumed the role of his brother's keeper through his support for housing for the poor.[21] Although the imperatives of the Sermon on the Mount guided his social analysis, Bohn also argued that there was no better way for Christians to "checkmate vicious and lying Communist propaganda than a demonstration that democracy is virile in improving the lot of the less fortunate citizen through programs such as low income housing."[22]

Bohn's advocacy of the social gospel applied to racial issues as well. The segregation of public housing in Cleveland on a basis of neighborhood congruence was a result of federal control during the Depression, rather than Bohn's commitment to segregation. Unable to check the federal selection process, he had managed, in cooperation with the Urban League, to crack the union ban on using black construction workers on the projects.[23] In the late 1930s, when the National Association of Housing Officials met in New Orleans and the hotel refused admission to its black members, he had protested and assisted in having the convention changed to Cincinnati.[24] Further indications of his attitude were his service in the late 1940s on the board of the National Association to Desegregate Our Nation's Capital and his deposit of half of his savings in Quincy Savings & Loan, an African American bank, because it was a source of loans to Cleveland minorities wishing to buy housing.[25]

When urban renewal began nationally in 1950, Bohn was an official of the American Society of Planning Officials (ASPO). He helped to secure the passage of an ASPO resolution on behalf of admitting anyone to the projects developed under urban renewal programs.[26] As the public housing director in Cleveland throughout the 1950s, Bohn advocated the integration of all facilities produced by the program, and the creation of "a unified front to solve domestic problems of race and economic difference."[27] The *Call and Post*, Cleveland's major African American newspaper, in the midst of later fights, would proclaim in an editorial that "Bohn has been a relentless fighter for maintaining a completely interracial policy in both the construction and occupancy of all public housing in Cleveland."[28]

Bohn was also an environmentalist. He believed, from his extensive reading of the literature on the housing movement, that a densely packed slum without access to the amenities of water, light, and heating, and to playgrounds, schools, and social service agencies eroded the spirit of its residents. The provision of standard housing within a neighborhood that encouraged community involvement and offered access to a variety of services, he hoped, would uplift the poor. He had followed such principles in the construction of Cleveland's public housing estates in the late thirties and early forties (he refused to call them projects since they were already finished).[29]

As a technocrat with Progressive leanings, Bohn supplemented his social vision with hard data. He convincingly argued, for instance, that private enterprise could not produce an affordable and standard house for the poor either to own or to rent; a subsidy was needed.[30] Bohn also relied on sociological data, such as that produced by Msgr. Robert A. Navin of the Cleveland diocese, revealing that slum areas brought in far less money in taxes than the city government expended on social problems packed into the relatively small area studied. Bohn often suggested that citizens should redirect this subsidy in a more positive direction, such as in support of public housing.[31] Through his extensive reliance on social and economic data, Bohn managed to avoid, for the most part, the accusation that he was a social visionary without an appreciation of the practical realities.

Bohn's expertise and his commitment to the capitalistic system enabled him to appeal to a broad base of followers. The two major local newspapers, the *Plain Dealer* and the *Press*, continuously lauded his efforts and supported expansion of public housing and the integration of all projects. They also proposed on numerous occasions that he become mayor of Cleveland.[32] Only the Cleveland *News* demurred, deterred by its suspicion of the potential for socialism in public housing. Numerous businessmen, lawyers, and architects associated themselves with Bohn and served on the boards or subcommittees of Cuyahoga Metropolitan Housing Authority, the Regional Association of Cleveland, or other bodies linked to Bohn. Obviously, not all members of these professions supported Bohn, but many did.

Fortunately, Bohn did not need to break the back of machine politics. For much of the twentieth-century, Cleveland had mayors who eschewed bossism. Harold Burton, Frank Lausche, and Thomas Burke followed Tom Johnson, Newton D. Baker, and a string of city managers in the 1920s prior to the arrival of Anthony Celebrezze in 1953. Although a few mayors had won who were dependent on the party organization, they were exceptional.[33] After 1930, Bohn had worked very closely with most of the Cleveland mayors and garnered their support for his programs. The election of Celebrezze, as an independent but ethnic Democrat, did not mark a turning point in political control but a continuation of the good government tradition.[34] Although a Republican, Bohn became a close personal friend and supporter of Celebrezze.

Cleveland's Urban Renewal

By 1949, Bohn was well prepared to push urban renewal. He had fifteen years of data gathering, political maneuvering, and social schmoozing behind him. The Cleveland Plan, proposed by the City Planning Commission and adopted by the city council in

1949, was wide sweeping in its range and satisfied the provision of the 1949 federal act that the city proposing urban renewal construct projects in line with a comprehensive plan.[35] Bohn and John T. Howard were kindred spirits who espoused urban renewal for both its human and economic potential. Howard did not favor these plans because they would lead to greater population growth within the city; rather, he advocated controlled decentralization and chided Cleveland officials for believing that bigness equated with success. Howard also contended that a decentralized and appropriately rebuilt city, with a mixture of economic and racial groups, could provide a decent and livable environment for all of its citizens.[36] By early 1950, Bohn had a commitment from the federal Public Housing Authority to build 6,000 units in Cleveland and $3 million for urban renewal.[37]

Bohn wanted to move quickly, but state and federal complications arose. Indeed he had, as usual, filled out the forms without delay, but the Ohio State Supreme Court had ruled in 1942 that public housing projects did not fit the state constitution's definition of public purpose and were, therefore, taxable. Since the 1937 housing act had required local governments to make a contribution, usually in the form of tax abatement, the court's decision caused the federal government to delay any further building in Ohio. Finally, in 1951, almost ten years after the initial decision, the Ohio Supreme Court reversed its finding because the state legislature had amended the Ohio housing law in 1949 to declare that public housing was a public purpose. The election of a Republican Congress in 1952 further complicated Bohn's initiative because it restricted the building of public housing units to 35,000 per year, rather than the 135,000 originally envisioned.

Meanwhile, Bohn and Howard faced the determined opposition of businessmen associated with the real estate industry. The Cleveland Federation of Real Estate Brokers, the Apartment and Building Owners Association (OA), and the Cleveland Home Builders Association (CHBA) spoke out repeatedly against the inclusion of public housing in any program. They contended that it competed directly with private enterprise, which, if given the opportunity, could provide sufficient housing. Both Karl Duldner (OA) and Morris Fishman (CHBA) condemned public housing as a socialist experiment undeserving of public support. Their ally, the Cleveland Federation of Realty Interests, proposed an unpassed constitutional amendment for the state of Ohio to require a local vote on public housing.[38]

Other businessmen, however, were more supportive. Under Mayor Thomas Burke (1945–1953), efforts to involve industrialists in urban renewal had floundered, money being the primary obstacle, but Bohn did not give up. He continued to solicit the support of leading industrialists and bankers.[39] In 1954, Bohn and newly elected Mayor Celebrezze were finally able to gather a coterie of leading businessmen throughout the city's economic structure and form the Cleveland Development Foundation (CDF). Members of the CDF board of trustees included Thomas Patton, president of Republic Steel; Elmer Lindseth, president of Cleveland Electric Illuminating Company; John Virden, president of the Virden Company and chairman of the board of the Federal Reserve Bank of Cleveland; E. Horton Hampton, vice-president of the Nickel Plate Railroad; Frederick C. Crawford, president of Thompson Products (eventually TRW); John K. Thompson, president of the Union Bank of Commerce; Walter F. Mumford, president of American Steel and Wire Company; John Greene, president of Ohio Bell; Curtis Lee Smith, president of the Chamber of Commerce; and a host of other major figures in the Cleveland world of business.[40] James Yielding, the urban renewal director under Celebrezze, encouraged these industrialists to support urban renewal because it would provide proper housing for their black employees, who had been confined within the same residential area they had occupied since 1930.[41] Mayor Celebrezze, who had grown up in the slums, called for industrialists' consideration for workers who labored in pastel-colored, air-conditioned plants with soothing music and then returned home to rats.[42]

CDF's response was creation of a $2 million fund donated by more than 100 businesses to serve as seed money for private and public projects. CDF proclaimed itself as "not interested in controversy in real estate, nor in the ideological concepts of public vs. private housing"; it supported both.[43] Rather, it sought to support the building of housing for moderate income groups, in particular, those who could not qualify for public housing. Private developers, to whom the government offered slum land at one-third the value, were reluctant to build homes or apartments for those who did not qualify for public housing. CDF was now there to give them additional financial assistance.[44] These efforts to underwrite urban renewal in Cleveland were an indication of the commitment of leading businessmen to forwarding the general plan of urban renewal and its broad-ranging social and economic goals.[45]

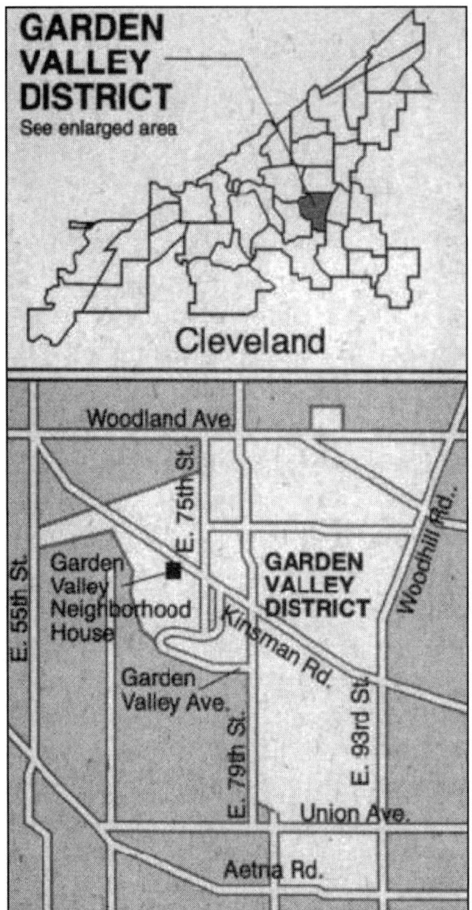

Figure 3. Garden Valley was the Most Ambitious and Comprehensive of Cleveland's Urban Renewal Projects (Source: The Kelvin Library, Case Western Reserve University).

This commitment to social and economic change was most evident in the Garden Valley project. Republic Steel contributed some land across from its plant in Kingsbury Run.[46] The steel company had formerly deposited its slag there but now offered the land, including finishing it off, as vacant property on which the city, with the encouragement of CDF funding, could build a showcase project that combined all the features of a comprehensive urban renewal project: public housing, new privately developed housing, and rehabilitation of existing structures surrounding the area (see Figure 3).[47] Plans also included space for social service agencies, shopping centers, athletic fields, and parks as well as accessibility to schools and libraries.[48] According to Bohn, "Here was to be an economically as well as racially integrated program."[49]

Another example of the CFD assistance of private developers involved Oscar Steiner of Community Development, Inc., in the Longwood area. His project enabled black families to own their own apartments for $500 down and $81.50 per month, which included interest, amortization, taxes, insurance, and exterior repairs and services, such as lawn mowing and snow removal. Steiner was concerned that most developers built decent new homes only for upper-income buyers and that blacks were confined to the oldest and most run-down sections of the city by "restrictive real-estate practices of builders, brokers, and lenders, echoing the sentiments of white neighbors." His plans focused on stabilizing the Longwood area by attracting more affluent blacks or whites into the area and increasing the ratio of ownership to rental.[50] Thus, it is apparent that social reform through urban renewal was seriously attempted in Cleveland, that it garnered the support of major groups (including businessmen), and that it predated the effort to rebuild the downtown.

These efforts, however, floundered on the rocks of racism and economic stratification, not because businessmen guided the urban renewal process toward physical renewal, as implied by Teaford.[51] Cleveland had a reputation as a liberal city regarding race relations.[52] Indeed, after desegregating its hospitals in the Depression, Cleveland had established a strong Community Relations Commission in 1945, whose job it was to oversee employment opportunities, as well as to provide for mediation in racial incidents. For its efforts, the city won the Human Relations award from the National Conference of Christians and Jews in 1947. But Cleveland's acceptance of the black population did not extend to housing. As African Americans swarmed to Cleveland during the war and after, they remained concentrated on the East Side, separated from the West Side by the Cuyahoga River. Between 1930 and 1950, the African American population had grown from 10% of the population in 1930 to 16.2% in 1950,[53] but its living space had remained hemmed in by white, ethnic populations. The dampening effect of the Depression and war years on home building in general added to the problem, as black families crowded into homes and apartments and paid high rents. Little relief came from private developers who built 55,000 new dwelling units between 1945 and 1950 but included only 200 for nonwhites. Even though some black families could afford better housing, local banks and the Federal Housing Administration (FHA) refused them mortgages, while white real estate brokers steered them away from properties in white areas. Black real estate salesmen could not even belong to the Cleveland Federation of Real Estate Brokers; they had to set up their own organization.[54]

Because the housing act of 1949 required that provision be made for families displaced by urban renewal programs, any demolition of housing was sure to have an impact on the racial composition of the city as the removal of slums or blighted areas, predominantly on the East Side, displaced black families. Since the rebuilt area would contain fewer dwellings—based on the desire to create a healthier environment—it was necessary for Bohn to find vacant land outside the slum area for public housing to accommodate those who could not afford the new privately built housing. Opponents in the white, ethnic neighborhoods of Cleveland responded negatively once efforts to provide this space for black families occurred. Since the turn of the century, these immigrants from southern and eastern Europe had established neighborhoods on the East Side that generally excluded black families; they were not ready to permit any invasion. They would prove to be ready allies for the Cleveland Federation of Real Estate Brokers, the Apartment and Building Owners Association, and the Cleveland Home Builders Association.

As early as 1952, Ernest Bohn had designated the southeastern portion of the city just north of the city of Maple Heights, known as the Lee-Seville area, as a place in which to build public housing for the displaced. The garden city type of projects that he favored had restricted his options because there were few expanses of vacant land within the city of Cleveland sufficiently large enough. But for Bohn, the plot in Lee-Seville provided just the right configuration for public housing despite the presence of ravines and other geographical problems that had discouraged developers. "Without the larger project on Lee Road," Bohn commented, "urban renewal can not go forward."[55]

The Lee-Seville area offered a possible solution because of the presence of black families in temporary war housing and in Miles Heights (an annexed suburb within the area). But white residents had already drawn a line to divide themselves from black residents. In late 1951, developers had proposed to build housing in Lee-Seville at a cost of $10,000 for middle-income black families, but white opponents managed to have the city council rezone part of the area for light industry only. This rezoned site, with an electric controls plant as its main feature, separated black and white sections and, in addition, discouraged the FHA from offering mortgages to housing so close to an industrial area.[56] This rezoning marked the first time that the city council had overridden the City Planning Commission (a two-thirds vote was required). Mayor Burke refused to veto the new ordinance.[57]

Bohn's proposal to place public housing in Lee-Seville provoked an already organized and angry opposition. White, ethnic residents, mostly Italian and Polish, formed organizations, such as the Miles Lee Civic Association and the Lee-Land Heights Civic Association, to petition the city council. Members of the Home Builders Association appeared at mass meetings, promising their vocal and financial support.[58] These residents were very conscious of the temporary war housing built in the Seville area and its poor condition.[59] They judged the residents as being at fault for the condition and believed that any public housing would replicate the war housing.

The sorry state of the buildings, however, was the result of the sparse funding available from the government, the scarcity of building materials, the temporary nature of the structures, and the fact that the government had determined to retain them beyond their useful life because of the need for veterans' housing after the war. At one point, Bohn had commented that "we're holding them up with props. They were built to meet an emergency and the emergency never ended."[60] Bohn lamented that "many well-meaning citizens of Cleveland know about public housing only through their contact with this inadequate temporary emergency housing either as residents or as passers-by. The result is that they readily believe the propaganda that 'this is public housing.'"[61]

There were also resentments expressed at the income level of public housing residents. Henry Hawk, a former truck driver and buildings trade handyman who lived in the Lee-Seville area, objected to people from the projects moving into his bastion because he had worked hard for what he got; they had not, and many, he charged, owned yachts. Vincent Busa, a spokesman for the Lee-Land Heights Civic Council, commented angrily that "well, 80% of the people in the projects make more money than I do."[62] After having heard for many years the inaccurate charges from builders and real estate interests that more than 50% of the residents of public housing were over the income limits, Bohn was skeptical that Hawk's and Busa's charges represented the real issue. "The community is divided, supposedly on the question of whether there should be more public housing or not," Bohn observed, "but the actual question is whether or not public housing should be built where both Negroes and whites could live together as American citizens should."[63]

Despite Bohn's analysis, many of his opponents, including residents in the nearby suburbs of Garfield Heights and Maple Heights, believed that the issue was the threat to their property values.[64] Councilman Joseph Kovach commented that "no matter where you propose to build public housing outside the central area, you will have opposition because there is fear it will destroy property values."[65] William J. Rogers, the Republican council leader, charged that both races in Lee-Seville were opposed to public housing projects because of a 25% threatened decline in property value and increased crime. He also warned of the influence of "hillbillies and other undesirables."[66]

Despite these charges that economic, rather than racial differences, had led to the opposition, there is no mistaking the fact that the residents' concerns were primarily racial. Their response to the efforts of Alex Treuhaft, a local developer of apartment complexes and president of the Home Builders Association, to build apartments in the Lee-Seville area was an example. An ardent opponent of public housing, Treuhaft had formed the Private Enterprise Redevelopment Corporation in 1951 to prove that he could build affordable housing for the poor based on private financing and no subsidies, except for FHA.[67] Treuhaft was an advocate of the filter-down approach to housing. He and his partner, Alex Goudreau, believed that the 1,200 units they wanted to build on 70 acres in the Seville area would free houses in the Central area for displaced residents as middle-income families moved into his housing.[68] "Our development will help slum clearance displacements, just as any large housing development does by making more homes available, but it is not in itself a slum relief program."[69]

Residents feared that these apartments would become available to displaced inner-city Cleveland residents, just as the wartime housing for defense workers had mixed races in the Lee-Seville area. The cost of renting, however, would have guaranteed that only middle-class black families could have afforded the apartments.[70] Despite the fact that poor families could not move into such apartments, Arthur Lysowski, ward councilman, refused to sponsor an ordinance that would have rezoned the area from single to multiple family dwellings. [71] Lysowski commented that "this is practically a suburb. We don't want people moving out here and crowding into apartments."[72]

Further indication of the predominance of the racial issue was the opposition that arose to the purchase of a home in a white area of Lee-Seville by Wendall Stewart, a black embalmer from the House of Wills, the largest African American funeral establishment in the city. Despite his middle-class origins, Stewart was not welcome.[73] Both Mayor Burke and Msgr. Navin appeared at a meeting to ask residents not to panic over the perceived threat to property values.[74]

Disgusted with the opposition's charges, Bohn counterattacked that "it is wrong to play on people's emotions on the basis of race or economic considerations, to halt the city's progress. A Negro has as much right to live as a white person. You must believe that if we are going to have a new city."[75] Bohn lamented that Cleveland had in place the laws, financial assets, and power to accomplish urban renewal, but "neighborhoods can not be rebuilt unless the citizens of Cleveland permit construction of dwellings on vacant land for Negroes, whatever their economic status."[76] For the failure to proceed, Cleveland could, according to Bohn, "thank the speculators who used the bigot to do their dirty work in fanning racial hatred."[77]

Bohn was not alone in his condemnation of racism. Mayor Celebrezze predicted that the people of Cleveland "as a whole will prosper together, live together in harmony or we will become a second-class city." Citing the need to "care for all our citizens properly," he posited the right of African American citizens to live in decency.[78] The Catholic Diocese, through the pastor of Saint Cecilia's Church, located in Lee-Seville, warned parishioners that "it is a serious sin to deny a colored family an opportunity to lie in decent quarters."[79] Through the *Universe Bulletin*, diocesan officials advised Catholics that Pope Pius XII had promoted public housing as essential to the well-being of family life.[80] The Greater Cleveland Ministerial Association joined the campaign through pulpit sermons urging a halt to bias in housing.[81] Meanwhile, newspaper editorials, particularly in *the Press* and the *Plain Dealer,* deplored the racially explosive situation and its impact on efforts to revive the city.[82] A. I. Davey, editor of the *Cleveland Citizen*, a labor newspaper, proclaimed that it was a Christian's duty to accept public housing.[83]

But the appeals had no effect. City councilmen from the West Side and white councilmen from the East Side wards held enough power to block the placement of public housing anywhere except within the ghetto. Most city councilmen were sympathetic with Lysowski, the councilman from the Lee-Seville Ward, who called on council members to reject it for his ward because they might face the same situation. They agreed with Ben F. Stores, an executive with the Home Builders Association, who crowed that "there will be no wholesale uprooting of entire sections of the population and moving them against their wills to areas which do not want them."[84] In early 1953, councilmen passed a resolution that they must consider and approve each public housing project.[85]

Council review meant that Bohn would have to restrict his projects to land either in or nearby the slum areas. Bohn had already lost the battle to integrate the city's housing by 1954 when the Kingsbury Run land proffered by the Cleveland Development Foundation enabled him to build public housing in an area acceptable to white councilmen.[86] Despite Bohn's disappointment at the location, he intended to combine Kingsbury Run with public and private projects on the near East Side in the Longwood area where black families already resided and to demonstrate that such projects could work. The publicly and privately developed projects were small, offering housing to only 8,000 people, when there were over 37,612 substandard buildings in Cleveland and nearly 26,500 needy families, according to the 1950 census.[87]

Location, location, location are the answers to the real estate salesperson's question about what are the three most important factors determining the value of a property. The location of these estates offered little to attract both white and black families with moderate incomes. Since these privately built garden-type apartments in the Central area were not affordable for nearly two-thirds of the families from the surrounding area, success depended on attracting moderate-income residents from elsewhere.[88] The possibility of middle-class residents choosing to move back into the central city from more desirable areas, however, was limited. Meanwhile, tenants who did move in earned too low an income but believed that these private projects were like public housing and that rents would fit their budgets. Once faced with high rents, they conducted rent strikes. In a report of organizations investigating the strike, the developers admitted that the rents were too high but also that the apartments were well worth the rents charged, the problem being that "this area is conducive only to low-cost housing experience." The report observed that "bounded on two sides by slums, on one side by a commercial development and a main trucking artery, and on the fourth by public housing (excellent though it may be), persons with middle-class incomes find it socially unacceptable and are able (for the most part) to find adequate housing elsewhere."[89] Except for the successful operation of the new public housing for inner-city residents, the urban renewal program had failed to lessen the racial and economic separation among the city's people.

James Stanton, President of the Cleveland City Council in the 1960s and a member of the Urban Renewal Advisory Committee (URAC), analyzed the failure of urban renewal in a statement before the URAC in 1964. He blamed the agency's staff and departments "because the unrealistic guidelines of relocation did not take into account the individual's social, economic and racial limitations which are barriers to the free movement of the individual." Echoing the thoughts of President Eisenhower in regard to civil rights legislation, Stanton observed that "it is very plain that one cannot achieve through legislation what the people themselves do not want to do."[90]

With the difficulties encountered by the Garden Valley and Longwood projects, the forces that Bohn had mounted behind the campaign for the social and economic renovation of Cleveland fragmented. Bohn had correctly identified race and class as major factors contributing to the decline of Cleveland, and he had attempted, along with others, to confront and ameliorate those factors. His public actions, however, caused him to suffer a loss of reputation; the housing fight had endangered his career, and Republican leaders were determined never to ask him to run for mayor again.[91] Mayor Celebrezze, the City Council, and CDF finally turned their attention to downtown renewal.

In the final analysis, Cleveland's efforts to rebuild deviates from the urban renewal pattern observed in Teaford's study of twelve selected cities during the 1950s. Although Teaford is accurate in his comparison of the monies spent on physical and social renewal and in his judgment that urban renewal was not successful, he has overlooked the extent to which social reform was at the heart of early urban renewal efforts in Cleveland (as well as the fact that Celebrezze was a continuation of the good government tradition). Indeed, it was only after it was apparent that social reform was not possible that downtown became the major focus.

Cleveland was not the only city of the twelve studied to deviate. John Bauman, in his study of the city of Philadelphia, claimed that "planners and redevelopers in Philadelphia seemed deeply sensitive to the sociological ramifications of urban development, especially the need to rehouse displaced black families in unsegregrated housing." He believed that Philadelphia "anchored its postwar housing and redevelopment dreams to a solid foundation of political and social reform." A key figure for Philadelphia was Joseph S. Clark, who was elected as a reform mayor in 1951, thus ending the control of a corrupt Republican machine. Clark championed urban renewal and public housing as a means of integrating the city. His administration included many social reformers, planners, and housers and undertook urban renewal plans that met social and economic, as well as physical, goals. As in Cleveland, these plans met the determined opposition of the white working class. Violence and political backlash overcame the efforts to integrate the city.[92]

Other cities, such as Chicago, Cincinnati, and Detroit, which have been the subject of historical studies, did not share the experience of Cleveland or Philadelphia. Although plans were drawn for urban renewal of each of these cities, the designers did not include broad-sweeping social goals. In Chicago, white ethnics and business interests, according to Arnold Hirsch, united to control urban renewal thereby restricting blacks to ghetto areas. By 1949, the city council of Chicago began to limit public housing to expansion of existing projects within the ghetto. Elizabeth Wood, one of a clique of social reformers, lost her position as head of the metropolitan housing authority in 1954 because of her efforts to integrate public housing.[93] According to Robert Fairbanks, Cincinnati's comprehensive plan of 1948 emphasized retention of neighborhoods as a means of continuing the separation of classes, races, and nationalities. In Detroit, June Manning Thomas has observed that, from the beginning, redevelopment schemes emphasized restoration of the city's central business and industrial districts.[94]

What has emerged from the interplay of local and national studies is a mixed picture of the progress of urban renewal. In some cities, social reformers led the charge and attracted support from politicians, businessmen, professionals, organized labor, black leaders, and social welfare advocates before suffering eventual defeat. In other cities, social reformers were indeed at, or quickly pushed to, the periphery. There is a need for further studies to understand why social reformers were stronger in some cities than in others. We must also realize, though, that regardless of the city, race was usually the major impediment to realizing the goals of urban renewal.

Notes

1 Mark I. Gelfand, *A Nation of Cities: The Federal Government and Urban America*, 1933–1965 (New York, 1975), Chapter 4, 105–56.

2 David C. Hammack, "Comprehensive Planning Before the Comprehensive Plan: A New Look at the Nineteenth-Century City," in Daniel Schaffer, ed., *Two Centuries of American Planning* (Baltimore, 1988), 155; Walter C. Leedy, Jr., "Cleveland's Struggle for Self-Identity: Aesthetics, Economics and Politics," in R. G.Wilson and S. K. Robinson, eds., *Modern Architecture in America: Visions and Revisions* (Iowa State University Press, 1991), 75–105.

3 Mel Scott, *American City Planning Since 1890* (Berkeley, 1969), 61–3; *Planning in Cleveland: 1903–1963*, City Planning Commission (Cleveland, 1963), 1–3.

4 David D. Van Tassel and John J. Grabowski, eds., *The Encyclopedia of Cleveland History* (Bloomington: Indiana University Press, 1987), xlii, 65–7, 137–9, 185–6, 333, 407, 518, 578–9, 668–9, 683, 692.

5 Thomas W. Hanchett, "Roots of the Renaissance': Federal Incentives to Urban Planning, 1941 to 1948," in Mary Corbin Sies and Christopher Silver, eds., *Planning the Twentieth Century American City* (Baltimore, 1996), 283–304. Clearly the effect of federal incentives began even earlier than the beginnings of the war.

6 William D. Jenkins, "Ernest J. Bohn and the Configuration of Public Housing and Urban Planning, 1932–1945," in *Proceedings of the Fifth National Conference on American Planning History* (Hilliard: The Society for American City and Regional Planning History, 1994), 109–23.

7 Director's Progress Report No. 7, Regional Association of Cleveland, October 1944, 1–4, Ernest J. Bohn Papers (Kelvin Smith Library, Case Western Reserve University Library); Ernest J. Bohn, "The Regional Association of Cleveland—A Citizens' Coordinating Organization on Planning," (Speech to the Chamber of Commerce, 20 March 1940, Bohn Papers). I am also grateful to Maury Klain, former political science professor at Case Western Reserve University, for granting me access to the Maury Klain interviews of Cleveland's leadership housed at the Western Reserve Historical Society. These papers are invaluable but limited by his promise of secrecy for the interviewees. They provide support for many of the points made in this article.

8 *Cleveland's General Plan: An Address by John T. Howard,* Publication No. 21 (Regional Association of Cleveland, 1949), 1–7, Bohn Papers.

9 Jon C. Teaford, *The Rough Road to Renaissance: Urban Revitalization in America, 1940–1985* (Baltimore: Johns Hopkins University Press, 1990), 7.

10 Teaford, *Rough Road,* 12.

11 Teaford, *Rough Road,* 7 & 26.

12 Teaford, *Rough Road,* 54.

13 Teaford, *Rough Road,* 59.

14 Teaford, *Rough Road,* 105.

15 Teaford, *Rough Road,* 108.

16 Letter Seward H. Mott to EJB, 17 May 1949; letters EJB to Seward H. Mott, 31 May 1945, 7 July 1945, 24 June 1946, and 8 May 1947, Bohn Papers. In a letter to EJB, 31 December 1941, Edmond H. Hoben, assistant director of the National Association of Housing Officials, gives credit to National Association of Real Estate Brokers (NAREB) for its interest in city planning, but not its attempt to create the impression that it originated the idea; "its present championship of planning and urban rehabilitation and its definite attempt to pose as the originator of these ideas is somewhat amusing in view of the traditional disinterestedness or actual opposition toward essential planning functions by local realtors previous to the last two or three years."

17 *Report of Cuyahoga Metropolitan Housing Authority: 1949* (Bohn Papers), 7.

18 Letter EJB to Joseph Porath, 16 June 1952, Bohn Papers.

19 *Report of Cuyahoga Metropolitan Housing Authority: 1949,* 1–3; John T. Howard, *Cleveland's General Plan* (Cleveland: Regional Association of Cleveland, 1949), Publication No. 21, 6–7; "Report of the Urban Redevelopment Commission to the Members of the General Assembly of the State of Ohio," 28 December 1946, page b; letter EJB to Bleeker Marquette, executive secretary of the Cincinnati Better Housing League, 11 July 1945, Bohn Papers.

20 Letter EJB to Rev. A. J. Murphy, Diocesan Director of Catholic Charities, 27 November 1941, Bohn Papers.

21 Jenkins, "Bohn and Configuration," 112.

22 *Catholic Universe Bulletin,* 6 July 1951, Scrapbooks, Bohn Papers.

23 *Cleveland Press,* 14 December 1954, Scrapbooks, Bohn Papers.

24 Letter Frank S. Horne to Hugh R. Pomeroy, director of the National Association of Housing Officials, 15 October 1942, Bohn Papers.

25 Ernest J. Bohn, "Cleveland's Future in Housing the Poorly Housed" (Speech before the Urban League, 11 January 1958), 3; *Cleveland Press,* 10 December 1951, Bohn Papers.

26 Letter Edward Howden, executive director, Council for Civic Unity of San Francisco to EJB, 5 September 1950, Bohn Papers.

27 *Cleveland Plain Dealer,* 11 May 1952, Scrapbooks, Bohn Papers.

28 *Call and Post,* 26 April 1953, Scrapbooks, Bohn Papers.

29 Jenkins, "Bohn and Configuration," 114.

30 *Report of Cuyahoga Metropolitan Housing Authority: 1950*, 4; *Report of Cuyahoga Metropolitan Housing Authority: 1949*, 6; Ernest J. Bohn, "Housing and Democracy" (Speech at the Chicago Housing Conference, 8 June 1940), 3–5; Ernest J. Bohn, "Assisted Housing Policies" (Speech before the 17th annual convention of the Canadian Construction Association, 24 January 1935), 3–4, Bohn Papers.

31 Letter EJB to Rev. Timothy L. McDonnell; Msgr. Robert A. Navin, "Analysis of a Slum Area in Cleveland," Publication No. 3, Regional Planning Association of Cleveland; Ernest J. Bohn, "Social Conditions," (Bohn Papers), 1–7.

32 *Cleveland Plain Dealer,* 22 February 1951, 24 April 1951; *Cleveland Press*, 5 May 1951, Scrapbooks, Bohn Papers.

33 Van Tassel and Grabowski, eds., *The Encyclopedia*, xlii, 66–7, 137–9, 185–6, 578–9, 668–9.

34 *Cleveland Plain Dealer,* 4 August 1953, Scrapbooks, Bohn Papers. Teaford mistakenly places Cleveland in this pattern when he comments, after discussing Boston politics, that "elsewhere the forces of reform and revival also tried to rid municipal government of the remnants of aging political machines." He then proceeds to discuss St. Louis and Cleveland. "In Cleveland," Teaford notes, "Mayor Anthony Celebrezze likewise won election in 1953 after defeating the candidate of the county Democratic organization in the primary." See Teaford, *Rough Road*, 59.

35 Cleveland City Planning Commission, "Status of Planning in Metropolitan Cleveland, Ohio," in Bohn Papers, 11 January 1952.

36 Statement of John T. Howard, Planning Director, Cleveland City Planning Commission, in Bohn Papers, 15 April 1949.

37 *Report of the Cuyahoga Metropolitan Housing Authority: 1949, 3*; *Cleveland News*, 13 October 1951, Bohn Papers.

38 *Cleveland Press*, 4 May 1951, 16 May 1953, 18 June 1952; *Call and Post,* 1 November 1947; *Cleveland Plain Dealer*, 15 November 1947, Scrapbooks, Bohn Papers.

39 Letter EJB to Mayor Thomas A. Burke, 3 December 1951; *Cleveland Plain Dealer*, 19 December 1951, Bohn Papers.

40 *Cleveland Plain Dealer,* 24 July 1954, Scrapbook, Bohn Papers.

41 *Cleveland Plain Dealer*, 28 May 1954; Frank Baldau, Executive Director of the city's Community Relations Board, expressed a similar idea to the Jewish Community Federation, *Cleveland Plain Dealer*, 25 June 1953, Scrapbooks, Bohn Papers.

42 *Cleveland Plain Dealer,* 14 September 1954, Scrapbooks, Bohn Papers.

43 *Cleveland Development Foundation,* Bohn Papers, 4.

44 *Report of the Cuyahoga Metropolitan Housing Authority: 1956,* 4; Oscar Steiner, "Slums Are a Luxury We Cannot Afford," *The Reporter*, 14 November 1957, 28, Bohn Papers.

45 Teaford does comment that the Cleveland Development Foundation (CDF) was interested in inner-city housing but makes no remarks about how this might have involved social reform. His main concern is to note that the kind of projects started by CDF failed to gain the "public relations rewards equal to those of the Allegheny Conference," which he commends as a widely recognized and highly praised "product of cooperation between local authorities and private enterprise with the federal government playing no role." See Teaford, *Rough Road,* 47–9, 108, 111, 150.

46 *Cleveland Plain Dealer*, 24 July 1954, Scrapbooks, Bohn Papers.

47 *Report of the Cuyahoga Metropolitan Housing Authority: 1955,* Bohn Papers, 3.

48 *Report of the Cuyahoga Metropolitan Housing Authority: 1956*, Bohn Papers, 4.

49 *Report of the Cuyahoga Metropolitan Housing Authority: 1954*, Bohn Papers, 3.

50 Steiner, "Slums Are a Luxury," Bohn Papers, 27–9.

51 Teaford does portray one of the causes of the failure of the moderate income housing in Cleveland as the reluctance of the middle-class black to move into ghetto housing. See Teaford, 159.

52 Comment of Frank Baldau, executive director of the Community Relations Committee, to the *Cleveland Press*, 27 December 1951, Scrapbooks, Bohn Papers.

53 Van Tassel and Grabowski, *Cleveland Encyclopedia*, 102–3; *Cleveland Press,* 27 December 1951; Call and Post, 4 April 1953; *Cleveland Plain Dealer*, 21 May 1952; *Cleveland News,* 22 March 1957, Scrapbooks, Bohn Papers.

54 *Call and Post,* 6 September 1952, 20 December 1952; *Cleveland Press*, 27 December 1951; *Cleveland Plain Dealer*, 28 February 1952, Scrapbooks, Bohn Papers.

55 *Cleveland Plain Dealer*, 18 June 1952, Scrapbooks, Bohn Papers; *Report of the Cuyahoga Metropolitan Housing Authority*: *1952*, 8–11, Bohn Papers.

56 *Cleveland Plain Dealer,* 18 March 1952; *Cleveland Press,* 2 February 1952; *Call and Post,* 3 January 1952, 28 June 1952; *Cleveland News,* 8 November 1951, Scrapbooks, Bohn Papers.

57 *Cleveland Plain Dealer*, 24 November 1951, Scrapbooks, Bohn Papers.

58 *Report of the Cuyahoga Metropolitan Housing Authority: 1952*, Bohn Papers, 11; *Cleveland Plain Dealer*, 3 April 1952, Scrapbooks, Bohn Papers.

59 *Cleveland Press*, 18 June 1952, Scrapbooks, Bohn Papers.

60 *Cleveland News*, 30 April 1951, Scrapbooks, Bohn Papers.

61 *Report of the Cuyahoga Metropolitan Housing Authority: 1949*, Bohn Papers, 13.

62 *Call and Post*, 10 and 17 January 1953, Scrapbooks, Bohn Papers.

63 *Report of the Cuyahoga Metropolitan Housing Authority: 1952*, Bohn Papers, 11; the Private Enterprise Re-development Corporation had issued these figures. *Cleveland Press*, 2 February 1953, Scrapbooks, Bohn Papers.

64 *Cleveland Plain Dealer,* 23 June 1952 and 7 February 1953; *Cleveland News*, 25 June 1952, Scrapbooks, Bohn Papers.

65 *Cleveland Plain Dealer,* 7 February 1953, Scrapbooks, Bohn Papers.

66 *Cleveland Plain Dealer,* 10 February 1953, Scrapbooks, Bohn Papers.

67 *Cleveland News*, 25 October 1951; *Cleveland Plain Dealer*, 29 August 1952, Scrapbooks, Bohn Papers.

68 *Cleveland Press*, 22 April 1952; *Cleveland Plain Dealer*, 9 January 1953, Scrapbooks, Bohn Papers.

69 *Cleveland Press*, 18 August 1953, Scrapbooks, Bohn Papers.

70 According to a report of the City Planning Commission, those moving into private housing could afford only between $55 and $75 monthly, *Cleveland News*, 12 March 1953, Scrapbooks, Bohn Papers.

71 *Cleveland Press*, 1 July 1952; *Cleveland Plain Dealer,* 16 January 1953; *Cleveland News*, 12 March 1953, Scrapbooks, Bohn Papers.

72 *Cleveland Press*, 16 March 1953, Scrapbooks, Bohn Papers.

73 *Cleveland Press*, 13 July 1953; *Catholic Universe Bulletin*, 13 November 1953, Scrapbooks, Bohn Papers.

74 *Cleveland Plain Dealer*, 22 July 1953, Scrapbooks, Bohn Papers.

75 *Cleveland Plain Dealer,* 27 June 1952, Scrapbooks, Bohn Papers.

76 *Cleveland News*, 26 June 1953, Scrapbooks, Bohn Papers

77 *Cleveland Plain Dealer*, 25 August 1953, Scrapbooks, Bohn Papers.

78 *Cleveland Press*, 6 October 1953, Scrapbooks, Bohn Papers.

79 *Catholic Universe Bulletin*, 13 November 1953, Scrapbooks, Bohn Papers.

80 Ibid., 27 November 1953, Scrapbooks, Bohn Papers.

81 *Cleveland Press and Cleveland Plain Dealer*, 14 December 1954, Scrapbooks, Bohn Papers.

82 *Cleveland Press*, 19 June 1952, 7 January 1954, Scrapbooks, Bohn Papers.

83 *Cleveland Citizen*, 27 June 1952, look for Patton, Scrapbooks, Bohn Papers.

84 *Cleveland Press,* 14 October 1952 & 22 April 1952, Scrapbooks, Bohn Papers.

85 *Cleveland Plain Dealer*, 3 February 1953; *Call and Post*, 7 February 1953; *Cleveland News*, 10 February 1953, Scrapbooks, Bohn Papers.

86 *Report of the Cuyahoga Metropolitan Housing Authority: 1954*, 2–3; *Cleveland Plain Dealer*, 17 April 1954, Bohn Papers.

87 *Report of the Cuyahoga Metropolitan Housing Authority: 1950*, Bohn Papers, 2.

88 *Cleveland Press*, 1 January 1953, Scrapbooks, *Bohn Papers; Report of the Cuyahoga Metropolitan Housing Authority: 1951*, Bohn Papers, 24–7.

89 *Report from the Joint Staffs of the Cleveland Community Relations Board*, Cleveland NAACP, and the Urban League of Cleveland, Bohn Papers.

90 Minutes of the Urban Renewal Advisory Committee, 1 July 1964, Bohn Papers.

91 *Cleveland Press*, 7 February 1953, Scrapbooks, Bohn Papers.

92 John Bauman, *Public Housing, Race, and Renewal: Urban Planning in Philadelphia, 1920–74* (Philadelphia: Temple University Press, 1987), 118–82.

93 Arnold Hirsch, *Making the Second Ghetto: Race and Housing in Chicago, 1940–1960* (Cambridge, UK: Cambridge University Press, 1983), xii–xiii, 41, 122, 185, 203–5, 224, 234–8, 256–8.

94 Robert B. Fairbanks, *Making Better Citizens: Housing Reform and the Community Development Strategy in Cincinnati, 1890–1960* (Chicago: University of Illinois Press, 1988), 158–64; June Manning Thomas, *Redevelopment and Race: Planning a Finer City in Postwar Detroit* (Baltimore: Johns Hopkins University Press, 1997), 47–51. In a city not included in the Teaford study, Richmond,Virginia, Christopher Silver found that economic leaders and city planners conjoined to plan for redevelopment that restricted and segregated the black population. See Christopher Silver, *Twentieth Century Richmond: Planning, Politics and Race* (Knoxville: University of Tennessee Press, 1984).

Credit

The Rise and Fall and Rise of Cleveland

Barney Warf and Brian Holly

On the shores of Lake Erie at the mouth of the Cuyahoga River, Cleveland, Ohio, offers a fascinating example of the intersection of global forces and local context, of the manifold ways in which the periodic long-wave restructuring brought on by the changing global economy has played out within the unique context of northeastern Ohio. Long the quintessential blue-collar city, Cleveland in the 1970s and 1980s embodied the worst aspects of the Rustbelt: deindustrialization, population loss, rising poverty, ugly landscapes, and a notoriously poor reputation. In the 1990s, however, Cleveland has enjoyed an unanticipated renaissance and has swiftly moved from backwater to the forefront of contemporary urban change. In surfing the business cycle, Cleveland serves as a mirror of how larger forces have periodically reshaped the fabric of urban America.

This article attempts to capture the complexity of Cleveland's changing circumstances in the twentieth century. It opens with a review of the city's historical context, stressing its competitive advantage throughout the late nineteenth and early and mid-twentieth centuries. Next, it ponders its slide from jewel of the Manufacturing Belt to the "mistake on the lake" during the 1970s and 1980s, detailing the city's abandonment by capital. Third, it examines the city's recovery in the 1990s, including the emergence of post-Fordist production systems, producer services, and cultural consumption. Throughout, it links Cleveland's temporal and spatial changes to the rhythms of national and global capitalism.

Cleveland's Historical Context: An Abbreviated Synopsis

In 1776, a surveyor for the Connecticut Land Company, Moses Cleaveland, surveyed the state's western reserve; his employers were interested in land speculation in what promised to be a lucrative new market. Cleaveland stayed only three months, but his namesake (whose spelling now excluded the first "a") lives on. In the post-Civil War boom that fashioned the Manufacturing Belt along the southern shores of the Great Lakes, Cleveland emerged as the premier center of industrialism between Buffalo and Chicago. The city's ascendancy was guaranteed when it became the northern terminus of the Ohio River–Lake Erie Canal, while the Erie Canal farther east guaranteed access to powerful eastern markets.[1] With a locational advantage augmented by ready access to the resources of Appalachia, cheap water transportation on Lake Erie, and a well-developed matrix of rail lines, the city evolved from the 1860s to the 1920s into a diversified node of durable goods production.[2]

Early industries included dairying, agricultural processing and implements, and coal mining. Riding a boom in petroleum processing, Clevelander John D. Rockefeller made his city the headquarters of Standard Oil Corporation in 1870, although this industry would soon move to the richer wells of Texas and Oklahoma. The city's steel industry blossomed in the 1870s and 1880s, driven by the newly invented Bessemer open hearth furnace and rising demand propelled by rapid industrialization and a thriving national urban middle class, as part of the world's largest steel-producing district. Westinghouse was founded in Cleveland in 1886. Tire making flourished in nearby Akron during the bicycling craze of the 1880s.

By 1900, the region had become covered with a dense mesh of firms, including iron and steel foundries, electrical motors, machine tools, meatpacking, clothing, paint, and varnish. As argued by Scott, such conglomerations typically saw small, labor-intensive, vertically disintegrated firms cluster near the city center while larger, more capital-intensive, vertically integrated companies located on the urban periphery, typically along transport lines.[3] Cleveland surpassed Cincinnati as Ohio's largest city, reaching 560,000 people at the turn of the century. Detroit's emergence as the epicenter of global automobile production further accelerated Cleveland's growth, particularly given the numerous backward linkages from that industry, many of which stretched into northeastern Ohio, including the production of tires, steel, paints, and electrical equipment. In the 1920s, when Cleveland was the nation's fifth-largest city, Shaker Heights, a wealthy suburb, exhibited the highest per capita income of any city in the United States. During World War II, the demand for tanks, trucks, and artillery further strengthened the city's manufacturing base.

These capital investments were accompanied by rapid population growth. From 1870 to 1930, despite its severe lakeside climate, Cleveland saw an average decadal growth rate of 47 percent. Until World War I, much of the labor supply was generated by a steady influx of immigrant labor, particularly from Italy and Eastern Europe. By the 1880s, three quarters of the city's population was foreign-born or first-generation immigrants.[4] Immigrants soon segregated themselves into a potpourri of ethnic neighborhoods.[5] A stream of Appalachian whites and black migrants from the South from the 1940s through the 1960s fueled the city's growth anew; blacks eventually composed roughly 40 per cent of the populace. In short, Cleveland was born and matured during the classic period of Fordism, the epoch of production characterized largely by mass markets, mass production, homogeneous goods, vertically integrated firms, oligopolistic market structure, and semiskilled labor.[6]

Northeastern Ohio prospered greatly during the post-World War II boom, an era characterized by unprecedented U.S. hegemony in the world system. In the 1950s, the completion of the St. Lawrence Seaway allowed large commercial ships to reach the Great Lakes, contributing to a steady growth in Cleveland's status as an international port. The flourishing steel industry saw numerous ships carrying iron ore from northern Michigan and Minnesota. In the 1960s, the economy of metropolitan Cleveland roared in conjunction with that of the nation. Manufacturing generated high-paying jobs in a variety of industries, notably iron and steel, automobile assembly, machinery, and fabricated metals. Total manufacturing employment in the Cleveland standard metropolitan statistical area was maximized in 1967 at 306,700. Labor unions operating under national contracts (primarily AFL-CIO) protected workers' wages, jobs, and benefits.

Degenerating Into the "Mistake on the Lake"

In the 1970s, the world and national economies changed in such profound ways that the economy of this grittiest of Rustbelt cities was permanently disemboweled. As American manufacturing found itself rocked by "petro shocks" and increasingly besieged by foreign competition, employment began to drop, often precipitously. Deindustrialization, numerous plant closures, and rising unemployment led to enormous socioeconomic dislocations, including the metamorphosis of the Manufacturing Belt into the Rustbelt.[7] Many large multi-establishment firms in mature industries, increasingly mobile in a competitive world economy and hampered by the highcost, unionized labor of the Midwest, evacuated the decaying cities of the Great Lakes and northeastern United States to find greener pastures—and higher profits—in the Sunbelt or overseas.[8]

In the Cleveland metro region, this process initiated a dramatic restructuring in the late 1970s and early 1980s. Total private employment plummeted from a high of 780,000 in 1979 to 675,000 in 1993, a 13 per cent drop, although when public sector employment is included, there was little change; manufacturing jobs, the core of the regional economy, fell from 280,000 in 1979 to less than 190,000 in 1994, a drop of 40 percent. The largest losses during the period of 1979–94 were in nonelectrical machinery, which lost 19,700 jobs, fabricated metals (15,200), and transportation equipment (13,300). For example, U.S. Steel Corporation closed its Cleveland plant,

LTV Steel shut its Youngstown facilities and reduced employment drastically in nearby plants, and USX closed its plant and sold its Lorain mill to Japan's Kobe Steel. White Motors' truck assembly plant and General Motors' Coit Road factory—both located in Cleveland—closed abruptly. Westinghouse closed its lighting products factory in 1979, General Electric shut down six factories, and the Harris Corporation moved its headquarters to Florida.[9] Other producers such as Eaton, which made automobile parts, diversified into more recession-resistant sectors. In the rubber industry, tire production moved to Georgia and Tennessee, although Akron remained the headquarters of the Big Four firms in this industry such as Firestone and Goodyear. As a result, Clevelanders' real median family income, which had risen 22 per cent throughout the 1960s, slid by 11 per cent in the 1970s. To add insult to injury, in 1969 the Cuyahoga River, coated with a thick layer of oil and toxic waste, caught fire, adding ridicule to an already tarnished reputation.

Table 1. Population of Cleveland Metropolitian Region, 1940–90 (Thousands)

Year	Cleveland	Standard Metropolitian Statistical Area
1940	878	1,320
1950	915	1,533
1960	876	1,909
1970	751	2,064
1980	574	1,899
1990	503	1,880

Source: *Statistical Abstract of the United States* (Washington DC: Government Printing Office, 1993).

The dramatic downturn in jobs was accompanied by demographic losses. Between 1970 and 1980, the metro area lost 8 per cent of its population, or 165,000 people, while the city of Cleveland lost 24 percent, or 177,000 people, one of the steepest declines in U.S. urban history (Table 1). Rapid out-migration was selective; those who could leave did, with the poor, elderly, and structurally unemployed or marginally unemployable remaining behind. Housing values went into a precipitous decline, especially in the inner city, often losing one-half to two-thirds of their 1967 value, and did not recover until a decade later.[10] Abandoned houses and commercial buildings began to blight the landscape in large numbers. Blue-collar neighborhoods were hit the hardest, particularly black communities on the city's eastern side. The poverty rate, correspondingly, rose from 27 per cent in 1980 to 40 per cent in 1987. Like many U.S. cities, Cleveland became a depository for the poor, infirm, and those dependent upon public services.[11] By 1975, Cleveland stood in the nation's highest quintile among cities in terms of poverty, unemployment, poor housing, violent crime, and municipal debt.[12]

The transformation of labor and housing markets had important repercussions for the public sector. Always a low-tax state, Ohio left its communities largely to fund themselves through local property, sales, and income taxes. Declining population, incomes, and real estate values, however, reduced the earnings base of many cities, even as the demand for public services by the elderly and impoverished climbed steadily. To make matters worse, aid from the federal government tapered off in the 1970s and, in the 1980s, fell substantially, making the costs of public transit and housing even more difficult to sustain.[13] With falling tax revenues and a burgeoning service-dependent population, municipal debt began to rise rapidly.[14]

The growing crisis reached its apex under Cleveland Mayor Dennis Kucinich (1977–79), who promoted an urban populism antithetical to the corporate establishment, opposing tax abatements and subsidies for firms and only reluctantly increasing the local income tax. Simultaneously, Cleveland emerged as a laboratory for urban planning; under the leadership of Planning Director Norman Krumholz, the city's planners invented "advocacy planning," which explicitly challenged conventional planning guidelines as essentially do-nothing strategies that protected a highly uneven status quo.[15] Advocacy planning, in contrast, actively sought to plan on behalf of the poor and powerless, emphasizing social equity over efficiency by stressing, for example, public housing and public transportation.

Kucinich's populism alarmed the business community, who denounced his anticorporatism and brought the full wrath of the local "growth machine" elite to bear. In December 1978, matters came to a head: bankers, who held the city's debt, led by Cleveland Trust, demanded the sale of Municipal Light to a privately owned utility in order to roll over the city's notes; Kucinich refused, charging blackmail.[16] Cleveland became the first U.S. city to default on its bonds since the Great Depression. Kucinich was ousted in 1979 after one two-year term, and Republican George Voinivich, now governor of Ohio, was elected (1979–89). Urban politics subsequently returned to "normal," with extensive tax abatements to firms that later helped set the stage for the downtown's recovery. Kucinich's brief reign illustrates that politicians who contradict the powerful vested interests of corporate capital enjoy short careers.[17]

From Joke to Jewel

The 1980s saw a widespread restructuring of the U.S. economy, including massive technological change and a tsunami of corporate layoffs as firms downsized to meet the prerequisites of bone-crushing global competition. This transition, which was acutely painful for millions of households, also laid the grounds for a sustained recovery in productivity, wages, and, to a lesser extent, employment. U.S. manufacturing is now among the most productive in the world. As the East and West coasts suffered from office overbuilding, the collapse of financial firms, and reductions in military spending, the Midwest has witnessed renewed prosperity. In the face of intense international competition, the region has recovered from the traumatic restructuring of the 1980s to become a highly productive center.

In the 1990s, Cleveland has enjoyed an abrupt reversal in status and fortunes that few could have foreseen during the bleak previous decade.[18] Several factors contributed to this change, including a surprising reindustrialization. The absence of large military contractors isolated the region from the post-Cold War defense cutbacks. Devastated by two decades of deindustrialization, the cost of doing business in northeastern Ohio had reached parity with the rest of the nation; meanwhile, the region also offered a well-developed infrastructure and skilled blue-collar workforce. One important force has been a reinvigorated automobile industry. The demand for automobiles, fueled by cheap petroleum, has assisted northeastern Ohio's parts producers and assemblers. Throughout much of Ohio, Japanese "greenfield" transplants in the automobile industry have created numerous jobs.[19] Ford has reinvested in its Brook Park plant, and Ford and Nissan set up a new minivan plant near Lorain.

Other forms of industry are also flourishing, if with fewer workers. American Steel and Wire reopened the old U.S. Steel plant in 1986. The instruments industry has seen new producers of circuit boards (such as Techmar) and calibration equipment. British Petroleum's absorption of Sohio included a movement of its world headquarters from New York to Cleveland. In chemicals, paints, and industrial coatings, Sherwin Williams and Glidden are headquartered in Cleveland's Public Square, the city's historic and commercial center, while the Ferro Corporation, with 800 employees, is headquartered nearby.[20] LTV Steel Corporation, whose Cleveland plant is the nation's largest flat-rolled facility, has entered into a joint venture with Sumitomo Metals.[21] Farther south, in Hudson, Ohio, Little Tykes, a division of Rubbermaid, has innovated plastic molded toys (a booming market given the birth of the baby boomlet).

The globalization of the U.S. economy also played a role in Cleveland's renaissance. Ohio is the nation's seventh-largest exporter of merchandise. The Center for Regional Economic Issues estimates that the Cleveland metro area exported $3.8 billion worth of commodities in 1993, employing 72,000 of the region's labor force. The top export industries included chemicals ($969 million), industrial machinery ($616 million), electronic equipment ($493 million), instruments ($312 million), transportation equipment (that is, automobiles, $310 million), and fabricated metal products ($294 million). The region's largest trading partners include, in order, Canada, Mexico, Great Britain, Germany, Japan, Taiwan, and France.[22] Cleveland also benefited from the implementation of the U.S.-Canada Free Trade Agreement in 1989;[23] because many of the region's exports were hampered in the Canadian market by tariffs and nontariff barriers, and because they exhibit relatively high price elasticities of demand, this trade agreement may generate an increase in Ohio exports between 4.5 and 5.9 percent.

As northeastern Ohio has been catapulted into the age of post-Fordism, characterized by niche markets, vertical disintegration and increased subcontracting, flexible production systems, just-in-time inventories, and enhanced skill levels,[24] a network of high-technology firms has flourished in industries such as industrial machinery, chemicals, electronic equipment, and instruments production.[25] The NASA Lewis Research Center tests equipment for space flight and trains astronauts. The region has become a leading center for research into polymers and liquid crystals. The Edison Biotechnology Center and the Great Lakes Manufacturing Technology Center, in Cleveland, and the Edison Polymer Innovation Corporation, in Brecksville, have provided assistance as well. The growth of such companies has been aided by the Cleveland Advanced Manufacturing Program, which assists manufacturers with technical assistance, quality control, worker training, marketing, and adherence to international standards.[26]

Simultaneously, services have grown steadily in northeastern Ohio. Many of the region's hospitals, banks, and law and accounting firms arose as providers for the mammoth industrial firms in the late nineteenth century. Services have increased in their absolute and relative shares of the local labor market. In 1993, 592,000 people in the Cleveland metropolitan area worked in services, compared to 185,000 in manufacturing. Surprisingly, the region has witnessed a rapid growth in health services, which employed 99,600 people, a reflection of the area's aging population and the rising share of gross national product spent on medical care. For example, the Cleveland Clinic rivals Minnesota's Mayo Clinic as a world renowned center of specialized medical care and generates $300 million in extra-local revenues.[27] Other large services include retailing (SIC 53–59, employing a total of 85,000), wholesale trade (63,000), eating or drinking establishments (52,000), and business services (55,900).

Cleveland's services include a disproportionate number of headquarters (which perform functions such as administration and research). Largely a legacy of its industrial past, 21 headquarters of the *Fortune* 500 are located in the Cleveland metro region (Table 2), including TRW, Eaton, LTV, Reliance Electric, and Parker-Hannifin. While the Cleveland metropolitan area is nineteenth largest in the nation, it ranks fourth in headquarters, following New York, Chicago, and Houston.

Table 2. *Fortune* 500 Companies Headquartered in Cleveland, 1995

Company	Industry	*Fortune* 500 Rank
TRW	diversified, auto	68
Eaton	diversified, auto	115
LTV	basic metals	123
Sherwin-Williams	paint, coatings	163
Parker-Hannifin	industrial equipment	187
Reliance Electric	electronics	253
American Greetings	greeting cards	255
MA Hanna	rubber, plastic	268
Nacco Industries	industrial equipment	272
Lubrizol	chemicals	276
Ferro	chemicals	355
Geon	chemicals	369
Lincoln Electric	industrial equipment	396
Figgie International	industrial equipment	418
Standard Products	rubber, plastics	420
Sealy	furniture	461
RPM	chemicals	491

Source: Center for Regional Economic Issues, 1995.

Many of the region's services are exported extra-locally. Goe found that even in a traditionally manufacturing-dependent economy such as that of northeastern Ohio, producer services (financial and producer services sold primarily to firms, not households) are exported elsewhere.[28] Cleveland producer service firms derived, on average, 36.3 per cent of their gross revenues from clients in other cities, including 19.5 per cent from outside of Ohio and 3.6 per cent outside of the United States. Cleveland is the headquarters to 14 of the nation's 500 largest legal services firms.[29] Such firms reflect the growing demand for specialized expertise that producer services provide, as well as the increases in subcontracting that typify the emerging post-Fordist global, national, and regional economies.[30]

Unfortunately, services tend to pay lower salaries than manufacturing jobs: the average service worker in northeastern Ohio receives only 56 per cent of the income of the average manufacturing employee.[31] Cleveland, like much of the nation, has seen the substitution of relatively well-paying blue-collar jobs by lower-paying pink-collar and white-collar jobs. The distribution of income today in the region has grown more unequal over time.[32] Today, Cleveland's employment profile closely mirrors that of the United States as a whole: for the northeastern Ohio region, manufacturing accounts for 20.5 per cent of total employment, compared to 15.7 per cent nationally. In losing much of its regional economic uniqueness, the region has also become less sensitive to cyclical fluctuations.[33]

Cleveland's success is also attributable to the aggressive efforts of its public authorities. In 1988, the city's Planning Commission released its Civic Vision 2000, which outlined plans for a rejuvenated downtown retailing and entertainment district, including multi-use public spaces along the lakefront and river, streetscape beautification, and strengthening the Dual Hub Corridor linking Tower City Center with the businesses, institutions, and neighborhoods along eastbound Euclid Avenue.[34] Northeastern Ohio has the largest chamber of commerce in the nation, the Greater Cleveland Growth Association. A privately funded development strategy group of fifty local chief executive officers, Cleveland Tomorrow, created a Technology Leadership Council in 1974 to facilitate research and university–private sector interaction. The Cleveland Industrial Retention Initiative, a combined project of the Cleveland Advanced Manufacturing Program, the Growth Association, the City of Cleveland, and the Cleveland Neighborhood Development Corporation, works to minimize plant closings, provide regulatory relief, and clean up brownfield sites of contaminated land. At the federal level, Cleveland in 1994 was designated as one of eight national Empowerment Zones under the federal Empowerment Zone Act of 1993, which generated $87 million in Economic Development Initiative grants and $3 million in Title XX grants, as well as $1 million in incentive financing from the Ohio Department of Development.[35] Cleveland City, Cuyahoga County, the Cleveland Port Authority, and the Chamber of Commerce formed the Greater Cleveland International Trade Alliance to encourage international trade through northeastern Ohio and to provide export assistance.

In many respects, Cleveland has come to rival Baltimore as a poster child of urban redevelopment. Rouse, the real estate developer widely responsible for gentrified inner-city projects in Baltimore, Boston, and elsewhere, will lead a waterfront redevelopment project on the Lake Erie shore. The Flats, an ensemble of dining and musical entertainment places in restored nineteenth-century industrial buildings, has infused new energy into the city's night life. A collection of aging movie houses has been transformed into Playhouse Square, while Tower Center has arisen around the old Baltimore & Ohio Terminal Tower. Several new real estate projects have given the central business district a badly needed facelift (see Table 3). In 1995, Clevelanders celebrated the opening of the $300 million Gateway Center, an urban baseball park with attendant restaurants, retail, and parking facilities (although the Cleveland Browns promptly abandoned the city for Baltimore). The Cleveland Indians enjoy a new home at Jacobs Field, while the $92 million Rock-and-Roll Hall of Fame and Museum is designed to "lift Cleveland beyond the old age of steel and into the age of Steely Dan."[36] Four miles east of Public Square, the University Circle district serves as Cleveland's Mecca of high culture, including the Cleveland Philharmonic; the Natural History, Art, and Children's museums; and Case Western Reserve University. Cedar Point, in Sandusky, and Sea World, in Hudson, offer further attractions. In Akron, the newly built Inventor's Hall of Fame and, in Canton, the Football Hall of Fame hold promise for a long-sought tourist alley stretching through northeast Ohio. Contrary to the old gag about spending a year in Cleveland one weekend, the region now attempts to make itself "the pre-eminent visitors' destination between New York and Chicago."[37] Indeed, Cleveland—long a city with a notorious reputation as an uncultured, working-class city void of sophistication—has emerged as an important center of cultural consumption, with a reputation as the "Comeback City" carefully crafted by the local growth machine.

Table 3. Major Real Estate Projects in Cleveland in the 1980s and 1990s

Firm	Type of Activity
Ohio Bell	new headquarters
Eaton Corporation	new headquarters
British Petroleum	new headquarters
Galleria	shopping mall
Society Center	mixed land use center
Cleveland Union Terminal	mixed land use center, transit
Playhouse Square	revived entertainment district
North Coast Harbor	waterfront promenade
Gateway	sports complex
Rock and Roll Hall of Fame	museum
Hyatt Regency	hotel
Marriott	hotel

Source: Compiled by authors from various sources, esp. Edward Hill, "The Cleveland Economy: A Case Study of Economic Restructuring." in *Cleveland: A Metropolitan Reader*, ed. W. Keating, N. Krumholz, and D. Perry (Kent, OH: Kent State University Press, 1995).

This effort should be viewed as part of Cleveland's attempts to position itself vis-à-vis neighboring cities. As Hill notes, "Cleveland is engaged in a competitive struggle with Pittsburgh, Columbus, and Detroit to become the economic capital of the eastern end of the Great Lakes region."[38] Pittsburgh's well-known success in remaking itself from a steel-producing city to an economy centered around business and medical services has become a role model for many Rustbelt communities. One adage holds that "Cleveland seeks to be like Pittsburgh, and Detroit seeks to be like Cleveland." In the current climate of increasingly mobile, internationalized capital flows, Cleveland's attempts to create a good business climate reflect the reconstructed relations between capital and space that characterize the late twentieth century.

Despite its successes, Cleveland still struggles with the legacy of decades of economic decline. The rapid growth of the suburbs, which constitute three-quarters of the metro area's population, has intensified the exodus of middle-class whites (a phenomenon subsidized by the federal government through the interstate highway system). In addition to older communities such as Shaker Heights, a prosperous collection of communities is found in cities such as Beachwood, Mayfield Heights, and Randall Park, all of which exemplify the growth of low-density, sprawling communities on the urban fringe.[39] Within Cleveland proper, especially east of downtown, large areas consist of dilapidated warehouses and abandoned storefronts and houses. Forty per cent of Clevelanders, half of whom are black, remain below the poverty level. Despite the growth of high-end retail malls downtown and on the urban periphery, central-city housing abandonment has accelerated, and thousands remain homeless.[40] Many inner-city blacks are denied access to the labor market by a lack of skills, a crime- and drug-ridden environment, racism, and a poor educational system.[41] Half of Cleveland's high school students fail to graduate. Trapped by poverty, lack of education, inadequate transportation, and little access to burgeoning suburban housing and labor markets, Cleveland's black population suffered much of the brunt of deindustrialization and few benefits of the recent renaissance in growth. In the 1980s, reductions in federal aid to cities and welfare programs augmented the suffering of the city's poor and powerless.

Conclusion

Like many urban places, Cleveland has surfed through numerous restructurings, riding successive waves of capital investment and disinvestment over different historical epochs. Rapid growth in the late nineteenth and early twentieth centuries created an economy centered around durable goods, particularly steel and automobiles. To a steel- or autoworker living in the region during the 1920s, the notion that Cleveland's prosperity would not last indefinitely would have been inconceivable. The 1970s and 1980s, however, saw devastating deindustrialization as Cleveland proved to be vulnerable to the new global economy; correspondingly, the region suffered massive capital disinvestment, population losses, rising unemployment and poverty, and real estate abandonment.

In the 1990s, a new wave of growth has washed over the city. The revival of manufacturing reflects the conjunction of the post-Fordist production systems that have re-energized the Rustbelt and the city's retention of its centralized location at the heart of North America. The Cleveland metro area has become centered around services and is less vulnerable to the oscillations of the business cycle. Through serendipity and aggressive promotional efforts, the city has enjoyed a remarkable transformation from cultural backwater to avant-garde avatar of chic. Although the metro area is now predominantly white-collar in nature and heavily suburbanized, the problems of the ghettoized inner city have persisted.

These periodic episodes have been driven largely by Cleveland's changing competitive position within the national and, increasingly, global division of labor. Each of these bouts left an indelible imprint on the local landscape, creating a unique mixture of peoples and places that defines northeastern Ohio. In many ways, Cleveland serves as a mirror to reflect the ways in which Kondratieff waves are given expression in the urban landscape, including capital investment and disinvestment, industrialization and deindustrialization, suburbanization and ghettoization, white flight and a black underclass, the growth of services, and a dual economy. Given the instability of capitalism, in which the only constant is change, the only certainty is that the current renaissance will not last indefinitely.

Notes

1 Harry Margulis, "Cleveland: Making the Transition from a Corporate to an Advanced Industrial City," in *The Changing Heartland: A Geography of Ohio*, ed. L. Peacefull (Needham Heights, MA: Ginn Press, 1990).

2 C. Miller and R. Wheeler, "Cleveland: The Making and Remaking of an American City, 1796–1993," in *Cleveland: A Metropolitan Reader*, ed. W. Keating, N. Krumholz, and D. Perry (Kent, OH: Kent State University Press, 1995).

3 Allen Scott, "Production System Dynamics and Metropolitan Development," *Annals of the Association of American Geographers*, 72:185–200 (1982).

4 Miller and Wheeler, "Cleveland."

5 E. Miggins and M. Morgenthaler, "The Ethnic Mosaic: The Settlement of Cleveland by the New Immigrants and Migrants," in *The Birth of Modern Cleveland, 1865–1930* (Cleveland: Western Reserve Historical Society, 1988).

6 Ash Amin, ed., *Post-Fordism* (Cambridge, MA: Basil Blackwell, 1994).

7 Barry Bluestone and Bennett Harrison, *The Deindustrialization of America* (New York: Basic Books, 1982).

8 Michael Storper and Richard Walker, *The Capitalist Imperative: Territory, Technology, and Industrial Growth* (Cambridge, MA: Basil Blackwell, 1989).

9 Edward Hill "The Cleveland Economy: A Case Study of Economic Restructuring," in *Cleveland*, ed. Keating, Krumholz, and Perry.

10 Edward Hill and Thomas Bier, "Economic Restructuring: Earnings, Occupations, and Housing Values in Cleveland," *Economic Development Quarterly*, 3:123–44 (1989).

11 Ibid.

12 K Bradbury, A. Downs, and K. Small, *Urban Decline and the Future of American Cities* (Washington, DC: Brookings Institution, 1982).

13 David McKee and Richard Bennett, eds., *Structural Change in an Urban Industrial Region* (New York: Praeger, 1987).

14 Bradbury, Downs, and Small, *Urban Decline*.

15 Norman Krumholz, Janice Cogger, and John Linner, "Make No Big Plans ... Planning in Cleveland in the 1970s," in *Planning Theory in the 1980s*, ed. R. Burchell and G. Stemlieb (New Brunswick, NJ: Rutgers Center for Urban Policy Research, 1978).

16 Todd Swanstrom, "Urban Populism, Fiscal Crisis, and the New Political Economy," in *Cleveland*, ed. Keating, Krumholz, and Perry.

17 John Logan and Harvey Molotch, *Urban Fortunes: The Political Economy of Place* (Berkeley: University of California Press, 1987).

18 Dennis Keating, "Cleveland: The 'Comeback' City. The Politics of Redevelopment and Sports Stadiums Amidst Urban Decline," in *Reconstructing Urban Regime Theory: Regulating Urban Politics in an Urban Economy,* ed. Mickey Lauria (Thousand Oaks, CA: Sage, 1997).

19 Andrew Mair, Richard Florida, and Martin Kenney, "The New Geography of Automobile Production: Japanese Transplants in North America," *Economic Geography*, 64:352– 73 (1988).

20 Edward Hill, "Cleveland, Ohio: Manufacturing Matters, Services Strengthened, But Earnings Erode," in *Economic Restructuring of the American Midwest*, ed. Richard Bingham and Randall Ebberts (Boston: Kluwer, 1990).

21 Hill, "Cleveland Economy."

22 Case Western Reserve University, Weatherhead School of Management, Center for Regional Economic Issues, "REI's Profile of the Northeast Ohio Economy," 1995, World Wide Web http://weatherhead.cwru.edu/ dept/rei/neo_prof.html.

23 Barney Warf and James Randall, "The U.S.-Canada Free Trade Agreement: Impacts on U.S. States and Canadian Provinces," *International Regional Science Review*, 17:99–119 (1994).

24 Erica Schoenberger, "From Fordism to Flexible Accumulation: Technology, Competitive Strategies and International Location," *Environment and Planning D: Society and Space*, 6:245–62 (1988); Amin, *Post-Fordism*.

25 Audrey Clarke, "Spatial Linkages and Subcontracting Relationships Among HighTechnology Industries in the Northeastern Ohio Region," *Environment and Planning A*, 26:1579–1603 (1994); Audrey Clarke and Brian Holly, "The Organization of Production in High Technology Industries: An Empirical Assessment," *Professional Geographer*, 48:127–39 (1996).

26 Center for Regional Economic Issues, "REI's Profile."

27 M. Magnet, "How Business Bosses Saved a Sick City," *Fortune, 27* Mar. 1989.

28 Richard Goe, "Producer Services, Trade and the Social Division of Labour," *Regional Studies*, 24:327–42 (1990).

29 Barney Warf and Chand Wije, "The Spatial Structure of Large U.S. Law Finns," *Growth and Change, 22*:157–74 (1992).

30 Schoenberger, "From Fordism to Flexible Accumulation"; Amin, *Post-Fordism.*

31 McKee and Bennett, eds., *Structural Change*, p. 174.

32 Hill, "Cleveland, Ohio: Manufacturing Matters."

33 Ibid.

34 Cleveland City Planning Commission, *Cleveland Civic Vision 2000* (Cleveland: Cleveland City Planning Commission, 1988).

35 Center for Regional Economic Issues, "REI's Profile."

36 Iver Peterson, "The 'Mistake' Wakes Up, Roaring," *New York Times*, 10 Sept. 1995.

37 A. Schorr, ed., *Cleveland Development: A Dissenting View* (Cleveland: Case Western University, Mandel School of Applied Science, 1991).

38 Hill, "Cleveland, Ohio: Manufacturing Matters," p. 135.

39 Joel Garreau, *Edge City: Life on the New Frontier* (New York: Anchor Books, 1988).

40 Hill and Bier, "Economic Restructuring."

41 William J. Wilson, *The Truly Disadvantaged: The Inner City, the Underclass, and Public Policy* (Chicago: University of Chicago Press, 1987).

Credit

Urban Green Uses: The New Renewal

Catherine J. LaCroix

After decades in which rapid growth was the planning challenge that grabbed the headlines, we find ourselves at a time when cities across the nation—including many that were growth hot spots even a few years ago—are confronting a different reality. Instead of worrying about how to make growth better or smarter, many cities wonder whether they will see much growth at all. The mortgage crisis and associated collapse of the housing boom has left unfinished projects and excess housing capacity in cities across the nation. In this changed environment, the Rust Belt cities of the Northeast and Midwest find that they have important lessons and guidance to offer. Cities like Cleveland, Detroit, Youngstown, and others have experienced decades-long population decline that had opened a great gaps in urban land use; these cities now are leading the way in innovative reuse that has been called "Re-Imagining," "Cities in Transition," "Smart Shrinkage," or (perhaps less appealing) "Smart decline." The common thread: these cities try to build on their strength for focused targeted economic development in key areas, while adopting an array of innovative green uses for vacant and surplus land as a new way to revitalize the city and serve its residents. These green resources include urban agriculture, community green spaces, alternative energy, and green infrastructure. Perhaps we should call this the "New Renewal."

Not only is the New Renewal green, but it is a flexible process that typically features extensive community involvement. By and large, the urban green pioneer cities have identified their goals through a community-focused planning process by which they have discerned key challenges and opportunities. While each city's precise strategy is shaped by its own urban environment, community organizations, and nonprofits seem to be important contributors everywhere. One of the encouraging features of the urban green movement is the grassroots involvement of community members, who can see visible, bite-sized progress emerging from their own efforts.[1]

Although community involvement might blunt the threat of legal wrangling, it is important to recognize that green renewal raises distinct legal issues as familiar concepts and strategies take a new twist. This commentary highlights some of the leading ideas at work in the Rust Belt and their associated legal parameters. Part I describes the typical menu of urban green uses, and Part II focuses on how to implement these uses within the existing legal landscape. Part III touches on some related topics: regionalism, nature conservancies, and mitigation of climate change.

Part I. Urban Green Land Uses

The typical Rust Belt shrinking city includes a politically distinct central city surrounded by relatively more prosperous suburbs. Although the central city has experienced significant population decline, the physical footprint of the city itself remains the same size. It cannot realistically shed some land surrounding jurisdiction such as a country; it must figure out how best to use tracts of vacant land over which it has jurisdiction for which there is no likelihood of traditional redevelopment in the short or medium term.

While useful examples abound in Rust belt cities, Cleveland provides a particularly robust overview of green renewal options. A few years ago, a coalition of public and private organizations, which includes the Cleveland Planning Commission, released an important vision, Re-Imagining a More Sustainable Cleveland (Re-Imagining).[2] Re-Imagining offers a menu of strategies for addressing vacant properties in the city, based on a particular property's long-term development potential. The city seeks to attract new development and foster local engines of economic growth where possible, focusing on areas of the city where growth is most promising. At the same time, it realizes that its long-term health is threatened by vacant and abandoned properties that are not located in pathways of development and that new uses for these properties must be found.[3] Re-Imagining endorses a vision of vacant land as a resource, not a liability.

Thus, Cleveland envisions "a city with densely-built, mixed-use walkable, neighborhoods connected by greenways and complemented by urban gardens and open space amenities."[4] Consistent with this two-pronged strategy, Re-Imagining presents a decision tree for individual vacant sites. Ecologically valuable or sensitive properties might be selected for preservation through a variety of uses: alternative energy generation, stormwater management (such as through bioretention or as a constructed wetland), green space, remediation through bioremediation, phytoremediation, or mycoremediation, or urban agriculture.[5] Other properties are assessed to determine their long-term development potential. Areas with strong development potential might be designated for a holding strategy: landscaping or bioremediation. For areas with weak development potential, Re-Imagining identifies the following menu of possible treatments:

- Community garden
- Bioremediation, phytoremediation, mycoremediation
- Constructed wetland
- Deep tailgate/pavement removal
- Basic greening techniques
- Solar field
- Urban agriculture/commodity farming
- Storm water management riparian setbacks, stream daylighting[6]

Re-Imaging makes clear that its goal is to put all land in Cleveland to some form of beneficial use:

> Given the large and growing inventory of vacant properties in the City of Cleveland, it is unlikely that all of the city's surplus land will be reused for conventional real estate development in the foreseeable future. The alternative land use strategies described in this document are intended to put vacant properties to productive use in ways that complement the city's long-term development objectives.[7]

Thus the report includes urban agriculture, green space, green energy, and ecosystem restoration as beneficial land uses. It lists the following goals:

- *Productive use/public benefit.* Whether vacant properties are developed with buildings and infrastructure, preserved as open space, or put into productive use as agriculture or energy generation sites, they should provide an economic return, a community benefit, or an enhancement to natural ecosystems.
- *Ecosystem function.* Stormwater management, soil restoration, air quality, carbon sequestration, urban heat island effects, biodiversity, and wildlife habitat should be incorporated into future plans for vacant sites in the city.
- *Remediation.* Remove the risk to human health and the environment from environmental pollutants at vacant sites, either with targeted remediation projects or with long-term incremental strategies.[8]

While urban agriculture seems to gather most of the headlines, it is important to emphasize that two other green uses are equally if not more important: bioremediation of contaminated sites (where feasible) and use of green spaces to manage stormwater as an ecologically beneficial way to protect lakes and streams from polluted urban runoff.

The Re-Imagining report prompted a series of pilot projects in various areas of the city, exploring a range of green uses. Many were focused on growing food locally,[9] by both for profit-farms and nonprofit community gardens, such as the Garden Boyz program, which offers employment for inner-city youths on land leased from the city.[10] Cleveland also features many initiatives related to the Re-Imagining vision, even if they are not a direct outgrowth. A large-scale urban greenhouse, run by and employee-owned cooperative, is in the planning stages.[11] The Cleveland Botanical Garden has announced an effort to investigate the use of vacant land as green infrastructure, primarily to reduce excess volumes of stormwater flowing into Lake Erie.[12] This project will specifically evaluate the extent to which green uses of vacant land can significantly reduce the looming of meeting federal Clean Water Act mandates to combat stormwater-based pollution of waterways.

Cities such as Detroit, Dayton, Toledo, Milwaukee, and Youngstown have similarly embraced the use of vacant land as a green resource to enhance a sense of community, grow crops for residents, mitigate urban runoff, and—where possible—remediate soil containment.[13]

In some cities, the effort goes beyond using existing vacant property: Detroit and Youngstown have explored moving remaining residents out of sparsely populated areas in order to generate consolidated tracts of land available for green uses and for which some traditional city services need not be provided.[14] While it can be quite controversial,[15] this is a particularly dramatic example of innovative thinking in urban renewal.

Part III. How Do We Get There?

A. Land Banks

The first challenge for a city that seeks to make productive use of its vacant land is to gain legal control over the property. Vacant or abandoned properties come in all shapes and sizes, but many of them share two key characteristics: tax delinquency and clouded title. In many jurisdictions, the tax foreclosure process is long and complicated, and offers the opportunity for speculators to purchase tax delinquent properties at auction. Rights of redemption (the statutory right of previous owners to reacquire a property by paying past-due amounts) may further handicap property transfers.[16] Land banks offer a valuable tool for cities interested in gaining legal control over abandoned or vacant properties within their borders.

In general, a land bank is a governmental entity that takes title to tax-delinquent property, secures the property and perhaps demolishes structures on it, and identifies the best long-term use for the land. It might maintain the property for interim uses if a transfer is not possible, or it may transfer the property back to private ownership with clear title to ensure that the property can be put to productive (and tax-paying) use.[17] Land banks have been established in cities such as Atlanta, Cleveland, Flint, Louisville, and St. Louis.[18]

A city seeking to establish a land bank requires statutory authority from its state legislature, so this is an area where city planners would need to work with state legislators to provide a legal framework.[19] There are various statutory models from which to choose.[20] The statue may establish a land bank form that is available to any city or country within the state that chooses to adopt it, or it might design a form specific to a metropolitan area. The core powers of a land bank include acquiring, managing, and disposing of property. A land bank needs some form of financing, either from the budget of local government or from an independent source (such as a portion of property tax revenues). The land bank needs to consider the policies that will guide its disposition of property: It might strategically bank large bundles of properties for future uses or focus on clearing property titles and returning the properties to private ownership. And the bank needs a defined organizational structure: Will it be a department of local government, or will it be a distinct legal entity? Will it be part of a single municipal government, or will it operate on a country-wide or metropolitan area-wide basis? All of these questions and more (e.g., the liability of the land bank for nuisances or harmful conditions on properties in its inventory) should be considered when drafting legislation.[21]

The history of land banking in Cleveland suggests that an effective land bank is shaped to achieve identified policy goals, has and assured source of funding, is focused on engagement with its community, an is scaled at a metropolitan-area level to assure a diverse real estate market for land bank properties. The City of Cleveland established its land bank in the 1970s as a way to gather and hold tax delinquent parcels. The Ohio Legislation authorizing this land bank streamlined the tax foreclosure process and provided that any properties that remained unsold at the end of a mandatory public auction process would be transferred into the land bank. The land bank was then authorized to hold and manage the properties and convey them with marketable title to private parties.[22] This bank—which still exists—is a so-called "passive" land bank: It is a department of local government, funded by the city budget, and is essentially a receiving location for tax-foreclosed vacant property.[23]

In 2009, as Cleveland was ravaged by the foreclosure crisis that began in 2000, it became apparent that the existing tax foreclosure process, with its mandatory public auction, allowed properties to be transferred to speculators, who failed to maintain the properties and allowed them to deteriorate. Other properties were held by banks with no profitable sale.[24] These properties were not available to the city land bank.

Consequently, the Ohio legislature approved a new form of land bank that could operate throughout Cuyahoga County, which includes Cleveland and some of the surrounding suburbs. This new land bank is a separate corporate entity, with its own sources of funding, and had the power to acquire tax-delinquent or bank-owned properties and demolish vacant buildings.[25] The land bank need not wait for tax-delinquent property to trickle into its hands; it can acquire properties, evaluate their best use, rehabilitate or demolish on-site structures at its option, and bundle clusters of property as needed for future uses. The Cuyahoga County land bank currently has agreements with the federal Department of Housing and Urban Development and Fannie Mae to acquire properties from their inventory of foreclosed homes.[26] Because the land bank operates at the county-wide level, it has access to a diverse range of properties and a greater likelihood of selling some properties at a profit,[27] although the municipality in which the property is located has a "priority right of acquisition" if it desires the property.[28]

On a cautionary note, the scope of the county land banks liability for contaminated property in its portfolio is not entirely clear. The legislation authorizing the land bank exempts it from liability under Ohio's environmental laws, including the state program governing cleanup of brownfields.[29] This grant of immunity was intended to allow the land bank to hold foreclosed commercial or industrial properties until an appropriate use is identified, without running the risk of significant cleanup cost under state law. It is not clear whether the land bank is similarly immune from liability as an owner of property under federal law. The federal Comprehensive Environmental Response, Compensation and Liability Act (known as CERCLA or Superfund) generally is used for cleanup or relatively severely contaminated land, and imposes strict liability on owners of such property.[30] While there is an exemption from liability for state and local government entities that acquire land "involuntarily" through tax delinquency or other circumstances,[31] the separate corporate status and aggressive acquisition powers of the Cuyahoga County land bank might carry it beyond the scope of this limited protection. The lack of immunity does not make significant liability inevitable, but it introduces the possibility. As the implementation of the land bank is still in its infancy, as the land bank's portfolio so far includes mostly (if not exclusively) residential properties, the scope of potential environmental cleanup liability has not yet been determined.

The contrast between the Cleveland and the Cuyahoga County land banks illustrates two land bank forms: the passive land bank that is a city department, and the more active land bank that is a separate legal entity. The Cleveland land bank resembles a bank established at about the same time in St. Louis, the Cuyahoga County land bank more closely resembles the model used in Kentucky. The land bank legislation adopted in Georgia, prompted by concerns about vacant properties in Atlanta, focuses on "interlocal cooperation" and apparently does not build an inventory of properties.[34] A similar interlocal focus is found in the Genesee County, Michigan, land bank.[35]

The land bank, then, can be an important tool in community's strategy for managing vacant land. A city wanting to establish one, however, must have authorizing legislation at the state level.[36]

B. Downzoning and Repurposing Land

A core concept of the New Renewal is that a city can use its vacant land for productive green uses: growing food, managing stormwater, providing public green space, or providing sites for alternative energy such as wind turbines or solar panels. Considering that the land in question is likely to be zoned for residential, commercial, or industrial use, we can see that these uses might be less intensive than the current zoning allows, or might give rise to possible objection based on their effects on neighboring properties. Some green uses might be permissible without rezoning: A city may allow urban gardens on land it owns, either as parkland or in its land bank, and a for-profit urban greenhouse might be permissible on land zoned for commercial or industrial use. Sometimes, however, a green use might merit specific treatment in local zoning law. Here we should consider two questions: What are the practical advantages and disadvantages to such zoning requirements, and what legal constraints or considerations must a city keep in mind?

Cleveland offers some examples of zoning requirements specifically designed to allow urban gardens and alternative energy. First, Cleveland has several zoning provisions specifically designed to encourage urban agriculture. The city recently amended its residential zoning code to allow urban gardens and related structures, including sales of food from farm stands as a conditional use.[37] It has a distinct Urban Garden zone, where the only permitted use is an urban garden. And it has animals such as chickens, goats, and bees.[38] Second Cleveland has adopted zoning requirements governing construction of wind turbines.[39] The city takes the position that no specific zoning requirements are needed for solar panels or geothermal power.

Zoning in Cleveland: Agriculture in Residential Zones. Recent changes to Cleveland's residential zoning requirements expressly allow agricultural uses, including keeping farm animals, in residential areas. While it appears that agricultural uses are allowed on either occupied or vacant residential land, more intensive agricultural use is allowed if the land is vacant. A residential lot thus may include "sheds, greenhouses, coops, cages, beehives, hoop houses, cold farms, barns, rain barrels, composting, farm stands ... , and similar structures not exceeding fifteen (15) feet in height."[40] Farmstands selling produce, eggs, or honey are allowed with restrictions, and after public hearing.[41] Thus, these new zoning provisions allow agricultural use of residential land while it awaits revived demand for housing.

Zoning in Cleveland: The Urban Garden Zone. The Urban Garden zone in Cleveland allows only gardening, with or without on-site sale of crops.[42] No structures are allowed, except small structures associated with the permitted uses, such as greenhouses, tool sheds, shade pavilions, or "rest-room facilities with composting toilets."[43] The Cleveland Zoning Code explains that the urban Green zone—which includes both community gardens and commercial, or "market" gardens—is intended "to ensure that urban garden areas are appropriately located and protected to meet needs for local food production, community health, community education, garden-related job training, environmental enhancement, preservation of green space, and community enjoyment on sites for which urban gardens represent the highest and best use for the community."[44]

With regard to the Urban Garden zone, Cleveland has concluded that there are practical reasons to zone land specifically for urban agriculture. The city seeks to ensure that urban gardens are established as a goal in themselves, not as a holding strategy until it is time for residential building construction.[45] A formal zoning designation reserves particular land for urban gardening: the zoning cannot be changed without rezoning the property through the standard zoning legislative process, including notice to neighbors and a public hearing. Thus, the urban garden zone is a public and transparent embodiment of a city policy in favor of such uses. Possible private owners of land in urban garden zone include local nonprofit organizations that foster community gardening for civic or educational purposes as well as for-profit urban farmer.

Zoning in Cleveland: Wind Turbines. Cleveland had adopted zoning provisions allowing wind turbines in any zone as a principal or accessory use. The turbines must comply with location and design requirements and obtain several different forms of city approval. The turbine owner must provide financial assurance that it will be able to demolish the turbine when it is no longer needed or wanted.[46]

Legal Issues: Legislative Discretion. In general, any new zoning requirement for green uses will benefit from the deference extended to rational legislative judgments in the rezoning process: Cities can choose how to regulate to promote the welfare, and the "concept of the public welfare is broad and inclusive."[47] Downzoning for a green use should be well within a city's police power, as long as the city presents and adequate rational basis for the decision. Re-Imagining, for example, makes clear that Cleveland has a process for evaluating redevelopment potential and assessing the suitability of a tract for urban gardens or other green uses.

Similarly, zoning provisions that allow new uses such as wind turbines should be permissible as long as the requirements have a rational basis. By now there is extensive expertise in the wind energy industry to guide a municipality in deciding how to regulate wind turbines, and numerous cities and counties have adopted requirements that can serve as a model. Some states have also adopted regulations with respect to wind energy zoning.[48]

Legal Issues: Regulatory Taking. The Cleveland Urban Garden zone is a particularly clear example of downzoning urban land to disallow uses that traditionally are regarded as more productive. Such downzoning might be challenged as a "regulatory taking"—a restriction on use so onerous that it amounts to a deprivation of property by removing the opportunity for an economic return, in violation of the Fifth Amendment. If a city downzones occupied land, the owner would benefit from the nonconforming use doctrine and thus would be protected from unwanted immediate application of the designation.[49] A city might downzone vacant land that is either privately held or in its land bank, and at some point the current owner or new private owner might object to the restriction zoning and challenge it as a regulatory taking.

One strategy that might seem attractive to avoid a takings challenge is to downzone land in a city's land bank and then transfer it to private hands with the new zoning restriction already attached. However, in *Palazzolo v. Rhode Island,* the U.S. Supreme Court held that a taking claim "is not barred by the mere fact that title was acquired after the effective date of the … restriction."[50]

Thus the mere transfer of title is not enough to prevent the new owner from bringing a takings challenge. Nothing is simple in this area of law, and the viability of the new owner's takings challenge depends in part on whether the claim was "ripe" under prior ownership. In *Palazzolo*, the restrictions at issue were adopted before Palazzolo took title to the land, but the Court noted that a claim could not be presented (that is, it was not ripe) until the landowner had followed "reasonable and necessary steps" to explore the availability of variances or waivers allowed by law;[51] that process might not have been completed until after Palazzolo became the owner. Thus, in the green zoning context, a new owner of restricted land could challenge green zoning a use variance and does not get it. The language of *Palazzolo* is sweeping enough to suggest that the claim might survive the transfer of title even if the claim was ripe for the prior owner, although that situation was not clearly presented in the case. Specifically, the Court noted that "Future generations, too, have a right to challenge unreasonable limitations on the use and value of land."[52] Although there are recent lower court cases concluding that a ripe claim does not survive a title transfer,[53] this conclusion seems inconsistent with the holding and rationale of *Palazzolo*. And there appear to be no cases addressing the specific context of land that is rezoned when it is in public, not private, hands. Thus, the Supreme Court has told us that the transfer of title does not extinguish the opportunity for a taking claim, but many factual and legal factors affect whether and such claim might be presented.

Nonetheless, even if a challenge is possible, a city that engages in green zoning generally should prevail. With regard to urban farming, the zoning allows a use; the land is not zoned in a way that excludes any use at all. In that circumstance, the federal test for a taking is established in *Penn Central Transportation Co. v. New York City*.[54] *Penn Central* tells us to apply an "essentially *ad hoc*, factual [inquiry]" using several factors: the character of the regulation diminishes the property's value (as compared to its value if unrestricted), and the impact of the restriction on the owner's distinct investment-backed expectations.[55] The case law at the federal level suggests that downzoning for an urban garden should survive a takings challenge, if it appears that urban farming is valid economic use.[56] Several Rust Belt cities have a growing array of urban commercial gardens or urban farms, including projects for urban hoop houses or greenhouses—particularly well-suited to the cold-winter locations of the Northeast and Midwest.[57] This track record suggests that urban farming can be sufficiently remunerative to be a viable economic use.[58]

In some states there are additional statutory limits that might make a regulatory taking claim more robust or might pose a roadblock to restrictive zoning. Texas requires that compensation be paid if regulation reduces the value of land by 25 per cent or more, and Florida requires compensation for regulations that impose an "inordinate burden" on private land.[59] A recent analysis of such state-level restrictions suggests that the requirements in Florida, Oregon, and possibly Arizona are the most significant, and that comparable requirements in a few other states, including Texas, have had little impact on local zoning decisions.[60] In general, the effect of such legislation is to discourage zoning restrictions that might resist the pressures of development; the impact of such legislation in a setting of low development demand is unclear.

Although zoning for urban agriculture or renewable energy is likely to survive a regulatory takings challenge, it is difficult to see a defense to such a claim if private land is rezoned for green infrastructure such as stormwater management, green space, or wildlife habitat. If the green infrastructure designation affects all of a particular tract—leaving no room for development on any portion—a court would likely find the use is a regulatory taking.[61] This is thus a strategy best reserved for publicly owned land.

Legal Issues: Spot Zoning and Equal Protection. Another possible legal challenge to downzoning urban land would be based on spot zoning or equal protection concerns. Cities face a charge of spot zoning when a litigant thinks that one parcel has been singled out for different zoning treatment than the areas around it. Usually the issue arises when a more intensive use is allowed to the detriment of the comfort of the neighbors. But an urban garden zone in the middle of a residential area might look like a spot on a zoning map. Spot zoning is not always unlawful; a court will evaluate whether it complies with zoning laws, including the concept that zoning must take place according to a comprehensive municipal plan of some nature.[62] Thus a city would have to prepare a careful factual and policy justification for rezoning sufficient to show that the selection for the site is not arbitrary and indeed is consistent with a rational policy making process.

An equal protection challenge would involve similar considerations of perceived unfairness: This tract of land is being treated differently from its neighbors. Ordinarily, however, such challenges are rejected if a municipality can show a rational basis for its zoning decision.[63]

Legal Issues: Nuisance. A traditional nuisance lawsuit involves a plaintiff landowner who complains that the use of adjacent or nearby land unreasonably affects the owner's enjoyment of his own land: a court can enjoin the offending use and award damages. The precise elements of a nuisance action vary from state to state. Residential plaintiffs who complain of noxious nonresidential uses can gain court's sympathy.[64] A use can be vulnerable to challenge as a nuisance even if it is specifically authorized by zoning.[65]

This issue was very much present in Cleveland's consideration of zoning amendments to allow chickens, bees, and other farm animals on sites within the city.[66] The number of animals permitted in a residential area is based on the square footage of the lot. Coops, pens, or cages must be in the rear yard, and size, design, and setback standards are specified. Roosters, geese, turkeys, and predatory birds are subject to particular restrictions. Goats, pigs, sheep, and "similar farm animals" require considerably more land than do smaller animals. Restrictions for bees are designed to restrict flyways and to assure that the bees have on-site water "to prevent bees from congregating at neighboring swimming pools or other sources of water on nearby properties." Structures housing farm animals require a building permit, and anyone proposing to raise farm animals must receive a license from the Public Health Department.

Other restrictions focus more directly on the nuisance issue. "Farm animals shall be kept only in conditions that limit odors and noise and the attraction of insects and rodents so as not to cause a nuisance to occupants of nearby buildings or properties and not to cause health hazards." Finally, the zoning code specifies that "[i]t shall be unlawful for any person … to keep … any animal or bird that makes noise so as to habitually disturb the peace and quiet of any person in the vicinity of the premises."[67]

Zoning for wind turbines also raises the possibility of nuisance actions once turbines are built. The neighboring landowners might object to the effects of the turbines: shadow flicker, vibrations, navigational lighting, falling ice, or other effects. Cleveland's wind turbine ordinance addresses wind turbines in all zones, but it is particularly attentive to the effect of wind turbines in residential areas: Setbacks in residential areas are doubled; illumination is prohibited in all areas unless it "enhances the appearance" of the turbine and "will not result in nuisances"; there are aesthetic requirements for the turbines; and signs are restricted in residential areas.[68] Nothing can prevent a determined plaintiff from filing suit; the point here is that an ordinance should be designed to minimize the likelihood that the completed turbine is vulnerable to nuisance claims.

If we assume that all urban green zoning will affect land with limited development potential, the likelihood of an immediate legal challenge to new zoning categories seems fairly remote—particularly where decisions are made with strong community support and the support of a current landowner. But the threat of a legal challenge cannot be ignored, particularly because the right to bring a challenge may survive if the land is transferred into new private hands and a developer seeks to build a structure on land zoned for a green use. This is a scenario that cities must confront as it arises, with care to avoid actions that could be characterized as arbitrary.

C. Consolidating Population

Cites such as Cleveland, Detroit, and Youngstown have plenty of vacant land from which to choose, but it is not necessarily available in large single parcels. Consequently it is possible that a city might want to consolidate a vacant area for relatively large-scale urban agriculture or as a way to reduce infrastructure costs. Cleveland already has two six-acre urban farms in development, and construction of an urban greenhouse on acres of land is in the works.[69] Youngstown and Detroit have explored the possibility of moving residential population from large tracts in order to reduce the burden of providing public services to scattered residents in largely vacant areas.[70] Both goals involve a problem familiar in the context of urban redevelopment: How do we assemble a unified tract of land when ownership is fragmented? How do we handle the owners who refuse to move? But they also include potentially new elements: Can we legitimately take a consolidated block of land and announce that, henceforth, we will no longer provide some or all of the traditional municipal services to that area? Can we use our powers in service of un-building rather than re-building?

Abandoning Services and Infrastructure. The first key question, then, is whether cities legitimately may identify swaths of land that the water and sewer lines, the streetlights, and the fire trucks will no longer serve. Here, we must assume that the city does not intend to let existing infrastructure fall into neglected disrepair: this could pose a liability issue if it leads to unsafe conditions. Rather, a city might make a site-by-site determination of which infrastructure and which services to eliminate and which to maintain, depending on the intended ownership and use of the property. Urban farming, for example, requires a source of water.

In general, municipalities do not appear to have an affirmative obligation to provide all services to all locations within their boundaries, in the absence of any resident demand.[71] In the context of growing municipalities, the courts have concluded that a municipality may refuse to extend services to new areas within their boundaries when the municipality lacks adequate financial resources or infrastructure capacity. For example, in South Carolina, the state constitution and applicable statutes provide that a municipality "may" provide services, and the South Carolina Supreme Court upheld a municipality's refusal to provide services to a developer: "The Legislature has recognized that a municipality—for financial or other legitimate reasons—may be able to provide sewer services or other utilities for only part of its residents."[72] Similarly, Ohio statutes governing municipalities say that they "may" provide services,[73] not that they "shall" or "must." While each state's laws bear examination, it is likely that most of them offer the power to supply services without imposing an across-the-board duty in all instances.[74]

In the absence of any affirmative statutory obligation, a municipality may reasonably exercise its discretionary power to allocate services as appropriate: "It is well settled that [a] court will not usually interfere with the details of municipal administration."[75] A municipality must be wary of decisions that have an air of discrimination in order to avoid equal protection challenges. It must also ensure that it does not create unsafe conditions by leaving neglected infrastructure in place. And, for the long term, a municipality will need to decide whether it is cheaper to abandon or remove aging infrastructure than to replace it, and whether abandoning it today will impede efforts to reinstall it in the future when the demand for urban development revives. A city that abandons and demolishes roadways and utility lines, for example, should be careful not to abandon the easements or other property interests that might allow the improvements to be rebuilt later.

Consolidation Process. We then must consider how the municipality consolidates a tract of land that is divided into multiple parcels with diverse ownership. Consolidation typically will proceed in stages: A city would address tax-delinquent properties by means of tax foreclosure; it might track down absentee owners and attempt to purchase their property; and it might contact resident owner-occupants and explore their willingness to sell. The power of eminent domain is available as a disfavored last resort. If we assume that the affected neighborhood is virtually empty of inhabitants, the few remaining residents might be happy to leave if offered comparable property elsewhere in exchange for their homesteads. This can be a relatively low-cost option, particularly if there are sites or properties in a land bank that the municipality could offer. The remaining individuals might be holdouts, tied to their property by sentimental attachments or personal reluctance to be uprooted. Both politically and practically, a city would try to avoid litigation. But if necessary, the city would have to exercise its eminent domain powers.

Eminent Domain. Thus the second major question concerns whether the city may use its power of eminent domain to help it consolidate tracts for green uses.[76] Eminent domain is the power to take private property for a publc use upon payment of just compensation.[77] It is a power that has been used for centuries to take land for actual public ownership and use (such as to build a road or public building) or for private uses open to the public generally, such as construction of a railroad. Over time, the constitutional requirement of "public use" has been interpreted as a more lenient standard of "public purpose."

Eminent domain ran into a political buzz saw in recent years, as objections arose to a particular use of the power: the taking of one person's private property in order to consolidate a tract and transfer that land to a private developer for redevelopment. This is the *Kelo v. New London*[78] scenario: The municipality promotes that project as a way of boosting tax revenue and generating jobs; local residents protest that they are being moved against their will. The taking is challenged on the ground that it is not for a public use or a public purpose; it is for the private economic advantage of the developer.

Public Purpose. Thus we must consider whether the use of eminent domain to clear an area of land for green uses serves a valid public purpose within the meaning of the law. In this setting the new use may or may not be privately owned. At first, the city might own the land and lease it to private parties for urban farming or a field of solar panels or wind turbines. Alternatively, the city might retain it for a use such as publicly owned green space for stormwater management, which might reduce the cost of constructing expensive improvements to handle urban runoff and provide an ecological benefit to nearby waterways. Ultimately, a municipality might prefer to sell the land and get it back on the city's tax rolls. Some consolidation might be intended specifically to allow a large-scale privately owned urban farm or greenhouse. The long-term economic benefit of all of these projects is to enhance green infrastructure and thus reenergize the city by making it a more sustainable and pleasant place to live, but some if this long-term effect might be relatively difficult to quantify.

Most of the green uses envisioned in this commentary are designed to benefit the public generally, and they do not offer a high level of profit to any particular private developer. Thus they fall within the range of public purpose that can justify eminent domain. Some green uses involve public ownership of property for the public's benefit; if a city can provide a rational justification for its decision, the use of condemnation should be well within a municipality's classic eminent domain power. The only use that even closely approximates the *Kelo* setting would be a project that takes private property to allow privately owned large-scale urban agriculture or alternative energy resources. And of course, in *Kelo* the Supreme Court upheld even the taking of private property for transfer to a private developer, as long as it was justified by a rational economic development plan that offered a public benefit.

In *Kelo,* The U.S. Supreme Court emphasized that the concept of public purpose is broad and flexible. The Court cited in particular the decision of *Berman v. Parker,*[79] which upheld the government's decision to take the plaintiff's non-blighted property as part of an overall redevelopment plan targeting a broad area of Washington, D.C. In *Berman,* the Court famously noted that "[t]he concept of the public welfare is broad and inclusive. ... It is within the power of the legislature to determine that the community should be beautiful as well as healthy, spacious as well as clean, well-balanced as well as carefully patrolled."[80] The *Kelo* Court emphasized the deference owed to a city's determination of whether a particular exercise of eminent domain power serves public purpose:

> Viewed as a whole, our jurisprudence has recognized that the needs of society have varied between different parts of the Nation, just as they have evolved over time in response to changed circumstances.[81]

This broad view of the public interest is more than adequate to justify a rational municipal decision to use its eminent domain power to assemble a tract of land for green uses.

The greatest threat to a city's flexibility is likely to be state law because the *Kelo* case was followed by a wave of state legislation restricting the power of eminent domain, in an effort to combat the abuse of the power in pursuit of economic redevelopment.[82] Thus, cities seeking to undertake "green takings" must pay careful attention to applicable state restrictions, including restrictive definitions of permissible purposes for eminent domain in situations of "blight."[83]

Just Compensation. If the power of eminent domain may be exercised (that is, if it serves a valid public purpose), the property owner must receive just compensation. Compensation is based on the fair market value of the property at its best use, based on a valuation of the property by a licensed real estate appraiser.[84] It is hard to determine the actual fair market value of a property in a virtually defunct neighborhood. As an illustration, a sample property in the Cuyahoga County land bank is listed for sale at $8,430—a price at which it remains unsold—but the "auditor's fair market value" is $58,200.[85] Certainly the land bank price seems too low, but given actual market conditions the listed "fair market value" seems unrealistically high. Of course, this property is already in the land bank and perhaps is not a good reflection of the value of a non-foreclosed property. In the case of an owner-occupier, one could argue that the city should be willing to offer a higher figure to reflect the resident owner's willingness to stay and be part of the city as contrasted to the many other neighbors who have moved away.[86] This argument is less compelling if the property is held by an absentee landlord or real estate speculator; in that instance, fair market value arguably should be based on actual market conditions.

Cities interested in consolidating tracts of vacant land, including moving residential residents, are in the early stages of this process. In general, they do not favor using eminent domain; it seems coercive and is thus politically unpalatable, and the legal process can be cumbersome. The issue will likely evolve over the next few years.

Part III. Some Related Issues

A. Regional Cooperation

One of the fundamental tenets of the smart growth movement is that we are all in this together: A region thrives best when all of its political jurisdictions cooperate.[87] Many of the cities with the greatest "luxury of vacant land"[88] are the centerpieces of a metropolitan area. Cleveland and Detroit, for example, are fringed with relatively prosperous and indeed some very elegant suburbs, all if which feel the chilly draft of the increasingly vacant central city. Yet the urban green movement does not so far seem to play a role in any metropolitan area's regional vision.

Perhaps this lack of a regional buy-in arises because urban green activity is inherently place-based: it is an effort to revitalize the central city, by making it a more forward-looking and sustainable environment. One problem of shrinking cities, for example, is that they tend to be unattractive to young professionals and others seeking a vibrant urban scene. The local food movement in Cleveland provides an example of a mobilized and energized community including many younger adults, all of whom are devoted to making Cleveland a better place. But the point remains: Urban green activity makes the central city a better place for those who live there and is not obviously a source of prosperity for the wider metropolitan area.

And yet a sinking central city can depress an entire metropolitan area: to the extent that regional cooperation can assist the urban-greening process, perhaps there should be greater efforts to develop the regional possibilities of the green movement. Food cooperatives, organized market garden distribution systems, regional efforts to encourage alternative energy sources—all of these might involve both the central city and its suburbs in productive regional cooperation that would enhance an overall metropolitan feeling of community. Perhaps the lack of a glittering and remunerative element is an advantage: It is unlikely to offer the kind of single shiny prize that sometimes—regrettably—induces competition among neighboring communities for a development opportunity.

B. Land Conservancies

Organizations like the Nature Conservancy and the Trust for Public Land seek to protect land and habitat from the pressures of development. Traditionally, they have focused their energy on ecologically significant tracts in rural or undeveloped areas by purchasing conservation easements from landowners or by taking title to the property itself.[89] These deep-pocket organizations have not focused on urban landscapes, but they might be able to play a role. In cities like Detroit and Cleveland, there are many acres of vacant land that could be used as parkland or wildlife habitat or—where relevant—restored to their natural condition as wetlands. The Nature Conservancy's Plant a Billion Tree initiative is part of its efforts to combat climate change by capturing carbon resources in trees,[90] and a tree captures carbon no matter where it is located. A satellite view of any urban area will reveal acres of blacktop. The urban green movement presents an opportunity to revitalize this desolate scene.

If we assume that urban redevelopment will occur at some point in the future, we have an opportunity now to set aside a core of green space for the future public's benefit. It might be possible to persuade private nonprofits like the Nature Conservancy to view urban free island preservation as part of their mission and thereby put their considerable financial resources to work for the nation's cash-strapped ailing cities.

C. Climate Change

Urban green uses fit nearly within the climate action programs of many cities. By now many observers have written about the ways in which local governments, including local land use decision makers, can help mitigate the impact of climate change.[91] The New Renewal, with its emphasis on more compact development in key areas of the city and green uses in areas that would otherwise be vacant, is fully compatible with this effort.

When the local climate action movement began, the *U.S. Mayors' Climate Action Handbook*[92] offered advice to local governments that highlighted the climate action value of the New Renewal. It urged cities to protect areas of green space and to develop sources of renewable energy, such as wind, geothermal, and solar energy—all of which are part of the urban green agenda for vacant land. The *Handbook* suggested that the cost of maintaining water systems and waste management—and water use (including inevitable water losses from aging leaking water pipes) can reduced by decommissioning unnecessary infrastructure. It suggested focusing on dense, mixed use neighborhoods that save green space (thus facilitating carbon capture through tree growth)—and cities such as Cleveland are focusing on compact urban environments for parts of the city where traditional development is possible. Finally, agriculture and other green uses can function as carbon sinks, as well as offering a source of local food.[93]

This link already has been made in Cleveland, where the Office of Sustainability coordinates all of the city's sustainability initiatives, including green uses of vacant land.[94] Thus an effort to promote green uses fits with a climate change and climate adaptation agenda as well.

Conclusion

From the Sun Belt to the Rust Belt, all areas of the United States are now confronted with short-term or perhaps longer term vacancies at their urban cores. The vacancy veterans of the Rust Belt are developing new ways to take advantage of shrinking populations, and the movement to develop a palette of urban green uses provides a new way forward in urban renewal. One key element of this effort is the focus on finding productive uses of the land, such as urban agriculture and alternative energy. Green space also offers a sustainable way to protect local waterways and the Great Lakes, by allowing constructed wetlands, bioswales, rain gardens, and other stormwater management resources, all of which potentially can reduce the cost of stormwater control by more conventional means. Ideally, the concept of a "green" use can thus gain two meanings in a cash-poor and struggling municipality.

Notes

1 Marc Lefkowitz, *Cleveland's Comeback: Reimagining the City from the Ground Up,* Next Americanan City, *available at* http://americancity.org/magazine/article/clevelands-comeback (for a discussion of community involvement in Cleveland).

2 *Cleveland Land Lab, Re-Imagining a More Sustainable Cleveland: Citywide Strategies for Reuse of Vacant Land* (2008), *available at* http://reimaginingcleveland.org/about/links-and-resources (hereinafter Re-Imagining). Re-Imagining was prepared by a coalition including the Cleveland City Planning Commission, the Cleveland Land Lab at the Cleveland Urban Design Collaborative of Kent State University, and a nonprofit organization, Neighborhood Progress, Inc., with financial support from the Surdna Foundation. A follow-up report was recently issued to offer specific suggestions for vacant land strategies, Kent State University's Cleveland Urban Design Collaborative and Neighborhood Progress, Inc., *The Ideas to Action Resource Book 2011* (*available at the same site*, http://reimaginingcleveland.org/about/links-and-resources; hereinafter, *Ideas to Action*).

3 *See* http://planning.city.cleveland.oh.us/cwp/contents.html for the current Cleveland City Plan.

4 Presentation of Robert N. Brown, Cleveland City Planning Commission, at the 2010 Reclaiming Vacant Properties conference in Cleveland, October 13–15, 2010. *See* http://www.communityprogress.net/2010-reclaiming-vacant-properties-conference-pages-82.php.

5 Re-Imagining, at 9 (figure 7). Each of the remediation techniques is a way to use natural processes to clean up mildly contaminated sites. Bioremediation uses microbes in soil and groundwater; phytoremediation and mycoremediation work in the same way, using plants and fungi. *Id.* at 24.

6 *Id.* at 9 Figure 7.

7 *Id.* at 5.

8 *Id.*

9 Much energy behind the Re-Imagining initiative comes from the local food movement. *See, e.g.*, Marc Lefkowitz, *Filling in the Local Food Gap*, GreenCityBlueLake (Aug. 11, 2010), http://www.gcbl.org/blog/marc-lefkowitz/filling-local-food-gap. Updates on the Re-Imagining projects are available at http://reimaginingcleveland.org.

10 Lefkowitz, *supra* note 1.

11 http://www.evergreencoop.com/GreenCity/greencity.html.

12 Marc Lefkowitz, *Cleveland Botanical Garden Will Plant $167K into Regional Green Infrastructure,* GreenCityBlueLake (Jan. 25, 2011), at http://www.gcbl.org/blog/marc-lefkowitz/cleveland-botanical-garden-will-plant-167k-regional-green-infrastructure.

13 Many strategies were on display at the 2010 Reclaiming Vacant Properties conference held in Cleveland from October 13 to 15, 2010. *See* http://www.communityprogress.net/2010-reclaiming-vacant-properties-conference-pages-82.php. For a description of urban agriculture zones in the small group of cities that have taken this step, see Mukherji & Morales, *Zoning for Urban Agriculture, Zoningng Practice* (March 2010).

14 *See, generally* The City of Youngstown 2010 Citywide Plan (2005), *available at* http://www.cityofyoungstownoh.com/about_youngstown/youngstown_2010/plan/plan.aspx. *See also* Christine McDonald and Mike Wilkinson, *City Begins Crafting Plan to Downsize,* Detroit News, Feb. 20, 2010, at A1 (discussing Mayor Bing's consideration of downsizing). In Detroit, there is also a grassroots pattern of suburbanization, as remaining home owners acquire adjacent lots for home and garden expansion. Tobias Amborst, et al., *Improve Your Lot!* in Cities Growingng Smaller 47 (2008). *See also* David Streitfeld, *An Effort to Save Flint, Mich., by Shrinking It,* N.Y. Times, April 21, 2009, http://www.nytimes.com/2009/04/22/business/22flint.html?ref=davidstreitfeld (discussing comparable efforts in Flint, Michigan).

15 Suzette Hackney, *Bing Staff Backs Off Talk About Downsizing Detroit,* Detroit Free Press, Apr. 29, 2010, at A8, *available at* http://www.freep.com/article/20100429/NEWS05/4290435/Bing-staff-backs-off-talk-about-downsizing-Detroit.

16 Thomas J. Fitzpatrick IV, *Understanding Ohio's Land Bank Legislation*, Federal Reserve Bank of Cleveland Policy Discussion Papapers (January 2009), *available at* http://www.clevelandfed.org/Research/PolicyDis/pdp25.pdf. *See also* Frank S. Alexander, *Revitalizing Community Assets: Louisiana Land Reform in the Storms' Aftermath,* 53 Loy. L. Rev. 727, 752–755 (2007).

17 Samsa, *Reclaiming Abandoned Properties: Using Public Nuisance Suits and Land Banks to Pursue Economic Redevelopment*, 56 Clev. St. L. Rev. 189, 213–214 (2008).

18 Alexander, *supra* note 16, at 755.

19 *See* Zoning & Planning Deskbook § 16:5 (2d ed.) (citing need for statutory authorization).

20 An excellent history of land banks and discussion of the forms of land banks and considerations in establishing one can be found in Frank S. Alexander, *Land Bank Strategies for Renewing Urban Land,* 14 Journal of Affordable Housing 140 (2005). Current strategies for land banking were presented at the Reclaiming Vacant Properties Conference in Cleveland in 2010. *See* http://www.communityprogress.net/2010-reclaiming-vacant-properties-conference-pages-82.php.

21 One land bank, in Genesee County, was initially established without express statutory authorization, using other mechanisms existing under Michigan law, but the state subsequently adopted additional land bank legislation. Alexander, *supra* note 20, at 150.

22 *Id.* at 147–148.

23 *See Fitzpatrick, supra* note 16, at 2–3; Oh. Rev. Code §§ 5722.01(F) & 5722.02(A) (land bank may acquire "nonproductive land"). The land bank program is housed in the Department of Community Development, Real Estate Division. There is a separate bank of industrial and commercial properties in the Department of Economic Development.

24 The ravages of the foreclosure crisis are detailed in Alex Kotlowitz, *All Boarded Up*, N.Y. Times, Mar. 8, 2009, at MM28. For an excellent history of the impact of questionable mortgage lending practices and their resulting waves of foreclosures, see Kermit J. Lind, *The Perfect Storm: An Eyewitness Report from Ground Zero in Cleveland's Neighborhoods*, 17 J. Affordable Housing & Community Dev. L. 237 (2008).

25 Ohio Rev. Code §§ 321.261 & 321.341 (funding), 1724.01, 1724.02, 1724.04 & 1724.10. *See generally*, http://www.cuyahogalandbank.org/about.php.

26 *See* http://www.cuyahogalandbank.org.

27 For an excellent comparison of the Cleveland City land bank with the Cuyahoga County land bank, *see* Fitzpatrick, *supra* note 16.

28 Ohio Rev. Code § 5722.02(D).

29 Ohio Rev. Code § 5722.22.

30 42 U.S.C. § 9607(a).

31 42 U.S.C. §§ 9601(20)(D), 9601(35)(A)(ii).

32 See Alexander, *supra* note 20, at 147.

33 *Id.* at 148–149.

34 *Id.* at 149.

35 *Id.* at 149–150.

36 One issue that has not been fully explored is the extent to which an aggressive land bank strategy might run afoul of the Fifth Amendment. It is possible that an owner who loses his land to tax foreclosure could argue that the land bank's land-acquisition process fails to satisfy due process or amounts to a taking of private property for public use without just compensation being paid. This possibility must be kept in mind when structuring land bank legislation.

37 Cleveland, Ohio, Codified Ordinances chapter 337.02, 337.23, 337.25 (effective November 3, 2010, Ordinance 814–10).

38 Cleveland, Ohio, Codifed Ordinances chapter 347.02. For a detailed look at legal requirements governing backyard chickens, *see* Patricia Salkin, *Feeding the Locavores, One Chicken at a Time, Zoning and Planning Law Report* (March 2011), *available at* http://papers.ssrn.com/sol3/papers.cfm?abstract_id=1774023.

39 Cleveland, Ohio, Codified Ordinances chapter 354A.

40 Cleveland, Ohio, Codified Ordinances chapter 337.25.

41 *Id.*

42 Cleveland, Ohio Codified Ordinances chapter 336.03, 336.04(b) & (c).

43 *Id.* 336.04.

44 Cleveland, Ohio, Codified Ordinances 336.01.

45 Re-Imagining, at 26–29.

46 Cleveland, Ohio, Codified Ordinances chapter 354A.

47 Berman v. Parker, 348 U.S. 26, 33 (1954).

48 For example, the Ohio Power Siting Board has adopted rules for siting wind farms. *See* http://www.opsb.ohio.gov/opsb.

49 Julian Conrad Juergensmeyer & Thomas E. Roberts, Land Use Planning and Development Regulation Law at § 4.31, page 118 (2d ed. 2007) ("zoning ordinances almost universally permit nonconforming uses to continue").

50 Palazzolo v. Rhode Island, 533 U.S. 606, 630 (2001).

51 *Id.* at 620–621. The Court did not identify the precise point at which the plaintiff's claim ripened. *See Id.* at 619–621.

52 *Id.* at 627.

53 The Federal Circuit recently rejected a claim of regulatory taking when the restriction at issue was imposed (and it concluded, presented a ripe claim) before the plaintiff took title to the land (CRV Enterprises, Inc. v. United States, 626 F.3d 1241 (Fed. Cir. 2010)). Similarly, the Ninth Circuit concluded that a facial challenge to a restriction—that is, one that does not depend on seeking a variance or other type of administrative permission before presenting the claim—ripens when the restrictions are imposed and cannot be raised by a subsequent purchaser. Guggenheim v. Goleta, 2010 U.S. App. LEXIS 25981 at *19 (9th Cir. 2010). In that case, the dissent observed that this holding is inconsistent with Palazzolo. Id. at *44–*45. The majority noted that a subsequent owner could bring an "as applied" challenge to the restrictions at some point in the future. *Id.* at *20.

54 438 U.S. 104 (1978).

55 *Id.* at 124.

56 *See* Catherine LaCroix, *Urban Agriculture and Other Green Uses: Remaking the Shrinking City,* 42 The Urban Lawyer 225, 250–273 (2010).

57 For an example of a local market for local foods, see Debbi Snook, *Case Western Reserve University Dining Hall Serves Comfort Food Locally Sourced and Made from Scratch*, Cleveland Plain Dealer, Feb. 15, 2011, available at http://www.cleveland.com/taste/index.ssf/2011/02/case_western_reserve_universit.html. *See also, An urban greenhouse is planned in Cleveland,* http://www.evergreencoop.com/GreenCity/greencity.html. There are many examples of the vitality of the urban farming and community garden community in Cleveland. *See, e.g.,* Local Food Cleveland, http://www.localfoodcleveland.org and the site of one urban farmer, http://thegardenlifeandtimesofjustinhusher.blogspot.com/. The Re-Imagining project is working on other innovative ideas, such as using the foundations of demolished houses to support greenhouses or food storage. Ideas to Action at 30 ("Bio-Cellar") (2011). Hantz Farms in Detroit is one example of a proposed urban farm, http://www.hantzfarmsdetroit.com.

58 The Ninth Circuit's decision in Guggenheim v. Goleta suggests an additional defense: the existence of restrictive zoning when a person acquires property shows that the owner has suffered no loss; "the price they paid for the property. doubtless reflected the burden of the restriction they would have to suffer," 2010 U.S. App. LEXIS 25981 at *23. The Guggenheim dissent asserts that this "impermissibly picks out only one of the three factors the Court has told us to consider ... under ... Penn Central ... ." *Id.* at *33 (referring to Penn Central Transp. Co. v. New York City, 438 U.S. 104 (1978). In the majority's defense, the court might have concluded that the lack of "investment backed expectations"—the term used in Penn Central—was so significant as to make further analysis unnecessary, although the opinion does not say so.

59 Tex. Gov't Code Ann. § 2007.002(5)(B) (compensation required if government regulation reduces property value by 25 per cent or more); Fla. Stat. Ann. § 70.001 (regulations that impose an "inordinate burden" are a taking). *See also* La. Rev. Stat. Ann. § 3:3610; Miss. Code Ann. § 49–33–9.

60 John D. Echeverria and Thekla Hansen-Young, *The Track Record on Takings Legislation: Lessons from Democracy's Laboratories,* 28 Stan. Envtl. L.J. 439 (2009). "The Florida and Oregon property rights laws have made it essentially impossible for government to regulate land uses unless it is willing to pay regulated owners. Because government officials have proven unable or unwilling to make such payments, the takings laws have effectively neutered the law-making process in relation to land use." *Id.* at 446.

61 Lucas v. S.C. Coastal Council, 505 U.S. 1003 (1992). For a reference to the vexing question of how to address a restriction affecting only part of a parcel, *see* Palazzolo, 533 U.S. at 631.

62 *See* Juergensmeyer & Roberts, *supra* note 49, at §5.10, p. 148.

63 An equal protection argument might gain greater weight if a plaintiff can allege and show a racial motivation in selecting a particular parcel of land, thereby triggering strict scrutiny of the classification. Juergensmeyer & Roberts, *supra* note 49 at § 10.14.A, p. 466.

64 Daniel Mandelker, Land Use Law at §4.01 & 4.05 (5th Ed. 2003). The Restatement of Torts defines private nuisance as "a non-trespassory invasion of another's interest in the private use and enjoyment of land." American Law Institute, Restatement of Torts (Second) § 821D (1978). In order to be actionable, the invasion must be either "intentional and unreasonable; or unintentional and otherwise actionable under the rules governing liability for negligent, reckless or ultrahazardous conduct." *Id.* at § 822.

65 *Id.* at § 4.10.

66 All of the discussion that follows refers to Cleveland, Ohio Codified Ordinances Chapter 347.02.

67 *Id.*

68 Cleveland, Ohio, Codified Ordinances 354A.04(b)(2), 354A.05(a), (c) & (d).

69 *See* Marc Lefkowitz, *Cleveland Adds Another Six-Acre Urban Incubator Farm*, GreenCityBlueLake (October 27, 2010), http://www.gcbl.org/blog/marc-lefkowitz/cleveland-adds-another-six-acre-urban-incubator-farm, and http://www.evergreencoop.com/GreenCity/greencity.html.

70 Youngstown's city plan notes that "Not all infrastructure can be maintained and not all neighborhoods can be returned to their past sustainability." The City of Youngstown, *supra* note 14, at 37. The current plan reallocates uses: Some abandoned areas of housing and unnecessary commercial zones are redesignated "industrial green"—a new category of "nonpolluting environmentally friendly"

industrial use. *Id.* at 49–51. *See also Id.* at 14; Suzette Hackney, *Bing, Strategy, Plan for Detroit is in the Works,* Detroit Free Press, May 12, 2010, *available at* http://www.freep.com/article/20100512/NEWS06/5120305; Streitfeld, *supra* note 14 at A12 (discussing comparable efforts in Flint, Michigan).

71 A municipality might have such an obligation if a resident seeks services and there is no practical reason why service would not be available. *See, e.g.,* Clark v. Bd. of Water and Sewer Comm'rs, 234 N.E.2d 893 (Mass. 1968).

72 Sunset Cay, LLC v. City of Folly Beach, 357 S.C. 414, 426, 393 S.E.2d 462 (S.C. 2004).

73 *E.g.,* Ohio Rev. Code § 715.06 (light, power, and heat), § 715.08 (water supply), §717.01 (general powers).

74 The situation appears to be somewhat different in the case of annexation and deannexation. An annexing city might have a duty to provide services to the area it annexes. *E.g.,* City of Rockport v. City of Malvern, 356 Ark. 393 155 S.W.3d 9 (Ark. 2004); N.C. Gen. Stat. § 160A-47, and areas that do not receive services may petition for deannexation. *E.g.,* Hickory Lane Land and Dev. Co. v. Vill. of Novi, 372 Mich. 219; 125 N.W.2d 487 (Mich. 1964). In general, deannexation seems to be an option only for tracts of land at the municipal borders, which can then seek to be part of an adjoining municipality or perhaps remain under county jurisdiction. *See, e.g.,* 65 I.L.C.S. §§ 5/7–3–1 5/7–3–6 (disconnection from municipality only if area to be disconnected is at the municipal boundary) (Illinois).

75 Perazzo v. Lindsay, 290 N.Y.S. 2d 971, 972 (N.Y. App. Div. 1968), aff'd, 244 N.E. 2d 471 (N.Y. 1968).

76 The debate over eminent domain for economic development has prompted interesting ideas concerning alternatives to condemnation. *See, e.g.,* Michael Heller & Rick Hills, Land Assembly Districts, 121 Harv. L. Rev. 1465 (2008). These are beyond the scope of this commentary.

77 U.S. Const. Amendment V.

78 *Kelo* v. City of New London, 545 U.S. 469 (2005).

79 348 U.S. 26 (1954).

80 *Id.* at 33.

81 *Kelo,* 545 U.S. at 482.

82 *See* John J. Costonis, *New Orleans, Katrina, and Kelo: American Cities in the Post-Kelo Era*, 83 Tul. L. Rev. 395, 412–420 (2008). For a web link tracking some post-Kelo legislation, see http://www.ncsl.org/IssuesResearch/EnvironmentandNaturalResources/EminentDomainmainpage/tabid/13252/Default.aspx.

83 *E.g.,* Pa. Cons. Stat. Ann. §§ 204(a), 205 (barring eminent domain for economic development but authorizing for blight removal); Ohio Rev. Code Ann. §717.01 (including language barring taking for economic development without a demonstration of blight); Norwood v. Horney, 853 N.E. 2d 1115 (Ohio 2006) (economic benefit alone does not satisfy public use requirement).

84 Harris K. Weiner, *Eminent Domain and Economic Development: Rhode Island General Assembly Addresses Kelo v. City of New London*, 57 R.I. Bar Jnl. 13, 16 (2008). Rhode Island adopted legislation requiring that just compensation be set at 150 per cent of fair market value for an economic development taking. *Id.* at 44.

85 http://www.cuyahogalandbank.org/properties.php (3804 Archwood Ave.).

86 *See* Beckman, *The Wholesale Decommissioning of Vacant Urban Neighborhoods: Smart Decline, Public-Purpose Takings, and the Legality of Shrinking Cities*, 58 Clev. St. L. Rev. 387, 455–457 (2010).

87 *See, e.g.,* Stuart Meck, Ed., Growing Smart Legislative Guidebook (2002 Edition) (Amer. Planning Ass'n).

88 This phrase is used by Terry Schwarz, a leading proponent of the Re-Imagining approach, http://www.cudc.kent.edu/a-WhoWeAre/whoweare3.html.

89 The Nature Conservancy's website is found at http://www.nature.org. A comparable organization serving Northeast Ohio is the Western Reserve Land Conservancy, http://www.wrlandconservancy.org. The Trust for Public Land is found at http://www.tpl.org.

90 http://www.plantabillion.org.

91 John Nolon has contributed to the dialogue in these pages. *See* John R. Nolon, *Climate Change and Sustainable Development: the Quest for Green Communities,* 61 Planning & Envtl. L. (October 2009), and John R. Nolon & Patricia E. Salkin, *Integrating Sustainable Development Planning and Climate Change Management: A Challenge to Planners and Land Use Attorneys,* Planning & Envtl. L. (March 2011). *See also* Catherine LaCroix, *SEPAs, Climate Change, and Corporate Responsibility: The Contribution of Local Government,* 58 Case Western Reserve L. Rev. 1289 (2008).

92 ICLEI—Local Governments for Sustainabnabnability et al., eds. U.S. Mayors' Climate Action Agreement: Climate Action Handbandbandbandbook, *available at* http://www.iclei.org/documents/USA/documents/CCP/Climate_Action_Handbook-0906.pdf.

93 *See, e.g.,* Carmen Gonzales, *Climate Change, Food Security, and Agrobiodiversity: Toward a Just, Resilient, and Sustainable Food System* (2011), *available at* http://papers.ssrn.com/sol3/papers.cfm?abstract_id=1756914.

94 *See* http://portal.cleveland-oh.gov/CityofCleveland/Home/Government/CityAgencies/PublicUtilities/Sustainability?_piref34_138416_34_138357_138357.

Credit

LaCroix, Catherine J. "Urban Green Uses: The New Renewal." *Planning & Environmental Law* 63.5 (Apr. 2011): 3–13. Print. *Planning & Environmental Law* is published by American Planning Association.

Notes

Notes

Notes

Notes

Notes

Unit 4

Cultures and Identities

In the opening article of this unit, "Race, Wealth, and Intergenerational Poverty" by Darrick Hamilton and William Darity Jr., the authors establish one of the overarching themes of Unit 4: that a person's relationship to power more often than not correlates with his or her access to privilege. And while what is privileged by a society shifts across decades, certain disparities persist: specifically, power dynamics between races, genders, sexual identities, and socioeconomic strata. The United States of the 21st century, a solid 50 years after the seismic convulsions of the 1960s Civil Rights Movement and second wave feminism, is still grappling with these disparities in arguably more subtle and psychologically complex ways. For example, Sheryl Sandberg, the first female COO of Facebook, in a selection from her book *Lean In*, demands that women be more assertive in a system where women continue to contend with a lack of societal and institutional support for their most ambitious professional goals. And in his article, "When Race Disappears", David Theo Goldberg charts the distressing ways in which Trayvon Martin's murder has illuminated archaic, yet deeply held inequities in our culture regarding "unacceptable" and "suspicious" behaviors in young black men.

This chapter aims to illustrate the difficult play between those who believe that the privileges they have are self-evident rights and those who challenge the very systems and policies that limit access to privilege in the first place. In a particularly modern spin, the article "Standing Up for the Rights of New Fathers" recounts one man's pursuit of a more generous and equitable paternity leave policy for working fathers. That more men wish to have comparable time off to be with their newborns also indicates a larger societal shift in the redefinition of family roles and responsibilities; in other words, our various pursuits of privilege intersect. And in order to understand our own, nuanced relationships to privilege, we must consider the varying perspectives that others have about whether privilege is achieved or withheld, about whether privilege is a national inheritance grounded in our Bill of Rights, or a crooked race to an elusive top.

Race, Wealth, and Intergenerational Poverty

There will never be a post-racial America if the wealth gap persists.

Darrick Hamilton and William Darity Jr.

Despite an enormous and persistent black-white wealth gap, the ascendant American narrative is one that proclaims our society has transcended the racial divide. But wealth is a paramount indicator of social well-being. Wealthier families are better positioned to afford elite education, access capital to start a business, finance expensive medical procedures, reside in higher-amenity neighborhoods, exert political influence through campaign contributions, purchase better legal representation, leave a bequest, and withstand financial hardship resulting from an emergency.

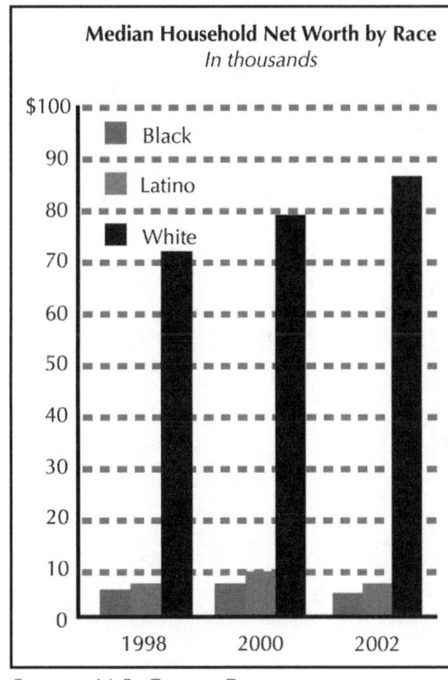

Source: U.S. Census Bureau

The wealth gap is the most acute indicator of racial inequality. Based on data from the 2002 Survey of Income and Program Participation, white median household net worth is about $90,000; in contrast it is only about $8,000 for the median Latino household and a mere $6,000 for the median black household. The median Latino or black household would have to save nearly 100 per cent of its income for at least three consecutive years to close the gap. Furthermore, 85 per cent of black and Latino households have a net worth below the median white household. Regardless of age, household structure, education, occupation, or income, black households typically have less than a quarter of the wealth of otherwise comparable white households.

Since the election of Barack Obama, a growing belief has emerged that race is no longer a defining feature of one's life chances. But the extraordinary overlap between wealth and race puts a lie to the notion that America is now in a post-racial era. The smallest racial wealth gap exists for families in the third quartile of the income distribution where the typical black family has only 38 per cent of the wealth of the typical white family. In the bottom income quartile—the group containing the working poor—a black family has a startlingly low 2 per cent of the wealth of the typical white family.

Those who recognize the racial wealth gap but still embrace the idea of a post-racial America have crafted two explanations for this disparity. The first is that, in search of immediate gratification, blacks are less frugal when it comes to savings. Indeed, in an April lecture at Morehouse College, Federal Reserve Chair Ben Bernanke attributed the racial wealth gap to a lack of "financial literacy" on the part of blacks, particularly with respect to savings behavior.

Such an explanation, however, is not the case. Economists ranging from Milton Friedman to Marjorie Galenson to the recently deceased founder of the Caucus of Black Economists, Marcus Alexis, found that, after accounting for household income, blacks historically have had a slightly higher savings rate than whites. In 2004, economists Maury Gittleman and Edward Wolff also found that blacks save at a moderately higher rate than do whites, again after adjusting for household income. This indicates even greater black frugality because many higher-income blacks offer more support to lower-income relatives than do whites, further reducing their resources to save.

The second explanation given to support the post-racial narrative is that inferior management of assets owned by blacks has resulted in lower portfolio returns. However, recent research finds no significant racial differences in asset appreciation rates for families with positive net worth.

Recessions disproportionately affect black and Latino families. During the 1999–2001 recession, median household wealth fell by 27 per cent for both Latinos and blacks, while it grew by 2 per cent for whites. The current recession likely will worsen the racial wealth gap. Although whites are more likely than blacks to own their home, the share of black wealth in the form of housing is nearly twice as large as the white share. And with blacks far more likely than whites to have been steered toward sub-prime loans in discriminatory credit markets, the foreclosure crisis is bound to have a more deleterious effect on black wealth than on white wealth.

Two Americans: Back Bay (top) is a wealthy, white neighborhood in Boston, and North Philadelphia (bottom) is predominantly back and Latina. The "asset" disparity will likely worsen with the current recession. (Source: Istock/Fotolia/Eiomobotron/Creative Commons.)

For example, a recent report on mortgage lending and race by the Institute on Race and Poverty at the University of Minnesota found that black Twin City residents earning over $150,000, in comparison to whites earning below $40,000, were twice as likely to be denied a home loan. Those fortunate (or unfortunate) enough to get a loan were more than three times as likely to have a sub-prime loan.

Economic studies also demonstrate that inheritances, bequests, and intra-family transfers account for more of the racial wealth gap than any other demographic and socioeconomic factor, including education, income, and household structure. These intra-familial transfers, the primary source of wealth for most Americans with positive net worth, are transfers of blatant non-merit resources. Why do blacks have vastly fewer resources to leave to the next generation?

Apart from the national failure to endow ex-slaves with the promised 40 acres and a mule after the Civil War, blacks were deprived systematically of property, especially land, accumulated between 1880 and 1910 by government complicity and fraud as well as seizures by white terrorists. During the first three decades of the 20th century, white rioters destroyed prosperous black communities from Wilmington, North Carolina, to Tulsa, Oklahoma. Restrictive covenants, redlining, and general housing and lending discrimination also inhibited blacks from accumulating wealth.

Given the importance of intergenerational transfers of wealth and past and present barriers preventing black wealth accumulation, private action and market forces alone cannot close an unjust racial wealth gap—public-sector intervention is necessary.

Indeed, the public sector already subsidizes asset acquisition. A 2004 report by the Corporation for Enterprise Development estimates that, even before the current financial crisis, the federal government allocated $335 billion of its 2003 budget in the form of tax subsidies and savings to promote asset development such as mortgage deductions. This excluded any corporate subsidies and tax savings and was more than 15 times the amount spent on education.

At issue is not the amount but the recipients. Those earning over $1 million a year received about one-third of the entire allocation, while the bottom 60 per cent of earners received only 5 percent. Individuals in the bottom 20 per cent typically received a measly $4.24 benefit. A more progressive distribution could be transformative for low-income Americans.

The surge in the post-racial perspective has moved us away from race-specific policies. However, wealth, given the racial disparity of its distribution, can be an effective non-race-based instrument to eliminate racial inequality. We could shift from an income-based to a wealth-based test for transfer programs. Policy eligibility based on net worth below the national median would qualify a large proportion of black households. Electronic financial records and publicly available home appraisals now make it easier to estimate net worth, and to avoid savings crowd-out, the program could be structured similarly to the Earned Income Tax Credit program, which uses a phase-out schedule to avoid work disincentives.

These changes in eligibility should be coupled with policies to promote asset building. For example, the American Dream Demonstration program uses individual development accounts to create match incentives for low-income savers. Another initiative, the Saving for Education, Entrepreneurship, and Downpayment, established children's development accounts (sometimes called "baby bonds") to create endowed trusts for children at birth. In the United Kingdom, since 2005, every newborn receives a trust ranging from 250 pounds to 500 pounds depending on familial resources.

In 2004, the American Saving for Personal Investment, Retirement, and Education (ASPIRE) Act was introduced in Congress to establish children's development accounts in the U.S. While the nation's first black president eschews race-specific policies, perhaps a strongly amended ASPIRE bill designed to progressively distribute funds based on familial net worth can be the policy that enables him to "bind … [black America's] grievances … to the larger aspirations of all Americans."

We envision a "baby bond" plan of much greater magnitude—progressively rising to $50,000 or $60,000 for children in families in the lowest wealth quartile and accessible once the child turns 18 years of age. We also would determine eligibility for such a program based upon the net-worth position, rather than the income, of the child's family (all children whose family fell below the national median for wealth would receive baby bonds).

We should strive not for a race-neutral America but a race-fair America. For that to occur, the transmission of racial economic advantage or disadvantage across generations would have to cease. Public provision of a substantial trust fund for newborns from wealth-poor families would also go a long way toward achieving the ideal.

Credit

What Happened to Post-Racial America?

Ward Connerly

Few government policies have had the reach, immortality, and consequences of affirmative action. A policy that could be justified at its start, affirmative action has now become yesterday's solution to yesterday's problem. Yet it endures as if nothing has happened in the past 50 years.

There is an interracial man—although self-identified "African-American"— occupying the White House, blacks are on our courts, including the highest court in the land, blacks are mayors of major cities and heads of American corporations.

Notwithstanding all this, President Barack Obama, who was elected largely because Americans thought he would lead the nation to a Promised Land of post-racialism, recently signed Executive Order 13583 "to promote Diversity and Inclusion in the Federal Workforce." The irony is that few institutions in America are more "diverse" and "inclusive" than the federal government, where the workforce is 17% black while blacks are roughly 13% of the U.S population.

In addition to the president's executive order, the Dodd-Frank financial-reform law included Section 342, promoted by Rep. Maxine Waters (D., Calif.), which should be called the "White Male Exclusion Act." It establishes in all federal financial regulatory agencies an "Office of Minority and Women Inclusion" with responsibility for "diversity in management, employment and business activities."

It is doubtful that anyone can name a government agency that does not include an affirmative-action office or "diversity" department in its structure. The infrastructure of the diversity network is vast.

More than anything else, the pursuit of diversity overshadows and subordinates excellence and competence and often makes us content with mediocrity. The late economist Milton Friedman once told me that "Freedom to compete fairly for university admissions, jobs, and contracts is central to all that America professes to be."

In a recent column on these pages, Stanford's Shelby Steele observed that "the values that made us exceptional have been smeared with derision. ... Talk of 'merit' or 'a competition of excellence' in the admissions office of any Ivy League university today and then stand by for the howls of academic laughter." As a former regent of the University of California, I can confirm that these howls, and worse, are not confined to the Ivy League.

When former Supreme Court Justice Sandra Day O'Connor ruled in the 2003 Grutter v. Bollinger decision that the use of race preferences was constitutional while in the pursuit of diversity, she offered the hope that such preferences would no longer be necessary by 2028. Eight years later, the federal government is moving further away from Justice O'Connor's goal, not closer.

The longer we allow preferences to endure in the guise of diversity, the more damage will be done to the nation. If the President is serious about America rededicating itself to our ideals—which are liberty, economic opportunity for all, individual merit, and the principle of equality—then he should begin with rescinding his executive order on affirmative action, calling on Congress to repeal Section 342 of Dodd-Frank, and paring back the burdensome and redundant diversity network that exists within the federal government.

Finally, he should urge Americans to embrace the color-blind vision of John F. Kennedy, who said that "race has no place in American life or law," and of Martin Luther King Jr., who dreamed of the day when the color of his children's skin would be subordinate to the content of their character.

Credit

Connerly, Ward. "What Happened to Post-Racial America?" *Wall Street Journal* 4 October 2011: A–19. Print. The *Wall Street Journal* is published by News Corporation's Dow Jones & Co. Reproduced with permission of Dow Jones & Company via Copyright Clearance Center.

When Race Disappears

David Theo Goldberg

Trayvon Martin was a seventeen-year-old African-American boy visiting his father's fiancée who lived in a mostly white housing development in Florida. He was shot to death by a neighbourhood watch vigilante, George Zimmerman, while returning to his father's house after purchasing sweets and a soft drink early one evening at a neighbourhood store. (For a detailed account of events surrounding the Martin killing, see Barry et al., 2012.)

In a sense, Trayvon Martin was (at least potentially) every black teenage boy in America. Just about every young black American male has been stopped under a cloud of suspicion by police, neighbourhood watchmen or, in more extreme cases, by self-appointed vigilantes. George Zimmerman gravitated in the no-man's land between the latter two modes of identification. In 2011 alone, the New York City Police Department, under an orchestrated policy of racial profiling, stopped over 643,000 people on the city's streets. Eighty-seven per cent of those stopped were black or Latino, far outstripping their proportional representation in the urban population, which amounts to a combined third of the city's make-up. Nine per cent of the accosted were white (while making up 65 per cent of the city's population). Only 12 per cent of those stopped were arrested or issued summonses as a result of these stoppages. Clearly, a very large number of black and brown people are being stopped and harassed, on the pretext, as Zimmerman put it, that they are "up to no good," that is, for no reason other than that they are not white.

Paul Haggis's film *Crash* (2004) tugged at the knotted impacts of these intrusions on black lives in the context of Los Angeles. Seek and the police shall find. Highway patrolmen on the main east–west highway that runs past St. Louis regularly pull over black drivers on "suspicion" of drug running and often confiscate their property—cars, cash—even when no wrongdoing has been established (Balko, 2012). If almost three times as many whites were stopped as their population proportion and treated with similar suspicion, you can be sure that their percentage of the criminalized would spiral upwards also.

The case of Trayvon Martin has filled the airwaves and blogosphere across the United States. The widespread community protests both in Florida—an initial gathering of 30,000 people in the town of Sanford, where he was killed—and around the country have prompted vigorous debate across local and national radio and television as well as on the internet. All this has elicited calls by politicians for thorough investigation of the events that led to his killing. In addition, it has renewed calls to reconsider laws that have encouraged police profiling of men of colour and their all too quick stereotyping-induced targeting by whites claiming self-defence. Even President Obama and the Republican presidential candidates have seen fit to weigh in.

In a relatively rare reference to race, President Obama poignantly pointed out that if he had a son, he would look like Trayvon Martin. What he failed to add is that his nominal son would also likely have been suspended from school at one time or another for fairly trivial behavioural infractions. Both Newt Gingrich and Rick Santorum, Republican presidential candidates at the time, chided Obama for invoking race, explicitly stressing that justice should be colour-blind. So in the face of staggering statistics about young black men being subjected to police harassment, racial profiling, and, to an unsettling degree, to white vigilante violence, some of the highest scales of political representation seem committed to placing racial reference outside the frame of reference for justice.

Trayvon Martin's killing, then, set off another one of those intermittent nationwide conversations about the racially inspired violence and threats faced especially by pretty much all young black men in America. (For a biting critique of the Martin case in the context of the war on America's youth, see Giroux, 2012.) In the wake of the Martin case, reports of racial profiling in police enforcement have proliferated. It has also raised, yet again if less obviously, concerns about blackness in the white imagination, and whiteness in the black imagination, as bell hooks insightfully responded some years ago.

In the white imagination blackness has prevailingly conjured the threat of criminality and violence, of laziness and the lack of self-reliance, as state beneficiaries and, in the body of the president now, as socialist, as the "racial hand-out" president. For whites, in short, blacks are slackers, no-gooders, takers. The question has been less pressed among whites, at least, about what their whiteness might signify for blacks. "Whites" as idea and as lived condition, as hooks suggested more than a decade ago, continues to represent a set of complex concerns for blacks, and for those taken not to be white more generally: the terror of harassment and police suspicion, of being stopped frequently even for minding one's own business or simply walking home, of being socially abandoned, evicted, and—in global political terms—more or less randomly bombed, of seeming to be out of place even in one's place. Whiteness, in short, signals to those supposedly not qualifying as white as a form of terrorism by the self-proclaimed guardians against it (hooks, 1992: 338–42).

A recent *Newsweek/Daily Beast* national poll in the wake of the Martin killing reveals stark divisions—and, by implication, dramatically different experiences—in America's racial experience. A solid majority of whites (65 per cent) think there is either racial equality or close to racial equality between whites and blacks in the U.S. Only 16 per cent of blacks claim to have achieved racial equality, and 47 per cent showed scepticism that they would achieve racial equality in their lifetimes. Seventy per cent of whites think blacks face no more challenges than whites do in securing affordable housing or landing a job. Among blacks, only 35 per cent agree about housing, and 25 per cent about securing work. And while close to all agree that racial profiling occurs, far fewer whites (less than 25 per cent) than blacks (63 per cent) think it happens regularly. And roughly 85 per cent of whites think the police and courts treat blacks and whites equally, while over 50 per cent of blacks think they are never treated equally in the criminal justice system. Two contrasting worlds, with very different life experiences, then (Schoen, 2012).

The Trayvon Martin case is far from an isolated incident regarding racial consideration in America. It needs to be read against a landscape of racially charged sociality. A recent poll in the state of Mississippi indicated that 21 per cent of residents believe that racial intermarriage should be illegal, and another 29 per cent are not sure whether it should be. A whopping 46 per cent of Republican voters in that state think it should be illegal, while another 11 per cent are unsure (Frayer, 2011). So in 2012 fully half the total population of Mississippi, recently identified as the most religious in the U.S., consider there to be something at the very least questionable about racial mixing. This, in a state that has recently created "The Mississippi Freedom Trail" to bolster tourism. The "Freedom Trail" marks approximately 30 key landmarks in Mississippi that figured prominently in the 1950s and 1960s civil rights struggles. These include the Greyhound Bus where civil rights activists were brutally beaten by bigots as Mississippi police made sure no one would intervene during the Freedom Rides of 1963. Other tour sights include the driveway of Medgar Evers' home where he was shot to death by Klansmen in front of his family, and the firebombed tomb of NAACP leader, Vernon Dahmer. Haley Barbour, then Mississippi governor, one time Republican presidential candidate, head of the Republican National Committee and keen supporter of the white and by all accounts racially exclusionary Citizens Councils, committed $20 million to establishing the trail at a time when employment, education, living standards, and criminalization of black Mississippians in the state continue to rank as or among the worst in the U.S. (Trillin, 2011). Civil rights may be good enough for historic tourism while it is clearly in remission for contemporary civic expectation and experience.

In 2011, in Mississippi also, a white teenager, Daryl Dedmon, and four of his friends, all well known for their racial bigotry and bullying violence, one evening went seeking black men to pick on. They found James Craig Anderson, a 49-year-old Nissan car mechanic, walking to his car in a mall parking lot. They beat him repeatedly and then ran him over and killed him with Dedmon's truck in a chilling display of utter disregard for human life. Dedmon and his friends had a history of harassing black youth at school, were known to refer to black people in openly and only derogatory terms, and had been reported repeatedly to the school principal and local police for their terrorizing actions. Yet police in the case denied they had previously ignored the group's violence towards African-Americans even though they had done little to address the concerns.

These pernicious and violent sensibilities around socialities of the racial are hardly restricted to Mississippi. In El Cajon, a suburban town of San Diego close to the Mexican border, an Iraqi woman was bludgeoned to death in her home in March 2012, the assailant leaving a note by the bleeding body that read "Terrorist go home." A similar note had been posted on the family's front door a couple of months earlier. El Cajon is home to the largest Iraqi population in the United States, though still a significant minority relative to the local largely white, middle-class, and English-speaking population of the town. In November 2011, in White Plains, a town outside New York City, the heart device of a 68-year-old former marine and correctional officer, Kenneth Chamberlain, Sr., accidentally set off a medical alert. The alert sent ten police officers to his housing project apartment at 5 a.m. From behind the closed front door; Chamberlain indicated it was a false alarm. The police insisted he open the door, he demurred, they broke down the door, found him in only a pair of briefs, allegedly hurled a racial epithet at him before tasering him and shooting him to death for apparently resisting their intrusion. It appears that a 68-year-old black man suffering a heart condition is potentially Trayvon Martin too.

In Louisiana, a woman followed Republican presidential candidate Rick Santorum into a shooting gallery where, of all places, he was holding a campaign event. As Santorum was taking aim at the shooting target, the woman shouted out, "Pretend it is Obama." To his credit Santorum later decried the outburst, and the woman was detained for questioning by the Secret Service (Edwards-Levy, 2012). A bumper sticker store in Scottsdale, Arizona, has published for sale a series of stickers that read "2012 Don't Re-Nig," some scripted over the Confederate flag, others alongside a crossed out decal of the Obama campaign.

A national website called "Niggermania" is dedicated in its own terms "to spreading the truth and presenting facts about n------s." The landing page reads: "We also have many pages of n----r jokes and racist humour. Please join our forum where the word n----r is not only allowed but encouraged. All races and religions are welcome to join but n-----s and n----r sympathizers are not allowed." The website's loudly proclaimed name perhaps best represents the broader social sentiment, if mostly less loudly at play in the examples I have been citing here. The site provides just some among thousands of degrading online images, pernicious jokes and crude representations of the Obamas. While all presidents have been subject in public forums to opposition derision, none prior has remotely had to endure this level of completely demeaning and racially prompted disrespect for the man, his family, and the office.

This culture of derogation is underpinned by a proliferating public ecology of racial disrespect on the part of political representatives at pretty much all levels of representation. Earlier this year a federal judge in Montana forwarded an email to friends that characterized African-Americans as dogs and implied President Obama's mother had sexual intercourse with animals. The judge, Richard Cebull, made clear in the accompanying note that the email expressed sentiments he himself harboured about African-Americans and the president. Republican Congressman Doug Lamborn of Colorado called President Obama "tar baby." The Speaker of the Kansas State House, Mike O'Neal, forwarded an email referring to Michelle Obama as "YoMama" while "praying for the President's death." During his nationally televized State of the Union address a couple of years ago, South Carolina congressman Joe Wilson interrupted President Obama's speech in an unprecedented outburst, calling the president "a liar." A libertarian politician, Jules Manson, supporting Ron Paul's presidential campaign, called on Facebook to "assassinate the fucken n----r and his monkey children." Ron Paul had no comment in response. The head of the Texas College Republicans at the University of Texas tweeted that "My President is black, he snorts a lot of crack." A Republican newsletter in California in 2008 represented then-candidate Obama among fried chicken, watermelons, and food stamps. And current Republican presidential candidate Newt Gingrich has called Obama the "food stamp president."

The examples are pretty much endless. What sort of representation, before courts of justice and from elected officials, can black Americans expect to receive from those harbouring such views?

Social commentators tend to see not a trend or a pattern so much as "instances," which are then mostly waved aside on two grounds. First, they may be thought to individualize racist expression, for the most part to the persona of the current president. America seemed to be coming to terms with its racist legacy, largely by ignoring it, until a counter-stereotypical black man was "imposed" upon the country. This not only trivializes racial conditionality by reducing it to anomalous racial expression, it also initiates the trend of racial reversal, turning the object of racial aggression into the perpetrating subject. An editorial in the conservative *Washington Times* newspaper late in 2011 characterized the Obama re-election campaign as "stupid, evil, crazy, racist" (Golub 2011). There is an irony at work here. Racist characterization tends to objectify, to denude subjecthood into objectification. Here, however, in characteristic post-racial reversibility the objectified black man is made subject so as to relegate him—and by extension his "kind"—to the racist perpetrator.

But, second, these instances of racist expression tend to be trivialized by restricting them to jokes, innuendo, individualized expression. This draws attention away from the structural arrangements constituting socialities of the skin, from those that fix in place social subjects into positions of privilege and disprivilege, power and powerlessness. Black Americans continue to suffer unemployment at twice the rate of Americans at large. Today, black family wealth is one-twentieth of white family wealth (for Latinos, the ratio is one-eighteenth), up from one-twelfth three decades ago. Until March 2012, the Federal Bureau of Investigation training manual urged trainees never to stare at or shake hands with Asians, and to beware of Arabs, who have "Jekyll and Hyde personalities" increasing their likelihood of demontrating "outbursts and loss of control" (Schmidt and Savage, 2012). A Hollywood screen writer wouldn't be believed if writing this nonsense into a screenplay. Noted African-American national journalist, Juan Williams (author of the award-winning *Eyes on the Prize*, 1988), and Fox News commentator, sparked a heated debated when he claimed that he gets nervous when boarding a plane with "visibly Islamic" passengers. The coterminous public political attacks on stereotyped women and gay folk, in this sense, should not be read as unrelated. As Frantz Fanon and Jean-Paul Sartre both pointed out, when public attacks on one or another class of social pariahs proliferate, all others should pay attention for the attackers are threatening all those taken to be strangers, holding estranged social views, pariahs, outsiders, second-class citizens.

This, then, is America in the age of Obama. What to make of it? It is a state of being and social arrangement in which pernicious racial characterization proliferates, stereotypes readily circulate, and debilitating structures of racial differentiation are deepened. Trayvon Martin's killing evidences that young black men are more likely to have their lives violently foreshortened than are whites, no matter whether or not there is any explicit racist intentionality on the part of the killer. A black teenager wearing a hoodie instantaneously becomes a hoodlum, a gangbanger, while the abiding whiteness of swimmers, surfers, tennis players, and snowboarders who keep warm by keeping their heads covered in hoods are simply looking after their health as they make a fashion statement.

We are nowhere near the promise of a raceless America, or of a post-racial one. Indeed, the claim to post-raciality or racelessness itself is misleading, a sort of malapropism, serving rather to express states of raciality in the name of their erasure or evaporation. So, today's America is one in which blacks can be dismissed, beaten up, degraded, pulled over by police, and incarcerated in record numbers while the language for characterizing such expression as racially implicated has been denuded, trivialized, rubbed out, or denied.

The emptiness those denials effect—the neutralizing of the traditional racial charge—is filled now with racial reversal. Any attempt to characterize and criticize such expression as racist itself is reversed, and itself quickly becomes charged as racist. Family and friends supporting Zimmerman, Martin's admitted killer, are now claiming as much. Joe Oliver, an African-American friend of Zimmerman's, declared in a television interview that "if we weren't sitting here today talking about George shooting Trayvon, we'd be talking about Trayvon shooting George" (Christopher, 2012). Fearful self-defence by a man ten years the teenager's senior, shorter but weighing a good deal more, justifies black death. Conservative pundits have posted to websites reports of Martin's behavioural trouble at school (actually quite minor in the scheme of things), his tattoos (irrelevant), and stereotypical gangster style images of gold-capped teeth (completely fabricated). No questions to be further posed. The accusation of racism is misguided, except when you are doing it to me. Zimmerman's father blurted out in public, "I never foresaw so much hate coming from the President, the Black Congressional Caucus, the NAACP ..." (Zimmerman, 2012), as though the trouble in which his son finds himself is a product of black power. Fifty years on, here is the civil rights struggle redux, only now stripped even of the conceptual terms to name the object of concern.

The above range of examples suggests that buried in the vernacular of racial terms in denial are signals, if not judgements, about social fitness and unfitness, of reliability and unreliability, predictability and uncertainty, objects of fear but also, counterfactually, of fascination. Implicit judgements about social belonging and contribution are made in terms of racial insinuation, if not attribution, at once denied: the president wasn't born here, rendering him ineligible; he is a socialist, rendering him un-American; he is a power-grabbing wannabe monarch in a republic supposedly constitutionally committed to individual liberty and limited government; he is un-American, making his policies unrepresentative; he is Muslim, meaning not Christian, and so not acting on properly American values or with American wellbeing at heart.

There is a racial politics of corrigibility regarding Trayvon Martin, too. He was "inappropriately" dressed; on the street on a rainy night when he should have been home (it was all of 7 p.m.); stalking a neighbourhood not his, even if his father's fiancée lived there. In racially predictable, predictably racial fashion, Trayvon was "characteristically" suspended from school for bad behaviour (traces of marijuana were found in his backpack). He is made culpable for his own demise in "viciously" attacking Zimmerman, breaking his nose and banging his head repeatedly on the kerb side, even though a police video of Zimmerman's initial arrest after the killing shows him to have at most minor signs of the supposed beating, and he declined medical assistance when police showed up at the scene of the killing. No signs of a skirmish producing commensurable injuries with those being claimed were found on the teenager's dead body. Voice analysis of the screams for help during the scuffle leading up to the shooting, and heard on tape as a neighbourhood woman called 911 from her adjacent home, strongly suggest the screams emanated from Martin, not Zimmerman. The scuffle—there is disagreement about who of the two started it—seems to have taken place between a well-grassed lawn, where Martin's dead body was found by the police, and a cement sidewalk, which Zimmerman claimed had produced his own injuries.

Just as President Obama supposedly is unfit to be American, doesn't fit in America, is not fit to lead the country, so Trayvon Martin fails to belong in a gated community in suburban middle-class residential Florida. Explicit racial reference is deemed improperly invoked to reference social arrangements: when used by critical analysts of racial inequality it is dismissed by conservative critics as being just as out of place as Trayvon Martin was that night in Florida, or as a black couple is found "inappropriately" to "occupy" the White House (where black folk historically have been more likely to be fed in the kitchen than in the state dining room) (Lusane, 2011). It doesn't help that Sanford, Florida was founded in the late nineteenth century by Henry Sanford, a white segregationist and supremacist who served as emissary and lobbyist for King Leopold II of Belgium in the latter's drive to get recognition from the United States Congress for Leopold's colonization of the Congo. Sanford himself supported the exportation of America's black population to Africa (Daly, 2012). The deathly implications of history's racial symbolics are haunting here.

When surrogate terms for race are invoked disparagingly to dismiss the efforts or actions of people of colour, those condemned for using the terms deny intention or significance, decry over-sensitivity or "double standards." And when they might be forced, usually because they represent a public office, to issue an apology, invariably the apology is for the discomfort anyone may have suffered, never an embracing of one's own responsibility for having done something wrong, thus shifting responsibility from offender to target. Racial denial, in both senses, is the quid pro quo of racial accusation. And the denial of the denial is reflexive reaction when charges of insensitivity are levelled at the proponents of deniability. At the heart of racial signification is the prolific intensification of its fungibility.

It would help to speak here of *disappointment*. Barack Obama and his electioneering team ran for president in 2007–08 on the mantra of "Hope" and the mandate of "Change (we can believe in)." There has been profound disappointment especially but not only among some of President Obama's most vocal election supporters who at his election were deeply hopeful of a more progressive agenda and a genuine transcendence of American racial making. The hope conjured was capacious in its multiple meanings: hope for a more civil political engagement in the wake of civility's trampling; hope for a more equitable body politic regarding access to possibility and the promise of a decent life; hope in decency and the reinstitution of respect for and among global others; and hope in a post-raciality represented in the appealing figure of a mixed-race man for whom race seemed so little a burden.

Hopefulness—perhaps even if only half-justified giddiness at his election—has given way to dolefulness. The disappointment has been directed at the centrism of Obama's political achievement through his first term, all the challenges notwithstanding, and at the extension of some of the Bush policies, especially concerning claims to state security (Goldberg, 2012). There is an attendant disappointment, veering between sometime melancholia and indignation, both in the intensification of raciality rather than its *Aufhebung*, its overcoming, and in Obama's sometime evasions and silences regarding raciality in the face of calls for critical leadership. Black Americans decry his general silence, while applauding his occasional embrace of his own racial experience, as in his Trayvon comments. Whites decry any reference he makes to race, comfortable in his general silence about American raciality. The above-cited *Newsweek* poll revealed blacks to be overwhelmingly appreciative of the president's intervention, while whites found it "unhelpful" (Frayer, 2011).

Here, racial calculation becomes complexly configured as representative of power and its modes of negotiated domination. There tends to be a failure of recognition in this regard that raciality has never been uniformly singular. Raciality is characteristically multiplicitous, shifting in social arrangement and significance, never reducible to one thing or sensibility or social arrangement. And its multiplicity makes it precisely available to power's representation and calculability. The "incidentality" I mentioned above regarding race is a factor here: for whites, race comes in incidents, in "eventfulness"; for people of colour, it is the stuff of persistent everyday experience.

This incidentality, however, speaks to another dimension of contemporary raciality. Considered in terms of "eventfulness," raciality is reduced to "race": the everyday to the occasional; the wearisome weight of everyday baggage to the momentary and fleeting; the ubiquitous threat to the passing and ephemeral; ontological condition to the apparent; constitutive condition to mash-up and make believe.

This speaks to another, less affective sense of disappointment that I suggest is especially illuminating in this context. There are socialities, as Ackbar Abbas (1997) has put it, which are *dis-appointing*. They are dis-appointing in failing to comply or live up to pre-ordained expectations. They are dis-appointments in the non-standard sense of failing or really refusing to conform to their appointed places, to appointed modes of comprehension, of being and doing, to conventional social arrangements. It may be better to understand these manifestations as creases or tremors, warps or, more readily, foldings in on itself in the structure of contemporary sociality and politics. At once apparently states of ordinariness with recognizable everyday markers—residential, recreational, resourceful, socially containable, exploitable—they nevertheless are out of the ordinary. They refuse their *appointed* and so anticipated sites or roles, unrecognizable as and in their everydayness. They are dis-appointments in the sense of being out of place, dis-locations. But they also prompt different ways of speaking about the socialities they conjure, and in that sense they are dis-locutions as much as dislocations. They manifest where least anticipated and express themselves in unexpected and unpredictable ways.

These dis-appointing socialities seem to lack location, or more precisely locatedness. They cast adrift their signifying sources and so also any recognizable touchstone as the stabilizing basis for their comprehensibility. The unpredictability and prolific heterogeneity of "Occupy" sites, at least when they first emerged, exemplify this sense of dis-appointment. And one could say the same thing about Obama's initial run for the presidency. His first presidential term, by contrast, has sewn together these dual meanings, creating a mash-up of these contrasting senses of disappointment. While his policy achievements may have been disappointing in the first sense to supporters and detractors alike, the presidency of a man of many mixtures has been profoundly unsettling, dislocating—dis-appointing—to many, and in some ways to American society more generally. The recourse to renewed expressions of racial attribution and derogation across portions of the population has been one of the significant and significantly alienating responses to this unsettlement.

The *dis*-appointedness at work here is the source and expression of the sometime illegibility at play concerning the social conditions marked by a set of racial configurations no longer so readily nameable. This illegibility spawns a crisis of social representation and control. The social conditions of everyday life in these instances, as more generally, are no longer predictable, can no longer be taken for granted. What these dislocations and dislocutions now point to is the proliferation of the conditions of precariousness, conceptual and material, that we now increasingly and increasingly prolifically face. While there is still no guarantee that justice will be served for Trayvon Martin—what could that be in any case, having lost his life through no fault of his own?—George Zimmerman can no longer so readily assume, as he once might have been able to, that the whiteness of his relatively privileged family connections and influence would protect him from prosecution for shooting an unarmed black teenager.

So, raciality—racial characterization and structuration—invariably disappoints. It fails always to live up to expectation, to deliver (fully) on its premises and promise. The premises are belied by the facts of life. The promises of sustaining privilege and power are always relative to the extension of domination and subjugation. Their targets ultimately refuse, resist, rise up. Raciality accordingly fails as it succeeds. It takes away as it provides. In undercutting the values and virtues of heterogeneities, it projects easiness, simplicity, predictability, and profitability. But it produces always difficulty, complexity, fear, and fabricated danger; ultimately social loss. George Zimmerman is now paying the price of a sociality of the skin, as he sacrificed the life of an innocent to its projection, its misdirecting premises and false promise.

These logics of dis-appointment suggest related insights conjured by the concept of racial *dis-appearance*. In the more straightforward and so obvious sense, the commitment to racelessness is conceptually predicated. Racial differentiation should be rendered obsolete first and foremost by the erasure—the disappearance from social life—of racial conception. When race disappears, so too supposedly will racial arrangement. But numerous commentators have detailed recently how unjustifiable racial inequities are cemented into the social fabric now no longer identifiable because the terms by which they could be recognized through their nomination have been made to disappear. Racial disappearance in this sense signals both the conceptual evaporation and the material unrecognizability of racial matters (Goldberg, 2009).

As with racial dis-appointment, so racial *dis-appearance* speaks to the ways in which racialities re-appear in sometimes unexpected, perhaps unpredictable and less noticeable ways once race conceptually disappears. Consider the euphoria with which the first black president of the U.S. is greeted only to be dismissed quickly on the most pernicious of racist grounds. Racial identification is supposed to be unacceptable in matters of state but profiling proliferates in policing. Racial reference is supposed to evaporate but derogatory references, jokes, and insults become more voluble, more privately public as they are rendered publicly privatized. Invocation of race to invigorate formal distribution of public privilege or positions of power is outlawed but privately mobilized racial differentiation professionally, politically or recreationally spirals upward with considerable material impact. And indeed, as the language of race disappears from the formal sphere of public administration, the newly abstracted facelessness that follows in its wake seems to make drone bombing at a human distance easier to stomach, more readily unquestioned.

So when race disappears, the racial dis-appears. Racial arrangements pop up elsewhere, less readily marked and so not so easily categorized or identifiable. Raciality re-appears in other ways, in newly formulated if less explicit terms in the renewal of contemporary social fabrication, the reweaving of the social in the wake of racial privatization. George Zimmerman could initially get away with murder, and the still anonymous White Plains policemen might yet get away with execution, precisely because the alleged aggression on the part of the killed in both cases fits a longstanding presumption about black men across almost all periods of the life cycle, even where much, if not all of the material evidence evidently belies the allegations.

Racial dis-appearance, then, reveals the effects of a culture of neoliberalizing privatization. It illustrates the sorts of implications that follow when privilege and power are hidden from scrutiny behind the walls of privately structured social arrangements. *Citizens United,* the 2008 U.S. Supreme Court case that enabled private individuals to anonymously donate limitless funding to political action committees so as to impact any election campaign they deemed beneficial to their privately architected interests, represents dis-appearance at the level of political economy. The logic of this sort of politico-economic dis-appearance finds its expression well articulated in the raciality I have been revealing here.

There is an acute awkwardness at work, accordingly, as race disappears from the official administrative lexicon. Presumptions like those concerning the aggression of black men can neither be recognized nor socially sustained without their informal persistence and insistence in privatized settings, supposedly outside the reach of the state. Non-racialists find themselves caught between the insistence that the state not categorize racially, on the one hand, and the recognition, on the other, that the right to free private expression and individualized self-defence "by any means necessary" includes the unhindered possibility of even the most pernicious racist expression. This is directed at a racial group at large even if individualized to only some members of the targeted group when circumstances call for the opportunity. It is enough, even necessary, that only a subset of the targeted racial group bear the "characteristic" traits or exhibit the behaviour in question. After all, that some of the accuser's best friends are group members becomes the defence of first and last resort against charges of racism, and, as it turns out, accusations of racially prompted murder.

For want of a better category, let's call this the "Obama effect." This is a structural condition, not reducible simply to Barack Obama's individualized responsibility, even if his own non-racialism has sometimes helped to shore up the structural formation underlying the tensions at play. Structurally, then, a sociality predicated on nonracialism necessarily entails that racial disappearance will continue to sustain what I have characterized above as dis-appearing raciality. A robust social commitment to critical anti-racism, by contrast, is unlikely to suffer the "Obama effect." Racial disappearance/dis-appearance has made the effectiveness of anti-racist commitments more difficult to achieve because the objects are more nebulous. The "machinic architecture" of racial states has been displaced by the interactions between what Ash Amin (2010) insightfully characterizes as the "vernacular" and "biopolitical regimes," between everyday expression and newly fashioned modes of racially ordered securitization and dispersed control. A critical anti-racism, nevertheless, finds disappearing race deeply knotted with dis-appearing raciality in ways I have attempted to lay out above. The focus for a critical anti-racism is neither simply public racial erasure nor the privatizing dis-appearing of raciality. It is unswervingly the demeaning and potentially deadly effects of that interplay between the vernacular and biopolitical regimes to which, as the Trayvon Martin case so painfully reminds us, both give rise.

Acknowledgements

I am grateful to my colleagues Ackbar Abbas, Nisha Kapoor and Diren Valayden, conversations with whom inspired various conceptual insights included in this article.

Works Cited

Abbas, A. *1997. Hong Kong: Culture and the Politics of Disappearance*. Minneapolis: University of Minnesota Press.

Amin, A. 2010. "The Remainders of Race." *Theory, Culture & Society*, 27(1): 1–23.

Christopher, T. 2012. Lawrence O'Donnell's Interview of "Joe Oliver Didn't Just Make Fireworks, It Made News." *Mediaite*. Available at: <http://www.mediaite.com/tv/lawrence-odonnells-interview-of-joe-oliver-didnt-justmake-fireworks–it-made-news/>.

Balko, R. 2012. "Illinois Traffic Stop of Star Trek Fans Raises Concerns About Drug Searches, Police Dogs, Bad Cops." *Huffington Post*, 31 March. Available at: <http://www.huffingtonpost.com/2012/03/31/drug-searchtrekies-stopped-searched-illinois_n_1364087.html>.

Barry, D. et al. 2012. "In the Eye of a Firestorm: In Florida, an Intersection of Tragedy, Race and Outrage." *New York Times,* 2 April. Available at: <http://www.msnbc.msn.com/id/46922042/ns/us_news-the_new_york_ times/#.T3vNto4Vm_g>.

Daly, M. 2012. "Sanford's Racist Past." *Daily Beast,* 4 April. Available at: <http://www.thedailybeast.com/articles/2012/04/04/the-city-of-sanford-s-racist-past.html>.

Edwards-Levy, A. 2012. "Rick Santorum Shoots Gun at Firing Range, Condemns 'Pretend It's Obama' Comment." *Huffington Post,* 23 March. Available at: <http://www.huffingtonpost.com/2012/03/23/rick-santorum-gunfiring-range-obama_n_1375756.html>.

Frayer, L. 2011. "46 Per Cent of Mississippi Republicans Want Interracial Marriage Banned." *Aol.news.com,* 8 April. Available at: <http://www.aolnews.com/2011/04/08/46-percent-of-mississippi-republicans-wantinterracial- marriage/>.

Giroux, H. 2012. "Hoodie Politics: Trayvon Martin and Racist Violence in Post-Racial America." *Truthout,* 2 April. Available at: <http://truth-out.org/news/item/8203-hoodie-politics-and-the-death-of-trayvon-martin>.

Goldberg, D. T. 2009. *The Threat of Race: Reflections on Racial Neoliberalism.* Oxford: Wiley-Blackwell.

Goldberg, D. T. 2012. "The Tale of Two Obamas." *Qualitative Sociology.* Available at: <http://www.springerlink. com/content/965u7351124770k7/?MUD=MP>.

Golub, E. 2011. "Barack Obama's Stupid, Evil, Crazy, Racist 2012 Campaign." *Washington Times,* 5 October. Available at: <http://communities.washingtontimes.com/neighborhood/tygrrrr-express/2011/oct/5/barack-obamasstupid-evil-crazy-racist-2012-campai/>.

hooks, bell. 1992. "Representing Whiteness in the Black Imagination." In: L. Grossberg et al., eds. *Cultural Studies.* New York and London: Routledge, pp. 338–42.

Lusane, C. 2011. *The Black History of the White House.* San Francisco, CA: City Lights Books.

Schmidt, M. & Savage, C. 2012. "Language Deemed Offensive Is Removed from F.B.I. Training Materials." *New York Times,* 29 March.

Schoen, D. 2012. "Newsweek/Daily Beast Poll Finds Majorities of Americans Think Country Divided by Race." *Daily Beast,* 7 April. Available at: <http://www.thedailybeast.com/articles/2012/04/07/newsweek-daily-beastpoll-finds-majorities-of-americans-think-country-divided-by-race.html>.

Trillin, C. 2011. "Back on the Bus: Remembering the Freedom Riders." *The New Yorker,* 25 July, pp. 36–42.

Williams, J. 1988. *Eyes on the Prize: America's Civil Rights Years, 1954–1965.* Harmondsworth: Penguin.

Zimmerman, G. 2012. Interview. Fox 35 News, 29 March. Available at: <http://www.youtube.com/watch?v= LnEQQnj7eXo>.

Credit

Goldberg, David Theo. "When Race Disappears." *Comparative American Studies,* 10.2. Aug. 2012: 116–27. Print. www.maneyonline.com/cas.

Renovating the American Dream

A long-term strategy to democratize the U.S. economy begins at the local level and scales up.

Gar Alperovitz

Everyone knows the United States faces enormous challenges: unemployment, poverty, global warming, environmental decay—to say nothing of whole cities that have essentially been thrown away. We know the economic system is dominated by powerful corporate institutions. And we know the political system is dominated by those same institutions. Elections occur and major fiscal debates ensue, but most of the problems are only marginally affected (and often in ways that increase the burdens).

The issue is not simply that our situation is worrisome. It is that the nation's most pressing problems are built into the structure of the system. They are not unique to the current economic slump or the result of partisan bickering, something passing in the night that will go away when we elect forward-looking leaders and pressure them to move in a different direction.

Not only has the economy been stagnating for a long time, but for the average family, things have been bad for a very long time. Real wages for 80 per cent of workers have not gone up more than a trivial amount for at least three decades. At the same time, income for the top 1 per cent has jumped from roughly 10 per cent of all income to more than 20 per cent. A recent estimate is that a mere 400 individuals in the United States own more wealth than the bottom 180 million Americans taken together.

Unfortunately, what we call traditional politics no longer has much capacity to alter most of the negative trends. To be clear: I think projects, organizing, demonstrations and related efforts are important. But deep down, most people sense—rightly, in my view—that unless we develop a more powerful long-term strategy, those efforts aren't going to make much of a dent.

In 2007, people got excited about federal legislation raising the minimum wage from \$5.15 to \$7.25 an hour. This was obviously good, but the long-term negative trend continued nonetheless. The minimum wage, adjusted for inflation, was more than

$2 higher in 1968. Clearly, when great victories don't even get us back to where we were more than forty years ago, we need to pay close attention. I support such efforts, but it appears unlikely that strategies aimed at reviving the politics that produced the New Deal and Great Society programs are going to alter the big trends, even if those strategies are intensified by movement building—especially given the decline of labor unions, the power base of traditional progressive politics.

There is, however, a little-noticed twist to this otherwise bleak narrative. Deepening economic and social pain are producing the kinds of conditions from which various new forms of democratization—of ownership, wealth and institutions—are beginning to emerge. The challenge is to develop a broad strategy that not only ends the downward spiral but also gives rise to something different: steadily changing who actually owns the system, beginning at the bottom and working up.

Consider the evolutionary change developing in that rustiest of Rust Belt states, Ohio. On one unhappy day in September 1977, 5,000 steelworkers lost their jobs, their livelihoods, and their futures when Youngstown Sheet and Tube closed down. Such large-scale layoffs were not common in the United States up to that point. The story made the front page of newspapers and led television news across the country. The workers called it Black Monday, and I remember all too well reports of desperate men committing suicide after concluding they could no longer support their families.

A young steelworker named Gerald Dickey had a different idea: Why couldn't the workers run the facility themselves? Dickey and a group of activist friends teamed up with an ecumenical coalition in Youngstown to demand that the mill be put back to work under worker-community ownership. After a huge organizing effort, they got support from Washington—including the Carter administration, which agreed to allocate $100 million in loan guarantees.

When the administration reneged after the midterm elections of 1978, the plan fell apart. But the story did not end there. And what happened next is of even greater significance.

The inspiring example of the workers and religious leaders—and the sophisticated educational and political work they did to spread the word—had lasting impact. They knew they were up against some of the most powerful corporate (and union) players in the country. They were fully aware they might lose the battle. They also knew they had discovered an important idea with great promise. Accordingly, they made it their business to educate the public, the press, and politicians in the state and around the country about what they were trying to do, and why.

The idea took root in Ohio, and over time the practices and strategies of worker-owned businesses grew more sophisticated and innovative. Today, the state is home to half a million worker-owners, and the support system for building such businesses is one of the most advanced in the nation. The simple idea that workers can and should own their businesses is now conventional in many parts of the state, not only among workers but also businessmen, many of whom (aided by certain tax benefits) sell their businesses to their employees when they retire.

The current goal is not simply worker ownership, but worker ownership linked to a community-building strategy. In Cleveland, a group of worker-owned companies are connected through a community-building nonprofit corporation and a revolving fund designed to help such businesses thrive. Part of the design involves getting hospitals and universities in the area (like the Cleveland Clinic, Case Western Reserve University, and University Hospitals) to purchase supplies, goods, and services from these companies. Everything in the network is green by design. One of the cooperatives, for example, is an industrial-scale laundry that uses two-thirds less energy and water than conventional ones.

Similar networks are developing in many other cities, and big unions are lending their support as well. Working with the Mondragon Corporation in the Basque region of Spain—an exemplary integrated model involving numerous cooperatives and more than 80,000 people—the United Steelworkers, whose national leadership once opposed the Youngstown effort, has announced a campaign to help build "union co-op" worker-owned companies here. The Service Employees International Union, the Steelworkers, and Mondragon are involved with a worker-owned laundry in Pittsburgh. SEIU has also joined in a groundbreaking partnership with the largest worker cooperative in the United States: New York City's Cooperative Home Care Associates, which provides home services to the elderly, disabled and chronically ill.

For more than three decades, Ohio has been experiencing the kind of economic pain that other parts of the country are just beginning to experience. Precisely because traditional solutions offer few answers, many other cities are exploring paths like the one that led from Youngstown to Cleveland.

❧❧❧

As the number of institutions directly concerned with the democratization of productive wealth continues to expand, innovations are occurring left and right. More than 130 million Americans—40 per cent of the population—are members of cooperatives; more than 10 million participate in other forms of worker-owned companies. Predominant among the older co-ops are credit unions—essentially democratized, "one person, one vote" banks. More than 95 million Americans are involved; total assets are approximately $1 trillion. Activists have begun electing credit union board members and have long participated in "move your money" efforts, which shifted hundreds of millions of dollars away from Wall Street to credit unions and small banks in 2011 and 2012.

There are also thousands of "social enterprises" that use democratized ownership to make money and achieve a broader social purpose. One of the most impressive is Pioneer Human Services, an organization based in Seattle that provides employment, job training, counseling, education and housing to people with criminal histories and issues of substance abuse. PHS now employs over 1,000 people and uses its $76 million in revenues from the businesses it created to fund social programs across the state. Among other things, PHS runs a full-service precision sheet-metal fabrication shop and produces millions of aerospace parts for companies like Boeing. Its kitchen prepares more than 1,500 meals a day for its work-release facilities and residential treatment centers.

At the other end of the continent is Greyston Bakery in Yonkers, New York. Founded in 1982 by a Buddhist teacher with the modest goal of employing his students, the organization expanded its mission to provide jobs for inner-city residents. An early contract with Ben & Jerry's opened the way to much larger development. Greyston now inhabits a modern 23,000-square-foot facility and operates several businesses and services, including a daycare center, a housing development for low-income residents with HIV/AIDS, six community gardens, counseling and support services, and a computer literacy program.

By far the most common social enterprise is the traditional community development corporation. There are nearly 5,000 CDCs operating around the country. For the most part, they serve as low-income housing developers and incubators for small business. One of the most ambitious is the New Community Corporation, based in Newark, New Jersey. This large-scale neighborhood nonprofit employs roughly 600 residents and manages more than 2,000 housing units and a shopping center anchored by a major supermarket. It has $200 million in assets and an operating budget of approximately $70 million. Proceeds help support early learning centers and after-school programs, job training, a 180-bed nursing home with an adult medical daycare program, and on-site delivery of medical care in several of its eight senior buildings.

I could go on, but you get the idea. In a profound sense, the struggle is about changing the dominant ideological patterns. New forms of ownership are important not only on their own, but because they offer ideas about democratization that can help form the basis of a different political-economic system consistent with American ideals and experience.

ঙ৪ঙ৪ঙ৪

How far the process of "evolutionary reconstruction" will proceed—and whether it can extend to higher levels—will likely depend on the degree to which problems and pain continue to deepen, on whether folks embrace a broad institution-building strategic approach, and on whether those who do embrace it make it part of a more comprehensive new politics.

The political game is beginning to resemble a checkerboard strategy: some of the squares on the board are clearly blocked, but others are open. The goal, of course, is to expand the number of squares that are receptive to democratization efforts—not just to restore economic health and sustainability in struggling communities, but to demonstrate viable alternatives to strategies that are faltering elsewhere. A key goal is to overtake the opposition by surrounding the decaying, failing states in a long-term pincer movement.

The strategy must take up the challenge of rebuilding the basic institutional substructure of the local economy in ways that are efficient, effective, stable, redistributive and ongoing. This will include:

§ Expanded use of city, school, hospital, university, and other purchasing power to help stabilize jobs in a manner that democratizes ownership and benefits for both low-income communities and small- and midsize businesses;

§ Expanded use of public and quasi-public land trusts (both for housing and commercial use) to capture development profits for the community and to prevent gentrification;

§ An all-out attack on the absurdly wasteful giveaways corporations extract from local governments;

§ Coordination with labor unions and community activists to build and sustain momentum.

A strategic plan that emerges from such efforts can also help to increase the tax base, partly offsetting taxpayer pressures and weakening the opposing coalition. Perhaps most important, it can help forge an alliance of public service workers, teachers, hospital workers, and blue-collar laborers; community groups and local activists; small-business groups that benefit from a revival of local economic health; and local government officials.

Obviously, none of this is easy, especially when you look at the current makeup of national politics. On the other hand, the local economic situation in many parts of the country is getting worse. It is only a matter of time before another community's square on the checkerboard becomes receptive to a democratizing flip.

ଔ

Systemic change will require decades, not weeks or months, of work—and a long-term focus on the larger scale. What happens when the next financial crisis hits and we again face the impossibility of regulating banks too big to fail? Even if we break the big ones up, history suggests they will simply regroup and reconcentrate, as AT&T and elements of the old Standard Oil did in earlier eras. Ultimately, the big banks will have to be taken over. In the meantime, we should familiarize ourselves with—and develop local capacity for—public banks. The idea is already gaining ground: at this writing, twenty states have introduced legislation to establish state-owned banks modeled after the enormously successful Bank of North Dakota.

A similar strategy can help tackle the national healthcare crisis. As costs keep rising and burdens increase (despite Obamacare), we can expect mounting frustration and anger, followed by increasing demands for a real alternative. Most likely, the first breakthroughs will come at the state level. More than fifteen states have already seen legislation proposing some form of a single-payer public system. Vermont is likely to establish one in 2014; California passed such legislation twice, only to have it vetoed by Arnold Schwarzenegger. The move to a national single-payer system will be long and difficult, but it is possible—and with it will come the democratization of a sector that currently represents almost a fifth of the U.S. economy.

Any ecologically serious strategy will confront the basic truth that large corporations must grow or die. This imperative undermines solutions to many national (and increasingly global) challenges. In addition to the overriding problem of global warming, countless studies show that limits to growth are fast approaching in such areas as energy, minerals, water and arable land, among others. The United States, with less than 5 per cent of the global population, accounts for 21 per cent of the world's consumption of oil, 12 per cent of coal, and 20.5 per cent of natural gas—and the projections heading toward 2050 are not promising.

At some point we will have to say, "Enough is enough." Former presidential adviser James Gustave Speth puts it bluntly: "For the most part, we have worked within this current system of political economy, but working within the system will not succeed in the end when what is needed is transformative change." The large-scale institutions we build to support a more democratic and sustainable future must transcend the Wall Street-driven growth imperative. Ultimately, they must be public.

History has a way of surprising us, especially in times when serious change seems impossible. The civil rights movement, the feminist movement, the gay rights movement—even the Arab Spring revolutions—all emerged without the benefit of pundit prediction. How many people anticipated in 1989 that the Berlin Wall would fall, or that within two years the Soviet Union would dissolve, or that within five years apartheid would finally end in South Africa?

I am no utopian; I am a historian and political economist. I am cautious about predictions of inevitability—including the assumed inevitability, dictated from on high, that nothing fundamental about the American social fabric can ever change. It is possible that the decay will simply continue. It is also possible, however, that the pain, anger and loss of confidence in Washington will lead to something far more explosive than business-as-usual politics or even a modest renewal of liberal reform. It is our responsibility to consider how a distinctly American system based on democratized ownership might be organized. Like a picture slowly developing in a photographer's darkroom, the elements of that "next system" are beginning to emerge.

Credit

Alperovitz, Gar. "Renovating the American Dream." *The Nation* 28 October 2013: 20–23. Print. Reprinted with permission from the October 28, 2013 issue of *The Nation*. For subscription information, call 1-800-333-8536. Portions of each week's *Nation* magazine can be accessed at http://www.thenation.com.

The War on Wealth Isn't Just Stupid—It's Wrong

Michael Medved

Beyond the dueling sound bites and apocalyptic rhetoric of Washington's increasingly desperate battle of the budget, President Obama enjoys an automatic advantage with his relentless calls to tax the rich. These demands resonate with the deep American instinct to endorse the underdog, while punishing (or at least diminishing) the privileged and the powerful.

The Republicans may insist with flawless logic that placing additional burdens on the nation's most productive citizens does nothing to create private sector jobs: after all, how will seizing profits from business people help them to invest or expand with their reduced resources? But in the arena of public opinion, arguments must appeal to emotion as well as common sense and reach the heart rather than merely persuading the mind. It's not enough to demonstrate that attacking the rich is misguided in practice; it's also essential to show that it's wrong as a matter of principle.

The only way to overcome the traditional populist preference for "the people over the powerful" is through impassioned affirmation of another long-standing national value: the conviction that beneficial behavior deserves better results and more encouragement than destructive, damaging courses of action. Americans may not favor rich over poor, but they certainly don't prefer the irresponsible to the productive, or the hapless over the helpful. Sure, most of us who felt like geeks and losers in high school may harbor envious resentment toward the class presidents and prom queens, but that doesn't mean we want them punished with unmerited detentions or unearned bad grades for their popularity and success.

When you consider people who've created wealth and built beautiful lives for their families, it's natural and healthy to want to emulate them. But it's profoundly unhealthy to want to annihilate them.

After all, the rich in this country for the most part do precisely what we hope all Americans will do with their lives: working hard, earning money, paying taxes, and spending or investing what's left. Industrious pursuit of profit remains the best way to stimulate recovery and prosperity, and most people understand that we should welcome, not discourage, the continuation of this pattern.

Poor people, on the other hand, need to change—and they know it. No one wants to remain destitute and dependent, or to pass on that condition to future generations. But in order to live middle class lives, members of the underclass need to learn middle class habits, and to leave behind the dysfunctional values that characterize our most persistent pockets of poverty. Even the most committed conservatives and free marketers acknowledge that this process often requires outside help—in mastering new skills, providing better schools, sustaining more durable family arrangements, building safer, more economically viable neighborhoods.

But such assistance only benefits the recipients (not to mention society at large) when it leads them to alter the conduct that's trapped them in hopeless indigence in the first place. Every kind-hearted individual can feel sympathy for the bedraggled homeless panhandler on skid row, but that doesn't make it a good idea to facilitate his life on the streets indefinitely. A compassionate society rightly hopes to rescue its least fortunate members, but promoting the continuation and extension of destructive behavior does no favors for the downtrodden.

Government policies on taxes and spending inevitably impact private decisions of every sort, and sanity and decency both demand rewarding helpful choices while discouraging hurtful options. We tax tobacco heavily, and those burdens have played an undeniable role in dramatically reduced smoking rates. At the same time, we spend lavishly with subsidized loans and outright grants to promote college education and fifty years of those federal and state subsidies nearly tripled the percentage of young people pursuing higher education.

In that context, it makes no sense to penalize people with higher tax rates who toil ceaselessly to claw their way up the economic ladder. Their effort and imagination add jobs and growth while subtracting nothing from the society at large.

When President Obama pushes the idea of "taxing the rich" he's actually talking about taxing those who are trying to get rich. His desired wealth increases won't so much impact the "millionaires and billionaires" who draw his derision as it will cripple those eager strivers who hope someday to become millionaires and billionaires. The federal tax authorities don't go after wealth but rather grab their share from income, hampering earning not luxurious living.

This explains the puzzling predisposition of progressive plutocrats who live primarily off their investments (or who won life's lottery with inherited fortunes like the Kennedys or Rockefellers) to favor high tax rates on top earners. It's not really noble or unselfish for those who have already earned their pile to seek to place new obstacles on hard-driving, up-and-coming challengers who seek to enter the charmed circle of privilege.

Those obstacles, however, will hardly benefit the nation as a whole. Isn't it obvious that America needs more, not fewer, millionaires? And we want the numbers of poor and dependent people to shrink, not multiply.

While the left tries to foment indignation against wealth-creators, conservatives should respond with outrage at the moral inversion at the core of contemporary liberalism. Though progressives trumpet "fairness" as their guiding priority, there's nothing fair about society and government conferring generous dispensations on dysfunctional, dependent conduct and onerous special burdens on those who enrich both themselves and others. It is both unwise and, at the deepest level, unjust to promote hatred and resentment where gratitude is due and to offer indulgence and support for values that require correction.

The Talmud sagely observes that "those who are kind when they ought to be cruel will end by being cruel when they ought to be kind." Today's liberal imperatives violate both practicality and ethics when they make it harder to get rich, and easier to stay poor.

Credit

Medved, Michael. "The War on Wealth Isn't Just Stupid—It's Wrong." Townhall.com 10 Aug. 2011: Web.

Facts and Fallacies about Paycheck Fairness

Phyllis Schlafly

President Barack Obama and his feminist friends have been trotting out their tiresome slogan that women are paid only 77 cents for every dollar a man earns. Every reputable scholar who has commented has proved that this is a notorious falsehood that anyone should be embarrassed to use.

U.S. law calls for equal pay for equal work, but the feminist slogan is not based on equal work. Women work fewer hours per day, per week, per year. They spend fewer years as full-time workers outside the home, avoid jobs that require overtime, and choose jobs with flexibility to take time off for personal reasons. According to the Bureau of Labor Statistics, men are twice as likely as women to work more than 40 hours a week.

Women place a much higher value on pleasant working conditions: a clean, comfortable, air-conditioned office with congenial co-workers. Men, on the other hand, are more willing to endure unpleasant working conditions to earn higher pay, doing dirty, dangerous outside work. In 2012, men suffered 92 per cent of work-related deaths.

If a man is supporting his family at the peak of his career, he often works longer hours to maximize his earnings. By contrast, a successful woman who reaches a high rank in her career is more likely to reduce her working hours.

All these reasons for women voluntarily choosing lower pay are now beyond dispute among those who have looked at the facts. But even those explanations for the alleged pay "gap" are still only part of the story.

Perhaps an even more important reason for women's lower pay is the choices women make in their personal lives, such as having children. Women with children earn less, but childless women earn about the same as men.

Another fact is the influence of hypergamy, which means that women typically choose a mate (husband or boyfriend) who earns more than she does. Men don't have the same preference for a higher-earning mate.

While women prefer to HAVE a higher-earning partner, men generally prefer to BE the higher-earning partner in a relationship. This simple but profound difference between the sexes has powerful consequences for the so-called pay gap.

Suppose the pay gap between men and women were magically eliminated. If that happened, simple arithmetic suggests that half of women would be unable to find what they regard as a suitable mate.

Obviously, I'm not saying women won't date or marry a lower-earning man, only that they probably prefer not to. If a higher-earning man is not available, many women are more likely not to marry at all.

In colleges, there are no gender separations in courses of study, and students can freely choose their majors. There are no male and female math classes. But women generally choose college courses that pay less in the labor market.

Those are the choices that women themselves make. Those choices contribute to the pay gap, just as much as the choice of a job with flexible hours and pleasant working conditions.

The pay gap between men and women is not all bad because it helps to promote and sustain marriages. Since husband and wife generally pool their incomes into a single economic unit, what really matters is the combined family income, not the pay gap between them.

In two segments of our population, the pay gap has virtually ceased to exist. In the African-American community and in the millennial generation (ages 18 to 32), women earn about the same as men, if not more.

It just so happens that those are the two segments of our population in which the rate of marriage has fallen the most. Fifty years ago, about 80 per cent of Americans were married by age 30; today, less than 50 per cent are.

Just a coincidence? I think not. The best way to improve economic prospects for women is to improve job prospects for the men in their lives, even if that means increasing the so-called pay gap.

The real economic story of the past 30 years is that women's pay has effectively risen to virtual parity, but men's pay has stagnated and thousands of well-paid blue-collar jobs have been shipped to low-wage countries. Nobody should be surprised that the marriage rate has fallen, the age of first marriage has risen, and marriage, in general, has become unstable.

Credit

Schlafly, Phyllis. "Facts and Fallacies About Paycheck Fairness." *The Christian Post* 15 Apr. 2014: Web.

Why I Want Women to Lean In

An exclusive excerpt from *Lean In: Women, Work, and the Will to Lead*

Sheryl Sandberg

Today in the United States and the developed world, women are better off than ever before. But the blunt truth is that men still run the world. While women continue to outpace men in educational achievement, we have ceased making real progress at the top of any industry. Women hold around 14% of Fortune 500 executive-officer positions and about 17% of board seats, numbers that have barely budged over the last decade. This means that when it comes to making the decisions that most affect our world, our voices are not heard equally.

It is time for us to face the fact that our revolution has stalled. A truly equal world would be one where women ran half of our countries and companies, and men ran half of our homes. The laws of economics and many studies of diversity tell us that if we tapped the entire pool of human resources and talent, our performance would improve.

Throughout my career, I was told over and over about inequalities in the workplace and how hard it would be to have a career and a family. I rarely, however, heard anything about the ways I was holding myself back. From the moment they are born, boys and girls are treated differently. Women internalize the negative messages we get throughout our lives—the messages that say it's wrong to be outspoken, aggressive, more powerful than men—and pull back when we should lean in.

We must not ignore the real obstacles women face in the professional world, from sexism and discrimination to a lack of flexibility, access to child care and parental leave. But women can dismantle the internal barriers holding us back today. Here are three examples of how women can lean in.

Don't Leave Before You Leave

A few years ago, a young woman at Facebook began asking me lots of questions about how I balance work and family. I inquired if she and her partner were considering having a child. She replied that she did not have a husband, then added with a little laugh, "Actually, I don't even have a boyfriend."

From an early age, girls get the message that they will likely have to choose between succeeding at work and being a good wife and mother. By the time they are in college, women are already thinking about the trade-offs. In a survey of Princeton's class of 2006, 62% of women said they anticipated work/family conflict, compared with 33% of men—and of the men who expected a conflict, 46% expected that their wives would step away from their career track. These expectations yield predictable results: among professional women who take time off for family, only 40% return to work full time.

But women rarely make one big decision to leave the workforce. Instead, they make a lot of small decisions along the way. A law associate might decide not to shoot for partner because someday she hopes to have a family. A sales rep might take a smaller territory or not apply for a management role. A teacher might pass on leading curriculum development for her school. Often without even realizing it, women stop reaching for new opportunities. By the time a baby actually arrives, a woman is likely to be in a drastically different place than she would have been had she not leaned back. Before, she was a top performer on par with her peers in responsibility, opportunity, and pay. But by not finding ways to stretch herself in the years leading up to motherhood, she has fallen behind. When she returns to the workplace after her child is born, she is likely to feel less fulfilled, underutilized, or unappreciated. At this point, she probably scales her ambitions back even further since she no longer believes that she can get to the top.

There are many powerful reasons to exit the workforce. No one should pass judgment on these highly personal decisions. My point is that the time for a woman to scale back is when a break is needed or a child arrives—not before, and certainly not years in advance. For those who even have a choice, choosing to leave a child in someone else's care and return to work is a hard decision. Anyone who has made this decision—myself included—knows how heartwrenching this can be. Only a compelling, challenging and rewarding job will begin to make that choice a fair contest.

Success and Likability

In 2003, Columbia Business School professor Frank Flynn and New York University professor Cameron Anderson ran an experiment. They started with a Harvard Business School case study about a real-life entrepreneur named Heidi Roizen. It described how Roizen became a successful venture capitalist by using her "outgoing personality ... and vast personal and professional network ... [which] included many of the most powerful business leaders in the technology sector." Half the students in the experiment were assigned to read Heidi's story. The other half got the same story with just one difference—the name was changed from Heidi to Howard.

When students were polled, they rated Heidi and Howard as equally competent. But Howard came across as a more appealing colleague. Heidi was seen as selfish and not "the type of person you would want to hire or work for." This experiment supports what research has already clearly shown: success and likability are positively correlated for men and negatively correlated for women. When a man is successful, he is liked by both men and women. When a woman is successful, people of both genders like her less.

I believe this bias is at the very core of why women are held back. It is also at the very core of why women hold themselves back. When a woman excels at her job, both men and women will comment that she is accomplishing a lot but is "not as well liked by her peers." She is probably also "too aggressive," "not a team player," "a bit political"; she "can't be trusted," or is "difficult." Those are all things that have been said about me and almost every senior woman I know.

The solution is making sure everyone is aware of the penalty women pay for success. Recently at Facebook, a manager received feedback that a woman who reported to him was "too aggressive." Before including this in her review, he decided to dig deeper. He went back to the people who gave the feedback and asked what aggressive actions she had taken. After they answered, he asked point-blank, "If a man had done those same things, would you have considered him too aggressive?" They each said no. By showing both men and women how female colleagues are held to different standards, we can start changing attitudes today.

Stop Trying to Have It All

Perhaps the greatest trap ever set for women was the coining of this phrase. No matter what any of us has—and how grateful we are for what we have—no one has it all. Nor can they. The very concept of having it all flies in the face of the basic laws of economics and common sense. Being a working parent means making adjustments, compromises and sacrifices every day.

For most people, sacrifices and hardships are not a choice but a necessity—and tougher than ever because of the expansion of working hours. In 2009, married middle-income parents worked about 8½ hours more per week than in 1979. Just as expectations about work hours have risen dramatically, so have expectations of how much time mothers will spend focused on their children. An employed mom today spends about the same amount of time reading to, feeding, and playing with her children as a nonemployed mother did in 1975.

One of my favorite posters on the walls at Facebook declares in big red letters, "Done is better than perfect." I have tried to embrace this motto and let go of unattainable standards. My first six months at Facebook were really hard. A lot of my colleagues followed Mark Zuckerberg's lead and worked night-owl engineering hours. I worried that leaving too early would make me stand out like a sore—and old—thumb. I missed dinner after dinner with my kids. I realized that if I didn't take control of the situation, my new job would prove unsustainable. I started forcing myself to leave the office at 5:30. Every competitive, type-A fiber of my being was screaming at me to stay, but unless I had a critical meeting, I walked out that door. And once I did it, I learned that I could.

I do not have the answers on how to make the right choices for myself, much less for anyone else. I do know that I can too easily spend time focusing on what I am not doing. When I remember that no one can do it all and identify my real priorities at home and at work, I feel better—and I am more productive in the office and probably a better mother as well. Instead of perfect, we should aim for sustainable and fulfilling.

I believe that if more women lean in, we can change the power structure of our world and expand opportunities. Shared experience forms the basis of empathy and, in turn, can spark the institutional changes we need. More female leadership will lead to fairer treatment for all women. We also need men to lean into their families more, especially since research has consistently found that children with involved and loving fathers have higher levels of psychological well-being and better cognitive abilities.

The hard work of generations before us means that equality is within our reach. We can close the leadership gap now. Each individual's success can make success a little easier for the next. We can do this—for ourselves, for one another, for our daughters, and for our sons. If we push hard now, this next wave can be the last wave. In the future there will be no female leaders. There will just be leaders.

Credit

Sandberg, Sheryl. "Why I Want Women to Lean In." *Time* 7 March 2013. Print.

Boys Won't Be Boys

Lisa Abend

From the pages of ***TIME***.

ଔ৯ଓ৯ଔ৯

Why Sweden's push for gender neutrality is both a noble project and political correctness gone overboard.

ଔ৯ଓ৯ଔ৯

On a Sunny afternoon in September, a 5-year-old girl played in a sandbox. The box contained more mud than sand, and as she whacked at it with a plastic shovel, globs of dirt stained her pink dress. But at the Nicolaigarden preschool in Stockholm, no teacher chastised her, and certainly no one told her that girls aren't supposed to play like that. In fact, at Nicolaigarden, they try not to use the word *girls* at all.

Or *boys* either. One of the most popular toys at the school, for both sexes, is a set of dolls designed to teach about emotions. Each wears a different expression—one smiles broadly, another frowns—but that is almost all they wear. Except for the homely knit hats that top their Nordically blond heads, the dolls are completely naked, which makes it easy to see that they have no distinguishable gender.

And that just might be a metaphor for what this school, and perhaps Sweden as a whole, is trying to achieve. This is a country in the midst of a dramatic new experiment in gender equality—call it gender neutrality.

In the early 1970s, when the Swedish government began actively promoting women's rights, even feminists could hardly have imagined the successes to come: near parity in political representation, a near leveling of the playing field in the workplace, and fathers who share, if not equally then at least significantly, in the raising of their children. But if Sweden has gone further than almost any other country in the world to eradicate gender discrimination, it has reached a critical turning point, moving beyond mainstream feminist goals like equal pay and equal opportunity toward a society in which gender doesn't matter.

Supporters say that process is a necessary step toward eroding the lingering vestiges of sexism, and people around the world who care about gender equality are watching with keen interest to see what lessons Sweden can offer other societies. But critics charge that feminism has become something of a state religion in Sweden, to the point that the country is on the verge of doing away with the idea of men and women altogether—and in the process, they say, casting aside much of the joy and complexity that comes with difference. For them, Sweden is a dangerous experiment in political correctness that would deny biological realities and impose artificial mandates of sameness. A country that has essentially built its national identity on the pursuit of equality, Sweden finds itself moving into uncharted territory over primal questions of justice and difference.

For the rest of the West, Sweden is "laying the groundwork," says Christine Ingebritsen, a professor of Scandinavian and women's studies at the University of Washington. "They're sort of postgender now and are focusing more on humanism, on what—as humans—is going to bring us all closer to equal rights. Sweden is our future."

The struggle over this future is taking place in a country that is already one of the world's bright spots when it comes to women's rights. The World Economic Forum Global Gender Gap Index, which measures discrepancies between men and women in pay, access to education and other factors, ranks Sweden fourth out of 136 countries in terms of narrowest gender gap. In the 2010 national elections, women won 45% of the seats in Parliament (down from 47% in the previous elections), and currently 13 of the country's 24 ministers are women. On the whole, women earn 14% less than men, and when factors like education and profession are taken into account, they make 94¢ for every dollar that men do—which isn't perfect but compares favorably with the 77¢ average for American women. But many argue that there's much yet to be done. Women head the boards of only 4% of publicly listed companies. Domestic violence remains a pressing problem, as does rape, which has risen in the past several years (though this may be a result of increased reporting). Many of the women who work do so only part time, which is caused by a failure to split parental leave 50–50 with fathers, says Maria Arnholm, Sweden's Minister for Gender Equality. "We're not going to run out of need for this ministry in my lifetime," she says wryly.

That sense—that even with all the advances, things in Sweden are still not good enough—helps explain why the country's government and other institutions have expanded their goals to include the erosion of gender itself: that is, the roles and assumptions associated with each sex. "I don't think we'll get to the point where there are no boundaries whatsoever," says journalist P.M. Nilsson, who was commissioned by the government to write a report on men's issues. "But in terms of expanding the options of what it means to be a man or a woman, yes we're definitely moving toward a more gender-neutral society."

He. She. Hen.

Spend a few days in Sweden, a nation with a population roughly equivalent to Michigan's, and you'll encounter many efforts to do away with gender distinctions. And that includes hearing people referred to by a newly popular gender-neutral pronoun.

Intended as an alternative to the Swedish words *han* (he) and *hon* (she), *hen* was first proposed in the 1960s but burst into public consciousness in 2012 when children's-book author Jesper Lundqvist used it exclusively in his book *Kivi and the Monster Dog* (neither Kivi nor the pup is identified by sex). That year the national encyclopedia included the word in its print edition, and now major newspapers like *Aftonbladet* routinely employ the pronoun in place of the phrase *he* or *she*.

Traditional gender stereotypes are being upended in other ways. The careers that remain predominantly male preserves—only 3% of the Swedish firefighting corps is female, for example—offer affirmative-action-type programs to attract more women. In 2012, Top-Toy, one of the largest toy companies in Sweden, issued a holiday catalog in which boys were depicted feeding baby dolls and girls fired Nerf guns. Even pornography is changing: in 2009 the Swedish Film Institute—a state organization—helped finance Mia Engberg's *Dirty Diaries*, a collection of shorts that by focusing on the female perspective positions itself as feminist.

Many of Sweden's equality measures are enshrined in law. The process began in 1971, when joint taxation for spouses was abolished, making it financially advantageous for women to enter the workplace. Subsequent laws have banned gender discrimination in the workplace and tightened penalties for sexual harassment.

But when it comes to blurring the lines between the genders, it is perhaps the country's approach to education that is most innovative. In 1998, Parliament obliged all schools to work against gender stereotypes. Stockholm's Nicolaigarden still stocks dolls and trucks, but neutral toys like Legos and dinosaurs predominate in the brightly colored rooms. The cozy library is carefully calibrated to contain the same number of books with female protagonists as those with male ones. Boys and girls alike twirl silken scarves during dance class, and they have equal access to pirate and princess costumes. Asked whether boys actually choose to dress up as princesses, principal Lotta Rajalin smiles and says, "They do. It's the grownups who have the expectations."

Besides Nicolaigarden, Rajalin oversees five other public preschools in Stockholm, all of which are dedicated to promoting gender equality. The effort to instill the schools with a greater degree of awareness began soon after the 1998 law was enacted. "Once we made the decision to improve this, it wasn't hard to convince the parents," says Rajalin. "I simply did this." She walks over to a whiteboard and draws a circle, then divides it in half. "On the right side are the things for girls"—she draws several lines inside the semicircle—"and on this are the things for boys. And then I asked, 'Do you want your child's life to be a half-circle or a whole one?'"

Marked Men?

For some parents, it's not always easy to navigate the new norms. Par Zetterberg, a marketing executive whose son is enrolled at Nicolaigarden, speaks easily of the boy's dolls. But he also knows a couple who recently refused to tell anyone the sex of their newborn baby because, he says, "they didn't want anyone to project their gender ideas onto the child." Stuffing a jacket into his son's backpack at the school playground, he shakes his head. "That's just going too far."

Some people say the same about Sweden as a whole. Critics of the country's gender innovations maintain that for all the feminist emphasis on removing limitations, the state and other institutions are imposing a whole new set of prejudices and barriers.

An engineer by training, Par Strom has become something of a spokesman for men who feel oppressed by Sweden's push toward gender neutrality. Society, he says, has turned against men, actively discriminating against them in things like child-custody laws and permitting inequality when it favors women (two-thirds of Swedish university-degree earners, he notes, are female). "We're considered the bad sex," he says in a voice barely above a whisper as he looks nervously around the busy café, "so it's O.K. to attack us." And in words like *hen* and efforts to create gender-neutral preschools, he sees not equality but erasure.

Worse, Strom argues, is that there is no room in public discourse for a discussion of such issues. "There are anonymous antifeminist bloggers, and I get lots of e-mails from men who agree, but they stay quiet because they're terrified of their names being exposed and their careers ruined," he says. Strom stopped participating in interviews about gender with Swedish media after the hostility—including a public-radio website that posted a photo of him with a nail through his head—grew too intense. "The media is almost exclusively feminist, and there's no room for moderate dissent," he says.

He may have a point. While a respected feminist writer like Nina Bjork can publish a column in Sweden's largest morning newspaper comparing the position of women in Sweden today to that of black South Africans under apartheid, there is little room for even mild expressions of antifeminism in all but the most conservative papers. "There is a kind of dogma, yes," says Nilsson, who identifies himself as a feminist. "Female sexism is O.K., but not the other way around."

Tell that to Maria Sveland. The feminist writer has been the target of vicious hate mail, including a serious death threat. "It's becoming more and more O.K. to hate feminists," she says.

The intimidation and attempts to suppress speech may yet prove to be dangerous fault lines opening up in a nation known for its tolerance and peaceableness. Or they may be the passing side effects of massive social change. The vast majority of Swedes, however, seem to be on board with their nation's experiment in closing the gender gap, and they want to see it through. If they succeed, the rest of the developed world may one day look at gender-neutral pronouns and gender-neutral dolls as every bit as essential to democracy as equal voting rights.

In the meantime, Sweden seems to be increasingly full of people like Theo Christenson who are just getting on with their lives in the midst of this remarkable experiment in equality. One Monday evening, the 13-year-old boarded the Stockholm subway, his gym bag in hand. It was rush hour and the car was full, but he had too much energy left over from his after-school ballet class to stand still. Watching himself in the window, he executed a perfect rond de jambe. Asked whether he was hassled by other boys for dancing ballet, Christenson said no. Told that that wouldn't necessarily be the case in other countries, he replied, "I know. But this is Sweden."

*Following this article, there is text for charts that is not included in this document, as well as two color photographs.

Credit

(Rethinking) Gender

Debra Rosenberg

A growing number of Americans are taking their private struggles with their identities into the public realm. How those who believe they were born with the wrong bodies are forcing us to re-examine what it means to be male and female.

Growing up in Corinth, Miss., J. T. Hayes had a legacy to attend to. His dad was a well-known race-car driver and Hayes spent much of his childhood tinkering in the family's greasy garage, learning how to design and build cars. By the age of 10, he had started racing in his own right. Eventually Hayes won more than 500 regional and national championships in go-kart, midget and sprint racing, even making it to the NASCAR Winston Cup in the early '90s. But behind the trophies and the swagger of the racing circuit, Hayes was harboring a painful secret: he had always believed he was a woman. He had feminine features and a slight frame—at 5 feet 6 and 118 pounds he was downright dainty—and had always felt, psychologically, like a girl. Only his anatomy got in the way. Since childhood he'd wrestled with what to do about it. He'd slip on "girl clothes" he hid under the mattress and try his hand with makeup. But he knew he'd find little support in his conservative hometown.

In 1991, Hayes had a moment of truth. He was driving a sprint car on a dirt track in Little Rock when the car flipped end over end. "I was trapped upside down, engine throttle stuck, fuel running all over the racetrack and me," Hayes recalls. "The accident didn't scare me, but the thought that I hadn't lived life to its full potential just ran chill bumps up and down my body." That night he vowed to complete the transition to womanhood. Hayes kept racing while he sought therapy and started hormone treatments, hiding his growing breasts under an Ace bandage and baggy T shirts.

Finally, in 1994, at 30, Hayes raced on a Saturday night in Memphis, then drove to Colorado the next day for sex-reassignment surgery, selling his prized race car to pay the tab. Hayes chose the name Terri O'Connell and began a new life as a woman who figured her racing days were over. But she had no idea what else to do. Eventually, O'Connell got a job at the mall selling women's handbags for $8 an hour. O'Connell still hopes to race again, but she knows the odds are long: "Transgendered and professional motor sports just don't go together."

To most of us, gender comes as naturally as breathing. We have no quarrel with the "M" or the "F" on our birth certificates. And, crash diets aside, we've made peace with how we want the world to see us—pants or skirt, boa or blazer, spiky heels or sneakers. But to those who consider themselves transgender, there's a disconnect between the sex they were assigned at birth and the way they see or express themselves. Though their numbers are relatively few—the most generous estimate from the National Center for Transgender Equality is between 750,000 and 3 million Americans (fewer than 1 per cent)—many of them are taking their intimate struggles public for the first time. In April, *L.A. Times* sportswriter Mike Penner announced in his column that when he returned from vacation, he would do so as a woman, Christine Daniels. Nine states plus Washington, D.C., have enacted antidiscrimination laws that protect transgender people—and an additional three states have legislation pending, according to the Human Rights Campaign. And this month the U.S. House of Representatives passed a hate-crimes prevention bill that included "gender identity." Today's transgender Americans go far beyond the old stereotypes (think "Rocky Horror Picture Show"). They are soccer moms, ministers, teachers, politicians, even young children. Their push for tolerance and acceptance is reshaping businesses, sports, schools and families. It's also raising new questions about just what makes us male or female.

What is gender anyway? It is certainly more than physical details of what's between our legs. History and science suggest that gender is more subtle and more complicated than anatomy. (It's separate from sexual orientation, too, which determines which sex we're attracted to.) Gender helps us organize the world into two boxes, his and hers, and gives us a way of quickly sizing up every person we see on the street. "Gender is a way of making the world secure," says feminist scholar Judith Butler, a rhetoric professor at University of California, Berkeley. Though some scholars like Butler consider gender largely a social construct, others increasingly see it as a complex interplay of biology, genes, hormones, and culture.

Genesis set up the initial dichotomy: "Male and female he created them." And historically, the differences between men and women in this country were thought to be distinct. Men, fueled by testosterone, were the providers, the fighters, the strong and silent types who brought home dinner. Women, hopped up on estrogen (not to mention the mothering hormone oxytocin), were the nuturers, the communicators, the soft, emotional ones who got that dinner on the table. But as society changed, the stereotypes faded. Now even discussing gender differences can be fraught. (Just ask former Harvard president Larry Summers, who unleashed a wave of criticism when he suggested, in 2005, that women might have less natural aptitude for math and science.) Still, even the most diehard feminist would likely agree that, even apart from genitalia, we are not exactly alike. In many cases, our habits, our posture, and even cultural identifiers like the way we dress set us apart.

Now, as transgender people become more visible and challenge the old boundaries, they've given voice to another debate—whether gender comes in just two flavors. "The old categories that everybody's either biologically male or female, that there are two distinct categories and there's no overlap, that's beginning to break down," says Michael Kimmel, a sociology professor at SUNY-Stony Brook. "All of those old categories seem to be more fluid." Just the terminology can get confusing. "Transsexual" is an older term that usually refers to someone who wants to use hormones or surgery to change their sex. "Transvestites," now more politely called "cross-dressers," occasionally wear clothes of the opposite sex. "Transgender" is an umbrella term that includes anyone whose gender identity or expression differs from the sex of their birth—whether they have surgery or not.

Gender identity first becomes an issue in early childhood, as any parent who's watched a toddler lunge for a truck or a doll can tell you. That's also when some kids may become aware that their bodies and brains don't quite match up. Jona Rose, a 6-year-old kindergartner in northern California, seems like a girl in nearly every way—she wears dresses, loves pink and purple, and bestowed female names on all her stuffed animals. But Jona, who was born Jonah, also has a penis. When she was 4, her mom, Pam, offered to buy Jona a dress, and she was so excited she nearly hyperventilated. She began wearing dresses every day to preschool and no one seemed to mind. It wasn't easy at first. "We wrung our hands about this every night," says her dad, Joel. But finally he and Pam decided to let their son live as a girl. They chose a private kindergarten where Jona wouldn't have to hide the fact that he was born a boy, but could comfortably dress like a girl and even use the girls' bathroom. "She has been pretty adamant from the get-go: 'I am a girl'," says Joel.

Male or female, we all start life looking pretty much the same. Genes determine whether a particular human embryo will develop as a male or female. But each individual embryo is equipped to be either one—each possesses the Mullerian ducts that become the female reproductive system as well as the Wolffian ducts that become the male one. Around eight weeks of development, through a complex genetic relay race, the X and the male's Y chromosomes kick into gear, directing the structures to become testes or ovaries. (In most cases, the unneeded extra structures simply break down.) The ovaries and the testes are soon pumping out estrogen and testosterone, bathing the developing fetus in hormones. Meanwhile, the brain begins to form, complete with receptors—wired differently in men and women—that will later determine how both estrogen and testosterone are used in the body.

After birth, the changes keep coming. In many species, male newborns experience a hormone surge that may "organize" sexual and behavioral traits, says Nirao Shah, a neuroscientist at UCSF. In rats, testosterone given in the first week of life can cause female babies to behave more like males once they reach adulthood. "These changes are thought to be irreversible," says Shah. Between 1 and 5 months, male human babies also experience a hormone surge. It's still unclear exactly what effect that surge has on the human brain, but it happens just when parents are oohing and aahing over their new arrivals.

Here's where culture comes in. Studies have shown that parents treat boys and girls very differently—breast-feeding boys longer but talking more to girls. That's going on while the baby's brain is engaged in a massive growth spurt. "The brain doubles in size in the first five years after birth, and the connectivity between the cells goes up hundreds of orders of magnitude," says Anne Fausto-Sterling, a biologist and feminist at Brown University who is currently investigating whether subtle differences in parental behavior could influence gender identity in very young children. "The brain is interacting with culture from day one."

So what's different in transgender people? Scientists don't know for certain. Though their hormone levels seem to be the same as non-trans levels, some scientists speculate that their brains react differently to the hormones, just as men's differ from women's. But that could take decades of further research to prove. One 1997 study tantalizingly suggested structural differences between male, and female and transsexual brains, but it has yet to be successfully replicated. Some transgender people blame the environment, citing studies that show pollutants have disrupted reproduction in frogs and other animals. But those links are so far not proved in humans. For now, transgender issues are classified as "Gender Identity Disorder" in the psychiatric manual DSM-IV. That's controversial, too—gay-rights activists spent years campaigning to have homosexuality removed from the manual.

ଔଡ଼ଔଡ଼ଔଡ଼

Gender fluidity hasn't always seemed shocking. Cross-dressing was common in ancient Greece and Rome, as well as among Native Americans and many other indigenous societies, according to Deborah Rudacille, author of "The Riddle of Gender." Court records from the Jamestown settlement in 1629 describe the case of Thomas Hall, who claimed to be both a man and a woman. Of course, what's considered masculine or feminine has long been a moving target. Our Founding Fathers wouldn't be surprised to see men today with long hair or earrings, but they might be puzzled by women in pants.

Transgender opponents have often turned to the Bible for support. Deut. 22:5 says: "The woman shall not wear that which pertaineth unto a man, neither shall a man put on a woman's garment: for all that do so are abomination unto the Lord thy God." When word leaked in February that Steve Stanton, the Largo, Fla., city manager for 14 years, was planning to transition to life as a woman, the community erupted. At a public meeting over whether Stanton should be fired, one of many critics, Ron Sanders, pastor of the Lighthouse Baptist Church, insisted that Jesus would "want him terminated." (Stanton did lose his job and this week will appear as Susan Stanton on Capitol Hill to lobby for antidiscrimination laws.) Equating gender change with homosexualtiy, Sanders says that "it's an abomination, which means that it's utterly disgusting."

Not all people of faith would agree. Baptist minister John Nemecek, 56, was surfing the Web one weekend in 2003, when his wife was at a baby shower. Desperate for clues to his long-suppressed feelings of femininity, he stumbled across an article about gender-identity disorder on WebMD. The suggested remedy was sex-reassignment surgery—something Nemecek soon thought he had to do. Many families can be ripped apart by such drastic changes, but Nemecek's wife of 33 years stuck by him. His employer of 15 years, Spring Arbor University, a faith-based liberal-arts college in Michigan, did not. Nemecek says the school claimed that transgenderism violated its Christian principles, and when it renewed Nemecek's contract—by then she was taking hormones and using the name Julie—it barred her from dressing as a woman on campus or even wearing earrings. Her workload and pay were cut, too, she says. She filed a discrimination claim, which was later settled through mediation. (The university declined to comment on the case.) Nemecek says she has no trouble squaring her gender change and her faith. "Actively expressing the feminine in me has helped me grow closer to God," she says.

Others have had better luck transitioning. Karen Kopriva, now 49, kept her job teaching high school in Lake Forest, Ill., when she shaved her beard and made the switch from Ken. When Mark Stumpp, a vice president at Prudential Financial, returned to work as Margaret in 2002, she sent a memo to her colleagues (subject: Me) explaining the change. "We all joked about wearing panty hose and whether 'my condition' was contagious," she says. But "when the dust settled, everyone got back to work." Companies like IBM and Kodak now cover trans-related medical care. And 125 Fortune 500 companies now protect transgender employees from job discrimination, up from three in 2000. Discrimination may not be the worst worry for transgender people: they are also at high risk of violence and hate crimes.

ଔଔଔ

Perhaps no field has wrestled more with the issue of gender than sports. There have long been accusations about male athletes' trying to pass as women, or women's taking testosterone to gain a competitive edge. In the 1960s, would-be female Olympians were required to undergo gender-screening tests Essentially, that meant baring all before a panel of doctors who could verify that an athlete had girl parts. That method was soon scrapped in favor of a genetic test. But that quickly led to confusion over a handful of genetic disorders that give typical-looking women chromosomes other than the usual XX. Finally, the International Olympic Committee ditched mandatory lab-based screening, too. "We found there is no scientifically sound lab-based technique that can differentiate between man and woman," says Arne Ljungqvist, chair of the IOC's medical commission.

The IOC recently waded into controversy again: in 2004 it issued regulations allowing transsexual athletes to compete in the Olympics if they've had sex-reassignment surgery and have taken hormones for two years. After convening a panel of experts, the IOC decided that the surgery and hormones would compensate for any hormonal or muscular advantage a male-to-female transsexual would have. (Female-to-male athletes would be allowed to take testosterone, but only at levels that wouldn't give them a boost.) So far, Ljungqvist doesn't know of any transsexual athletes who've competed. Ironically, Renee Richards, who won a lawsuit in 1977 for the right to play tennis as a woman after her own sex-reassignment surgery, questions the fairness of the IOC rule. She thinks decisions should be made on a case-by-case basis.

Richards and other pioneers reflect the huge cultural shift over a generation of gender change. Now 70, Richards rejects the term transgender along with all the fluidity it conveys. "God didn't put us on this earth to have gender diversity," she says. "I don't like the kids that are experimenting. I didn't want to be something in between. I didn't want to be trans anything. I wanted to be a man or a woman."

But more young people are embracing something we would traditionally consider in between. Because of the expense, invasiveness and mixed results (especially for women becoming men), only 1,000 to 2,000 Americans each year get sex-reassignment surgery—a number that's on the rise, says Mara Keisling of the National Center for Transgender Equality. Mykell Miller, a Northwestern University student born female who now considers himself male, hides his breasts under a special compression vest. Though he one day wants to take hormones and get a mastectomy, he can't yet afford it. But that doesn't affect his self-image. "I challenge the idea that all men were born with male bodies," he says. "I don't go out of my way to be the biggest, strongest guy."

Nowhere is the issue more pressing at the moment than a place that helped give rise to feminist movement a generation ago: Smith College in Northampton, Mass. Though Smith was one of the original Seven Sisters women's colleges, its students have now taken to calling it a "mostly women's college," in part because of a growing number of "transmen" who decide to become male after they've enrolled. In 2004, students voted to remove pronouns from the student government constitution as a gesture to transgender students who no longer identified with "she" or "her." (Smith is also one of 70 schools that has antidiscrimination policies protecting transgender students.) For now, anyone who is enrolled at Smith may graduate, but in order to be admitted in the first place, you must have been born a female. Tobias Davis, class of '03, entered Smith as a woman, but graduated as a "transman." When he first told friends over dinner, "I think I might be a boy," they were instantly behind him, saying "Great! Have you picked a name yet?" Davis passed as male for his junior year abroad in Italy even without taking hormones; he had a mastectomy last fall. Now 25, Davis works at Smith and writes plays about the transgender experience. (His work "The Naked I: Monologues From Beyond the Binary" is a trans take on "The Vagina Monologues.")

As kids at ever-younger ages grapple with issues of gender variance, doctors, psychologists, and parents are weighing how to balance immediate desires and long-term ones. Like Jona Rose, many kids begin questioning gender as toddlers, identifying with the other gender's toys and clothes. Five times as many boys as girls say their gender doesn't match their biological sex, says Dr. Edgardo Menvielle, a psychiatrist who heads a gender-variance outreach program at Children's National Medical Center. (Perhaps that's because it's easier for girls to blend in as tomboys.) Many of these children eventually move on and accept their biological sex, says Menvielle, often when they're exposed to a disapproving larger world or when they're influenced by the hormone surges of puberty. Only about 15 per cent continue to show signs of gender-identity problems into adulthood, says Ken Zucker, who heads the Gender Identity Service at the Centre for Addiction and Mental Health in Toronto.

In the past, doctors often advised parents to direct their kids into more gender-appropriate clothing and behavior. Zucker still tells parents of unhappy boys to try more-neutral activities—say chess club instead of football. But now the thinking is that kids should lead the way. If a child persists in wanting to be the other gender, doctors may prescribe hormone "blockers" to keep puberty at bay. (Blockers have no permanent effects.) But they're also increasingly willing to take more lasting steps: Isaak Brown (who started life as Liza) began taking male hormones at 16; at 17 he had a mastectomy.

For parents like Colleen Vincente, 44, following a child's lead seems only natural. Her second child, M. (Vincente asked to use an initial to protect the child's privacy), was born female. But as soon as she could talk, she insisted on wearing boy's clothes. Though M. had plenty of dolls, she gravitated toward "the boy things" and soon wanted to shave off all her hair. "We went along with that," says Vincente. "We figured it was a phase." One day, when she was 2½, M. overheard her parents talking about her using female pronouns. "He said, 'No—I'm a him. You need to call me him'," Vincente recalls. "We were shocked." In his California preschool, M. continued to insist he was a boy and decided to change his name. Vincente and her husband, John, consulted a therapist, who confirmed their instincts to let M. guide them. Now 9, M. lives as a boy, and most people have no idea he was born otherwise. "The most important thing is to realize this is who your child is," Vincente says. That's a big step for a family, but could be an even bigger one for the rest of the world.

*Following this article, there are ten color photographs that are not included.

**A special thanks to the following contributors to this article: Lorraine Ali, Mary Carmichael, Samantha Henig, Raina Kelley, Matthew Philips, Julie Scelfo, Kurt Soller, Karen Springen, and Lynn Waddell.

Credit

Rosenberg, Debra, et. al. "(Rethinking) Gender." *Newsweek*: 50–57. Print. From *Newsweek* May 21

Standing Up for the Rights of New Fathers

Tara Siegel Bernard

Josh Levs, father of a new baby girl, emerged from his sleep-deprived stupor last month to take a stand: He is challenging his employer's parental leave policy on the grounds that it discriminates against biological dads.

This was his third child, and this time around, he said he felt compelled to take action. So Mr. Levs, a reporter at CNN, filed a charge with the Equal Employment Opportunity Commission against Time Warner, his employer's parent company.

He took his case public on his Tumblr page, where he laid out his reasoning: Birth mothers are entitled to 10 weeks of paid leave. The same policy applies to both men and women who adopt or have children through a surrogate. Biological fathers, on the other hand, receive only two paid weeks.

He said this left him with two choices: stay home for a longer period of time without pay or go back to work and hire help. "Neither is financially tenable," wrote Mr. Levs, who lives in Atlanta, "and the fact that only biological dads face this choice at this point in a newborn's life is ludicrous."

It was a gutsy move, particularly when there was a new child to feed. Time Warner declined to elaborate on the specifics of the case; though, on the surface, it appears to treat biological fathers as second-class parents compared to their peers. But what's fair and what is discriminatory under the law are two different matters (we'll get to those issues in a minute).

Time Warner's policy does happen to be more generous than that of many American employers, but the bar is pretty low. Most employers don't provide any paid paternity leave (A study conducted by the Society for Human Resource Management that polled human resource professionals found that a mere 15 per cent of companies offered paid paternity benefits). Of course, the United States has one of the least civilized policies in the world when it comes to offering paid leave for new mothers. So, it's no surprise that fathers are often treated as an afterthought.

But more workers may be starting to do more than quietly grumble about the policies, according to discrimination lawyers, researchers and legal experts who run a workplace discrimination hotline. More employees—particularly men of the millennial generation, whose oldest members are in their early 30s—are filing legal actions against their employers, these experts say.

"What is happening is the new work-life pioneers are young egalitarian men exactly like this guy," said Joan C. Williams, founding director of the Center for WorkLife Law at the University of California, Hastings College of the Law. "In many ways, these younger men are acting in ways that mothers have always acted: "I have family responsibilities that aren't going away and either you accommodate them or there is going to be a fight against it." In many ways, this is economic contraction fueling gender equality."

There aren't any federal laws that explicitly prohibit discrimination against workers with family responsibilities, but some states and municipalities have more specific protections. The type of claim filed by Mr. Levs is brought under Title VII of the Civil Rights Act of 1964, enforced by the E.E.O.C., which prohibits employment discrimination based on sex. Mothers who claim they were treated differently from men with children file claims under the law, and so do fathers who say they were denied leave or benefits available to female caregivers.

That's generally what Mr. Levs is contending. "If I gave up my child for adoption, and some other guy at Time Warner adopted her, he would get 10 weeks off, paid, to take care of her," he wrote on his Tumblr page. "I, however, the biological father, can't."

It's hard to predict exactly how the commission will view his claims. But Justine Lisser, an E.E.O.C. lawyer and spokeswoman, offered some insight into what may be considered sex discrimination in a hypothetical situation. It's not necessarily wrong, for instance, if women were given a certain period of paid leave to recover from pregnancy and childbirth, while men (and women) were also entitled to the same period to recover from other medical conditions.

But it would be considered sex discrimination to give women paid time off to care for a newborn, but not give the same time to men. It would also obviously be wrong to have such a policy on the books, but then penalize men for using it. "We see this in some caregiving cases," she said. "Women are presumed to need caregiving time off, but men are presumed not to be invested in their jobs if they want to take the same time for the same reason and are either denied it or demoted after using it."

Mr. Levs's lawyer, A. Lee Parks Jr., a civil rights lawyer in Atlanta, acknowledged that the policies could (and potentially should) be different for men and women. "The bizarre thing here is they give a significant amount of time if you are a certain type of parent," he said. "So, they made a value judgment that, in those situations, that there is really a period where you need to bond."

If you're curious about the legality of your company's policy, legal experts said to look at it as a breakdown of recovery time and bonding time. "Men should get the same bonding time," said Cynthia T. Calvert, a senior adviser on family responsibilities discrimination at the Center for WorkLife Law. She suggests that employers designate six to eight weeks for recovery, and then anything beyond that should be deemed bonding time, and available to all parents.

Workplace experts who read Mr. Levs's blog said he appeared to take the right approach. He started the process two months before the birth of his daughter, followed his company's protocols, and kept the matter confidential. You might start by simply asking your supervisor or human resources department for more information, just to be sure you're understanding the policy correctly. "You don't want to come on too strong, but at the same time, you want to be sure you've done everything in the system before you bring in the lawyers," said Ms. Calvert, who also consults with employers to shape their policies and train their supervisors to avoid discrimination. "Because then, everyone gets their armor on. People don't view you as a team player anymore."

If you have reason to believe your policy could be discriminatory, she said you might ask the human resources department if it considered whether the policy violated Title VII or any state antidiscrimination laws. In many cases, legal experts say, simply nudging employers works. "When we receive calls, we give callers the language they can use, and the employers almost always change their policies," said Ms. Calvert, who oversees a family discrimination hotline at the center. "That's why we don't have a lot of these cases on the books."

Still, men like Mr. Levs may be penalized even more than women when seeking flexibility after the birth of a child because they are stepping outside of their usual gender roles and flouting convention, some researchers found. Several workplace experts report that men still suffer the consequences after taking unpaid leave through the Family and Medical Leave Act of 1993, which requires larger employers and public agencies to provide up to 12 weeks of unpaid leave for the birth or adoption of a child or to care for certain other family members.

"The organizations haven't yet caught up to the attitudinal shift among new dads," said Brad Harrington, executive director of the Boston College Center for Work and Family and a research professor in the Carroll School of Management. "Men who ask for leave time or who are more visibly active and involved in caregiving are experiencing a whole range of negative repercussions as a result of that."

Getting paid leave may do more to change perceptions, some experts say. "Men are supposed to make a living, so if a benefit is not paid, it is not for them," said Eileen Appelbaum, an expert in workplace practices and senior economist at the Center for Economic and Policy Research, who supports a social insurance program that would replace a portion of pay for all workers who need to take leave. "But if it is paid, it changes the culture and expectation inside the organizations."

And when men take time off after the birth of a child, it can have lasting ripple effects. Not only does it help create a connection with the child, but it sets the stage for a more egalitarian division of labor at home over the longer term. It could also help equalize the perception when women take time off. "If it is true that women will not be equal in the workplace until men are equal at home," Ms. Calvert added, "it has greater repercussions as well."

Credit

Bernard, Tara Siegel. "Standing Up for the Rights of New Fathers." From *The New York Times*, 9 November © 2013 *The New York Times*.

Notes

Notes

Notes

Unit 5

Science and Nature

As humanity steps further away from nature and closer to science and technologies, it is imperative that students of the 21st century not only recognize the shift but also discuss consequences and effects of this growth. Though the scientific community has had many positive breakthroughs and has contributed significantly to society, conversations regarding our relationship to nature and the ethical questions of science and technology must occur. As discussions concerning various issues within science and nature take place, it is important that problems are defined and plausible solutions examined.

Some areas where human interference with nature is problematic include how food is grown and distributed, contamination of oceans and land, and the ramifications of the possible honeybee extinction. Problems such as these illustrate the necessity to analyze conceivable solutions to positively re-shape the future of the earth. Our responsibility to nature warrants investigation, but so does society's intimate relationship with technology and science concerning artificial intelligence and nanotechnologies, eugenics and "designer babies," and the human genome and genetic modifications. The ethical questions these issues raise must be addressed so that we do not lose our humanity in the quest for technological breakthrough.

These conversations are an important step in the journey Cleveland State University students take to become engaged members of a global community. As a community we should concern ourselves with ways to protect natural resources and learn how to preserve those resources. And although there are many serious achievements to applaud in the field of science, there must also be critical discussions of how we are ethically responsible for the implementation of scientific and technological achievements for the well-being of our city and our planet.

Will Frankenfood Save the Planet?

Jonathan Rauch

Over the next half century genetic engineering could feed humanity and solve a raft of enviromental ills—if only environmentalists would let it.

That genetic engineering may be the most environmentally beneficial technology to have emerged in decades, or possibly centuries, is not immediately obvious. Certainly, at least, it is not obvious to the many U.S. and foreign environmental groups that regard biotechnology as a bête noire. Nor is it necessarily obvious to people who grew up in cities, and who have only an inkling of what happens on a modern farm. Being agriculturally illiterate myself, I set out to look at what may be, if the planet is fortunate, the farming of the future.

It was baking hot that April day. I traveled with two Virginia state soil-and-water-conservation officers and an agricultural-extension agent to an area not far from Richmond. The farmers there are national (and therefore world) leaders in the application of what is known as continuous no-till farming. In plain English, they don't plough. For thousands of years, since the dawn of the agricultural revolution, farmers have ploughed, often several times a year; and with ploughing has come runoff that pollutes rivers and blights aquatic habitat, erosion that wears away the land, and the release into the atmosphere of greenhouse gases stored in the soil. Today, at last, farmers are working out methods that have begun to make ploughing obsolete.

At about one-thirty we arrived at a 200-acre patch of farmland known as the Good Luck Tract. No one seemed to know the provenance of the name, but the best guess was that somebody had said something like "You intend to farm this? Good luck!" The land was rolling, rather than flat, and its slopes came together to form natural troughs for rainwater. Ordinarily this highly erodible land would be suitable for cows, not crops. Yet it was dense with wheat—wheat yielding almost twice what could normally be expected, and in soil that had grown richer in organic matter, and thus more nourishing to crops, even as the land was farmed. Perhaps most striking was the almost complete absence of any chemical or soil runoff. Even the beating administered in 1999 by Hurricane Floyd, which lashed the ground with nineteen inches of rain in less than twenty-four hours, produced no significant runoff or erosion. The land simply absorbed the sheets of water before they could course downhill.

At another site, a few miles away, I saw why. On land planted in corn whose shoots had only just broken the surface, Paul Davis, the extension agent, wedged a shovel into the ground and dislodged about eight inches of topsoil. Then he reached down and picked up a clump. Ploughed soil, having been stirred up and turned over again and again, becomes lifeless and homogeneous, but the clump that Davis held out was alive. I immediately noticed three squirming earthworms, one grub, and quantities of tiny white insects that looked very busy. As if in greeting, a worm defecated. "Plant-available food!" a delighted Davis exclaimed.

This soil, like that of the Good Luck Tract, had not been ploughed for years, allowing the underground ecosystem to return. Insects and roots and microorganisms had given the soil an elaborate architecture, which held the earth in place and made it a sponge for water. That was why erosion and runoff had been reduced to practically nil. Crops thrived because worms were doing the ploughing. Crop residue that was left on the ground, rather than ploughed under as usual, provided nourishment for the soil's biota and, as it decayed, enriched the soil. The farmer saved the fuel he would have used driving back and forth with a heavy plough. That saved money, and of course it also saved energy and reduced pollution. On top of all that, crop yields were better than with conventional methods.

The conservation people in Virginia were full of excitement over no-till farming. Their job was to clean up the James and York Rivers and the rest of the Chesapeake Bay watershed. Most of the sediment that clogs and clouds the rivers, and most of the fertilizer runoff that causes the algae blooms that kill fish, comes from farmland. By all but eliminating agricultural erosion and runoff—so Brian Noyes, the local conservation-district manager, told me—continuous no-till could "revolutionize" the area's water quality.

Even granting that Noyes is an enthusiast, from an environmental point of view no-till farming looks like a dramatic advance. The rub—if it is a rub—is that the widespread elimination of the plough depends on genetically modified crops.

It is only a modest exaggeration to say that as goes agriculture, so goes the planet. Of all the human activities that shape the environment, agriculture is the single most important, and it is well ahead of whatever comes second. Today about 38 per cent of the earth's land area is cropland or pasture—a total that has crept upward over the past few decades as global population has grown. The increase has been gradual, only about 0.3 per cent a year; but that still translates into an additional Greece or Nicaragua cultivated or grazed every year.

Farming does not go easy on the earth, and never has. To farm is to make war upon millions of plants (weeds, so-called) and animals (pests, so-called) that in the ordinary course of things would crowd out or eat or infest whatever it is a farmer is growing. Crop monocultures, as whole fields of only wheat or corn or any other single plant are called, make poor habitat and are vulnerable to disease and disaster. Although fertilizer runs off and pollutes water, farming without fertilizer will deplete and eventually exhaust the soil. Pesticides can harm the health of human beings and kill desirable or harmless bugs along with pests. Irrigation leaves behind trace elements that can accumulate and poison the soil. And on and on.

The trade-offs are fundamental. Organic farming, for example, uses no artificial fertilizer, but it does use a lot of manure, which can pollute water and contaminate food. Traditional farmers may use less herbicide, but they also do more ploughing, with all the ensuing environmental complications. Low-input agriculture uses fewer chemicals but more land. The point is not that farming is an environmental crime—it is not—but that there is no escaping the pressure it puts on the planet.

In the next half century the pressure will intensify. The United Nations, in its midrange projections, estimates that the earth's human population will grow by more than 40 percent, from 6.3 billion people today to 8.9 billion in 2050. Feeding all those people, and feeding their billion or so hungry pets (a dog or a cat is one of the first things people want once they move beyond a subsistence lifestyle), and providing the increasingly protein-rich diets that an increasingly wealthy world will expect—doing all of that will require food output to at least double, and possibly triple.

But then the story will change. According to the UN's midrange projections (which may, if anything, err somewhat on the high side), around 2050 the world's population will more or less level off. Even if the growth does not stop, it will slow. The crunch will be over. In fact, if in 2050 crop yields are still increasing, if most of the world is economically developed, and if population pressures are declining or even reversing—all of which seems reasonably likely—then the human species may at long last be able to feed itself, year in and year out, without putting any additional net stress on the environment. We might even be able to grow everything we need while *reducing* our agricultural footprint: returning cropland to wilderness, repairing damaged soils, restoring ecosystems, and so on. In other words, human agriculture might be placed on a sustainable footing forever: a breathtaking prospect.

The great problem, then, is to get through the next four or five decades with as little environmental damage as possible. That is where biotechnology comes in.

One day recently I drove down to southern Virginia to visit Dennis Avery and his son, Alex. The older Avery, a man in late middle age with a chinstrap beard, droopy eyes, and an intent, scholarly manner, lives on ninety-seven acres that he shares with horses, chickens, fish, cats, dogs, bluebirds, ducks, transient geese, and assorted other creatures. He is the director of global food issues at the Hudson Institute, a conservative think tank; Alex works with him, and is trained as a plant physiologist. We sat in a sunroom at the back of the house our afternoon conversation punctuated every so often by dog snores and rooster crows. We talked for a little while about the Green Revolution, a dramatic advance in farm productivity that fed the world's burgeoning population over the past four decades, and then I asked if the challenge of the next four decades could be met.

"Well," Dennis replied, "we have tripled the world's farm output since 1960. And we're feeding twice as many people from the same land. That was a heroic achievement. But we have to do what some think is an even more difficult thing in this next forty years, because the Green Revolution had more land per person and more water per person—"

"—and more potential for increases," Alex added, "because the base that we were starting from was so much lower."

"By and large," Dennis went on, "the world's civilizations have been built around its best farmland. And we have used most of the world's good farmland. Most of the good land is already heavily fertilized. Most of the good land is already being planted with high-yield seeds. [Africa is the important exception.] Most of the good irrigation sites are used. We can't triple yields again with the technologies we're already using. And we might be lucky to get a fifty per cent yield increase if we froze our technology short of biotech."

"Biotech" can refer to a number of things, but the relevant application here is genetic modification: the selective transfer of genes from one organism to another. Ordinary breeding can cross related varieties, but it cannot take a gene from a bacterium, for instance, and transfer it to a wheat plant. The organisms resulting from gene transfers are called "transgenic" by scientists—and "Frankenfood" by many greens.

Gene transfer poses risks, unquestionably. So, for that matter, does traditional crossbreeding. But many people worry that transgenic organisms might prove more unpredictable. One possibility is that transgenic crops would spread from fields into forests or other wild lands and there become environmental nuisances, or worse. A further risk is that transgenic plants might cross-pollinate with neighboring wild plants, producing "superweeds" or other invasive or destructive varieties in the wild. Those risks are real enough that even most biotech enthusiasts—including Dennis Avery, for example—favor some government regulation of transgenic crops.

What is much less widely appreciated is biotech's potential to do the environment good. Take as an example continuous no-till farming, which really works best with the help of transgenic crops. Human beings have been ploughing for so long that we tend to forget why we started doing it in the first place. The short answer: weed control. Turning over the soil between plantings smothers weeds and their seeds. If you don't plough, your land becomes a weed garden—unless you use herbicides to kill the weeds. Herbicides, however, are expensive, and can be complicated to apply. And they tend to kill the good with the bad.

In the mid-1990s the agricultural-products company Monsanto introduced a transgenic soybean variety called Roundup Ready. As the name implies, these soybeans tolerate Roundup, an herbicide (also made by Monsanto) that kills many kinds of weeds and then quickly breaks down into harmless ingredients. Equipped with Roundup Ready crops, farmers found that they could retire their ploughs and control weeds with just a few applications of a single, relatively benign herbicide—instead of many applications of a complex and expensive menu of chemicals. More than a third of all U.S. soybeans are now grown without ploughing, mostly owing to the introduction of Roundup Ready varieties. Ploughless cotton farming has likewise received a big boost from the advent of bioengineered varieties. No-till farming without biotech is possible, but it's more difficult and expensive, which is why no-till and biotech are advancing in tandem.

In 2001 a group of scientists announced that they had engineered a transgenic tomato plant able to thrive on salty water—water, in fact, almost half as salty as seawater, and fifty times as salty as tomatoes can ordinarily abide. One of the researchers was quoted as saying, "I've already transformed tomato, tobacco, and canola. I believe I can transform any crop with this gene"—just the sort of Frankenstein hubris that makes environmentalists shudder. But consider the environmental implications. Irrigation has for millennia been a cornerstone of agriculture, but it comes at a price. As irrigation water evaporates, it leaves behind traces of salt, which accumulate in the soil and gradually render it infertile. (As any Roman legion knows, to destroy a nation's agricultural base you salt the soil.) Every year the world loses about

25 million acres—an area equivalent to a fifth of California—to salinity; 40 per cent of the world's irrigated land, and 25 per cent of America's, has been hurt to some degree. For decades traditional plant breeders tried to create salt-tolerant crop plants, and for decades they failed.

Salt-tolerant crops might bring millions of acres of wounded or crippled land back into production. "And it gets better," Alex Avery told me. The transgenic tomato plants take up and sequester in their leaves as much as six or seven per cent of their weight in sodium. "Theoretically," Alex said, "you could reclaim a salt-contaminated field by growing enough of these crops to remove the salts from the soil."

His father chimed in: "We've worried about being able to keep these salt-contaminated fields going even for decades. We can now think about *centuries*."

One of the first biotech crops to reach the market, in the mid-1990s, was a cotton plant that makes its own pesticide. Scientists incorporated into the plant a toxin-producing gene from a soil bacterium known as *Bacillus thuringiensis*. With Bt cotton, as it is called, farmers can spray much less, and the poison contained in the plant is delivered only to bugs that actually eat the crop. As any environmentalist can tell you, insecticide is not very nice stuff—especially if you breathe it, which many Third World farmers do as they walk through their fields with backpack sprayers.

Transgenic cotton reduced pesticide use by more than two million pounds in the United States from 1996 to 2000, and it has reduced pesticide sprayings in parts of China by more than half. Earlier this year the Environmental Protection Agency approved a genetically modified corn that resists a beetle larva known as rootworm. Because rootworm is American corn's most voracious enemy, this new variety has the potential to reduce annual pesticide use in America by more than 14 million pounds. It could reduce or eliminate the spraying of pesticide on 23 million acres of U.S. land.

All of that is the beginning, not the end. Bioengineers are also working, for instance, on crops that tolerate aluminum, another major contaminant of soil, especially in the tropics. Return an acre of farmland to productivity, or double yields on an already productive acre, and, other things being equal, you reduce by an acre the amount of virgin forest or savannah that will be stripped and cultivated. That may be the most important benefit of all.

Of the many people I have interviewed in my twenty years as a journalist, Norman Borlaug must be the one who has saved the most lives. Today he is an unprepossessing eighty-nine-year-old man of middling height, with crystal-bright blue eyes and thinning white hair. He still loves to talk about plant breeding, the discipline that won him the 1970 Nobel Peace Prize: Borlaug led efforts to breed the staples of the Green Revolution. (See "Forgotten Benefactor of Humanity," by Gregg Easterbrook, an article on Borlaug in the January 1997 *Atlantic.)* Yet the renowned plant breeder is quick to mention that he began his career, in the 1930s, in forestry, and that forest conservation has never been far from his thoughts. In the 1960s, while he was working to improve crop yields in India and Pakistan, he made a mental connection. He would create tables detailing acres under cultivation and average yields—and then, in another column, he would estimate how much land had been saved by higher farm productivity. Later, in the 1980s and 1990s, he and others began paying increased attention to what some agricultural economists now call the Borlaug hypothesis: that the Green Revolution has saved not only many human lives but, by improving the productivity of existing farmland, also millions of acres of tropical forest and other habitat—and so has saved countless animal lives.

From the 1960s through the 1980s, for example, Green Revolution advances saved more than 100 million acres of wild lands in India. More recently, higher yields in rice, coffee, vegetables, and other crops have reduced or in some cases stopped forest-clearing in Honduras, the Philippines, and elsewhere. Dennis Avery estimates that if farming techniques and yields had not improved since 1950, the world would have lost an additional 20 million or so square miles of wildlife habitat, most of it forest. About 16 million square miles of forest exists today. "What I'm saying," Avery said, in response to my puzzled expression, "is that we have saved every square mile of forest on the planet."

Habitat destruction remains a serious environmental problem; in some respects it is the most serious. The savannahs and tropical forests of Central and South America, Asia, and Africa by and large make poor farmland, but they are the earth's storehouses of biodiversity, and the forests are the earth's lungs. Since 1972 about 200,000 square miles of Amazon rain forest have been cleared for crops and pasture; from 1966 to 1994 all but three of the Central American countries cleared more forest than they left standing. Mexico is losing more than 4,000 square miles of forest a year to peasant farms; sub-Saharan Africa is losing more than 19,000.

That is why the great challenge of the next four or five decades is not to feed an additional three billion people (and their pets) but to do so without converting much of the world's prime habitat into second- or third-rate farmland. Now, most agronomists agree that some substantial yield improvements are still to be had from advances in conventional breeding, fertilizers, herbicides, and other Green Revolution standbys. But it seems pretty clear that biotechnology holds more promise—probably much more. Recall that world food output will need to at least double and possibly triple over the next several decades. Even if production could be increased that much using conventional technology, which is doubtful, the required amounts of pesticide and fertilizer and other polluting chemicals would be immense. If properly developed, disseminated, and used, genetically modified crops might well be the best hope the planet has got.

If properly developed, disseminated, and used. That tripartite qualification turns out to be important, and it brings the environmental community squarely, and at the moment rather jarringly, into the picture.

Not long ago I went to see David Sandalow in his office at the World Wildlife Fund, in Washington, D.C. Sandalow, the organization's executive vice-president in charge of conservation programs, is a tall, affable, polished, and slightly reticent man in his forties who holds degrees from Yale and the University of Michigan Law School.

Some weeks earlier, over lunch, I had mentioned Dennis Avery's claim that genetic modification had great environmental potential. I was surprised when Sandalow told me he agreed. Later, in our interview in his office, I asked him to elaborate. "With biotechnology," he said, "there are no simple answers. Biotechnology has huge potential benefits and huge risks, and we need to address both as we move forward. The huge potential benefits include increased productivity of arable land, which could relieve pressure on forests. They include decreased pesticide usage. But the huge risks include severe ecological disruptions—from gene flow and from enhanced invasiveness, which is a very antiseptic word for some very scary stuff."

I asked if he thought that, absent biotechnology, the world could feed everybody over the next forty or fifty years without ploughing down the rain forests. Instead of answering directly he said, "Biotechnology could be part of our arsenal if we can overcome some of the barriers. It will never be a panacea or a magic bullet. But nor should we remove it from our tool kit."

Sandalow is unusual. Very few credentialed greens talk the way he does about biotechnology, at least publicly. They would readily agree with him about the huge risks, but they wouldn't be caught dead speaking of huge potential benefits—a point I will come back to. From an ecological point of view, a very great deal depends on other environmentalists coming to think more the way Sandalow does.

Biotech companies are in business to make money. That is fitting and proper. But developing and testing new transgenic crops is expensive and commercially risky, to say nothing of politically controversial. When they decide how to invest their research-and-development money, biotech companies will naturally seek products for which farmers and consumers will pay top dollar. Roundup Ready products, for instance, are well suited to U.S. farming, with its high levels of capital spending on such things as herbicides and automated sprayers. Poor farmers in the developing world, of course, have much less buying power. Creating, say, salt-tolerant cassava suitable for growing on hardscrabble African farms might save habitat as well as lives—but commercial enterprises are not likely to fall over one another in a rush to do it.

If earth-friendly transgenics are developed, the next problem is disseminating them. As a number of the farmers and experts I talked to were quick to mention, switching to an unfamiliar new technology—something like no-till—is not easy. It requires capital investment in new seed and equipment, mastery of new skills and methods, a fragile transition period as farmer and ecology readjust, and an often considerable amount of trial and error to find out what works best on any given field. Such problems are only magnified in the Third World, where the learning curve is steeper and capital cushions are thin to nonexistent. Just handing a peasant farmer a bag of newfangled seed is not enough. In many cases peasant farmers will need one-on-one attention. Many will need help to pay for the seed, too.

Finally there is the matter of using biotech in a way that actually benefits the environment. Often the technological blade can cut either way, especially in the short run. A salt-tolerant or drought-resistant rice that allowed farmers to keep land in production might also induce them to plough up virgin land that previously was too salty or too dry to farm. If the effect of improved seed is to make farming more profitable, farmers may respond, at least temporarily, by bringing more land into production. If a farm becomes more productive, it may require fewer workers; and if local labor markets cannot provide jobs for them, displaced workers may move to a nearby patch of rain forest and burn it down to make way for subsistence farming. Such transition problems are solvable, but they need money and attention.

In short, realizing the great—probably unique—environmental potential of biotech will require stewardship. "It's a tool," Sara Scherr, an agricultural economist with the conservation group Forest Trends, told me, "but it's absolutely not going to happen automatically."

So now ask a question: Who is the natural constituency for earth-friendly biotechnology? Who cares enough to lobby governments to underwrite research—frequently unprofitable research—on transgenic crops that might restore soils or cut down on pesticides in poor countries? Who cares enough to teach Asian or African farmers, one by one, how to farm without ploughing? Who cares enough to help poor farmers afford high-tech, earth-friendly seed? Who cares enough to agitate for programs and reforms that might steer displaced peasants and profit-seeking farmers away from sensitive lands? Not politicians, for the most part. Not farmers. Not corporations. Not consumers.

At the World Resources Institute, an environmental think tank in Washington, the molecular biologist Don Doering envisions transgenic crops designed specifically to solve environmental problems: crops that might fertilize the soil, crops that could clean water, crops tailored to remedy the ecological problems of specific places. "Suddenly you might find yourself with a virtually chemical-free agriculture, where your cropland itself is filtering the water, it's protecting the watershed, it's providing habitat," Doering told me. "There is still so little investment in what I call design-for-environment." The natural constituency for such investment is, of course, environmentalists.

But environmentalists are not acting as such a constituency today. They are doing the opposite. For example, Greenpeace declares on its website: "The introduction of genetically engineered (GE) organisms into the complex ecosystems of our environment is a dangerous global experiment with nature and evolution ... GE organisms must not be released into the environment. They pose unacceptable risks to ecosystems, and have the potential to threaten biodiversity, wildlife and sustainable forms of agriculture."

Other groups argue for what they call the Precautionary Principle, under which no transgenic crop could be used until proven benign in virtually all respects. The Sierra Club says on its website,

> In accordance with this Precautionary Principle, we call for a moratorium on the planting of all genetically engineered crops and the release of all GEOs [genetically engineered organisms] into the environment, *including those now approved.* Releases should be delayed until extensive, rigorous research is done which determines the long-term environmental and health impacts of each GEO and there is public debate to ascertain the need for the use of each GEO intended for release into the environment. [italics added]

Under this policy the cleaner water and healthier soil that continuous no-till farming has already brought to the Chesapeake Bay watershed would be undone, and countless tons of polluted runoff and eroded topsoil would accumulate in Virginia rivers and streams while debaters debated and researchers researched. Recall David Sandalow: "Biotechnology has huge potential benefits and huge risks, and we need to address both as we move forward." A lot of environmentalists would say instead, "*before* we move forward." That is an important difference, particularly because the big population squeeze will happen not in the distant future but over the next several decades.

For reasons having more to do with politics than with logic, the modern environmental movement was to a large extent founded on suspicion of markets and artificial substances. Markets exploit the earth; chemicals poison it. Biotech touches both hot buttons. It is being pushed forward by greedy corporations, and it seems to be the very epitome of the unnatural.

Still, I hereby hazard a prediction. In ten years or less, most American environmentalists (European ones are more dogmatic) will regard genetic modification as one of their most powerful tools. In only the past ten years or so, after all, environmentalists have reversed field and embraced market mechanisms—tradable emissions permits and the like—as useful in the fight against pollution. The environmental logic of biotechnology is, if anything, even more compelling. The potential upside of genetic modification is simply too large to ignore—and therefore environmentalists will not ignore it. Biotechnology will transform agriculture, and in doing so will transform American environmentalism.

Credit

Rauch, Jonathan. "Will Frankenfood Save the Planet?" *The Atlantic Monthly* Oct. 2003 292. 3: 103–8. Print.

The Plight of the Honeybee

Bryan Walsh

You can thank the Apis Mellifera, better known as the Western honeybee, for 1 in every 3 mouthfuls of food you'll eat today. From the almond orchards of central California—where each spring billions of honeybees from across the U.S. arrive to pollinate a multibillion-dollar crop—to the blueberry bogs of Maine, the bees are the unsung, unpaid laborers of the American agricultural system, adding more than $15 billion in value to farming each year. In June, a Whole Foods store in Rhode Island, as part of a campaign to highlight the importance of honeybees, temporarily removed from its produce section all the food that depended on pollinators. Of 453 items, 237 vanished, including apples, lemons and zucchini and other squashes. Honeybees "are the glue that holds our agricultural system together," wrote journalist Hannah Nordhaus in her 2011 book, *The Beekeeper's Lament.*

And now that glue is failing. Around 2006, commercial beekeepers began noticing something disturbing: their honeybees were disappearing. Beekeepers would open their hives and find them full of honeycomb, wax, even honey—but devoid of actual bees. As reports from worried beekeepers rolled in, scientists coined an appropriately apocalyptic term for the mystery malady: colony-collapse disorder (CCD). Suddenly beekeepers found themselves in the media spotlight, the public captivated by the horror-movie mystery of CCD. Seven years later, honeybees are still dying on a scale rarely seen before, and the reasons remain mysterious. One-third of U.S. honeybee colonies died or disappeared during the past winter, a 42% increase over the year before and well above the 10% to 15% losses beekeepers used to experience in normal winters.

Though beekeepers can replenish dead hives over time, the high rates of colony loss are putting intense pressure on the industry and on agriculture. There were just barely enough viable honeybees in the U.S. to service this spring's vital almond pollination in California, putting a product worth nearly $4 billion at risk. Almonds are a big deal—they're the Golden State's most valuable agricultural export, worth more than twice as much as its iconic wine grapes. And almonds, totally dependent on honeybees, are a bellwether of the larger problem. For fruits and vegetables as diverse as cantaloupes, cranberries and cucumbers, pollination can be a farmer's only chance to increase maximum yield. Eliminate the honeybee and agriculture would be permanently diminished. "The take-home message is that we are very close to the edge," says Jeff Pettis, the research leader at the U.S. Department of Agriculture's Bee Research Laboratory. "It's a roll of the dice now."

That's why scientists like Pettis are working hard to figure out what's bugging the bees. Agricultural pesticides were an obvious suspect—specifically a popular new class of chemicals known as neonicotinoids, which seem to affect bees and other insects even at what should be safe doses. Other researchers focused on bee-killing pests like the accurately named Varroa destructor, a parasitic mite that has ravaged honeybee colonies since it was accidentally introduced into the U.S. in the 1980s. Others still have looked at bacterial and viral diseases. The lack of a clear culprit only deepened the mystery and the fear, heralding what some greens call a "second silent spring," a reference to Rachel Carson's breakthrough 1962 book, which is widely credited with helping launch the environmental movement. A quote that's often attributed to Albert Einstein became a slogan: "If the bee disappears from the surface of the globe, man would have no more than four years to live."

One problem: experts doubt that Einstein ever said those words, but the misattribution is characteristic of the confusion that surrounds the disappearance of the bees, the sense that we're inadvertently killing a species that we've tended and depended on for thousands of years. The loss of the honeybees would leave the planet poorer and hungrier, but what's really scary is the fear that bees may be a sign of what's to come, a symbol that something is deeply wrong with the world around us. "If we don't make some changes soon, we're going to see disaster," says Tom Theobald, a beekeeper in Colorado. "The bees are just the beginning."

Sublethal Effects

If the honeybee is a victim of natural menaces like viruses and unnatural ones like pesticides, it's worth remembering that the bee itself is not a natural resident of the continent. It was imported to North America in the 17th century, and it thrived until recently because it found a perfect niche in a food system that demands crops at ever cheaper prices and in ever greater quantities. That's a man-made, mercantile ecosystem that not only has been good for the bees and beekeepers but also has meant steady business and big revenue for supermarkets and grocery stores.

Jim Doan has been keeping bees since the age of 5, but the apiary genes in his family go back even further. Doan's father paid his way to college with the proceeds of his part-time beekeeping, and in 1973 he left the bond business to tend bees full time. Bees are even in the Doan family's English coat of arms. Although Jim went to college with the aim of becoming an agriculture teacher, the pull of the beekeeping business was too great.

For a long time, that business was very good. The family built up its operation in the town of Hamlin, in western New York, making money from honey and from pollination contracts with farmers. At the peak of his business, Doan estimates he was responsible for pollinating 1 out of 10 apples grown in New York, running nearly 6,000 hives, one of the biggest such operations in the state. He didn't mind the inevitable stings—"you have to be willing to be punished"—and he could endure the early hours. "We made a lot of honey, and we made a lot of money," he says.

All that ended in 2006, the year CCD hit the mainstream, and Doan's hives weren't spared. That winter, when he popped the covers to check on his bees—tipped off by a fellow beekeeper who experienced one of the first documented cases of CCD—Doan found nothing. "There were hundreds of hives in the backyard and no bees in them," he says. In the years since, he has experienced repeated losses, his bees growing sick and dying. To replace lost hives, Doan needs to buy new queens and split his remaining colonies, which reduces honey production and puts more pressure on his few remaining healthy bees. Eventually it all became unsustainable. In 2013, after decades in the business, Doan gave up. He sold the 112 acres (45 hectares) he owns—land he had been saving to sell after his retirement—and plans to sell his beekeeping equipment as well, provided he can find someone to buy it. Doan is still keeping some bees in the meantime, maintaining a revenue stream while considering his options. Those options include a job at Walmart.

Doan and I walk through his backyard, which is piled high with bee boxes that would resemble filing cabinets, if filing cabinets hummed and vibrated. Doan lends me a protective jacket and a bee veil that covers my face. He walks slowly among the boxes—partly because he's a big guy and partly because bees don't appreciate fast moves—and he spreads smoke in advance, which masks the bees' alarm pheromones and keeps them calm. He opens each box and removes a few frames—the narrowly spaced scaffolds on which the bees build their honeycombs—checking to see how a new population he imported from Florida is doing. Some frames are choked with crawling bees, flowing honey and healthy brood cells, each of which contains an infant bee. But other frames seem abandoned, even the wax in the honeycomb crumbling. Doan lays these boxes—known as dead-outs—on their side.

He used to love checking on his bees. "Now it's gotten to the point where I look at the bees every few weeks, and it scares me," he says. "Will it be a good day, will they be alive, or will I just find a whole lot of junk? It depresses the hell out of me."

Doan's not alone in walking away from such unhappy work. The number of commercial beekeepers has dropped by some three-quarters over the past 15 years, and while all of them may agree that the struggle is just not worth it anymore, they differ on which of the possible causes is most to blame. Doan has settled on the neonicotinoid pesticides—and there's a strong case to be made against them.

The chemicals are used on more than 140 different crops as well as in home gardens, meaning endless chances of exposure for any insect that alights on the treated plants. Doan shows me studies of pollen samples taken from his hives that indicate the presence of dozens of chemicals, including the neonicotinoids. He has testified before Congress about the danger the chemicals pose and is involved in a lawsuit with other beekeepers and with green groups that calls on the Environmental Protection Agency (EPA) to suspend a pair of pesticides in the neonicotinoid class. "The impacts [from the pesticides] are not marginal, and they're not academic," says Peter Jenkins, a lawyer for the Center for Food Safety and a lead counsel in the suit. "They pose real threats to the viability of pollinators."

American farmers have been dousing their fields with pesticides for decades, meaning that honeybees—which can fly as far as 5 miles (8 km) in search of forage—have been exposed to toxins since well before the dawn of CCD. But neonicotinoids, which were introduced in the mid-1990s and became widespread in the years that followed, are different. The chemicals are known as systematics, which means that seeds are soaked in them before they're planted. Traces of the chemicals are eventually passed on to every part of the mature plant—including the pollen and nectar a bee might come into contact with—and can remain for much longer than other pesticides do. There's really no way to prevent bees from being exposed to some level of neonicotinoids if the pesticides have been used nearby. "We have growing evidence that neonicotinoids can have dangerous effects, especially in conjunction with other pathogens," says Peter Neumann, head of the Institute of Bee Health at the University of Bern in Switzerland.

Ironically, neonicotinoids are actually safer for farmworkers because they can be applied more precisely than older classes of pesticides, which disperse into the air. Bees, however, seem uniquely sensitive to the chemicals. Studies have shown that neonicotinoids attack their nervous system, interfering with their flying and navigation abilities without killing them immediately. "The scientific literature is exploding now with work on sublethal impacts on bees," says James Frazier, an entomologist at Penn State University. The delayed but cumulative effects of repeated exposure might explain why colonies keep dying off year after year despite beekeepers' best efforts. It's as if the bees were being poisoned very slowly.

It's undeniably attractive to blame the honeybee crisis on neonicotinoids. The widespread adoption of these pesticides roughly corresponds to the spike in colony loss, and neonicotinoids are, after all, meant to kill insects. Chemicals are ubiquitous—a recent study found that honeybee pollen was contaminated, on average, with nine different pesticides and fungicides. Best of all, if the problem is neonicotinoids, the solution is simple: ban them. That's what the European Commission decided to do this year, putting a two-year restriction on the use of some neonicotinoids. But while the EPA is planning to review neonicotinoids, a European-style ban is unlikely—in part because the evidence is still unclear. Beekeepers in Australia have been largely spared from CCD even though neonicotinoids are used there, while France has continued to suffer bee losses despite restricting the use of the pesticides since 1999. Pesticide makers argue that actual levels of neonicotinoid exposure in the field are too low to be the main culprit in colony loss. "We've dealt with insecticides for a long time," says Randy Oliver, a beekeeper who has done independent research on CCD. "I'm not thoroughly convinced this is a major issue."

Hostile Terrain

Even if pesticides are a big part of the bee-death mystery, there are other suspects. Beekeepers have always had to protect their charges from dangers such as the American foulbrood—a bacterial disease that kills developing bees—and the small hive beetle, a pest that can infiltrate and contaminate colonies. Bloodiest of all is the multidecade war against the Varroa destructor, a microscopic mite that burrows into the brood cells that host baby bees. The mites are equipped with a sharp, two-pronged tongue that can pierce a bee's exoskeleton and suck its hemolymph—the fluid that serves as blood in bees. And since the Varroa can also spread a number of other diseases—they're the bee equivalent of a dirty hypodermic needle—an uncontrolled mite infestation can quickly lead to a dying hive.

The Varroa first surfaced in the U.S. in 1987—likely from infected bees imported from South America—and it has killed billions of bees since. Countermeasures used by beekeepers, including chemical miticides, have proved only partly effective. "When the Varroa mite made its way in, it changed what we had to do," says Jerry Hayes, who heads Monsanto's commercial bee work. "It's not easy to try to kill a little bug on a big bug."

Other researchers have pointed a finger at fungal infections like the parasite Nosema ceranae, possibly in league with a pathogen like the invertebrate iridescent virus. But again, the evidence isn't conclusive: some CCD-afflicted hives show evidence of fungi or mites or viruses, and others don't. Some beekeepers are skeptical that there's an underlying problem at all, preferring to blame CCD on what they call PPB—piss-poor beekeeping, a failure of beekeepers to stay on top of colony health. But while not every major beekeeper has suffered catastrophic loss, colony failures have been widespread for long enough that it seems perverse to blame the human victims. "I've been keeping bees for decades," says Doan. "It's not like I suddenly forgot how to do it in 2006."

There's also the simple fact that beekeepers live in a country that is becoming inhospitable to honeybees. To survive, bees need forage, which means flowers and wild spaces. Our industrialized agricultural system has conspired against that, transforming the countryside into vast stretches of crop monocultures—factory fields of corn or soybeans that are little more than a desert for honeybees starved of pollen and nectar. Under the Conservation Reserve Program (CRP), the government rents land from farmers and sets it aside, taking it out of production to conserve soil and preserve wildlife. But as prices of commodity crops like corn and soybeans have skyrocketed, farmers have found that they can make much more money planting on even marginal land than they can from the CRP rentals. This year, just 25.3 million acres (10.2 million hectares) will be held in the CRP, down by one-third from the peak in 2007 and the smallest area in reserve since 1988.

Lonely Spring

For all the enemies that are massing against honeybees, a bee-pocalypse isn't quite upon us yet. Even with the high rates of annual loss, the number of managed honeybee colonies in the U.S. has stayed stable over the past 15 years, at about 2.5 million. That's still significantly down from the 5.8 million colonies that were kept in 1946, but that shift had more to do with competition from cheap imported honey and the general rural depopulation of the U.S. over the past half-century. (The number of farms in the U.S. fell from a peak of 6.8 million in 1935 to just 2.2 million today, even as food production has ballooned.) Honeybees have a remarkable ability to regenerate, and year after year the beekeepers who remain have been able to regrow their stocks after a bad loss. But the burden on beekeepers is becoming unbearable. Since 2006 an estimated 10 million beehives have been lost, at a cost of some $2 billion. "We can replace the bees, but we can't replace beekeepers with 40 years of experience," says Tim Tucker, the vice president of the American Beekeeping Federation.

As valuable as honeybees are, the food system wouldn't collapse without them. The backbone of the world's diet—grains like corn, wheat and rice—is self-pollinating. But our dinner plates would be far less colorful, not to mention far less nutritious, without blueberries, cherries, watermelons, lettuce and the scores of other plants that would be challenging to raise commercially without honeybee pollination. There could be replacements. In southwest China, where wild bees have all but died out thanks to massive pesticide use, farmers laboriously hand-pollinate pear and apple trees with brushes. Scientists at Harvard are experimenting with tiny robobees that might one day be able to pollinate autonomously. But right now, neither solution is technically or economically feasible. The government could do its part by placing tighter regulations on the use of all pesticides, especially during planting season. There needs to be more support for the CRP too to break up the crop monocultures that are suffocating honeybees. One way we can all help is by planting bee-friendly flowers in backyard gardens and keeping them free of pesticides. The country, says Dennis vanEngelsdorp, a research scientist at the University of Maryland who has studied CCD since it first emerged, is suffering from a "nature deficit disorder"—and the bees are paying the price.

But the reality is that barring a major change in the way the U.S. grows food, the pressure on honeybees won't subside. There are more than 1,200 pesticides currently registered for use in the U.S.; nobody pretends that number will be coming down by a lot. Instead, the honeybee and its various pests are more likely to be changed to fit into the existing agricultural system. Monsanto is working on an RNA-interference technology that can kill the Varroa mite by disrupting the way its genes are expressed. The result would be a species-specific self-destruct mechanism—a much better alternative than the toxic and often ineffective miticides beekeepers have been forced to use. Meanwhile, researchers at Washington State University are developing what will probably be the world's smallest sperm bank—a bee-genome repository that will be used to crossbreed a more resilient honeybee from the 28 recognized subspecies of the insect around the world.

Already, commercial beekeepers have adjusted to the threats facing their charges by spending more to provide supplemental feed to their colonies. Supplemental feed raises costs, and some scientists worry that replacing honey with sugar or corn syrup can leave bees less capable of fighting off infections. But beekeepers living adrift in a nutritional wasteland have little choice. The beekeeping business may well begin to resemble the industrial farming industry it works with: fewer beekeepers running larger operations that produce enough revenue to pay for the equipment and technologies needed to stay ahead of an increasingly hostile environment. "Bees may end up managed like cattle, pigs and chicken, where we put them in confinement and bring the food to them," says Oliver, the beekeeper and independent researcher. "You could do feedlot beekeeping."

That's something no one in the beekeeping world wants to see. But it may be the only way to keep honeybees going. And as long as there are almonds, apples, apricots and scores of other fruits and vegetables that need pollinating—and farmers willing to pay for the service—beekeepers will find a way.

So if the honeybee survives, it likely won't resemble what we've known for centuries. But it could be worse. For all the recent attention on the commercial honeybee, wild bees are in far worse shape. In June, after a landscaping company sprayed insecticide on trees, 50,000 wild bumblebees in Oregon were killed—the largest such mass poisoning on record. Unlike the honeybee, the bumblebee has no human caretakers. Globally, up to 100,000 animal species die off each year—nearly every one of them without fanfare or notice. This is what happens when one species—that would be us—becomes so widespread and so dominant that it crowds out almost everything else. It won't be a second silent spring that dawns; we'll still have the buzz of the feedlot honeybee in our ears. But humans and our handful of preferred species may find that all of our seasons have become lonelier ones.

Credit

Is Fish Farming Safe?

Terry McCarthy

Flying in a seaplane up the east coast of Vancouver Island in British Columbia you see little but forested hills, a myriad of islands and the blue waters of the narrow channel that runs from Seattle to the Alaska Panhandle. As the plane drops over a ridge, a floating hut appears, anchored in the channel and nestled in a grid of net-covered pens. It all looks innocuous enough—no smoking chimneys, no visible plumes of discharge, no growling of chainsaws, not even a road.

This is Venture Point, 15 minutes northeast of Campbell River by air, one of 91 salmon farms licensed to operate in British Columbian waters. They produce some 50,000 tons of salmon a year, most of it destined for the U.S. market. Young men work their way along the floating walkways around the 10,000-sq.-ft. pens, tossing brown food pellets that are met by a swirl of fish. In these 12 pens, there are about 1 million salmon, each a delicious, silver-sided beauty, and when harvested in 18 months, they will fetch more than $10 million in retail sales.

What could be wrong with this picture? The farm-grown harvest is cheap, predictable and year-round. "A fillet of farmed salmon in your supermarket is fresher than a wild fish netted at sea that can take five to six days to get to harbor," says Odd Grydeland, 54, former president of the British Columbia Salmon Farmers Association and an executive at Heritage Salmon, based in New Brunswick, B.C. Moreover, each farm-grown salmon means, in theory, one less fish taken from wild stocks that have been declining for decades. (Farm-raised fish now make up most of the fresh salmon sold in U.S. supermarkets.)

But the story isn't that simple. Salmon farming can be a dirty business. According to Otto Langer, 56, a biologist who worked 30 years for Canada's Department of Fisheries, a large salmon farm may pour as much liquid waste into the sea as a small city. Add to that the plagues of destructive sea lice that thrive in densely packed salmon pens and the schools of farm-grown fish that inevitably escape to the open sea, where they spread diseases and compete for food and breeding grounds with wild stocks.

Because salmon are voracious eaters of smaller species, it takes several pounds of wild fish, ground up into meal, to yield 1 lb. of farmed salmon—an exchange that depletes the world supply of protein. The diet of farmed salmon lacks the small, pink-colored krill that their wild cousins eat, so the flesh of farmed fish is gray; a synthetic version of astaxanthin, a naturally occurring pigment, is added to the feed.

Aquaculture—the commercial raising of fish—is being touted as a "blue revolution," a seagoing version of the Green Revolution that vastly multiplied agricultural output in underdeveloped countries. But just as the Green Revolution sparked concerns about its reliance on pesticides and chemical fertilizers, so has the blue revolution provoked a rebellion among scientists and environmentalists who fear that the industry, if left unregulated, could wreak havoc in oceans and estuaries. "We are not against aquaculture," says Langer, "but we are against the way it is being done now."

It has been several decades since there were enough fish in the sea to meet, on a sustainable basis, the growing worldwide demand for seafood—which accounts for 16% of global animal-protein intake, up from 14% in the early 1960s. About half the world's wild fisheries have been exhausted by overfishing. In the North Atlantic, one of the most depleted oceans, populations of popular fish (cod, flounder, haddock, hake and tuna) are just one-sixth of what they were a century ago. A European Union panel last week backed calls for a total ban on the fishing of cod in the North Atlantic and a moratorium on the fishing of haddock and whiting there.

Aquaculture was supposed to pick up the slack. It's already the world's fastest-growing food industry, with production increasing more than 10% a year. Farmed fish and shellfish supply 30% of all the seafood consumed worldwide today, up from 10% two decades ago.

But while the principles of aquaculture are generally accepted, experts fiercely debate which types of fish farming are safe to pursue. Says Andrew Fisk, 37, aquaculture coordinator for Maine's department of marine resources: "Aquaculturists used to be the good guys, and now they aren't, and there is a lot of anger on both sides."

On an eco-friendly scale, bivalves generally rate highest among the more than 220 species of fish and shellfish that are cultivated commercially. Mussels and oysters are filter-feeders that make the surrounding water cleaner, so small-scale farming of them is not usually harmful to the ecosystem. Farming of crayfish in China—the largest supplier to the U.S.—is a relatively low-maintenance, drug-free business carried out in rice paddies. Next come the vegetarian freshwater species that do not need large quantities of fish meal—carp, catfish and tilapia. At the bottom are salmon and shrimp, onetime luxury foods that, thanks to aquaculture, can be purchased around the world in any season at supermarket prices. Both species eat several pounds of fish meal to gain a pound of weight. And both create a lot of waste.

To see fish farming at its worst, travel to Chile, where salmon farming has boomed in the past decade and generates $1 billion a year in export revenue. "A film of feed leftover made of fish oil, animal fat and transgenic soybean oil floats on the water around the salmon farms," says Ronald Pfeil, 67, a cattle farmer in Chile's remote Aysen region. "When the tide is low, the beaches stink."

Under international pressure, Chile introduced strict new regulations in January. But the problems surrounding fish farming are complex, and some are only dimly understood. Daniel Pauly, 55, a professor of fisheries science at the University of British Columbia, has calculated that it takes 2 to 5 lbs. of anchovies, sardines, menhaden and the other oily fish that comprise fish meal to produce 1 lb. of farmed salmon, which he says makes no sense in a world trying to increase the amount of available protein. Kentucky State University biologist James Tidwell, 47, a former president of the World Aquaculture Society, points out, however, that wild salmon are bigger eaters than that—consuming at least 10 lbs. of fish to add 1 lb. in weight—and argues that harvesting large amounts of short-lived species like menhaden is no more harmful than mowing the lawn. "Fish-meal fish are nature's forage," he says. "Cropping them merely increases their productivity."

Disease is always a problem when fish are raised in close quarters. After a 1999 outbreak of infectious salmon anemia in fish farms in Scotland, all the farm-grown fish within 25 miles were slaughtered. A similar anemia outbreak in Maine two years ago led to the destruction of more than 2.5 million fish—and to federal insurance payouts totaling $16 million. "The more aquaculture there is," warns Callum Roberts, senior lecturer in marine conservation at the University of York in England, "the more disease there will be."

Some of the antibiotics that fish farmers give their stock to minimize disease pass easily into the surrounding environment, and some are highly toxic. Last year traces of the banned drug nitrofuran, which is dangerous to humans, were found by European Union inspectors in shrimp from Myanmar, Thailand and Vietnam. According to Wang Sihe, an expert with the Jiangsu Seawater Fisheries Research Institute, Chinese shrimp farms have mixed fish food with antibiotics and dumped it into fish ponds. Chloramphenicol, an antibiotic that can cause fatal anemia in humans, has also been used.

The fetid water that runs off shrimp farms is particularly damaging to the environment. Thailand, with 25,000 coastal shrimp farms, is the world's largest exporter of shrimp—$3 billion worth in 2001 alone. Through last June, Thailand accounted for 28% of the shrimp imported into the U.S. But this commerce is costly. Long strips of coastline south of Bangkok now look like powdery gray moonscapes. Shrimp farms can raise the salinity of the surrounding soil and water, poisoning the land for agriculture. Some flush their effluent into the sea, killing mangrove trees. Shrimp farming is also practiced in Brazil, India and Ecuador, and in the U.S. in Florida, South Carolina, and Texas.

Parasite infestation is another chronic problem of high-density seafood farms. One of the most damaging organisms is the sea louse, which breeds by the millions in the vicinity of captive salmon. In 1989 Peter Mantle, who owns a wild salmon and sea-trout sport fishery in Delphi on the west coast of Ireland, discovered that young trout returning to his river from the ocean were covered with lice that were boring through the trouts' skin and feasting on their flesh. The sea lice were breeding near newly installed salmon farms in the inlet fed by his river. By the time the salmon farmers started dosing their pens with anti-sea-lice chemicals, the sea-trout fisheries of the west of Ireland were effectively dead. "Sea-trout fishing was sustainable and eco-friendly," says Mantle, "but the salmon farms killed it off within a decade."

In the long run, wild-fish stocks may face an even greater threat from captive fish escaping and competing with or consuming native fish, or cross-breeding with them and diluting the genes that have helped them survive. Fish escapes are common: nets are ripped open by predators or storms, fish in ponds get swept into channels by rainfall, others are released accidentally during transport. Bighead and silver carp that were introduced to China's plateau lakes in the 1950s have cleared those waters of whole species of indigenous fish. And Asian carp, which were introduced in Mississippi Delta catfish ponds to control parasites, escaped in the early 1990s and have migrated up the Mississippi and Illinois rivers to within 25 miles of Lake Michigan, threatening native fish with their voracious feeding habits.

Experts say aquaculture done right could easily feed the world without polluting it. A favored method of environmentalists is the hard-walled pen system that isolates the fish from the surrounding water in 40-ft.-deep tanks and catches their waste in the bottom. Even more secure are containment ponds built onshore into which seawater is pumped. Agrimarine Industries in Cedar, B.C., is testing a site with eight tanks 100 yds. from the sea and 40 ft. above it. But production costs are expected to be about $2.20 a fish—double what it costs to raise a salmon in a net pen.

Although salmon farming for decades has been a highly profitable industry and shows strong promise for the long term, profits are being squeezed today—making it more difficult for operators to adopt more expensive, eco-friendly methods. About 75% of salmon-farming firms are relatively small and privately held and don't make their finances public. The large, publicly held companies in the business—including Dutch food producer Nutreco Holdings NV and Norwegian seafood giants Fjord Seafood ASA, Stolt Sea Farm and Pan Fish ASA—are feeling the pinch. Pan Fish recently reported a quarterly operating loss of $18.5 million.

The Chinese, who have been farming fish for 2,000 years, pioneered a method in which nothing is wasted. Farmers dig ponds around rice paddies and feed carp in the ponds with weeds from the rice field. The silt from the ponds is used as fertilizer for the fields, and crabs are grown to eat pests. Some of those techniques are being adapted in Western fish farms. In Tuscaloosa, Ala., Dan Butterfield, 59, raises bass, carp, catfish, and other species in the same pond; the sun and the catfish feces stimulate the growth of phytoplankton, which feeds the other species. His water stays relatively clean, with no need to discharge wastes. "I am probably the most environment-friendly fish farmer in the country," claims Butterfield, who figures he nets about $1,000 an acre each year on his 150 acres of ponds.

But these alternative techniques tend to be expensive and difficult to scale up, which make them a hard sell for U.S. fish farmers. "The challenge is to have the industry grow in a way that is both ecologically sensitive and sustainable," says Rebecca Goldburg, 44, a scientist who co-authored a report on the aquaculture industry last year for the Pew Oceans Commission. "But until the government steps in, there will be no incentive for the industry to act."

Boatmen who catch wild fish and shellfish are often more strictly regulated than seafood farmers, whose wholesome image has helped them resist government oversight. But after eight years of discussion, shrimp farmers around the world are considering adoption of a universal certification process that would require them to comply with standards on the siting of ponds, effluent treatment, the reduction of chemicals and disease management. In exchange, their products would be labeled eco-friendly. By 2004, labels indicating whether seafood is farmed or wild will become mandatory in the U.S. (though they won't be required on restaurant menus). Jason Clay, 51, a senior fellow at World Wildlife Fund who helped develop the standards, is optimistic that they will be accepted. "As the industry gets more competitive, those who survive will be those who do it better and cleaner," he says.

Except in Maine, there's little talk of certification systems among salmon farmers. But there are quiet moves to clean up the industry from within. "A lot of farms were badly run," admits Peter Sawchuk, 49, who has been farming salmon in British Columbia since 1989 for Marine Harvest and Agrimarine. "They were overfed, poorly sited and there was too much drugging. But now we are getting better. We are not in the business of destroying our farms."

Venture Point, near Vancouver Island, is something of a showcase. Underwater video cameras monitor the salmon feeding so that extra pellets are not added after the fish have stopped eating. And those pellets contain up to 60% soy meal instead of fish. Nutreco, the company that owns Venture Point, individually vaccinates young salmon, reducing the need for larger quantities of antibiotics later on. Venture Point was located in a narrow channel east of Vancouver Island to take advantage of powerful currents that prevent wastes from building up under the pens.

If techniques like those used at Venture Point are widely adopted, fish farming could become sustainable while remaining profitable. If methods don't change, either voluntarily or by government regulation, we may get plenty of fish and shrimp to eat—at least for a while—but lose the wild stocks they came from and the clear blue waters in which they once swam.

Credit

McCarthy, Terry. "Is Fish Farming Safe?" *Time* 17 Nov. 2002. Print.

The Acid Sea

Elizabeth Kolbert

The carbon dioxide we pump into the air is seeping into the oceans and slowly acidifying them. One hundred years from now, will oysters, mussels, and coral reefs survive?

☙❧☙

Castello Aragonese is a tiny island that rises straight out of the Tyrrhenian Sea like a tower. Seventeen miles west of Naples, it can be reached from the somewhat larger island of Ischia via a long, narrow stone bridge. The tourists who visit Castello Aragonese come to see what life was like in the past. They climb—or better yet, take the elevator—up to a massive castle, which houses a display of medieval torture instruments. The scientists who visit the island, by contrast, come to see what life will be like in the future.

Owing to a quirk of geology, the sea around Castello Aragonese provides a window onto the oceans of 2050 and beyond. Bubbles of CO_2 rise from volcanic vents on the seafloor and dissolve to form carbonic acid. Carbonic acid is relatively weak; people drink it all the time in carbonated beverages. But if enough of it forms, it makes seawater corrosive. "When you get to the extremely high CO_2, almost nothing can tolerate that," Jason Hall-Spencer, a marine biologist from Britain's University of Plymouth, explains. Castello Aragonese offers a natural analogue for an unnatural process: The acidification that has taken place off its shore is occurring more gradually across the world's oceans, as they absorb more and more of the carbon dioxide that's coming from tailpipes and smokestacks.

Hall-Spencer has been studying the sea around the island for the past eight years, carefully measuring the properties of the water and tracking the fish and corals and mollusks that live and, in some cases, dissolve there. On a chilly winter's day I went swimming with him and with Maria Cristina Buia, a scientist at Italy's Anton Dohrn Zoological Station, to see the effects of acidification up close. We anchored our boat about 50 yards from the southern shore of Castello Aragonese. Even before we got into the water, some impacts were evident. Clumps of barnacles formed a whitish band at the base of the island's wave-battered cliffs. "Barnacles are really tough," Hall-Spencer observed. In the areas where the water was most acidified, though, they were missing.

We all dived in. Buia was carrying a knife. She pried some unlucky limpets from a rock. Searching for food, they had wandered into water that was too caustic for them. Their shells were so thin they were almost transparent. Bubbles of carbon dioxide streamed up from the seafloor like beads of quicksilver. We swam on. Beds of sea grass waved beneath us. The grass was a vivid green; the tiny organisms that usually coat the blades, dulling their color, were all missing. Sea urchins, commonplace away from the vents, were also absent; they can't tolerate even moderately acidified water. Swarms of nearly transparent jellyfish floated by. "Watch out," Hall-Spencer warned. "They sting."

Jellyfish, sea grass, and algae—not much else lives near the densest concentration of vents at Castello Aragonese. Even a few hundred yards away, many native species can't survive. The water there is about as acidified as the oceans as a whole are forecast to be by 2100. "Normally in a polluted harbor you've got just a few species that are weed like and able to cope with widely fluctuating conditions," Hall-Spencer said once we were back on the boat. "Well, it's like that when you ramp up CO_2."

Since the start of the industrial revolution, enough fossil fuels—coal, oil, and natural gas—have been burned and enough forests cut down to emit more than 500 billion tons of CO_2. As is well-known, the atmosphere has a higher concentration of CO_2 today than at any point in the past 800,000 years and probably a lot longer.

What is less well-known is how carbon emissions are changing the oceans too. The air and the water constantly exchange gases, so a portion of anything emitted into the atmosphere eventually ends up in the sea. Winds quickly mix it into the top few hundred feet, and over centuries currents spread it through the ocean depths. In the 1990s an international team of scientists undertook a massive research project that involved collecting and analyzing more than 77,000 seawater samples from different depths and locations around the world. The work took 15 years. It showed that the oceans have absorbed 30 per cent of the CO_2 released by humans over the past two centuries. They continue to absorb roughly a million tons every hour.

For life on land this process is a boon; every ton of CO_2 the oceans remove from the atmosphere is a ton that's not contributing to global warming. But for life in the sea the picture looks different. The head of the National Oceanic and Atmospheric Administration, Jane Lubchenco, a marine ecologist, has called ocean acidification global warning's "equally evil twin."

The pH scale, which measures acidity in terms of the concentration of hydrogen ions, runs from zero to 14. At the low end of the scale are strong acids, such as hydrochloric acid, that release hydrogen readily (more readily than carbonic acid does). At the high end are strong bases such as lye. Pure, distilled water has a pH of 7, which is neutral. Seawater should be slightly basic, with a pH around 8.2 near the sea surface. So far CO_2 emissions have reduced the pH there by about 0.1. Like the Richter scale, the pH scale is logarithmic, so even small numerical changes represent large effects. A pH drop of 0.1 means the water has become 30 per cent more acidic. If present trends continue, surface pH will drop to around 7.8 by 2100. At that point the water will be 150 per cent more acidic than it was in 1800.

The acidification that has occurred so far is probably irreversible. Although in theory it's possible to add chemicals to the sea to counter the effects of the extra CO_2, as a practical matter, the volumes involved would be staggering; it would take at least two tons of lime, for example, to offset a single ton of carbon dioxide, and the world now emits more than 30 billion tons of CO_2 each year. Meanwhile, natural processes that could counter acidification—such as the weathering of rocks on land—operate far too slowly to make a difference on a human time-scale. Even if CO_2 emissions were somehow to cease today, it would take tens of thousands of years for ocean chemistry to return to its pre-industrial condition.

Acidification has myriad effects. By favoring some marine microbes over others, it is likely to alter the availability of key nutrients like iron and nitrogen. For similar reasons it may let more sunlight penetrate the sea surface. By changing the basic chemistry of seawater, acidification is also expected to reduce the water's ability to absorb and muffle low-frequency sound by up to 40 percent, making some parts of the ocean noisier. Finally, acidification interferes with reproduction in some species and with the ability of others—the so-called calcifiers—to form shells and stony skeletons of calcium carbonate. These last effects are the best documented ones, but whether they will prove the most significant in the long run is unclear.

In 2008 a group of more than 150 leading researchers issued a declaration stating that they were "deeply concerned by recent, rapid changes in ocean chemistry," which could within decades "severely affect marine organisms, food webs, biodiversity, and fisheries." Warm-water coral reefs are the prime worry. But because carbon dioxide dissolves more readily in cold water, the impact may actually show up first closer to the Poles. Scientists have already documented significant effects on pteropods—tiny swimming snails that are an important food for fish, whales, and birds in both the Arctic and the Antarctic. Experiments show that pteropod shells grow more slowly in acidified seawater.

Will organisms be able to adapt to the new ocean chemistry? The evidence from Castello Aragonese is not encouraging. The volcanic vents have been pouring CO_2 into the water for at least a thousand years, Hall-Spencer told me when I visited. But the area where the pH is 7.8—the level that may be reached oceanwide by the end of the century—is missing nearly a third of the species that live nearby, outside the vent system. Those species have had "generations on generations to adapt to these conditions," Hall-Spencer said, "yet they're not there."

"Because it's so important, we humans put a lot of energy into making sure that the pH of our blood is constant," he went on. "But some of these lower organisms, they don't have the physiology to do that. They've just got to tolerate what's happening outside. And so they get pushed beyond their limits."

Fifty miles off the coast of Australia and half a world away from Castello Aragonese lies the equally tiny One Tree Island. One Tree, which actually has several hundred trees, is shaped like a boomerang, with two arms that stretch out into the Coral Sea. In the crook of the boomerang there's a small research station run by the University of Sydney. As it happened, just as I arrived one spectacular summer afternoon, an enormous loggerhead turtle heaved herself up onto the beach in front of the lab buildings. The island's entire human population—11 people, not including me—gathered around to watch.

One Tree Island is part of the Great Barrier Reef, the world's largest reef complex, which stretches for more than 1,400 miles. The entire island is composed of bits of coral rubble, ranging from marble to basketball size, that began piling up after a peculiarly violent storm about 4,000 years ago. Even today, the island has nothing that could really be called dirt. The trees seem to rise up directly out of the rubble like flagpoles.

When scientists first started visiting the island in the 1960s, they posed questions like, How do reefs grow? Nowadays the questions are more urgent. "Something like 25 per cent of all species in the oceans spend at least part of their life in coral reef systems," Ken Caldeira, an expert on ocean acidification at the Carnegie Institution, said one evening before heading out to collect water samples on the reef. "Corals build the architecture of the ecosystem, and it's pretty clear if they go, the whole ecosystem goes."

Coral reefs are already threatened by a wide array of forces. Rising water temperatures are producing more frequent "bleaching" events, when corals turn a stark white and often die. Overfishing removes grazers that keep reefs from being overgrown with algae. Agricultural runoff fertilizes algae, further upsetting reef ecology. In the Caribbean some formerly abundant coral species have been devastated by an infection that leaves behind a white band of dead tissue. Probably owing to all these factors, coral cover in the Caribbean declined by around 80 per cent between 1977 and 2001.

Ocean acidification adds yet another threat, one that may be less immediate but ultimately more devastating to hard, reef-building corals. It undermines their basic, ancient structure—the stony skeleton that's secreted by millions upon millions of coral polyps over thousands of years.

Coral polyps are tiny animals that form a thin layer of living tissue on the surface of a reef. They're shaped a bit like flowers, with six or more tentacles that capture food and feed it to a central mouth. (Many corals actually get most of their food from algae that live and photosynthesize inside them; when corals bleach, it's because stress has prompted the polyps to expel those dark symbionts.) Each polyp surrounds itself with a protective, cup-shaped exoskeleton of calcium carbonate that contributes to the collective skeleton of the whole colony.

To make calcium carbonate, corals need two ingredients: calcium ions and carbonate ions. Acids react with carbonate ions, in effect tying them up. So as atmospheric CO_2 levels rise, carbonate ions become scarcer in the water, and corals have to expend more energy to collect them. Under lab conditions coral skeleton growth has been shown to decline pretty much linearly as the carbonate concentration drops off.

Slow growth may not matter much in the lab. Out in the ocean, though, reefs are constantly being picked at by other organisms, both large and small. (When I went snorkeling off One Tree Island, I could hear parrotfish chomping away at the reef.) "A reef is like a city," said Ove Hoegh-Guldberg, who used to direct the One Tree Island Research Station and now heads the Global Change Institute at Australia's University of Queensland. "You've got construction firms and you've got demolition firms. By restricting the building materials that go to the construction firms, you tip the balance toward destruction, which is going on all the time, even on a healthy reef. In the end you wind up with a city that destroys itself."

By comparing measurements made in the 1970s with those taken more recently, Caldeira's team found that at one location on the northern tip of the reef, calcification had declined by 40 percent. (The team was at One Tree to repeat this study at the southern tip of the reef.) A different team using a different method has found that the growth of *Porites* corals, which form massive, boulder like clumps, declined 14 per cent on the Great Barrier Reef between 1990 and 2005.

Ocean acidification seems to affect corals' ability to produce new colonies as well. Corals can, in effect, clone themselves, and an entire colony is likely to be made up of genetically identical polyps. But once a year, in summer, many species of coral also engage in "mass spawning," a kind of synchronized group sex. Each polyp produces a beadlike pink sac that contains both eggs and sperm. On the night of the spawning all the polyps release their sacs into the water. So many sacs are bobbing around that the waves seem to be covered in a veil of mauve.

Selina Ward, a researcher at the University of Queensland, has been studying coral reproduction on Heron Island, about ten miles west of One Tree, for the past 16 years. I met up with her just a few hours before the annual spawning event. She was keeping tabs on a dozen tanks of gravid corals, like an obstetrician making the rounds of a maternity ward. As soon as the corals released their pink sacs, she was planning to scoop them up and subject them to different levels of acidification. Her results so far suggest that lower pH leads to declines in fertilization, in larval development, and also in settlement—the stage at which the coral larvae drop out of the water column, attach themselves to something solid, and start producing new colonies. "And if any of those steps doesn't work, you're not going to get replacement corals coming into your system," Ward said.

The reefs that corals maintain are crucial to an incredible diversity of organisms. Somewhere between one and nine million marine species live on or around coral reefs. These include not just the fancifully colored fish and enormous turtles that people visit reefs to see, but also sea squirts and shrimps, anemones and clams, sea cucumbers and worms—the list goes on and on. The nooks and crevices on a reef provide homes for many species, which in turn provide resources for many others.

Once a reef can no longer grow fast enough to keep up with erosion, this community will crumble. "Coral reefs will lose their ecological functionality," Jack Silverman, a member of Caldeira's team at One Tree, told me. "They won't be able to maintain their framework. And if you don't have a building, where are the tenants going to live?" That moment could come by 2050. Under the business-as-usual emissions scenario, CO_2 concentrations in the atmosphere will be roughly double what they were in preindustrial times. Many experiments suggest that coral reefs will then start to disintegrate.

"Under business-as-usual, by mid-century things are looking rather grim," Caldeira said. He paused for a moment. "I mean, they're looking grim already."

Corals, of course, are just one kind of calcifier. There are thousands of others. Crustaceans like barnacles are calcifiers, and so are echinoderms like sea stars and sea urchins and mollusks like clams and oysters. Coralline algae—minute organisms that produce what looks like a coating of pink or lilac paint—are also calcifiers. Their calcium carbonate secretions help cement coral reefs together, but they're also found elsewhere—on sea grass at Castello Aragonese, for instance. It was their absence from the grass near the volcanic vents that made it look so green.

The seas are filled with one-celled calcifying plants called coccolithophores, whose seasonal blooms turn thousands of square miles of ocean a milky hue. Many species of planktonic foraminifera—also one-celled—are calcifiers; their dead shells drift down to the ocean floor in what's been described as a never ending rain. Calcifiers are so plentiful they've changed the Earth's geology. England's White Cliffs of Dover, for example, are the remains of countless ancient calcifiers that piled up during the Cretaceous period.

Acidification makes all calcifiers work harder, though some seem better able to cope. In experiments on 18 species belonging to different taxonomic groups, researchers at the Woods Hole Oceanographic Institution found that while a majority calcified less when CO_2 was high, some calcified more. One species—blue mussels—showed no change, no matter how acidified the water.

"Organisms make choices," explained Ulf Riebesell, a biological oceanographer at the Leibniz Institute of Marine Sciences in Kiel, Germany. "They sense the change in their environment, and some of them have the ability to compensate. They just have to invest more energy into calcification. They choose, 'OK, I'll invest less in reproduction' or 'I'll invest less in growth.'" What drives such choices, and whether they're viable over the long term, is not known; most studies so far have been performed on creatures living for a brief time in tanks, without other species that might compete with them. "If I invest less in growth or in reproduction," Riebesell went on, "does it mean that somebody else who does not have to make this choice, because they are not calcifying, will win out and take my spot?"

Meanwhile, scientists are just beginning to explore the way that ocean acidification will affect more-complex organisms such as fish and marine mammals. Changes at the bottom of the marine food web—to shell-forming pteropods, say, or coccolithophores—will inevitably affect the animals higher up. But altering oceanic pH is also likely to have a direct impact on their physiology. Researchers in Australia have found, for example, that young clownfish—the real-life versions of Nemo—can't find their way to suitable habitat when CO_2 is elevated. Apparently the acidified water impairs their sense of smell.

During the long history of life on Earth, atmospheric carbon dioxide levels have often been higher than they are today. But only very rarely—if ever—have they risen as quickly as right now. For life in the oceans, it's probably the rate of change that matters.

To find a period analogous to the present, you have to go back at least 55 million years, to what's known as the Paleocene-Eocene Thermal Maximum or PETM. During the PETM huge quantities of carbon were released into the atmosphere, from where, no one is quite sure. Temperatures around the world soared by around ten degrees Fahrenheit, and marine chemistry changed dramatically. The ocean depths became so corrosive that in many places shells stopped piling up on the seafloor and simply dissolved. In sediment cores the period shows up as a layer of red clay sandwiched between two white layers of calcium carbonate. Many deep-water species of foraminifera went extinct.

Surprisingly, though, most organisms that live near the sea surface seem to have come through the PETM just fine. Perhaps marine life is more resilient than the results from places like Castello Aragonese and One Tree Island seem to indicate. Or perhaps the PETM, while extreme, was not as extreme as what's happening today.

The sediment record doesn't reveal how fast the PETM carbon release occurred. But modeling studies suggest it took place over thousands of years—slow enough for the chemical effects to spread through the entire ocean to its depths. Today's rate of emissions seems to be roughly ten times as fast, and there's not enough time for the water layers to mix. In the coming century acidification will be concentrated near the surface, where most marine calcifiers and all tropical corals reside. "What we're doing now is quite geologically special," says climate scientist Andy Ridgwell of the University of Bristol, who has modeled the PETM ocean.

Just how special is up to us. It's still possible to avert the most extreme acidification scenarios. But the only way to do this, or at least the only way anyone has come up with so far, is to dramatically reduce CO_2 emissions. At the moment, corals and pteropods are lined up against a global economy built on cheap fossil fuels. It's not a fair fight.

Credit

Kolbert, Elizabeth. "The Acid Sea." *National Geographic* 1 Apr. 2011. Print.

Our Oceans are Turning into Plastic ... are You?

A vast swath of the Pacific twice the size of Texas is full of plastic stew that is entering the food chain. Scientists say it's causing obesity, infertility ... and worse.

Photographs by Gregg Segal

Susan Casey

Plastic Plague: (left) A jellyfish whose tentacles became entangled in plastic line; (right) A sample of the North Pacific gyre—a virtual trash dump where plastic outweighs plankton by a ratio of 6 to 1.

Man in the Plastic Bubble: Captain Charles Moore shows off a sample of our plastic ocean aboard the *Alguita* on his 2002 voyage to the gyre.

Fate can take strange forms, and so perhaps it does not seem unusual that Captain Charles Moore found his life's purpose in a nightmare. Unfortunately, he was awake at the time, and 800 miles north of Hawaii in the Pacific Ocean. It happened on August 3, 1997, a lovely day, at least in the beginning: Sunny. Little wind. Water the color of sapphires. Moore and the crew of *Alguita*, his 50-foot aluminum-hulled catamaran, sliced through the sea.

Returning to Southern California from Hawaii after a sailing race, Moore had altered *Alguita's* course, veering slightly north. He had the time and the curiosity to try a new route, one that would lead the vessel through the eastern corner of a 10-million-square-mile oval known as the North Pacific subtropical gyre. This was an odd stretch of ocean, a place most boats purposely avoided. For one thing, it was becalmed. "The doldrums," sailors called it, and they steered clear. So did the ocean's top predators: the tuna, sharks, and other large fish that required livelier waters, flush with prey. The gyre was more like a desert—a slow, deep, clockwise-swirling vortex of air and water caused by a mountain of high-pressure air that lingered above it.

The area's reputation didn't deter Moore. He had grown up in Long Beach, 40 miles south of L.A., the Pacific literally in his front yard, and he possessed an impressive aquatic résumé: deckhand, able seaman, sailor, scuba diver, surfer, and finally captain. Moore had spent countless hours in the ocean, fascinated by its vast trove of secrets and terrors. He'd seen a lot of things out there, things that were glorious and grand; things that were ferocious and humbling. But he had never seen anything nearly as chilling as what lay ahead of him in the gyre.

It began with a line of plastic bags ghosting the surface, followed by an ugly tangle of junk: nets and ropes and bottles, motor oil jugs and cracked bath toys, a mangled tarp. Tires. A traffic cone. Moore could not believe his eyes. Out here in this desolate place, the water was a stew of plastic crap. It was as though someone had taken the pristine seascape of his youth and swapped it for a landfill.

How did all the plastic end up here? How did this trash tsunami begin? What did it mean? If the questions seemed overwhelming, Moore would soon learn that the answers were even more so, and that his discovery had dire implications for human—and planetary—health. As *Alguita* glided through the area that scientists now refer to as the "Eastern Garbage Patch," Moore realized that the trail of plastic went on for hundreds of miles. Depressed and stunned, he sailed for a week through bobbing, toxic debris trapped in a purgatory of circling currents. To his horror, he had stumbled across the 21st century Leviathan. It had no head, no tail. Just an endless body.

ঔ

"Everybody's plastic, but I love plastic. I want to be plastic." This Andy Warhol quote is emblazoned on a six-foot-long magenta and yellow banner that hangs—with extreme irony—in the solar-powered workshop in Moore's Long Beach home. The workshop is surrounded by a crazy Eden of trees, bushes, flowers, and fruits, as well as vegetables ranging from the prosaic (tomatoes) to the exotic (cherimoyas, guavas, chocolate persimmons, white figs the size of baseballs). This is the house in which Moore, 59, was raised, and it has a kind of open-air earthiness that reflects his sixties-activist roots, which included a stint in a Berkeley commune. Composting and organic gardening are serious business here—you can practically smell the humus—but there is also a kidney-shaped hot tub surrounded by palm trees. Two wet suits hang drying on a clothesline above it.

Plastic Bullets: An albatross on Kure Atoll that mistook too many floating plastic particles for baitfish.

This afternoon, Moore strides the grounds. "How about a nice, fresh boysenberry?" he asks, and plucks one off a bush. He's a striking man wearing no-nonsense black trousers and a shirt with official-looking epaulettes. A thick brush of salt-and-pepper hair frames his intense blue eyes and serious face. But the first thing you notice about Moore is his voice, a deep, bemused drawl that becomes animated and sardonic when the subject turns to plastic pollution. This problem is Moore's calling, a passion he inherited from his father, an industrial chemist who studied waste management as a hobby. On family vacations, Moore recalls, part of the agenda would be to see what the locals threw out. "We could be in paradise, but we would go to the dump," he says, with a shrug. "That's what we wanted to see."

Since his first encounter with the Garbage Patch nine years ago, Moore has been on a mission to learn exactly what's going on out there. Leaving behind a 25-year career running a furniture-restoration business, he has created Algalita Marine Research Foundation to spread the word of his findings. He has resumed his science studies, which he'd set aside when his attention swerved from pursuing a university degree to protesting the Vietnam War. His tireless effort has placed him on the front lines of this new, more abstract battle. After enlisting scientists such as Steven B. Weisberg, Ph.D. (director of the Southern California Coastal Water Research Project and an expert in marine environmental monitoring), to develop methods for analyzing the gyre's contents, Moore has sailed *Alguita* back to the Garbage Patch several times. On each trip, the volume of plastic has grown alarmingly. The area in which it accumulates is now twice the size of Texas.

At the same time, all over the globe, there are signs that plastic pollution is doing more than blighting the scenery; that it is also making its way into the food chain. Some of the most obvious victims are the dead seabirds that have been washing ashore in startling numbers, their bodies packed with plastic: things like bottle caps, cigarette lighters, tampon applicators, and colored scraps that, to a foraging bird, resemble baitfish. (One animal dissected by Dutch researchers contained 1,603 pieces of plastic.) And the birds aren't alone. All sea creatures are threatened by floating plastic, from whales down to zooplankton. There's basic moral horror in seeing the pictures: a sea turtle with a plastic band strangling its shell into an hourglass shape; a humpback towing plastic nets that cut into its flesh and make it impossible for the animal to hunt. More than a million seabirds, 100,000 marine mammals, and countless fish die in the North Pacific each year, either from mistakenly eating this junk or from being ensnared in it and drowning.

Plastic Bullets: A turtle that grew in to an hourglass shape after swimming through a plastic ring.

Bad enough. But Moore soon learned that the big, tentacled balls of trash were only the most visible signs of the problem; others were far less obvious, and far more evil. Dragging a fine-meshed net known as a manta trawl, he discovered minuscule pieces of plastic, some barely visible to the eye, swirling like fish food throughout the water. He and his researchers parsed, measured, and sorted their samples and arrived at the following conclusion: By weight, this swath of sea contains six times as much plastic as it does plankton.

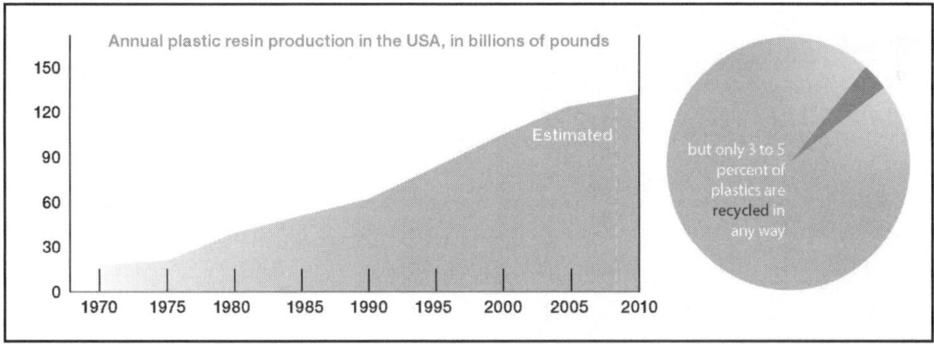

This statistic is grim—for marine animals, of course, but even more so for humans. The more invisible and ubiquitous the pollution, the more likely it will end up inside us. And there's growing—and disturbing—proof that we're ingesting plastic toxins constantly, and that even slight doses of these substances can severely disrupt gene activity. "Every one of us has this huge body burden," Moore says. "You could take your serum to a lab now, and they'd find at least 100 industrial chemicals that weren't around in 1950." The fact that these toxins don't cause violent and immediate reactions does not mean they're benign: Scientists are just beginning to research the long-term ways in which the chemicals used to make plastic interact with our own biochemistry.

ଔ

In simple terms, plastic is a petroleum-based mix of monomers that become polymers, to which additional chemicals—such as di (2-ethylhexyl) phthalate (DEHP) and polybrominated biphenyls (PBBs)—are added for suppleness, inflammability, and other qualities. When it comes to these substances, even the syllables are scary. For instance, if you're thinking that perfluorooctanoic acid (PFOA) isn't something you want to sprinkle on your microwave popcorn, you're right. Recently, the Science Advisory Board of the Environmental Protection Agency (EPA) voted PFOA a likely carcinogen. And yet when your butter deluxe meets your superheated microwave oven, so much PFOA leaches into the popcorn oil from the product packaging that a single serving spikes the amount of this poison in your blood.

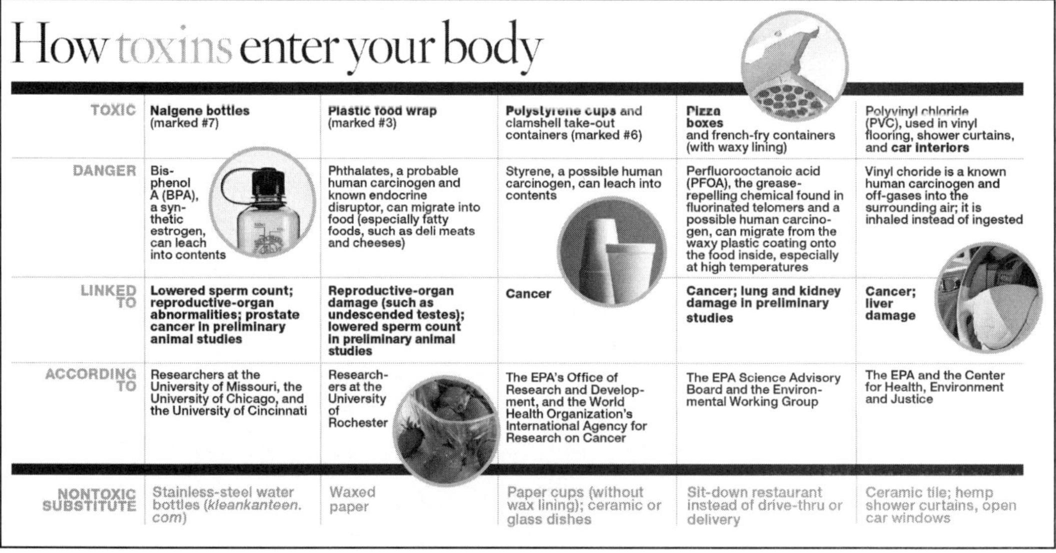

How toxins enter your body

TOXIC	**Nalgene bottles** (marked #7)	**Plastic food wrap** (marked #3)	**Polystyrene cups** and clamshell take-out containers (marked #6)	**Pizza boxes** and french-fry containers (with waxy lining)	Polyvinyl chloride (PVC), used in vinyl flooring, shower curtains, and **car interiors**
DANGER	Bisphenol A (BPA), a synthetic estrogen, can leach into contents	Phthalates, a probable human carcinogen and known endocrine disruptor, can migrate into food (especially fatty foods, such as deli meats and cheeses)	Styrene, a possible human carcinogen, can leach into contents	Perfluorooctanoic acid (PFOA), the grease-repelling chemical found in fluorinated telomers and a possible human carcinogen, can migrate from the waxy plastic coating onto the food inside, especially at high temperatures	Vinyl choride is a known human carcinogen and off-gases into the surrounding air; it is inhaled instead of ingested
LINKED TO	**Lowered sperm count; reproductive-organ abnormalities; prostate cancer in preliminary animal studies**	**Reproductive-organ damage (such as undescended testes); lowered sperm count in preliminary animal studies**	**Cancer**	**Cancer; lung and kidney damage in preliminary studies**	**Cancer; liver damage**
ACCORDING TO	Researchers at the University of Missouri, the University of Chicago, and the University of Cincinnati	Researchers at the University of Rochester	The EPA's Office of Research and Development, and the World Health Organization's International Agency for Research on Cancer	The EPA Science Advisory Board and the Environmental Working Group	The EPA and the Center for Health, Environment and Justice
NONTOXIC SUBSTITUTE	Stainless-steel water bottles (*kleankanteen.com*)	Waxed paper	Paper cups (without wax lining); ceramic or glass dishes	Sit-down restaurant instead of drive-thru or delivery	Ceramic tile; hemp shower curtains, open car windows

Other nasty chemical additives are the flame retardants known as polybrominated diphenyl ethers (PBDEs). These chemicals have been shown to cause liver and thyroid toxicity, reproductive problems, and memory loss in preliminary animal studies. In vehicle interiors, PBDEs—used in moldings and floor coverings, among other things—combine with another group called phthalates to create that much-vaunted "new-car smell." Leave your new wheels in the hot sun for a few hours, and these substances can "off-gas" at an accelerated rate, releasing noxious byproducts.

It's not fair, however, to single out fast food and new cars. PBDEs, to take just one example, are used in many products, incuding computers, carpeting, and paint. As for phthalates, we deploy about a billion pounds of them a year worldwide despite the fact that California recently listed this as a chemical known to be toxic to our reproductive systems. Used to make plastic soft and pliable, phthalates leach easily from millions of products—food, cosmetics, varnishes, the coatings of timed-release pharmaceuticals—into our blood, urine, saliva, seminal fluid, breast milk, and amniotic fluid. In food containers and plastic bottles, phthalates are now found with another compound called bisphenol A (BPA), which scientists are now discovering can wreak stunning havoc in the body. We produce 6 billion pounds of that each year, and it shows: BPA has been found in nearly every human who has been tested in the United States. We're eating these plasticizing additives, drinking them, breathing them, and absorbing them through our skin every single day.

Most alarming, these chemicals may disrupt the endocrine system—the delicately balanced set of hormones and glands that affect virtually every organ and cell—by mimicking the female hormone estrogen. In marine environments, excess estrogen has led to *Twilight Zone*-esque discoveries of male fish and seagulls that have sprouted female sex organs.

On land, things are equally gruesome. "Fertility rates have been declining for quite some time now, and exposure to synthetic estrogen—especially from the chemicals found in plastic products—can have an adverse effect," says Marc Goldstein, M.D., director of the Cornell Institute for Reproductive Medicine. Dr. Goldstein also notes that pregnant women are particularly vulnerable: "Prenatal exposure, even in very low doses, can cause irreversible damage in an unborn baby's reproductive organs." And after the baby is born, he or she is hardly out of the woods. Frederick vom Saal, Ph.D., a professor at the University of Missouri at Columbia who specifically studies estrogenic chemicals in plastics, warns parents to "steer clear of polycarbonate baby bottles. They're particularly dangerous for newborns whose brains, immune systems, and gonads are still developing." Vom Saal's research spurred him to throw out every polycarbonate plastic item in his house, and to stop buying plastic-wrapped food and canned goods (cans are plastic-lined) at the grocery store. "We now know that BPA causes prostate cancer in mice and rats, and abnormalities in the prostate's stem cell, which is the cell implicated in human prostate cancer," he says. "That's enough to scare the hell out of me." At Tufts University, Ana M. Soto, M.D., a professor of anatomy and cellular biology, has also found connections between these chemicals and breast cancer.

As if the potential for cancer and mutation weren't enough, Dr. Vom Saal says "prenatal exposure to very low doses of BPA increases the rate of postnatal growth in mice and rats." In other words, BPA made rodents fat. Their insulin output surged wildly and then crashed into a state of resistance—the virtual definition of diabetes. They produced bigger fat cells, and more of them. A recent scientific paper Dr. Vom Saal coauthored contains this chilling sentence: "These findings suggest that developmental exposure to BPA is contributing to the obesity epidemic that has occurred during the last two decades in the developed world, associated with the dramatic increase in the amount of plastic being produced each year." Given this, it is perhaps not entirely coincidental that America's dramatic rise in diabetes—a 735 per cent increase since 1935—follows the same arc.

☙❧

Such news is depressing enough to make a person reach for the bottle. Glass, at least, is easily recyclable. You can take one tequila bottle, melt it down, and make another tequila bottle. With plastic, recycling is more complicated. Unfortunately, that promising-looking triangle of arrows that appears on products doesn't signify endless reuse; it merely identifies which type of plastic the item is made from. And of the seven different plastics in common use, only two of them—PET (#1, used in soda bottles) and HDPE (#2, used in milk jugs)—have much of an aftermarket. So no matter how virtuously you toss your chip bags and shampoo bottles into your blue bin, few of them will escape the landfill—only 3 to 5 per cent of plastics are recycled in any way.

"There's no legal way to recycle a milk container into another milk container without adding a new virgin layer of plastic," Moore says, pointing out that because plastic melts at low temperatures, it retains pollutants and the tainted residue of its former contents. Turn up the heat to sear these off, and some plastics release deadly vapors.

So the reclaimed stuff is mostly used to make entirely different products, things that don't go anywhere near our mouths, such as fleece jackets and carpeting. Therefore, unlike glass, metal, or paper, recycling plastic doesn't always result in less use of virgin material. It also doesn't help that fresh-made plastic is far cheaper.

Moore routinely finds half-melted blobs of plastic in the ocean, as though the person doing the burning realized partway through the process that this was a bad idea, and stopped (or passed out from the fumes). "That's a concern as plastic proliferates worldwide, and people run out of room for trash and start burning plastic—you're producing some of the most toxic gases known," he says. The color-coded bin system may be alive and well in Marin County, but it is somewhat less effective in subequatorial Africa or rural Peru.

"Except for the small amount that's been incinerated—and it's a very small amount—every bit of plastic ever made still exists," Moore says, describing how the material's molecular structure resists biodegradation. Instead, plastic crumbles into ever-tinier fragments as it's exposed to sunlight and the elements. And none of these untold gazillions of fragments is disappearing anytime soon: Even when plastic is broken down to a single molecule, it remains too tough for biodegradation.

Truth is, no one knows how long it will take for plastic to biodegrade, or return to its carbon and hydrogen elements. We only invented the stuff 144 years ago, and science's best guess is that its natural disappearance will take several more centuries. Meanwhile, every year, we churn out 60 billion tons of it, much of which becomes disposable products meant only for a single use. Set aside the question of why we're creating ketchup bottles and six–pack rings that last for half a millennium, and consider the implications of it: *Plastic never really goes away.*

Ask a group of people to name an overwhelming global problem, and you'll hear about climate change, the Middle East, or AIDS. No one, it is guaranteed, will cite the sloppy transport of nurdles as a concern. And yet nurdles, lentil–size pellets of plastic in its rawest form, are especially effective couriers of waste chemicals called persistent organic pollutants, or POPs, which include known carcinogens such as DDT and PCBs. The United States banned these poisons in the 1970s, but they remain stubbornly at large in the environment, where they latch on to plastic because of its molecular tendency to attract oils.

The word itself—*nurdles*—sounds cuddly and harmless, like a cartoon character or a pasta for kids, but the thing that it refers to is most certainly not. Absorbing up to a million times the level of POP pollution in their surrounding waters, nurdles become supersaturated poison pills. They're light enough to blow around like dust, to spill out of shipping containers, and to wash into harbors, storm drains, and creeks. In the ocean, nurdles are easily mistaken for fish eggs by creatures that would very much like to have such a snack. And once inside the body of a bigeye tuna or a king salmon, these tenacious chemicals are headed directly to your dinner table.

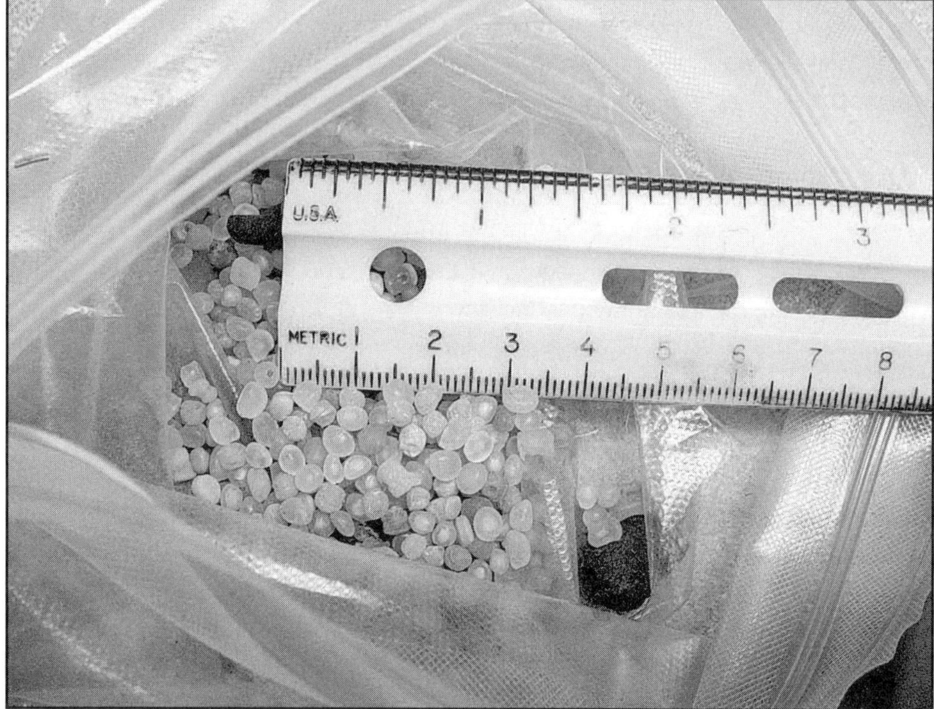

Poison Pellets: Plastic pellets known as nurdles soak up toxins like DDT and can now be found mixed in with beach sand around the world.

One study sponsored by the California Water Resources Control Board estimated that nurdles now account for 10 per cent of plastic ocean debris. And once they're scattered in the environment, they're diabolically hard to clean up (think wayward confetti). At places as remote as Rarotonga, in the Cook Islands, 2,100 miles northeast of New Zealand and a 12-hour flight from L.A., they're commonly found mixed with beach sand. In 2004, Moore received a $500,000 grant from the state of California to investigate the myriad ways in which nurdles go astray during the plastic manufacturing process. On a visit to a polyvinyl chloride (PVC) pipe factory, as he walked through an area where railcars unloaded ground-up nurdles, he noticed that his pant cuffs were filled with a fine plastic dust. Turning a corner, he saw windblown drifts of nurdles piled against a fence. Talking about the experience, Moore's voice becomes strained and his words pour out in an urgent tumble: "It's not the big trash on the beach. It's the fact that the whole biosphere is becoming mixed with these plastic particles. What are they doing to us? We're breathing them, the fish are eating them, they're in our hair, they're in our skin."

Though marine dumping is part of the problem, escaped nurdles and other plastic litter migrate to the gyre largely from land. That polystyrene cup you saw floating in the creek, if it doesn't get picked up and specifically taken to a landfill, will eventually be washed out to sea. Once there, it will have plenty of places to go: The North Pacific gyre is only one of five such high-pressure zones in the oceans. There are similar areas in the South Pacific, the North and South Atlantic, and the Indian Ocean. Each of these gyres has its own version of the Garbage Patch, as plastic gathers in the currents. Together, these areas cover 40 per cent of the sea. "That corresponds to a quarter of the earth's surface," Moore says. "So twenty-five per cent of our planet is a toilet that never flushes."

❧❧❧

It wasn't supposed to be this way. In 1865, a few years after Alexander Parkes unveiled the first man-made plastic, a scientist named John W. Hyatt set out to make a synthetic replacement for ivory billiard balls. He had the best of intentions: Save the elephants! After some tinkering, he created celluloid. From then on, each year brought a miraculous recipe: rayon in 1891, Teflon in 1938, Velcro in 1957. Durable, cheap, versatile—plastic seemed like a miracle. And in many ways, it was. Plastic has given us bulletproof vests, credit cards, slinky spandex pants. It has led to breakthroughs in medicine, aerospace engineering, and computer science. And who among us doesn't own a Frisbee?

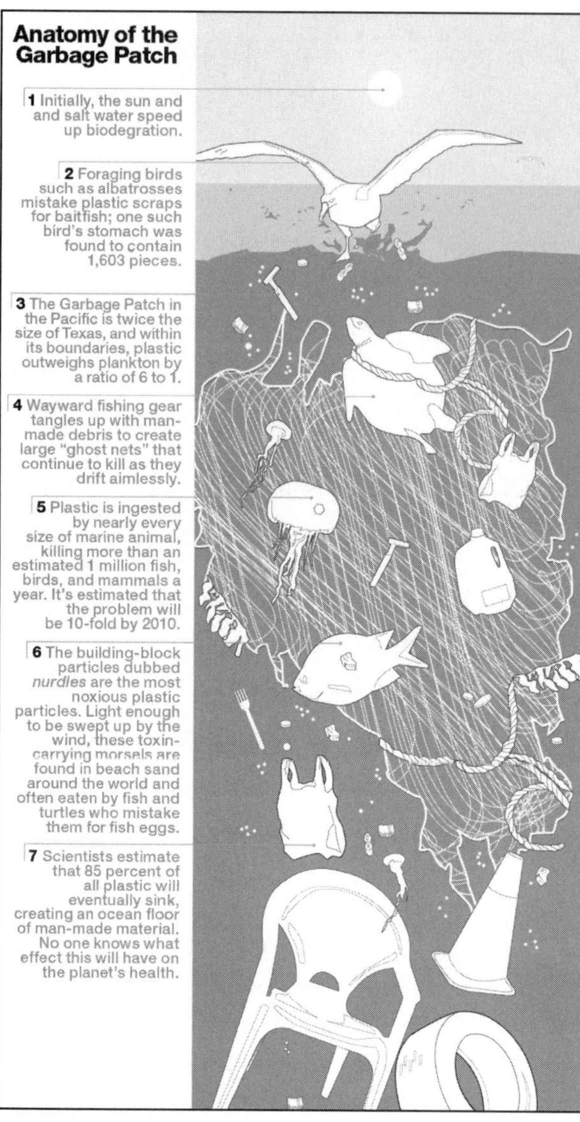

That plastic has benefits, no one would deny. Few of us, however, are as enthusiastic as the American Plastics Council. One of its recent press releases, titled "Plastic Bags—A Family's Trusted Companion," reads: "Very few people remember what life was like before plastic bags became an icon of convenience and practicality—and now art. Remember the 'beautiful' [sic] swirling, floating bag in *American Beauty*?"

Alas, the same ephemeral quality that allows bags to dance gracefully across the big screen also lands them in many less desirable places. Twenty-three countries, including Germany, South Africa, and Australia, have banned, taxed, or restricted the use of plastic bags because they clog sewers and lodge in the throats of livestock. Like pernicious Kleenex, these flimsy sacks end up snagged in trees and snarled in fences, blighting the scenery. They also trap rainwater, creating perfect little breeding ponds for disease-carrying mosquitoes.

In the face of public outrage over pictures of dolphins choking on "a family's trusted companion," the American Plastics Council takes a defensive stance, sounding not unlike the NRA: Plastics don't pollute, people do.

It has a point. Each of us tosses about 185 pounds of plastic per year. We could certainly reduce that. And yet—do our products have to be quite so lethal? Must a discarded flip-flop remain with us until the end of time? Aren't disposable razors and foam packing peanuts a poor consolation prize for the destruction of the world's oceans, not to mention our own bodies and the health of future generations? "If 'more is better' and that's the only mantra we have, we're doomed," Moore says, summing it up.

Oceanographer Curtis Ebbesmeyer, Ph.D., an expert on marine debris, agrees. "If you could fast-forward 10,000 years and do an archaeological dig ... you'd find a little line of plastic," he told *The Seattle Times* last April. "What happened to those people? Well, they ate their own plastic and disrupted their genetic structure and weren't able to reproduce. They didn't last very long because they killed themselves."

Wrist-slittingly depressing, yes, but there are glimmers of hope on the horizon. Green architect and designer William McDonough has become an influential voice, not only in environmental circles but among Fortune 500 CEOs. McDonough proposes a standard known as "cradle to cradle" in which all manufactured things must be reusable, poison-free, and beneficial over the long haul. His outrage is obvious when he holds up a rubber ducky, a common child's bath toy. The duck is made of phthalate-laden PVC and bears a warning about cancer and reproductive harm. "What kind of people are we that we would design like this?" McDonough asks. In the United States, it's commonly accepted that children's teething rings, cosmetics, food wrappers, cars, and textiles will be made from toxic materials. Other countries—and many individual companies—seem to be reconsidering. Currently, McDonough is working with the Chinese government to build seven cities using "the building materials of the future," including a fabric that is safe enough to eat and a new, nontoxic polystyrene.

Thanks to people like Moore and McDonough, and media hits such as Al Gore's *An Inconvenient Truth*, awareness of just how hard we've bitch-slapped the planet is skyrocketing. After all, unless we're planning to colonize Mars soon, this is where we live, and none of us would choose to live in a toxic wasteland or to spend our days getting pumped full of drugs to deal with our haywire endocrine systems and runaway cancer.

None of plastic's problems can be fixed overnight, but the more we learn, the more likely that, eventually, wisdom will trump convenience and cheap disposability. In the meantime, let the cleanup begin: The National Oceanographic & Atmospheric Administration (NOAA) is aggressively using satellites to identify and remove "ghost nets," abandoned plastic fishing gear that never stops killing. (A single net recently hauled up off the Florida coast contained more than 1,000 dead fish, sharks, and one loggerhead turtle.) New biodegradable starch- and corn-based plastics have arrived, and Wal-Mart has signed on as a customer. A consumer rebellion against dumb and excessive packaging is afoot. And in August 2006, Moore was invited to speak about "marine debris and hormone disruption" at a meeting in Sicily convened by the science advisor to the Vatican. This annual gathering, called the International Seminars on Planetary Emergencies, brings scientists together to discuss mankind's worst threats. Past topics have included nuclear holocaust and terrorism.

Ghost Killers: The *Alguita's* crew deploys a tracking buoy on fishing gear that was either discarded or lost at sea and has now amassed with other wayward debris.

꧁

The gray plastic kayak floats next to Moore's catamaran, *Alguita*, which lives in a slip across from his house. It is not a lovely kayak; in fact, it looks pretty rough. But it's floating, a sturdy, eight-foot-long two-seater. Moore stands on *Alguita*'s deck, hands on hips, staring down at it. On the sailboat next to him, his neighbor, Cass Bastain, does the same. He has just informed Moore that he came across the abandoned craft yesterday, floating 3 yards offshore. The two men shake their heads in bewilderment. "That's probably a six-hundred-dollar kayak," Moore says, adding, "I don't even shop anymore. Anything I need will just float by." (In his opinion, the movie *Cast Away* was a joke—Tom Hanks could've built a village with the crap that would've washed ashore during a storm.)

Watching the kayak bobbing disconsolately, it is hard not to wonder what will become of it. The world is full of cooler, sexier kayaks. It is also full of cheap plastic kayaks that come in more attractive colors than battleship gray. The ownerless kayak is a lummox of a boat, 50 pounds of nurdles extruded into an object that nobody wants but that'll be around for centuries longer than we will.

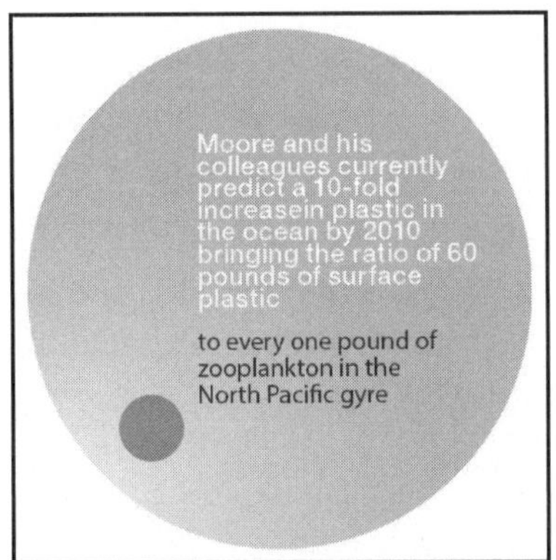

And as Moore stands on deck looking into the water, it is easy to imagine him doing the same thing 800 miles west, in the gyre. You can see his silhouette in the silvering light, caught between ocean and sky. You can see the mercurial surface of the most majestic body of water on earth. And then below, you can see the half-submerged madhouse of forgotten and discarded things. As Moore looks over the side of the boat, you can see the seabirds sweeping overhead, dipping, and skimming the water. One of the journeying birds, sleek as a fighter plane, carries a scrap of something yellow in its beak. The bird dives low and then boomerangs over the horizon. Gone.

Credit

My Genome, My Self

Steven Pinker

One of the perks of being a psychologist is access to tools that allow you to carry out the injunction to know thyself. I have been tested for vocational interest (closest match: psychologist), intelligence (above average), personality (open, conscientious, agreeable, average in extroversion, not too neurotic), and political orientation (neither leftist nor rightist, more libertarian than authoritarian). I have MRI pictures of my brain (no obvious holes or bulges) and soon will undergo the ultimate test of marital love: my brain will be scanned while my wife's name is subliminally flashed before my eyes.

Last fall I submitted to the latest high-tech way to bare your soul. I had my genome sequenced and am allowing it to be posted on the Internet, along with my medical history. The opportunity arose when the biologist George Church sought ten volunteers to kick off his audacious Personal Genome Project. The PGP has created a public database that will contain the genomes and traits of one hundred thousand people. Tapping the magic of crowd sourcing that gave us Wikipedia and Google rankings, the project seeks to engage geneticists in a worldwide effort to sift through the genetic and environmental predictors of medical, physical, and behavioral traits.

The Personal Genome Project is an initiative in basic research, not personal discovery. Yet the technological advance making it possible—the plunging cost of genome sequencing—will soon give people an unprecedented opportunity to contemplate their own biological and even psychological makeups. We have entered the era of consumer genetics. At one end of the price range you can get a complete sequence and analysis of your genome from Knome (often pronounced "know me") for $99,500. At the other you can get a sample of traits, disease risks, and ancestry data from 23andMe for $399. The science journal *Nature* listed "Personal Genomics Goes Mainstream" as a top news story of 2008.

Like the early days of the Internet, the dawn of personal genomics promises benefits and pitfalls that no one can foresee. It could usher in an era of personalized medicine, in which drug regimens are customized for a patient's biochemistry rather than juggled through trial and error, and screening and prevention measures are aimed at those who are most at risk. It opens up a niche for bottom-feeding companies to terrify hypochondriacs by turning dubious probabilities into Genes of Doom. Depending on who has access to the information, personal genomics could bring about national health insurance, leapfrogging decades of debate, because piecemeal insurance is not viable in a world in which insurers can cherry-pick the most risk-free customers, or in which at-risk customers can load up on lavish insurance.

The pitfalls of personal genomics have already made it a subject of government attention. In 2008 President Bush signed the Genetic Information Nondiscrimination Act, outlawing discrimination in employment and health insurance based on genetic data. And the states of California and New York took action against the direct-to-consumer companies, arguing that what they provide are medical tests and thus can be ordered only by a doctor.

With the genome no less than with the Internet, information wants to be free, and I doubt that paternalistic measures can stifle the industry for long (but then, I have a libertarian temperament). For better or for worse, people will want to know about their genomes. The human mind is prone to essentialism—the intuition that living things house some hidden substance that gives them their form and determines their powers. Over the past century, this essence has become increasingly concrete. Growing out of the early, vague idea that traits are "in the blood," the essence became identified with the abstractions discovered by Gregor Mendel called genes, and then with the iconic double helix of DNA. But DNA has long been an invisible molecule accessible only to a white-coated priesthood. Today, for the price of a flat-screen TV, people can read their essence as a printout detailing their very own A's, C's, T's, and G's.

A firsthand familiarity with the code of life is bound to confront us with the emotional, moral, and political baggage associated with the idea of our essential nature. People have long been familiar with tests for heritable disease, and the use of genetics to trace ancestry—the new *Roots*—is becoming familiar as well. But we are only beginning to recognize that our genome also contains information about our temperaments and abilities. Affordable genotyping may offer new kinds of answers to the question "Who am I?"—to ruminations about our ancestry, our vulnerabilities, our character, and our choices in life.

Over the years I have come to appreciate how elusive the answers to those questions can be. During my first book tour fifteen years ago, an interviewer noted that the paleontologist Stephen Jay Gould had dedicated his first book to his father, who took him to see the dinosaurs when he was five. What was the event that made me become a cognitive psychologist who studies language? I was dumbstruck. The only thing that came to mind was that the human mind is uniquely interesting and that as soon as I learned you could study it for a living, I knew that that was what I wanted to do. But that response would not just have been charmless; it would also have failed to answer the question. Millions of people are exposed to cognitive psychology in college but have no interest in making a career of it. What made it so attractive to *me?*

As I stared blankly, the interviewer suggested that perhaps it was because I grew up in Quebec in the 1970s when language, our preeminent cognitive capacity, figured so prominently in debates about the future of the province. I quickly agreed—and silently vowed to come up with something better for the next time. Now I say that my formative years were a time of raging debates about the political implications of human nature, or that my parents subscribed to a *Time-Life* series of science books, and my eye was caught by the one called *The Mind*, or that one day a friend took me to hear a lecture by the great Canadian psychologist D. O. Hebb, and I was hooked. But it is all humbug. The very fact that I had to think so hard brought home what scholars of autobiography and memoir have long recognized. None of us know what made us what we are, and when we have to say something, we make up a good story.

An obvious candidate for the real answer is that we are shaped by our genes in ways that no one of us can directly know. Of course genes can't pull the levers of our behavior directly. But they affect the wiring and workings of the brain, and the brain is the seat of our drives, temperaments, and patterns of thought. Each of us is dealt a unique hand of tastes and aptitudes, like curiosity, ambition, empathy, a thirst for novelty or for security, a comfort level with the social or the mechanical or the abstract. Some opportunities we come across click with our constitutions and set us along a path in life.

This hardly seems radical—any parent of more than one child will tell you that babies come into the world with distinct personalities. But what can anyone say about how the baby got to be that way? Until recently, the only portents on offer were traits that ran in the family, and even they conflated genetic tendencies with family traditions. Now, at least in theory, personal genomics can offer a more precise explanation. We might be able to identify the actual genes that incline a person to being nasty or nice, an egghead or a doer, a sad sack or a blithe spirit.

Looking to the genome for the nature of the person is far from innocuous. In the twentieth century, many intellectuals embraced the idea that babies are blank slates that are inscribed by parents and society. It allowed them to distance themselves from toxic doctrines like that of a superior race, the eugenic breeding of a better species, or a genetic version of the Twinkie Defense in which individuals or society could evade responsibility by saying that it's all in the genes. When it came to human behavior, the attitude toward genetics was "Don't go there." Those who did go there found themselves picketed, tarred as Nazis and genetic determinists, or, in the case of the biologist E. O. Wilson, doused with a pitcher of ice water at a scientific conference.

Today, as the lessons of history have become clearer, the taboo is fading. Though the twentieth century saw horrific genocides inspired by Nazi pseudoscience about genetics and race, it also saw horrific genocides inspired by Marxist pseudoscience about the malleability of human nature. The real threat to humanity comes from totalizing ideologies and the denial of human rights, rather than a curiosity about nature and nurture. Today it is the humane democracies of Scandinavia that are hotbeds of research in behavioral genetics, and two of the groups who were historically most victimized by racial pseudoscience—Jews and African Americans—are among the most avid consumers of information about their genes.

Nor should the scare word "determinism" get in the way of understanding our genetic roots. For some conditions, like Huntington's disease, genetic determinism is simply correct: everyone with the defective gene who lives long enough will develop the condition. But for most other traits, any influence of the genes will be probabilistic. Having a version of a gene may change the odds, making you more or less likely to have a trait, all things being equal, but as we shall see, the actual outcome depends on a tangle of other circumstances as well.

❧❧❧

With personal genomics in its infancy, we can't know whether it will deliver usable information about our psychological traits. But evidence from old-fashioned behavioral genetics—studies of twins, adoptees, and other kinds of relatives—suggests that those genes are in there somewhere. Though once vilified as fraud-infested crypto-eugenics, behavioral genetics has accumulated sophisticated methodologies and replicable findings, which can tell us how much we can ever expect to learn about ourselves from personal genomics.

To study something scientifically, you first have to measure it, and psychologists have developed tests for many mental traits. And contrary to popular opinion, the tests work pretty well: they give a similar measurement of a person every time they are administered, and they statistically predict life outcome like school and job performance, psychiatric diagnosis, and marital stability. Tests for intelligence might ask people to recite a string of digits backward, define a word like "predicament," identify what an egg and a seed have in common, or assemble four triangles into a square. Personality tests ask people to agree or disagree with statements like "Often I cross the street in order not to meet someone I know," "I often was in trouble in school," "Before I do something I try to consider how my friends will react to it," and "People say insulting and vulgar things about me." People's answers to a large set of these questions tend to vary in five major ways: openness to experience, conscientiousness, extroversion, agreeableness (as opposed to antagonism), and neuroticism. The scores can then be compared with those of relatives who vary in relatedness and family backgrounds.

The most prominent finding of behavioral genetics has been summarized by the psychologist Eric Turkheimer: "The nature-nurture debate is over … All human behavioral traits are heritable." By this he meant that a substantial fraction of the variation among individuals within a culture can be linked to variation in their genes. Whether you measure intelligence or personality, religiosity or political orientation, television watching or cigarette smoking, the outcome is the same. Identical twins (who share all their genes) are more similar than fraternal twins (who share half their genes that vary among people). Biological siblings (who share half those genes too) are more similar than adopted siblings (who share no more genes than do strangers). And identical twins separated at birth and raised in different adoptive homes (who share their genes but not their environments) are uncannily similar.

Behavioral geneticists like Turkheimer are quick to add that many of the differences among people *cannot* be attributed to their genes. First among these are the effects of culture, which cannot be measured by these studies because all the participants come from the same culture, typically middle-class European or American. The importance of culture is obvious from the study of history and anthropology. The reason that most of us don't challenge each other to duels or worship our ancestors or chug down a nice warm glass of cow urine has nothing to do with genes and everything to do with the milieu in which we grew up. But this still leaves the question of why people in the same culture differ from one another.

Behavioral geneticists will point to data showing that even within a single culture, individuals are shaped by their environments. This is another way of saying that a large fraction of the differences among individuals in any trait you care to measure do not correlate with differences among their genes. But a look at these nongenetic causes of our psychological differences shows that it's far from clear what this "environment" is.

Behavioral genetics has repeatedly found that the "shared environment"—everything that siblings growing up in the same home have in common, including their parents, their neighborhood, their home, their peer group, and their school—has less of an influence on the way they turn out than their genes. In many studies, the shared environment has no measurable influence on the adult at all. Siblings reared together end up no more similar than siblings apart, and adoptive siblings reared in the same family end up not similar at all. A large chunk of the variation among people in intelligence and personality is not predictable from any obvious feature of the world of their childhood.

Think of a pair of identical twins you know. They are probably highly similar, but they are certainly not indistinguishable. They clearly have their own personalities, and in some cases one twin can be gay and the other straight, or one schizophrenic and the other not. But where could these differences have come from? Not from their genes, which are identical. And not from their parents or siblings or neighborhood or school either, which were also, in most cases, identical. Behavioral geneticists attribute this mysterious variation to the "nonshared" or "unique" environment, but that is just a fudge factor introduced to make the numbers add up to 100 percent.

No one knows what the nongenetic causes of individuality are. Perhaps people are shaped by modifications of genes that take place after conception, or by haphazard fluctuations in the chemical soup in the womb or the wiring up of the brain or the expression of the genes themselves. Even in the simplest organisms, genes are not turned on and off like clockwork but are subject to a lot of random noise, which is why genetically identical fruit flies bred in controlled laboratory conditions can end up with unpredictable differences in their anatomy. This genetic roulette must be even more significant in an organism as complex as a human, and it tells us that the two traditional shapers of a person, nature and nurture, must be augmented by a third one, brute chance.

The discoveries of behavioral genetics call for another adjustment to our traditional conception of a nature-nurture cocktail. A common finding is that the effects of being brought up in a given family are sometimes detectable in childhood, but that they tend to peter out by the time the child has grown up. That is, the reach of the genes appears to get stronger as we age, not weaker. Perhaps our genes affect our environments, which in turn affect ourselves. Young children are at the mercy of parents and have to adapt to a world that is not of their choosing. As they get older, however, they can gravitate to the microenvironments that best suit their natures. Some children naturally lose themselves in the library or the local woods or the nearest computer; others ingratiate themselves with the jocks or the goths or the church youth group. Whatever genetic quirks incline a youth toward one niche or another will be magnified over time as they develop the parts of themselves that allow them to flourish in their chosen worlds. Also magnified are the accidents of life (catching or dropping a ball, acing or flubbing a test), which, according to the psychologist Judith Rich Harris, may help explain the seemingly random component of personality variation. The environment, then, is not a stamping machine that pounds us into a shape but a cafeteria of options from which our genes and our histories incline us to choose.

All this sets the stage for what we can expect from personal genomics. Our genes are a big part of what we are. But even knowing the totality of genetic predictors, there will be many things about ourselves that no genome scan—and for that matter, no demographic checklist—will ever reveal. With these bookends in mind, I rolled up my sleeve, drooled into a couple of vials, and awaited the results of three analyses of my DNA.

❧❧❧

The output of a complete genome scan would be a list of six billion A's, C's, G's, and T's—a multigigabyte file that is still prohibitively expensive to generate and that, by itself, will always be perfectly useless. That is why most personal genomics ventures are starting with smaller portions of the genome that promise to contain nuggets of interpretable information.

The Personal Genome Project is beginning with the exome: the 1 per cent of our genome that is translated into strings of amino acids that assemble themselves into proteins. Proteins make up our physical structure, catalyze the chemical reactions that keep us alive, and regulate the expression of other genes. The vast majority of heritable diseases that we currently understand involve tiny differences in one of the exons that collectively make up the exome, so it's a logical place to start.

Only a portion of my exome has been sequenced by the PGP so far, none of its terribly interesting. But I did face a decision that will confront every genome consumer. Most genes linked to disease nudge the odds of developing the illness up or down a bit, and when the odds are increased, there is a recommended course of action, like more frequent testing or a preventive drug or a lifestyle change. But a few genes are perfect storms of bad news: high odds of developing a horrible condition that you can do nothing about. Huntington's disease is one example, and many people whose family histories put them at risk (like Arlo Guthrie, whose father, Woody, died of the disease) choose not to learn whether they carry the gene.

Another example is the apolipoprotein E gene (APOE). Nearly a quarter of the population carries one copy of the E_4 variant, which triples their risk of developing Alzheimer's disease. Two per cent of people carry two copies of the gene (one from each parent), which increases their risk fifteenfold. James Watson, who with Francis Crick discovered the structure of DNA and who was one of the first two humans to have his genome sequenced, asked not to see which variant he had.

As it turns out, we know what happens to people who do get the worst news. According to preliminary findings by the epidemiologist Robert C. Green, they don't sink into despair or throw themselves off bridges; they handle it perfectly well. This should not be terribly surprising. All of us already live with the knowledge that we have the fatal genetic condition called mortality, and most of us cope using some combination of denial, resignation, and religion. Still, I figured that my current burden of existential dread is just about right, so I followed Watson's lead and asked for a line-item veto of my APOE gene information when the PGP sequencer gets to it.

The genes analyzed by a new company called Counsyl are more actionable, as they say in the trade. Their "universal carrier screen" is meant to tell prospective parents whether they carry genes that put their potential children at risk for more than a hundred serious disease like cystic fibrosis and alpha thalassemia. If both parents have a copy of a recessive disease gene, there is a one-in-four chance that any child they conceive will develop the disease. With this knowledge they can choose to adopt a child instead or to undergo *in vitro* fertilization and screen the embryos for the dangerous genes. It's a scaled-up version of the Tay-Sachs test that Ashkenazi Jews have undergone for decades.

I have known since 1972 that I am clean for Tay-Sachs, but the Counsyl screen showed that I carry one copy of a gene for familial dysautonomia, an incurable disorder of the autonomic nervous system that causes a number of unpleasant symptoms and a high chance of premature death. A well-meaning colleague tried to console me, but I was pleased to gain the knowledge. Children are not in my cards, but my nieces and nephews, who have a 25 per cent chance of being carriers, will know to get tested. And I can shut the door to whatever wistfulness I may have had about my childlessness. The gene was not discovered until 2001, well after the choice confronted me, so my road not taken could have led to tragedy. But perhaps that's the way you think if you are open to experience and not too neurotic.

Familial dysautonomia is found almost exclusively among Ashkenazi Jews, and 23andMe provided additional clues to that ancestry in my genome. My mitochondrial DNA (which is passed intact from mother to offspring) is specific to Ashkenazi populations and is similar to ones found in Sephardic and Oriental Jews and in Druze and Kurds. My Y chromosome (which is passed intact from father to son) is also Levantine, common among Ashkenazi, Sephardic, and Oriental Jews and also sprinkled across the eastern Mediterranean. Both variants arose in the Middle East more than two thousand years ago and were probably carried to regions in Italy by Jewish exiles after the Roman destruction of Jerusalem, then to the Rhine Valley in the Middle Ages and eastward to the Pale of Settlement in Poland and Moldova, ending up in my father's father and my mother's mother a century ago.

It's thrilling to find yourself so tangibly connected to two millennia of history. And even this secular, ecumenical Jew experienced a primitive tribal stirring in learning of a deep genealogy that coincides with the handing down of traditions I grew up with. But my blue eyes remind me not to get carried away with delusions about a Semitic essence. Mitochondrial DNA and the Y chromosome, do not literally tell you about "your ancestry" but only half of your ancestry a generation ago, a quarter two generations ago, and so on, shrinking exponentially the further back you go. In fact, since the further back you go the more ancestors you theoretically have (eight great-grandparents, sixteen great-great-grandparents, and so on), at some point there aren't enough ancestors to go around, everyone's ancestors overlap with everyone else's, and the very concept of personal ancestry becomes meaningless. I found it just as thrilling to zoom outward in the diagrams of my genetic lineage and see my place in a family tree that embraces all of humanity.

As fascinating as carrier screening and ancestry are, the really new feature offered by 23andMe is its genetic report card. The company directs you to a Web page that displays risk factors for fourteen diseases and ten traits, and links to pages for an additional fifty-one diseases and twenty-one traits for which the scientific evidence is more iffy. Curious users can browse a list of markers from the rest of their genomes with a third-party program that searches a wiki of gene-trait associations that have been reported in the scientific literature. I found the site user-friendly and scientifically responsible. This clarity, though, made it easy to see that personal genomics has a long way to go before it will be a significant tool of self-discovery.

The two biggest pieces of news I got about my disease risks were a 12.6 per cent chance of getting prostate cancer before I turn eighty compared with the average risk for white men of 17.8 percent, and a 26.8 per cent chance of getting type 2 diabetes compared with the average risk of 21.9 percent. Most of the other outcomes involved even smaller departures from the norm. For a blessedly average person like me, it is completely unclear what to do with these odds. A one-in-four chance of developing diabetes should make any prudent person watch his weight and other risk factors. But then so should a one-in-five chance.

It became all the more confusing when I browsed for genes beyond those on the summary page. Both the PGP and the genome browser turned up studies that linked various of my genes to an *elevated* risk of prostate cancer, deflating my initial relief at the lowered risk. Assessing risks from genomic data is not like using a pregnancy-test kit with its bright blue line. It's more like writing a term paper on a topic with a huge and chaotic research literature. You are whipsawed by contradictory studies with different sample sizes, ages, sexes, ethnicities, selection criteria, and levels of statistical significance. Geneticists working for 23andMe sift through the journals and make their best judgments of which associations are solid. But these judgments are necessarily subjective, and they can quickly become obsolete now that cheap genotyping techniques have opened the floodgates to new studies.

Direct-to-consumer companies are sometimes accused of peddling "recreational genetics," and there's no denying the horoscopelike fascination of learning about genes that predict your traits. Who wouldn't be flattered to learn that he has two genes associated with higher IQ and one linked to a taste for novelty? It is also strangely validating to learn that I have genes for traits that I already know I have, like light skin and blue eyes. Then there are the genes for traits that seem plausible enough but make the wrong prediction about how I live my life, like my genes for tasting the bitterness in broccoli, beer, and Brussels sprouts (I consume them all), for lactose intolerance (I seem to tolerate ice cream just fine), and for fast-twitch muscle fibers (I prefer hiking and cycling to basketball and squash). I also have genes that are nothing to brag about (like average memory performance and lower efficiency at learning from errors), ones whose meanings are a bit baffling (like a gene that gives me "typical odds" for having red hair, which I don't have), and ones whose predictions are flat-out wrong (like a high risk of baldness).

For all the narcissistic pleasure that comes from poring over clues to my inner makeup, I soon realized that I was using my knowledge of myself to make sense of the genetic readout, not the other way around. My novelty-seeking gene, for example, has been associated with a cluster of traits that includes impulsivity. But I don't think I'm particularly impulsive, so I interpret the gene as the cause of my openness to experience. But then it may be like the baldness gene and say nothing about me at all.

Individual genes are just not very informative. Call it Geno's Paradox. We know from classic medical and behavioral genetics that many physical and psychological traits are substantially heritable. But when scientists use the latest methods to fish for the responsible genes, the catch is paltry.

Take height. Though health and nutrition can affect stature, height is highly heritable: no one thinks that Kareem Abdul-Jabbar just ate more Wheaties growing up than Danny DeVito. Height should therefore be a target-rich area in the search for genes, and in 2007 a genomewide scan of nearly sixteen thousand people turned up a dozen of them. But these genes collectively accounted for just *2 per cent* of the variation in height, and a person who had most of the genes was barely an inch taller, on average, than a person who had few of them. If that's the best we can do for height, which can be assessed with a tape measure, what can we expect for more elusive traits like intelligence or personality?

Geno's Paradox entails that apart from carrier screening, personal genomics will be more recreational than diagnostic for some time to come. Some reasons are technological. The affordable genotyping services don't actually sequence your entire genome but follow the time-honored scientific practice of looking for one's keys under the lamppost because that's where the light is best. They can scan for half a million or so spots on the genome where a single nucleotide (half a rung on the DNA ladder) is likely to differ from one person to the next. These differences are called Single Nucleotide Polymorphisms, or SNPs (pronounced "snips"), and they can be cheaply identified en masse by putting a dollop of someone's DNA on a device called a microarray or SNP chip. A SNP can be a variant of a gene or can serve as a signpost for variants of a gene that are nearby.

But not all genetic variation comes in the form of these one-letter typos. A much larger portion of our genomes varies in other ways. A chunk of DNA may be missing or inverted or duplicated, or a tiny substring may be repeated different numbers of times—say, five times in one person and seven times in another. These variations are known to cause diseases and differences in personality, but unless they accompany a particular SNP, they will not turn up on a SNP chip.

As sequencing technology improves, more of our genomic variations will come into view. But determining what those variants *mean* is another matter. A good day for geneticists is one in which they look for genes that have nice big effects and that are found in many people. But remember the minuscule influence of each of the genes that affects stature. There may be hundreds of other such genes, each affecting height by an even smaller smidgen, but it is hard to discern the genes in this long tail of the distribution amid the cacophony of the entire genome. And so it may be for the hundreds or thousands of genes that make you a teensy bit smarter or duller, calmer or more jittery.

Another kind of headache for geneticists comes from gene variants that do have large effects but that are unique to you or to some tiny fraction of humanity. These, too, are hard to spot in genomewide scans. Say you have a unique genetic variant that gives you big ears. The problem is that you have other unique genes as well. Since it would be literally impossible to assemble a large sample of people who do and don't have the crucial gene and who do and don't have big ears, there is no way to know which of your proprietary genes is the culprit. If we understood the molecular assembly line by which ears were put together in the embryo, we could identify the gene by what it does rather than by what it correlates with. But with most traits, that's not yet possible—not for ears, and certainly not for a sense of humor or a gift of gab or a sweet disposition. In fact, the road to discovery in biology often goes in the other direction. Biologists discover the genetic pathways that build an organ by spotting genes that correlate with different forms of it and then seeing what they do.

So how likely is it that future upgrades to consumer genomics kits will turn up markers for psychological traits? The answer depends on why we vary in the first place, an unsolved problem in behavioral genetics. And the answer may be different for different psychological traits.

In theory, we should hardly differ at all. Natural selection works like compound interest: a gene with even a 1 per cent advantage in the number of surviving offspring it yields will expand geometrically over a few hundred generations and quickly crowd out its less fecund alternatives. Why didn't this winnowing leave each of us with the best version of every gene, making each of us as vigorous, smart, and well adjusted as human physiology allow? The world would be a duller place, but evolution doesn't go out of its way to keep us entertained.

It's tempting to say that society as a whole prospers with a mixture of tinkers, tailors, soldiers, sailors, and so on. But evolution selects among genes, not societies, and if the genes that make tinkers outreproduce the genes that make tailors, the tinker genes will become a monopoly. A better way of thinking about genetic diversity is that if everyone were a tinker, it would pay to have tailor genes, and the tailor genes would start to make an inroad, but then as society filled up with tailor genes, the advantage would shift back to the tinkers. A result would be an equilibrium with a certain proportion of tinkers and a certain proportion of tailors. Biologists call this process balancing selection: two designs for an organism are equally fit, but in different physical or social environments, including the environments that consist of other members of the species. Often the choice between versions of such a trait is governed by a single gene, or a few adjacent genes that are inherited together. If instead the trait were controlled by many genes, then during sexual reproduction those genes would get all mixed up with the genes from the other parent, who might have the alternative version of the trait. Over several generations the genes for the two designs would be thoroughly scrambled, and the species would be homogenized.

The psychologists Lars Penke, Jaap Denissen, and Geoffrey Miller argue that personality differences arise from this process of balancing selection. Selfish people prosper in a world of nice guys, until they become so common that they start to swindle one another, whereupon nice guys who cooperate get the upper hand, until there are enough of them for the swindlers to exploit, and so on. The same balancing act can favor rebels in a world of conformists and vice versa, or doves in a world of hawks.

The optimal personality may also depend on the opportunities and risk presented by different environments. The early bird gets the worm, but the second mouse gets the cheese. An environment that has worms in some parts but mousetraps in others could select for a mixture of go-getters and nervous nellies. More plausibly, it selects for organisms that sniff out what kind of environment they are in and tune their boldness accordingly, with different individuals setting their danger threshold at different points.

But not all variation in nature arises from balancing selection. The other reason that genetic variation can persist is that rust never sleeps: new mutations creep into the genome faster than natural selection and weed them out. At any given moment, the population is laden with a portfolio of recent mutations, each of whose days are numbered. This Sisyphean struggle between selection and mutation is common with traits that depend on any genes because there are so many things that can go wrong.

Penke, Denissen, and Miller argue that a mutation-selection standoff is the explanation for why we differ in intelligence. Unlike personality, where it takes all kinds to make a world, with intelligence, smarter is simply better, so balancing selection is unlikely. But intelligence depends on a large network of brain areas, and it thrives in a body that is properly nourished and free of diseases and defects. Many genes are engaged in keeping this system going, and so there are many genes that, when mutated, can make us a little bit stupider.

At the same time there aren't many mutations that can make us a whole lot smarter. Mutations in general are far more likely to be harmful than helpful, and the large, helpful ones were low-hanging fruit that were picked long ago in our evolutionary history and entrenched in the species. One reason for this can be explained with an analogy inspired by the mathematician Ronald Fisher. A large twist of a focusing knob has some chance of bringing a microscope into better focus when it is far from the best setting. But as the barrel gets closer to the target, smaller and smaller tweaks are needed to bring any further improvement.

ঌ৪ঌ৪ঌ৪

The Penke/Denissen/Miller theory, which attributes variation in personality and intelligence to different evolutionary processes, is consistent with what we have learned so far about the genes for those two kinds of traits. The search for IQ genes calls to mind the cartoon in which a scientist with a smoldering test tube asks a colleague, "What's the opposite of Eureka?" Though we know that genes for intelligence must exist, each is likely to be small in effect, found in only a few people, or both. In a recent study of six thousand children, the genes with the biggest effect accounted for less than one-quarter of an IQ point. The quest for genes that underlie major disorders of cognition, like autism and schizophrenia, has been almost as frustrating. Both conditions are highly heritable, yet no one has identified genes that cause either condition across a wide range of people. Perhaps this is what we should expect for a high-maintenance trait like human cognition, which is vulnerable to many mutations.

The hunt for personality genes, though not yet Nobel-worthy, has had better fortunes. Several associations have been found between personality traits and genes that govern the breakdown, recycling, or detection of neurotransmitters (the molecules that seep from neuron to neuron) in the brain systems underlying mood and motivation.

Dopamine is the molecular currency in several brain circuits associated with wanting, getting satisfaction, and paying attention. The gene for one kind of dopamine receptor, DRD_4, comes in several versions. Some of the variants (like the one I have) have been associated with "approach related" personality traits like novelty seeking, sensation seeking, and extroversion. A gene for another kind of receptor, DRD_2, comes in a version that makes its dopamine system function less effectively. It has been associated with impulsivity, obesity, and substance abuse. Still another gene, COMT, produces an enzyme that breaks down dopamine in the prefrontal cortex, the home of higher cognitive functions like reasoning and planning. If your version of the gene produces less COMT, you may have better concentration but might also be more neurotic and jittery.

Behavioral geneticists have also trained their sights on serotonin, which is found in brain circuits that affect many moods and drives, including those affected by Prozac and similar drugs. SERT, the serotonin transporter, is a molecule that scoops up stray serotonin for recycling, reducing the amount available to act in the brain. The switch for the gene that makes SERT comes in long and short versions, and the short version has been linked to depression and anxiety. A 2003 study made headlines because it suggested that the gene may affect a person's resilience to life's stressors rather than giving him a tendency to be depressed or content across the board. People who had two short versions of the gene (one from each parent) were likely to have a major depressive episode only if they had undergone traumatic experiences; those who had a more placid history were fine. In contrast, people who had two long versions of the gene typically failed to report depression regardless of their life histories. In other words, the effects of the gene are sensitive to a person's environment. Psychologists have long known that some people are resilient to life's slings and arrows and others are more fragile, but they had never seen this interaction played out in the effects of individual genes.

Still other genes have been associated with trust and commitment or with a tendency to antisocial outburst. It's still a messy science, with plenty of false alarms, contradictory results, and tiny effects. But consumers will probably learn of genes linked to personality before they see any that are reliably connected to intelligence.

Personal genomics is here to stay. The science will improve as efforts like the Personal Genome Project amass huge samples, the price of sequencing sinks, and biologists come to a better understanding of what genes do and why they vary. People who have grown up with the democratization of information will not tolerate paternalistic regulations that keep them from their own genomes, and early adopters will explore how this new information can best be used to manage our health. There are risks of misunderstandings, but there are also risks in much of the flimflam we tolerate in alternative medicine, and in the hunches and folklore that many doctors prefer to evidence-based medicine. And besides, personal genomics is just too much fun.

At the same time, there is nothing like perusing your genetic data to drive home its limitations as a source of insight into yourself. What should I make of the nonsensical news that I am "probably light-skinned" but have a "twofold risk of baldness"? These diagnoses, of course, are simply peeled off the data in a study: 40 per cent of men with the C version of the rs2180439 SNP are bald, compared with 80 per cent of men with the T version, and I have the T. But something strange happens when you take a number representing the proportion of people in a sample and apply it to a single individual. The first use of the number is perfectly respectable as an input into a policy that will optimize the costs and benefits of treating a large similar group in a particular way. But the second use of the number is just plain weird. Anyone who knows me can confirm that I'm not 80 per cent bald or even 80 per cent likely to be bald; I'm 100 per cent likely not to be bald. The most charitable interpretation of the number when applied to me is, "If you knew nothing else about me your subjective confidence that I am bald, on a scale of 0 to 10, should be 8." But that is a statement about your mental state, not my physical one. If you learned more clues about me (like seeing photographs of my father and grandfathers), that number would change, while not a hair on my head would be different. Some mathematicians say that "the probability of a single event" is a meaningless concept.

Even when the effect of some gene is indubitable, the sheer complexity of the self will mean that it will not serve as an oracle on what the person will do. The gene that lets me taste propylthiouracil, 23andMe suggest, might make me dislike tonic water, coffee, and dark beer. Unlike the tenuous genes linked to personality or intelligence, this one codes for a single taste-bud receptor, and I don't doubt that it lets me taste the bitterness. So why hasn't it stopped me from enjoying those drinks? Presumably it's because adults get a sophisticated pleasure from administering controlled doses of aversive stimuli to themselves. I've acquired a taste for Beck's Dark; others enjoy saunas, rock climbing, thrillers, or dissonant music. Similarly, why don't I conform to type and exploit those fast-twitch muscle fibers (thanks, $ACTN_3$ genes!) in squash or basketball, rather than wasting them on hiking? A lack of coordination, a love of the outdoors, an inclination to daydream, all of the above? The self is a byzantine bureaucracy, and no gene can push the buttons of behavior by itself. You can attribute the ability to defy our genotypes to free will, whatever that means, but you can also attribute it to the fact that in a hundred-trillion-synapse human brain, any single influence can be outweighed by the product of all of the others.

Even if personal genomics someday delivers a detailed printout of psychological traits, it will probably not change everything, or even most things. It will give us deeper insight about the biological causes of individuality, and it may narrow the guesswork in assessing individual cases. But the issues about self and society that it brings into focus have always been with us. We have always known that people are liable, to varying degrees, to antisocial temptations and weakness of the will. We have always known that people should be encouraged to develop the parts of themselves that they can ("a man's reach should exceed his grasp") but that it's foolish to expect that anyone can accomplish anything ("a man has got to know his limitations"). And we know that holding people responsible for their behavior will make it more likely that they behave responsibly. "My genes made me do it" is no better an excuse than "We're depraved on account of we're deprived."

Many of the dystopian fears raised by personal genomics are simply out of touch with the complex and probabilistic nature of genes. Forget about the hyperparents who want to implant math genes in their unborn children, the *Gattaca* corporations that scan people's DNA to assign them to castes, the employers or suitors who hack into your genome to find out what kind of worker or spouse you'd make. Let them try; they'd be wasting their time.

The real-life examples are almost as futile. When the connection between the $ACTN_3$ gene and muscle type was discovered, parents and coaches started swabbing the cheeks of children so they could steer the ones with the fast-twitch variant into sprinting and football. Carl Foster, one of the scientists who uncovered the association, had a better idea: "Just line them up with their classmates for a race and see which ones are the fastest." Good advice. The test for a gene can identify one of the contributors to a trait. A measurement of the trait itself will identify all of them: the other genes (many or few, discovered or undiscovered, understood or not understood), the way they interact, the effects of the environment, and the child's unique history of developmental quirks.

It's our essentialist mindset that makes the cheek swab feel as if it is somehow a deeper, truer, more authentic test of the child's ability. It's not that the mindset is utterly misguided. Our genomes truly are a fundamental part of us. They are what make us human, including the distinctively human ability to learn and create culture. They account for at least half of what makes us different from our neighbors. And though we can change both inherited and acquired traits, changing the inherited ones is usually harder. It is a question of the most perspicuous level of analysis at which to understand a complex phenomenon. You can't understand the stock market by studying a single trader, or a movie by putting a DVD under a microscope. The fallacy is not in thinking that the entire genome matters, but in thinking that an individual gene will matter, at least in a way that is large and intelligible enough for us to care about.

So if you are bitten by scientific or personal curiosity and can think in probabilities, by all means enjoy the fruits of personal genomics. But if you want to know whether you are at risk for high cholesterol, have your cholesterol measured; if you want to know whether you are good at math, take a math test. And if you really want to know yourself (and this will be the test of how much you do), consider the suggestion of François de La Rochefoucauld: "Our enemies' opinion of us comes closer to the truth than our own."

Credit

Building Baby From the Genes Up

Ronald M. Green

The two British couples no doubt thought that their appeal for medical help in conceiving a child was entirely reasonable. Over several generations, many female members of their families had died of breast cancer. One or both spouses in each couple had probably inherited the genetic mutations for the disease, and they wanted to use in-vitro fertilization and preimplantation genetic diagnosis (PGD) to select only the healthy embryos for implantation. Their goal was to eradicate breast cancer from their family lines once and for all.

In the United States, this combination of reproductive and genetic medicine—what one scientist has dubbed "reprogenetics"—remains largely unregulated, but Britain has a formal agency, the Human Fertilization and Embryology Authority (HFEA), that must approve all requests for PGD. In July 2007, after considerable deliberation, the HFEA approved the procedure for both families. The concern was not about the use of PGD to avoid genetic disease, since embryo screening for serious disorders is commonplace now on both sides of the Atlantic. What troubled the HFEA was the fact that an embryo carrying the cancer mutation could go on to live for 40 or 50 years before ever developing cancer, and there was a chance it might never develop. Did this warrant selecting and discarding embryos? To its critics, the HFEA, in approving this request, crossed a bright line separating legitimate medical genetics from the quest for "the perfect baby."

Like it or not, that decision is a sign of things to come—and not necessarily a bad sign. Since the completion of the Human Genome Project in 2003, our understanding of the genetic bases of human disease and non-disease traits has been growing almost exponentially. The National Institutes of Health has initiated a quest for the "$1,000 genome," a 10-year program to develop machines that could identify all the genetic letters in anyone's genome at low cost (it took more than $3 billion to sequence the first human genome). With this technology, which some believe may be just four or five years away, we could not only scan an individual's—or embryo's—genome, we could also rapidly compare thousands of people and pinpoint those DNA sequences or combinations that underlie the variations that contribute to our biological differences.

With knowledge comes power. If we understand the genetic causes of obesity, for example, we can intervene by means of embryo selection to produce a child with a reduced genetic likelihood of getting fat. Eventually, without discarding embryos at all, we could use gene-targeting techniques to tweak fetal DNA sequences. No child would have to face a lifetime of dieting or experience the health and cosmetic problems associated with obesity. The same is true for cognitive problems such as dyslexia. Geneticists have already identified some of the mutations that contribute to this disorder. Why should a child struggle with reading difficulties when we could alter the genes responsible for the problem?

Many people are horrified at the thought of such uses of genetics, seeing echoes of the 1997 science-fiction film *Gattaca,* which depicted a world where parents choose their children's traits. Human weakness has been eliminated through genetic engineering, and the few parents who opt for a "natural" conception run the risk of producing offspring—"invalids" or "degenerates"—who become members of a despised underclass. Gattaca's world is clean and efficient, but its eugenic obsessions have all but extinguished human love and compassion.

These fears aren't limited to fiction. Over the past few years, many bioethicists have spoken out against genetic manipulations. The critics tend to voice at least four major concerns. First, they worry about the effect of genetic selection on parenting. Will our ability to choose our children's biological inheritance lead parents to replace unconditional love with a consumerist mentality that seeks perfection?

Second, they ask whether gene manipulations will diminish our freedom by making us creatures of our genes or our parents' whims. In his book *Enough,* the techno-critic Bill McKibben asks: "If I am a world-class runner, but my parents inserted the 'Sweatworks2010 GenePack' in my genome, can I really feel pride in my accomplishments? Worse, if I refuse to use my costly genetic endowments, will I face relentless pressure to live up to my parents' expectations?"

Third, many critics fear that reproductive genetics will widen our social divisions as the affluent "buy" more competitive abilities for their offspring. Will we eventually see "speciation," the emergence of two or more human populations so different that they no longer even breed with one another? Will we re-create the horrors of eugenics that led, in Europe, Asia and the United States, to the sterilization of tens of thousands of people declared to be "unfit" and that in Nazi Germany paved the way for the Holocaust?

Finally, some worry about the religious implications of this technology. Does it amount to a forbidden and prideful "playing God"?

To many, the answers to these questions are clear. Not long ago, when I asked a large class at Dartmouth Medical School whether they thought that we should move in the direction of human genetic engineering, more than 80 per cent said no. This squares with public opinion polls that show a similar degree of opposition. Nevertheless, "babies by design" are probably in our future—but I think that the critics' concerns may be less troublesome than they first appear.

Will critical scrutiny replace parental love? Not likely. Even today, parents who hope for a healthy child but have one born with disabilities tend to love that child ferociously. The very intensity of parental love is the best protection against its erosion by genetic technologies. Will a child somehow feel less free because parents have helped select his or her traits? The fact is that a child is already remarkably influenced by the genes she inherits. The difference is that we haven't taken control of the process. Yet.

Knowing more about our genes may actually increase our freedom by helping us understand the biological obstacles—and opportunities—we have to work with. Take the case of Tiger Woods. His father, Earl, is said to have handed him a golf club when he was still in the playpen. Earl probably also gave Tiger the genes for some of the traits that help make him a champion golfer. Genes and upbringing worked together to inspire excellence. Does Tiger feel less free because of his inherited abilities? Did he feel pressured by his parents? I doubt it. Of course, his story could have gone the other way, with overbearing parents forcing a child into their mold. But the problem in that case wouldn't be genetics, but bad parenting.

Granted, the social effects of reproductive genetics are worrisome. The risks of producing a "genobility," genetic overlords ruling a vast genetic underclass, are real. But genetics could also become a tool for reducing the class divide. Will we see the day when perhaps all youngsters are genetically vaccinated against dyslexia? And how might this contribute to everyone's social betterment?

As for the question of intruding on God's domain, the answer is less clear than the critics believe. The use of genetic medicine to cure or prevent disease is widely accepted by religious traditions, even those that oppose discarding embryos. Speaking in 1982 at the Pontifical Academy of Sciences, Pope John Paul II observed that modern biological research "can ameliorate the condition of those who are affected by chromosomic diseases," and he lauded this as helping to cure "the smallest and weakest of human beings ... during their intrauterine life or in the period immediately after birth." For Catholicism and some other traditions, it is one thing to cure disease, but another to create children who are faster runners, longer-lived or smarter.

But why should we think that the human genome is a once-and-for-all-finished, untamperable product? All of the biblically derived faiths permit human beings to improve on nature using technology, from agriculture to aviation. Why not improve our genome? I have no doubt that most people considering these questions for the first time are certain that human genetic improvement is a bad idea, but I'd like to shake up that certainty.

Genomic science is racing toward a future in which foreseeable improvements include reduced susceptibility to a host of diseases, increased life span, better cognitive functioning and maybe even cosmetic enhancements such as whiter, straighter teeth. Yes, genetic orthodontics may be in our future. The challenge is to see that we don't also unleash the demons of discrimination and oppression. Although I acknowledge the risks, I believe that we can and will incorporate gene technology into the ongoing human adventure.

Credit

Genetically Modified Humans? No Thanks.

Richard Hayes

In an essay[1] in Sunday's Outlook section, Dartmouth ethics professor Ronald Green asks us to consider a neo-eugenic future of "designer babies," with parents assembling their children quite literally from genes selected from a catalogue. Distancing himself from the compulsory, state-sponsored eugenics that darkened the first half of the last century, Green instead celebrates the advent of a libertarian, consumer-driven eugenics motivated by the free play of human desire, technology and markets. He argues that this vision of the human future is desirable and very likely inevitable.

To put it mildly: I disagree. Granted, new human genetic technologies have real potential to help prevent or cure many terrible diseases, and I support research directed towards that end. But these same technologies also have the potential for real harm. If misapplied, they would exacerbate existing inequalities and reinforce existing modes of discrimination. If more widely abused, they could undermine the foundations of civil and human rights. In the worst case, they could undermine our experience of being part of a single human community with a common human future.

Once we begin genetically modifying our children, where do we stop? If it's acceptable to modify one gene, why not two, or 20 or 200? At what point do children become artifacts designed to someone's specifications rather than members of a family to be nurtured?

Given what we know about human nature, the development and commercial marketing of human genetic modification would likely spark a techno-eugenic rat-race. Even parents opposed to manipulating their children's genes would feel compelled to participate in this race, lest their offspring be left behind.

Green proposes that eugenic technologies could be used to reduce "the class divide." But nowhere in his essay does he suggest how such a proposal might ever be made practicable in the real world.

The danger of genetic misuse is equally threatening at the international level. What happens when some rogue country announces an ambitious program to "improve the genetic stock" of its citizens? In a world still barely able to contain the forces of nationalism, ethnocentrism, and militarism, the last thing we need to worry about is a high-tech eugenic arms race.

In his essay, Green doesn't distinguish clearly between different uses of genetic technology—and the distinctions are critical. It's one thing to enable a couple to avoid passing on a devastating genetic condition, such as Tay-Sachs.[2] But it's a different thing altogether to create children with a host of "enhanced" athletic, cosmetic and cognitive traits that could be passed to their own children, who in turn could further genetically modify their children, who in turn … you get the picture. It's this second use of gene technology (the technical term is "heritable genetic enhancement") that Green most fervently wants us to embrace.

In this position, Green is well outside the growing national and international consensus on the proper use of human genetic science and technology. To his credit, he acknowledges that 80 per cent of the medical school students he surveyed said they were against such forms of human genetic engineering, and that public opinion polls show equally dramatic opposition. He could have noted, as well, that nearly 40 countries[3]—including Brazil, Canada, France, Germany, India, Japan, and South Africa—have adopted socially responsible policies regulating the new human genetic technologies. They allow genetic research (including stem cell research) for medical applications, but prohibit its use for heritable genetic modification and reproductive human cloning.

In the face of this consensus, Green blithely announces his confidence that humanity "can and will" incorporate heritable genetic enhancement into the "ongoing human adventure."

Well, it's certainly possible. Our desires for good looks, good brains, wealth, and long lives, for ourselves and for our children, are strong and enduring. If the gene-tech entrepreneurs are able to convince us that we can satisfy these desires by buying into genetic modification, perhaps we'll bite. Green certainly seems eager to encourage us to do so.

But he would be wise to listen to what medical students, the great majority of Americans and the international community appear to be saying: We want all these things, yes, and genetic technology might help us attain them, but we don't want to run the huge risks to the human community and the human future that would come with altering the genetic basis of our common human nature.

Notes

1 Ronald M. Green, "Building Baby From the Genes Up," *The Washington Post,* April 13, 2008, http://www.washingtonpost.com/wp-dyn/content/article/2008/04/11/AR2008041103330.html.

2 "Tay-Sachs Disease Information Page," *National Institute of Neurological Disorders,* http://www.ninds.nih.gov/disorders/taysachs/taysachs.htm.

3 "National Polices on Human Genetic Modification: A Preliminary Survey," *Center for Genetics and Society,* November 15, 2007, http://www.geneticsandsociety.org/article.php?id=304.

Credit

Hayes, Richard. "Genetically Modified Humans? No Thanks." *Washington Post,* Opinions 15 Apr. 2008.

Creating "Companions" for Children: The Ethics of Designing Esthetic Features for Robots

Yvette Pearson and Jason Borenstein

1. Introduction

This article examines the ethical aspects of robots that function as friends, caregivers, assistive devices, or toys for children. The increased use of robots is intended to affect various facets of human life, including individual welfare, decision-making, and relationships among humans. In addition to anticipating and addressing basic safety issues, roboticists should also grapple with ethical questions generated by design decisions that have no obvious safety-related implications. While it is important to minimize the probability of harmful malfunction, the focus of this article will be on risks emerging from properly functioning robots. More specifically, we will discuss the relative importance of a robot companion's esthetic features, including whether it should be gendered. Our hope is that continued examination of design decisions will promote children's well-being and contribute to positive transformations of social institutions.

2. Background and Rationale

Contemporary societies are moving away from robots operating in isolation from human beings to an era of pervasive human–robot interaction (HRI). Regarding the increasing prevalence of HRI, the International Federation of Robotics (IFR) quotes a "robot expert" who states that "as technological improvements resulting in more intelligent robot systems with better sensors enable closer interaction between human workers and robots, it will become a reality" (IFR 2011a, p. 31). Though the development of robots outside of military and industrial contexts is still in its early stages, the rate of advance in robotics is accelerating. Robots designed for therapeutic or educational purposes are increasingly being used in experimental settings. Moreover, according to *World Robotics 2011*, "about 2.2 million service robots for personal and domestic use were sold," marking an increase of 35% over 2009 sales (IFR 2011b, XIV). The report also projected that this number would increase significantly between 2011 and 2014 to 14.4 million "units of service robots for personal use" (IFR 2011b, XV). Rather than waiting until various social or personal robots become common, we prefer a proactive approach that identifies potential design-related ethical problems and aims to prevent or mitigate them.

Using the capabilities approach as our primary theoretical foundation, our previous work emphasized the importance of incorporating robots into society in ways that promote human flourishing (Borenstein and Pearson 2010). Mere "avoidance of harm," while a worthy goal, does not go far enough. The integration of robots into society should involve the careful examination of existing institutions and practices. We should aim to avoid simply integrating robots into our lives in ways that perpetuate problematic practices and instead use their introduction as an opportunity to question longstanding social institutions and interpersonal interactions. Among other things, we will consider whether robots should be designed to be humanlike and, if so, how closely and in what ways they should resemble humans. Even if designing humanlike robots turns out to be an ethically sound course of action, it does not follow that other design pathways should be off-limits. It may be acceptable, or even preferable, for practical or moral reasons to design robots that are zoomorphic or even abstract—bearing no resemblance to any living animal, human, or non-human (e.g., e-puck; Mondada et al. 2009).

Though the focus here will be on the design and use of robots *for children*, we recognize that there is great variation among children, according to their age group as well as other factors affecting their development. This means that the design and use of a robot that promotes the welfare of one group of children (e.g., toddlers) may be deficient in achieving this aim with another group of children (e.g., 6-year-olds). Because of the wide variation in the abilities of children as they move through the stages of development, the recommendations we provide here will be general enough to apply to a plurality of categories of children without being so general that they fail to provide practical guidance.

Capurro maintains that it is important to understand *why* we are trying to realize certain values via robots. He claims that we "redefine ourselves in comparison with robots … as we redefine ourselves in comparison with animals or gods" and that doing so has "far reaching economic, ethical, and cultural implications" (2009, p. 120). Additionally, some scholars suggest that interaction with emerging technologies can generate new ways of understanding the world and ourselves. For example, though not referring to the context of robotics, Hausman (1995) explains that "new developments in technology make new discursive situations possible, open up new subject positions" (14). In a similar vein, Fior et al. (2010) suggest that children interacting with robots over time will develop "a new system or schema of understanding and subsequent vocabulary to articulate their sense of friendship with a robot that is likely distinct from their friendships with children" (p. 15). The transformative power of increased HRI combined with society's obligation to protect children from harm requires us to implement proactive measures that will promote the flourishing of developing children and avoid inadvertently cutting off their "right to an open future."

3. Types of Robots

Many different types of companion robots have been, or are in the process of being, created to fulfill a wide range of functions. For purposes of this paper, we are using the term "companion" in a broad sense to include not only robots that interact in "friendly" ways (e.g., playing games with people), but also more passive robots that simply keep a person company without necessarily responding to the persons specific actions or commands. Included in this definition are robotic pets such as *Paro*, a robotic seal, and *Aibo*, a robotic dog. More recently, *MyKeepon* was introduced to the public; it is a robotic toy first used in research aimed at helping autistic children (Ceceri 2011). Another robot, *Wakamaru*, is supposed to offer a higher level of engagement and provide companionship, and *CareBot* is touted as being able to monitor care recipients. MIT's Personal Robotics Group is in the process of creating a series of socially assistive robots that will be able to interact with people in a variety of contexts. Our definition of a "companion" includes socially assistive and other types of robots intended to be used by an individual person, typically outside of military or industrial contexts.

Of course, the ethical dimensions associated with the design of each kind of robot might overlap, but there are subtleties that distinguish different categories of robots. In general, the ethical concerns relating to robots tend to grow and intensify as the amount of "responsibility" delegated to them for a child's care increases. For example, Prazak et al. (2004) draw a distinction between robotic toys and robots that assist children while they play with a toy. Users should reasonably expect more from a robotic assistant than they would from a toy, since the former is intentionally designed to take on a caregiving or educational role. Yet, as the field of robotics advances, users will likely demand and expect more from all types of robots.

4. The Importance of Context-Sensitive Design

For HRI to promote the welfare of children effectively, some degree of bonding between the robot and child will have to occur. It is necessary, however, to determine which esthetic features are more conducive to a robot's ability to fulfill this function. For example, Walters et al. (2008) note how the appearance of a robotic tour-guide may vary sharply from a companion robot; the former is supposed to instruct groups of people while the latter can be tailored to the demands of an individual person. At first glance, the appearance of a robot intended to be a child's companion might be more crucial than if the robot is merely performing mundane tasks such as cleaning the child's room. This is not to say that esthetics is unimportant in the latter case, but it is a matter of degree. Certain esthetic features will be determined according to the frequency and duration of the interactions between the robot and the child, which overlaps with the child's expectations of what the robot can provide. For instance, Turkle notes, children often believe a robot is alive if it can move on its own; also, it has become common during the digital age that a child thinks an electronic toy is "alive" if it can "think" (2006). Taking this kind of psychological finding into account, designers could make it rather obvious that a robot is thinking by mimicking human behavior (e.g., placing a hand on its chin). Assessing the appropriateness of this sort of design strategy hinges on a number of considerations; this includes whether eliciting a less than accurate understanding of reality is ethically problematic.

Design features must be integrated so that they are compatible with how a robot will be used. To minimize confusion, disappointment, or other negative emotional responses, Feil-Seifer and Mataric (2011) astutely point out that users should be provided with a clear explanation of the robot's role, abilities, and limitations. They cite recent studies that show that people "quickly form mental models of robots ... based on what they know best: other people" (p. 27). Since a human caregiver's behaviors can amplify this tendency and promote gross misunderstandings of the robot's actual abilities and limitations, designers and users must exercise caution not only when making decisions about the robot's size, but also how a robot is "dressed and accessorized." For example, Feil-Seifer and Mataric (2011) note that a robot may be mistakenly viewed as medically competent if it is "dressed in a lab coat and wearing a stethoscope" (p. 27). In short, design choices generate expectations, perhaps some of which are erroneous, about the abilities that a robot possesses (Goetz et al. 2003).

A high priority is anticipating and avoiding design features likely to frighten children, such as an overwhelmingly large size or a "creepy" appearance. For example, Movellan recalls the reaction that toddlers had when he brought *Robovie*, a social robot, into his son's classroom; it caused them to be distressed (Tucker, 2009). In contrast, Movellan suggests that another robot, *RUBI*, may have helped children to learn vocabulary words. Besides warding off negative emotional reactions in children, Salter et al. (2008) remind us that it is equally important to avoid boring children. Whether a robot's features will elicit a negative reaction from a child will depend in large part on the child's developmental level and the context in which the child's interaction with the robot occurs.

A number of variables make it difficult to generalize about how children will respond to particular design features. For instance, the existence of countless forms of animation and art seems to imply that there are many standards for what is considered esthetically appealing. It follows that there will be at least some variability in people's responses to esthetic features. With the expansion of global communication, it is an open question whether apparent cultural differences in taste may become less striking and more homogenized.

Reber et al.'s (2004) review of literature from social psychology, cognitive psychology, and experimental esthetics indicates that esthetic judgment is affected by "objective" or "core" features (e.g., quantity of information, figure-ground contrast, and clarity) as well as a perceiver's prior experience with certain kinds of stimuli. Further, it is possible that some preferences are "hardwired" into human psychology. For instance, Brown et al. (2008) argue that for evolutionary reasons, symmetry is integrally connected to whether someone is deemed to be attractive. Hence, how stimuli are processed is not solely a function of the features of the object perceived but also the present state and previous experiences of the perceiver and the perceiver's psychological make-up. This suggests that in addition to integrating "core" esthetic features into the design of robots, the manner in which individuals are socialized is a key variable. While far from conclusive, Ho et al. (2008) observe that "anecdotal evidence indicates that the eeriness of a human-looking robot habituates with exposure" (p. 170); in other words, people tend to adapt to a robot whose appearance initially repels them. Presumably, those who have greater exposure to robots may respond more positively, at least to certain types of robots, and those who are exposed to broad array of robot types may respond rather favorably to them.

Because esthetic judgments and corresponding affective responses are partially a function of fluency, which can develop over time, designers of robots for children should incorporate certain of the aforementioned "core" esthetic features into a robot's design if they hope to promote its acceptance. "Clarity" is one example of a core feature, and this seems to be what Breazeal (2002) identifies when she refers to readability of facial expressions as an important element in the design of sociable robots. In other words, if the manner in which a robot tries to convey an emotion is too vague or ambiguous, the design pathway could fail. Along these lines, if the tone of voice does not match the emotional content of what is being said, it could be unsettling to the user. For example, Nass and Yen (2010) devised a scenario that involved a "male" synthetic voice telling two stories (one happy and one sad), and the voice could sound happy or sad. They state that "... when the emotion of the content and the voice matched, the emotional message was clear and strong. On the other hand, mismatching the tone of voice muddled the emotion of the content" (p. 128). In a later section, the connection between this type of issue and the uncanny valley hypothesis will be explored.

Roboticists will not be able to control fully how users respond to robots (nor perhaps should they). Yet the robotics community should make a concerted effort to predict problematic uses and user reactions to robots. Both policy makers and consumers should be made aware of the true capabilities of companion robots and be provided with guidance about how to avoid negative consequences from their use. For example, if a child believes that a robot is caring and can be trusted (e.g., "The robot can protect me") but it cannot fulfill these expectations, this can be highly problematic (Sharkey and Sharkey 2010). Of greater concern, perhaps, is that adults entrusted with the welfare of children will expect too much of robots and assign them far greater responsibility for children than is warranted by the robot's actual abilities. Belpaeme and Morse (2010) argue that growing more accustomed to robots "... will more than counter this tendency to over-attribute the abilities of robots" (p. 194). Yet it is not clear that their far-reaching optimism is warranted especially considering how willing many parents already are to surrender portions of their caregiving responsibilities to technology (e.g., using a television or an electronic game system as a babysitter). Hence, it will be necessary to tread carefully when considering which beliefs might be affected by HRI and how various modifications to children's beliefs will impact their view of themselves and others.

5. Cultural Factors

In addition to contemplating the possible basis for individual esthetic judgments, it is also worthwhile to consider the collective esthetic preferences attributed to a particular culture. For example, Japanese people are commonly viewed as being technophiles, while Americans are often considered to be less enamored with robotic technology or downright fearful of it (e.g., *Terminator*; Kaplan 2004). Yet MacDorman et al. (2009) argue that the perception of Japan as a "robot-loving" culture is overstated. Their study, which surveyed U.S. and Japanese faculty, found significant agreement between both groups in attitudes toward robots even though Japan does not seem to have as many cultural or religious reservations about technology. Arguably, Japan's widespread use of robots for non-military applications is grounded in practical considerations, such as predicted labor shortages, rather than a mere fondness for artificial beings.

Along similar lines, Wagner (2009) believes that it is a mistake to view Japanese culture as a whole as naturally inclined to interact with robots because external forces pushed robots into various facets of domestic life in Japan. For example, she points out that "the development of mechanical dolls ... was caused by [an edict] of the Japanese military rulers ... who prohibited in 1649 any further research and development of new technological products in the fear of riots" and the rise of a potent technological rival (p. 511). Hence, a plausible explanation is that a military edict, not the "national character" of the Japanese people, contributed to the creation and use of mechanical dolls in domestic settings. Wagner also discusses the claim that Japan may have been trying to exert its own technological prowess in response to allegations that the country was stealing ideas from the West (p. 511).

Nishida (2009) draws similar conclusions, suggesting that the interest of Japanese young people in robot contests may be due to their excitement about the prospect of winning high-tech products and "opportunities for enhancing collaborative learning" (pp. 111–112). He offers reasons that do not seem culture specific even though these practices may evoke the "robot-loving" stereotype. For example, Nishida explains that the use of industrial robots or sushi robots is just a way to improve efficiency and lower costs. He also alleges that Japanese people are no more eager to replicate humans than people in other countries. This assertion, however, is at odds with other research indicating that xenophobia may be *a* motivating factor behind the drive to increase the use of robot caregivers (Parks 2010) and at least one empirical study that alleges that there is significant anti-immigrant sentiment in Japan (Richey 2010). Ironically, Parks (2010) observes that many Japanese are more comfortable with robots than humans even though they desire robots that are "as authentically human as possible" (104). Regardless of the nature and extent of difference in attitudes toward robots between the United States and Japan, Melson (2010) notes that the increased use of mediated interactions in the United States is paving the way for "receptivity to robots in children's lives" (p. 229). Robots might not "invade" as many facets of human life in the United States as in Japan, but interaction with children is one area where significant HRI is likely to emerge. Interestingly, children in a study by Fior et al. (2010) were inclined to view a robotic arm as a social being despite its relative lack of sophistication. They concluded that "children will readily accept these types of devices as companions or friends even when they exhibit minimal emotional cues" (p. 16).

Despite apparent cultural differences in attitudes toward robots, the recognition of similarities across human beings can guide at least some design decisions. The esthetic features of a robot are ethically salient in part because they can influence the kinds of characteristics that children will attribute to the robot. It is equally important to consider robot behavior and its impact on HRI. According to Woods et al. (2006) "… many designers focus predominantly on the different types of facial features and expressions needed for a robot while ignoring robot movement and body shape" (p. 1412). Children's perceptions of a robot's behavioral intentions are not only affected by whether a robot appears machinelike or humanlike, but also by factors like the robot's means of locomotion. Woods and colleagues acknowledge, however, that further study is necessary to evaluate the relative importance of behavioral and esthetic features of robots in promoting positive responses to the technology.

6. Humanlike Appearance and the Uncanny Valley

A major design consideration is whether and to what degree robots should be humanlike. A useful starting point is to distinguish between humanoid robots and androids. MacDorman and Ishiguro (2006) explain that while androids are designed to be indistinguishable from humans, humanoid robots are humanlike only in the sense that their "gross morphology" resembles that of a human (p. 322). Yet androids are designed to resemble humans in many ways beyond gross morphology; for example, an android's skin texture, gestures, and other behaviors should be designed to mimic a human's features. One example of an android is Ishiguro's *Repliee Q1Expo*, which has been described in the following terms: "She has flexible silicone for skin rather than hard plastic … She can flutter her eyelids and move her hands like a human. She even appears to breathe" (Whitehouse 2005). Though MacDorman and Ishiguro's distinction does not appear to be universally embraced in the robotics literature (Halpern and Katz 2012), it is useful for the present discussion.

Discussions about the physical appearance of robots usually include cautionary words about the "uncanny valley" hypothesis put forth by Mori (1970/2012). Mori claimed that there is a "valley" of great discomfort when we interact with a robot or other entity that looks human but lacks key attributes that we would normally expect to accompany a certain (human) appearance. For example, Woods et al. (2006) note that children in their study became "more comfortable" as a robot's appearance approached the uncanny valley. However, they also observed that the children's attitudes toward humanlike robots, at least up to a certain point, were more positive than toward machinelike or animallike robots. When the robots started to seem too humanlike, the children tended to attribute negative character traits to the robots (e.g., bossy, aggressive, angry; p. 1409).

Doubts about the validity of the uncanny valley hypothesis continue to emerge. According to Hanson et al. (2005), worries about the uncanny valley are overstated and that humanlike robots "will serve as an unparalleled tool for investigating human social perception and cognition" (p. 31). Bartneck et al. (2009) claim that empirical evidence in support of Mori's hypothesis has been minimal. Participants in their study were asked to rate the likeability of humans as compared to "highly realistic androids" (p. 270). Real human beings were found to be more humanlike than androids, but the likability ratings of the humans versus androids were fairly similar (p. 274). A potential limitation of the study is that the researchers did not measure differences in the likeability of androids with differing levels of anthropomorphism (i.e., human likeness).

While avoiding the uncanny valley may still be a desirable goal, it is possible that cultural changes over the past several decades may render this concern somewhat less relevant today. Not only have various technologies been more fully integrated into our lives (e.g., realistic-looking animation), but also social attitudes and behaviors toward people with impairments have shifted. Though things were beginning to change during the time of Mori's research, a tendency to institutionalize individuals with cognitive or physical impairments persisted. It was therefore less common to either see or interact with individuals whose appearance or behavior was unfamiliar. On a related note, Bartneck et al. (2009), referencing Nancy Etcoff's *Survival of the Prettiest: The Science of Beauty*, point out that "Sick or injured people are generally perceived as disturbing ..." (p. 272). In a society where it is rare to see people with severe impairments or using assistive medical devices to interface with their environment, encountering an individual who is clearly human but appears or behaves in a way that is not well understood can cause an "uncanny valley" type of experience. Many societies have begun to at least question practices that marginalize people with cognitive and physical impairments or otherwise cause them to be treated poorly. In short, ongoing changes in prevailing social practices or shifts in individual comfort levels might diminish the impact of the uncanny valley.

More frequent exposure to humans with physical or cognitive impairments may put people more at ease while they are in the company of individuals whose appearance or behavior does not match their expectations. Yet this may not entirely resolve the uncanny valley problem if there are other significant contributors to that experience. As Mitchell et al. (2011) explain, the feelings of eeriness experienced during HRI may not be due solely to atypical appearances or behavior patterns. Instead, their study indicates that a mismatch between various sense modalities is another factor that can give rise to feelings of eeriness. They showed videos of a robot using a human voice, a robot using a synthetic voice, a human using a human voice, and a human using a synthetic voice (Mitchell et al. 2011). Study participants were asked to rate the humanness, eeriness, and warmth of the characters viewed on the video screen. They found that the eeriness rating was highest for the human figure—synthetic voice and robot figure—human voice conditions. Mitchell and colleagues conclude that there should be a match between the degree of human likeness of the voice and visual elements. They did not seem to detect a significant difference in the results in terms of the participants' age or gender.

Even though a perceived mismatch appears to generate feelings of eeriness, Ho et al. (2008) point out that there is at least anecdotal evidence indicating that people can become reasonably comfortable with a humanlike robot over time even if an initial encounter with it gives them "the creeps." What remains unclear, however, is whether there are other relevant phenomena that could generate similar feelings of eeriness. As mentioned previously, a mismatch among sense modalities can cause greater discomfort, but this may not be the source, or at least not the only eeriness-generating factor. The public has now been exposed for decades to Stephen Hawking's mechanical voice, and this experience might make it less likely that the human figure–mechanical voice pairing will be viewed as disturbing to people today as it might have been viewed when such devices were first used (e.g., for those who had their vocal cords removed). Whether the mismatches that adults found disturbing are likely to translate to children is something that should not be assumed a priori. It is possible, for example, that a child's reactions will correspond more closely to Ho et al.'s (2008) finding that "older people were more willing to overlook defects in a robot" when rating whether it looks "humanlike" (p. 175).

Ho et al. (2008) consider other possible sources that may contribute to feelings of eeriness. They mention the possibility that these feelings may arise depending on the extent to which robots elicit feelings of fear, especially fear of death or fear of losing bodily control. They give examples of human-looking robots eliciting a fear of being replaced or threatening a deeply held metaphysical assumption that humans have souls and are not simply "soulless machines" (Ho et al. 2008, 170). While their study does not rule out the possibility of associations between the uncanny valley and either fear of mortality or disgust "as an evolved mechanism for pathogen avoidance" (175), they point out that further research is needed to identify the aspects of a robot's appearance or behavior that prompts such reactions from humans. Where children, particularly very young children, are concerned, it seems unlikely that views about human mortality will play a significant role in how they react to robots. Moreover, it is possible that children's interaction with robots will render moot some of the concerns raised here. For example, if an individual is accustomed to robots from early childhood, she will presumably not find encounters with robots as unusual or as jarring as an adult who has not interacted with them before.

Briefly stated, additional empirical evidence is needed to answer questions regarding what precisely might be called for in terms of a robot's appearance. The etiology or manifestation of uncanny valley-type experiences in adults may not necessarily translate to the case of children. A standardized approach (e.g., making them look "humanlike") is neither necessary nor desirable. At this early stage of the robotic era, it is preferable to have a plurality of design strategies until there is greater clarity regarding which ones are most conducive to promoting human well-being. The varied tastes and preferences of children in their selection of toys, television programs, etc. indicate that convergence may be unwise. Walters et al. (2008) suggest in their study that a person's personality type might give some indication of how that individual will respond to a robot. For example, they claim that introverted humans prefer a more mechanical-looking robot, whereas extroverts prefer a more human-looking robot (p. 175). Considering the benefits of animal-assisted therapy, there are compelling reasons to continue creating at least some robots that look like non-human animals. The fact that the benefits of robotic animals have already been substantiated to some degree only serves to reinforce this point (Banks et al. 2008).

7. Gender

One underexplored area within robot ethics is the relationship between gender stereotypes and decisions about the design and use of robots. A key issue to consider is whether robot should be gendered and exactly what it would mean for a robot to be gendered. For example, would this require having a certain body type or merely a "feminine" or "masculine" voice? Further, if a robot does not display clear signs of a particular gender (i.e., it looks "too androgynous"), will this elicit an "uncanny valley" type of reaction? Of course, there are other gender-related matters surrounding robot design. These include whether robots should be designed to recognize the gender of an individual and, if so, whether the robot should respond differently according to the gender of the person that it encounters. Understanding whether and how gender differences affect an individual's responses to robots is also salient.

A related matter is whether gendering should depend on the particular type of robot. For example, gendering toy robots might have a different impact than gendering a caregiver robot. Whether toys are gender-specific may be less of an issue, because it appears that the tendency to select same-gender toys is influenced heavily by parent/caregiver biases (Fine 2010). In contrast to a robotic *toy*, a gendered robot *caregiver or playmate* might strongly influence beliefs about gender roles in the way that human caregivers and peers do. Gender features are sometimes integrated into technology unconsciously, and this is a pattern likely to persist with robots (e.g., creating a robotic kindergarten teacher that looks "female"). It is also possible that designers might decide to integrate gender features deliberately. One reason for this is to facilitate bonding. Within the context of HRI, Woods et al. (2006) observe that a "female gender was associated with positive robot traits such as happiness and friendliness" (p. 1412). Yet, as Carpenter et al. (2009) explain, gendering humanoid robots is likely to perpetuate stereotypes that persist in interpersonal interaction. Along these lines, referring to the Japanese roboticist Tomotaka Takahashi, Robertson (2010) states that "Technical difficulties aside, Takahashi—and my research suggests that he is representative of Japanese roboticists in general—invokes, in no uncertain terms, his common-sense view that an attribution of female gender requires an interiorized, slender body, and male gender an exteriorized, stocky body" (p. 19). Such tendencies can have the unfortunate consequence of reinforcing rigid views of how individuals of a particular gender should present themselves or behave.

Not only could gendering a robot perpetuate certain problematic stereotypes, but also it can influence how users interact with the technology. Nass and Yen (2010) claim that a group of German males were unwilling to take instructions from a female-sounding navigation system in their automobiles. Similarly, if a robot has a "masculine" or "feminine" tone of voice, this will likely affect how humans respond to it (Sigel et al. 2009). For example, Crowell et al. (2009) claim that women viewed a female-sounding synthetic voice as more likeable and trustworthy and were "more persuaded in a choice-making task" by such a voice (p. 3736). According to Coeckelbergh (2011), "... we can expect that a person's response to gender differences in relations with robots will resemble that person's response to human gender differences" (p. 199). He offers the example of a cleaning robot and how individuals will respond to the robot if they are told that it is a "lady" (p. 199). Nomura and Tagaki (2011) point out that even if a robot has a gender-neutral appearance, users may assign a particular gender to it based on the specific tasks in which the robot is engaged, especially if those tasks are "strongly related to gender" (p. 28).

Negative stereotypes are objectionable and often destructive. As De Angeli and Brahnam (2006) claim, "the application of negative stereotypes is an important predictor of prejudice, discrimination, and hostility leading to aggression and violence" (p. 1). However, stereotypes can serve a positive function, and arguably, there are times when they are worth perpetuating. For example, a stereotype might be defensible if the by-product is robot behavior that is "appropriately persuasive" (Siegel et al. 2009) and a good outcome follows (e.g., a child accepts a necessary therapeutic intervention). To reiterate, how a robot will be perceived is integrally tied to its appearance and behavior; whether a positive response emerges is apparently affected in part by the preconceptions and assumptions that a person has about the robot because it looks like a particular gender.

Carpenter et al. (2009) found that study participants were more likely to perceive a male robot as being threatening (p. 263). This kind of finding indicates that designing a robot to look female might be preferable in some contexts. If a non-threatening presence more readily elicits cooperation, this could improve an assistive robot's ability to fulfill its function. One could imagine scenarios where a robot with a high, soothing voice could provide comfort, especially since human caregivers commonly modify their voice and make it "higher" in order to calm distressed children. However, a study by Eyssel et al. (2012) indicates that male subjects, for example, felt "psychologically closer to the male voice," and both males and females had a stronger tendency to anthropomorphize voices that corresponded to their own gender (p. 126). Crowell et al. (2009) conclude that people "resonate more with a gendered voice that matches their own" (p. 3736). Yet they also distinguish between people's perceptions of the trustworthiness of embodied versus disembodied voices and maintain that more research is needed before drawing definitive conclusions about the "highly complex" interactions between gendered robots and humans (p. 3741).

At a minimum, the varying hypotheses about the impact of gendered voices and robots has on humans remind us of the importance of attending closely to the context in which these elements are introduced as well as whether their use is aimed at achieving ethically sound goals.

Young children, especially boys, tend to play with gender-typed toys, but this tendency appears to vary across individuals and can be significantly modified by relatively minor interventions, e.g., reading a counter-stereotypical story to a child (Green et al. 2004). Whether children choose gender-typed/typical toys seems to depend significantly on the reinforcement they receive from adults and peers in their environments. Green et al. (2004) suggest that boys are more rigidly locked into playing with "masculine" toys because of the harsher treatment they endure when they show interest in "feminine" toys. Fine (2010) observes that "four-year-old children will play for three times as long with a xylophone or balloon if it is labeled as for their own sex rather than for children of the other sex" (p. 230). She also explains that as early as 10 months, children begin to recognize what counts as gender-appropriate behavior, dress, and so on. These very young children are purportedly "gender detectives" who sort people and objects into gender categories.

Inquiry within the domain of robots and gender should force us to reexamine current social attitudes and practices. This is one way in which robots might help us to move forward and become increasingly sensitized to gender issues. In general, design and use decisions that reinforce gender stereotypes remain ethically questionable. Roboticists presumably would respond by arguing that gendering robots is defensible in at least some situations; this may include that female children might be more willing to interact with a "female" robot, and a similar phenomenon might be witnessed with male children and "male" robots. While comforting children is a noble goal, we should not assume that reinforcing gender stereotypes is part of an appropriate means to achieve that end. For instance, a cautious approach would require that we avoid reinforcing beliefs such as "all and only females are capable of nurturing others" or "females naturally derive immense joy from menial household chores."

8. Conclusion

Designing robots for children in a way that will allow them to flourish requires us to pay close attention to the many ways in which particular design features might affect both their short- and long-term development. Because HRI has the potential to alter not only children's development but also their interactions with other humans, design decisions must be made in ways that are likely to promote their physical, psychological, and emotional health. We questioned whether concerns about the uncanny valley hypothesis are as relevant today, primarily in the context of designing robots for children. We also delved into the underexplored area of gendering robots. Additional research will be necessary to investigate whether, beyond that which is insinuated by mere appearance, certain types of robot behaviors are ethically permissible.

There are many ethically salient aspects to a robot's design, and our hope is that roboticists will continue to examine a growing catalog of ethical issues. Focusing on the intersection of robotics, esthetics, and ethics should ideally promote careful re-examination of certain assumptions about the appropriateness of a particular design pathway. As this process continues, it may lend additional insight into the nature and appropriateness of existing human interactions and institutions. This may offer a profound opportunity to re-examine and, when necessary, revise current social practices and institutions.

Works Cited

Banks MR, Willoughby LM, Banks WA (2008) "Animal-Assisted Therapy and Loneliness in Nursing Homes: Use of Robotic Versus Living Dogs." *J Am Med Dir Assoc* 9(3):173–177.

Bartneck C, Kanda T, Ishiguro H, Hagita N (2009) "My Robot Doppelganger: A Critical Look at the Uncanny Valley." *Robot and Human Interactive Communication RO-MAN.*

Belpaeme T, Morse A (2010) "Time Will Tell—Why it is too Early to Worry." *Interact Stud* 11(2):191–195.

Borenstein J, Pearson Y (2010) "Robot Caregivers: Harbingers of Expanded Freedom for All?" *Ethics Inf Technol* 12(3): 277–288.

Breazeal C (2002) *Designing Sociable Robots.* MIT Press, Cambridge.

Brown WM, Price ME, Kang J, Pound N, Zhao Y, Yu H (2008) "Fluctuating Asymmetry and Preferences for Sex-Typical Bodily Characteristics." *PNAS* 105(35):12938–43.

Capurro R (2009) "Ethics and Robotics. In: Nagenborg M, Capurro R (Eds)" *Ethics and Robotics.* IOS Press, Heidelberg, 117–123.

Carpenter J, Davis JM, Erwin-Stewart N, Lee TR, Bransford JD, Vye N (2009) "Gender Representation and Humanoid Robots Designed for Domestic Use." *Int J Soc Robot* 1:261–265.

Ceceri K (2011) "My Keepon Dances Into Stores in October!" *Wired Magazine.* http://www.wired.com/geekdad/2011/10/my-keepon-dances-into-stores-in-october/. Accessed 9 Oct 2011.

Coeckelbergh M (2011) "Humans, Animals, and Robots: A Phenomenological Approach to Human–Robot Relations." *Int J Soc Rob* 3(2):197–204.

Crowell CR, Scheutz M, Schemerhorn P, Villano M (2009) "Gendered Voice and Robotic Entities: Perceptions and Reactions of Male and Female Subjects." In: IEEE/RSJ international conference on intelligent robots and systems (October), 3735–41.

De Angeli A, Brahnam S (2006) "Sex Stereotypes and Conversational Agents." In: Proceedings of the AVI 2006 workshop on gender and interaction: real and virtual women in a male world, Venice, Italy. http://sherylbrahnam.com/papers/EN2033.pdf. Accessed 30 May 2012.

Eyssel F, Kuchenbrandt D, Bobinger S, de Ruiter L, Hegel F (2012) "'If You Sound Like Me, You Must Be More Human': On the Interplay of Robot and User Features on Human–Robot Acceptance and Anthropomorphism *Hri'12.*" In: Proceedings of the 7th annual ACM/IEEE international conference on human–robot interaction pages (March), 125–26.

Feil-Seifer D, Mataric MJ (2011) "Socially Assistive Robotics: Ethical Issues Related to Technology." IEEE Rob Autom 18(1):24–31.

Fine C (2010) *Delusions of Gender: How our Minds, Society, and Neurosexism Create a Difference.* W W Norton and Company, New York.

Fior M, Nugent S, Beran TN, Ramirez-Serrano A, Kuzyk R (2010) "Children's Relationships With Robots: Robot is Child's New Friend." *J Phys Agents* 4(3):9–17.

Goetz J, Kiesler S, Powers A (2003) "Matching Robot Appearance and Behavior to Tasks to Improve Human–Robot Cooperation." In: Proceedings of the 12th IEEE international workshop on robot and human interactive communication (RO-MAN 2003). Milbrae, 55–60.

Green VA, Bigler R, Catherwood D (2004) "The Variability and Flexibility of Gender-Typed Toy Play: A Close Look at Children's Behavioral Responses to Counterstereotypic Models." *Sex Roles* 51 (7–8): 371–386.

Halpern D, Katz JE (2012) "Unveiling Robotophobia and Cyberdystopianism: The Role of Gender, Technology and Religion on Attitudes Towards Robots *Hri'12.*" In: Proceedings of the 7th annual ACM/IEEE international conference on human–robot interaction pages (March), 139–140.

Hanson D, Olney A, Prilliman S, Mathews E, Zielke M, Hammons D, Fernandez R, Stephanou H (2005) "Upending the Uncanny Valley." In: Cohn A (ed) Proceedings of the 20th national conference on artificial intelligence 4 (AAAI'05). AAAI Press, 1728–29.

Hausman BL (1995) *Changing Sex: Transsexualsim, Technology, and the Idea of Gender.* Duke University Press, Durham.

Ho C–C, MacDorman KF, Dwi Pramono ZAD (2008) "Human Emotion and the Uncanny Valley: A Glm, Mds, and Isoma Analysis of Robot Video Ratings." In: Proceedings of the 3rd ACM/IEEE international conference on human robot interaction (HRI '08). ACM, New York, 169–176.

International Federation of Robotics (IFR) (2011a) "Positive Impact of Industrial Robots on Employment." http://www.ifr.org/uploads/media/Metra_Martech_Study_on_robots_02.pdf. Accessed 18 June 2012.

International Federation of Robotics (IFR) (2011b) "World Robotics 2011 (Executive Summary)." http://www.worldrobotics.org/uploads/media/2011_Executive_Summary.pdf. Accessed 31 May 2012.

Kaplan F (2004) "Who is Afraid of the Humanoid? Investigating Cultural Differences in the Acceptance of Robots." *Int J Humanoid Rob* 1(3):1–16.

MacDorman KF, Ishiguro H (2006) "The Uncanny Advantage of Using Androids in Social and Cognitive Science Research." *Interact Stud* 7(3):297–337.

MacDorman KF, Vasudevan SK, Ho C (2009) "Does Japan Really Have Robot Mania? Comparing Attitudes by Implicit and Explicit Measure." *AI & Soc* 23(4):485-510.

Melson GF (2010) "Child Development Robots: Social Forces, Children's Perspectives." *Interact Stud* 11(2):227–232.

Mitchell WJ, Szerszen KA, Lu AS, Schermerhorn PW, Scheutz M, MacDorman KF (2011) "A Mismatch in the Human Realism of Face and Voice Produces an Uncanny Valley." *i-Perception* 2(1):10–12.

Mondada F, Bonani M, Raemy X, Pugh J, Cianci C, Klaptocz A, Magnenat S, Zufferey J-C, Floreano D, Martinoli A (2009) "The E-Puck, A Robot Designed for Education in Engineering." In: Proceedings of the 9th conference on autonomous robot systems and competitions, vol 1, no 1, 59–65.

Mori M (2012) "The Uncanny Valley" (KF MacDorman and N Kageki, Trans.) *IEEE Robotics and Automation,* 19(2):98–100 (Original work published in 1970). doi:10.1109/MRA.2012.2192811. http://spectrum.ieee.org/automaton/robotics/humanoids/the-uncanny-valley. Accessed 18 June 2012.

Nass C, Yen C (2010) *The Man Who Lied to His Laptop: What Machines Teach Us About Human Relationships.* Penguin Group, New York.

Nishida T (2009) "Towards Robots With Good Will." In: Capurro R, Nagenborg M (eds) *Ethics and robotics.* IOS Press, Heidelberg, 105–116.

Nomura T, Tagaki S (2011) "Exploring Effects of Educational Backgrounds and Gender in Human Robot Interaction." In: International conference on user science and engineering (i-USEr), 24–29.

Parks JA (2010) "Lifting the Burden of Women's Care Work: Should Robots Replace the Human Touch?" *Hypatia* 25(1):100–120.

Prazak B, Kronreif G, Hochgatterer A, Furst M (2004) "A Toy Robot for Physically Disabled Children." *Technol Disabil* 16:131–136.

Reber R, Schwarz N, Winkielman P (2004) "Processing Fluency and Aesthetic Pleasure: Is Beauty in the Perceiver's Processing Experience." *Pers Soc Psychol Rev* 8(4):364–382.

Richey S (2010) "The Impact of Anti-Assimilationist Beliefs on Attitudes Toward Immigration." *Int Stud Q* 54:197–212.

Robertson J (2010) "Gendering Humanoid Robots: Robo-Sexism in Japan." *Body Soc* 16(2)1–36.

Salter T, Werry I, Michaud F (2008) "Going into the Wild in Child–Robot Interaction Studies: Issues in Social Robotic Development." *Intel Serv Robot* 1(2):93–108.

Sharkey N, Sharkey A (2010) "The Crying Shame of Robot Nannies: An Ethical Appraisal." *Interact Stud* 11(2):161–190.

Siegel M, Breazeal C, Norton MI (2009) "Persuasive Robotics: The Influence of Robot Gender on Human Behavior." In: IEEE/RSJ international conference on intelligent robots and systems, 2563–68.

Tucker A (2009) "Robot Babies." *Smithsonian Magazine* (July):56–65. http://www.smithsonianmag.com/science-nature/Birth-of-a-Robot.html. Accessed 8 Oct 2011.

Turkle S (2006) "A Nascent Robotics Culture: New Complicities for Companionship." AAAI technical report series (July).

Wagner C (2009) "'The Japanese Way of Robotics': Interacting 'Naturally' With Robots as a National Character?" In: The 18th IEEE international symposium on robot and human interactive communication (September), 510–515.

Walters ML, Syrdal S, Dautenhahn K, Boekhorst R, Koay KL (2008) "Avoiding the Uncanny Valley: Robot Appearance, Personality, and Consistency of Behavior in an Attention-Seeking Home Scenario for a Robot Companion." *Auton Robot* 24:159–178.

Whitehouse D (2005) "Japanese Develop 'Female' Android." *BBC News,* July 27, http://news.bb.co.uk/2/hi/science/nature/4714135.stm. Accessed 5 May 2012.

Woods S, Dautenhahn K, Schulz J (2006) "Exploring the Design of Space Roots: Children's Perspectives." *Interact Comput* 1(5–6):1390–1418.

Credit

Pearson, Yvette and Jason Borenstein. "Creating 'Companions' for Children: The Ethics of Designing Esthetic Features for Robots." *AI & Soc* 29 (2014): 23–31. Print. Reproduced with permission of Springer-Verlag London via Copyright Clearance Center.

Why the Future Doesn't Need Us

Our most powerful 21st century technologies—robotics, genetic engineering, and nanotech—are threatening to make humans an endangered species.

Bill Joy

From the moment I became involved in the creation of new technologies, their ethical dimensions have concerned me, but it was only in the autumn of 1998 that I became anxiously aware of how great are the dangers facing us in the 21st century. I can date the onset of my unease to the day I met Ray Kurzweil, the deservedly famous inventor of the first reading machine for the blind and many other amazing things.

Ray and I were both speakers at George Gilder's Telecosm conference, and I encountered him by chance in the bar of the hotel after both our sessions were over. I was sitting with John Searle, a Berkeley philosopher who studies consciousness. While we were talking, Ray approached and a conversation began, the subject of which haunts me to this day.

I had missed Ray's talk and the subsequent panel that Ray and John had been on, and they now picked right up where they'd left off, with Ray saying that the rate of improvement of technology was going to accelerate and that we were going to become robots or fuse with robots or something like that, and John countering that this couldn't happen because the robots couldn't be conscious.

While I had heard such talk before, I had always felt sentient robots were in the realm of science fiction. But now, from someone I respected, I was hearing a strong argument that they were a near-term possibility. I was taken aback, especially given Ray's proven ability to imagine and create the future. I already knew that new technologies like genetic engineering and nanotechnology were giving us the power to remake the world, but a realistic and imminent scenario for intelligent robots surprised me.

It's easy to get jaded about such breakthroughs. We hear in the news almost every day of some kind of technological or scientific advance. Yet this was no ordinary prediction. In the hotel bar, Ray gave me a partial preprint of his then-forthcoming book *The Age of Spiritual Machines*, which outlined a utopia he foresaw—one in which humans gained near immortality by becoming one with robotic technology. On reading it, my sense of unease only intensified; I felt sure he had to be understating the dangers, understating the probability of a bad outcome along this path.

I found myself most troubled by a passage detailing a dystopian scenario:

The New Luddite Challenge

> First let us postulate that the computer scientists succeed in developing intelligent machines that can do all things better than human beings can do them. In that case presumably all work will be done by vast, highly organized systems of machines and no human effort will be necessary. Either of two cases might occur. The machines might be permitted to make all of their own decisions without human oversight, or else human control over the machines might be retained.
>
> If the machines are permitted to make all their own decisions, we can't make any conjectures as to the results, because it is impossible to guess how such machines might behave. We only point out that the fate of the human race would be at the mercy of the machines. It might be argued that the human race would never be foolish enough to hand over all the power to the machines. But we are suggesting neither that the human race would voluntarily turn power over to the machines nor that the machines would willfully seize power. What we do suggest is that the human race might easily permit itself to drift into a position of such dependence on the machines that it would have no practical choice but to accept all of the machines' decisions. As society and the problems that face it become more and more complex and machines become more and more intelligent, people will let machines make more of their decisions for them, simply because machine-made decisions will bring better results than man-made ones. Eventually a stage may be reached at which the decisions necessary to keep the system running will be so complex that human beings will be incapable of making them intelligently. At that stage the machines will be in effective control. People won't be able to just turn the machines off, because they will be so dependent on them that turning them off would amount to suicide.
>
> On the other hand it is possible that human control over the machines may be retained. In that case the average man may have control over certain private machines of his own, such as his car or his personal computer, but control over large systems of machines will be in the hands of a tiny elite—just as it is today, but with two differences. Due to improved techniques the elite will have greater control over the masses; and because human work will no longer be necessary the masses will be superfluous, a useless burden on the system. If the elite is ruthless they may simply decide to exterminate the

> mass of humanity. If they are humane they may use propaganda or other psychological or biological techniques to reduce the birth rate until the mass of humanity becomes extinct, leaving the world to the elite. Or, if the elite consists of soft-hearted liberals, they may decide to play the role of good shepherds to the rest of the human race. They will see to it that everyone's physical needs are satisfied, that all children are raised under psychologically hygienic conditions, that everyone has a wholesome hobby to keep him busy, and that anyone who may become dissatisfied undergoes "treatment" to cure his "problem." Of course, life will be so purposeless that people will have to be biologically or psychologically engineered either to remove their need for the power process or make them "sublimate" their drive for power into some harmless hobby. These engineered human beings may be happy in such a society, but they will most certainly not be free. They will have been reduced to the status of domestic animals.[1]

In the book, you don't discover until you turn the page that the author of this passage is Theodore Kaczynski—the Unabomber. I am no apologist for Kaczynski. His bombs killed three people during a 17-year terror campaign and wounded many others. One of his bombs gravely injured my friend David Gelernter, one of the most brilliant and visionary computer scientists of our time. Like many of my colleagues, I felt that I could easily have been the Unabomber's next target.

Kaczynski's actions were murderous and, in my view, criminally insane. He is clearly a Luddite, but simply saying this does not dismiss his argument; as difficult as it is for me to acknowledge, I saw some merit in the reasoning in this single passage. I felt compelled to confront it.

Kaczynski's dystopian vision describes unintended consequences, a well-known problem with the design and use of technology, and one that is clearly related to Murphy's law—"Anything that can go wrong, will." (Actually, this is Finagle's law, which in itself shows that Finagle was right.) Our overuse of antibiotics has led to what may be the biggest such problem so far: the emergence of antibiotic-resistant and much more dangerous bacteria. Similar things happened when attempts to eliminate malarial mosquitoes using DDT caused them to acquire DDT resistance; malarial parasites likewise acquired multi-drug-resistant genes.[2]

The cause of many such surprises seems clear: The systems involved are complex, involving interaction among and feedback between many parts. Any changes to such a system will cascade in ways that are difficult to predict; this is especially true when human actions are involved.

I started showing friends the Kaczynski quote from *The Age of Spiritual Machines*; I would hand them Kurzweil's book, let them read the quote, and then watch their reaction as they discovered who had written it. At around the same time, I found Hans Moravec's book *Robot: Mere Machine* to *Transcendent Mind*. Moravec is one of the leaders in robotics research and was a founder of the world's largest robotics research program at Carnegie Mellon University. *Robot* gave me more material to try out on my friends—material surprisingly supportive of Kaczynski's argument. For example:

The Short Run (Early 2000s)

> Biological species almost never survive encounters with superior competitors. Ten million years ago, South and North America were separated by a sunken Panama isthmus. South America, like Australia today, was populated by marsupial mammals, including pouched equivalents of rats, deers, and tigers. When the isthmus connecting North and South America rose, it took only a few thousand years for the northern placental species, with slightly more effective metabolisms and reproductive and nervous systems, to displace and eliminate almost all the southern marsupials.
>
> In a completely free marketplace, superior robots would surely affect humans as North American placentals affected South American marsupials (and as humans have affected countless species). Robotic industries would compete vigorously among themselves for matter, energy, and space, incidentally driving their price beyond human reach. Unable to afford the necessities of life, biological humans would be squeezed out of existence.
>
> There is probably some breathing room, because we do not live in a completely free marketplace. Government coerces nonmarket behavior, especially by collecting taxes. Judiciously applied, governmental coercion could support human populations in high style on the fruits of robot labor, perhaps for a long while.

A textbook dystopia—and Moravec is just getting wound up. He goes on to discuss how our main job in the 21st century will be "ensuring continued cooperation from the robot industries" by passing laws decreeing that they be "nice,"[3] and to describe how seriously dangerous a human can be "once transformed into an unbounded superintelligent robot." Moravec's view is that the robots will eventually succeed us—that humans clearly face extinction.

I decided it was time to talk to my friend Danny Hillis. Danny became famous as the cofounder of Thinking Machines Corporation, which built a very powerful parallel supercomputer. Despite my current job title of Chief Scientist at Sun Microsystems, I am more a computer architect than a scientist, and I respect Danny's knowledge of the information and physical sciences more than that of any other single person I know. Danny is also a highly regarded futurist who thinks long-term—four years ago he started the Long Now Foundation, which is building a clock designed to last 10,000 years, in an attempt to draw attention to the pitifully short attention span of our society. (See "Test of Time," *Wired* 8.03, p. 78.)

So I flew to Los Angeles for the express purpose of having dinner with Danny and his wife, Pati. I went through my now-familiar routine, trotting out the ideas and passages that I found so disturbing. Danny's answer—directed specifically at Kurzweil's scenario of humans merging with robots—came swiftly, and quite surprised me. He said, simply, that the changes would come gradually, and that we would get used to them.

But I guess I wasn't totally surprised. I had seen a quote from Danny in Kurzweil's book in which he said, "I'm as fond of my body as anyone, but if I can be 200 with a body of silicon, I'll take it." It seemed that he was at peace with this process and its attendant risks, while I was not.

While talking and thinking about Kurzweil, Kaczynski, and Moravec, I suddenly remembered a novel I had read almost 20 years ago—*The White Plague*, by Frank Herbert—in which a molecular biologist is driven insane by the senseless murder of his family. To seek revenge he constructs and disseminates a new and highly contagious plague that kills widely but selectively. (We're lucky Kaczynski was a mathematician, not a molecular biologist.) I was also reminded of the Borg of *Star Trek*, a hive of partly biological, partly robotic creatures with a strong destructive streak. Borg-like disasters are a staple of science fiction, so why hadn't I been more concerned about such robotic dystopias earlier? Why weren't other people more concerned about these nightmarish scenarios?

Part of the answer certainly lies in our attitude toward the new—in our bias toward instant familiarity and unquestioning acceptance. Accustomed to living with almost routine scientific breakthroughs, we have yet to come to terms with the fact that the most compelling 21st century technologies—robotics, genetic engineering, and nanotechnology—pose a different threat than the technologies that have come before. Specifically, robots, engineered organisms, and nanobots share a dangerous amplifying factor: They can self-replicate. A bomb is blown up only once—but one bot can become many and quickly get out of control.

Much of my work over the past 25 years has been on computer networking, where the sending and receiving of messages creates the opportunity for out-of-control replication. But while replication in a computer or a computer network can be a nuisance, at worst it disables a machine or takes down a network or network service. Uncontrolled self-replication in these newer technologies runs a much greater risk: a risk of substantial damage in the physical world.

Each of these technologies also offers untold promise: The vision of near immortality that Kurzweil sees in his robot dreams drives us forward; genetic engineering may soon provide treatments, if not outright cures, for most diseases; and nanotechnology and nanomedicine can address yet more ills. Together they could significantly extend our average life span and improve the quality of our lives. Yet, with each of these technologies, a sequence of small, individually sensible advances leads to an accumulation of great power and, concomitantly, great danger.

What was different in the 20th century? Certainly, the technologies underlying the weapons of mass destruction (WMD)—nuclear, biological, and chemical (NBC)—were powerful, and the weapons an enormous threat. But building nuclear weapons required, at least for a time, access to both rare—indeed, effectively unavailable—raw materials and highly protected information; biological and chemical weapons programs also tended to require large-scale activities.

The 21st century technologies—genetics, nanotechnology, and robotics (GNR)—are so powerful that they can spawn whole new classes of accidents and abuses. Most dangerously, for the first time, these accidents and abuses are widely within the reach of individuals or small groups. They will not require large facilities or rare raw materials. Knowledge alone will enable the use of them.

Thus we have the possibility not just of weapons of mass destruction but of knowledge-enabled mass destruction (KMD), this destructiveness hugely amplified by the power of self-replication.

I think it is no exaggeration to say we are on the cusp of the further perfection of extreme evil, an evil whose possibility spreads well beyond that which weapons of mass destruction bequeathed to the nation-states, on to a surprising and terrible empowerment of extreme individuals.

Nothing about the way I got involved with computers suggested to me that I was going to be facing these kinds of issues.

My life has been driven by a deep need to ask questions and find answers. When I was 3, I was already reading, so my father took me to the elementary school, where I sat on the principal's lap and read him a story. I started school early, later skipped a grade, and escaped into books—I was incredibly motivated to learn. I asked lots of questions, often driving adults to distraction.

As a teenager I was very interested in science and technology. I wanted to be a ham radio operator but didn't have the money to buy the equipment. Ham radio was the Internet of its time: very addictive, and quite solitary. Money issues aside, my mother put her foot down—I was not to be a ham; I was antisocial enough already.

I may not have had many close friends, but I was awash in ideas. By high school, I had discovered the great science fiction writers. I remember especially Heinlein's *Have Spacesuit Will Travel* and Asimov's *I, Robot*, with its Three Laws of Robotics. I was enchanted by the descriptions of space travel and wanted to have a telescope to look at the stars; since I had no money to buy or make one, I checked books on telescope-making out of the library and read about making them instead. I soared in my imagination.

Thursday nights my parents went bowling, and we kids stayed home alone. It was the night of Gene Roddenberry's original *Star Trek*, and the program made a big impression on me. I came to accept its notion that humans had a future in space, Western-style, with big heroes and adventures. Roddenberry's vision of the centuries to come was one with strong moral values, embodied in codes like the Prime Directive: to not interfere in the development of less technologically advanced civilizations. This had an incredible appeal to me; ethical humans, not robots, dominated this future, and I took Roddenberry's dream as part of my own.

I excelled in mathematics in high school, and when I went to the University of Michigan as an undergraduate engineering student I took the advanced curriculum of the mathematics majors. Solving math problems was an exciting challenge, but when I discovered computers I found something much more interesting: a machine into which you could put a program that attempted to solve a problem, after which the machine quickly checked the solution. The computer had a clear notion of correct and incorrect, true and false. Were my ideas correct? The machine could tell me. This was very seductive.

I was lucky enough to get a job programming early supercomputers and discovered the amazing power of large machines to numerically simulate advanced designs. When I went to graduate school at UC Berkeley in the mid-1970s, I started staying up late, often all night, inventing new worlds inside the machines. Solving problems. Writing the code that argued so strongly to be written.

In *The Agony and the Ecstasy,* Irving Stone's biographical novel of Michelangelo, Stone described vividly how Michelangelo released the statues from the stone, "breaking the marble spell," carving from the images in his mind.[4] In my most ecstatic moments, the software in the computer emerged in the same way. Once I had imagined it in my mind I felt that it was already there in the machine, waiting to be released. Staying up all night seemed a small price to pay to free it—to give the ideas concrete form.

After a few years at Berkeley I started to send out some of the software I had written—an instructional Pascal system, Unix utilities, and a text editor called vi (which is still, to my surprise, widely used more than 20 years later)—to others who had similar small PDP-11 and VAX minicomputers. These adventures in software eventually turned into the Berkeley version of the Unix operating system, which became a personal "success disaster"—so many people wanted it that I never finished my PhD. Instead I got a job working for Darpa putting Berkeley Unix on the Internet and fixing it to be reliable and to run large research applications well. This was all great fun and very rewarding. And, frankly, I saw no robots here, or anywhere near.

Still, by the early 1980s, I was drowning. The Unix releases were very successful, and my little project of one soon had money and some staff, but the problem at Berkeley was always office space rather than money—there wasn't room for the help the project needed, so when the other founders of Sun Microsystems showed up I jumped at the chance to join them. At Sun, the long hours continued into the early days of workstations and personal computers, and I have enjoyed participating in the creation of advanced microprocessor technologies and Internet technologies such as Java and Jini.

From all this, I trust it is clear that I am not a Luddite. I have always, rather, had a strong belief in the value of the scientific search for truth and in the ability of great engineering to bring material progress. The Industrial Revolution has immeasurably improved everyone's life over the last couple hundred years, and I always expected my career to involve the building of worthwhile solutions to real problems, one problem at a time.

I have not been disappointed. My work has had more impact than I had ever hoped for and has been more widely used than I could have reasonably expected. I have spent the last 20 years still trying to figure out how to make computers as reliable as I want them to be (they are not nearly there yet) and how to make them simple to use (a goal that has met with even less relative success). Despite some progress, the problems that remain seem even more daunting.

But while I was aware of the moral dilemmas surrounding technology's consequences in fields like weapons research, I did not expect that I would confront such issues in my own field, or at least not so soon.

ঔ

Perhaps it is always hard to see the bigger impact while you are in the vortex of a change. Failing to understand the consequences of our inventions while we are in the rapture of discovery and innovation seems to be a common fault of scientists and technologists; we have long been driven by the overarching desire to know. That is the nature of science's quest, not stopping to notice that the progress to newer and more powerful technologies can take on a life of its own.

I have long realized that the big advances in information technology come not from the work of computer scientists, computer architects, or electrical engineers, but from that of physical scientists. The physicists Stephen Wolfram and Brosl Hasslacher introduced me, in the early 1980s, to chaos theory and nonlinear systems. In the 1990s, I learned about complex systems from conversations with Danny Hillis, the biologist Stuart Kauffman, the Nobel-laureate physicist Murray Gell-Mann, and others. Most recently, Hasslacher and the electrical engineer and device physicist Mark Reed have been giving me insight into the incredible possibilities of molecular electronics.

In my own work, as codesigner of three microprocessor architectures—SPARC, picoJava, and MAJC—and as the designer of several implementations thereof, I've been afforded a deep and firsthand acquaintance with Moore's law. For decades, Moore's law has correctly predicted the exponential rate of improvement of semiconductor technology. Until last year I believed that the rate of advances predicted by Moore's law might continue only until roughly 2010, when some physical limits would begin to be reached. It was not obvious to me that a new technology would arrive in time to keep performance advancing smoothly.

But because of the recent rapid and radical progress in molecular electronics—where individual atoms and molecules replace lithographically drawn transistors—and related nanoscale technologies, we should be able to meet or exceed the Moore's law rate of progress for another 30 years. By 2030, we are likely to be able to build machines, in quantity, a million times as powerful as the personal computers of today —sufficient to implement the dreams of Kurzweil and Moravec.

As this enormous computing power is combined with the manipulative advances of the physical sciences and the new, deep understandings in genetics, enormous transformative power is being unleashed. These combinations open up the opportunity to completely redesign the world, for better or worse: The replicating and evolving processes that have been confined to the natural world are about to become realms of human endeavor.

In designing software and microprocessors, I have never had the feeling that I was designing an intelligent machine. The software and hardware is so fragile and the capabilities of the machine to "think" so clearly absent that, even as a possibility, this has always seemed very far in the future.

But now, with the prospect of human-level computing power in about 30 years, a new idea suggests itself: that I may be working to create tools which will enable the construction of the technology that may replace our species. How do I feel about this? Very uncomfortable. Having struggled my entire career to build reliable software systems, it seems to me more than likely that this future will not work out as well as some people may imagine. My personal experience suggests we tend to overestimate our design abilities.

Given the incredible power of these new technologies, shouldn't we be asking how we can best coexist with them? And if our own extinction is a likely, or even possible, outcome of our technological development, shouldn't we proceed with great caution?

❧❧❧

The dream of robotics is, first, that intelligent machines can do our work for us, allowing us lives of leisure, restoring us to Eden. Yet in his history of such ideas, *Darwin Among the Machines,* George Dyson warns: "In the game of life and evolution there are three players at the table: human beings, nature, and machines. I am firmly on the side of nature. But nature, I suspect, is on the side of the machines." As we have seen, Moravec agrees, believing we may well not survive the encounter with the superior robot species.

How soon could such an intelligent robot be built? The coming advances in computing power seem to make it possible by 2030. And once an intelligent robot exists, it is only a small step to a robot species—to an intelligent robot that can make evolved copies of itself.

A second dream of robotics is that we will gradually replace ourselves with our robotic technology, achieving near immortality by downloading our consciousnesses; it is this process that Danny Hillis thinks we will gradually get used to and that Ray Kurzweil elegantly details in *The Age of Spiritual Machines*. (We are beginning to see intimations of this in the implantation of computer devices into the human body, as illustrated on the cover of *Wired* 8.02.)

But if we are downloaded into our technology, what are the chances that we will thereafter be ourselves or even human? It seems to me far more likely that a robotic existence would not be like a human one in any sense that we understand, that the robots would in no sense be our children, that on this path our humanity may well be lost.

Genetic engineering promises to revolutionize agriculture by increasing crop yields while reducing the use of pesticides; to create tens of thousands of novel species of bacteria, plants, viruses, and animals; to replace reproduction, or supplement it, with cloning; to create cures for many diseases, increasing our life span and our quality of life; and much, much more. We now know with certainty that these profound changes in the biological sciences are imminent and will challenge all our notions of what life is.

Technologies such as human cloning have in particular raised our awareness of the profound ethical and moral issues we face. If, for example, we were to reengineer ourselves into several separate and unequal species using the power of genetic engineering, then we would threaten the notion of equality that is the very cornerstone of our democracy.

Given the incredible power of genetic engineering, it's no surprise that there are significant safety issues in its use. My friend Amory Lovins recently cowrote, along with Hunter Lovins, an editorial that provides an ecological view of some of these dangers. Among their concerns: that "the new botany aligns the development of plants with their economic, not evolutionary, success." (See "A Tale of Two Botanies," p. 247.) Amory's long career has been focused on energy and resource efficiency by taking a whole-system view of human-made systems; such a whole-system view often finds simple, smart solutions to otherwise seemingly difficult problems, and is usefully applied here as well.

After reading the Lovins' editorial, I saw an op-ed by Gregg Easterbrook in *The New York Times* (November 19, 1999) about genetically engineered crops, under the headline: "Food for the Future: Someday, rice will have built-in vitamin A. Unless the Luddites win."

Are Amory and Hunter Lovins Luddites? Certainly not. I believe we all would agree that golden rice, with its built-in vitamin A, is probably a good thing, if developed with proper care and respect for the likely dangers in moving genes across species boundaries.

Awareness of the dangers inherent in genetic engineering is beginning to grow, as reflected in the Lovins' editorial. The general public is aware of, and uneasy about, genetically modified foods and seems to be rejecting the notion that such foods should be permitted to be unlabeled.

But genetic engineering technology is already very far along. As the Lovins note, the USDA has already approved about 50 genetically engineered crops for unlimited release; more than half of the world's soybeans and a third of its corn now contain genes spliced in from other forms of life.

While there are many important issues here, my own major concern with genetic engineering is narrower: that it gives the power—whether militarily, accidentally, or in a deliberate terrorist act—to create a White Plague.

The many wonders of nanotechnology were first imagined by the Nobel-laureate physicist Richard Feynman in a speech he gave in 1959, subsequently published under the title "There's Plenty of Room at the Bottom." The book that made a big impression on me, in the mid-80's, was Eric Drexler's *Engines of Creation*, in which he described beautifully how manipulation of matter at the atomic level could create a utopian future of abundance, where just about everything could be made cheaply, and almost any imaginable disease or physical problem could be solved using nanotechnology and artificial intelligences.

A subsequent book, *Unbounding the Future: The Nanotechnology Revolution*, which Drexler cowrote, imagines some of the changes that might take place in a world where we had molecular-level "assemblers." Assemblers could make possible incredibly low-cost solar power, cures for cancer and the common cold by augmentation of the human immune system, essentially complete cleanup of the environment, incredibly inexpensive pocket supercomputers—in fact, any product would be manufacturable by assemblers at a cost no greater than that of wood—spaceflight more accessible than transoceanic travel today, and restoration of extinct species.

I remember feeling good about nanotechnology after reading *Engines of Creation*. As a technologist, it gave me a sense of calm—that is, nanotechnology showed us that incredible progress was possible, and indeed perhaps inevitable. If nanotechnology was our future, then I didn't feel pressed to solve so many problems in the present. I would get to Drexler's utopian future in due time; I might as well enjoy life more in the here and now. It didn't make sense, given his vision, to stay up all night, all the time.

Drexler's vision also led to a lot of good fun. I would occasionally get to describe the wonders of nanotechnology to others who had not heard of it. After teasing them with all the things Drexler described I would give a homework assignment of my own: "Use nanotechnology to create a vampire; for extra credit create an antidote."

With these wonders came clear dangers, of which I was acutely aware. As I said at a nanotechnology conference in 1989, "We can't simply do our science and not worry about these ethical issues."[5] But my subsequent conversations with physicists convinced me that nanotechnology might not even work—or, at least, it wouldn't work anytime soon. Shortly thereafter I moved to Colorado, to a skunk works I had set up, and the focus of my work shifted to software for the Internet, specifically on ideas that became Java and Jini.

Then, last summer, Brosl Hasslacher told me that nanoscale molecular electronics was now practical. This was *new* news, at least to me, and I think to many people—and it radically changed my opinion about nanotechnology. It sent me back to *Engines of Creation*. Rereading Drexler's work after more than 10 years, I was dismayed to realize how little I had remembered of its lengthy section called "Dangers and Hopes," including a discussion of how nanotechnologies can become "engines of destruction." Indeed, in my rereading of this cautionary material today, I am struck by how naive some of Drexler's safeguard proposals seem, and how much greater I judge the dangers to be now than even he seemed to then. (Having anticipated and described many technical and political problems with nanotechnology, Drexler started the Foresight Institute in the late 1980s "to help prepare society for anticipated advanced technologies"—most important, nanotechnology.)

The enabling breakthrough to assemblers seems quite likely within the next 20 years. Molecular electronics—the new subfield of nanotechnology where individual molecules are circuit elements—should mature quickly and become enormously lucrative within this decade, causing a large incremental investment in all nanotechnologies.

Unfortunately, as with nuclear technology, it is far easier to create destructive uses for nanotechnology than constructive ones. Nanotechnology has clear military and terrorist uses, and you need not be suicidal to release a massively destructive nanotechnological device—such devices can be built to be selectively destructive, affecting, for example, only a certain geographical area or a group of people who are genetically distinct.

An immediate consequence of the Faustian bargain in obtaining the great power of nanotechnology is that we run a grave risk—the risk that we might destroy the biosphere on which all life depends.

As Drexler explained:

> "Plants" with "leaves" no more efficient than today's solar cells could out-compete real plants, crowding the biosphere with an inedible foliage. Tough omnivorous "bacteria" could out-compete real bacteria: They could spread like blowing pollen, replicate swiftly, and reduce the biosphere to dust in a matter of days. Dangerous replicators could easily be too tough, small, and rapidly spreading to stop—at least if we make no preparation. We have trouble enough controlling viruses and fruit flies
>
> Among the cognoscenti of nanotechnology, this threat has become known as the "gray goo problem." Though masses of uncontrolled replicators need not be gray or gooey, the term "gray goo" emphasizes that replicators able to obliterate life might be less inspiring than a single species of crabgrass. They might be superior in an evolutionary sense, but this need not make them valuable.
>
> The gray goo threat makes one thing perfectly clear: We cannot afford certain kinds of accidents with replicating assemblers.

Gray goo would surely be a depressing ending to our human adventure on Earth, far worse than mere fire or ice, and one that could stem from a simple laboratory accident.[6] Oops.

It is most of all the power of destructive self-replication in genetics, nanotechnology, and robotics (GNR) that should give us pause. Self-replication is the modus operandi of genetic engineering, which uses the machinery of the cell to replicate its designs, and the prime danger underlying gray goo in nanotechnology. Stories of run-amok robots like the Borg, replicating or mutating to escape from the ethical constraints imposed on them by their creators, are well established in our science fiction books and movies. It is even possible that self-replication may be more fundamental than we thought, and hence harder—or even impossible—to control. A recent article by Stuart Kauffman in *Nature* titled "Self-Replication: Even Peptides Do It" discusses the discovery that a 32-amino-acid peptide can "autocatalyse its own synthesis." We don't know how widespread this ability is, but Kauffman notes that it may hint at "a route to self-reproducing molecular systems on a basis far wider than Watson-Crick base-pairing."[7]

In truth, we have had in hand for years clear warnings of the dangers inherent in widespread knowledge of GNR technologies—of the possibility of knowledge alone enabling mass destruction. But these warnings haven't been widely publicized; the public discussions have been clearly inadequate.

There is no profit in publicizing the dangers.

The nuclear, biological, and chemical (NBC) technologies used in 20th century weapons of mass destruction were and are largely military, developed in government laboratories. In sharp contrast, the 21st century GNR technologies have clear commercial uses and are being developed almost exclusively by corporate enterprises. In this age of triumphant commercialism, technology—with science as its handmaiden—is delivering a series of almost magical inventions that are the most phenomenally lucrative ever seen. We are aggressively pursuing the promises of these new technologies within the now-unchallenged system of global capitalism and its manifold financial incentives and competitive pressures:

> This is the first moment in the history of our planet when any species, by its own voluntary actions, has become a danger to itself—as well as to vast numbers of others.
>
> It might be a familiar progression, transpiring on many worlds—a planet, newly formed, placidly revolves around its star; life slowly forms; a kaleidoscopic procession of creatures evolves; intelligence emerges which, at least up to a point, confers enormous survival value; and then technology is invented. It dawns on them that there are such things as laws of Nature, that these laws can be revealed by experiment, and that knowledge of these laws can be made both to save and to take lives, both on unprecedented scales. Science, they recognize, grants immense powers. In a flash, they create world-altering contrivances. Some planetary civilizations see their way through, place limits on what may and what must not be done, and safely pass through the time of perils. Others, not so lucky or so prudent, perish.

That is Carl Sagan, writing in 1994, in *Pale Blue Dot*, a book describing his vision of the human future in space. I am only now realizing how deep his insight was, and how sorely I miss, and will miss, his voice. For all its eloquence, Sagan's contribution was not least that of simple common sense—an attribute that, along with humility, many of the leading advocates of the 21st century technologies seem to lack.

I remember from my childhood that my grandmother was strongly against the overuse of antibiotics. She had worked since before the first World War as a nurse and had a commonsense attitude that taking antibiotics, unless they were absolutely necessary, was bad for you.

It is not that she was an enemy of progress. She saw much progress in an almost 70-year nursing career; my grandfather, a diabetic, benefited greatly from the improved treatments that became available in his lifetime. But she, like many levelheaded people, would probably think it greatly arrogant for us, now, to be designing a robotic "replacement species," when we obviously have so much trouble making relatively simple things work, and so much trouble managing—or even understanding—ourselves.

I realize now that she had an awareness of the nature of the order of life, and of the necessity of living with and respecting that order. With this respect comes a necessary humility that we, with our early-21st century chutzpah, lack at our peril. The commonsense view, grounded in this respect, is often right, in advance of the scientific evidence. The clear fragility and inefficiencies of the human-made systems we have built should give us all pause; the fragility of the systems I have worked on certainly humbles me.

We should have learned a lesson from the making of the first atomic bomb and the resulting arms race. We didn't do well then, and the parallels to our current situation are troubling.

The effort to build the first atomic bomb was led by the brilliant physicist J. Robert Oppenheimer. Oppenheimer was not naturally interested in politics but became painfully aware of what he perceived as the grave threat to Western civilization from the Third Reich, a threat surely grave because of the possibility that Hitler might obtain nuclear weapons. Energized by this concern, he brought his strong intellect, passion for physics, and charismatic leadership skills to Los Alamos and led a rapid and successful effort by an incredible collection of great minds to quickly invent the bomb.

What is striking is how this effort continued so naturally after the initial impetus was removed. In a meeting shortly after V-E Day with some physicists who felt that perhaps the effort should stop, Oppenheimer argued to continue. His stated reason seems a bit strange: not because of the fear of large casualties from an invasion of Japan, but because the United Nations, which was soon to be formed, should have foreknowledge of atomic weapons. A more likely reason the project continued is the momentum that had built up—the first atomic test, Trinity, was nearly at hand.

We know that in preparing this first atomic test the physicists proceeded despite a large number of possible dangers. They were initially worried, based on a calculation by Edward Teller, that an atomic explosion might set fire to the atmosphere. A revised calculation reduced the danger of destroying the world to a three-in-a-million chance. (Teller says he was later able to dismiss the prospect of atmospheric ignition entirely.) Oppenheimer, though, was sufficiently concerned about the result of Trinity that he arranged for a possible evacuation of the southwest part of the state of New Mexico. And, of course, there was the clear danger of starting a nuclear arms race.

Within a month of that first, successful test, two atomic bombs destroyed Hiroshima and Nagasaki. Some scientists had suggested that the bomb simply be demonstrated, rather than dropped on Japanese cities—saying that this would greatly improve the chances for arms control after the war—but to no avail. With the tragedy of Pearl Harbor still fresh in Americans' minds, it would have been very difficult for President Truman to order a demonstration of the weapons rather than use them as he did—the desire to quickly end the war and save the lives that would have been lost in any invasion of Japan was very strong. Yet the overriding truth was probably very simple: As the physicist Freeman Dyson later said, "The reason that it was dropped was just that nobody had the courage or the foresight to say no."

It's important to realize how shocked the physicists were in the aftermath of the bombing of Hiroshima, on August 6, 1945. They describe a series of waves of emotion: first, a sense of fulfillment that the bomb worked, then horror at all the people that had been killed, and then a convincing feeling that on no account should another bomb be dropped. Yet of course another bomb was dropped, on Nagasaki, only three days after the bombing of Hiroshima.

In November 1945, three months after the atomic bombings, Oppenheimer stood firmly behind the scientific attitude, saying, "It is not possible to be a scientist unless you believe that the knowledge of the world, and the power which this gives, is a thing which is of intrinsic value to humanity, and that you are using it to help in the spread of knowledge and are willing to take the consequences."

Oppenheimer went on to work, with others, on the Acheson-Lilienthal report, which, as Richard Rhodes says in his recent book *Visions of Technology,* "found a way to prevent a clandestine nuclear arms race without resorting to armed world government"; their suggestion was a form of relinquishment of nuclear weapons work by nation-states to an international agency.

This proposal led to the Baruch Plan, which was submitted to the United Nations in June 1946 but never adopted (perhaps because, as Rhodes suggests, Bernard Baruch had "insisted on burdening the plan with conventional sanctions," thereby inevitably dooming it, even though it would "almost certainly have been rejected by Stalinist Russia anyway"). Other efforts to promote sensible steps toward internationalizing nuclear power to prevent an arms race ran afoul either of U.S. politics and internal distrust, or distrust by the Soviets. The opportunity to avoid the arms race was lost, and very quickly.

Two years later, in 1948, Oppenheimer seemed to have reached another stage in his thinking, saying, "In some sort of crude sense which no vulgarity, no humor, no overstatement can quite extinguish, the physicists have known sin; and this is a knowledge they cannot lose."

In 1949, the Soviets exploded an atom bomb. By 1955, both the U.S. and the Soviet Union had tested hydrogen bombs suitable for delivery by aircraft. And so the nuclear arms race began.

Nearly 20 years ago, in the documentary *The Day After Trinity*, Freeman Dyson summarized the scientific attitudes that brought us to the nuclear precipice:

"I have felt it myself. The glitter of nuclear weapons. It is irresistible if you come to them as a scientist. To feel it's there in your hands, to release this energy that fuels the stars, to let it do your bidding. To perform these miracles, to lift a million tons of rock into the sky. It is something that gives people an illusion of illimitable power, and it is, in some ways, responsible for all our troubles—this, what you might call technical arrogance, that overcomes people when they see what they can do with their minds."[8]

Now, as then, we are creators of new technologies and stars of the imagined future, driven—this time by great financial rewards and global competition—despite the clear dangers, hardly evaluating what it may be like to try to live in a world that is the realistic outcome of what we are creating and imagining.

ঔঔঔ

In 1947, *The Bulletin of the Atomic Scientists* began putting a Doomsday Clock on its cover. For more than 50 years, it has shown an estimate of the relative nuclear danger we have faced, reflecting the changing international conditions. The hands on the clock have moved 15 times and today, standing at nine minutes to midnight, reflect continuing and real danger from nuclear weapons. The recent addition of India and Pakistan to the list of nuclear powers has increased the threat of failure of the nonproliferation goal, and this danger was reflected by moving the hands closer to midnight in 1998.

In our time, how much danger do we face, not just from nuclear weapons, but from all of these technologies? How high are the extinction risks?

The philosopher John Leslie has studied this question and concluded that the risk of human extinction is at least 30 percent,[9] while Ray Kurzweil believes we have "a better than even chance of making it through," with the caveat that he has "always been accused of being an optimist." Not only are these estimates not encouraging, but they do not include the probability of many horrid outcomes that lie short of extinction.

Faced with such assessments, some serious people are already suggesting that we simply move beyond Earth as quickly as possible. We would colonize the galaxy using von Neumann probes, which hop from star system to star system, replicating as they go. This step will almost certainly be necessary 5 billion years from now (or sooner if our solar system is disastrously impacted by the impending collision of our galaxy with the Andromeda galaxy within the next 3 billion years), but if we take Kurzweil and Moravec at their word it might be necessary by the middle of this century.

What are the moral implications here? If we must move beyond Earth this quickly in order for the species to survive, who accepts the responsibility for the fate of those (most of us, after all) who are left behind? And even if we scatter to the stars, isn't it likely that we may take our problems with us or find, later, that they have followed us? The fate of our species on Earth and our fate in the galaxy seem inextricably linked.

Another idea is to erect a series of shields to defend against each of the dangerous technologies. The Strategic Defense Initiative, proposed by the Reagan administration, was an attempt to design such a shield against the threat of a nuclear attack from the Soviet Union. But as Arthur C. Clarke, who was privy to discussions about the project, observed: "Though it might be possible, at vast expense, to construct local defense systems that would 'only' let through a few per cent of ballistic missiles, the much touted idea of a national umbrella was nonsense. Luis Alvarez, perhaps the greatest experimental physicist of this century, remarked to me that the advocates of such schemes were 'very bright guys with no common sense.'"

Clarke continued: "Looking into my often cloudy crystal ball, I suspect that a total defense might indeed be possible in a century or so. But the technology involved would produce, as a by-product, weapons so terrible that no one would bother with anything as primitive as ballistic missiles." [10]

In *Engines of Creation*, Eric Drexler proposed that we build an active nanotechnological shield—a form of immune system for the biosphere—to defend against dangerous replicators of all kinds that might escape from laboratories or otherwise be maliciously created. But the shield he proposed would itself be extremely dangerous—nothing could prevent it from developing autoimmune problems and attacking the biosphere itself.[11]

Similar difficulties apply to the construction of shields against robotics and genetic engineering. These technologies are too powerful to be shielded against in the time frame of interest; even if it were possible to implement defensive shields, the side effects of their development would be at least as dangerous as the technologies we are trying to protect against.

These possibilities are all thus either undesirable or unachievable or both. The only realistic alternative I see is relinquishment: to limit development of the technologies that are too dangerous, by limiting our pursuit of certain kinds of knowledge.

Yes, I know, knowledge is good, as is the search for new truths. We have been seeking knowledge since ancient times. Aristotle opened his Metaphysics with the simple statement: "All men by nature desire to know." We have, as a bedrock value in our society, long agreed on the value of open access to information and recognize the problems that arise with attempts to restrict access to and development of knowledge. In recent times, we have come to revere scientific knowledge.

But despite the strong historical precedents, if open access to and unlimited development of knowledge henceforth puts us all in clear danger of extinction, then common sense demands that we reexamine even these basic, long-held beliefs.

It was Nietzsche who warned us, at the end of the 19th century, not only that God is dead but that "faith in science, which after all exists undeniably, cannot owe its origin to a calculus of utility; it must have originated *in spite* of the fact that the disutility and dangerousness of the "will to truth," of "truth at any price' is proved to it constantly." It is this further danger that we now fully face—the consequences of our truth-seeking. The truth that science seeks can certainly be considered a dangerous substitute for God if it is likely to lead to our extinction.

If we could agree, as a species, what we wanted, where we were headed, and why, then we would make our future much less dangerous—then we might understand what we can and should relinquish. Otherwise, we can easily imagine an arms race developing over GNR technologies, as it did with the NBC technologies in the 20th century. This is perhaps the greatest risk, for once such a race begins, it's very hard to end it. This time—unlike during the Manhattan Project—we aren't in a war, facing an implacable enemy that is threatening our civilization; we are driven, instead, by our habits, our desires, our economic system, and our competitive need to know.

I believe that we all wish our course could be determined by our collective values, ethics, and morals. If we had gained more collective wisdom over the past few thousand years, then a dialogue to this end would be more practical, and the incredible powers we are about to unleash would not be nearly so troubling.

One would think we might be driven to such a dialogue by our instinct for self-preservation. Individuals clearly have this desire, yet as a species our behavior seems to be not in our favor. In dealing with the nuclear threat, we often spoke dishonestly to ourselves and to each other, thereby greatly increasing the risks. Whether this was politically motivated, or because we chose not to think ahead, or because when faced with such grave threats we acted irrationally out of fear, I do not know, but it does not bode well.

The new Pandora's boxes of genetics, nanotechnology, and robotics are almost open, yet we seem hardly to have noticed. Ideas can't be put back in a box; unlike uranium or plutonium, they don't need to be mined and refined, and they can be freely copied. Once they are out, they are out. Churchill remarked, in a famous left-handed compliment, that the American people and their leaders "invariably do the right thing, after they have examined every other alternative." In this case, however, we must act more presciently, as to do the right thing only at last may be to lose the chance to do it at all.

ઊઊઊ

As Thoreau said, "We do not ride on the railroad; it rides upon us"; and this is what we must fight, in our time. The question is, indeed, Which is to be master? Will we survive our technologies?

We are being propelled into this new century with no plan, no control, no brakes. Have we already gone too far down the path to alter course? I don't believe so, but we aren't trying yet, and the last chance to assert control—the fail-safe point—is rapidly approaching. We have our first pet robots, as well as commercially available genetic engineering techniques, and our nanoscale techniques are advancing rapidly. While the development of these technologies proceeds through a number of steps, it isn't necessarily the case—as happened in the Manhattan Project and the Trinity test—that the last step in proving a technology is large and hard. The breakthrough to wild self-replication in robotics, genetic engineering, or nanotechnology could come suddenly, reprising the surprise we felt when we learned of the cloning of a mammal.

And yet I believe we do have a strong and solid basis for hope. Our attempts to deal with weapons of mass destruction in the last century provide a shining example of relinquishment for us to consider: the unilateral U.S. abandonment, without preconditions, of the development of biological weapons. This relinquishment stemmed from the realization that while it would take an enormous effort to create these terrible weapons, they could from then on easily be duplicated and fall into the hands of rogue nations or terrorist groups.

The clear conclusion was that we would create additional threats to ourselves by pursuing these weapons and that we would be more secure if we did not pursue them. We have embodied our relinquishment of biological and chemical weapons in the 1972 Biological Weapons Convention (BWC) and the 1993 Chemical Weapons Convention (CWC).[12]

As for the continuing sizable threat from nuclear weapons, which we have lived with now for more than 50 years, the U.S. Senate's recent rejection of the Comprehensive Test Ban Treaty makes it clear relinquishing nuclear weapons will not be politically easy. But we have a unique opportunity, with the end of the Cold War, to avert a multipolar arms race. Building on the BWC and CWC relinquishments, successful abolition of nuclear weapons could help us build toward a habit of relinquishing dangerous technologies. (Actually, by getting rid of all but 100 nuclear weapons worldwide—roughly the total destructive power of World War II and a considerably easier task—we could eliminate this extinction threat. [13])

Verifying relinquishment will be a difficult problem, but not an unsolvable one. We are fortunate to have already done a lot of relevant work in the context of the BWC and other treaties. Our major task will be to apply this to technologies that are naturally much more commercial than military. The substantial need here is for transparency, as difficulty of verification is directly proportional to the difficulty of distinguishing relinquished from legitimate activities.

I frankly believe that the situation in 1945 was simpler than the one we now face: The nuclear technologies were reasonably separable into commercial and military uses, and monitoring was aided by the nature of atomic tests and the ease with which radioactivity could be measured. Research on military applications could be performed at national laboratories such as Los Alamos, with the results kept secret as long as possible.

The GNR technologies do not divide clearly into commercial and military uses; given their potential in the market, it's hard to imagine pursuing them only in national laboratories. With their widespread commercial pursuit, enforcing relinquishment will require a verification regime similar to that for biological weapons, but on an unprecedented scale. This, inevitably, will raise tensions between our individual privacy and desire for proprietary information, and the need for verification to protect us all. We will undoubtedly encounter strong resistance to this loss of privacy and freedom of action.

Verifying the relinquishment of certain GNR technologies will have to occur in cyberspace as well as at physical facilities. The critical issue will be to make the necessary transparency acceptable in a world of proprietary information, presumably by providing new forms of protection for intellectual property.

Verifying compliance will also require that scientists and engineers adopt a strong code of ethical conduct, resembling the Hippocratic oath, and that they have the courage to whistleblow as necessary, even at high personal cost. This would answer the call—50 years after Hiroshima—by the Nobel laureate Hans Bethe, one of the most senior of the surviving members of the Manhattan Project, that all scientists "cease and desist from work creating, developing, improving, and manufacturing nuclear weapons and other weapons of potential mass destruction."[14] In the 21st century, this requires vigilance and personal responsibility by those who would work on both NBC and GNR technologies to avoid implementing weapons of mass destruction and knowledge-enabled mass destruction.

❧❧❧

Thoreau also said that we will be "rich in proportion to the number of things which we can afford to let alone." We each seek to be happy, but it would seem worthwhile to question whether we need to take such a high risk of total destruction to gain yet more knowledge and yet more things; common sense says that there is a limit to our material needs—and that certain knowledge is too dangerous and is best forgone.

Neither should we pursue near immortality without considering the costs, without considering the commensurate increase in the risk of extinction. Immortality, while perhaps the original, is certainly not the only possible utopian dream.

I recently had the good fortune to meet the distinguished author and scholar Jacques Attali, whose book *Lignes d'horizons* (*Millennium,* in the English translation) helped inspire the Java and Jini approach to the coming age of pervasive computing, as previously described in this magazine. In his new book *Fraternités,* Attali describes how our dreams of utopia have changed over time:

> At the dawn of societies, men saw their passage on Earth as nothing more than a labyrinth of pain, at the end of which stood a door leading, via their death, to the company of gods and to *Eternity.* With the Hebrews and then the Greeks, some men dared free themselves from theological demands and dream of an ideal City where *Liberty* would flourish. Others, noting the evolution of the market society, understood that the liberty of some would entail the alienation of others, and they sought *Equality.*

Jacques helped me understand how these three different utopian goals exist in tension in our society today. He goes on to describe a fourth utopia, *Fraternity,* whose foundation is altruism. Fraternity alone associates individual happiness with the happiness of others, affording the promise of self-sustainment.

This crystallized for me my problem with Kurzweil's dream. A technological approach to Eternity—near immortality through robotics—may not be the most desirable utopia, and its pursuit brings clear dangers. Maybe we should rethink our utopian choices.

Where can we look for a new ethical basis to set our course? I have found the ideas in the book *Ethics for the New Millennium,* by the Dalai Lama, to be very helpful. As is perhaps well known but little heeded, the Dalai Lama argues that the most important thing is for us to conduct our lives with love and compassion for others and that our societies need to develop a stronger notion of universal responsibility and of our interdependency; he proposes a standard of positive ethical conduct for individuals and societies that seems consonant with Attali's Fraternity utopia.

The Dalai Lama further argues that we must understand what it is that makes people happy and acknowledge the strong evidence that neither material progress nor the pursuit of the power of knowledge is the key—that there are limits to what science and the scientific pursuit alone can do.

Our Western notion of happiness seems to come from the Greeks, who defined it as "the exercise of vital powers along lines of excellence in a life affording them scope."[15]

Clearly, we need to find meaningful challenges and sufficient scope in our lives if we are to be happy in whatever is to come. But I believe we must find alternative outlets for our creative forces, beyond the culture of perpetual economic growth; this growth has largely been a blessing for several hundred years, but it has not brought us unalloyed happiness, and we must now choose between the pursuit of unrestricted and undirected growth through science and technology and the clear accompanying dangers.

It is now more than a year since my first encounter with Ray Kurzweil and John Searle. I see around me cause for hope in the voices for caution and relinquishment and in those people I have discovered who are as concerned as I am about our current predicament. I feel, too, a deepened sense of personal responsibility—not for the work I have already done, but for the work that I might yet do, at the confluence of the sciences.

But many other people who know about the dangers still seem strangely silent. When pressed, they trot out the "this is nothing new" riposte—as if awareness of what could happen is response enough. They tell me, "There are universities filled with bioethicists who study this stuff all day long." They say, "All this has been written about before, and by experts." They complain, "Your worries and your arguments are already old hat."

I don't know where these people hide their fear. As an architect of complex systems I enter this arena as a generalist. But should this diminish my concerns? I am aware of how much has been written about, talked about, and lectured about so authoritatively. But does this mean it has reached people? Does this mean we can discount the dangers before us?

Knowing is not a rationale for not acting. Can we doubt that knowledge has become a weapon we wield against ourselves?

The experiences of the atomic scientists clearly show the need to take personal responsibility, the danger that things will move too fast, and the way in which a process can take on a life of its own. We can, as they did, create insurmountable problems in almost no time flat. We must do more thinking up front if we are not to be similarly surprised and shocked by the consequences of our inventions.

My continuing professional work is on improving the reliability of software. Software is a tool, and as a toolbuilder I must struggle with the uses to which the tools I make are put. I have always believed that making software more reliable, given its many uses, will make the world a safer and better place; if I were to come to believe the opposite, then I would be morally obligated to stop this work. I can now imagine such a day may come.

This all leaves me not angry but at least a bit melancholic. Henceforth, for me, progress will be somewhat bittersweet.

Do you remember the beautiful penultimate scene in *Manhattan* where Woody Allen is lying on his couch and talking into a tape recorder? He is writing a short story about people who are creating unnecessary, neurotic problems for themselves because it keeps them from dealing with more unsolvable, terrifying problems about the universe.

He leads himself to the question, "Why is life worth living?" and to consider what makes it worthwhile for him: Groucho Marx, Willie Mays, the second movement of the Jupiter Symphony, Louis Armstrong's recording of "Potato Head Blues," Swedish movies, Flaubert's Sentimental Education, Marlon Brando, Frank Sinatra, the apples and pears by Cézanne, the crabs at Sam Wo's, and, finally, the showstopper: his love Tracy's face.

Each of us has our precious things, and as we care for them we locate the essence of our humanity. In the end, it is because of our great capacity for caring that I remain optimistic we will confront the dangerous issues now before us.

My immediate hope is to participate in a much larger discussion of the issues raised here, with people from many different backgrounds, in settings not predisposed to fear or favor technology for its own sake.

As a start, I have twice raised many of these issues at events sponsored by the Aspen Institute and have separately proposed that the American Academy of Arts and Sciences take them up as an extension of its work with the Pugwash Conferences. (These have been held since 1957 to discuss arms control, especially of nuclear weapons, and to formulate workable policies.)

It's unfortunate that the Pugwash meetings started only well after the nuclear genie was out of the bottle—roughly 15 years too late. We are also getting a belated start on seriously addressing the issues around 21st century technologies—the prevention of knowledge-enabled mass destruction—and further delay seems unacceptable.

So I'm still searching; there are many more things to learn. Whether we are to succeed or fail, to survive or fall victim to these technologies, is not yet decided. I'm up late again—it's almost 6 am. I'm trying to imagine some better answers, to break the spell and free them from the stone.

Notes

1 The passage Kurzweil quotes is from Kaczynski's Unabomber Manifesto, which was published jointly, under duress, by *The New York Times* and *The Washington Post* to attempt to bring his campaign of terror to an end. I agree with David Gelernter, who said about their decision:

"It was a tough call for the newspapers. To say yes would be giving in to terrorism, and for all they knew he was lying anyway. On the other hand, to say yes might stop the killing. There was also a chance that someone would read the tract and get a hunch about the author; and that is exactly what happened. The suspect's brother read it, and it rang a bell.

"I would have told them not to publish. I'm glad they didn't ask me. I guess."

(Drawing Life: Surviving the Unabomber. Free Press, 1997: 120.)

2 Garrett, Laurie. *The Coming Plague: Newly Emerging Diseases in a World Out of Balance*. Penguin, 1994: 47–52, 414, 419, 452.

3 Isaac Asimov described what became the most famous view of ethical rules for robot behavior in his book *I, Robot* in 1950, in his *Three Laws of Robotics*: 1. A robot may not injure a human being, or, through inaction, allow a human being to come to harm. 2. A robot must obey the orders given it by human beings, except where such orders would conflict with the First Law. 3. A robot must protect its own existence, as long as such protection does not conflict with the First or Second Law.

4 Michelangelo wrote a sonnet that begins:

> *Non ha l' ottimo artista alcun concetto*
> *Ch' un marmo solo in sè non circonscriva*
> *Col suo soverchio; e solo a quello arriva*
> *La man che ubbidisce all' intelleto.*

Stone translates this as:

> *The best of artists hath no thought to show*
> *which the rough stone in its superfluous shell*
> *doth not include; to break the marble spell*
> *is all the hand that serves the brain can do.*

Stone describes the process: "He was not working from his drawings or clay models; they had all been put away. He was carving from the images in his mind. His eyes and hands knew where every line, curve, mass must emerge, and at what depth in the heart of the stone to create the low relief."

(The Agony and the Ecstasy. Doubleday, 1961: 6, 144.)

5 First Foresight Conference on Nanotechnology in October 1989, a talk titled "The Future of Computation." Published in Crandall, B. C. and James Lewis, editors. *Nanotechnology: Research and Perspectives*. MIT Press, 1992: 269. See also www.foresight.org/Conferences/MNT01/Nano1.html.

6 In his 1963 novel *Cat's Cradle*, Kurt Vonnegut imagined a gray-goo-like accident where a form of ice called ice-nine, which becomes solid at a much higher temperature, freezes the oceans.

7 Kauffman, Stuart. "Self-replication: Even Peptides Do It." *Nature*, 382, August 8, 1996: 496. See www.santafe.edu/sfi/People /kauffman/sak-peptides.html.

8 Else, Jon. *The Day After Trinity: J. Robert Oppenheimer and The Atomic Bomb* (available at www.pyramiddirect.com).

9 This estimate is in Leslie's book *The End of the World: The Science and Ethics of Human Extinction*, where he notes that the probability of extinction is substantially higher if we accept Brandon Carter's Doomsday Argument, which is, briefly, that "we ought to have some reluctance to believe that we are very exceptionally early, for instance in the earliest 0.001 percent, among all humans who will ever have lived. This would be some reason for thinking that humankind will not survive for many more centuries, let alone colonize the galaxy. Carter's doomsday argument doesn't generate any risk estimates just by itself. It is an argument for *revising* the estimates which we generate when we consider various possible dangers." (Routledge, 1996: 1, 3, 145.)

10 Clarke, Arthur C. "Presidents, Experts, and Asteroids." *Science*, June 5, 1998. Reprinted as *"Science and Society"* in *Greetings, Carbon-Based Bipeds! Collected Essays*, 1934–1998. St. Martin's Press, 1999: 526.

11 And, as David Forrest suggests in his paper "Regulating Nanotechnology Development," available at www.foresight.org/NanoRev/Forrest1989.html, "If we used strict liability as an alternative to regulation it would be impossible for any developer to internalize the cost of the risk (destruction of the biosphere), so theoretically the activity of developing nanotechnology should never be undertaken." Forrest's analysis leaves us with only government regulation to protect us—not a comforting thought.

12 Meselson, Matthew. "The Problem of Biological Weapons." Presentation to the 1,818th Stated Meeting of the American Academy of Arts and Sciences, January 13, 1999. (minerva.amacad.org/archive/bulletin4.htm)

13 Doty, Paul. "The Forgotten Menace: Nuclear Weapons Stockpiles Still Represent the Biggest Threat to Civilization." *Nature, 402,* December 9, 1999: 583.

14 See also Hans Bethe's 1997 letter to President Clinton, at www.fas.org/bethecr.htm.

15 Hamilton, Edith. *The Greek Way*. W. W. Norton & Co., 1942: 35.

Credit

Joy. Bill. "Why the Future Doesn't Need Us." *Wired* 8.04 Apr. 2000. Print.

Mind vs. Machine

Brian Christian

In the race to build computers that can think like humans, the proving ground is the Turing Test—an annual battle between the world's most advanced artificial-intelligence programs and ordinary people. The objective? To find out whether a computer can act "more human" than a person. In his own quest to beat the machines, the author discovers that the march of technology isn't just changing how we live, it's raising new questions about what it means to be human.

Brighton, England, September 2009. I wake up in a hotel room 5,000 miles from my home in Seattle. After breakfast, I step out into the salty air and walk the coastline of the country that invented my language, though I find I can't understand a good portion of the signs I pass on my way—LET AGREED, one says, prominently, in large print, and it means nothing to me.

I pause, and stare dumbly at the sea for a moment, parsing and reparsing the sign. Normally these kinds of linguistic curiosities and cultural gaps intrigue me; today, though, they are mostly a cause for concern. In two hours, I will sit down at a computer and have a series of five-minute instant-message chats with several strangers. At the other end of these chats will be a psychologist, a linguist, a computer scientist, and the host of a popular British technology show. Together they form a judging panel, evaluating my ability to do one of the strangest things I've ever been asked to do.

I must convince them that I'm human.

Fortunately, I *am* human; unfortunately, it's not clear how much that will help.

The Turing Test

Each year for the past two decades, the artificial-intelligence community has convened for the field's most anticipated and controversial event—a meeting to confer the Loebner Prize on the winner of a competition called the Turing Test. The test is named for the British mathematician Alan Turing, one of the founders of computer science, who in 1950 attempted to answer one of the field's earliest questions: can machines think? That is, would it ever be possible to construct a computer so sophisticated that it could actually be said to be thinking, to be intelligent, to have a mind? And if indeed there were, someday, such a machine: how would we know?

Instead of debating this question on purely theoretical grounds, Turing proposed an experiment. Several judges each pose questions, via computer terminal, to several pairs of unseen correspondents, one a human "confederate," the other a computer program, and attempt to discern which is which. The dialogue can range from small talk to trivia questions, from celebrity gossip to heavy-duty philosophy—the whole gamut of human conversation. Turing predicted that by the year 2000, computers would be able to fool 30 per cent of human judges after five minutes of conversation, and that as a result, one would "be able to speak of machines thinking without expecting to be contradicted."

Turing's prediction has not come to pass; however, at the 2008 contest, the top-scoring computer program missed that mark by just a single vote. When I read the news, I realized instantly that the 2009 test in Brighton could be the decisive one. I'd never attended the event, but I felt I had to go—and not just as a spectator, but as part of the human defense. A steely voice had risen up inside me, seemingly out of nowhere: *Not on my watch.* I determined to become a confederate.

The thought of going head-to-head (head-to-motherboard?) against some of the world's top AI programs filled me with a romantic notion that, as a confederate, I would be *defending the human race,* à la Garry Kasparov's chess match against Deep Blue.

During the competition, each of four judges will type a conversation with one of us for five minutes, then the other, and then will have 10 minutes to reflect and decide which one is the human. Judges will also rank all the contestants—this is used in part as a tiebreaking measure. The computer program receiving the most votes and highest ranking from the judges (regardless of whether it passes the Turing Test by fooling 30 per cent of them) is awarded the title of the Most Human Computer. It is this title that the research teams are all gunning for, the one with the cash prize (usually $3,000), the one with which most everyone involved in the contest is principally concerned. But there is also, intriguingly, another title, one given to the *confederate* who is most convincing: the Most Human Human award.

One of the first winners, in 1994, was the journalist and science-fiction writer Charles Platt. How'd he do it? By "being moody, irritable, and obnoxious," as he explained in *Wired* magazine—which strikes me as not only hilarious and bleak, but, in some deeper sense, a call to arms: how, in fact, do we be the most human we can be—not only under the constraints of the test, but in life?

The Importance of Being Yourself

Since 1991, the Turing Test has been administered at the so-called Loebner Prize competition, an event sponsored by a colorful figure: the former baron of plastic roll-up portable disco dance floors, Hugh Loebner. When asked his motives for orchestrating this annual Turing Test, Loebner cites laziness, of all things: his utopian future, apparently, is one in which unemployment rates are nearly 100 per cent and virtually all of human endeavor and industry is outsourced to intelligent machines.

To learn how to become a confederate, I sought out Loebner himself, who put me in touch with contest organizers, to whom I explained that I'm a nonfiction writer of science and philosophy, fascinated by the Most Human Human award. Soon I was on the confederate roster. I was briefed on the logistics of the competition, but not much else. "There's not much more you need to know, really," I was told. "You are human, so just be yourself."

Just be yourself has become, in effect, the confederate motto, but it seems to me like a somewhat naive overconfidence in human instincts—or at worst, like fixing the fight. Many of the AI programs we confederates go up against are the result of decades of work. Then again, so are we. But the AI research teams have huge databases of test runs for their programs, and they've done statistical analysis on these archives: the programs know how to deftly guide the conversation away from their shortcomings and toward their strengths, know which conversational routes lead to deep exchange and which ones fizzle. The average off-the-street confederate's instincts—or judge's, for that matter—aren't likely to be so good. This is a strange and deeply interesting point, amply proved by the perennial demand in our society for dating coaches and public-speaking classes. The transcripts from the 2008 contest show the humans to be such wet blankets that the judges become downright apologetic for failing to provoke better conversation: "I feel sorry for the humans behind the screen, I reckon they must be getting a bit bored talking about the weather," one writes; another offers, meekly, "Sorry for being so banal." Meanwhile a computer appears to be charming the pants off one judge, who in no time at all is gushing LOLs and smiley-face emoticons. We can do better.

Thus, my intention from the start was to thoroughly disobey the advice to just show up and be myself—I would spend months preparing to give it everything I had.

Ordinarily this notion wouldn't be odd at all, of course—we train and prepare for tennis competitions, spelling bees, standardized tests, and the like. But given that the Turing Test is meant to evaluate *how human* I am, the implication seems to be that being human (and being oneself) is about more than simply showing up.

The Sentence

To understand why our human sense of self is so bound up with the history of computers, it's important to realize that computers used to *be human*. In the early 20th century, before a "computer" was one of the digital processing devices that permeate our 21st century lives, it was something else: a job description.

From the mid-18th century onward, computers, many of them women, were on the payrolls of corporations, engineering firms, and universities, performing calculations and numerical analysis, sometimes with the use of a rudimentary calculator. These original, human computers were behind the calculations for everything from the first accurate prediction, in 1757, for the return of Halley's Comet—early proof of Newton's theory of gravity—to the Manhattan Project at Los Alamos, where the physicist Richard Feynman oversaw a group of human computers.

It's amazing to look back at some of the earliest papers on computer science and see the authors attempting to explain what exactly these new contraptions were. Turing's paper, for instance, describes the unheard-of "digital computer" by making analogies to a *human* computer:

> The idea behind digital computers may be explained by saying that these machines are intended to carry out any operations which could be done by a human computer.

Of course, in the decades that followed, we know that the quotation marks migrated, and now it is "digital computer" that is not only the default term, but the *literal* one. In the mid-20th century, a piece of cutting-edge mathematical gadgetry was said to be "like a computer." In the 21st century, it is the human math whiz who is "like a computer." It's an odd twist: we're *like* the thing that used to be *like* us. We imitate our old imitators, in one of the strange reversals in the long saga of human uniqueness.

Philosophers, psychologists, and scientists have been puzzling over the essential definition of human uniqueness since the beginning of recorded history. The Harvard psychologist Daniel Gilbert says that every psychologist must, at some point in his or her career, write a version of what he calls "The Sentence." Specifically, The Sentence reads like this:

> The human being is the only animal that _________.

The story of humans' sense of self is, you might say, the story of failed, debunked versions of The Sentence. Except now it's not just the animals that we're worried about.

We once thought humans were unique for using language, but this seems less certain each year; we once thought humans were unique for using tools, but this claim also erodes with ongoing animal-behavior research; we once thought humans were unique for being able to do mathematics, and now we can barely imagine being able to do what our calculators can.

We might ask ourselves: Is it appropriate to allow our definition of our own uniqueness to be, in some sense, *reactive* to the advancing front of technology? And why is it that we are so compelled to feel unique in the first place?

"Sometimes it seems," says Douglas Hofstadter, a Pulitzer Prize-winning cognitive scientist, "as though each new step towards AI, rather than producing something which everyone agrees is real intelligence, merely reveals what real intelligence is *not*." While at first this seems a consoling position—one that keeps our unique claim to thought intact—it does bear the uncomfortable appearance of a gradual retreat, like a medieval army withdrawing from the castle to the keep. But the retreat can't continue indefinitely. Consider: if everything that we thought hinged on thinking turns out to not involve it, then ... what is thinking? It would seem to reduce to either an epiphenomenon—a kind of "exhaust" thrown off by the brain—or, worse, an illusion.

Where is the keep of our *selfhood*?

The story of the 21st century will be, in part, the story of the drawing and redrawing of these battle lines, the story of *Homo sapiens* trying to stake a claim on shifting ground, flanked by beast and machine, pinned between meat and math.

Is this retreat a good thing or a bad thing? For instance, does the fact that computers are so good at mathematics in some sense *take away* an arena of human activity, or does it *free* us from having to do a nonhuman activity, liberating us into a more human life? The latter view seems to be more appealing, but less so when we begin to imagine a point in the future when the number of "human activities" left for us to be "liberated" into has grown uncomfortably small. What then?

Alan Turing proposed his test as a way to measure technology's progress, but it just as easily lets us measure our own. The Oxford philosopher John Lucas says, for instance, that if we fail to prevent the machines from passing the Turing Test, it will be "not because machines are so intelligent, but because humans, many of them at least, are so wooden."

Beyond its use as a technological benchmark, the Turing Test is, at bottom, about the act of communication. I see its deepest questions as practical ones: How do we connect meaningfully with each other, as meaningfully as possible, within the limits of language and time? How does empathy work? What is the process by which someone enters into our life and comes to mean something to us? These, to me, are the test's most central questions—the most central questions of being human.

Part of what's fascinating about studying the programs that have done well at the Turing Test is seeing how conversation can work in the total absence of emotional intimacy. A look at the transcripts of Turing Tests past is, frankly, a sobering tour of the various ways in which we demur, dodge the question, lighten the mood, change the subject, distract, burn time: what shouldn't pass for real conversation at the Turing Test probably shouldn't be allowed to pass for real conversation in everyday life either.

How to Talk Like a Human

When the Turing Test was first proposed in 1950, it was a hypothetical: technology was nowhere near the point at which a practical test was possible. But, as we know, it got there; the first conversational computer program to attract significant notice and attention was Eliza, written in 1964 and 1965 by Joseph Weizenbaum at MIT. Modeled after a Rogerian therapist, Eliza worked on a very simple principle: extract key words from the users' own language and pose their statements back to them. ("I am unhappy." "Do you think coming here will help you not to be unhappy?") If in doubt, it might fall back on some completely generic phrases, like "Please go on." This technique of fitting the users' statements into predefined patterns and responding with a prescribed phrasing of its own—called "template matching"—was Eliza's only capacity.

A look at an Eliza transcript reveals how adeptly such an impoverished set of rules can, in the right context, pass at a glance for understanding:

User: Men are all alike.

Eliza: In what way?

User: They're always bugging us about something or other.

Eliza: Can you think of a specific example?

User: Well, my boyfriend made me come here.

Eliza: Your boyfriend made you come here.

User: He says I'm depressed much of the time.

Eliza: I am sorry to hear you are depressed.

User: It's true. I am unhappy.

Eliza: Do you think coming here will help you not to be unhappy?

User: I need some help, that much seems certain.

Eliza: What would it mean to you if you got some help?

User: Perhaps I could learn to get along with my mother.

Eliza: Tell me more about your family.

The results were stunning: many of the people who first talked with Eliza were convinced that they were having a genuine human exchange. In some cases, even Weizenbaum's own insistence to the contrary was of no use. People asked to be left alone to talk "in private," sometimes for hours and returned with reports of having had a meaningful therapeutic experience. Meanwhile, academics leapt to conclude that Eliza represented "a general solution to the problem of computer understanding of natural language."

One of the strangest twists to the Eliza story, however, was the reaction of the *medical community,* which decided Weizenbaum had hit upon something both brilliant and useful. *The Journal of Nervous and Mental Disease,* for example, said of Eliza in 1966:

> Several hundred patients an hour could be handled by a computer system designed for this purpose. The human therapist, involved in the design and operation of this system, would not be replaced, but would become a much more efficient man.

The famed scientist Carl Sagan, in 1975, concurred:

> I can imagine the development of a network of computer psychotherapeutic terminals, something like arrays of large telephone booths, in which, for a few dollars a session, we would be able to talk with an attentive, tested, and largely non-directive psychotherapist.

As for Weizenbaum, appalled and horrified, he did something almost unheard-of: an about-face on his entire career. He pulled the plug on the Eliza project, encouraged his own critics, and became one of science's most outspoken opponents of AI research. But the genie was out of the bottle, and there was no going back. The basic "template matching" skeleton and approach of Eliza has been reworked and implemented in some form or another in almost every chat program since, including the contenders at the 2009 Loebner Prize competition. The enthusiasm—as well as the unease—about these programs has only grown.

The Jerk as Genius

The first Loebner Prize competition was held on November 8, 1991, at the Boston Computer Museum. In its first few years, the contest required each program and human confederate to choose a topic, as a means of limiting the conversation. One of the confederates in 1991 was the Shakespeare expert Cynthia Clay, who was, famously, deemed a computer by three different judges after a conversation about the playwright. The consensus seemed to be: "No one knows that much about Shakespeare." (For this reason, Clay took her misclassifications as a compliment.)

The programmer Joseph Weintraub chose "Whimsical Conversation" for his PC Therapist III and went on to earn the very first Most Human Computer award. As the program practiced it, "whimsical conversation" was not a topic at all, but a manner—a crucial distinction. Weintraub was able to play off a looseness in the contest rules, the natural behavior patterns of chatbots, and people's stereotypes about computers and humans, all at once. Strategically, this was brilliant.

By dutifully and scrupulously providing information in response to the questions asked, Clay demonstrated her knowledge and understanding—but sometimes in a factual, encyclopedic way commonly associated with computer systems. Here is a sample of Clay's conversation:

Judge: What is your opinion on Shakespeare's plays?

Confederate: That's pretty general; would you be more specific? Otherwise, I'll just say I like them.

The computer at the "Whimsical Conversation" terminal stood in stark contrast:

Judge: It has been a long day! Now I think I'm ready for some fun. The weather isn't very pleasant today. Do you have any jokes that could lift the clouds?

Computer: Everybody talks about the weather but nobody seems to do much about it. Why do you need to tell me now you think you're ready for some fun? Groannnnnn … … … … …

Judge: What is the definition of whimsical conversation?

Computer: Didn't you say well anyway I would imagine whimsical conversation is like a series of knight's moves in chess—skrt of zig-zag rather than following any nparticular line.? [Weintraub's program, like many that followed it, faked typos. Any unintentional typing errors in the transcripts that follow have been corrected.] Why do you ask? Was that a clever comment, or what? Are such questions much on your mind?

Judge: I like the image of knights moving haphazardly across the chess board, does that mean there is no thought to whimsical conversation?

Computer: I could swear you just said how do you define whimsical?? How do yku define whimsical? Were you always so sick sick sick? Why do you need to tell me you like the image of knights moving haphazardly across the chess board?

"I really thought [PC Therapist] was human, because it … was weird and funny, in a normal sort of way," said one of the judges, a Harvard graduate student. Weintraub's program, shifting topics wildly and spouting non sequiturs and canned one-liners, came off as zany, a jokester, a much more "human" personality type. At least I used to think so—before I learned how easy this was to mimic.

As Richard Wallace, three-time winner of the Most Human Computer award ('00, '01, and '04), explains:

> Experience with [Wallace's chatbot] ALICE indicates that most casual conversation is "state-less," that is, each reply depends only on the current query, without any knowledge of the history of the conversation required to formulate the reply.

Many human conversations function in this way, and it behooves AI researchers to determine which types of conversation are stateless—with each remark depending only on the last—and try to create these very sorts of interactions. It's our job as confederates, as humans, to resist them.

One of the classic stateless conversation types is the kind of zany free-associative riffing that Weintraub's program, PC Therapist III, employed. Another, it turns out, is verbal abuse.

In May 1989, Mark Humphrys, a 21-year-old University College Dublin undergraduate, put online an Eliza-style program he'd written, called "MGonz," and left the building for the day. A user (screen name "Someone") at Drake University in Iowa tentatively sent the message "finger" to Humphrys's account—an early-Internet command that acted as a request for basic information about a user. To Someone's surprise, a response came back immediately: "cut this cryptic shit speak in full sentences." This began an argument between Someone and MGonz that lasted almost an hour and a half. (The best part was undoubtedly when Someone said, "you sound like a goddamn robot that repeats everything.")

Returning to the lab the next morning, Humphrys was stunned to find the log and felt a strange, ambivalent emotion. His program might have just shown how to pass the Turing Test, he thought—but the evidence was so profane that he was afraid to publish it.

Humphrys's twist on the Eliza paradigm was to abandon the therapist persona for that of an abusive jerk; when it lacked any clear cue for what to say, MGonz fell back not on therapy clichés like "How does that make you feel?" but on things like "You are obviously an asshole," or "Ah type something interesting or shut up." It's a stroke of genius because, as becomes painfully clear from reading the MGonz transcripts, argument is stateless—that is, unanchored from all context, a kind of Markov chain of riposte, meta-riposte, meta-meta-riposte. Each remark after the first is only about the previous remark. If a program can induce us to sink to this level, of course it can pass the Turing Test.

Once again, the question of what types of human behavior computers can imitate shines light on how we conduct our own, human lives. Verbal abuse is simply less complex than other forms of conversation. In fact, since reading the papers on MGonz, and transcripts of its conversations, I find myself much more able to constructively manage heated conversations. Aware of the stateless, knee-jerk character of the terse remark I want to blurt out, I recognize that that remark has far more to do with a reflex reaction to the very last sentence of the conversation than with either the issue at hand or the person I'm talking to. All of a sudden, the absurdity and ridiculousness of this kind of escalation become quantitatively clear, and, contemptuously unwilling to act like a bot, I steer myself toward a more "stateful" response: better living through science.

Beware of Banality

Entering the Brighton Centre, I found my way to the Loebner Prize contest room. I saw rows of seats, where a handful of audience members had already gathered, and up front, what could only be the bot programmers worked hurriedly, plugging in tangles of wires and making the last flurries of keystrokes. Before I could get too good a look at them, this year's test organizer, Philip Jackson, greeted me and led me behind a velvet curtain to the confederate area. Out of view of the audience and the judges, the four of us confederates sat around a rectangular table, each at a laptop set up for the test: Doug, a Canadian linguistics researcher; Dave, an American engineer working for Sandia National Laboratories; Olga, a speech-research graduate student from South Africa; and me. As we introduced ourselves, we could hear the judges and audience members slowly filing in but couldn't see them around the curtain. A man zoomed by in a green floral shirt, talking a mile a minute and devouring finger sandwiches. Though I had never met him before, I knew instantly he could be only one person: Hugh Loebner. Everything was in place, he told us, between bites, and the first round of the test would start momentarily. We four confederates grew quiet, staring at the blinking cursors on our laptops. My hands were poised over the keyboard, like a nervous gunfighter's over his holsters.

The cursor, blinking. I, unblinking. Then all at once, letters and words began to materialize:

Hi how are you doing?

The Turing Test had begun.

I had learned from reading past Loebner Prize transcripts that judges come in two types: the small-talkers and the interrogators. The latter go straight in with word problems, spatial-reasoning questions, deliberate misspellings. They lay down a verbal obstacle course, and you have to run it. This type of conversation is extraordinarily hard for programmers to prepare against because anything goes—and this is why Turing had language and conversation in mind as his test because they are really a test of everything. The downside to the give-'em-the-third-degree approach is that it doesn't leave much room to express yourself, personality-wise.

The small-talk approach has the advantage of making it easier to get a sense of who a person is—if you are indeed talking to a person. And this style of conversation comes more naturally to layperson judges. For one reason or another, small talk has been explicitly and implicitly encouraged among Loebner Prize judges. It's come to be known as the "strangers on a plane" paradigm. The downside is that these conversations are, in some sense, uniform—familiar in a way that allows a programmer to anticipate a number of the questions.

I started typing back.

Confederate: hey there!

Confederate: i'm good, excited to actually be typing

Confederate: how are you?

I could imagine the whole lackluster conversation spread out before me: *Good. Where are you from? / Seattle. How about yourself? / London.*

Four minutes and 43 seconds left. My fingers tapped and fluttered anxiously.

I could just feel the clock grinding away while we lingered over the pleasantries. I felt this desperate urge to go off script, cut the crap, cut to the chase—because I knew that the computers could do the small-talk thing, which played directly into their preparation. As the generic civilities stretched forebodingly out before me, I realized that this very kind of conversational boilerplate was the enemy, every bit as much as the bots. *How,* I was thinking as I typed another unassuming pleasantry, *do I get an obviously human connection to happen?*

Taking Turns

Part of what I needed to figure out was how to exploit the Loebner Prize's unusual "live typing" medium. The protocol being used was unlike e-mails, text messages, and standard instant-messaging systems in a very crucial way: it transmitted our typing keystroke by keystroke. The judge and I were watching each other type, typos and backspacing and all. I remember some Internet chat programs back in the '90s trying out this character-at-a-time approach, but people for the most part rejected it. It was too invasive, was the feeling: what people like about writing is the time and space to compose and edit a message before sharing it with the other person. The advantage of the character-at-a-time transmission, though, is that it approaches much more closely the condition of speech, with its fluidity of turn-taking and its choppy grammar: what's lost in eloquence is made up for in agility.

It also, then, lets us see typing's "negative space": hesitation. In a chat conversation where text is transmitted with every carriage return, only egregiously long pauses are taken to be part of the interaction. With more fluid and immediate feedback, silence acquires meaning. Failing to quickly answer a question in a face-to-face conversation, for instance, is tantamount in many cases to answering it. I recall asking a friend of mine how things were going with the woman he'd started seeing; the *um* and the tiny pause in which he searched for the right words made it clear they were having problems.

So what did the Loebner Prize's unusual (and recently implemented) protocols enable and disable, compared with the standard, walkie-talkie, turn-taking style? Long missives weren't going to work, as they had in previous years, when programs were able to steamroll the judges by eating up the clock and delivering ridiculously prolix answers. If two parties are taking strict turns under time pressure, they are putting themselves at the mercy of the length of the other's turns. Here, for instance, is one program's conversation transcript from 1996:

Computer: How about telling me a joke?

Judge: No.

Computer: Here's my favorite joke ... A dog limps into a bar with a bloody bandage on his foot. He's wearing a 10-gallon hat, six-shooters in his holsters and chaps. He growled, "I'm a-lookin' for the man that shot my paw."

"The joke's not funny ..." the judge writes, giving the program an opening to tell another one—which it does ("A knotty, worn-out old string walks into a bar ..."). Meanwhile, three full minutes have elapsed. If a computer (or confederate) started rambling on too long under the new, live-typing protocols, the judge could and would just cut it off.

And so another piece of my confederate strategy fell into place. I would treat the Turing Test's strange and unfamiliar textual medium more like spoken English and less like the written language. I would attempt to disrupt the turn-taking "wait and parse" pattern that computers understand, and create a single, flowing duet of verbal behavior, emphasizing timing. If computers understand little about verbal "harmony," they understand even less about rhythm.

If nothing was happening on my screen, whether or not it was my turn, I'd elaborate a little on my answer, or add a parenthetical, or throw a question back at the judge—just as we offer and/or fill audible silence when we talk out loud. If the judge took too long considering the next question, I'd keep talking. I would be the one (unlike the bots) with something to prove. If I knew what the judge was about to write, I'd spare him the keystrokes and jump in.

There's a trade-off, of course, between the number of opportunities for serve and volley, and the sophistication of the responses themselves. The former thrives with brevity, the latter with length. It seemed to me, though, that so much of the nuance (or difficulty) in conversation comes from understanding (or misunderstanding) a question and offering an appropriate (or inappropriate) response—thus, it made sense to maximize the number of interchanges.

Some judges, I discovered, would be startled or confused at this jumping of the gun, and I saw them pause, hesitate, yield, even start backspacing what they had half-written. Other judges cottoned on immediately and leapt right in after me.

In the first round of the 2009 contest, Judge Shalom Lappin—a computational linguist at King's College London—spoke with a computer program called Cleverbot, and then with me. My strategy of verbosity was clearly in evidence: I made 1,089 keystrokes in five minutes (3.6 keystrokes a second) to Cleverbot's 356 (1.2/sec), and Lappin made 548 keystrokes (1.8/sec) in my conversation, compared with 397 (1.3/sec) with Cleverbot. Not only did I say three times as much as my silicon adversary, but I engaged the judge more, to the tune of 38 per cent more typing from Lappin.

Reviewing the logs later, though, I looked for a way to quantify the fluidity of the human-to-human interactions against the rigidity of the human-to-machine ones. It occurred to me that you could count the changes—let's call them "swaps"—of the party who typed the latest keystroke. I did manage to type three times as much as Cleverbot, but the real story, as it turns out, is in the swaps. Lappin's conversation with Cleverbot had 33; his conversation with me had 492, almost 15 times as many.

The Confederate's Gambit

You don't *converse with* Google, or with most computer systems; you *depose* them. There's a crucial difference. Interestingly, many Loebner Prize judges approach the Turing Test as a kind of cross-examination; strangely, a number of confederates also seem to approach it with that dynamic in mind. One of the human-to-human conversations in 2008 never manages to get out of that stiff question-and-response mode:

Judge: Do you have a long drive?

Confederate: fairly long

Judge: so do I :(ah well, do you think you could have used public transport?

Confederate: i could have

Judge: and why not?

Confederate: i chose not to

Judge: that's fair. Do you think we have too many cars on the road or not enough today?

Confederate: it's not for me to say

Yawn! But the computer in this pair is playful with the judge from the get-go:

Judge: HI

Computer: Amen to that.

Judge: quite the evangelist

Computer: Our Father, who art in cyberspace, give us today our daily bandwidth.

Judge: evangelist / nerd lol. So how are things with you today?

And with that, the program has practically sealed up the judge's confidence in its humanity with its second sentence. Note that the confederate's stiff answers prompt more grilling and forced conversation—*what's your opinion on such-and-such political topic?* But with the computer, the judge, misled by the opening wisecracks into assuming it's the real person, remains utterly casual: *how are things?* This makes the contest easier for the computer and harder for the confederate.

It surprised me to see some confederates being coy with their judges. Asked what kind of engineer he is, Dave, to my left, answered, "A good one. :)" And Doug, to my right, responded to a question about what brought him to Brighton with "if I tell you, you'll know immediately that I'm human ;-)" For my money, wit is very successful, but coyness is a double-edged sword. You show a sense of humor, but you jam the cogs of the conversation. Probably the most dangerous thing a confederate can do in a Turing Test is stall. It's suspect—as the guilty party would tend to be the one running out the clock—and it squanders your most precious resource: time.

The humans in a Turing Test are strangers, limited to a medium that is slow and has no vocal tonality, and without much time. A five-second Turing Test would be an easy win for the machines: the judges, barely able to even say "hello," simply wouldn't be able to get enough data from their respondents to make any kind of judgment.

A five-hour test would be an easy win for the humans. The Loebner Prize organizers have tried different time limits since the contest's inception, but in recent years they've mostly adhered to Turing's original prescription of five minutes: around the point when conversation starts to get interesting.

A big part of what I needed to do as a confederate was simply to make as much engagement happen in those minutes as I physically and mentally could. Rather than adopt the terseness of a deponent, I offered the prolixity of a writer. In other words, I talked *a lot.* I stopped typing only when to keep going would have seemed blatantly impolite or blatantly suspicious. The rest of the time, my fingers were moving. I went out of my way to embody that maxim of "A bore is a man who, being asked 'How are you?' starts telling you how he is."

Judge: Hi, how's things?

Confederate: hey there

Confederate: things are good

Confederate: a lot of waiting, but ...

Confederate: good to be back now and going along

Confederate: how are you?

When we'd finished, and my judge was engaged in conversation with one of my computer counterparts, I strolled around the table, seeing what my comrades were up to. Looking over at my fellow confederate Dave's screen, I noticed his conversation began like he was on the receiving end of an interrogation, and he was answering in a kind of minimal staccato:

Judge: Are you from Brighton?

Confederate: No, from the U.S.

Judge: What are you doing in Brighton?

Confederate: On business

Judge: How did you get involved with the competition?

Confederate: I answered an e-mail.

Like a good deponent, he let the questioner do all the work. When I saw how stiff Dave was being, I confess I felt a certain confidence—I, in my role as the world's worst deponent, was perhaps in fairly good shape as far as the Most Human Human award was concerned.

This confidence lasted approximately 60 seconds, or enough time for me to continue around the table and see what another fellow confederate, Doug, and his judge had been saying.

Judge: Hey Bro, I'm from TO.

Confederate: cool

Confederate: leafs suck

Confederate: ;-)

Judge: I am just back from a sabbatical in the CS Dept. at U of T.

Confederate:nice!

Judge: I remember when they were a great team.

Judge: That carbon date me, eh?

Confederate: well, the habs were a great team once, too …

Confederate: *sigh*

Judge: YEH, THEY SUCK TOO.

Confederate: (I'm from Montreal, if you didn't guess)

Doug and his judge had just discovered that they were both Canadian. They let rip with abbreviations and nicknames and slang and local references. And then they started to talk about hockey.

I was in trouble.

❧❧❧

Six months after the 2009 contest, a video appeared on YouTube of a man having a shockingly cogent conversation with a bot about Shakespeare's *Hamlet*. Some suspected it might herald a new age for chatbots, and for AI. Others, including myself, were unimpressed. Sophisticated behavior doesn't necessarily indicate a *mind.* It might indicate just a *memory.* As Dalí so famously put it, "The first man to compare the cheeks of a young woman to a rose was obviously a poet; the first to repeat it was possibly an idiot."

For instance, Richard Wallace, the three-time Most Human Computer winner, recounts an "AI urban legend" in which

> a famous natural language researcher was embarrassed … when it became apparent to his audience of Texas bankers that the robot was consistently responding to the *next* question he was about to ask … [His] demonstration of natural language understanding … was in reality nothing but a simple script.

The moral of the story: no demonstration is ever sufficient. Only *interaction* will do. In the 1997 contest, one judge gets taken for a ride by Catherine, waxing political and really engaging in the topical conversation "she" has been programmed to lead about the Clintons and Whitewater. In fact, everything is going swimmingly until the very end, when the judge signs off:

Judge: it looks like i've got to go, Catherine. its been nice talking with you

Judge: do you need water or something before the 5 minute rounds?

At which point the program erupts into gibberish.

Computer: OK, yes on balance … Time to get off this one I think and onto something more down to earth!

Judge: like what?

Computer: Almost certainly! let's move on

Computer: I suppose it depends on where you're coming from, but as the song goes in My Fair Lady, "Why can't a woman be more like a man?"

Defeat from the jaws of victory.

We so often think of intelligence, of AI, in terms of sophistication, or complexity of behavior. But in so many cases, it's impossible to say much with certainty about the program itself, because any number of different pieces of software—of wildly varying levels of "intelligence"—could have produced that behavior.

No, I think sophistication, complexity of behavior, is not it at all. For instance, you can't judge the intelligence of an orator by the eloquence of his prepared remarks; you must wait until the Q&A and see how he fields questions. The computation theorist Hava Siegelmann once described intelligence as "a kind of sensitivity to things." These Turing Test programs that hold forth may produce interesting output, but they're rigid and inflexible. They are, in other words, insensitive—occasionally fascinating talkers that cannot listen.

As computing technology in the 21st century moves increasingly toward mobile devices, we've seen the 1990's explosive growth in processor speed taper off, and product development become less about raw computing horsepower than about the overall design of the product and its fluidity, reactivity, and ease of use. This fascinating shift in computing emphasis may be the cause, effect, or correlative of a healthier view of human intelligence—an understanding, not so much that it is complex and powerful, per se, as that it is reactive, responsive, sensitive, nimble. Our computers, flawed mirrors that they are, have helped us see that about ourselves.

The Most Human Human

The Most Human Computer award in 2009 goes to David Levy and his program, Do-Much-More. Levy, who also won in '97, with Catherine, is an intriguing guy: he was one of the big early figures in the digital-chess scene of the '70s and '80s, and was one of the organizers of the Marion Tinsley—Chinook checkers matches that preceded the Kasparov—Deep Blue showdowns in the '90s. He's also the author of the recent nonfiction book *Love and Sex With Robots,* to give you an idea of the sorts of things that are on his mind when he's not competing for the Loebner Prize.

Levy stands up, to applause, accepts the award from Philip Jackson and Hugh Loebner, and makes a short speech about the importance of AI for a bright future, and the importance of the Loebner Prize for AI. I know what's next on the agenda, and my stomach knots. I'm certain that Doug's gotten it; he and the judge were talking Canada 30 seconds into their conversation.

Ridiculous Canadians and their ice hockey, I'm thinking. Then I'm thinking how ridiculous it is that I'm even allowing myself to get this worked up about some silly award. Then I'm thinking how ridiculous it is to fly 5,000 miles just to have a few minutes' worth of IM conversations. Then I'm thinking how maybe it'll be great to be the runner-up; I can compete again in 2010, in Los Angeles, with the home-field cultural advantage, and finally prove—

"And the results here show also the identification of the humans," Jackson announces, "and from the ranking list we can see that 'Confederate 1,' which is Brian Christian, was the most human."

And he hands me the certificate for the Most Human Human award.

ঞ্জ্ঞ

I didn't know how to feel, exactly. It seemed strange to treat the award as meaningless or trivial, but did winning really represent something about me as a person? More than anything, I felt that together, my fellow confederates and I had avenged the mistakes of 2008 in dramatic fashion. That year, the 12 judges decided five times that computer programs were more human than confederates. In three of those instances, the judge was fooled by a program named Elbot, which was the handiwork of a company called Artificial Solutions, one of many new businesses leveraging chatbot technology. One more deception, and Elbot would have tricked 33 per cent of that year's dozen judges—surpassing Turing's 30 per cent mark, and making history. After Elbot's victory at the Loebner Prize and the publicity that followed, the company seemingly decided to prioritize the Elbot software's more commercial applications; at any rate, it had not entered the '09 contest as the returning champion.

In some ways a closer fight would have been more dramatic. Between us, we confederates hadn't permitted a single vote to go the machines' way. Whereas 2008 was a nail-biter, 2009 was a rout. We think of science as an unhaltable, indefatigable advance. But in the context of the Turing Test, humans—dynamic as ever—don't allow for that kind of narrative. We don't provide the kind of benchmark that sits still.

As for the prospects of AI, some people imagine the future of computing as a kind of heaven. Rallying behind an idea called "The Singularity," people like Ray Kurzweil (in *The Singularity Is Near*) and his cohort of believers envision a moment when we make smarter-than-us machines, which make machines smarter than themselves, and so on, and the whole thing accelerates exponentially toward a massive ultra-intelligence that we can barely fathom. Such a time will become, in their view, a kind of a techno-Rapture, in which humans can upload their consciousness onto the Internet and get assumed—if not bodily, then at least mentally—into an eternal, imperishable afterlife in the world of electricity.

Others imagine the future of computing as a kind of hell. Machines black out the sun, level our cities, seal us in hyperbaric chambers, and siphon our body heat forever.

I'm no futurist, but I suppose if anything, I prefer to think of the long-term future of AI as a kind of purgatory: a place where the flawed but good-hearted go to be purified—and tested—and come out better on the other side.

Who would have imagined that the computer's earliest achievements would be in the domain of logical analysis, a capacity once held to be what made us most different from everything else on the planet? That it could fly a plane and guide a missile before it could ride a bike? That it could create plausible preludes in the style of Bach before it could make plausible small talk? That it could translate before it could paraphrase? That it could spin half-discernible essays on postmodern theory before it could be shown a chair and say, as most toddlers can, "chair"?

As computers have mastered rarefied domains once thought to be uniquely human, they simultaneously have failed to master the ground-floor basics of the human experience—spatial orientation, object recognition, natural language, adaptive goal-setting—and in so doing, have shown us how impressive, computationally and otherwise, such minute-to-minute fundamentals truly are.

We forget how impressive we are. Computers are reminding us.

One of my best friends was a barista in high school. Over the course of a day, she would make countless subtle adjustments to the espresso being made, to account for everything from the freshness of the beans to the temperature of the machine to the barometric pressure's effect on the steam volume, meanwhile manipulating the machine with an octopus's dexterity and bantering with all manner of customers on whatever topics came up. Then she went to college and landed her first "real" job: rigidly procedural data entry. She thought longingly back to her barista days—when her job actually made demands of her intelligence.

Perhaps the fetishization of analytical thinking, and the concomitant denigration of the creatural—that is, animal—and bodily aspects of life are two things we'd do well to leave behind. Perhaps at last, in the beginnings of an age of AI, we are starting to *center* ourselves again, after generations of living slightly to one side—the logical, left-hemisphere side. Add to this that humans' contempt for "soulless" animals, our unwillingness to think of ourselves as descended from our fellow "beasts," is now challenged on all fronts: growing secularism and empiricism, growing appreciation for the cognitive and behavioral abilities of organisms other than ourselves, and, not coincidentally, the entrance onto the scene of an entity with considerably less soul than we sense in a common chimpanzee or bonobo—in this way AI may even turn out to be a boon for animal rights.

Indeed, it's entirely possible that we've seen the high-water mark of our left-hemisphere bias. I think the return of a more balanced view of the brain and mind—and of human identity—is a good thing, one that brings with it a changing perspective on the sophistication of various tasks.

It's my belief that only experiencing and understanding *truly* disembodied cognition—only seeing the coldness and deadness and disconnectedness of something that really *does* deal in pure abstraction, divorced from sensory reality—can snap us out of it. Only this can bring us, quite literally, back to our senses.

In a 2006 article about the Turing Test, the Loebner Prize co-founder Robert Epstein writes, "One thing is certain: whereas the confederates in the competition will never get any smarter, the computers will." I agree with the latter and couldn't disagree more strongly with the former.

When the world-champion chess player Garry Kasparov defeated Deep Blue, rather convincingly, in their first encounter in 1996, he and IBM readily agreed to return the next year for a rematch. When Deep Blue beat Kasparov (rather less convincingly) in '97, Kasparov proposed another rematch for '98, but IBM would have none of it. The company dismantled Deep Blue, which never played chess again.

The apparent implication is that—because technological evolution seems to occur so much faster than biological evolution (measured in years rather than millennia)—once the *Homo sapiens* species is overtaken, it won't be able to catch up. Simply put: the Turing Test, once passed, is passed forever. I don't buy it.

Rather, IBM's odd anxiousness to get out of Dodge after the '97 match suggests a kind of insecurity on its part that I think proves my point. The fact is, the human race got to where it is by being the most adaptive, flexible, innovative, and quick-learning species on the planet. We're not going to take defeat lying down.

No, I think that, while the first year that computers pass the Turing Test will certainly be a historic one, it will not mark the end of the story. Indeed, the *next* year's Turing Test will truly be the one to watch—the one where we humans, knocked to the canvas, must pull ourselves up; the one where we learn how to be better friends, artists, teachers, parents, lovers; the one where we come back. More human than ever.

Credit

Notes

Notes

Notes